THE COMPLETE SERMONS OF
RALPH WALDO EMERSON

THE COMPLETE SERMONS OF RALPH WALDO EMERSON IN FOUR VOLUMES

Chief Editor: Albert J. von Frank

Editors: Ronald A. Bosco
Andrew H. Delbanco
Wesley T. Mott
Teresa Toulouse

Contributing Editors: David M. Robinson
Wallace E. Williams
Douglas E. Wilson

THE COMPLETE SERMONS OF RALPH WALDO EMERSON

VOLUME 3

Edited by Ronald A. Bosco

UNIVERSITY OF MISSOURI PRESS
COLUMBIA AND LONDON

The publication of this volume was made possible in part by a grant
from the National Endowment for the Humanities, an independent
federal agency.

5 4 3 2 1   95 94 93 92 91

Library of Congress Cataloging-in-Publication Data
(Revised for volume 3)

Emerson, Ralph Waldo, 1803–1882.
  The complete sermons of Ralph Waldo Emerson.

  Vol. 3: Edited by Ronald A. Bosco.
  Includes index.
    1. Unitarian churches—Sermons.   2. Sermons, American.
I. Von Frank, Albert J.   II. Title.
BX9843.E487C66   1989   252'.08   88-4834
ISBN 0-8262-0681-6 (v. 1 : alk. paper)
ISBN 0-8262-0746-4 (v. 2 : alk. paper)

PREFACE

Since the appearance of the first volumes of the *Journals and Miscellaneous Notebooks* and the *Early Lectures* in the 1960s, Emersonians have come to recognize (and indeed to take some satisfaction in the fact) that editions of Emerson's writings are essentially collaborative works, regardless of the editor's name that appears on the title page. Certainly, this volume is no exception.

The sermons belonging to volume 3 presented extraordinary textual challenges, which, although not wholly unexpected, no one could have taken completely upon himself. The difficulties of the manuscript clearly reflect the turmoil in Emerson's private life during the thirteen months in which they were written, a turmoil occasioned by the declining health of his wife, Ellen Tucker Emerson, who died on February 8, 1831. Although Emerson's feelings are reflected in a number of his discourses, culminating in the consolatory Sermon CVII, the state of his mind is in some ways best expressed in the textual situations themselves, which can only be described as tortured.

For permission to publish the sermons, I am indebted to the Ralph Waldo Emerson Memorial Association and the Houghton Library. The staffs of the Houghton and Widener libraries at Harvard University were, as always, gracious and cooperative. For their collaborative efforts and assistance of various kinds on this volume, I gratefully acknowledge fellow Emerson editors Wesley T. Mott, Joel Myerson, Ralph H. Orth, the late Wallace E. Williams, and Douglas Emory Wilson. I would also like to thank Rich Haswell of Washington State University and Hugh N. Maclean, Rudolph Nelson, and David C. Redding, colleagues at the State University of New York at Albany. Because it cannot be adequately acknowledged in the notes, I recognize here the bibliocritical work of William B. Barton, Kenneth Walter Cameron, Gene Irey, and Arthur Cushman McGiffert, Jr.

My greatest debt, however, is to Albert J. von Frank, Chief Editor of this series, who verified my transcription of genetic and clear texts and my notes, and prepared the chronology that appears in the opening pages of the volume. His friendship, good humor, and encouragement over many years have always been cheering.

R.A.B.
January 1991

CONTENTS

Abbreviations of Works Frequently Cited

CW   *The Collected Works of Ralph Waldo Emerson.* Edited by Joseph
         Slater et al. 5 vols. to date. Cambridge: Harvard University Press,
         1971–.

EL   *The Early Lectures of Ralph Waldo Emerson.* Edited by Stephen E.
         Whicher, Robert E. Spiller, and Wallace E. Williams. 3 vols. Cam-
         bridge: Harvard University Press, 1959–1972.

J   *Journals of Ralph Waldo Emerson.* Edited by Edward Waldo Emer-
         son and Waldo Emerson Forbes. 10 vols. Boston and New York:
         Houghton Mifflin Co., 1909–1914.

JMN   *The Journals and Miscellaneous Notebooks of Ralph Waldo Emer-
         son.* Edited by William H. Gilman et al. 16 vols. Cambridge: Har-
         vard University Press, 1960–1982.

L   *The Letters of Ralph Waldo Emerson.* Edited by Ralph L. Rusk. 6
         vols. New York: Columbia University Press, 1939. Continued under
         the editorship of Eleanor M. Tilton. 1 vol. to date (vol. 7). New
         York: Columbia University Press, 1990.

MHS   Massachusetts Historical Society. Papers of the Second Church,
         Boston.

OFL   *One First Love: The Letters of Ellen Louisa Tucker to Ralph Waldo
         Emerson.* Edited by Edith W. Gregg. Cambridge: Harvard Univer-
         sity Press, 1962.

RWEMA   Manuscript owned by the Ralph Waldo Emerson Memorial Asso-
         ciation (Houghton Library).

W   *The Complete Works of Ralph Waldo Emerson.* Edited by Edward
         Waldo Emerson. Centenary Edition. 12 vols. Boston and New York:
         Houghton Mifflin Co., 1903–1904.

THE COMPLETE SERMONS OF
RALPH WALDO EMERSON

VOLUME 3

TEXTUAL INTRODUCTION

Sermons XCI through CXXXV are presented here in accordance with the textual principles set forth in the introductions to the preceding volumes—that is to say, in an annotated clear-text format with full textual notes in the back matter. Wesley T. Mott has performed an independent reading of the computer transcript against the manuscripts, and his readings were made available to the volume editor for cross-checking. Albert von Frank, as General Editor, has verified the accuracy of the entire volume and assisted with the annotations.

Textual Notes

The textual notes give the manuscript reading in every case of authorial insertion, deletion, substitution, transposition, and variant reading. With the exception of the categories of silent emendation listed below, the notes also record every instance in which a word or part of a word has been editorially supplied or deleted (for example, to correct Emerson's accidental doubling of words), or in which punctuation has been altered for clarity. No editorial emendations, silent or otherwise, occur in the textual notes, the purpose of which in each instance is to give the manuscript form using such standard symbols as are necessary to describe the situation. (A key to these symbols appears at the head of the Textual and Manuscript Notes.) Thus, a textual note might take this form:

our ⟨beliefs⟩ ↑Xty↓.

The symbols indicate that Emerson canceled "beliefs" and inserted "Xty". Although abbreviations in the edited text are regularly and silently expanded (the clear text would in this instance read "our Christianity."), the textual note is always bound to reproduce the manuscript form. Because the expansion of abbreviations is treated in this edition as a *silent* emendation (see the list below), no textual note is provided when Emerson uses "Xty" or any other abbreviation in the course of a sentence he did not revise. Put another way, the occasion for the textual note in the example above is not the abbreviation, but Emerson's substitution of one word for another.

Silent Emendations

1. Citations for biblical texts at the head of each sermon are given in regularized form, spelling out the book of the Bible, which Emerson often abbreviates, and giving chapter and verse in arabic numerals, which Emerson does

1

not consistently use. Emerson often quotes the Bible, as indeed he quotes other sources, from memory; inexact quotations are not corrected.

2. The following abbreviations are expanded: altho' (although), & (and), bro't (brought), ch. (chapter), Xt (Christ), Xdom (Christendom), Xn or Chr^n (Christian), Xty (Christianity), ch. (church), cd. (could), eno' (enough), eveg. (evening), gov^t (government), hist. (history), mt. (might), m.f. (my friends), nt. (not), N.T. or N. Testament (New Testament), pd. (paid), relig. (religious), Rev. (Revelation), sd. (said), servt (servant), shd. (should), y^e (the), y^{rs} (there's), tho't (thought), tho'tless (thoughtless), v. (verse), wd. (would), wro't (wrought), yrself (yourself).

3. Numbers and numerical terms are spelled out: e.g., 1 (one), 3^d (third).

4. Missing punctuation is supplied when undoubtedly called for, as periods at the ends of sentences, commas or semi-colons in series, commas or colons to introduce quotations, and question marks at the ends of rhetorical questions (silently emended from a period when necessary). Periods are supplied for the abbreviation "St."—as in "St. James." Emerson's use of single and double quotation marks is preserved without imposing uniformity, but omitted marks in a pair are supplied (a textual note describes the situation if there is any doubt about where a quotation ends). Apostrophes have been supplied where necessary; if there is any doubt whether singular or plural possessive is intended, the manuscript form is given in a note.

5. Words beginning a sentence (following Emerson's period) have been capitalized; capitalized words following Emerson's semicolons (but not his colons) have been reduced to lowercase.

6. Terminal punctuation consisting of a period followed by a dash has been retained within paragraphs when it seems to have the force of a semicolon. The dash is silently omitted when it falls at the end of a paragraph.

7. Emerson's usual practice is to put commas and periods inside his quotation marks. Contrary instances in the manuscript seem to be the result of haste and carelessness, and are therefore silently regularized.

Variants, Transpositions, and Other Reported Emendations

1. Emerson occasionally inserts an alternate word or phrase above the uncanceled corresponding word or phrase in his initial inscription. This situation is always reported in the textual notes, where it takes the form /first/second/. The clear text regularly adopts the second inscription in a pair of variants unless doing so results in a reading that is objectionable on the grounds of grammar or sense.

2. Emerson's usual method of indicating transposition is to label the relevant sentences, phrases, or words with subscript numbers 1 and 2 (or, more rarely, a and b) and to mark off the material to be transposed with square brackets. In a few instances, three elements are designated for transposition. The clear text reflects the transposed order; the original order is given (with Emerson's numbers or letters represented as superscript) in a textual note.

3. Misspelled words are corrected and the misspellings reported in the textual notes. Inconsistency in the use of British and American forms is not regularized. No attempt has been made to revise odd spellings when Emerson's version occurs in dictionaries of the period or when contemporary authority for it has been found in the *Oxford English Dictionary.*

4. Emerson's erratic punctuation has been altered in the few instances when it is likely to cause confusion. All such instances are recorded in the textual notes. All ambiguous instances in which *missing* punctuation has been supplied are recorded in the textual notes.

5. Words that Emerson accidentally omitted or that are illegible or lost through damage to the manuscript are supplied without editorial brackets in the clear text and the situation described in the textual notes. Accidentally doubled words (as well as a few deliberately used catchwords) are corrected and reported in the textual notes.

6. Notes by Emerson—either footnotes or parenthetical notes—that briefly identify the source of a quotation are given in the editor's explanatory footnotes, where they are identified as Emerson's; they do not otherwise appear in the text or textual notes. Emerson's notations of hymn and scripture selections, often appearing at the top of the first manuscript page, will be reported in tabular form as an appendix to the final volume of this edition. Emerson's notations concerning the date and place of delivery, irregularly given on the last manuscript page, are incorporated in the information supplied in the first explanatory footnote for each sermon as well as in the Chronology; they do not otherwise appear in the text or textual notes.

7. Emerson's use of square brackets is always reported in the textual notes (with curved brackets to distinguish them from editorial remarks), though they do not appear in the clear text. In addition to setting off the elements in a transposition, they are frequently used to identify the limits of an inserted passage. Emerson also used them to set off paragraphs or larger blocks of text, most likely to indicate that the portions thus bracketed could be omitted in a particular delivery. Emerson was not consistent in the form of his square brackets, and while we believe we have consistently been able to distinguish them from Emerson's parentheses, we have freely interpreted as square brackets a range of crooked and angled lines that manifestly serve the same function.

Editorial Annotations

Editorial annotations, which appear as footnotes to the text, have been kept to a minimum. For each sermon, the unnumbered first note supplies what is known about its composition and, drawing on Emerson's manuscript Preaching Record and notations on the sermon manuscript itself, information about when and where it was delivered. If substantial draft passages relating to the sermon exist in the *Journals and Miscellaneous Notebooks,* that fact is given in the first note; otherwise, the existence of briefer draft passages is indicated in the appropriate place in subsequent notes. Biblical and other allusions are identified in the numbered notes, as are Emerson's uses of sermon material in lectures and other later compositions.

Emerson's repetitions of the main Bible text in each sermon are not annotated. Phrases of common occurrence in the King James Version of the Bible, such as "the second death" and "the ends of the earth," for example, belong to Emerson's generally biblical rhetoric in the sermons and are not annotated. An effort has also been made to annotate passages that occur only in the textual notes, primarily to have as full a record as possible of Emerson's use of the Bible; these allusions have been included in the index along with the other annotations.

AN EMERSON CHRONOLOGY
October 1830 to November 1831

Note: When two sermons are listed as having been preached on a particular day, the first is the morning sermon, the second the afternoon sermon. A third sermon indicates a special Sunday evening service: he also delivered sermons for Thursday (or other weekday) lectures, Fast Days, Thanksgiving, and Christmas.

While Emerson (and others) often referred to Boston's Second Church as the "North Church" or the "Old North Church," it is here always identified as the Second Church. It should not be confused with another "Old North," the Anglican church associated with Paul Revere's ride; that church, which Emerson referred to as the "New North," was at this time led by Francis Parkman, father of the historian. Similarly, Nathaniel Frothingham's First Church was popularly known as "Chauncy (or Chauncey) Place"; to avoid confusion, it is regularly identified in the following Chronology as the First Church.

1830

Oct. 3	Preaches XC (Second Church).
Oct. 10	Preaches XCI (Second Church) and XLIII (King's Chapel).
Oct. 17	Emerson does not preach.
Oct. 24	Preaches XCII and XLVII (Second Church).
Oct. 29	Journal entry used in Sermon XCIII (*JMN* 3:204–5).
Oct. 31	Preaches XCIII (Second Church) and LXXXV (Purchase St.).
Nov. 7	Preaches LXXXI and XCIII (Dedham, for Mr. Lawson).
Nov. 13	Completes XCV.
Nov. 14	Preaches XCIII (West Church) and XCV (Second Church). In the evening Emerson and his brother Charles hear Edward Taylor preach at the Seamen's Bethel, Boston.
Nov. 20	Completes XCIV.
Nov. 21	Preaches XCIV (Second Church) and XCV (Roxbury, for Eliphalet Porter).
Nov. 26	Preaches XXXVII, Friday Lecture (Second Church).
Nov. 27	Writes to John Gorham Palfrey: "I have promised to preach Dr Tuckermans Chapel Lecture tomorrow evg. I am now unexpectedly called to the funeral of a parishioner after

service—& so all my time sine qua non, taken away. I am now writing a sermon for the morng & tis Communion so can you not do me the great favor to preach at the Chapel . . ." (*L* 7:195).

Nov. 28 Preaches XCVI (Second Church), XCV (Federal St.) and X (Friend St. Chapel).

Dec. 2 Thanksgiving; preaches XCVII (Second Church).

Dec. 5 Preaches XCV (New North) and XCVIII (Second Church).

Dec. 6 Journal passage on temptation, subject of Sermon XCIX (*JMN* 3:213).

Dec. 11 Completes XCIX.

Dec. 12 Preaches XCIX (Second Church). Ezra Ripley preaches for Emerson in the afternoon.

Dec. 19 Preaches XCV and LXXXI (Charlestown, for James Walker).

Dec. 21 "The value of Xty. must be shown . . . by showing the amt. of truth it has brought. I am raised by the reception of a great principle, to its height. And he who communicates, & applies, & embodies, a great principle for me, is my redeemer from the evil to which the want of it would have led me . . ." (*JMN* 3:216–17).

Dec. 22 Forefather's Day. "The Saint knows best the truth of Christianity. . . . When the earth shall be Christianized every hand will act for God, every tongue speak for him. Now it is diseased; it meets with obstructions of self every where" (*JMN* 3:217–18).

Dec. 23 Sees Sampson Reed, who says it is ten years since he had known the fear of death (*L* 1:315). Journal entry continues this period of heightened religious speculation (*JMN* 3: 218–19).

Dec. 26 Preaches C and XLIX (Second Church).

Dec. 31 Preaches CI (Second Church, Watch Night service).

1831

Jan. 1 Completes CII.

Jan. 2 Preaches CII (Second Church) and XCIII (New South).

Jan. 9 Preaches LXXXV (South Congregational Church, for Mellish Motte) and LIII (Second Church).

Jan. 12 Preaches CIV for the Howard Benevolent Society (Old South).

Jan. 16 The Preaching Record indicates a severe snowstorm in the morning—no morning sermon; preaches XVIII (Second Church) in the afternoon.

Jan. 23	Preaches CIII and CV (Second Church).
Jan. 30	Preaches CVI (Second Church), XCV (Twelfth Church), and CIII as the Evening Lecture in South End, Boston.
Jan. 31	"My poor Ellen has been sadly sick &, we flatter ourselves, is a little better." Emerson and his wife hope soon to go south, though perhaps not before March. Charles Chauncy Emerson "has stirred up an Indian indignation in Cambridge & the meeting is tonight. Ashmun & the Danas, &c to speak perhaps the young Tully himself. His health is not so robust as his mind" (*L* 1:317).
Feb. 3	Preaches XC, Thursday Lecture (First Church).
Feb. 5	In the morning Charles visits, and finds Ellen near death, "her husband & mother without any hope of her recovery— . . . Waldo . . . is bowed down under his affliction, but he says 'it is like nothing, but an angel taking her flight to Heaven'" (*L* 1:318n).
Feb. 6	Charles Follen preaches for Emerson at the Second Church in the morning; Nathaniel Langdon Frothingham in the afternoon.
Feb. 8	Ellen dies at 9 A.M.
Feb. 13	Emerson does not preach.
Feb. 19	Completes CVII.
Feb. 20	Preaches CVII (Second Church).
Feb. 26	Completes CVIII.
Feb. 27	Preaches CVIII (Second Church).
Mar. 1	Emerson speaks at the dedication of the newly completed Second Church Vestry.
Mar. 5	Completes CIX.
Mar. 6	Preaches CIX and LVI (Second Church).
Mar. 8	Delivers first Vestry Lecture.[1]
Mar. 13	Preaches LXIV (Second Church) and CVIII (West Church, for Charles Lowell).
Mar. 15	Delivers second Vestry Lecture (MS missing).
Mar. 20	Preaches XCIII (New North), CX (Second Church), and XVIII (Friend St. Chapel).
Mar. 22	Delivers third Vestry Lecture.
Mar. 25	Preaches LXXIII, Monthly Lecture (Second Church).
Mar. 27	Preaches CXI (Second Church) and CX (First Church).

1. The Vestry Lectures reveal Emerson's immersion in contemporary biblical scholarship in ways that the sermons do not, and are therefore important documents for students of Emerson's theology. See Karen Kalenevitch, "Turning from the Orthodox: Emerson's Gospel Lectures," in *Studies in the American Renaissance: 1986*, Joel Myerson, ed. (Charlottesville, Va., 1986), 69–112; and Kenneth Walter Cameron, ed., *The Vestry Lectures and a Rare Sermon* (Hartford, 1984), reprinted from Cameron's *Transcendental Epilogue* (Hartford, 1965-1982), 2:721–39.

Mar. 29	Delivers fourth Vestry Lecture.
Apr. 3	Preaches CXII and LIX (Second Church).
Apr. 4	"The days go by, griefs, & simpers, & sloth, & disappointments. The dead do not return, & sometimes we are negligent of their image. Not of yours Ellen—I know too well who is gone from me. And here come on the formal duties which are to be formally discharged, and in our sluggish minds no sentiment rises to quicken them . . ." (*JMN* 3:244). Writes out a sketch of Sermon CXIII, defending the institution of the Fast (*JMN* 3:244–46).
Apr. 5	Delivers fifth Vestry Lecture.
Apr. 7	Fast Day. Preaches Sermon CXIII (New North and Second Church).
Apr. 10	Preaches LXIV (Cambridge, First Parish) and CX (Brattle St.).
Apr. 12	Delivers sixth Vestry Lecture (MS missing).
Apr. 13	Goes to hear Nathaniel W. Taylor in the evening at the Revival meetings. "He wisely identified his cause with the conscience & so made us subscribe to almost all he said" (*L* 1:321).
Apr. 17	Preaches LXIV and XCV (North Church, Salem). Charles T. Brooks hears Emerson preach in John Brazer's pulpit, Old North Church, Salem, in the afternoon: "His sermon was characterized by an earnest, calm eloquence. His text was, 'For we must all appear before the judgment-seat of Christ,' which he makes out to be the Christian religion, whose principles ever condemn the wrong-doer" (See Charles W. Wendte, "A Memoir," in Charles T. Brooks, *Poems* . . . [Boston, 1885], 17).
Apr. 19	Delivers seventh Vestry Lecture (MS missing).
Apr. 24	Preaches CXIV and XLVIII (Second Church).
Apr. 26	Delivers eighth Vestry Lecture.
Apr. 30	*Christian Register:* "the Course of Sunday Evening Lectures, at Messrs Emerson's and Motte's churches, for the present season, is concluded" (*L* 1:320n).
May 1	Preaches CXV and LVIII (Second Church).
May 3	Delivers ninth and last Vestry Lecture.
May 7	Charles Emerson: "We went the other evening to hear Dr. McAulay of N.Y. address the Mass. Bible Society on the subject of supplying all the destitute portions of the U.S. with bibles. Chas. G. Loring, A. H. Everett, & Mr. Gannett spoke—t'was a very interesting meeting" (RWEMA).
May 8	Preaches LXXII (Second Church), CXV (Hollis St.), and CV (Friend St. Chapel).

May 15	Preaches CXVI, Part I (Second Church).
May 18	Attends Sunday School meeting, where the question was discussed whether the instruction should be altogether of a religious nature. Emerson apparently does not speak, but records his thoughts later (*JMN* 3:253–54).
May 22	Preaches CXV and XCIII (Framingham, First Parish).
May 25	Ezra Ripley comes to town from Concord for the Election week conference of liberal ministers at the Berry Street vestry (*L* 1:323n).
May 29	Preaches CXVI, Part II, and CXVII (Second Church). Samuel J. May delivers an antislavery lecture at the Second Church (7:30 P.M.).
May 30	Leaves with Charles Emerson on a trip to Vermont, taking the stage to Keene, N.H.
June 5	Preaches X and LXIV (Burlington, Vt., for Mr. Ingersoll). During their stay in Burlington, they are introduced to President Marsh, the disciple of Coleridge.
June 12	Preaches XCIII and XCV (Northampton).
June 14	Emerson and his brother travel from Northampton and arrive home in the evening.
June 18	Completes CXVIII.
June 19	Preaches CXVIII and XXXIX (Second Church).
June 24	Preaches LXXVIII, Friday Lecture (Second Church).
June 26	Preaches CXIX (Second Church) and CXVIII (New North Church).
June 30	Preaches LXXV, Thursday Lecture (Second Church).
July 3	Preaches LXXVII and CXX (Second Church).
July 10	Preaches CXVIII (Charlestown, for James Walker) and LIV (Second Church). About this time writes "Gnothi Sueton" (*JMN* 3:290–94).
July 17	Preaches CXXI (Second Church) and CXVIII (Purchase St.).
July 24	Preaches CXXI (First Church) and CXXII (Second Church).
July 31	Preaches CXXIII and LXXXV (Second Church).
Aug. 7	Preaches CXXI and CXVIII (Dover, N.H., for Hubbard Winslow).
Aug. 13	Completes CXXIV.
Aug. 14	Preaches CXXIV and LXXXI (Second Church).
Aug. 21	Preaches CXXI and XXXIII (West Cambridge).
Aug. 26	Preaches LXXXVII, Friday Lecture (Second Church). The Preaching Record indicates that Emerson lent the sermon to his brother Edward.
Aug. 28	Preaches CXXV (Second Church) and LXXXI (Friend St.).
Sept. 4	Preaches LXIII and XLI (Second Church).

Sept. 10   Completes CXXVI.

Sept. 11   Preaches CXXVI (Second Church) and CXXI (Charles-
                town, for James Walker).

Sept. 18   Preaches CXXVII (Second Church) and CXXI (New North).

Sept. 23   Preaches CXXVIII (First Church) on the anniversary of the
                Female Asylum. Charles Emerson: "This afternoon Waldo
                speaks to the Female Asylum. He is going to tell them how
                they ought to educate their charge.—that the accomplish-
                ments commonly taught children, are not education, but
                the means of education." He adds later: "Waldo preached
                very well—& announced to the worthy managers, the sol-
                emn declaration of Pestalozzi after years of devotion to the
                care of children—'that he had found that the amelioration
                of outward condition might be the effect, but could never
                be the cause of mental & moral improvement'" (RWEMA).

Sept. 25   Preaches CXXIX in the afternoon (Second Church). The
                Preaching Record shows that Mr. Hale took the pulpit in
                the morning.

Oct. 1   Completes CXXX.

Oct. 2   Preaches CXXX and CXXXI (Second Church).

Oct. 9   Preaches CXXI and CXVIII (Concord, Mass.).

Oct. 16   Preaches CXVIII (Hollis St.) and CXXXII (Second Church).
                The Preaching Record indicates that the Second Church
                proprietors adopted the new hymn book.

Oct. 23   Preaches LXXXIX (Second Church) and XCV (New South).

Oct. 28   Preaches LXXXII, Friday Evening Lecture (Second Church).

Oct. 30   Preaches CXXXIII (Second Church).

Oct. 31   Preaches CXXVIII as the Evening Lecture at Derry, N.H.,
                in the course of which he mentions having attended some
                of the exercises put on by the students (cf. *JMN* 3:303–4).

Nov. 4   "I sit Friday night & note the first thought that rises. Pres-
                ently another, presently five or six—of all these I take the
                mean, as the subject for Saturday's sermon [i.e., the one he
                writes on Saturday for Sunday]" (*JMN* 3:303).

Nov. 6   Preaches CXXXIV and LXXXVIII (Second Church) and
                XCIX (Friend St. Chapel).

Nov. 13   Preaches CXVIII and LXXXI (Waltham).

Nov. 17   Preaches CXXIV, Thursday Lecture (Second Church).

Nov. 20   Preaches CXXXV (Second Church); in the afternoon Charles
                Lowell preaches at the Second Church.

THE SERMONS

The God of hope fill you with all joy and hope in believing.

ROMANS 15:13

If the gospel of Christ did not commend itself to our reason by its inherent truth we could not in any proper sense be said to be Christians. The miracles which were wrought to show its divine origin might be placed on a basis of evidence so firm that we could no more doubt of their having been performed than we doubt the existence of the Red Sea and the town of Jerusalem. But if the doctrines which these miracles were wrought to attest, had been assertions of incomprehensible facts, of facts which we could neither affirm nor deny, the miracle could add nothing to our faith. It would puzzle and perplex us. The miracle could not be controverted. We should see plainly that power superior to ours existed in the Universe but we should see it without any pleasure. It is necessary to the making a miracle answer any worthy end, that the purpose of it should fall in with our own nature, that it should not come to prove any thing trifling or any thing indifferent, but to prove what by the structure of our being was dear and great, to prove what to enlarged knowledge would prove itself, not to contradict reason, but to add something which reason could not quite reach. I like very much the view of Lessing that revelation announces truths that are in the natural path of the human mind but in its present state of sin and ignorance beyond its reach, that the same announcement of truth may be a revelation to one mind and not to another which by its greater freedom from sin and its greater diligence in seeking truth has anticipated the progress of the general human mind.[1]

Now I wish to invite your attention to a view of religion which brings a very strong evidence of the truth of Christianity. It is in the manner in which religion administers consolation to human suffering.

Manuscript dated October 10, 1830, and February 26, 1832. Preached twice: October 10, 1830, at the Second Church, Boston, and February 26, 1832, again at the Second Church.

1. Emerson may have gleaned this information from Madame de Staël's *Germany,* which he was reading at the time and which draws on Lessing's "The Education of the Human Race" for a chapter on "Religion and Enthusiasm" in Germany. Emerson's statement here is a succinct expression of one theme Lessing argues in the piece. See Mme. de Staël, *Germany,* 3 vols. (London, 1813), 3:267–77, and "The Education of the Human Race," in *Lessing's Theological Writings,* trans. Henry Chadwick (Stanford, Ca., 1957), 82–98.

A message from heaven to man, we should naturally expect, would contain some provision for human misery. Man is born to trouble as the sparks to fly upward.[2] There is no individual, let his situation be ever so much distinguished by pleasing conditions, who has not some defect, some pain, in every one of his enjoyments. The uncertainty that always rests on all external ones is the greatest of defects becau..e the ..iore valuable they are, the more the uneasiness from this source increases. Society is never rested from the stories of disaster occa-
:d by human passions or by the evils of nature—of quarrels in families or between individuals, of hard times in trade, or fires on shore or storms at sea, of gross mistakes in government by which towns and states suffer, or the madness of parties, and the cruel persecutions of the few by the many, of loss of office, of loss of fame. And not only the outward and inward evils that touch man, but the decay and demolition of man himself. Sickness comes and cripples his bodily and mental faculties and takes him out of the pleasant action of life and the sense of successful exertion for his family, and shuts him up in his chamber and then almost shuts him out from those who stand around his bed, in the gloom and debility of dise? How shall he be comforted? Then death comes and all mortal hopes are defeated and the house full of social comfort and hope is lonely and the rooms are darkened and the face and the heart are yet darker. How shall they be comforted? I have looked into the New Testament to find what considerations of comfort it offered to sickness and death, and though itself a message of consolation to human wo, I find the direct notices of these things very few and abstemious, reserved. It does not address itself to these evils in the direct way of removing the evils but it overcomes them by a great indirection. To make this plainer. Human consolation, the solace that men are accustomed to offer each other, under any misfortune, is always founded upon the circumstances of the case. Thus it says to one man, you have lost your property, but with it you have lost the care of it, or here are such prospects opened for you as may help to redeem it. You have lost your friend, or your son, or your father, but if he had lived, you would have seen him suffer. You have lost your parent, but he has left you what he labored to procure for you, a plentiful estate, and you are master of your own liberty.

You are sick with a chronick malady but it does not threaten life, and it will secure you from other dangers and give you leisure that you have long desired.

This is the consolation men offer each oth   This is the inference of a mere worldly prudence, and this is the heighı ıo · hich false religion can go. The religion of Mahomet spoke in this manner to circumstances. It said to the poor soldier, If you die in the field you go at once to the lap of all sensual pleasure, to games, to gardens, to endless revellings. The paganism of the North of Europe said the same thing, reminding the barbarian that when he died he should enter on spacious hunting-fields where he should always triumph and drink from the

2. Job 5:7.

skulls of his enemies. And precisely of this character were the fables of the classic mythology.[3]

Now the gospel of Christ takes a wholly different course. It does not meddle with the circumstances; it does not promise any alleviations to them; it does not tell what rewards await you; it goes directly to considerations wholly *from* the case; it neglects the event and speaks to the human character, and says, I will give you principles. It says, Contemn the flesh, and walk by the Spirit, and you shall find rest to your souls.[4] It does not say, if you will believe, your friend who is sick shall revive, but it says, Believe and you shall be changed,[5] and all events shall be indifferent to you, all shall be well to you. Listen to the words of Jesus himself. He did not attempt to beguile his followers with any hope of joining their worldly interest to his cause. He did not say, I will help you to your livelihood—or Come join your work with my work, but he said, Let the dead bury their dead.[6] Forsake all. Hate father and mother and sister and brother, and come follow me[7]—i.e., Love them not as means of earthly good, but as gifts of God.

This still is the language which he addresses to the human race. They come to him at his command, the weary and heavy laden with all their burden of griefs and wants,[8] and ask for consolation. And what are the consolations he presents to them? He saith to them all, Love the Lord your God with all your heart,[9] that is to say, Let your affections receive a new principle of arrangement. Love God first, and supremely, and keep his commandments, and love yourself and your father, and wife, and brother, and sister *from* God, in a manner consistent with your love of him. Let all your worldly possessions be held, let all your powers be used, under the direction of this primal love.

This language was justified by all the life of Christ and all the life of his apostles. They never speak of poverty as a great evil,—they endured it always; they do not speak of sickness or death as a great evil,—their hearts were so transformed by the power of this great principle which they enforced, the over-ruling idea of God, that in sickness, in privation, in imprisonment, in stripes, at the stake, they felt only the joy of fulfilling his will, the uplifting assurance of his approbation. And death was the door through which they entered into life. Principles and not circumstances were their consolation. Their souls were moved upon by a power so vast, were awakened from the sleep of sensual life to a self-examination and self-respect so cheering, that circumstances were indifferent and the flattering promises of this world were broken cisterns which could hold no water,[10] and its riches were ashes, and its glory was shame, when compared

---

3. Emerson repeats an argument from Sermon XXXVII (*Sermons* 1:286).
4. Cf. Romans 8:1, Galatians 5:16, and Matthew 11:29.
5. Cf. Acts 16:31 and I Corinthians 15:51–52.
6. Luke 9:60.
7. Luke 14:26.
8. Cf. Matthew 11:28.
9. Matthew 22:37, Mark 12:30, and Luke 10:27.
10. Jeremiah 2:13.

with the everlasting light that was just breaking on the human mind in the distinct revelation of immortality granted to the soul by its nature as the child of God.

The sum of this distinction then between the voice of man and of God, between the false religions and Christianity, is briefly this. They attempted to alleviate suffering by mending the circumstances of the sufferer, his character remaining the same. True religion proposes to change his character without any attention to the circumstances. This too is the explanation of all that stern language which our Saviour uses: I bring not peace, but a sword; I bring denial, crosses to the outward man, joy and peace to the soul.[11]

Is not this lofty and uncompromising tone taken by our Saviour and his apostles, which is at once so superior to the temporizing spirit of false religion and so in unison with the best state of the human soul which it has itself developed, is it not a very high evidence of the divine origin of the religion itself? This it is which places the teachers of the gospel above all suspicion of sinister motives, and this which gives that severe and holy dignity to the spirit of the New Testament above all other history and all other philosophy.

Let me add one or two practical reflexions.

1. What is this consolation which is got from loving God? It is not to be got by the world's giving us its pleasures in reward for our goodness. It is distinctly declared to be a peace which the world cannot give nor take away.[12] It is the health of the Soul. Happiness is the sense of well being that results from the soul's health, and there only can all its faculties revolve in their orbit and every inclination keep its place when God is in the centre of the system, the source of light and motion to all. It is the keeping of his commandments which is effect and cause of his love. It is the unfailing observance of right, the perpetual obedience to the feeling of Duty from the highest action down to the least, the continual recognition of the presence of God—down to the least. It is simply a more perfect mind. God would declare to us what, no doubt, sounds rather harshly in the ears of the flesh. The greatest possible good I can confer upon you is to make you better. The greatest blessing your obedience ensures to you is more perfect obedience. For as God made the Universe, so he makes it forever. As he formed our spirits at first, so is he the life of them always, and true health and true worship consist in a perpetual acknowledgment that we exist by him and from him. Then our faculties, then our thoughts and actions, assume at once their right place. Confusion gives way to order, and the pleasures of sin to the pleasures of virtue.

2. We are here provided with a measure of our own advancement in the church of Christ. Have you any of the objects of earthly regard? Have you house, lands, office, and plenty? Does it seem to you that in the event of their entire loss your whole means of happiness would be taken away? Then you have

11. Matthew 10:34; II Corinthians 4:16; Romans 14:17 and 15:13.
12. Cf. John 14:27.

made small proficiency in the kingdom of heaven. You have not yet known the true springs of spiritual comfort. You have not explored yourself. You have not understood the power and the love of God. You have not understood that all the worth of man is inward. You have faculties that you have never used.[13] There is much meaning in the Bible that has not yet dawned on your mind. Your soul is now a child, but it is capable of being trained into a being so great that all earthly shows and goods shall shrink by its side. Nor have you learned to regard those whom you love, husband, wife, children, father, mother, with the highest kind of love if their death will destroy your peace. The love of them must combine with the love of God; they must be to you in all the comfort they give you here the tokens only of God's kindness, their graces and virtues the faint types of God's perfections, that when they depart, you may feel they are not wholly gone, that when the earth shall claim its dust, the connexions of affection and virtue shall not cease, but shall revive and strengthen and be glorified—in the presence of God.

13. Cf. "'He that contemns &c has faculties which he has never used'" (*JMN* 3:167). See also Sermon LXXXII (*Sermons* 2:225). In both instances, the quotation appears without attribution.

XCII

We are of God. . . . Hereby know we the spirit of truth and the spirit of error.

I JOHN 4:6

It is much to be lamented that so much falsehood has corrupted the history of true religion in the world. Every lie is mischievous. When the old philosopher was asked what advantage could result to a man from falsehood, he answered, Not to be believed when he speaks the truth. The extreme dignity and importance of Christianity to us makes any discredit that attaches to it from this source a very serious calamity to mankind. The foolish exaggeration in which its defenders have often indulged in its praise has been so much dispraise, and this in two ways; first, by discrediting that which was true; and secondly, because every addition, however well meant, that is made to truth, is a deformity. They who have adventured it might have believed that God works better than man, and that every exaggeration will be less good than the truth. By these falsehoods, many wise and good men who should have been the warmest friends of the Christian faith have been filled with doubt and coldness towards it. And whatever defects beget distrust in minds distinguished for their endowments produce the same impression upon every man in proportion to what independence and discernment is in his mind.

We ought to feel that interest in religion which should lead us to examine, every one for himself, the grounds of our faith, and to make our faith practical and precious to us by a careful separation and rejection of all but the truth.

There are some respects in which Christianity is much misunderstood by those who love and honour it and whose life is guided by its light. No such misapprehension I conceive can be held without diminishing the value of the revelation to the soul and diminishing the strength of its faith to precisely the same degree. For I believe that the effectual faith of any mind in Revelation will be exactly measured by the excellence it perceives in it.

It has for ages been thought that there is some hostility between reason and faith. Many things are to be received which are not to be understood. I mean that Christianity teaches many things which we are not only not capable of

---

Manuscript dated October 24, 1830. Preached twice: October 24, 1830, at the Second Church, Boston, and February 18, 1838, in East Lexington.

comprehending, but that are contradictory to our reason. A false distinction has been set up that there is a justice in the mind of God which differs from justice in the mind of man, and that where this contradiction appears, it were irreverent in us to uphold our opinion against the Divine Will. We may flatter ourselves perhaps with having in some degree escaped from these errors, yet a portion of this darkness still rests on many minds.

There are to a great extent two common prejudices with regard to Christianity: that the morality of the gospel is something different in kind from the morality of heathens, and secondly that there is an influence unfavorable to freedom of thought, an inculcation of blind faith in the New Testament, which represses the speculation which is the dearest privilege of every active and virtuous mind. I wish to offer a few remarks upon both these prejudices.

I. The zeal with which Christianity has been defended has led to an undue contempt of pagan virtue, to exaggerations of human depravity without the light of the gospel.[1] Friends to revelation, men have been foes to reason, and seem to imagine that the nature of man is one thing and God's endowment of it another, instead of noticing that the gifts man has now received are as much in his nature as the gifts to which they were added. No one can look much into the history of Christianity without being struck with this disposition to depreciate the moral science of the heathen nations, ancient or modern, as if to show that human reason never could discover what revelation has disclosed. And this is not only in the formal discussions of divines, but something like this unfairness may be continually observed in conversation. There is an uneasiness felt if you extol the height to which the ancient philosophers carried the practice of virtue, as if you would say something derogatory to Christianity.

Now this surely is a way of thinking altogether unworthy of the nobleness of a Christian heart. It has the air at once of a jealousy of the goodness of others and of a dishonour to God's Providence. Is any thing gained by depreciating our reason? Is not one God the author of reason and of revelation? The best, the indispensable evidence of revelation is its entire agreement with reason. The perfection of the gospel is not one thing and the perfection of the human mind another,—but the gospel is only a confirmation and fuller disclosure of that which was already trembling on the tongues, and glowing in the hearts of the truly wise. There are no precepts in the gospel which the reason of man cannot receive and which are to be carried down by the awful authority alone of God exhibited in miracles. But the whole credit of the New Testament lies in the unexampled force of its addresses to the conscience, that is, the moral reason of man. It teaches nothing which any wise and good heathen would disapprove, but, on the contrary, what they would eagerly accept.

I would therefore look at the administration of God in a more becoming and just view. I would look at all virtue as his holy Cause, the same eternal nature, wherever in the universe its force is felt, flowing directly from him as its cause. I

1. Cf. II Corinthians 4:4.

would hail every intimation of sincere goodness, every clear perception of truth, every approach to the knowledge of Him, as imperfect revelations, as imperfect Christianity, whether in the garden of Eden in the beginnings of civilization, or in the better instructed communities of modern ages. I would feel that every where I was in my Father's house—among my brethren—and hail with affectionate interest every dim gleam of the light of nature, every step of progress in philosophy, every redeeming trait in the bloody history of savage nations, as a spark of God which might yet kindle to a flame that should light the world. I would be very jealous for my brother man that he should not be confounded with the beasts of the field. And I think the harshness of our judgments indicates a want of religion in our own souls. We are not yet so imbued with the spirit of Christ as to hold the human soul and every ray of truth and goodness in it in that anxious love that is due to them. When we are more Christians, we shall honour the poor pagans more. We have now too much of that Judaical spirit of exclusion which Jesus so often reproved, which he glanced at when he said to the Syro-Phenician woman, I have not found so great faith in Israel as in thee.² We have that Judaical spirit from which Peter was not yet redeemed when he said, Lord I cannot eat meats which thou givest me that are common and unclean, and from which he was redeemed when he said, I perceive that God is no respecter of persons, but in every nation he that feareth him, and worketh righteousness, is accepted with him.³

More than this, I think, brethren, that we should be more likely to honour our Christian profession if we would look a little into the lives and instructions of some of the old heathen Stoics. We should there find the picture of a life which would shame the common life we lead ourselves. It would reveal to us a most important truth, that the whole value of Christianity to us is prospective; that in time past whilst we have rested in its accidental advantages, it has not made us such good men as many heathens; that its superiority can only be shown by the adoption of its rules in practice, by living on earth with our Father in heaven. Certainly it is to our tempted and afflicted nature a far more suitable dependence and instructer than the purest precepts of ancient philosophy. For that was proud and this is humble; that taught men to rest on themselves, this makes love the great principle of action and leads them to God that we may lean with entire confidence upon the Infinite being and that we may feel our relation of kindness and usefulness to every being he has made.

It labored to overcome the world without, but it had no succor in its humility—no reference to God's strength. Who is he that overcometh the world but he that believeth that Jesus is the Son of God.⁴ One spoke only of the present time; the other by exercising all the highest parts of our nature awakens in the

2. The encounter between Jesus and the Syro-Phenician woman is recorded in Mark 7:25-30; however, the remark by Jesus that Emerson quotes here actually belongs to the exchange between Jesus and the centurion in Matthew 8:5-10.

3. Acts 10:14 and 10:34-35.

4. I John 5:5.

soul the belief of its relations to all the future. The Stoic was the forerunner of the Christian. And we ought to thank God for the new truth he has shown us and for the old truth to which it was added.

II. The second error which I notice and one more common and more injurious is the idea that Christianity is unfriendly to freedom of thought. There are a multitude of passages in the New Testament which rather point the way to truth than fully show it. The discourses of our Lord were for the most part addressed to persons whose ignorance of religion was so gross that perhaps he felt it was sufficient only to introduce them within the doors of the spiritual world. And perhaps he felt it to be more the way of God to supply man only with the rudiments, the seeds of truth, and let him plant and water and raise them to their fruit for himself, than to do all for him.[5]

Whatever the cause may be, the fact is manifest, that there is foundation in the gospel for every noble and delightful hope, and yet very little clear detailed explanation of those truths most interesting to men, as the nature and mode of existence of God, the condition and employments of the soul in the future state.

Now when Christianity has been in the world two thousand years, and the human mind, grown up under its cultivation, begins to follow out these questions suggested in the gospel, explores itself, and pursues every intimation of God's will and purposes, with pious hope and gratitude,—it is continually rebuked with admonitions of the sufficiency of the scriptures, of the danger of being wise beyond what is written, of the fallibility of human judgment, and other perversions of good texts and good sense.

Now this I consider a mischievous misapprehension of God's word. It is, I am afraid, very much misunderstood, as condemning *opinions;* I understand it only as condemning *sins.* It is, I believe, in all its spirit adverse to the hoodwinking of the mind. It is the only religion in history which has not inculcated a blind reception of its dogmas. But faith, faith it is said every where is inculcated. The apostles use this word as we would say, The power of Christianity, and not surely as a subscription to articles. It does not hold a man to any creed. I think any serious person who attends to the instructions of Jesus will become convinced that so far from insisting on certain speculative doctrines as essential to salvation, a man who faithfully acted upon the principles of the Christian religion would feel it his duty to refuse any doctrine which stood on mere authority. Let it be supposed that in any case he is clearly of opinion that St. Peter or St. Paul is mistaken, and positively lays down a false doctrine, the faith he follows has educated him, I say, to reject that doctrine. For he has been taught that with the heart only man believeth unto righteousness; that all his thoughts are known to God; that of them he is to render an account; that the pure in heart shall see God; that such as love the truth are free indeed, and dwell with Him; and that all liars and hypocrites and whatsoever loveth and maketh a lie are estranged from him; that we are spiritual; that whatsoever spirit of fear holdeth

5. Cf. Matthew 13:18–23 and I Corinthians 3:6–8.

us is not of God.[6] Now what is the direct tendency of these and a multitude of similar passages in the New Testament and whose truth we feel the assurance in our souls proportioned to the cultivation we have bestowed on our moral character,—What is the stress of all but this, that a man must walk before God in perfect singleness of heart, a thing not to be done by him who out of a spirit of fear holds a doctrine which he thinks impossible.

Let me state a simple consequence which, if we would weigh it well, would go far to stablish our minds in our faith that the gospel came from God, but not this interpretation of it. It is that this belief that the mind was not free but must receive willing or unwilling a system of doctrines straitly joined together from age to age—has produced all this bitter controversy betwixt church and church, between disciple and disciple, from the separation of Paul and Barnabas down to this day.[7] But the reception of the gospel as condemning our sins where it has been so received has never caused one injurious word, one hard thought of our neighbor, one criminal action, but love, penitence, and martyrdom instead, and if it always had been received would have entirely checked the evil influences of the first opinion.

I have offered these considerations to show that Christianity doth to its whole extent cherish virtue wherever it appears and doth cherish the freedom of the mind; that it hath no hostility to our moral nature on the one hand nor to our intellectual nature on the other, but doth give to both the most hearty and effectual support. The more faithfully it is obeyed, the more noble do our views of our nature and destiny become; and wherever degrading views are held of man, and any goodness is spoken of with disrespect, or any doctrines are taught which man cannot understand, there I am afraid the law is not practised which said, Love the Lord thy God with all thy heart and thy neighbor as thyself.[8]

Let us then accept it, brethren, not in outward profession only, but in that inward mind which shall implicitly obey its laws and live in its hope and work in its love and so open the kingdom of heaven in our own souls.

---

6. Romans 10:10; Psalms 94:11; Matthew 12:36, Romans 14:12; Matthew 5:8; John 8:32, 8:36; John 8:44–47, Revelation 22:15; II Timothy 1:7.

7. For the account of the separation of Paul and Barnabas, see Acts 15:36–41.

8. Matthew 22:37–39, Mark 12:30–31, and Luke 10:27.

XCIII

The kingdom of God cometh not by observation:
neither shall they say lo here or lo there
for behold the kingdom of God is within you.

Luke 17:20-21

The prominent fact presented in the New Testament is this; that, man hath a spiritual nature superior to his animal life and superior to his intellectual powers and comprehending them—which in the past state of the world has been neglected but which deserves his supreme attention and which Jesus came to establish in its rights. This plain truth is the key to all his discourses. The distinction he constantly draws is between the flesh and the spirit; between the light of the body and truth, the light of the mind; between bread and the bread of life; water and the water of life; between animal life and spiritual life; the power of this world, as, the Empire of Rome, the kingdom of Judea, and the kingdom of heaven; or, in another sense, the power of appetite and earthly passions over the mind of man, which he calls the kingdom of darkness and of Satan, and the power of truth and goodness, which in a phrase equally metaphorical is called the kingdom of heaven.[1]

It is the nature of the human mind to receive knowledge slowly, not to pass suddenly from ignorance to wisdom, but to intermix the first rays of truth which it receives with its own familiar errors. And Jesus seems always to have felt that what he said was very imperfectly comprehended by most of those who heard him, and he repeatedly declares to his disciples that a fuller understanding of his sayings awaits them, when a longer career of sincere devotion shall open their minds to the use of the truth.[2]

Manuscript dated October 31, 1830, and April 22, 1832. Preached ten times: October 31, 1830, at the Second Church, Boston; November 7 in Dedham; November 14 at the West Church, Boston; January 2, 1831, at the New South Church; March 20 at the New North Church; May 22 at the First Parish Church, Framingham; June 12 in Northampton; April 22, 1832, at the Second Church, Boston; April 19, 1835, in Acton; and September 4, 1836, in East Lexington. In *JMN* 3:205 Emerson summarized a theme treated "at large in Serm. 93": "Can it be . . . that there should not be a retribution to our actions if . . . our nature is single, & feels throughout the condition of every part?"

1. Cf. John 3:6; Matthew 6:22 and Luke 11:34; John 6:35; John 4:10-14; Mark 12:17; Matthew 12:25-26 and Luke 22:53.

2. Cf. John 16:12-13.

But it was hardly within the expectation of his faithful friends that they should sleep in the ground, that ages should roll away, and the doctrine he taught, should become honoured throughout the world, and yet the same ignorance which darkened their minds should darken ours, the same causes should operate to shut our eyes, lest we should see, and our ears, lest we should hear, and our hearts lest we should understand, and be converted, and God should heal us.[3]

Yet this has happened, and in the midst of the Christian Church the command is still as imperative as it was when it was given to preach the glad tidings of redemption, of salvation, of eternal life.[4]

For the doctrine is still a strange thing to our ears. This, its main distinction, that of being a *spiritual* faith, is very slowly received by us. For to measure the real power of the gospel in the world, ascertain what reception that great hope has found which it upholds to the obedient: i.e., let the reception of that hope be the measure of the reception of the gospel. Let any intelligent person ask himself, how many men understand the true nature of the future happiness promised by the gospel? Who knows what *the kingdom of heaven* means? Yet who can doubt that it will explain itself,—be known for what it is, as we enter it? To how few minds in any age, to how few minds in our age, is not this word a dark saying—"The kingdom of God is within you"? And the darkness that rests upon it condemns therefore tardy progress in the faith of Christ.

We are guessing at future things after the way of the world, instead of using that telescope which a practical Christian faith will give us. We do indeed believe partially, and I may say interruptedly in the immortality of the soul; and the kingdom of heaven we usually refer beyond the grave. But examine the common idea of heaven and of hell that prevails in Christendom, and you find we are looking for the state of the dead in a palace or in a prison, and it is the imagination instead of the heart that describes it to us. Certainly, my friends, he that receives the account of the vision of St. John in the Apocalypse as a literal description of heaven has been betrayed into the same error as the Jews who surrounded Jesus and whom he so often cautioned that his kingdom was not of this world.[5] Though we call it *spiritual,* because we refer it to the soul after death, yet it is substantially *carnal,* because it is an image of external goods, an image of thrones, and splendor, of bodily rest, and freedom from inconvenience and want.

There are many who disclaim such views with great warmth as puerile, who do not yet hold any that can be clearly distinguished from them; who think that heaven does not consist in bright light and sweet sound, yet if they push their speculations farther than the name, they hold out the idea that God shall yet add to them great gifts, (they do not promise themselves any thing very desir-

3. Matthew 13:15.
4. Luke 8:1.
5. Revelation 4 and John 18:36.

able, for they have no eagerness to go thither) but God, they think, will give them what they shall enjoy—It is, in every idea, something not now possessed, to come from God, something beyond virtue, to be the reward of virtue, something else than the love of God which is to crown that love—and this I conceive to be the essence of the mistake. I think Christ saith to all such expectations, "Some shall say, lo here! lo there! but the kingdom of God is within you." He teaches us that it is not something God shall give us but something God has given us power to do for ourselves. He teaches us that the kingdom of God is not meat and drink, but righteousness and peace and joy of the holy Ghost.[6] The whole emphasis of the New Testament is on this thought, that not in power, or pleasure, or place, or company,—not in any thing *external,* whether in this world or the same things referred to a future world, does heaven reside, but wholly in the character, and in that alone.

When will men wake to the belief that the *love of God*—an emotion whose name is familiar to us, but whose meaning is only dimly suspected by most minds, and which can only exist in a mind full of love to men,—and *virtue,* which is the keeping of his commandments;—that these are heaven, these and nothing more than these, according to the sublime saying of the Eastern moralist, "O Lord! what has thou left to the wicked? for thou hast given all things to the good, in making them good."[7]

There are nevertheless many illustrations of this great truth within our daily experience. Let me ask your attention to a few of those facts that go to show us that we should not look for our weal or woe beyond ourselves.

And first it may be noted that a man's improvement is by the development of his own mind. Our improvement is from within not from without. Each mind has its own laws and agrees with itself.

It has been observed that all the parts of a man's character have a common likeness so as to distinguish any action done by him from a similar action done by another. All his views are of a piece. If he is an ardent lover of freedom of conscience, he will probably be found not to have narrow speculative views of religion, he will be found to be a defender of a free press, of free principles in trade. On the contrary is he a bigot? he will also contract his views of education and of politics. This will be the case with a man's general opinions where interest does not bias him to either side. Now because of this great principle of association which binds together all his knowledge, the improvement that is made in any one part of his mind by the acquisition of any new information, is felt in every other part, as the light that shines on one object illuminates all parts of the room.

A man's daily occupation commonly furnishes his mind, and then his conversation, with those observations upon the general laws of things which make his

6. Romans 14:17.

7. *The Gulistan, or Flower-Garden of Shaikh Sadi of Shiraz,* trans. James Ross (London, 1823), 470. See *JMN* 9:39 and Sermon CII, n. 7.

most valuable convictions, and the more natural wisdom he may get from increase of skill or invention or extension of the processes of his business, the more will the spiritual wisdom which he gathers from it be augmented.

In the next place, you may observe that not only his ways of thinking but his motives of action are alike. You will commonly find about the same level in his actions. He does not today astonish you with his magnanimity, and tomorrow with his meanness. If you observe violent contrasts, it is probably because you do not see him near enough. If you come nearer and learn his ruling passion you will see that all these are natural results. You find that his unexpected generosity proceeded only from a little more extended calculation, if he is mean, or his apparent meanness from some hidden circumstances, if he is habitually charitable.

In these facts you may see that each mind has its own laws and must be benefitted, if at all, only through its own action. The mind of Luther does not thrive on the same nutriment as the mind of Calvin; the mind of Erasmus unfolds in a manner different from either. Outward events may furnish the occasion of its action, as the earth may give food and moisture to the seed, but the earth may be moist and rich a thousand years to no purpose unless the seed have life in itself and can send down its radicle to draw nourishment out of it. So all the stores of knowledge and enjoyment may be presented to the soul in vain unless by its own inward health it can draw happiness from them.

The next thing to be considered is that the state of mind is always agreeable or painful according to the moral character of the feelings we indulge. You hear a man in his conversation continually suggesting sinister motives for the actions of other men. He sneers at their weakness; he sneers at their goodness. Do you think he has an equal serenity of mind with Fenelon and Paley?[8] You have heard of a murderer whom the law could not convict. Did he walk in his impunity with the peace and cheerfulness of a man over whom religious principle has great power? On the contrary, every vice hath its sting. An ungovernable ambition is a raging fever. An army of mortifications attends it. What is more deplorable—what is more speedily punished—than lust? Avarice is a self tormentor. If we are selfish, envious, suspicious, revengeful, we are inevitably unhappy. And all external luxuries, the sweetest meats, the softest couch, the rarest music, will be only poison and thorns and strife to our depraved and sick perceptions. But courage and benevolence and magnanimity are happiness. Certainly it presents a far more lively image of heaven to say of a man that he forgave his mortal enemy and eagerly rendered him very important services, than to say that he was very glad. Certainly we come nearer to describing the state of an angel with God, when we say that a man tenderly loves his friends and lives to be their benefactor, than when we say that he was rich or healthy or learned.

A sincere love for the truth, a willingness to follow it meekly but firmly

8. François de Salignac de La Mothe-Fénelon (1651-1715), Archbishop of Cambray and author of *Télémaque,* supported the liberalization of women's education and the Semiquietist movement in France. William Paley (1743-1805), English theologian, utilitarian philosopher, and author of *Natural Theology* and *The Principles of Moral and Political Philosophy.*

wherever it may lead us, indicates a health of soul which is a guarantee of its well-being. Such a mind must be cheerful, for it is delivered from all the torment of fear. Such a mind will make progress, where progress is possible. And above all these, yet in close coincidence with all, the entire reference of the whole soul to the disposal of the great and good being who made us; the acceptance of all events with thanks as his choice for us; the sentiment, 'Thy Will be done'[9] carried out into every thought that passes unexpressed over the face of the mind, supplies an idea of well being for which happiness is a feeble name.

Well then, brethren, if thus all our intellectual powers are joined together, part with part, and all our moral powers, so that the whole man advances or recedes together; and if every good feeling is connected with its own joy, and every bad one with its pain, is there not plainly a strict retribution conjoined to all action? May we not receive literally our Saviour's doctrine, that God's kingdom, which flesh and blood, or the thoughts and wishes that belong to flesh and blood, cannot inherit, which the unrighteous, the extortioner, the liar, the whoremonger, the murderer, cannot inherit, is within us, is the state of holiness itself, and has no other happiness and asks no other than flows from the indulgence of its own majestic thoughts?[10] It is not to go abroad and seek God; God will come and dwell with those who truly do his will.[11] Blessed are the poor in spirit for theirs is the kingdom of heaven.[12] There is no heaven so high and glorious as a mind dedicated without any reserve to the love of God—to all the truth which is his nature and all the goodness which he imparts. There is no hell so deep and dark as the misery of a human spirit which wholly hates what is good, which hates his brother, and hates God; a soul that is lost.

Certainly it is not to be lost sight of that the event of death does operate a most essential and unknown change on our condition, and we cannot with the scanty light which has been furnished us speak with any positiveness of the mode of our future being. We naturally look forward to great facilities of action and of knowledge when we lose the incumbrance of the flesh. But this circumstance ought not diminish our confidence in the eternity of spiritual distinctions and in the fact that our condition will always be determined by our character.

I think the consideration of this subject of the greatest practical importance because it tends to undeceive us of all dangerous errors. The true doctrine as Christ taught it can only be received by each mind in proportion as it becomes virtuous, in proportion as the great work of regeneration goes on within it.— Only as far as we are good, can we know what heaven is. It is spiritual and must be spiritually discerned.[13] But whilst, on one hand, this truth opens wide the gates of happiness to every moral agent God hath made,—excluding not one,—

9. Matthew 6:9 and Luke 11:2.
10. Cf. I Corinthians 6:9-10.
11. Cf. Romans 8:5-11.
12. Matthew 5:3.
13. Cf. I Corinthians 2:14.

on the other hand, it cuts up by the roots every vain hope that God will have mercy on them who have no mercy on themselves. If heaven was a place, bad men might go there; but since heaven is goodness and the inseparable effects of goodness, there can be no hope but for repentance and reformation and justice and self-denial and love.

I wish, brethren, we might all be induced to read the gospel of St. John, where our Saviour's discourses are most fully recorded, with a constant effort to apply the phrase 'kingdom of God,' and 'kingdom of heaven,' to the state of the soul. It would, as is the effect of all truth, confirm and clear our convictions of the truth of Christianity. It would increase our trust in the world of peace and power and joy it has yet to reveal to us.

Wherefore, brethren, since we live by the spirit let us walk by the spirit.[14] Let us, in the clear view that the pure in heart now behold God,[15] and that heaven is begun wherever virtue is begun, let us see to it that every day and every hour we make some progress therein, that we help one another by the way, that every day we enter by the force of good purpose and good habit into interior mansions of the spiritual house of God.[16] Then when thy corruptible puts on incorruption,[17] when not only we are fitted for the society of the good but united to the society and restored to the blessed spirits of our friends departed from the earth, shall we ask any other good than the indulgence of our affections and the use of our immortal faculties.

14. Romans 8:1 and 8:4.
15. Matthew 5:8.
16. Cf. John 14:2.
17. Cf. I Corinthians 15:53.

He took part of the same (flesh and blood)
that through death he might destroy him that
had the power of death, that is, the devil,
and deliver them who through fear of death
were all their lifetime subject to bondage.

HEBREWS 2:14–15

The fear of death, which the Scriptures were written to remove, always throws a gloom over the mind that is not confirmed in its religious hope. The fear of death comes to him who builds a house, and makes its apartments gloomy to him by the thought that he builds for those who know him not, that truly social life shall rejoice within its walls, the board shall be duly covered, domestic cares shall please, they shall marry and be given in marriage,[1] children shall be born, their minds shall be trained, they shall be sent out of these doors to school and to play, and to youthful adventures—but to all this hum of life he shall be indifferent; he shall be dead in his place; his friends shall be laid beside him and strangers shall stand on his hearth stone.

The fear of death presents itself to him who heaps up wealth, who goes up and down on his affairs all day, and half the night, and denies himself meat and sleep,—when after many years of thrift he begins to reckon his interest, and to ask himself whether he has not enough, he sighs to think that life has been wasting whilst he has been preparing to live, and that a day which cannot be very far off will make him even with the beggar at his door. Naked came he out of his mother's womb and naked must he return to the earth.[2]

The fear of death comes to the Scholar when he surveys with newly awakened curiosity the vast region of knowledge, doubting where to begin and what to

---

Manuscript dated November 20, 1830; May 20, 1832; and November 17, 1833. Preached eleven times: November 21, 1830, at the Second Church, Boston; November 17, 1833, in New Bedford; June 8, 1834, at the Hollis Street Church; July 27 in Bangor, Maine; August 24 in Waltham; August 9, 1835, in Chelmsford; August 16 in Acton; August 23 in Lowell; January 31, 1836, in East Lexington; July 10 in Concord, Mass.; and November 20 in Weston. Notes and draft passages for this sermon occur in *JMN* 3:205–7.

1. Cf. Luke 20:34.
2. Job 1:21.

hope to accomplish, and fills him with gloom at the thought that he must read today, and read fast, for his study hours are already numbered, and few as they are will be subject to a thousand interruptions.

The fear of death comes to the sick man in every new symptom of his disease, and makes his face sad, and sends him on long journeys to escape from that which travels as fast as he by land and by water, and teaches him in warmer climates he has only come so far to seek a grave, which with better heart he could have found at home.

The fear of death is before the young and discourages them; and makes them diffident of their strength and shake in their purposes. It is a perpetual reproof to the mature, and gives a sour taste to every enjoyment. It is the age of the aged and gives new bitterness to every infirmity. It is the infirmity of the infirm. It touches us all. It checks our courage, it limits our plans. It tames our pride. It withers beauty, it saps strength. It threatens the intellect. And thus through fear of death we are all our lifetime subject to bondage.

Is not this a manifest defect in man? Surely he cannot boast to be sufficient unto himself whilst this capital evil—out of himself—murders his happiness. Whilst this sword hangs over him, nothing can be more absurd than his pretensions to an angelic or godlike condition.

Let us inquire, my friends, whether the fear of death can be overcome—whether Christianity has at all removed the yoke of this fear from the necks of men. And what we ought to do to redeem ourselves from it.

It has been said by Lord Bacon that there is no passion in the mind of man so weak, but it mates and masters the fear of death—revenge, love, honour, grief, fear, pity even, and niceness and satiety have continually prevailed over it.[3]

And we know that some men of no elevation of mind live in constant exposure to it without loss of cheerfulness. The savage in his woods meets death with no more complaint than the wolf. The sailor flies in its face every week and the soldier will march up against blazing artillery without emotion; and without the elevation that sometimes enters into these persons, we know that very ignorant men and women are dying every day with almost no exhibition of alarm.

Now when courage of this sort is spoken of, it ought to be distinguished from a higher kind. It has been observed that there are two kinds of ignorance; a childish ignorance before any knowledge has been got, and a learned ignorance which is the conclusion at which we arrive after years of study, that we can fully know nothing. So are there two kinds of courage or absence of fear, one merely passive and animal, proceeding from want of thought; and one wholly moral, proceeding from a conscious superiority to the cause of danger

---

3. Cf. "It is worthy the observing, that there is no passion in the mind of man so weak, but it mates and masters the fear of death; and therefore death is no such terrible enemy when a man hath so many attendants about him that can win the combat of him. Revenge triumphs over death; Love slights it; Honour aspireth to it; Grief flieth to it; Fear pre-occupateth it." See Bacon, "Of Death," *The Works of Francis Bacon,* ed. James Spedding et al. (London, 1857-1874), 6:379-80.

when it is fully known. The fear of death in every mind seems to consist in the doubt whether this being will not stop—an insufficient faith—the gloomy apprehension of annihilation;—the sun indeed will shine, and the universe resound as before with the melodies of joy, but we shall have no part in all that is done therein. The removal of this doubt, the acquisition of a perfect faith, is the only solid foundation for courage in the prospect of death. There is no thoughtful mind that would not overcome all other uneasiness if fully assured of this.

In the cases abovementioned, the indifference to death is not, I apprehend, a conquest of the fear, but a setting it aside. It is want of thought. It is not the victory over death promised to the Christian, but an inconsiderateness of the event of death, through a dogged attention to the facts immediately under the eye.

This unenviable courage is so far from being an excellence, that the first degrees of cultivation will probably weaken it. Those men who pay the most attention to the cultivation of their minds are apt to discover the most solicitude on this subject. A lively apprehension or a settled gloom joins itself in their minds to this thought. And the more delicate the structure of the mind, the stronger in general will this emotion become. Men of the finest genius have suffered the most from this cause.

Now this certainly deserves attention.

How should this be, that persons who have cultivated their minds, that is,— made some proficiency in spiritual life, should be more than others subject to this grievous bondage?

I conceive there are two reasons for it, *first,* because such persons, in losing life, have more to lose than others; and, *secondly,* because they are not yet spiritual enough to overcome the fear.

I. Certainly he who has learned that there is a richer pleasure in conversation, in reading, in meditation, in virtue, in prayer, than any the senses can furnish him, has made life more to him than it was before. Represent to your mind the soul of a man who once found all his gratification in dress and the pleasures of the table, and the vanities of fashionable life, but who is now engaged in the prosecution of profound scientific enquiries,—who has an interest in every discovery of chemistry, or geography, or mechanics, that is made from one side of the world to the other, and not only so, but who is engaged in a constant endeavor to improve character and lives in the daily exercise of the purest and most expanded affections, and more than this, has learned the serious pleasure of meditating on God and heaven; represent to your mind such a person, and ask yourself whether life is not worth to him more than it was—infinitely more than it is to the sensual and selfish. He lives in another earth than they; other heavens shine over his head. Life to him is a world of pure and pleasant thought, and the idea of losing it, (whenever it comes to his mind with any colour of probability,) is tremendous.

For this reason, it seems to me that in the partial effect which Christianity has hitherto had on the world, it has done much to increase the fear of death, by the degree of improvement it has produced in mankind as respects the love of knowledge and the refinement of social life; whilst it has yet failed to affect any large portion of society to that higher degree as to overcome the terror by convincing them of their immortal nature.

II. Secondly it seems to be the distinct voice of reason and of Scripture that the fuller effect of Christian principles upon the heart will be the disappearance of the fear of death. Men doubt of their immortality because they doubt whether their moral nature is really independent of their body. They suppose it to have an inseparable connexion with the animal life, and it is unavoidable that a man should think so whilst he sees that in himself and in others the spiritual nature is only disclosed to them in connexion with, in subordination to, the animal nature; whilst they see the soul made the servant of the body; and that all the great men of the world think deeply and speak strongly and act energetically to the end that they may live in palaces and have abundance of food and clothing and praise. Whilst they see this, that the flesh and its gratifications are the motive and the reward of the exertions of the soul, it is natural that they should fear that the thoughts of God, of goodness, of love, and the laws of moral nature as they appear to the mind, that all these may be only more delicate material phenomena created from the health of the body, and it and they may perish together. God grant this shall not always be so.

But, on the contrary, whenever our spiritual nature is *used,* whenever in the earnest love of truth and goodness, truth and goodness shall be sought, their reality and independence will distinctly appear. It is vain to describe the sentiment of love to him who has never felt it. The existence of love can only be believed by loving. Thought can only be known by thinking; and as the existence of the lightning is only made known by the fall of its fire, so our moral nature can never be seen to exist of itself except by the fact of executing its commandment in the life of the man.

There is much valuable experience to confirm this belief, that it is only by the use of our spiritual nature, that its eternal life can appear to us. Any one accustomed to much meditation upon moral and religious questions may notice that after he has been occupied with vigour for any length of time upon such subjects, as upon human liberty, upon the perfectness of the retributions that take place, or upon the the analysis of the affections,—or upon any question of simple right;—if, from the midst of these thoughts, he glances at the question of the separate being of the soul, he will have a far deeper conviction of his immortality than at other times. And this because these powers are at that moment quickened and enlarged by their own action.

There is a higher testimony that operates inwardly to prove the same doctrine—a life of purest devotion, which it is the direct object of Christianity to form in us. There are Christians who never doubt their immortality; and to see such persons does wonderfully refresh the soul. They are free from doubt by the mere purity and entireness of their devotion. The inheritance of faith bequeathed from age to age by the devout spirit of our ancestors is not wholly gone. New England yet savors of the rich piety of her saints. The country is full of anecdotes of the simple yet excellent people of the last and the former generation who, living in an age of few books, read almost none but their bible and hymnbook and had, burning within, a less rational yet a far more fervid piety than is commonly witnessed among us—and died not only without fear but with exultation even in the love of Christ.

We have heard and known of those who hungered and thirsted to be released from the flesh. Theirs was the spirit of the apostles who never speak of death with terror; to whom to live was Christ, and to die was gain; and who, living or dying, were the Lord's.[4]

III. I have spoken of the actual influence of Christianity upon the fear of death.

I proceed to speak of the manner in which Christianity removes the fear of death by the revelation of immortality. There is something quite peculiar in the manner in which this revelation is made.

Jesus, armed with miracles, teaches distinctly and with authority the immortality of the soul. Not a mystical existence of the soul absorbed into God, as some of the philosophers said, nor of resurrection after an interval of death, but a continuance of the individual being. God is the God of Abraham, he saith, and of Isaac, and of Jacob, and to Him they live;[5] that is, Abraham as Abraham, and Isaac as Isaac. This is plain: this is what we want.

But observe the fact that this information goes no further. It is most remarkable in this revelation that it has not answered one of the questions so embarrassing concerning the state and laws and employments of a disembodied soul, its modes of action and society, nor presented any interior view of the soul's abode.

More than this it does not insist explicitly, and in the manner of declaring a doctrine hitherto unknown, on the fact itself, that the soul shall live again. It is incidentally taught in the discourses of Jesus as well as in the recorded sermons of the apostles and in the Epistles. But instead of an express affirmation of this momentous truth, and instead of gratifying the curiosity of the mind on all these points, what does it say?—Repent and be converted. Love God: love thy brother: trample on your lusts; live above the world. Redeem the time, be just, be merciful, put off the lower nature; put on the higher nature.[6] Here is all the emphasis, and you are left to make the inference, the assurance of life eternal involved in these instructions. And it is true that these precepts are given with an air of passion and triumph as if they were themselves the annunciation of the

4. Philippians 1:21; Romans 14:8.
5. Matthew 22:31–32, Mark 12:26–27, and Luke 20:37–38. In speaking of "resurrection after an interval of death," Emerson is alluding to the mortalist heresy, the doctrine that the soul dies or "sleeps" until the Last Judgment. See also Sermon XLV (*Sermons* 2:30, n. 1). This entire paragraph is repeated in Sermon CXXVI; see Sermon CXXVI, n. 12. For Emerson's possible debt to Coleridge here and in his remarks on miracles in the sentence immediately above, see Kenneth Walter Cameron, *Emerson the Essayist* (Raleigh, N.C., 1945), 1:135 and 1:168.
6. Acts 3:19; Luke 10:27; I John 3:23; I Peter 2:11; Romans 12:2; Ephesians 5:16, and Luke 6:36.

splendid truth;—as if they were themselves the consolation, and the power, and the happiness, which the heart of man sought in a gospel opening the future life.

Now, brethren, I suppose there is a deep wisdom—a faithful truth in this mode of making known this great fact. First, I suppose it never was meant to be communicated or received as a splendid and solitary truth that the soul should exist for ages of ages. It was not meant to be taught that bare existence was a blessing—a vast waste of unprofitable time—but always this truth was to be communicated in connexion with, or rather as subordinate to, the lesson of the soul's duties. Duty is the object of the soul, and the question in their minds is not how long we must live, but how much is to be done. Not a single allusion is made by Jesus or Paul to the idea of simple eternity; they dwelt so fervently on the actual progress of the soul, its sanctification, its redemption from lust and pride and hatred and avarice and falsehood; and its edification in love, humility, pureness, and simplicity, that they only perceived the duration by implication in the divine nature of these things.[7] They wish to have it understood that it is to the mind as it becomes virtuous, not as it lives longer, as it approaches God, not as it dies out of this world, that the revelation is made that 'Time shall be no more.'[8]

Brethren, I do not much value the indifferency that does not fear to die because it has never inquired of itself what death is. I do value that clean conscience which, with a firm temperament, does not fear that death can bring any danger it cannot meet with decency, or any harm to its innocency. But I venerate that rare and high elevation which, dwelling with God and informed by his Will and spirit, has wholly rid itself of any apprehension of mortality through its own enjoyment of better life.

None can wholly part with the apprehension of mortality but by parting with sin. And whatever tends to the last effect tends to the first. Whenever, then, you resist the temptation of intemperate eating or drinking, or indolence, or lust; whenever you serve those who cannot serve you; whenever you forgive those who have offended you; whenever you pray in your closet;[9] whenever you direct your thought into good channels;—you are in that moment doing something not only to remove the fear of judgment but to eradicate the fear of death, to stablish your mind with the assurance that you are so united to God that you cannot die, though the universe were blotted out. It will not produce an ardent desire to die;—that is not a frame of mind consistent with well regulated powers and just performance of duty, but it will make the light of every day pleasant with more than the radiance of the Sun, and it will make the last day calm and great as the day before an eternity of knowledge and love and joy in the presence of God.

7. Cf. Matthew 5:1–11 and Philippians 4:8.
8. Revelation 10:6.
9. Cf. Matthew 18:21–22 and 6:6.

We must all appear before the judgment seat of Christ.

II CORINTHIANS 5:10

It seems no longer fit that men should be amused or distressed with fictions of the imagination, in the place of the solemn realities of religion. Whilst the mind of society is uninformed, gross errors may have more power over it than truth. The imposing shows of the Roman Catholic church may comfort or affright a very ignorant man; but when his understanding has been cultivated it will penetrate the form for a meaning, and if it does not find a full one, it will despise the form. Not only will forms thus perish but the imagery also in which religious truth has been contained, the idea of heaven as a kingdom; of God as a king; of hell as a pit of fire; of Jesus as a judge upon a bench[1]—these words must be pierced for the truth they contain as we desire to bring about any real efficiency from Religion over enlightened minds and sincere hearts. These images, these time honoured words, are like the leaves on which the Scriptures are written; though they may receive a passing reverence for the sake of their contents, they are poor and perishable materials, time shall wear them, fire burn them, the wind scatter them, but the truth of which they are the vehicle, is higher than heaven, deeper than hell, of the same nature as man and, like him, derived from God.

Let the great doctrines of the New Testament, of death, of judgement, of heaven and hell, be studied in this frame of mind which passes through the dead letter to the living spirit.[2] Let the New Testament be read by each of us with the constant effort to apply it to our own persons, to our business, to our relations in life, as husbands, wives, masters, parents, children,—to our temptations, to our desires,—to all that complex but peculiar thought, which, in each individual, constitutes himself. Then shall it speak not of Jews and Romans, of

---

Manuscript dated November 13, 1830. Preached fourteen times: November 14, 1830, at the Second Church, Boston; November 21 in Roxbury; November 28 at the Federal Street Church; December 5 at the New North Church; December 19 in Charlestown; January 30, 1831, at the Twelfth Church, Boston; April 17 at the North Church, Salem; June 12 at Northampton; October 23 at the New South Church, Boston; June 3, 1832, in Waltham; January 26, 1834, in New Bedford; November 27, 1836, in East Lexington; December 4 in Concord, Mass.; and March 26, 1837, in Lowell.

1. Revelation 9:12; II Corinthians 5:10 and Romans 14:10.
2. II Corinthians 3:6.

temples, and customs, that are passed away, but of familiar hopes and fears, of bosom sins, of what makes the heart beat, and the feet run, and the hands work, of what we are, and what we shall be.

Let us consider in what manner Christ shall judge the earth. The doctrine of the final Judgment is always preached by the Saviour and his apostles as an event of unspeakable joy to the good, of unspeakable sorrow to the sinner.

It means something. It means much of the last interest to us here and forever. But let us not weaken its importance by connecting its awful truth too closely with the figures and types by which it has been represented.

Let us consider what is meant by the expression, "We shall appear before the judgment seat of Christ," or, in another place, "God shall judge the world in righteousness by the man whom he hath ordained."[3] Before we give our attention to the nature of this judgment, it is important that we should consider a little the import that belongs to the name of Christ in this and similar expressions. Throughout the evangelists, it is used for the most part to denote the *bodily person* of Jesus. But it is used by the writers of the epistles, with much more latitude. In the expressions, *"To live, is Christ,"* "By Christ all became alive"[4]—there is obviously a very wide departure from this meaning, and none can understand the *body* of Christ to be meant, but his *religion*. It is precisely in this manner that he speaks of himself—"I am the light of the world,"—"I am the resurrection and the life."[5] What was the light? Not his *person,* certainly, but his *doctrines. He* was not the resurrection, but the spirit in him that could not die.

He uses his own name for his religion as he uses the name of Moses for the law of Moses: "Not I, but Moses accuseth you."[6]

So in all these passages: The law was a schoolmaster to bring us to Christ.[7] If Christ be in you, the body is dead because of sin.[8] I live, yet not I, but Christ liveth in me.[9] Till Christ be formed in you.[10] But ye have not so learned Christ.[11] Arise from the dead and Christ shall give you light.[12] When Christ, who is our life, shall appear.[13] Christ, the power of God and the wisdom of God.[14]

It is obvious that Christianity, or the religious truths brought by Christ to men, is meant. I understand, then, that the expression of the text is one of the same import, that *the truth which came by Jesus Christ shall judge the world.*

Let us consider how the religion of Christ doth erect a tribunal to judge the world, and every human soul.

3. Acts 17:31.
4. Philippians 1:21; I Corinthians 15:22.
5. John 8:12 and 11:25.
6. John 5:45.
7. Galatians 3:24.
8. Romans 8:10.
9. Galatians 2:20.
10. Galatians 4:19.
11. Ephesians 4:20.
12. Ephesians 5:14.
13. Colossians 3:4.
14. I Corinthians 1:24.

Every truth that is clearly known to men is a sort of tribunal by which other truth may be tried. For it is a maxim that every truth agrees with all truth.[15] Thus, after all experience has demonstrated the truth of the theory of Gravitation, if any theory should be proposed inconsistent with that law, we should pronounce it false at once. So every acquisition we make in any kind of knowledge is continually furnishing us with a better test for detecting the truth of other opinions. Especially may this be said of religious truth. Whenever a more excellent principle is presented, it condemns the less excellent.

In this manner, in a most real and effective sense, is *Christ the judge of the world*. He is the light that enlighteneth every man that cometh into the world.[16] The divine truth which his religion teaches, is the soul of our souls, is a sufficient law for all action. It literally *passes judgment* upon every thought, and every action, that is brought before it, and condemns every thing that will be displeasing to God, and hurtful to the peace of the soul. Every other rule of life is only partial and temporary, may regulate certain actions, may make specific directions respecting study, conversation, business, that will serve well enough for a little while, and for certain purposes,—but this infuses a living soul, this constitutes the man himself a judge of action. Thus one man may write from observations in a court, rules of manners, and another, from experience in affairs, may write rules of equity in trade; but Religion will furnish the sentiment of *love* from which good manners spring, and the sentiment of right, which will better regulate our commercial intercourse than any book of rules.

And there is not a corruption in the laws or practice of any people, but is inconsistent with the sentiments of the Christian spirit, that is to say, there is not one, which a more full understanding of the Christian religion would not expose.

But suffer me to speak a little more particularly to these two points, *first,* that Christ judges the world; *secondly,* that Christ judges every human soul.

I. Christ shall judge the world. The truth which Christ preached to mankind is eternal. It is as true now as it shall be at any time. The judgment that it passes upon the things of this world is not deferred but is now made manifest precisely in that degree in which this truth prevails. Wherever Christianity has been received into the hearts of men, it has denounced their sins. The progress of Christianity therefore may be as accurately measured by the cultivation of nations as the virtue of one man by his works. I ask if Christ has not already judged—is he not now judging the world by reproving and removing the old repute of many abominations? What was the Reformation, but the judgment of Christ upon the falsehood and crimes of the Romish Church? The force of Christ's truth in men's hearts condemned the institutions that bore his name. And now the progress of the same truth is reforming the Reformed Church.

The oppression of the ancient governments hath been judged by his righteousness, and has fallen to pieces in this quarter of the world, and is coming to an end every where. The ferocious usages of savage nations,—War, Duelling,

15. Omne verum vero consonat [Emerson's note]. The English translation also occurs in *JMN* 4:376, and the Latin in *JMN* 6:191 and in *Nature* (*CW* 1:28).
16. John 1:9.

Assassination, have been judged by him, and shall come to an end. Intemperance has been judged by him, and is beginning to disappear. Slavery has been judged by him and must be cut off root and branch.[17] It is now threatening those who are engaged in it, and us for our share in the guilt with accumulated evil.

These things are not known to be crimes where this religion is not known. And it is as inevitable an effect of the approach of his religion, that these crimes should be seen to be crimes, as that the light of the sun should distinguish the beasts that prowled in darkness.

Nor shall this judgment come to an end. As the Christian faith obtains a more solid possession of every community, it will expose more and more vices and expel them from the earth. "Neither do Christians in Parthia indulge in polygamy, though they be Parthians: nor do they marry their own daughters in Persia though they be Persians. Among the Bactrians and the Gauls they do not commit adultery but wheresoever they are they rise above the evil laws and customs of the country."[18]

II. We must all appear before the Judgment seat of Christ, secondly, *in our own proper persons*. Not only must the world be judged, and offences cease, but every soul of man must be judged according to its deeds. There is no proxy, there is no escape. In each of our hearts, my brethren, must judgment be passed upon all our life by the law of our Master. Each of our actions must be brought up to this light, and the light shall try it of what sort it is.[19] Our principles must be judged by his principles. His principle was *Thy will be done.*[20] Our principle is *My will be done,* and it is condemned by him. His principle was—Love your enemies. Can we bear to be tried by that? His principle was, Love all men, Be the servant of all; and all the hatred, the malice, the selfseeking that is in us, must shrink before the brightness of his law.[21] His principle was, to despise the flesh and its food and dress and accommodation and seek only the things of the spirit, the love of God in the obedience to his commandments.[22] But we are very careful to dress well, and to feed well, and to be surrounded with bodily accommodations, but it does not give us so much anguish as it should, to break the law and to lose the love of our Heavenly Father. Yet, brethren, for all these things we must enter into judgment. These great principles are the eternal law of our being and must be obeyed if we would be happy. To disobey them, is to seal our doom. To disobey them, is to incur the reproaches of our conscience,

17. Cf. Malachi 4:1.

18. (Bardesanes, in time of M. Antonine.) ap Eusebius [Emerson's note]. Bardesanes or Bardaisan (154–224?), Syrian poet, theologian, and author of *Dialogue of Destiny, or Book of the Laws of the Countries,* which contains the original of this quotation, is mentioned briefly by Eusebius in *The Ecclesiastical History.* However, because this statement is not quoted there, Emerson's actual source remains uncertain. See *The Ante-Nicene Fathers. Translations of the Writings of the Fathers down to* A.D. 325, 10 vols. (New York, 1890), 8:733.

19. I Corinthians 3:13.

20. Cf. Luke 22:42.

21. Cf. Matthew 5:43–46.

22. Cf. Matthew 6:28–30.

declaring beforehand to us the wrath of God. It is to encumber us with all moral disqualifications for happiness. It is to ruin our peace of mind. It is to waste the time and the means of grace. It is to trifle with God's goodness. It is to collect the materials and lay the pile, as the Scriptures speak, of the everlasting fire.[23]

I know not—no man knoweth—the nature of those changes that death shall bring to pass in us. But there is not a syllable in all the word of God, there is not the least breathing in all the voice of reason, that intimates any mitigation to come from that change, to the evils that are suffered in this world for sin. The consequences of sin in this world are painful thoughts, fear, further desire to sin, and a blindness which hides our interest and happiness from us, and, beyond this, the disapprobation and united opposition of all the rest of mankind. All these consequences may yet cleave to us, when the body is gone, and be far more intense causes of pain when the relief of bodily pleasure, and the shield of bodily insensibility, is withdrawn. And the satisfactions of virtue may by the same change be exalted. The connexions of friendship shall be more intimate, the pursuit of knowledge far more rapid and extensive, the joys of meditation, of devotion, shall be purified. The judgment of Christ, the judgment of the eternal Truth which he declared, upon our characters, shall be fully carried out in the spiritual world upon the good and the evil.

Brethren, let us not postpone this judgment, as in some measure we may, to a distant day. Beware lest any action is habitual to any of us, any language, any desire, that cannot stand before the judgment of the law of Christ. O consider most of all, whether the general habit of all our lives, the general level of our principles, may not be condemned by that law; whether the reason why our conscience doth not fill us with horror is that we skulk into the dark because our deeds are evil, and do not ever bring our principles to the trial. Be not deceived; God is not mocked. Whatsoever a man soweth that shall he also reap.[24]

23. Cf. Matthew 18:8 and 25:41.
24. Galatians 6:7.

XCVI

Thy will be done.
MATTHEW 6:10

When our Saviour was in the world he said, "Not my will, Father, but thine be done."[1] He not only prayed thus, but thus he practised. What is it that distinguishes his life in your memories from that of other good men? Is it not that you perceive this presence of a Superior Will to his own, or to that of any created being, in every one of his actions? His life was a body, if I may so speak, of this sentiment. And it is by the announcing of this law that he is our Saviour. He is not yet the Saviour of any soul to whom he has not brought this sentiment home. The soul is not saved that has not felt it. For it is the soul's law and health and end. Its sublimity consists in its truth. The history of the Creation, Let there be light and there was light,[2] does not so fill the mind as this. The laws of light and gravity and electricity are truly simple and grand, for they are the works of the same Artist, but they are his lower work, subservient to moral ends, and are only the temple of which this is the glory. But *Thy Will be done* is the Constitution of the spiritual world. It is the desire of angels. It is the love and the happiness of heaven.

But how slowly does this desire enter into the hearts of men. Self-love shuts it out.

The child grows up in the indulgence of his own will; he thinks that his toys are the best in the school, that his house is the best house, that his father and mother are better than other people, and when he enlarges his knowledge a little, that his town and his country are better than all others. He grows up. He crosses the sea, and visiting conspicuous towns, he discovers that his home was an obscure sterile spot no ways remarkable, that the geographer had quite overlooked it in his map, and learns to speak of it himself, perhaps, with an affected contempt in comparison with what he has elsewhere seen.

But our young men have travelled over Europe and seen many great places to little purpose if they have not found a better reason for undervaluing their earliest views of things than that they have seen London and Paris.

Manuscript dated November 28, 1830, and January 1, 1832. Preached four times: November 28, 1830, at the Second Church, Boston; January 1, 1832, again at the Second Church; December 13, 1835, in Waltham; and February 14, 1836, in East Lexington.

1. Cf. Luke 22:42.
2. Genesis 1:3.

But it is plain at the first glance that this thought neither in the religion of nature nor in the Revelation is an idle sentiment. It is a practical rule. We are not only to rejoice that things are ordered wisely and will issue well but we are to perceive why they are not well now; what it is that opposes the general well being; and then we shall perceive that it is self-will. Whilst we indulge joy that God protects us, whilst we embark in new periods of time and new walks of duty, it teaches us that this law protects only them that serve it.

The time shall come sooner or later in the history of every soul when the veil shall be torn from this truth,[3] that the happiness of all is involved in the voluntary performance of God's will, and who resists it, resists himself and man and God. And blessed is he who knows this in season.

'Thy Will be done' is the prayer of all Christendom. But when we use the words, do we really mean what we say? I invite your attention to three points of consideration: how God's will is ascertained, what it is, and how it should be sought by us.

What is God's will is easily ascertained in the outward creation, for there his will is done. It has no will of its own. The grass grows by laws imposed by omnipotence. The solid earth, the atmosphere, the sea observe his commandment in their place. Our perverse wills cannot reach the planets, and they have none of their own. Their glorious order is never disturbed by sin or imperfection. It might satisfy us that the will of God is good, that the laws of matter wherein always his will is done, are our symbols of usefulness and order and eternity. We never doubt that the sun will rise. We never doubt that any caprice or change will enter into the nature of water or air or heat.

A portion of this magnificence we behold, and it fills us, according to the measure of our wisdom, with confidence and delight in the wisdom that conducts the whole, until this great system comes athwart our diminutive interests. When a cloud lowers over our roof and the rain wets us, or the wind blows our ship out of its course, or we inhale disease from the infected air, or for want of industry and frugality we come to want, instantly we forget that our good is comprehended in God's great operations for all, and fret and charge him foolishly.[4]

What would become of us if for one hour the material world were released from its obedience to God's will and submitted to ours? How would the sun scorch the globe to gratify one man's whim and freeze it for another? Earth rent for gems, stript for spices—zones and winds and climates and minerals and the level of lands would start into chaos.[5] Here one man would pile the mountains on one hated nation, and the overflowing rivers would drown here a sect, the thunder would strike the kings to serve their subject and strike the people to wreak the kings' spite, and the tendency of every evil thought in innumerable men would add to the horror of the time. It would be a true picture of the

3. Cf. II Corinthians 3:16.
4. Cf. Job 1:22.
5. Emerson returned to this idea in 1849; see *JMN* 11:95 and "Fate" (*W* 6:48–49).

tendency of the evil heart of man that would then be painted in the outward world.

It is very natural that we should pray that God's will should hold these atoms and worlds in their beneficent places and uses. But these are not the main object of that petition inasmuch as their whole existence is dependent upon him, and any release from his will would shake the Universe to chaos. The true objects of that prayer are not material but moral natures, natures that have a Will capable of uniting with or opposing the divine Will. May thy Will be done in man. And here, how shall it be ascertained? No man hath seen God at any time,[6] and his works never speak to us with the voice of a man to communicate his will. It is not by any messenger that his will can be communicated. At least it needs more than a messenger. It is not by miracles that his will can be known. For if it were possible that one should come with miracles and bid us steal and murder, hate our brother or take our own life, and should work a miracle to prove his commission, it could not prove it. Or if a man should work a miracle in attestation of highest truths before sensual persons, they would not apprehend them. As Jesus himself declares: He says that sin had so blinded the eyes of the Jews and hardened their hearts that his works could not convince them, nor would they believe though one rose from the dead.[7] It is very remarkable that this teacher armed with miracles should deny their power to work conviction and appeal always to higher influence, namely, to the Heart of man, to a faith coming from obedience to commandments written in the Heart. If ye will do the will of my Father, ye shall know, he said, of my doctrine whether I speak of myself or from God.[8] So it seems they knew the will of God already, or had a commandment. It was the very same to which Moses appealed when he said, This Commandment is not far off—not in heaven—not beyond the sea, but in thy mouth and in thy heart.[9]

And so the united voice of all good men in every age and country has declared that the Will of God is coincident with the moral faculty. It is spoken by the Conscience. God is in our hearts, and it is the entire correspondence of the Word spoken by our Saviour with this heart that gives persuasion to his miracles and shows them and him divine. He may reveal what is already in the heart unknown to us. He may teach what is consistent with our being, but any thing else would not be intelligible to us, but lay hidden.

As in the laws of material nature, when we inquire the cause of gravity, we find it is God only, or what determines the growth of a seed?—God; or what power gives power to things, it is God;—beyond a few steps we come full upon God's agency,—so it is in man, when we inquire the cause of the cause, who gave or rather who is now giving this commandment to speak truth, to abstain from injustice, to be pure, we must answer, God. He is the substratum and

6. Cf. John 1:18.
7. Luke 16:31.
8. John 7:17.
9. Deuteronomy 30:14.

basis of every one of his works. This is the meaning of his omnipresence. He is present to all because he is the life and heart of all.

The will of God is to be ascertained, then, by listening to that inward voice which always communicates to him who listens to it so much of God's will as concerns his present exigency. 2. And what is it? Universal good. Natural and moral good. Not only the greatest good of the greatest number of his creatures,[10] but the perfection of all.

In the human heart to promote this great end the Will of God is felt in the form of a law. It teaches us how we should live toward others. It is mercy, truth, and righteousness. It is the good of others opposed to the desires of self. It is the good of the soul opposed to the good of the body, of eternity opposed to time.

It is manifest, then, since always the commandment issues from the heart itself, since the bible has no force but what it derives from within us, that the will of God is not a contest between ourselves and another; it is really a contest between a higher self and a lower self, between the spirit and the flesh, and that therefore we ourselves have really the highest interest in its authority.

Now he who seeks his own will in this lower sense must suffer, for he fights against the law of nature, he fights single handed against the Universe. Whatever belongs to such a Will is robbed from the whole Creation. All that he is, is an insult upon all other beings, and all others have a common interest to put him down. His acquisitions, his whole importance, is fitly represented by a robber's castle which is a scourge and an outrage to the country where it stands. It is what Tripoli and Algiers have been to the civilized world.[11] It is what a pirate is upon the high seas—an enemy of the human race.

And not only so that self-will fights against the world, but as it is opposed to God, on whom man immediately rests, it is cut off from all life. It is a wave raised in the air or a branch lopped from its tree or a fire without fuel, and having no life in itself must perish.

Every crime is the fruit of this low detestable love of self—Avarice, lust, ambition, hatred, envy: these murder. On the contrary, fortitude, generosity, self-devotion, self-denial, humility, love, are of God.

All laws are directed to enforce God's will, and it is self that always breaks them. If self was permitted to seek and gain its ends, it would turn the world into a hell. The abasing of self, the seeking of God's will by all men, would constitute heaven.

Let the principles be tried by their fruit.[12] Here is much complaint of the evils of Slavery. Would the man who sought not his own will enslave his brother? Here is great fear of an Aristocracy. Would the self-abaser crush the poor? Here is great instability of credit and trade. But he that preferred his brother and all

10. Francis Hutcheson, *An Inquiry into the Original of Our Ideas of Beauty and Virtue; In Two Treatises*, 2d ed. (London, 1726), 177; see Sermon LXXVII, n. 2 (*Sermons* 2:197).

11. America's war with Tripoli was concluded by treaty on June 4, 1805.

12. Cf. Matthew 7:16–20.

his brethren to himself would not endanger his brother by his enterprizes or his extravagance.

The will of God is seen by us to be infinitely good and desirable the moment we measure it by its effects on society.

III. How then should it be sought by us? Brethren, we ought to feel that Religion, that is, our eternal well being, our life, consists in the practical knowledge of God's Will,—in the renouncement of *my* will for *thine*. In the world, men's thoughts are arranged from the principle of self-love, and our neighbor is loved as he contributes to our advantage, and God is honoured for the bounty we expect from him. Religion changes entirely this order and puts God for self and teaches us to love ourselves only as we are parts and manifestations of him, and our neighbor as ourselves.[13] It refers every thing to God. We must worship him in all we do. He must be a party to our conversation, to our labor, to our traffic, to our meals, to our recreation, to our disappointments, to our distress—so that he shall oversee all, and nothing shall offend him. We must pray that his will be done with us, in us, and by us. *With us,* that is, with our possessions, our prospects, our healths, our lives. This is resignation. *In us,* that is, that sin be rooted out, that this needful revolution take place in all our motives and Will from self-love to godly love, that we be re-formed. *By us,* that is yet a higher strain than these. Let thy will be done by me implies that it be done with me and in me. It implies industry and courage and charity. It implies a conquest over the afflictions of life inasmuch as I am more part of God who does the act than I am of my outward felicity which suffers. Let us aim, my friends, to work this excellent change in ourselves. The bible speaks commandments that are echoed by the spirit within us, teaching us how this may be done. Let us consider what a heaven it were if all the wills of all free agents were as totally submitted to the will of God as is the material world. Let us consider how much it is the glory of a free agent to bring his will into a perfect sympathy and obedience to God's; it makes him divine,—as Jesus Christ is the Son of God because in him only among men was this obedience perfect. In his example, in his glowing benevolence, in the words of forgiveness that fell from him on the Cross, let us learn how to live and to die.[14]

13. Luke 10:27.
14. Luke 23:34.

XCVII

O that men would praise the Lord for his goodness and for his wonderful works to the children of men. . . . Whoso is wise and will observe these things, even they shall understand the lovingkindness of the Lord.

<small>Psalms 107:21, 43</small>

We are called on this returning anniversary, my Christian friends, by the civil authority to the duty of gratitude. The call is I trust welcome to every heart. There is no one whose lot is so low and hard, whose afflictions have been so severe and accumulated, that he can think of no blessing in the past twelve-month for which to say, 'Father, I thank thee.' To religious minds every dealing of Providence is full of sweetness and instruction; the common gifts of life, and the air, the sun, the senses, and every occupation of the body, and the mind, and every public event, and every domestic incident, instead of being disregarded as general, are received as particular bounty to their bosoms, and have as much force to persuade them to praise as if their names were inscribed on the gift. To those who love God it is an argument for gratitude that they are not distinguished in the diffusion of common mercy; that He sends rain to the unjust as well as the just and causes the sun to shine on the evil and the good.[1] They worship the more because these worship less. They worship the more the infinite love of God and the wisdom which knows how to multiply every blessing a thousand and a million fold by making it common to towns or to nations or to mankind. For whilst others receive with open arms the gift, they think more of the love.

To us who are here assembled I cannot think there is any deficiency in causes for praise and none, I hope, in the disposition.

Let us then consider our reasons for thanksgiving. Let us sing the earth's harvest hymn to the God of the harvest. Let us provoke one another to love and to praise by a careful review of the divine favors. We will unlock our treasure

---

Manuscript dated Thanksgiving Day, December 2, 1830. Preached twice: December 2, 1830, at the Second Church, Boston, and December 1, 1836, in East Lexington.

1. Matthew 5:45.

house and show our corn and wine, our advantages, our means—not to pride, as Hezekiah did to the Assyrian,[2] but to God, that we may make an offering of all we are and have to Him.

And first, brethren, consider whether each of us has not had some reason to acknowledge the special favor of God to himself. Twelve months are past. All nature with her countless contrivances for the pleasure of the eye, the gratification of all the senses, has fulfilled her year, and has she brought no fruit to your basket, from her harvest; no strength to your limbs from air and sun and food; no medicine in her herbs and balsams and drugs for your sickness? Has the cloud that fertilized every other field dropped no rain on yours, and the wind that favoured every other ship driven yours off her course? Have you not shared God's blessing? Have you not drank his water, and eat his bread, and been warmed at his fire? Has not the fleece of his flock clothed you, and the vine and the olive cheered you?

To him who knows how to live, to the man of benevolent affections, every thing ministers in its proper place. He loves the storm and he loves fair weather, solitude is agreeable and company not disagreeable, and nothing seems to him more splendid and festive than the shows of nature which other men have no pleasure in seeing.

> The humblest note that swells the gale
> The meanest floweret of the dale
> The common earth the air the skies
> To him are opening paradise.[3]

And has God done you no kindness in his Providence? Has there been no signal favor in your house? Has not the absent child or husband or brother been restored? Has not the sick been healed? Has not the apprehension that weighed on your spirit been removed? Has not the fear of death been removed? Has there been no mitigation to your real sufferings? Has no knowledge been imparted to your soul? Have you gained no increase of faith, no cheerful and elevating views of God? Have you had no hour of true worship, of soul-rejoicing communion with him? Have you not had the highest favor, any opportunity of doing good?—If you say *no* to all these, I am afraid you are wanting to your opportunities;—for there are two things needed for happiness—the blessing; and a heart fit to receive it.

Secondly. We have not only special favors done to us but we have general favors in which we share. As citizens of this metropolis and of New England we may congratulate ourselves on possessing advantages denied to far the largest portion of the human race. We are natives or inhabitants of this city of the

2. II Kings 20:12–17; Emerson corrected "Assyrian" to "Babylonian" for the second delivery of the sermon.

3. Emerson misquotes Thomas Gray, "Ode On the Pleasure Arising from Vicissitude," lines 49–52.

English pilgrims. We share in her fair fame. We joy in the two hundred years of this simple, useful, free, and Christian town. We inherit the reward of her goodness and greatness. We have worshipped in her churches. We have studied in her schools. We have used our franchise in her elections. We have obeyed her laws. We have wrought in her streets.

Compare our clear and unquestioned possession of our personal independence with those thronged regions of Europe where the same good is not obtained without frightful sacrifices. Where the harvest is burned on the day when the rights of man are declared, and the streets are soaked with native blood to keep the sworn contracts from being broken by her princes.

But we have made no sacrifice. We say to those patriots, At a great price you procured your freedom, but we are freeborn.

Akin to this blessing is that which is inseparably connected with it, and dearest of all that may be read in the present condition of our country to every true Christian heart. I mean the knowledge and love of what is right, which however far below the Christian standard, is yet nearer to it than in any other people known to us. The measure I have in my mind is this. We know that in most ages and countries the general level of moral principle has been so low that the appearance of any man of distinguished probity and piety has provoked men to rage, because such goodness reflected upon their evil ways, and has commonly been fatal to the peace and life of the possessor. History numbers many of these painful instances, as if devils in the shape of men cried out for the blood of the saints. I think it will be agreed that no such hostility would be exhibited among us to the highest strain of Christian excellence, but on the contrary that virtue would be hailed with an ardent affection. And this surely is a comprehensive advantage to call out our acknowledgments.

Thirdly. We not only share the general favors of our community, but as we are good and wise we have a property in the prosperity of the human race. A foolish man cares for nothing but himself, but a reasoning, affectionate man cares for all he knows. It is the glory of the human soul to embrace all knowledge in its apprehension and all men in its affection. Thus a benevolent man feels every event that tends to the redemption of African or Indian slavery with equal liveliness as a piece of good fortune in his own family or town. He occupies no more ground than another man, but he sympathizes with the North of Europe and the South of Europe, with the Cherokee in his camp and the Chinese by the Yellow Sea. And with the highest reason. "That man's soul is not dear to himself to whom the souls of his brethren are not dear." The world is the country of illustrious minds. The cause of the human soul is their cause; they feel that there are no seas and mountains in the spiritual world, no distinctions of skin and color; as Jesus said, that they who do his Father's will are his father and mother and sister and brother.[4]

It is then a rightful cause of thanksgiving to us which is suggested in the

4. Matthew 12:50.

public Proclamation that the light of Christianity has been admitted by reason of the French Conquest of Algiers into the North of Africa.[5] The Cross shall be lifted on the shore of the Mediterranean with better hope than when it was expelled thence before. A second day shall open upon Africa, where the grey dawn of learning and the fine arts is yet remembered by the sons of men.

An event of far greater interest is the recent revolution in France, itself a war of principle which after destroying the despotism stayed its hand and did not as in former revolutions destroy the principle.[6] An event which has done much to regenerate Europe and confirm the hearts of those who wish well to mankind. We have an old and dear bond of kindness with that family of the human race. Their hearts warmed to our desire when their kindness was fleets and armies to the cause of liberty, and we may reasonably include their success among the causes of this day's praise.

In short, brethren, there is no good in progress on the face of the globe; no discovery making; no power at work for the removal of any evil, or the production of any good; no wise man devising means of spreading knowledge; no benevolent man relieving misery but you and I and all men have a direct interest in it that increases with our wisdom and makes it a legitimate object for our joy and praise.

We have thus run over the general topics of gratitude. I desire now your attention to an important distinction among these topics of gratitude, which forces itself upon our minds, as we make this enumeration.

No man can be thankful but for those blessings which he has received, and it is very much to be feared that the very highest and the most accessible of all are the least in our account. For, do you not remark that the goods of which we take most account are secondary? that those advantages which we enumerate with most emphasis, and for which we really feel a warm gratitude, are but subsidiary to others which they point at?

The Earth has been covered with her robe of verdure and in due time a more abundant harvest than usual has been got off the ground. Now consider what a delicate and subtle process is required to bring to perfection a single blade of grass or an obscure mushroom, and then follow out the immense multiplication of this process through all the countless leaves and fruits of the forest and the field to an extent that oppresses the imagination to bring about this wondrous growth—Now what was it all for? to end in bearing fruit? Oh no—but this was subsidiary to a higher purpose, namely, to give bread to man and to the animals that serve him. And for what—to end there? to tickle his palate with sweet and flavored food? No—but to sustain him for the business of life.

5. The French conquest of Algiers occurred on July 5, 1830.
6. Emerson is referring to the French Revolution of 1830, which effectively commenced on July 26 with the passing of ordinances that restricted the press and restructured the French Chamber of Deputies. The ringing of Paris with barricades on July 27 contributed to general public panic on July 28–30, which was followed by the abdication of Charles X on August 2 and the installation of the Duke of Orleans as Louis Philippe I on August 7.

So we rejoice that man has made progress in the arts. We meet every where the action and hear the din of toiling enginery. The hammer, the saw, the forge, the windlass never stop. The mechanical genius of the age is directed to the improvement of travelling. Man is laid up in great palaces filled with every accommodation, and swims the rivers at a greater speed than the bark flies before the gale on the sea. And in the huge wagon selfmoved he whirls over an ironed road at a speed far greater than the steamboat—But what is the end of this extreme ingenuity? Not that of itself speedy is better than slow motion, but this has another end—to carry man quicker to the accomplishment of his purposes. This then is still a secondary good.

So also with those political objects sought with such terrible determination and at such a price of blood. The world is shaken by the changes of government. Portugal or Spain or Mexico draw the sword.[7] A kingdom is thrown into commotion. The trade, the pleasures, the worship of towns is stopped; the streets are filled with barricades and cannon and dragoons. Kingdoms are turned to desarts; a thousand or ten thousand brave and valuable men are slain. And why? for the war's sake? No; but for freedom and security of property; but why are these desired?—only that man may with more ease do his duty in the world. Thus even this blessing, great as it is, is not a principal but a subsidiary good. And so it is with almost all that class of events which we denominate blessings and which we account the proper themes of praise. They are not in themselves absolute good. They are only means. They point all to some higher end, to some end beyond which is good in itself.

When Pyrrhus prepared to make war with Rome, his counsellor Cineas asked him what use he meant to make of his victory. Pyrrhus replied, "To make himself master of Italy." "But after we have conquered Italy, sire?" said the counsellor. "To conquer Sicily to be sure," replied the king. "But is the conquest of Sicily the end of your ambition?" "By no means, but to get Lybia and Carthage and then recover Macedon." "But when we have conquered all, what then?" "Why then sit down and enjoy ourselves." "And what hinders us," said Cineas, "from doing this now?"[8]

This is the picture of man always devising a world of contrivances to get at an end that is close by him all the time, and forgetting the end in the means.

What is the chief good to which all things point? What is the end of man? What is the highest blessing for which not man only but all spirits give thanks? God,—the knowledge, the love, and the service of God is that which blesses our blessing and constitutes our perfection. This is an end which may be pursued in the pursuance of all the others and must crown the others. The true anthem of praise which makes music in the ear of God is the gratitude of a good heart for the love of himself. The mind is of the nature of God and whatsoever confor-

7. It is likely that Emerson is not referring to any specific event or events, since civil strife was the rule in Portugal, Spain, and Mexico from the mid-1820s to 1830.

8. Plutarch, "Life of Pyrrhus," in *The Lives*, ed. John and William Langhorne (New York, 1822), 3:324-35.

mity is in it to him becomes eternal. Whatever else he imparts and we render thanks for, must at one or another time be relinquished, but what of himself he imparts shall not be taken away.

There is a way of holding our blessings, such is the exquisite contrivance of the human soul, that they cannot be taken away without leaving a greater blessing in their place. If you hold your children or your health or your possessions as wholly God's, when they are taken away there may be in you a resignation, a calm and perfect love, which is a far more excellent spectacle to angels, and a far more precious good to your soul than children, or bodily vigour, or lands.

Let us then, brethren, praise God aright by holding all we have and all we are, from him and for his will. Let us now, as we have ability, testify this disposition by supplying something to the wants of the sick and the unfortunate and making them feel that we think God is our Father and they are our brothers and sisters in more than a name.

XCVIII _____

Perfect love casteth out fear.
I JOHN 4:18

Which of us is a stranger to fear? Life is full of danger. The young fear lest they shall grow old; the old fear lest they shall be deaf, and blind, and die. The rich man fears lest his cargo miscarry or his stocks depreciate, or his house be broken open, or his dealers get advantage of him in traffic. The poor fears lest the times grow to a worse pinch; lest his limbs fail him, and he shall want bread; the poor woman fears lest she shall not be so fortunate as others in securing friends; the poor fear hard winters, old age, rheums, lameness, and neglect. All fear fever, consumption, loss, and death. What a load of apprehension rests on the world, and on every bosom in it! Christianity comes to remove it. The first words in which it was announced by angels on the clouds of heaven were "Fear not."[1] Jesus is born, and the law that Jesus brought as a remedy for all human wo, was this, "Love God and love man."[2] And the apostle in our text joins these two together, the promise and the performance, by saying *Perfect love casteth out fear.*

In leading your attention to some practical views of this doctrine I put it to the consideration of every thinking person, whether (setting aside that species of love which is properly instinct) goodness is not the only natural object of love, and therefore perfect love can only be felt for perfect goodness, so that God is the only object of perfect love.

It will be said that the doctrine of the text is of no practical use. If perfect love is required to cast out fear, in what human bosom can the perfect love of God dwell? To love him perfectly requires a copy of his moral perfections in the human heart, for love is a perfect sympathy, a oneness of thought in two individuals.

I reply that all the commands of religion and morality are absolute but our performance necessarily imperfect and that a degree of reward is annexed to every degree of obedience. If we cannot perfectly love God we must love him as far as we can,—and in that degree we shall cast out fear.

Manuscript dated December 5, 1830. Preached three times: December 5, 1830, at the Second Church, Boston; January 29, 1832, as the Sunday Evening Lecture at the Friend Street Chapel; and November 6, 1836, in East Lexington.

1. Luke 1:30.
2. Luke 10:27.

Perfect love of God casteth out fear.

What is the love of God—is a question of great pertinence and interest but it is not to be told in a few sentences. Our life, in its best hours and in its richest experience, can only give an approximate answer. No man hath seen God at any time,[3] and almost we say no man hath known him at any time, so confessedly poor and confused are the ideas which at our best estate we obtain concerning him. Yet must not this surprize or daunt us. God is infinite, and it is for higher spirits to approach him. 'Tis true, we are made for this love. But our whole being—ages added to ages without end, is the time allowed for our study of God. And in this life we only begin to know how he is to be sought.

Yet it is a very important truth that we are fitted for his love by whatever acts make us like him, when yet we are unable to bring home any satisfactory idea of his nature to our mind. For the doctrine of the Scripture is that there must be something of God within us to discern the marks of God without us. As we form ourselves in his image and likeness by doing his known will, we are fitted to know and love him. It is not by increasing mere knowledge that God is known. Many men have learned all tongues and all sciences and have not found him.

It is not those who are distinguished by powerful minds and vigorous purposes, far less those who have power and wealth and influence—'Tis not the great that resemble God.[4] The great men of the world whose names have been most in men's mouths, the great robbers, the great murderers, the great defrauders of mankind, are more like the great Adversary than like God. But that soul knows God best and loves him most who is most like him. He who does good, in the moment that he does good, has some idea of God; he who repents of a sin and overcomes the returning temptation has at that moment an idea of God's approving presence. And every truth that replaces an error in our mind and every good habit that replaces a vicious one removes one obstruction more to our knowledge and to our love of God.

I. I remark then in the first place that a perfect love of God would cast out a fear of God, for it will be readily seen that a perfect love would remove all terror from our notion of Him. The reason why we tremble at the thought of his eye resting upon us is because it rests upon our sins. But perfect love cannot consist with the least disobedience to his laws, and before any such beatitude can dwell in our heart every sin must be passed out of it. Then the perception of perfect accordance between us and God will give us peace, will smooth the awful brow of the Almighty to the brow of a friend.

II. Perfect love casteth out the fear of man. Although perfect love may never be attained in this world, yet to every degree of it belongs a degree of the reward. Such imperfect love as has often been shown by men and such as may be shown by each of us casteth out in its degree the fear of man. And this in two

3. John 1:18.
4. Cf. I Corinthians 1:26-27.

ways; *first,* by *casting out sin.* The reason why we fear men is because we have sinned. Examine and see if it be not so. Violent outrages on life and property are rare. It is a blessed consequence of the progress of Christianity and the improvement of laws and manners among us that the word *enemy* is almost a word of romance and of rhetorick among us. The bloody quarrels which rise among savage and wicked places and which give history its shocking interest, are wholly unknown among us. Men of no more than ordinary excellence feel often that the prayer to forgive our enemies requires no very great stretch of generosity; they feel capable of it for they have no enemy—I know this is not universally true. There are *enemies* among us.

There are the representatives of savage life in the bosom of Christianity and New England. There are sometimes to be met with those unhappy individuals who hide their thoughts from the day, and take a diabolical pleasure in brooding over the injuries they have received and rendered. There are enmities that grow up in trade and in the settlement of estates as detestable and ferocious as the hatreds of cannibals. There are men and women who, in the face of the sun and nourished by the overflowing bounty of the benevolent Father, carry about a fire in their souls that seems to have been lighted from hell. Its coals and smoke are malice, slander, fraud, perjury, and murder. If you nourish any resentment examine yourself, for this, like other passions, is a very skilful deceiver. It persuades you that you are innocent, because you were not the first aggressor. I believe there is seldom a quarrel in which some portion of the blame does not fairly belong to both parties. Is there any person on whom you bestow that name, any whom you think has deeply wronged you, and has discovered a constant disposition to injure you, and whom you fear? You have probably retaliated that wrong in secret. You have injured him in your own mind by hard thoughts and by evil hopes, by silent curses; or very possibly your resentment has gone farther and has poisoned with prejudice the ear of his friends, and these thoughts weaken your courage at the mention of his name.

But there is none to whom you have feelings of declared hostility, you have no *enemy,* and yet there are those whom you fear. Who is it that you fear? Let us honestly put the question to our own breasts. You fear the person whom you have injured, or you fear the person who has detected you in a crime, or who has had reason to suspect you of one.

Perhaps you are not guilty, and have never been, of a gross crime, or any serious offence to the character or property of another. Yet you will fear a man who has far higher principles than yours, who sees your weakness, who from his higher ground of Christian life overlooks you and must feel you are sensible of some degree of scorn for your pitiful and unworthy way of life. This fear is ever the conviction of sin. Is the governor afraid of his people; is the representative afraid of his constituents; is the minister afraid of his parish; is the agent afraid of his employer; is the wife afraid of her husband? It is a bad mark for their faithfulness. They are not clear in their office.

It is their compunction that makes those whom they have wronged seem hostile to them. Their neighbor looks just as he did before but their compunction finds in his countenance an expression of reproach or contempt. Every good word sounds like a sentence of judgment, every good man wears the face of an accuser to a burdened conscience.

It is wonderful what power an evil conscience has to sour all our pleasures, to make the faces of our friends look suspicious, to make even a fine day seem disagreeable, to haunt our sleep with ugly dreams, indeed, to suck all the sweetness out of life, and leave nothing but bitterness. This is one of the ways in which God punishes sin. Sin causes all this fear and the love of God which casts out your sin will remove your anxiety.

Secondly, love of God casts out fear of man by *begetting the love of man.* He that loves God, and esteems all men as his offspring, and the human soul as his image,[5] discerns something amiable and excellent in all men. He picks out the grains and beginnings of virtue even in the worst. He looks at their vices as a greater calamity to themselves than offence to others and desires for God's sake and for their sake to raise every germ of goodness, to make the mustard seed grow to a tree and spread out its arms toward heaven. Now he that hath this love is armed against fear. It removes the danger of personal violence and where it cannot do that, removes all apprehension of it. Except a madman who can offer violence to that image of God—*perfect innocence with perfect love?* The Moravians who carried their missions into every quarter of the globe and almost into every savage tribe with no assistant but love, found no ferocity in the Savage. William Penn not only overcame all resistance by this single weapon in the settlement of Pennsylvania but long after when the Indians were treating with another Governor, they gave him the highest praise in saying, "We love you as William Penn himself."[6]

Indeed if you consider what a state of mind is produced by a strong love of mankind, you feel at once that nothing is more inconsistent with fear. It fills the soul to the exclusion of all other feeling. It is related of an Arabian sage that he was insulted and beaten by a worthless fellow at the gate of the mosque. He rose from the ground and wiping the dust from his face, said to his adversary, "If I were revengeful, I would return you blow for blow. If I were an informer I would carry you to the Caliph; but I prefer to go into the temple, and ask of God that he will make you enter the kingdom of heaven with me."[7] Can such a person fear personal violence? He has a salve for every sore. Who will wish to harm him and who can if he will? His treasure is his love and his obedience, and except by injuring that, I had almost said you cannot beat or rob or slay him.

A vulgar mind is fenced and walled in on every side with dislikes and prejudices; a virtuous mind takes delight in goodness wherever it appears.

Thus perfect love of God casteth out the fear of man by casting out sin and by

5. Genesis 1:26.

6. Keith [Emerson's note]. The reference is to Sir William Keith (1680–1749), lieutenant governor of Pennsylvania from 1717 to 1726. Emerson's source is *The Select Works of William Penn,* 3rd ed. (London, 1782), 1:lxxiii. See *JMN* 3:210.

7. Not located.

producing in us the love of man. Now let me, brethren, apply this two-fold aid to a particular case, that this Christian principle may throw light upon our duties. Our community is divided into great religious parties, and by a force not easily avoided every individual is ranked with one. In this compulsory assumption of sectarian colours it behoves every mind to be more than usually heedful of the first great principle of the Christian religion—love. It is not uncommon to hear men express a fear of the designs and of the growth of the Orthodox party. A fear of the Orthodox argues an imperfection in the faith of him that fears. It shows that he thinks they act from higher motives than himself. Here then it is a consciousness of sin. There is reason then in his fear. If they are purer they will prevail. And it seems to me that the reigning sects among us fear each other. The majority of individuals among them are conscious that however high the party banner may be borne, they have a spirit that must shrink before the spirit of Christ, which as it is not in them they think may be in the other. But when our eyes are purged by the spirit of love we shall clearly discern it is not these persons, it is not the clamorous majority, it is not even the distinguished zealots, whose whole influence seems devoted to the propagation of their tenets, that form the real strength of any sect. But in every one of these sects, in every sect of the Christian Church, there are some spirits that sit apart and tranquil, vexed with no fears, shaken by no doubts, in whom the flame of love to God has consumed every inferior passion, in whom love has shut out fear, who embrace all souls in their unbounded Charity. These are the strong instances which the unstable minds adduce to prove the sufficiency of their opinion. But it is not opinion, but love, has made them what they are.

We shall be instructed to join ourselves to these.

There is a selfsubsistency in a man of this temper which is very unlike and very superior to the dogmatism of the mere partisan. He is indeed founded on a Rock.[8] He is calm because he sees that his basis is as broad as the Universe. If a man sees that there is not in any part of his life a contrariety to God, if every part lies parallel to that great will, if wholly he is a pipe through which the breath of God blows unobstructed,[9] he does not fear controversy and sects, he does not think of them. He is after something better than controversy, but he is afflicted with no misgiving that he is wrong, when he meets another pious man of another education. Controversy shrinks from him. His life conquers for him wherever he goes. In some points very possibly he may hold wrong opinions, in some points every man does, but he is in the way to rectify them.

Scattered under all denominations, these are the select disciples of Jesus. It is

---

8. Cf. Matthew 16:18.

9. Emerson first developed this image in a journal entry dated February 20, 1824, in which, while summarizing a temperance lecture by George Bancroft, he recalls "the representation of the body as the corruptible & perishable 'channel thro' which flow for a season the streams of immortal thought" (*JMN* 2:221). Similar references occur in *JMN* 2:289, 2:402, 5:96, and 5:103, with the last *JMN* reference used in the lecture "The School," given on December 19, 1838 (*EL* 3:36). The image appears also in Emerson's poem "O what are heroes prophets men," printed as "Pan"; see *The Poetry Notebooks of Ralph Waldo Emerson,* ed. Ralph H. Orth et al. (Columbia, Mo., 1986), 59 and 880. See also *W* 9:360.

a thin partition that separates the pious Unitarian from the pious Calvinist. It is a wide gulf that separates the pious Unitarian from the sensual unitarian.

This true Christian is free from fear, because he is free from sin and because he is full of love. He cannot be a bondman of a party. Under whatever name he may be ranged by men his real party is the church universal. He is wedded to that by all the laws of his being. Do not then imagine, brethren, that any party are so closely marshalled as to hurt the State. Whatever sect may be feared, the true Christian in your own party shall tell you, I have stronger ties to them than they have to their party; there is a magnet in me which attracts a magnet in them, and that is love. I love them. Every soul which my Father hath made is my brother, and I will use every occasion that offers to promote his welfare and be sure, whilst the laws of our nature remain, he cannot resist and hate me.

Let me urge the consideration of this topic, brethren, as a practical principle. It does appear strange to us, in our best moments, (when the clouds disperse for a moment and show us a true view of our condition)—that men, ever eager to set themselves on the loftiest ground, and get every advantage of their neighbors, should be so slow to learn that the only ground which is not to be commanded, but must always be higher than any other principle, is this of unlimited benevolence. It is the majesty, and real superiority of the Saviour to all other teachers that he taught to love all men and distinctly announced this truth that *if any man would be greatest of all let him make himself the servant of all.*[10] It is the law of the Universe. God is love[11] and doth not disdain to feed the small emmet and preserve a race invisible to the naked eye. If he did not serve the wants of any, if he forsook the minutest member, he would not be God of that being. And this great principle is capable of immediate application to every action of life. He is always the superior of two beings who outdoes the other in love. If I prefer my own comfort to yours in any moment when both are in my hands, in that moment I degrade myself—if I prefer yours, I exalt myself. Our usefulness is the measure of our greatness. My friends, let us fix this one rule in our hearts. It is strange how many times in one day it will be forgotten. O carry it home and tonight and tomorrow Do as you would be done by,[12] and see how pleasant it is. St. John when he was old is reported to have been brought every day in a litter into the church at Ephesus and to have every day uttered only these words, "Little children, love one another."[13]

Let us keep his counsel. It will cast out fear. It will cast out the fear of losing our property by giving us a higher value for unfading riches. It will cast out the fear of sickness and death by convincing us of our hold on eternal life. It will cast out the fear of man by making us the friend of man. It will cast out the fear of God by making him our Friend.

10. Matthew 20:27.
11. I John 4:8.
12. Matthew 7:12.
13. Cf. I John 3:18-23 and 4:4-7.

XCIX

Watch and pray lest ye enter into temptation.
MARK 14:38

I. Evil and good grow together in the field of this world so closely, the presence of one always indicates the presence of the other. It was a very natural doctrine certainly which the fathers of the human race adopted in Asia, that the world was governed by two great principles which waged eternal war; one made light, the other, darkness; one caused happiness, the other turned it sour, one the author of all good, the other of evil. They thought moreover that the good principle should triumph at the last. It is a faithful representation of the intimate connexion in which good and ill subsist. Let a man consider where temptation is found and how it may be avoided. He will find that it is every where present; that whatsoever good he seeks, therewith it is combined; let him retire from the world, he will find it in private life; let him depart from friends, he will find it in his family; let him retire to his closet, he cannot shut himself up so close nor deny himself so scrupulously any outward gratification, but it shall slide in and nestle in his bosom. You might as well try to flee from yourself as flee from temptation. The truth is it is not to be avoided, it is to be *resisted,* and then there is some hope of parting company from this tenacious and dangerous companion.

It cannot be shunned. For see how it originates. You are hungry, and eat,—and the pleasure of the taste leads you on to eat too much. You are tired and sleep, and that you have slept warm makes the cold air and the prospect of hard work so disagreeable that you begin to sin by lingering in bed. Impelled by the law of your nature you work hard to get bread and clothes for yourself and your family, and the habit of aiming at this minor good makes you exclude all other good, and labor too long and too exclusively for the meat that perishes.[1]

Manuscript dated December 11, 1830. Preached four times: December 12, 1830, at the Second Church, Boston; November 6, 1831, as the Sunday Evening Lecture at the Friend Street Chapel; March 22, 1835, in Waltham; and January 31, 1836, in East Lexington. The idea for Sermon XCIX apparently occurred to Emerson on December 6, 1830, when he made this notation in his journal: "On Temptation. A man by reason of a good principle achieves a good deed or draws a hidden consequence into light & admiration. The fruit of his good principle becomes immediately a temptation to which the noble sometimes yields" (*JMN* 3:213). Although Emerson's remark hardly hints at the possibility of a necessary connection between good and evil, Sermon XCIX invokes the Manichean aspects of Zoroastrianism to show the reasonableness of the relation between them, and offers an early statement of themes developed in the essay "Fate."

1. John 6:27.

You seek even some *innocent good,* as the advantage of your health, and insensibly you are led to neglect the duties for which health is to be gained, and grow selfish and fretful.

You seek a *laudable good* like the improvement of your mind, and, in the curiosity that is excited there is danger of other good being omitted, that you read books when you ought to be taking your share in the family duties, or that a foolish pedantic display will be made of the books you have read.

You do more and better; you obtain by prayer and meditation the distinct knowledge of a great spiritual truth, and immediately selflove joins itself with this heavenly visitant and you become jealous and vain of your announcement of the truth. Great and good men sometimes quarrelled because one charged the other with stealing his words out of his mouth.

Or on some occasion, you display great self devotion or humility, and give way to pride because you have conquered pride, or to self-love that you have conquered self-love. It is related of an eminent divine that when on one occasion he had officiated with great success in a church one of his friends came to him and told him that he had made a heavenly prayer; he replied, My friend, the devil told me the same thing before I left the desk.

Thus out of the bosom of every good comes forth the hand of the Adversary of God and man beckoning us backward with pleasant invitations to give up the good we have so hardly bought. And hence it comes that the progress of a man towards heaven is so slow, and through so many interruptions and defeats and disgraces that he is made triumphant.

This fact that evil is everywhere found, has always been hard to be accounted for. But it deserves the best power of thought which any of us can give, whether it is not accounted for by the Christian doctrine that the soul is here placed for education; that the highest good can not be imagined by us as existing without evil; that without evil there can be no such thing as virtue, which consists in overcoming evil.

II. The next fact of great importance to us—next to the *universality* of temptation—is this, that we exercise a great influence upon the moral evils that touch us, that we make a great portion of our temptations—that we make the most and the worst of them.

We make our own temptations. It is in the nature of things, that every thing bad should lead to worse, and every good should lead to better. We are not tempted to desperate courses except in desperate fortunes, which are commonly the consequence of guilt or folly. It is a wise observation that "Prudence consists in avoiding the occurrence of difficult cases, and Virtue in doing our duty when they happen."[2] It may happen to a man to be compelled to choose between destroying his own life or that of his brother. It may happen to him to lie almost under a necessity to commit an enormous crime. But it is very seldom or never in the course of Providence that these dreadful alternatives present

---

2. Not located.

themselves to innocent persons. It is in bad places and in bad pursuits and by bad men that grievous provocations to sin are felt.

In war, which is a savage institution, the crime of manslaughter becomes inevitable. Where so criminal an institution as slavery exists, terrible examples of punishment may become necessary for the personal security of the master. And in the vices of individuals, it is not in the meeting house, nor in the court, nor in the workyard, nor round the fireside, it is in the nameless dens of intemperance and debauchery that violent passions lead men into violent temptations. Men get into harm because they first got into harm's way. They frequent the bar-room, and there learn the way to the gaming table and the brothel and the jail. Let it, I pray, be put home to the personal experience of every one of us, even of those who by the kindness of Providence have been furthest removed from the indulgence of gross vices, whether every one of our sorest temptations have not issued from our own fault. Every temptation to which we yield is the fruitful mother of a hundred more. Consider into how many trials a foolish compliance leads us. You have in the warmth of dispute or out of vanity been led to a false statement, a slander, for example. And presently when inquiry presses close the temptation to fortify your first assertion by a new lie was so strong that you could not resist. For what more mortifying than to go back and confess to those with whom you were angry or to whom you feel yourself superior, that you were guilty of so low a thing as a lie? The lie then must be maintained, cost what it will. Now lies have no legs.[3] It costs ten falsehoods probably to patch up the first, and every one is a new stab on your neighbor's reputation. But these irrecoverable words cannot be won back; they fly nimbly from tongue to tongue; they produce resentment and offences from the party you have injured against you, and every one is a fresh temptation, and a greater one. And presently you are involved in very serious difficulties where you find it very hard to go right with the best intentions, and for all which you can only thank yourself.

Perhaps your trials are different, or is your temptation that species of injustice which consists in going beyond your income in your expenses? If you examine any temptation you will find that a former indulgence created this want. A very little will supply our natural wants. Very few men think how little. An earthen lamp will give as much light as a silver one, but the love of uniformity when we have indulged in one expense which we can afford leads us to a great many which we cannot, and hence all costly luxuries come to be thought necessary to comfort. You have got a costly watch and must have costly ornaments. You have a good house and therefore the furniture must be good.

The embarrassed tradesman borrows new thousands to save his thousands in danger, and involves by successive faults himself and his creditors so deeply that the temptation to fraud continually grows stronger till he thinks he cannot do otherwise; but in all this, who but he made the temptation strong?

3. Cf. "A Lye has no Leg, but a Scandal has Wings." See Thomas Fuller, *Gnomologia* (London, 1732), 10.

Or is it sensual indulgence that is your bosom sin? The excess of yesterday created the appetite of today, and weakened the power of resistance by taking away the dignity that belongs only to temperance.

And thus it is in every sin. Let no man when he is tempted say I am tempted of God, for it is we ourselves that have laid out and digged and paved the downward road in which we go to destruction.[4]

But as it is the law of God that from him that hath not, shall be taken that which he hath, and he that is filthy shall be filthy still,—so is it his law that to him that hath shall be given, and he that is holy shall be holy still.[5] Good is the parent of good. Resist the devil and he shall flee from you.[6] By refusing an allowed morsel we keep farther off from the gout and indigestion and the repentance and the other appendages of the unallowed morsel. The way upward is as direct as the way downward. A virtuous exertion leads to a virtuous habit. A virtuous habit to an acquaintance with virtuous men. An acquaintance with a few to the encouraging and instructive society of many. These auxiliaries lead to higher merit; and this again to trusts and connexions which become obligations to perseverance in virtue and effectual barriers against whole classes of low temptations. What is a severe trial to one man's virtue may be so far from a temptation to another as to be wholly loathsome merely from the difference of progress.

It is true, as we stated before, that mount as high as we will, we never escape from temptation; but there is great difference betwixt the temptations of a good man and of a selfish man. They refine and rise. His conscience becomes more tender. He makes distinctions where before he made none. He attains to an inner life, to sources of happiness of which formerly he had no conception. He does not mourn that still he is tempted. It is a matter of consolation to an infinite being that the field is worthy of his force. As Alexander said he would have kings for competitors,[7] the soul is proved and sanctified by progressive and proportioned trials and increases her strength by the strength of her adversaries.

We have considered the universality of temptation and the help which we ourselves give it. Let us now in the third place consider the appointed cure.

III. The text furnishes us with the remedy to this universal disease. If thus our house, our business, the social circle, the street swarm with temptations, it becomes us to study how to encounter them. The answer is Watch and Pray. And I believe if we accept it we shall find it a perfect one.

Watch; for as the sin is very subtle and gains ground by imperceptible advances, you must watch from month to month the state of your soul, from day to day the progress you have made, from hour to hour the dangers that threaten you.

---

4. James 1:13; Matthew 7:13.

5. Matthew 13:12 and Revelation 22:11.

6. James 4:7.

7. "Alexander, when his father wished him to run for the prize of the race at the Olympian games, (for he was very swift,) said; *He would, if he might run with kings*." See "Apophthegms New and Old," no. 171, in *The Works of Francis Bacon* (London, 1857–1874), 7:148.

Do you fear your temper, or your appetite, or your vanity, or your love of gain or your indolence? Never let the eye of conscience shut upon the dangerous propensity. For sometimes when we are pleasing ourselves with our victory, we do the sin again.

Watch, for sin to be hated needs but to be seen.[8] There is no more perfect cure of the desire of vice than a distinct apprehension of the consequences of vice. Ask yourself if the whole amount of all the inconveniences and anxieties arising from any wrong action had been fully known to you at first would you have put your shoulder to that weary burden? "By always thinking unto it" was the mode of Newton's discoveries,[9] and by always thinking unto it is our appointed way of overcoming a sin.

Watch and pray, for the great temptation of most of us is not any particular evil so much as the general habit of our life; the misdirection of our love, that we are averse to God, addicted to the world. Watch then the things within and those without, the works of nature, the dealings of Providence, the voice of Christ—what is close to you yet unseen. Watch the wanderings of your own soul. Sin watches for us, God watches for us, and shall we not watch for ourselves?

Equally important is the other way, namely, praying. Pray; for if we would really destroy a temptation we must conquer it in God's name. If we conquer it in our own, if led by interest or pride we forsake a sin, it is likely that a worse may rise in its room. To *watch,* is to give all our strength; to *pray,* is to add a divine strength. To pray (in the best and highest sense of that word) describes the highest state of which human nature is capable. True prayer is a clear sight of our own wants and our own place in the universe. It is a wisdom from above.[10] It is a ceasing from thinking as men and a beginning to think as angels. What other state is desirable or great but this? What compared with this is the mind that marshals armies or combines campaigns, or the mind that legislates for an empire, or the wit that accumulates and wields vast knowledge, or the genius that commands you by its eloquence or that advances the kingdom of man over nature by discoveries? What is all that man has done or man can do compared with the state of that soul that truly rises to a sympathy with the Deity in prayer, yields itself to him and is heard and accepted by the Infinite Spirit? That mind is armed best against temptation for God has more part in it than man. Yet is there not one so low and ignorant but by faith and obedience may rise to this state.

Therefore, brethren, let us watch and pray lest we enter into temptation. Let us watch ourselves inasmuch as we make our temptations; and let us pray to God that he will deliver us from the evil that is in the world for which we are not

8. "Vice is a monster of so frightful mien, / As, to be hated, needs but to be seen." Alexander Pope, *Essay on Man,* II, 217-18.

9. "To one who had asked him on some occasion, by what means he had arrived at his discoveries, he replied, 'By always thinking unto them.'" See Jean Baptiste Biot, "Life of Sir Isaac Newton," trans. Howard Elphinstone, *Lives of Eminent Persons, The Library of Useful Knowledge* (London, 1833), 19. Cf. *JMN* 3:200.

10. Cf. James 3:17.

accountable.[11] We have each of us a deep interest in the matter. We have each of us real sins and well known to us. Whilst we spare them they are ruining us. And every indulgence leads, as we have seen, to a worse snare. If ever we hope—in all the future periods of our being—to gain any ground over our bosom sin, we must begin today. We must deny the temptation today. Now is the accepted time. Now is the day of salvation.[12]

11. Cf. Matthew 6:13 and Luke 11:4.
12. II Corinthians 6:2.

C

For God who commanded the light to shine out of darkness hath shined in our hearts to give the light of the knowledge of the glory of God in the face of Jesus Christ.

II CORINTHIANS 4:6

The year as it draws to its close calls the attention of Christendom to the festival of the Nativity of Christ. As the principles of Christianity are better understood and wider disseminated, a more deep yet more cheerful interest gathers round the religious system introduced by Jesus of Nazareth. The man who was born in Bethlehem in a stable increases his power amidst the rise and fall of states, the change of laws and principles of government, and steadily advances with the good of mankind, and is only opposed by the barbarism and the corruption of nations. They who have watched for his halting, they who have persecuted and slain his servants, have gone to their own graves, with the bitterness of crimes perpetrated in vain. The moral influence which he infused into the world has never lost one jot of its activity but has remained a permanent and indestructible element of human society, now shaking empires and institutions as ripe fruit to the ground, now building them up on solid foundations of righteousness, as strong when it was secret and in a few breasts, as when it sat in thrones. Not to be measured by the outward appearance, there yet are tokens that now it has greater sway in the world than at any former period.

It will be a much better celebration of the occasion to us if we shall in our minds make a single principle of the religion more distinct and so more effectual than, without this, would all the decoration and festivity and solemn pomps of Catholic and Episcopal Europe. The time invites us to consider the worth of the gift which it commemorates; to consider the value of the revelation brought by Jesus Christ to all men, and to us.

It is assailed, it is defended. It is claimed by one part of his followers as only

Manuscript dated December 26, 1830, and March 4, 1832. Preached three times: December 26, 1830, at the Second Church, Boston; March 4, 1832, again at the Second Church; and November 6, 1836, in East Lexington. Notes and draft passages for this sermon occur in *JMN* 3:216–19. On MS p. 2 Emerson drafted the following notes on his argument in the sermon: "Christianity exactly coincident with morals Its progress not opposed by infidelity but by sin It is the greatest good."

theirs. It is daily forgotten, betrayed, transgressed by the great multitude of those who bear his name and live in the hearing of his word. Let us improve the time by considering a few circumstances that, though not new to any of us, may yet serve, if weighed by us, to confirm our faith and bring our practice nearer to its rule.

I. It may sound like a trite remark but it is one which deserves the best attention of all, that Christianity is exactly coincident with morals. Christianity has been disobeyed, and, what is more strange, has been opposed. Yet is it to the whole extent of its teaching exactly coincident with the dictates of the common Conscience.

The conscience, though a familiar term, is used I know with great looseness. Yet all will agree that it differs in every man according to his knowledge. One man's conscience condemns that which another man's conscience allows. But give them the same light, and both will condemn the same thing. It varies in different individuals only by degrees of wisdom. Conscience strictly speaking is not the law of right and wrong, but only the sight of that law, and may be weak in one and strong in another. The law is fixed and eternal; the sight of it varies in every individual. But in general use Conscience signifies more, viz., not only the sight, but the authority, which when it is seen, commands its observance.

Now wherever Christianity has gone, it has coincided entirely with the conscience of cultivated persons, i.e., with the conscience of the most virtuous persons. It enjoins what that enjoins and condemns what that condemns. It commends every sober and elevating principle and militates against no man and no society and no interest and no motive that is desirable or safe. It condemns war and slavery and intemperance, and every vice, every unsocial and injurious practice.

Herein it differs from other systems pretending to come from God. The religion of Mahomet teaches what is contrary to the Conscience; it is sensual.

The religion of the Hindoos is a cruel violation of natural duties; and so are the religions of the savage nations of the North and South. The law of Christ alone is accurately consistent with the moral Constitution of man.

Further, Christianity is not only strictly coincident with what the Conscience teaches, but it enlightens and confirms the conscience or moral sight. It is a torch that casts a flood of light upon the obscure field of duty and along the dim boundary of right and wrong. The ancient moralist taught men to respect each other's rights. The Christian moralist shows whence men's rights flow out of a common parentage in God. The ancient moralist taught men to abstain from evil. The Christian moralist teaches men to abstain from evil *as sin*. The ancient moralist taught men to keep the commandments to avoid the wrath of heaven. The Christian moralist enjoins us by gratitude to the most wise, most tender, most holy Parent—to serve him in love. The love of God who is perfect and the desire of perfection in ourselves are the beginning and end of the gospel.

We claim for Christianity this praise, that it is coincident with the conscience in greatest advances that had made in the knowledge of the moral law and, further, that it carries the conscience on with it to a wider prospect of the moral law. Is not this the best proof that it came from the same hand from which human nature came?

If Christianity is thus one with man's nature,—if man's Constitution is thus Christian, why should it be rejected? Why should it be received thus tardily? What opposes it?

And this is the second point to which I beg your attention.

II. Christianity is opposed by our sins. Every thing that is good in us waits and hungers for its coming, and government, and increase. But what is evil in us instinctively hates and fears that which passes judgment upon it. Public sin opposes Christianity in states, private sin opposes it in men's bosoms. As long as a man's life is inconsistent with it, he will be hostile to it. He is insensible to its beauty according to the measure of his moral guilt. Certainly a man can have no other objection to a mild and salutary law strictly agreeable to the inward rule, except that it reproaches him. But that is the malignant nature of evil that it poisons all it touches. If I do wrong, I am prone to hate him who knows my offence, him who judges it, the law which condemns me, and all those whose better life accuses mine. Who ever heard of a faithful friend of truth and goodness who followed to the best of his light the commands of duty who was at the same time an enemy to Christianity or to one of its laws? If a man then finds any hostility in his disposition towards the revelation, would it not be reasonable to seek first if it does not come from some artful sin that lurks privily in his bosom? First cast out the beam that is in thine own eye, and then shalt thou see clearly to cast out the mote that is in thy brother's eye.[1]

III. The next consideration is a practical inference from the two former, that this revelation is the greatest external good of man, and it behoves us to hear and obey it with a diligence and devotion to which I fear most of us are strangers. The simplest facts are the most grand, and oft the most hidden. I put it to your reason, brethren, if it be not the noblest attribute in us, *that we are capable of being addressed on the ground of moral principles*? This fact is so close to the first fact of our *existence,* that like the circulation of the blood or the law of gravity it passes long unnoticed from the very circumstance of its omnipresence.

If you will feel as you ought that all external blessings are of less account, that it is not that you have a body of wondrous workmanship, that you have a tongue, and eye, and ear, the pleasures of the senses, or the power to raise about you houses, and decorate them with all accommodations; it is not these things that distinguish you; that they are dust and straw and all outward glory is like unto them, compared with the awful power that resides in you to know right and wrong, the sense of duty; this is your true distinction and to this God speaks—you will understand the price of the blessing better.

Without this distinction man is only an upright beast,—a beast that may

1. Matthew 7:5 and Luke 6:42.

speak,—and may entrap or slay other beasts, but add this, and you first impart the capacity of religion, the capacity of eternal life. He is on the direct road to God and Heaven. And this it is which Christianity addresses. The pain that a commandment gives us, by condemning our practice, ought even in that moment to give us joy beyond all the pleasures of sin, because it is a pledge and a measure of the good whereof we are capable,—of the excellency of our nature. It is the observation of an eminent moralist "that there is a sweetness even in remorse."[2] And there is reason for this pleasure. For see how it raises you. Let a principle come from heaven to man, such as Jesus presented, *that he should love and serve God.*[3] If I receive it into my soul, forthwith, from a poor necessitous sickly creature, occupying a spot of the earth, I become associated with God, I prosper in the prosperity of the Universe. Wherever truth and virtue thrive, there my interests are promoted; there is no star, or soul, or plant, or atom, but I have my part and use of it, by my love of its Maker, and my part in Him.

I am raised by the reception of a great principle to its height and have by it a being greater than my own. And he who communicates applies and embodies a great principle for me, is my redeemer from the evil to which the want of it would have led me. Jesus Christ addressed this moral nature and gave the soul these infinite principles. He taught man to live above himself; to seek the Kingdom of God first, and wholly to undervalue the whole world in comparison with the health of the soul, that is, purity, humility, love; that the end for which all things exist is the soul; that God is preparing the soul for himself, and designs that it should be tempted, and resist, and triumph; should feel the disease of wrong, and so seek the well being of right.

My friends, we think much and justly of the great men who have instructed our minds or established our rights. Men of Science never forget the greatness of Bacon who taught men to seek the progress of science in observation and so saved men from the consequences of pedantic speculation. We think much of Newton who disclosed some of the simplest laws of matter and so saved us from mistake in the study of daily laws. We love to praise the name of Leonidas, of Sidney, of Washington,—our political saviours, who established the principle of right to personal liberty. Yet this last, the greatest of all—what is it but a single corollary (valued by us because directly touching our worldly good) nothing but an inference flowing from the free agency of the soul implied in the great moral revelation of Jesus. The political freedom of man will always exist where Christianity is received; freedom to the subject and freedom to the slave will issue out of it. We think much of those who have found out one separate truth,— but the Divine Teacher of our souls, (in whose lesson all these truths are contained) we dishonour and grieve. He will lead us if we will follow him to a nobler freedom than the mere absence of external chains. He will break the chains of sin. He will teach us something better than the orbits of the planets

---

2. The quotation occurs without attribution in "Religion" (*EL* 2:87).
3. Luke 10:27.

and the order of systems; he will teach us to put our souls in harmony by introducing love to God and man.

The excellence of the truths which Jesus brought is that they are inexhaustible. Truth does not lose its use to us with its first appearance. It opens as it is examined, and discloses more worth as it is more used. The eldest angel has not found the end of God's love or wisdom. Sin loses its sweetness at once, but virtue never.

My friends, if we will consider these things: 1. that Christianity is strictly consistent with our moral nature; 2. that it is commonly opposed in ourselves and in others by sin; and 3. that really it is an infinite good to have a moral law, even though at present it should condemn us—if we will give these thoughts their full weight in our minds they will make us greet this gracious law with devout gratitude and love. We shall welcome in our soul this returning season. We shall echo the angels' song, Glory to God in the Highest, on earth Peace, good will to Man.[4]

We shall value as we ought God's unspeakable gift. We shall sympathize with the ardent apostle in his continual thankfulness, that God who commanded the light to shine out of darkness, hath shined in our hearts to give the light of the knowledge of the glory of God in the face of Jesus Christ.

---

4. Luke 2:14.

CI

How old art thou?

GENESIS 47:8

This is the inquiry which in the natural world may be made of all objects, for all are growing old. And old age is the approach of dissolution to animated and to inanimate beings. Every science is the record of the progressive changes or steps toward dissolution in the objects it considers. Geology shows us how the ball we dwell upon has been rent and its central beds of granite lifted to be the ragged peaks of the Andes and Alps; how these have been worn and crumbled into common soil; what races of vast and shapeless animals have roamed over the earth and been buried under new convulsions; how populous cities of men have been whelmed, now under floods of the sea, now under inundations of melted stone from volcanic hills, now have been swallowed by the yawning of the earth itself.

These are the great graveyards that entomb their thousands in a moment. But every moment is as fatal as these dreadful catastrophes; every moment kills some part of life in all the children of nature. In our own race it is plain enough. Every face, every feature we behold betrays marks of its destiny. All history is an epitaph. All life is but a progress toward death. It is computed that in ordinary times when the plague is stayed in Asia and War in Europe and only the common causes of mortality operate, 2400 of the human race die in an hour; so that almost every pulse is the knell of a brother. The world is but a large urn. The glorious sun itself, burning in his brightness at the heart of the system, and pouring out the incessant floods of heat and light, to all his tributary planets, seems but a funeral fire operating the destruction of all that he shines upon and lighting men and animals and plants to their graves.

All things are so constituted that they perish in using. The lamp burns out, the causes of destruction lie so thick and numberless that the gentlest wind that brings the perfume of the fields proves poisonous to some frame and checks the tides of the blood and sets the seed of fever or rheumatism.[1]

Manuscript dated December 31, 1830. Preached three times: December 31, 1830, as a lecture for the Watch Night service at the Second Church, Boston; January 1, 1837, in East Lexington; and January 13, 1839, in Concord, Mass. Notes for this sermon occur in *JMN* 3:220–21. The annual Watch Night service at the Second Church was initiated by Henry Ware, Jr.; for the occasion Emerson also preached Sermons LXI (on December 31, 1829) and CXXXIX (on December 31, 1831).

1. For images developed in this and the preceding paragraph, see the quotations Emerson

In this scene of wreck and fear the natural man hears on every side the question, How old art thou? that is to say, How soon is your turn to die?

The true asylum from these apprehensions of mortality is the church. It is the only refuge from this fear. In the mouldering of nature we flee to the gospel. The soul escapes to God affrighted by the decays of the Universe. (To the natural man all things decay and himself also. To the spiritual man all things are eternal and himself also in God.)

What is it that working ever in the soul of man has constrained him in every place to build his temple, altar, church, or meetinghouse? What is that grander nature which everywhere separates him at short periods from his day labor to think and to pray? A conviction swells in his heart, which all the decays of the senses will not put down, that, within this decay, there is a germ that decays not.

Whilst all things are thus flitting away there is a duration to which a century is but the turning of an hourglass. Whilst all perishes, there is a creation as fresh as it was in its morning prime, before the stars were launched on their orbits, and that shall be as fresh when they are swept out of the heaven. There is a natural world and there is a spiritual world.

My friends, the Church takes a different view of almost all seasons and events from that which is taken in the street or the exchange or the Statehouse. It surveys man and his life from quite another side.

There is a spiritual world which is immutable, the kingdom of love, of purity, of righteousness, of truth, the kingdom of God—which is incorruptible and cannot grow old. The cause of all order, the source of all good, it is in the world, and the world is made by it, yet the world knows it not.[2] But the soul of man must live in it or it hath no life. As the body was born into this world, so must the soul be born into that, not in some future time but now. This is the Scripture doctrine of the Regeneration.[3] The Scripture is the message from that world to the soul of man to call him to that, his true home. It teaches the necessity of this new birth. It teaches that in the closing the senses to the exclusive commerce with outward things and in the opening of the interior senses to the acknowledgment of this better kingdom does true life consist. In the spiritual world only can we live. In this world we die daily.[4] It calls nothing else, *life,* but that life. It calls the entering in that state by men, a *passage from death unto life.*[5] It looks round on men struggling in vain care and keen competitions of this world, the pursuit of fame and office, the labor for perishing meat as all laborious trifling, no better than the toys of children. It teaches the soul to seek for life in itself as the Father hath life in Himself.[6] And what is the life that Jesus means?

---

gathered on December 29, 1830, from Sir Thomas Browne's *Hydrotaphia,* beginning with "That great antiquity America lay buried for thousands of years. & a large part of the earth is still in the urn unto us" (*JMN* 3:219–20).

2. John 1:10
3. Cf. John 3:5–8.
4. I Corinthians 15:31.
5. John 5:24 and I John 3:14.
6. John 5:26.

His truth alone. "The words that I speak unto you," said he—"*they are Spirit and they are life.*"[7] That soul only has entered into life that has found out, that God's will is better than its own; that humility is better than pride; that to seek another's good is better than to seek its own; that to be good is to do good; that a perfect trust in God, gives more contentment than the greatest possessions. These facts are the years of the soul. Therefore as soon as a man has received these truths, not into his ear, for there they are mere sounds—not into his memory, for there also it may be a dead stock, but into his soul as a part of his soul; as we receive bread into our bodies and it becomes flesh, so when this has become mind and soul in us, then is his second life begun. Then does man emerge out of the finite into the infinite; out of time into eternity; then really does his life begin. Now, *How old art thou?* Judge by this measure. Let the question come home to each of us. Do not run back to the month nor the year when your parents say you were born; if you are in any true sense, *of age,* "ask yourself"; take the New Testament for your Almanack.

How long have you *lived*? that is to say, how long have you lived in any other way than to the senses? How long has the Word of God been to you any thing but a dull book? Has light begun to break forth from it? How long has Jesus Christ been the Son of God in your mind? Take the New Testament and read it thoughtfully and observe how many of its rules yet seem disagreeable to you. See if you do not stop with the first recorded teaching of the Lord, *Blessed are the poor in Spirit for theirs is the kingdom of heaven.*[8] I am afraid it will seem to you mean and unworthy, not finding through the darkness of your soul any correspondent sentiment reflecting it as a mirror in your mind. Read on—Find the summary of the new law. *Love the Lord your God with all your heart and strength and mind.*[9] Here is the great law of moral nature, and does it find its full echo in yours? Read the next, Love your neighbour as yourself.[10] Is this your rule? Have you shared your means and toil between the good of others and your own good? How many months have been filled with the love of others and how many have been spent upon yourself? Stop now and think—*how old is your soul*? Is it ten years old? Is it one year old? Is it one month old? Has it yet burst its bondage, has it yet awoke from the womb of worldly life to the light of Heaven, and the sight of the face of God? And yet twenty, thirty, forty, fifty, sixty ungrateful years of self love, of impurity, of sloth, of covetousness have been counted on the family register and every one has ample vouchers in the memories of your companions, perhaps in the too faithful imitation of your children.

My friends, we received the words of the gospel with our mothers' milk; we call ourselves Christians, that is to say, receivers of the word of God that came by Christ,—and yet if we deduct all those days of our life that have not been

7. John 6:63.
8. Matthew 5:3.
9. Mark 12:30 and Luke 10:27.
10. Mark 12:31 and Luke 10:27.

lived in this faith; if we reckon up only those hours that have proved our adherence to the truth, add up all the good, and take out all the evil, I am afraid these years that have been so busily spent and have brought us so near to the grave would shrink to a hand's breadth—the compass of a few hours—perhaps to less.

Honourable age is not that which standeth in length of time, nor that is measured by number of years, but wisdom is grey hair unto a man and unspotted life is old age.[11]

These principles must be the law of our action. Just as in the natural world we conform ourselves to natural laws and do not try to walk on the water, nor to fly into the air, nor to live without food or without motion, so in the spiritual world, if really we enter it by a new birth, we shall studiously conform ourselves to these principles which Jesus declared. I do not think we are old at all until the Christian law flows unobstructed through the channels of our life. It seems to me there should be no Christian who should not hold himself amenable for all his acts and words to every other Christian. I desire to do nothing that I cannot justify. If anything can be shown us in our practice inconsistent with what we receive as truth, we are bound to alter our action. It is the perfection of free agency to be as faithful to the law as brute matter is. We believe it impossible for God to do wrong because he is perfectly wise. There is not a leaf nor a fibre in all the vast economy of nature that breaks a law of matter, so neither should one thought in all the world of souls. When we are old truly, old in love, old in truth, old in God, we shall thus find our perfect freedom a perfect law and move "impelled by strict necessity along the path of order and of good."[12]

Now, brethren, that you have the plain Scripture for the truth of this doctrine, that you were born for the spirit and not for the flesh, now that he who does not live by a second birth, must die by the second death,—you will permit me in the last hour of a large portion of your term to press it upon you. That whole term is a span. Seventy or sixty or thirty such rounds as this make up human life. Twelve of those few years are taken up in childhood; then follow the heats and temptations of youth, that are apt to make the real life yet shorter, and so much of maturity is apt to be consumed in the cares of this world, that the main business of man is shoved aside from day to day and remains at the last undone. Now it is too soon. And then it is too late.

This delay has been the rock on which the former men have been shipwrecked. Our time is yet present. That span out of his measureless eternity which the Almighty Father allows to each, to be tried and instructed, to hear his name and to read his commandments, to make friends, to deal with men, to choose our part and make our character, that time which is nearly equal in all, (a few years making little difference when compared with the boundless duration out of which it rose and into which it recedes,)—is now ours. It is all that

---

11. Wisdom of Solomon 4:8.
12. William Wordsworth, *The Excursion,* IV, 1268-70.

the great and the wise have had. It is all that saints and heroes had. It is all that
Paul or Luther or Newton or Washington had, to lift themselves by humility and
the love of truth and sublime energy into the spiritual world and help the human
race. It is now our turn of life. It is a singular proof of the independence of
spiritual nature on space and time that this life is long enough for the vast
purposes to be answered by it. It is long enough for useful men to work their
ends. It is long enough to the wise to instruct men. It has been long enough for
tyrants to enslave men. It has been long enough for the patriots to free nations.
A truth may be announced in a moment that shall go down to all ages and affect
all human society. Finally it is long enough, as all experience shows, for men to
be saved or to be lost. And now it is our turn to make our election; all for which
the soul of a man can exist, the great things of eternity, the choice of all the
future, of the love of God, and of all souls, and unceasing advancement towards
the infinitude of wisdom and love, or the rejection of all these, are on the right
hand and on the left hand, of each of us. We are to choose principles for the rule
of our souls on the one part, or we are to prefer the little gratifications that begin
and end in this nook of earth where our bodies were born and where they will
moulder. This is our alternative. It is pressed on our minds at a season like this
with unwonted force.

Whilst the occasion calls us to the consideration, there is another fact that
may increase interest: the care God has manifested that we must make this
choice for ourselves. It is the stern law of his moral order that each must be wise
for himself. Every soul is jealously excluded from the salvation or the death of
the rest. The knowledge that has been accumulated by others is of no use until it
has been verified by us. For all the learning and sound judgment and rich experience that has been in the world, no man is wiser by one poor thought who is not
wise in himself. And yet more clear is this truth respecting another's virtue. He
is virtuous to himself. But whilst wisdom cannot pass into folly nor one man's
goodness into another who is vicious, yet these are means of helping those who
help themselves. To him that hath is given.[13] If it were not for this law, the vast
burden of evidence arising into one voice from the history of every individual
man, would teach every other that a Christian life leads to peace and a worldly
life to ruin, and leave no room for doubt. The convictions of all would be
accumulated on him and the gospel would be demonstrated in his faith. But
there is no such lazy wisdom allowed us. None can by any means redeem his
brother;[14] all past wisdom is nothing but as far as it is identified in our own.
Our own is nothing till our will directs it. But God is continually presenting
excitements, suggestions, to startle us into attention and beseech men as Christ
besought them to be reconciled to God.

One of these excitements, one of these occasions that are the trumpets and
thunders of God is this which now speaks to us. The shadows of the last hours

13. Matthew 13:12.
14. Psalms 49:7.

of the year are come upon us. They speak to us of change and death. They hush the passions, the worldly hopes, they outspeak our temptations even, and procure a moment's silence for their question. They ask if the time has any terror to you; if you have any fear of what time and death can do, or whether you have passed from death unto life through the power of that quickening truth which Jesus revealed. If you have any fear of death, it is a pretty plain mark that you have not yet read your title clear to a place in the new heavens and the new earth, wherein dwelleth righteousness;[15] that the flesh has yet a great part in you. Let us, my friends, not be deaf to this Voice; save these fleeting moments with a divine economy by making them bind us to God for the next year. Let us repent of our sins. Let us love one another; let us be humble; let us be resigned to God's will; let us sin no more.[16] These are the signs of the Regeneration, of our birth and adoption into that world, of which God is the everlasting light, where is no age but immortal youth and no change but from glory to glory.

15. Cf. Isaiah 65:17 and 66:22, II Peter 3:13, and Revelation 21:1.
16. John 8:11.

CII _____

As thy days, so shall thy strength be.

DEUTERONOMY 33:25

The new year is for the most part regarded as an hour fit for congratulation to all the members of the human family. It has been thought by many philosophers, that a very accurate comparison of the pain and the pleasure in every hour would show a far greater amount of suffering than of enjoyment in human life. The common sense of mankind seems to decide against this sour philosophy in the general practice of welcoming as a positive good, a new year. We welcome the New Year with all its hazards. We congratulate each other that the simplest goods are sufficiently desirable in themselves, counting reason and knowledge and affection a blessing even though they are to be enjoyed with serious drawbacks: with debt and hard labor, with hunger and pain and wet and cold. And if there were not a traditional faith in life after death, many of those who by reason of sickness and old age lose much of their desire to live would cling to life with a firmer grasp.

> To be no more, sad cure, for who would lose,
> Though full of pain, this intellectual being,
> These thoughts that wander through eternity.[1]

Who would lose the common consciousness to be rid of the common pain?

To the largest part of the community, to those who are in the years of usefulness or of hope, to those who are knit by numerous connexions to the human society, to those whose heads teem with projects that threescore years are not long enough to execute, nor the finite powers of man sufficient to compass; to the ambitious, to whom celebrity is very sweet; to the covetous who think that a great estate is a great happiness; to the laborer whose buoyant health and pressing business do not allow him to look much beyond the passing day; to the scholar who sees simple contentment for him in the walls of a library, and in the prospect of leisure to read and to write; to the young persons of ardent affections, who form no bolder expectation than the indulgence of these affections;—

Manuscript dated January 1, 1831. Preached three times: January 2, 1831, at the Second Church, Boston; January 1, 1835, as a lecture in Concord, Mass.; and January 3, 1836, in East Lexington.

1. Milton, *Paradise Lost,* II, 146–48.

to all these, the year is welcome; it is boon enough to live; and each promises himself, with undoubting confidence, that he shall be able to hew out of the quarry of so much time an ample satisfaction.

And these, I suppose, are the majority of men. This we should expect in a world proceeding from an intelligent Cause; that there should be some proportion observed between the powers of men and their gratifications; that the same hand that formed the animal creation with such attention to their enjoyment and especially provided it by blinding them to the future, would have remembered also the present welfare of man when he withdrew this veil from his eyes and made him to look before and after.

But it must not be forgotten, that however great is this happy multitude, the New Year does not rise in sunshine to all. There are many to whom the wishes of a happy year sound harsh and unfeeling; their sad convictions repel them. Or if they receive the kindness of the salutation they are persuaded in their hearts that the wish is vain. They see so clearly their own hard lot staring them in the face; they see difficulties, in contending with which they have worn out all their youthful strength and spirits, still to be freshly encountered; they are reminded by the time of what the last year took away, and no future year on earth can restore, and for which earth holds no equivalent; or they see troubles which have been hitherto unnoticed ripening into size and force for which they are all unprovided, that they begin the season with little cheerfulness and do not see how they shall make the ends of the year meet, in the common expression, that is, how the power shall overcome the difficulties of their situation.

Now to all these sufferers and to all of us, as far as we are sufferers, the word of God comes with a grave and parental rebuke, yet giving consolation far beyond its pain, and saith to them, 'You have overlooked the most important of all the facts in your estimate of the future: you have omitted to consider the source of all strength; you forget the eternal Providence which always adjusts your condition to your character, and which does never forsake any, not even those who forsake themselves. Trust in Him. 'As thy days so shall thy strength be.''

It will be a wholesome consideration to us and may prepare us all to begin with better heart and resolution our several appointed works to consider a little the manner in which God does thus proportion our burden to our strength.

I. And, first, he does it by his natural laws. I say *natural;* but who shall say what are the limits of the natural? Spiritual helps are natural; they are part of the nature with which every man is endowed and the life of all his nature. Trials often seem to make men strong, for they call out a strength that was hidden before, even to ourselves. As it is often observed in the history of nations that a great emergency seems to create great men, so it is true of individuals that in cases of extremity they will often behave with a discretion and greatness altogether unexpected. Many a hero, it is said, has been made by fear. And certainly many a sluggard has been made a workman by the very desperateness of the alternative before him. He must put out his might, or he must starve. And thus shall God protect and aid you, by yourself, by faculties now dormant which your necessities shall arouse. Thus your trial shall be a blessing. Is it a trial of poverty? it shall make you content with little, it shall sharpen your faculties and make you skilful and wise. Is it a severe trial of temper? It shall clothe you with a heavenly patience which before you had not numbered among the virtues. Is it a trial of pride? Your enemies shall prove your best friends. Are you forced to compliances that you are ashamed of, before people whom you have despised? It may inspire you with the humility of Jesus. Is it a trial of great affliction in the loss of a friend with whom you would have willingly given your own life? It may fix your affections on God, which will be more than a compensation for the loss of all friends. Is it a trial not of one kind but of all kinds, a life of most perplexed and painful sort? Even this may work out a better and more various excellence, it may arm the entire soul, it may form a perfect character. Never let us forget that in the Christian theory, all trials are disguised mercies. We are stronger than we seem. A man has deeper places in his heart, nobler faculties in his mind than he yet has believed; and a far greater variety of discipline must he enter before he can know himself.

By the help of God's spirit, in the multitude of your thoughts you may make the discovery that there is no low place; that where our duty calls us there is dignity, as much in a menial as in a commanding office. And when you have made this discovery, a light not of this world shall shine into the closets and corners of your dwelling.

Once more, as thy days shall thy strength be. It is a pleasing fact to observe that whilst the passage of time seems even to reach the soul by impairing in mature minds the cheerful imagination which in childhood and youth made all life a holiday, it does not less surely operate to develop other powers which are more than equivalent. It matures the judgment; it increases the love of truth with the acquisition of truth, and so tends to take off the false colors from things of sense and take off our minds from them.

And thus by natural laws God assists us against our trials.

II. In the second place, God assists us in our trials by foreign helps. The course of Providence operates in our favour, or, according to a good proverb, 'tempers the wind to the shorn lamb.'[2] Unexpected difficulties are encountered by means of unexpected auxiliaries. Extraordinary distress calls out extraordinary sympathy. But there is a little more than this. Most good men have seen in their lifetime, good reason for the saying of David—"I have been young and now am old; yet have I not seen the righteous forsaken, nor his seed begging bread."[3] If I speak to any pious heart who has been tried occasionally with more than the common hardships, and has, in all, kept its faith and hope in God, let it

2. "'God tempers the wind,' said Maria, 'to the shorn lamb.'" See Laurence Sterne, A Sentimental Journey through France and Italy (1768), ed. Gardner D. Stout, Jr. (Berkeley, Ca., 1967), 272. This French proverb, first collected in Henri Estienne, Prémices (Paris, 1594), is most commonly quoted in Sterne's version.

3. Psalms 37:25.

bear me witness, whether when the cloud was darkest, in the very hour when it seemed sorest beset, and cut off from every help, whether then help did not appear, and in some quarter to their eye the least likely to afford it, suggesting to their faith that prayer was answered. This will never seem strange to him who believes in the omnipresence of the Divine Being. A particular act of Providence will not seem wonderful to him who sees that every throb of his heart, every motion of his hand is wonderful and involves of necessity a Providence.

I will only specify one of the foreign helps whereby God most signally assists the human mind; that is, by friends. The poorest is not poor whilst he has a true friend. The richest is not rich who wants one. And if we look back upon our life, I think we shall see no such sweetness in it as that which has come out of the conversation, the counsel, and the love of a few individuals that have made a little light for us in the darkness of our path. Nor, I know you all will bear me witness, nor would any generous mind esteem any privation severe, any labor hard, that was to be lightened by the spiritual comfort of sincere, wise, and virtuous friends, loving and instructing us. Shall we then esteem corn and wine and oil the gift of God, and not esteem our friends as his special and highest gift? Or shall we trust his Providence that he will spread our table and cover our nakedness in the days to come, and not believe that he will more richly bless us with that inward strength which shall satisfy and exercise our affections?

III. There is yet a third way in which God strengthens us for our trials, and that is by the gift of an infinite nature. This consideration gives an extent of meaning to the promise that will infuse a mighty virtue into our souls. 'As thy days, shall thy strength be.' But the days of the soul are without end. When the sun of the spiritual world hath risen upon it, it can never fear a night. One day is as a thousand years.[4] So then, according to this intended duration is thy strength. God has formed us, as these affections and faculties may declare, not for seventy summers, but for day without night, for action without end.

Now if a man will attentively consider it, he will see that the reason why he is wretched, the reason why the New Year brings no joy to him, is that he misapplies these infinite powers with which he is furnished, to insignificant things; as if a giant should play with flies. The soul that was formed to act upon sublime principles cannot act habitually upon mean ones without suffering. The love that was meant for God and our fellow beings cannot be confined to our lower self without missing its satisfaction. The soul that was made to comprehend all truth cannot be shut out from all truth without eating on itself. If our strength was made infinite as our duration, we ought not to murmur if our abuse of it has caused us unhappiness. Let us rather enter into the views of our Father. Let us bring back the soul to its true objects. Let us judge less by custom and more by God's word and by our Conscience and we shall find many of our supposed trials not to be such, and many that are painful difficulties now to be very light and tolerable. We shall be armed too with a divine strength which now we are

4. II Peter 3:8.

apt least to reckon. We shall feel that the invisible world sympathizes with us. We shall be able to do all things through Christ that strengtheneth us.[5] We shall seek first the kingdom of God and his righteousness, and all lesser things shall be added unto us.[6] And if lesser things should be denied we shall feel that we can as well forego them. We shall see the noble sense of that ancient devout man who exclaimed, O Lord what hast thou left to the wicked, for thou hast given all things to the good in making them good.[7]

My friends, let us fortify our hearts with these thoughts against whatever discouraging circumstances exist in our knowledge. Especially let us apply it as Christian souls to the evil of sin. Not the failure of any earthly hope is so much to be deplored as the failure of our moral principles when exposed to daily temptations. And let us feel that there is no need that ever again we should do a wrong act, let the temptation be what it will. As our days and as our temptations, so shall our strength be. Let our resolution only cooperate with this promise and every day of this year shall instruct and raise us to an apprehension of the happiness of Heaven.

5. Philippians 4:13.
6. Matthew 6:33.
7. See Sermon XCIII, n. 7.

CIII

*The same came to Jesus by night, and said
unto him, Rabbi, We know that thou art a
teacher sent from God: for no man can do
these miracles that thou doest
except God be with him.*

JOHN 3:2

It is my present purpose to offer to your consideration a plain account of the reasons which make the miracles recorded in the New Testament credible. It will be readily seen that the evidence of any particular miracle must continually become less accessible with time, and let it have stood on whatever demonstration once, a thousand years must make it continually more difficult of proof. The point of importance in the question, therefore, has always been felt to be, to show that in some circumstances it is not unreasonable to expect a miracle and that such circumstances existed in the age of Jesus Christ.

I shall therefore proceed to consider first the considerations which show a miracle is not incredible.

I. The first consideration is, that a miracle is the only means by which God can make a communication to men, that shall be known to be from God. For to suppose that he should speak directly to each mind, is only to suppose millions of miracles instead of one. The speaking to each mind in any unusual way, would be a miracle, or else would not be believed by that mind, a peculiar communication from God. To deny therefore that there has ever been or ever can be any miracle, is to deny that there has ever been or ever can be any communication from God to men.

II. The second consideration requires more words in the statement. It is a certain want that arises from the nature of things to the human mind, and which only a miracle can supply. It seems to be the inevitable effect of the invariable order of God's operations, to withdraw the human mind from the contemplation of God. For the unceasing succession of events without any

---

Manuscript dated January 20, 1831. Preached twice: January 23, 1831, at the Second Church, Boston, and January 30, as the Sunday Evening Lecture in the South End, Boston. Notes and extensive draft passages for this sermon occur in *JMN* 3:214-17.

interruption, or any sign of intelligence beyond what the infinite beauty of the whole furnishes, without a hand outstretched, or a word spoken in heaven or on earth, makes man doubt the existence of a cause that is never shown to his senses. It is only the very thoughtful that see the necessity of something more. The multitude, seeing the laws of nature uniform, stop at the law and take that for cause enough. Now the only way by which men's attention can be aroused to the thought that there is a presiding Intelligence, is to startle them by a plain departure from the common order, as by causing the blind to see, and the dead to arise. There are thousands of men who if there were no histories and if the order of natural events had never been broken would never ask in the course of their lives for a secondary cause and never ask for a first. It is enough for them to say that a stone falls or the earth falls in its orbit *by Gravity;* that a man walks and speaks by reason of his Life, without asking whence Gravity and what is Life? But astonish them with a miracle and their minds instantly inquire why things keep one order rather than another, and the same inquiry instantly suggests itself to every mind who hears of the miracle.

Now does not this furnish a suitable occasion for the particular interposition of that Providence which consults always for the good of his offspring? If truth and religion are good for us, will not God interpose to prevent us from losing both?

III. Another consideration that makes a miracle not incredible, is this, that, it supposes no more power than we have already seen every day exerted in and around us, and no more inconceivable power. The existence of God is necessarily suggested to the reasoning man by what he now beholds and a miracle suggests no more. Does the unbeliever, who doubts of a miracle, suppose, that by giving up that superstition, he has made all plain, that he shall now be troubled by nothing for which he cannot assign a cause?

Far otherwise. To an instructed eye the most common facts are the most wonderful. It is not so surprising to a wise man that there should be volcanoes and earthquakes and meteors and cannibals and monsters, as that he himself should live from day to day. A wise man perceives that there is really nothing more incredible in the story that reason should be restored to an insane man by a word than that he himself should be able by a mere thought to raise his own arm; or that he can communicate such vibrations to the air by his tongue as shall make his thoughts known to another man; or that by an effort of recollection he can summon up events in which he took part twenty years ago. All our life is a miracle. Ourselves are the greatest wonder of all. Our own being is a far more astounding and inexplicable fact, than, after life has once been exercised, would be the resurrection of a man from the tomb.

The ordinary course of nature indicates an intelligence capable of the alleged works, for, it can require no greater power to suspend than to originate the operations of nature. In other words; I can believe a miracle, because I can raise my own arm. I can believe a miracle, because I can remember. I can believe it, because I can speak and be understood by you. I can believe a manifestation of power beyond my own, because I am such a manifestation.

IV. In the fourth place, as a miracle does not transcend the power, so neither does it depart from the character of the Intelligence that presides over ordinary nature, in being an evidence of a moral truth. Our Constitution is moral, and so is that of the universe. All things preach the moral law—that is to say, a life in conformity to nature is a moral life. Health is to be sought by temperance. Safety is got by abstaining to offend. The love of others is gained by loving them. All benevolent feelings are pleasant to him that exercises them. All malevolent feelings are painful. And the moral law with no essential variation reigns in the bosom of every man. The character of the Deity that presides over the world is thus ascertained to be moral. And therefore a miracle which is a special act of his power, *for a moral purpose* conforms with what we know of him.

I take notice of this fact that from the constitution of things we should expect that a miracle *would have a moral purpose,* because it seems to be necessary to the idea of a miracle that it should be *moral.* A miracle must be to a moral end, to have any effect. A miracle could not prove a falsehood. It cannot approve a vicious act. Let it be supposed that here before our eyes a man should pretend to declare from God that hatred and murder were agreeable to his will and should cause stones to speak or storms to rise to confirm his word,—it could never engage us to think that it was right to hate and kill men and that the messenger came from God. It might bewilder us with horrible doubts, but the miracle would be ascribed to an evil spirit and not to the same power which made our moral constitution. To make a miracle of any effect as evidence, it must accompany the revelation of a truth which when made known is agreeable to the laws of the mind. Then the truth and the miracle mutually confirm each other.

These considerations may serve to show in general the credibility of a miracle. The history of a particular miracle must always show to what degree of credit it is entitled.

We ought to weigh with extreme caution the evidence of any alleged miracle, for though a pious man will always be ready on good evidence to admit a miraculous agency yet we feel that the same wisdom which may sometimes interrupt its customary order, for the special benefit of man, will, for the same reason, very seldom interrupt it. Some may ask, if there have been miracles, why are they not common? Why have not I seen them? For this reason, that their often occurrence would be fatal to knowledge which the human mind stores up and reasons on the expectation of the permanence of the laws of nature. Any uncertainty in the operation of the laws of nature would defeat entirely the purposes of that wisdom which formed him and them. If it were in the least uncertain whether the sun would rise tomorrow or whether wheat on being sown should come up wheat or hemlock, all prudence, all experience would be of no use, and not only so but the order on which we found our belief of the unity and providence of the presiding cause would be broken. And not only so but the miracle, it is plain, would no longer answer the use of a miracle.

I wish now to speak of the peculiar credibility of the miracles of the New Testament. In so doing I shall confine myself to a single general consideration which seems to be conclusive on the subject, and that is, the claim to miraculous power considered in connexion with the nature of the revelation.

It ought to be considered that a miracle is a lower species of evidence. It speaks to unbelief. It speaks to ignorance. It is not, (even on the foundation, on which now it stands,) the favourite evidence of wise and pious Christians. Internal evidence far outweighs all miracles to the soul. A reasoning Christian would think himself injured by the fortifying too scrupulously the outward evidence of Christianity. If the whole history of the New Testament had perished and only its teachings remained, the discourses of our Lord, the authority, the holiness, and the heavenly standard of Jesus, the ardour and spirituality of Paul, the grave and selfexamining advice of James would take the same rank with me that now they do. I should say as now I say that this certainly is the greatest height to which the religious principle of human nature has ever been carried, and it has the total suffrage of my soul to its truth whether the miracle was wrought, as is pretended, or not.

The truth taught in the New Testament will stand by itself. In other words, many minds will not want the miracle but to all it is such truth as might be expected to be accompanied by miraculous power. Now we put the question to every reasoning mind whether the great peculiarity of the Christian miracles is not decisive in their favor—viz., that the moral truths which they are alleged to have accompanied are not utterly incompatible with the supposition of imposture in those who declared them and lived by them. There is nothing in the teaching of Jesus or of his apostles that would encourage what is called *pious frauds* but all that abhors them. They were teachers of sincerity, of contempt of worldly honour, of the fear of God and the fear of hurting the soul beyond any earthly evil, and they kept their own rules and exhibited the principle in practice. Yet these persons appeal distinctly to the knowledge of the persons they address respecting miracles done by their hands; and since I perceive the divine truth of the doctrine, I know the miracle must have been wrought which they say was wrought. This is an evidence so strong that I ask no other. It is impossible that the principles which these men reasoned out and lived out, as all external testimony declares, should permit the least imposture. To suppose it is to admit a miracle far more confounding than the miracle of the Resurrection.

There are many allowances to be made for any thing that seems improbable in the records of these transactions, which will always be considered by sincere seekers for truth. Thus it should be considered that the books of the Evangelists are not the revelation but the record of the Revelation and that many things may have come to their ears by common rumour which were false. One miracle performed will make a multitude credible, as one clap of thunder has a hundred echoes. I am not therefore made uneasy by any plausible account that gives a natural origin to an event related as miraculous, or to any number of such events. All I ask is a single miracle, a single fact to show that such power was evinced by the teachers of such wisdom.

The question to be asked concerning them (I now quote the words of an eloquent English writer, Mr. Coleridge,) is, "Was it an appropriate mean to a necessary end? Has it been attested by lovers of truth; has it been believed by lovers of wisdom? Do we see throughout all nature the occasional intervention of particular agencies in countercheck of universal laws? (And of what other definition is a miracle susceptible?) These are the questions, and if to these our answers must be affirmative, then we too will acquiesce in the traditions of humanity, and yielding as to a high interest of our own being, will discipline ourselves to the reverential and kindly faith that the guides and teachers of mankind were the hands of power no less than the voices of inspiration: and little anxious concerning the particular forms and circumstances of each manifestation, we will give an historic credence to the historic fact that men sent by God have come with signs and wonders on the earth."[1]

1. Coleridge, *The Friend,* 3 vols. (London, 1818), 3:257–58. In *JMN* 3:216 Emerson reminded himself, "See p. 258 of III Vol. of The Friend," and in his copy indexed "p. 103 & p. 257-8" under "Miracles." See Kenneth Walter Cameron, *Emerson the Essayist* (Raleigh, N.C., 1945), 1:122.

CIV

Thou shalt love the Lord thy God with all thy heart, and thy neighbor as thyself.

LUKE 10:27

It is my design in the present discourse to present the principle on which the great class of social duties depends. There is something at all times refreshing and elevating in the contemplation of the social duties. All selfish passions are mean and all social ones, that is, all that seek the good of another for his own sake, are noble.

The fear of death is unworthy of a man. Would you know the remedy? Go and see the death of one who spends the last breath in devoted serving of others and you see the ruins of human nature clothed with beauty and all the meanness of death taken away. It may be recommended to us as a practical rule, the golden rule of Christ, that when unawares we are surprized with any cowardice either in the apprehension of death or of evils on this side of it, let us take refuge in immediately applying ourselves to an active interest in the welfare of those persons who have the nearest claims upon us. It will bring more than angels to our side. It will bring courage and conscience and God to our aid.[1]

Especially should these thoughts reinforce us amidst anxious and difficult times. 'To keep yourself temperate at a feast,' says an old moralist, 'you have two expedients, to carve or to discourse.' And how shall you more gratefully awaken your heart and your conscience amid the present despondency than by reflexions on the perfection of that web of relations to all beings into which your own lot is woven, and which makes it impossible for you to act without affecting many more than one; which enables you to touch so many hearts with joy or

Manuscript dated January 1831 and February 9, 1834. Preached six times: January 12, 1831, a Wednesday, at the Old South Church, Boston, for the Howard Benevolent Society; February 9, 1834, in New Bedford; June 1 in Waltham; July 20 in Bangor, Maine; December 6, 1835, in East Lexington; and July 24, 1836, in Concord, Mass. Notes and draft passages for this sermon occur in *JMN* 3:222–24. In *JMN* 4:294, on the day after he preached the sermon in Waltham, Emerson's remarks suggest the sermon provoked him to wonder about the relation between the "genuine man," the preacher, and "the supposed advantages of Christian institutions," a relation he characterizes at one point as "discords." The Howard Benevolent Society, for whom this sermon was first preached, was an early Unitarian philanthropy, whose charitable endowments continued into this century.

1. Emerson used this paragraph again in Sermon CXL.

sorrow; which therefore teaches you that you are born to promote happiness; to add to the sum of good.

Let us proceed to consider the false answers and the true that have been offered to the question, What is the principle on which our duty to serve our fellow men depends?

I. In the first place, it has been answered that it flows from self-love, but a long sighted self-love. 'Benevolence,' according to a proverb of false philosophy, 'is self love well calculated.'[2] This is not true. Self-love short-sighted or long sighted is not benevolence. In any common use of the word self;—in any sense less than that infinite sense in which self-love loses itself in the love of God and the Universe, this answer is not true. Self-love and Benevolence may prompt the same outward act. They are not the same action, as is proved by its not having the same effect.

Self-interest never prompted a sincere service of others. From a polluted source a pure act cannot flow.

It is true indeed that it is the interest of man to be the friend of man. It was an early discovery of political economy that in no form could labor be exerted to less advantage than in an attempt to confine its fruits to the laborer. The man who should set himself to build his own house, weave his own clothes, make his own shoes, teach his own children and so prevent the price of these works from enriching his neighbors would presently find himself the poorest of all.[3]

It is easy to show that united men live easier, richer, and happier than hating men. A striking illustration of this may be seen in history whenever small contiguous countries have been united under one government. The small territories of England, Scotland, and Wales, included in the isle of Great Britain, were once separate nations and their continued separation cost them each a perpetual garrison upon all their frontier beside endless wars and all the expenditure of life, comfort, and virtue which war involves. It is all saved by the simple discovery that they can be one nation; a fact so cheap that it costs nothing. And in general it is easy to show that a well calculated self-love would dictate a punctual discharge of duty to others, as Pride is civil to others to keep others from treading upon its skirts; or as covetousness relieves the starving multitude with part of its store to hinder the starving multitude from relieving themselves, or as the wise statesman educates the lowest class of the population in order that God's restraints of knowledge and virtue may keep down the turbulence which an armed police cannot keep down.

It is true then that it is the interest of men to be benevolent. Is it therefore the true foundation of our duty to others? What a motive were this? I am to go to my brother with relief for his wants, with kind words in his distress, with

2. Emerson's source, as Kenneth Cameron suggests, is Coleridge's quotation of a French maxim in *The Friend:* "Amour *de moi-même, mais bien calculé*"; see *Emerson the Essayist* (Raleigh, N.C., 1945) 1:107.

3. This and the preceding sentence are taken from Sermon LXV (*Sermons* 2:133).

instruction in his ignorance and say, Brother, I find that such are the laws of Providence that I cannot get and keep all the bread without your aid. I therefore give you some. I find you can do me great mischief; I therefore speak you fair. I instruct you, to keep you from assailing my life or burning my barn, or being the pirate of my ship.

What sort of gratitude will this excite? What hatred rather will it not inflame? It is fear, it is concession, and deserves no honor or love and will find none.

It neither benefits you nor him. And in so far as it now operates, it begets the disposition which just this language would create in individuals. It exists and it creates that murmuring which is so often heard against the rich.

That the interest of the individual and of society are one is most true, and much more than this is true, and yet all together do not yet constitute the true motive of our social duty. It might be shown that it is an indispensable part of a finished character to comply with the law of charity. It might be shown that he who withholds his aid from his fellow man is more a loser than his fellow man from whom he withholds it, that the soul of man was made to act for others as much as his body was made to breathe the air, that speech and reason and knowledge and grace and beauty and power are all worthless whilst they are confined to one and were given to be communicated, that all his improvement is from a selfish to a social life—a development of power to act with and for others.

I look upon all these facts as of great importance, as illustrations of the perfect wisdom with which the world is framed, so that the good of others is promoted involuntarily and against his will by the most selfish man in his most selfish action, yet this is all their value to our present purpose. Let self-love be instructed and exalted as much as possible, it can never become the principle from which the good of others should be sought, nor can it be proposed to Christians by Christians as a proper motive.

II. Nor, in the second place, will it do to say that the manifest wants of our nature make the obligation to serve our fellowmen. It is not a sufficient reason. It needs a foundation itself. The question may still be asked, And why must I supply my neighbor's wants?

Nor can the love of our neighbor in that degree of strength in which the sentiment is ordinarily found, be safely trusted as the support of such various and incessantly returning duties as we owe to others. It is too capricious and discriminating—too selfish. It is to be considered that although love is a universal passion and no man can be found but his heart warms to some fellowbeing, yet very few men love all their fellowbeings.

Especially how is it to prompt us to that important part of duty we owe to the inferior and to the wretched? Would it do to trust the supply of the wants of the poor to this partial selecting passion? Some men hate the poor. Some men lock their gates and a great many lock their hearts against the poor.

We love the lovely, the modest, the good, the eloquent, the poetical, the well educated, the well mannered, the elegant.

But that class of persons who most need the assistance of their fellowmen are commonly unlovely, uneducated, many of them stupid, often vicious, offensive frequently from the filth of their habitations, and sometimes much more so from loathsome diseases,—as the Committee of this Society have abundant occasion to observe.[4] And the very fact of their wants is apt to make the selfishness of men hostile to them. The love of man in those who have no higher principle, the love of man in the atheist, would be a bad dispensary, I fear, to the sickly, hungry, shivering wretch who ventured to appeal to it. Who has not heard the oft repeated refusals of the selfish that the beggar is a nuisance; that all charity is a bounty to vice; there was mismanagement somewhere, or there never would be want; I am sorry they suffer, but follow it up and you shall find it was their own fault.[5]

The love of our neighbour is a principle of wonderful force where it really acts, as in the relations of parent and child, of husband and wife, of friend and friend, and will prompt the noblest actions and the greatest sacrifices, but it will not serve as a principle whereon to found the whole system of social duty.

III. It appears, then, that the love of self is not worthy and the love of the neighbour is not sufficient to be the principle on which our duty to our fellow creatures is built. The Scriptures, both in the old and new Testaments, furnish us with the true principle in the language of my text. Thou shalt love the Lord thy God, with all thy heart. The love of God is the principle on which the love of our neighbor stands. The reason why I must help him when I can, is because he is God's child, as I am. His claim on me is through God; God is my father, all I have is his and I am wholly bound to his will. His will is the good of the Universe, and that I must promote, and my neighbor's as a part of it.

Does this seem too vague and distant a principle for the motive of actions that are to be done every day?

The love of God, some will say, is a sublime theory which makes the happiness of heaven, but few men in this world attain to anything beyond low degrees of the sentiment, and certainly the duties of every hour ought to meet us with all the force of the plainest commandments. Yes, and it is because we are so much separated from God that we so ill understand our relation to our fellowmen and so poorly discharge our social duties. This objection which is continually made in the world, this awful distance at which God is placed from our minds, this uncertainty with which men speak of him, accuses our evil life and dims the evidence of the truth but cannot alter the truth itself. We are sad aliens from the heavenly life, we grievously break the commandments, if we are thus strangers to Him. The Scriptures teach us that nothing is more intimate than our relation to Him. They teach that we are God's children, not by any metaphor but in a far stricter sense than we are the children of men. We are made of him—we live but in him, as the leaf lives in the tree. "*Know ye not that*

4. Emerson refers to the committee, including himself, charged with disbursing the funds of the Evangelical Treasury to aid poor families in Boston.
5. The sentence is taken from Sermon XL (*Sermons* 1:303).

the spirit of God dwelleth in you? God worketh in us, both to will and to do, of his own good pleasure."[6] We are his children in a manner, that as we keep his commandments, shall all but identify us with him. We shall be parts of God, as the hand is part of the body, if only the hand had a will. We are made of God as the urn is made of clay, but separated from our great Parent by our free agency, and separated further from him by it perhaps day by day. Whenever we act from self, we separate ourselves from God; whenever we do right, we consent to his action by our hands.

When we do right, it is not our act, it is that we receive God into our souls and submit to be his organ. We are then conscious of acting upon a greater will and to a greater end than self-good. It is I that do wrong; it is God in me who does right. And it is the perception of thus living in God, that makes the propriety of the commandment to the Jews, Be you Holy because I am Holy, and that by Jesus Christ, Be you merciful as your Father is merciful. Be you perfect as your father in Heaven is perfect,[7] commandments which would be wholly incomprehensible but for the great truth that men, in the words of St. Peter, are partakers of the divine nature.[8]

This truth is so invaluable to the mind that I wish it may receive the consideration of every one who hears me. For all great souls when they have given themselves up to their duty have found this conviction grow in them, that in God only they had life. As Paul said, The spirit beareth witness with our spirit that we are the children of God.[9]

This great doctrine that God dwells in the human heart in a manner so intimate that it is because he there is present, that we exist—so that a man is not so much an individual as a manifestation of the Eternal and Universal One—is no new or peculiar doctrine. It does not belong to any church but to a certain elevation of mind in all churches. It is not the doctrine of any sect but of all devout Christians. I may say not the property of Christians but of men. For before Christ had declared the character of God and his relations to the human mind, humble and thoughtful men had yet communed with their Maker and rejoiced in the conviction that God dwelt within them. The pious men of the Stoic sect received this faith, saying that the wise man differed from God in nothing but duration.[10] It was also a maxim of their school that mind was God in man.

The devout Fenelon, a bishop of the Church of Rome, declares that God is in our souls as our soul is in our bodies.[11]

Archbishop Leighton, one of the most esteemed and one of the best divines of

6. I Corinthians 3:16 and Philippians 2:13.
7. Leviticus 19:2, Luke 6:36, and Matthew 5:48.
8. II Peter 1:4.
9. Romans 8:16.
10. "Bonus vir tempore tantum a Deo differt." Seneca, "De Providentia," *Moral Essays,* trans. John W. Besore (London and New York, 1928), 1:6; used in Sermons LVI (*Sermons* 2:90) and CLXV, "Ethical Writers" (*EL* 1:359), and "Plutarch" (*W* 10:312).
11. *Extracts from the Writings of Francis Fenelon,* ed. John Kendall (Philadelphia, 1804), 16.

the Church of England, writes that "by the love of God the soul is made divine and one with him," and quotes with approbation the language of St. Austin, If you love the earth, you become earth; if you love God—shall I not say you become God?[12]

And that great light of the Calvinistic Church, Henry Scougal, says in his sermon on the Excellency of the religious—"Learn to adore your nature."[13]

Now whilst I see this to be true in my nature I see that my fellow man is made in the same mould and of the same substance. Every man you meet seems to repeat yourself, to be another and the same. We never converse without seeking, if I may use the expression, to find ourselves in each other, guided always by the conviction that we were made to think alike. Especially as men are good do they understand each other, for then the spirit of God in them is less and less disguised and they feel that they are inspired by one soul.

Now is not this the principle of Charity? Is not this the principle that must regulate all our dealings with mankind? Is it not that we are every where to acknowledge the present God? Must not all my intercourse with my brother, poor or rich, be governed by this tender reverence for our mutual nature, divine in its origin, however disguised by selfishness in both of us? Are we not to deal with the most obscure and sinful wretch as only a perverted wreck and ruin of a mansion in which God has dwelt and perchance is already returning to dwell through these very storms of misery by which he is preparing his entrance? I see at once that there are nobler ends to be sought by me than giving him bread. I am not to relieve his wants as an end, but by means of relieving his wants I would justify myself to himself, or produce a full consent between God in him and God in me. I am to show him that I know and own this our sacred relation as children of one God. I would not forget the glorious attributes that are obscured by the necessities of his circumstances and by his sin; I would search for them under his rags and under his sin; I would love him as myself. I would love him for the same reason that can alone justify and regulate the love of myself, that, in both of us, is the spirit of the living God. It will be seen at once that this principle will exclude all selfishness. I shall be seeking, in every exertion, to benefit another, the good of the Universe, and it will serve in all places throughout the sphere of human action. It begins with the nearest relation and reaches to the farthest. It dictates our intercourse at the fireside and it reaches our conduct to our country, to other nations, and to the brute creation.

Let me add now a few remarks as to the extent of this claim. It lays its grasp on your whole being. It says you are bound to the will of God because all you are is from him. What hast thou which thou didst not receive?[14] There is not a

12. "According as the Love is, so is the Soul; it is made like to, yea, it is made one with that which it loves. By loving gross base Things, it becomes gross, and turns to Flesh, or Earth; and so, by the Love of God, is made divine, is one with him. *Si terram amas, terra es; si Deum amas, quid vis ut dicam, Deus es?* Aug." *Select Works of Robert Leighton,* 2 vols. (London, 1805), 1:257.

13. "The Superior Excellency of the Religious.—On Prov. xii. 26," in *The Works of the Rev. H[enry] Scougal* (Boston, 1831), 94.

14. I Corinthians 4:7.

man in the world, who has got a piece of bread for himself. He got it by the hands which he never made, and by the head he never made, and by aids that he never made. And if you should strip the most powerful and opulent and accomplished person on earth of all that he has received you would leave him nothing but his sins.

To the same extent then does the claim on us reach. In the eye of the Christian law, "No man liveth to himself and no man dieth to himself but whether living or dying we are the Lord's."[15] There is not an inch of ground in the Creation left for self-love to stand upon. We are not our own and our business is the love of all. We are to hold all our possessions and all our powers of body and mind *in trust* for the utmost good they can be made to accomplish.

The doctrine of the New Testament which I have endeavored to illustrate is that because God is our Father and all we are brethren, therefore we are dearly bound to seek each other's good. And to whom does it speak? to some Jews and Romans long departed from this world? or to our fathers who are also departed? or to us, to you and to me in whatever state we are,[16] of joy or sorrow, alone or in families? To you and to me does this sublime doctrine come home, and if we can open our eyes to see it, with such power of consolation and of command as to make adversity no longer adverse, the fears and vexations of time no disturbance of our peace, and human life a part of the Eternity of God. My friend (and I speak to each one in this house) have you never suspected a greater inmate in your frail body than a frail animal life? Have you never perceived that while all things change a soul possesses you which changes not; which amid doubts, doubts not; which amidst dejection, intimates that all will be well? A soul which amid the clamors of temptation, breathes the low thunders of his admonition, a soul which though disregarded and forgotten in the din of affairs still meets you again with its unruffled supremacy on its own occasions when you are alone. A soul before which you are known though you wear a mask to all the world. A soul which never participates in your guilt, but as God in Heaven beholds it all from an infinite superiority. A soul which assures you that integrity and truth and love can never be a loss, nor crime a gain.

My friend, have you this soul and has it never seemed to you that an Eternal voice speaks through it to you, and an Eternal Eye looks through it upon you? "Know you not that you are the Temple of the Holy Ghost, and that the spirit of God dwelleth in you?"[17] It commands you with the whole of its authority, to use all the occasions that are presented of serving your fellow man who is also a Temple, however disguised by evil influences and his own will, of the Divine Presence.

The manner of our being, the strange mystery of our greatness and our littleness, we may not understand, but these duties he hath written in light.

15. Romans 14:8.
16. Cf. Philippians 4:11.
17. I Corinthians 3:16.

Because God is, and for God's sake, let us love and serve his children, our fellowmen. In the name of God, if your brother has wronged you, forgive him; and so conspire with all that is good at the bottom of his own heart. And if you have entertained an unkind purpose against him, O see that it is a warfare against yourself and God in you. It is the suggestion of an evil spirit. Why should you make the happiness that is in the world less? O for our own sake let us be just; then, where we can, let us be merciful; and, with fixed resolutions to make others happier that we have lived, let us purchase by kind forgiving thoughts, and helping intercessions and affectionate wishes a little permanent happiness amid the sorrows and sins of this transitory life.

CV

And whatsoever ye do, do it heartily,
as to the Lord and not unto men.

<small>COLOSSIANS 3:23</small>

Every Christian who looks at society with the demands of the Christian law in his mind, cannot help being pained by observing how few comply with it in any great degree, and scarcely one complies with it even to all outward appearance. The great multitude of men seem to have no high standard of excellence; their notions of what is their duty, are got from custom and not from reflection; the Bible is heard or possibly read without application to the state of the soul; its principles are so high, so uncompromising, so inconsistent with their practice that in their darkened minds, it is an argument against the Bible, and not against themselves; their principles are low and their practice not so good as their principles, that the Christian is staggered with doubt when he would indulge the infinite hopes that grow out of his faith. It seems strange to him that a faith so sweet and so awful should be thus disgustful to the souls of men; he feels that there is a sore side to human nature; that men call evil good and good evil.

But it is yet a more painful feeling which arises from a view of the faults of the good. If we are pained by observing that the bad are very bad, it is yet a further wound to find that the good are not good enough. Those who know, if we may judge from their description, what spiritual life means, what is the beauty of holiness, what are the heavenly pleasures of believing, of praying, of praise, sometimes seem indifferent to the great discovery they have made. They who are born of God in the Regeneration, seem to have lost for a time the signs of their more excellent life. Their principles differ so widely from those of the world, that their practice should be as much marked. In childhood and youth our whole confidence in the reality and power of religion rests upon our reverence for a few eminent examples. God seems never to have left himself without witness to any nation, nor yet to any mind. A good man, a pious mother, or the well kept anecdotes of a holy ancestor are that *witness*. Such persons become associated in our minds with every commandment. We see their faces when we

Manuscript dated January 23, 1831. Preached three times: January 23, 1831, at the Second Church, Boston; May 8 at the Friend Street Chapel; and August 14, 1836, in East Lexington. A brief note on this sermon occurs in *JMN* 3:225.

read the bible. We ascribe one character, a kindred heart, to St. Paul and St. Peter with the godly men of the English and American churches and with these honoured individuals of our own name or blood. It is therefore a great shock to our souls when more knowledge of any good person discovers anything in him unworthy of this holy society. We feel as if fault in him were fault in all. We feel as if salt itself had lost its savour.[1] We say in our haste, *"all men are liars."*[2] We justify the too literal reading of the Calvinist that "there is none who doeth good, no, not one."[3]

This shock that is caused in us by the imperfection of the reputed good, is dangerous to us in proportion as our respect for virtue is a respect for it in others. If we have made no proficiency in religion ourselves, if we have never learned to think; if God is to us a historical being, of whom we read and talk as of one that is absent; in short, if our whole reverence for religion as a reality rests on the testimony of others, then in discovering unsoundness in the religion of others our whole belief in it falls down,—a total ruin.

For this reason when good men stumble, the bad exult. It seems to them a confirmation of unbelief. It arms them anew against the doubts that often goad them, the last strivings of the grieved spirit. It arms them with a strong argument to pull down the tottering faith of other men.

I have seen an old man of affectionate manners and clear head, not at all learned beyond a very intimate acquaintance with his bible and a few religious books, whose life was chiefly spent in hard labor in the fields but his soul ever on the wing, intent to draw the moral from what he heard and what he saw. This man never jested. But his heart was so impressed with the honour of God, that the expression of the feeling ran over in all he did. He never contemplated any considerable, hardly any trivial, action of his life without reference to God. His talk came back continually to this topic simply because he was not much interested in any thing else. He was just and obliging as if involuntarily. His faith had so cheerfully written itself out upon his face that wherever he went you thought of him as a God-believing mind.

That man to me is a moving argument of the immortality of the soul. He is what he is, by natural influences of this habit, nor can such a man be seen without respect or without greater confidence in the truth of the gospel which has made him what he is.

And truly, brethren, it is not an imagination but a sentiment which all men sometimes feel that the heart of man cannot be trusted to all the influences that act upon it without any other guide than whatever feeling is uppermost; it needs to be made fast by going voluntarily to its home, its centre, its regulator, by making fast to this Unchangeable Refuge.

But the pain caused by the discovery of imperfections in those esteemed religious is far less injurious when we have ourselves made progress in a holy

1. Cf. Matthew 5:13, Mark 9:50, and Luke 14:34.
2. Psalms 116:11.
3. Cf. Psalms 14:3 and 53:3.

life; when, as the apostle saith, we have faith to ourselves.[4] 'Experimental religion' is almost a cant word, and yet to many ears, it will convey the sense I mean. When we have thought anxiously upon our duties as they are declared in the Scriptures; when we have quitted passive following of other men and sincerely and meekly compared what they say, with what we see and feel; when we have once observed as with our own eye and found it no fable (and no common place) but plain truth, that nothing can confer peace but a good heart, and that every wrong step is a wound to our happiness; when we have learned to speak and to *think* even as in the presence of God—then our faith is no longer derivative, it is original in us—it holds directly on God and not on God through other persons. We have tasted pleasures of the spiritual world. We have felt pains of the spiritual world; and to us thenceforward the spiritual world begins to be felt to be real, and the material world begins to appear shadowy. We begin to think that our bread and meat—the house we live in, the streets we walk in—are things far less real and enduring than the soul. We begin to feel that truth and goodness never grow old whilst all material things perish. The more good a man grows the greater does his soul grow within him and the more sure he grows that it will never die. We know that God is, and that he is a rewarder of them that seek him.[5] When therefore we discover imperfections in the good or even gross unworthiness in those we had esteemed men of God, though it may fill us with sorrow, it cannot unteach us what we know; it cannot uncreate that new man in our minds. The rains may come, the winds may beat vehemently on the house, but the house that is founded on the rock, stands.[6]

That men's professions should be higher than their practice, or that men of irregular fervor should be overthrown, may find explanation and palliation also in our own experience in our slow and oft-retarded progress, and may fill us with wholesome alarm lest we also make shipwreck of a good conscience.

My friends, the gospel teaches us this lesson, which is enforced by the consideration I have now presented, that, no faith is good, that rests on any but God; and no character is good that is formed on any principle but the love of God; that, only we can have a well grounded hope of final salvation when all we do, is done as unto the Lord and not unto men.

This lesson is writ on every page of the New Testament, that the foundation of all goodness must be a regard to God and not to men; that virtue must be godliness. It is expressed or implied in all the teaching of Christ, and he himself lived by this principle. And so I say to every one of you, my friends, you are not a Christian whilst your good works are not done as unto the Lord, let your good works be as many and as great, as they may. You are not a Christian, for Christ did all unto the Lord. He did not come in his own name. He disclaims the doing of his own works. He disclaims the speaking of his own words, but gives all the glory, yea, all the will even, to God. 'I can of mine own self do

4. Cf. Romans 14:22.
5. Hebrews 11:6.
6. Cf. Luke 6:48.

nothing; as I hear, I judge, and my judgment is just because I seek not mine own will but the will of the Father which hath sent me.'[7] He sought no honour from men but directed all to God. 'How can ye believe,' he said to the Jews, 'who receive honour one from another, and seek not the honour which cometh from God only?'[8] All his instructions were directed to lead his disciples to fear God and not men and to give him the whole heart. Indeed, brethren, this is the essence of religion and it highly behoves us to apply this test to all our habits of thinking and acting. I shall therefore ask your attention to a few applications of the rule.

Let this rule be present to our minds and it will be a safe interpreter of every difficulty touching faith and works. Works done as unto the Lord and not unto men contain faith. Works not so done are not good. And this is the truth on which some Christians have stood when they say of an unregenerate person that all his good works are sin, which is often carried so far as to affirm that such a person's prayers are sinful. It may serve to illustrate the remark that all religious history illustrates, that the errors of sects are not unfounded falsehoods but exaggerations only of weak minds, and may in general be traced directly back to some spiritual truth from which they spring.

Thus apply the rule to what a worldly man calls his virtues. Here is a man who eats and drinks temperately. He is extremely scrupulous about gratifying his appetite. No luxury, no company, no solicitation can tempt him to excess. And why? Is it because he accounts his body a temple of God and will not displease him by gratifying his low desires? No such matter. If you examine the motive you find it is mere selfishness taking in this instance the form of a prudent care of his health, which intemperance has rendered necessary. It flows from the same motive that makes him uncharitable in one instance and refuse his bread to the hungry and dishonest in another in keeping his creditor for months out of his honest debt. Now this temperance I will not call sinful but surely it has no claim whatever to the name or the praise or the peace of virtue.

But this is a selfishness of which you do not feel guilty. You have never defrauded the rich. You have never refused alms to the poor. You love others. You do not bear false witness. You have no gross vices. In true dealing with your own heart you cannot help perceiving that you are better than other men are. And yet when you read the bible you do not find a perfect truth. It promises the faithful unspeakable joy and you are often unhappy.

The reason why we derive so little confidence and satisfaction from our freedom from sins which other people commit, is that we do not shun them *as sins*. We avoid them out of regard to men. A thousand and a thousand proofs of this may occur to each one. And hence too come our disappointments and secret unhappiness. The reason why you are out of sorts, of all disgusts at society and life, is a disgust at self. He that completely succeeds in the world,

7. John V.20 [Emerson's note]; i.e., John 5:30.
8. John 5:44.

loves the world. He that fails in it hates it. But the reason why he fails, is because he does not do his own duty. If he did it to the utmost, as unto the Lord and not unto men, he would be satisfied with his condition. The opposition and injuries he encountered would move his pity and benevolence and not make him cross. Consider then whether at any time your situation and duties in life appear odious to you. Pause at the moment and look back carefully upon the last three or four days and somewhere you will find lurking the secret cause of that disgust. Bring it to the light and you will be surprized to find it is not any evil of your condition, but an omission or transgression of your own. Take out that splinter and you will find the wound heal over, and soundness restored to the whole body of your condition.

Consider who is the most contented person you have ever known. I am sure it was a religious person.

Brethren, the apostle in presenting us with this rule of action has provided for every possible exigency into which the Providence of God may call us. The situations of those who now are in this house are widely various; our duties, our fears, our temptations, our prospects. Some of us are beginning life, some will shortly leave it. Some of us are entering on the spiritual life, some perhaps are declining from it. But there is not one who if he will open his understanding and his heart to this commandment will find it strictly suitable to his occasions and an everlasting benefit.[9]

And whatsoever you do, do it heartily as unto the Lord and not to men.

9. Despite the faulty syntax, Emerson means, of course, that people *will* find the commandment strictly suitable to their occasions.

CVI

Hast thou faith?
Have it unto thyself before God.

ROMANS 14:22

The strain of remark in the excellent passage from which the text is taken is upon the folly of disturbing the consciences of our brethren by insisting upon their reception of our views in unimportant things. Especially the apostle urges his friends not to shake the faith of the scrupulous by thrusting on their notice a boastful disregard of any opinion or practice which is to them sacred. The particular instance to which he speaks is the question whether it were lawful to buy and eat the broken meats sold in the markets that had been first offered in the heathen temples.

The general truth to be gathered from the chapter is that our faith has respect to God alone and should therefore be less social and dependent. Our works are due to our fellowmen, for to God we can bring no profit. Our brethren are his stewards to receive for him. But our faith, our religious life, must be from him and throughout its extent must be between him and us without society. Hast thou faith? Have it to thyself. I wish in continuance of the remarks offered by me last Sunday afternoon to consider and apply the instruction we gain from this passage.[1]

1. Have faith to thyself before God first in acts of worship. A good man needs no provocatives to piety, from the sympathy or the example of others. These are the crutches of weakness. It is matter of sad regret to see how low and dependent is the flame of devotion in us. How feeble is our faith—a mere infant's thought—in the spiritual life. Is it not true that a mere toy, a little noise, a new face, or a new dress, will catch the eye of many a person of mature age, and occupy his attention to the exclusion of all serious thought in the house of God? How many come up to the church and go away unchanged, untouched; without having once prostrated the soul in worship, without the application of one word to themselves, without having thought that they had the least stake, beyond their reputation for decorum, in the service which is here conducted? Does it never give such a person any terror, the thought that though his head may be

Manuscript undated. Preached once: January 30, 1831, at the Second Church, Boston.
    1. Emerson delivered Sermon CV the previous Sunday afternoon.

white with time, his soul is not yet mature, his soul is not yet born of God, and so has no hold on life, when in a short time his body dies?

But there are many whose attention has at sometime been aroused to the hopes and fears of the future life, who have sometime made a beginning of goodness, and seriously addressed themselves to their work, but the temptations did not stop when their prayers ended; their fervor grew cold; the fire went out. They suffer, they complain, under strange absences of God, and these feel the need of those forms of duty which they undertook when their religious feeling was new. Forms which once were mere expressions of their fervent soul, are now relied upon as marks of what they have done, and as anchors by which they seem to hold fast to the shore now that the waters ebb. These persons need sympathy; they need numbers; they need the example of those that are respectable for something besides spiritual growth.

They are confirmed by the adhesion of learned and powerful men to the cause of Christ and shaken by their alienation. They are looking for succour without. It can only come from within. Hast thou faith? Have it to thyself. They complain of their coldness and want of faith. I suppose, brethren, we ought rather to repent of our sins. We flattered ourselves the work was done, when it was only commenced. Indolent worship is none. We must watch and pray.[2] A good man does not have this mendicant faith. What is this but the virgins in the parable who begged oil of others, for their lamps were out? But they did not receive.[3] In the nature of things they cannot. Each must go and buy for himself. A truly devout man at church would not feel the interruption of trifles. He needs no aid from company.

Sufficient to him would be the presence of the Ommipresent. Not only these sights and sounds that engross others, pass unheeded, but the great sights and sounds that seem so important to mankind out of the church, great offices, great fortunes, great parties in the State, and all that is called most solid and valuable, seem to him a tinkling cymbal or a breath of mist.[4] In the heaven of his pure and humble thoughts where he worships God, he sees that truth and goodness are eternal, and that they are independent of body and bodily good, and that he shall make better progress in them when the deceptions of this life pass away from his eyes.

2. Not only in worship, but in its daily work, must the soul reject these alliances of flesh, and lean upon God alone. Faith is not a periodical visiter, it is the life of the soul. And therefore it is only genuine when it subordinates every act and thought to its great perceptions. Have it to yourself in your study and practice of your common duties. Have no master, no patron, no partner. Your faith must be a freehold. You must not live in it, a tenant at will of another.

Most men in society are dependent for their faith and so for their works good

2. Cf. Matthew 26:41, Mark 13:33 and 14:38, and I Peter 4:7.
3. Matthew 25:1–13.
4. Cf. I Corinthians 13:1.

or bad upon others. If they stand upright, it is because the pressure is equal on every side. Among those that are reckoned good men it is just the same. Custom governs in the church almost as absolutely as in the fashions of the world. We can hardly help searching for the eye of each other, and being pious after a pattern. We hallow in our memories one or two or a few characters and they are the mediums through which we look at the godly life. Two evils flow from this dependence. First, that you adopt their errors in speculation, and secondly, that you adopt their errors in practice.

We get our faith from others. That is the great evil of all religious history. Men allow the Church to regulate their faith. A church again asks of an eminent individual what it shall determine. Calvin thinks for thousands; and Wesley for thousands. And that office of thinking, of believing, which cannot be done for another, is done in appearance, and the worst consequences follow. Every false-hood which one of these leaders received is transmitted from church to church for ages. If each soul had been instructed that its first duty as a moral being was to reflect, to go alone before God with its prayer and its obedience, no errors would have been transmitted with authority.

And see the consequence in the distracted, bleeding, I had almost said,—the hating church of Christ; the Church of Christ, where only the *name* is found, and *he* is much a stranger; for it was said, "If ye have not the spirit of Christ, ye are none of his."[5] 'Behold how these Christians love one another!' is true no longer.[6] They magnify one another's faults. They misrepresent each other's faith. They organize the means and institutions of recrimination, until this horrible profanation—I can call it by no better name—of the gift of God has got to be so familiar to the eye that it causes no surprize and men that are called good engage in the warfare themselves. This is not the kingdom of God which is righteousness and peace and joy in the holy Ghost.[7] This is not agreeable to the description of the gospel principles in the prayer of St. Paul. "For this cause I bow my knees unto the Father of our Lord Jesus Christ (of whom the whole family in heaven and earth is named,) that he would grant you (according to the riches of his glory) to be strengthened with might by his spirit in the inner man, that Christ may dwell in your hearts by faith, that ye being rooted and grounded in love, may be able to comprehend with all saints, what is the breadth and length and depth and height, and to know the love of Christ, which passeth knowledge, that you might be filled with all the fulness of God."[8] *To be rooted and grounded in love,* was the beginning of the gospel which he had received; to know the love of Christ was the preparation for being filled with the fulness of

5. Romans 8:9.
6. "'See,' they say, 'how these Christians love one another,' for themselves hate one another; 'and how they are ready to die for each other,' for themselves will be readier to kill each other." Tertullian, *Apologeticus,* trans. Alexander Souter (Cambridge, 1917), 113. See *JMN* 3:288 and Sermon CXXX, n. 5.
7. Romans 14:17.
8. Eph. 3 14 [Emerson's note]; i.e., Ephesians 3:14-19.

God. This foundation which was the head of the corner the builders have again rejected.[9] It is time to examine the superstructure, to try the materials. It is time to forsake the interpreters, and go back again to the book itself. Hast thou faith? Have it to thyself before God.

Consider whether there is not any person among your acquaintance who holds and defends opinions which he is too good and too wise a man to receive if now they were proposed to the world for the first time.

3. We adopt the evil unworthy practices of others. When these corruptions get into the faith, when opinions are preferred to principles, it cannot be strange if the practice grows worse. And so I pray each of you, my friends, to consider whether never you have found a palliation for your offences in the sins of others. Have you not satisfied yourself with believing that your principles were sound and forborne to carry the principle into all your conversation and all your thoughts because other Christians do not? He that refuses the cross is not worthy of the crown. He that puts his hand to the plough and looks back is not worthy.[10] The apostle says to you, Hast thou faith? Have it to thyself before God.

There are some moments in the progress of the spiritual man, and those are the best of his life, when he is alone with God—when the Idea of his Maker is so clear to him that he feels that God is society enough. As a man advances in goodness, as he resists his appetites and overcomes his indolence, these times of refreshment from the presence of the Lord, once rare, become more frequent as they are more sought. As his obedience and love increases, his eyes see truly and his hands do right. They are not promised to our party spirit, nor to those who say, Lord, Lord, but do not keep the commandments,[11] but the pure in heart shall see God and the poor in spirit and those who have the spirit of Christ and are united to him as his disciples by the humble and thankful reception of his truth and his spirit, by prayer and by works and by faith.[12]

I am not so unreasonable as to undervalue the privilege of truly social worship. I know well that our religious feelings are wonderfully assisted by our love for each other, that among friends we worship more joyfully than among strangers, and that all strong affection leads as it were directly to religion.

All I urge upon you from the text, is, that your faith must have an independent connexion with God in the first instance. Else it is not faith, but a parrot's talk. But once having that union formed, all your friendships, all your affections for your brethren will increase it and be increased themselves.

9. Cf. Matthew 21:42 and Mark 12:10.
10. Cf. Luke 9:62.
11. Matthew 7:21.
12. Matthew 5:3 and 5:8.

CVII _____

*For we know that if our earthly house of
this tabernacle were dissolved, we have a
building of God, an house not made with
hands, eternal in the heavens.*

II Corinthians 5:1

The truth of God brought by Jesus Christ related to all our being, to all its changes, to life and death, to two worlds. Its main fact is the immortality of the human soul. It teaches us, that when we descend by age or disease to the tomb, it is a change and not a termination of our being;—that the Providence of God reaches through all space, and lasts through all time, and upholds this feeble spirit of man through that extent; and administers to it eternal justice; and makes it capable of receiving all truth, and all goodness. It is made of God, and it is made to find its perfection in resembling him, in knowing and doing his will.

But these sublime ends are begun to be sought with means how small! We have this treasure in earthen vessels.[1] The immortal soul is lodged in a dwelling most frail and painful, that in its greatest strength will last eighty summers,— sometimes not twenty—sometimes not one.

A thousand causes of pain beset every one in this great company of pilgrims and the heart aches to enumerate them. And to this child of sorrow and fear, this human soul imprisoned in flesh, God sends the consolation of the truth and promises of the New Testament.

My friends I wish to speak, though I fear very unworthily of my theme, of the consolation that Christianity offers to those who mourn. Let me speak as I feel. Let me give utterance, if I can, to some of those thoughts that crowd in succession into the heart of those who have seen the life that made their own life pleasant come to an end. Which of us has no interest in these consolations? Which of us has not needed them, or is not likely to need them?

Manuscript dated February 19, 1831. Preached once: February 20, 1831, at the Second Church, Boston. The occasion for Emerson's theme in this sermon—"the consolation that Christianity offers to those who mourn"—and for the moments of distraction evident in the sermon was the death of Ellen Tucker Emerson, at the age of nineteen, on February 8. The impact of her death on Emerson's ministry is reviewed in the Historical Introduction to the *Sermons* (1:12–14, 1:16–17). See Emerson's own account of Ellen's death in *JMN* 3:226–27.

1. II Corinthians 4:7.

And first, I cannot pass without notice one or two counsels that are habitually in men's mouths when they condole with the afflicted, but which in most cases are thrown away, because they are not founded in truth; and can only give unnecessary pain. It is usual to warn the bereaved man to be still, and not repine at the decree of the Almighty.

Let me say, that, *it never occurs* to a mind at all enlarged by religion, at all accustomed to observe and admire the uniform and universal provisions for good that, on every hand, reach far out of his sight, when he meets with a distressing event, *it never comes into his heart to murmur and repine.* To repine is to believe, that though he who reigns in all is called a God, it is only a man, ignorant, and severe, or partial, that administers events; and as a well ordered mind is incapable of receiving such an idea of the infinite Divinity, to charge him not to repine, is like telling him not to fly, or that he must not imagine the earth to be a plane, nor believe that the sun is annihilated when it sets, or any thing else which would never come into his thoughts. If called upon in that moment when grief has sharpened into anguish, when heaven and earth grow dark in his eye, because the life of his body is only regarded as the wall of separation that hinders him from his desires,—even in that moment, and often it returns, if called upon, he would bear witness with the same conviction as in his brightest hour, to the perfection of the Providence in which his only hope is, 'and feels even then that God even then is good.' Is it not plain that then more than ever he needs the whole support of that central faith? For except in that belief he has no prospect of relighting his extinguished lamp. And for the world he would not utter a word that could have a tendency to shake his own confidence in the Divine love.

Neither is there to a mind that seeks truth the least unkindness in its grief. Sorrow is called selfish, but it is because it is occupied at home, and not that it covets or reproaches the happiness of others. It cannot leave its own thought, it is out of the power of man when prostrated by calamity, to get up with cheerful social face, and interest himself to his usual degree in the condition of his friends and neighborhood. He is so entirely disheartened by an event which changes the whole aspect of life to him that he broods on that event, and has no spirit to act or to think. He is unstrung, debilitated by grief, and so neglects others as he neglects himself, but do not imagine that he who well deserves all your pity, nourishes a secret malevolence at pleasures which he cannot enjoy.

I have said that the mind that is used in all times to recognize God, and in any worthy degree to keep his commandments, will not charge God foolishly,[2] nor grieve at the happiness of others. But if this were all the peace the gospel brought, it would hardly touch the evil of sorrow. The truth and the resurrection of Christ have done more for his disciples. The blessing of the Christian hope enters with alleviation into every degree and every thought of sorrow. The Christian faith teaches us that the soul does not die but is separated from the

2. Job 1:22.

body and enters into a nearer relation to the Father of Spirits. The Christian faith teaches this, and the Christian soul, as it departs out of life, affirms it cheerfully to those who weep.

I proceed now to say that the Christian faith removes the dread from the grave, first, in regard to those who die, and then to those who survive.

1. The pure and the wise who leave this world receive the natural reward of goodness and wisdom, in the removal of all doubt as to the course and the end of their secret journey. We follow them down to the last gate of life but our unaided eye cannot explore one step into the gloom beyond. Yet they go in a courage not their own, and above nature. They follow their Lord. They are gone with him into the house, and the door is shut.

Jesus says, "My Father's house hath many mansions,"[3] and we easily believe that the 'mansion,' i.e., the happiness of every soul, will be different, and measured by the progress it has already made. Every element of evil it has indulged in itself is so much diminution of its peace. Every truth it has understood, every act of humility, of love, of devotion, is a new star in its crown.

All that part of man which we call *the character,* survives and ascends. Not a shade, not a thought of it cleaves to the cold clay we have put in the ground. And let me ask of those who have been called to part with some dear image of human worth, whether they find any difficulty in separating the soul from the body in their thought; whether the being that has been forming under their eye for years, acquiring truth, adopting habits, and beginning to disclose hints and glimmerings of an unknown abyss of thought within itself, putting forth the marks of magnanimity, of fortitude, of inexhaustible kindness, and lastly of a great trust in God,—I ask, if you think this being is one with the body, and all these are signs of corruption? If you think so,—you do not understand the language God speaks by his works to your soul, and you have not kept the commandments of Christ, for those who obey them, insensibly receive the thought of this happy future.

Yes, they teach us better—the pious dead—whose hope in God grew stronger as the heart it agitated, was ceasing to beat. They went down to the tomb with prayer and praise on their lips, and the thoughts of heaven found their way in to the convulsions of death. We will sing the hallelujahs of faith over their ashes. We will leave the soul with God, sure that his wisdom shall find action and enjoyment suited to the soul in the resurrection. A wise and good man may think he sees enough in this life, to suggest to him the satisfactions of an unbodied spirit. But far more gladly we trust the promise of the Scriptures, that "Eye hath not seen, nor ear heard, nor hath entered the heart of man, the glory that God has prepared for them that love him."[4]

2. The faith of Christ removes the dread of the grave, secondly, in regard to those who are yet alive in the body. It abolishes the power of death. It peoples

3. John 14:2.
4. I Corinthians 2:9.

every solitude; it animates every silence with the conviction on the mind of the mourner that the dead are present. They speak to him out of the darkness words of comfort which the living could never utter. He is assured of their sympathy, of their prayer, and of whatsoever aid the spirit out of the body can give to the spirit in the body. By the living he may be neglected, he may be affronted, he may be misunderstood; he appeals from their imperfect judgments with a swelling spirit to the clearer sight, to the unmixed and now glorified affection of the dead, and he finds comfort and increasing conviction in this invisible sympathy.

He may find temptations multiplied in his path, he may feel deeply his own unworthiness, his uselessness to his fellowmen, his guilt before God. But in this holy society which he finds in his closet or in the open day, with the virtuous dead, he is calmed and strengthened. They present the remembrance of a pure example, and the suggestions of approbation and succour to every good intention. They remind him, that he is not alone or unpitied when his house seems most lonely, and his duty most difficult; for the Father of all Spirits who made him at first the gift of these affections, and of their objects, has not lost sight of his afflicted child. Jesus will not forget a humble disciple, for his promise was, "Lo, I am with you alway even unto the end of the world."[5]

And, in these our friends who are gone, we now seem to possess a *personal interest of love, of intercession in the spiritual society.* The soul that has thought with us, and preferred our interest to its own, and known well what was in our heart, is now only a step removed from us, and, we believe, looks back with more than earthly love, mixing the recent knowledge of human wants, with the newness of the revelations now made to it by change of state. In a pure love for the departed it is very easy to bring home to the soul the vision of their joy and love.

And it is these contemplations which make what has been well called "the sublime attraction of the grave."[6] Soothed by these thoughts, we wonder how the grave was ever frightful to us. When we have explored our desolate house for what shall never there be seen we return with an eagerness to the tomb, as the only place of healing and peace. It seems to us that willingly—oh yes, joyfully, we would, if permitted, lay down our head also on the same pillow, so that God would restore us to the society we have lost.

But does any one say this is extravagant, unreasonable sorrow? This is a spirit of bitterness which would disqualify man for his place in society; the loss of a friend would then, by the indulgence of these fruitless desires, be the loss of usefulness to the survivor, and Death would be a far greater evil in the world than now it is. Does any one say this? So in our ear say the dead also. Reason and virtue do not change their language by change of state; the virtuous dead utter the same sentiment with the virtuous living. This is what I would chiefly

5. Matthew 28:20.
6. William Wordsworth, *The Excursion,* IV, 238.

observe in commending the blessedness of the Christian faith, that it does not permit even these holy affections to mislead us. It keeps *Duty, the soul's ever-lasting object, always uppermost.* When the love and desire of departed excellence makes us eager to quit the places and offices of earthly duty, the same love and desire corrects this disgust of life. It makes us consider that it is not death, but life that we are seeking, and that an inglorious quitting of our post, a neglect of any of our appointed trusts, a life of inaction, a death of grief, would disqualify us for that very happiness we aim at; would bring down upon us the displeasure and sorrow of those very friends who watch over us; would be unfaithful to their counsels and to their devoted love; would alienate us from their hearts instead of cementing us with them because the only true and enduring bond that can unite souls is the love of the same excellence, the love of truth and goodness—the love of God who is their source.

When therefore we first feel that the claims of others upon us are irksome, and are disposed to lie down in useless despondency, let us feel that then the eye of love begins to grow severe, that we are departing from the friendship of the pure, that the best tribute the living can offer to the dead is to be faithful in our place as they were faithful in theirs, to keep up the courage and good hope that will always spring from earnest endeavours to do right, even against the embarrassments of disappointment, of defeat, of reproach, of poverty, of sickness, of old age. Thus may the connexions of nature and friendship become yet more sacred and as may reasonably be thought, I hope, by Christians, the tie may really grow stronger between one on earth and one in heaven.

These are the feelings that by direct inference from the New Testament mix with our sad thoughts and lead them toward heaven. By them and by the spectacle of triumphant faith the dying chamber of youth where a thousand expectations are shattered may infuse more sweetness and joy into the soul than ever prosperity or praise could give. In the wreck of earthly good the goods of the soul show a lustre and permanence divine. Blessed be God, that there are these consolations, these remembrances, these hopes. Blessed be his name, that he has provided every soul among us in the truth of the New Testament with the means of depriving death of its sting.[7]

7. Cf. I Corinthians 15:55.

CVIII

Who is among you that feareth the Lord . . .
that walketh in darkness and hath no light?
Let him trust in the name of the Lord,
and stay upon his God.

ISAIAH 50:10

'Man is born to trouble,' saith the Scripture, 'as the sparks to fly upward.'[1] All his joy is dashed with a taste of grief, and the years that close and begin have a melancholy face. No one certainly will deny the innumerable contrivances to produce comfort and good that every where appear; none can point to a single contrivance in nature that seems to have been intended to produce pain as an end. Good seems every where to be the end;—pain an accident or a guard and warning and so a means for farther good. Yet neither will any one deny that now pain forms a very large part, perhaps the largest part of life—that whatever we may think of the brightness of the universe, we yet dwell in a cloud,—that what we suffer equals or exceeds what we enjoy. For there is in man a sort of appetite for pain that leads him to think more of the few evils than of the many advantages of his condition. All good availeth him nothing whilst some Mordecai sits in the king's gate.[2] The instances are many of prosperous men who have committed suicide.

These insatiable desires are so many signs of an immortal nature, but here they eat into the heart. Youth and strength and wisdom and virtue are not exempt from suffering. Every thing that increases a man's capacity of pleasure to the same extent increases his capacity of pain, as the larger the branches of the oak grow the more they invite the lightning, and the wind, and the worm. 'If a king,' says Jeremy Taylor, 'has an army of guards on the one side he has an army of mortifications on the other,'[3] and it has been

Manuscript dated February 26, 1831. Preached four times: February 27, 1831, at the Second Church, Boston; March 13 at the West Church, Boston; February 7, 1836, in Waltham; and March 13 in East Lexington.

1. Job 5:7.
2. See Esther 5:13.
3. Emerson misquotes Jeremy Taylor, *The Whole Works of the Right Reverend Jeremy Taylor, D. D.*, ed. Reginald Heber, 15 vols. (London, 1822), 3:430. See *JMN* 6:8 and 6:82.

pointedly said that "The man of pleasure is the man of pain."[4]

But there is no need of taking general views of human suffering. I need not go beyond the walls of this house for ample testimony. There is domestic, private, personal suffering; there is secret distress—griefs untold in any human ear. Do you think, brethren, if the hidden record of each of our hearts were disclosed to every other it would be all made up of pleasant anecdotes? How many prayers have gone up to God in this church that the lips never made audible? In the hundred years of this temple how many weary limbs have laboured up hither to worship that were fain to stretch themselves in the grave? How many young men and maidens whose years have not the hope that belongs to their season but who have borne the yoke in their youth and lost all elasticity before the age of man? How many mature and old men in whom sorrow had grown to be a habit strengthened and renewed by every new year's new freight of misfortunes?

But it is not these extreme cases, which need, and somewhere, I trust in God, are or shall be provided with strong remedies, 'tis not these that I wish now to consider. They all,—every pang of every human bosom,—find their medicine in God's parental love. But I wish to speak of that common measure of grief which every man has to receive and sustain, which each of us feels or must expect to feel because he is one of the human race. I wish to consider what are its uses and what are its consolations.

There are a great many persons over whom conscience has habitual influence, who are just and kind to men, and who walk humbly before God—who are yet far from enjoying what they desire in this life. They have met with misfortunes or their whole lot has not been disposed as they could wish, and though they do not openly complain of their condition and perhaps would freely own that their condition is better than their merits, yet all their views of this life are tinged with dissatisfaction. They believe they see something of peculiar disadvantage in their lot; opportunities which others misuse, never come to them. With hearts made for kindness they have wanted a friend. With a thirst for knowledge they have been compelled to drudge in business wholly disagreeable to them; blest with genius and virtue they languish under a hereditary malady; hating dependance, and eager to help themselves, they find every avenue to employment and competence closed upon them; or, happy in their own situation, life is rendered miserable by the guilt or by the misfortunes of their nearest friend; or having none of these afflictions, and conscious themselves of superior powers, they yet labour under some constitutional defect, some coldness of manners, or slowness of speech, or want of self-command, that baffles them in every exertion to do what they ought and to place themselves where they think they ought to stand.

To these and to all who suffer and to every one according to his trial, let the gospel speak. The paternal character of God is the central fact of the Christian

4. Edward Young, *Night Thoughts,* "Night VIII," line 793.

religion. Let them find a reproof and a comfort to every despondency in the two first words of the prayer of Jesus: *"Our Father."*[5] Receive these words of Jesus, your elder brother, who brought the truth in kindness and not in wrath. Receive this message of the Most High into your heart, whoever you are and whatever your griefs may be. Is it not an adequate relief to your afflictions—and I will not dispute that they may be sore beyond the reach of sympathy—that the whole course, and all the particulars, of your fate are ordered by one who has more interest in you, than you have in your children. In a pious and docile temper, try to comprehend all the fulness of this consolation, and you shall find it overruns the measure of your griefs.

Let me apply this thought particularly to the condition of the young, in whom when the ardour of youthful hopes is checked by the straitness of their circumstances this chilling discontent is very apt to appear.

You go along the street to your daily work and feel in the thickest throng as if you were forsaken. You feel that the eyes of men look coldly on you, and that you possess noble desires and principles which ought to be rewarded by their esteem and they know it not, and slight you. You know that you have done good actions, and projected generous schemes for your fellow man; you feel that you are capable of giving your life for your country; that you are incapable of the crimes that others commit, that you are habitually making sacrifices that blow no trumpet before them;[6]—and they know it not, and slight you. When these thoughts swell your bosom, Oh receive the cheering truth that not a pang of the heart, not a regret at its solitude, its defeats, its reproach, its poverty, but God perceives from the beginning to the end; that his Eye is fastened upon you, full of affection as it is of wisdom. "Who is he that feareth the Lord and walketh in darkness having no light?" Let him trust in the name of the Lord and stay upon his God. Is not the eye of God society enough?

This doctrine contains all the reproof and all the comfort your case requires. Let us consider some of the particulars.

A little consideration in a humble spirit will always remove the blame from Providence and lay it upon our own hasty judgments. God does not immediately reward you and relieve you, and so your little faith grows less. Remember the words of Jesus, Thinkest thou I could not now pray to my Father and he would send me ten legions of angels?[7] God has ample means of relieving you. Your wants could be cheaply supplied, and so doubtless if forty or eighty years constituted your whole existence, you would be instantly relieved; but his means throughout the Creation are proportioned in the speed as well as the force of their operation, to the whole condition of the object affected. The mushroom may grow up in a night. The bud of the aloes requires a hundred years to mature it. So the virtues of the human soul, the heir of eternity, need not hurry to their satisfactions but may wait the operation of moral laws.

5. Matthew 6:9.
6. Cf. Matthew 6:2.
7. Matthew 26:53.

In the figurative language of Scripture God may be said to wait to see if your virtue is like to live. A virtue that hath no life in itself, that is born of the breath of others, a tide waiting virtue—a praise loving virtue—a virtue that warms only to be loved and applauded and will shrink and die the moment it is neglected is good for nothing. Nothing can prove yours sincere but this very trial—these frosts of neglect—these rude rubs of enmity. If you decline them, if in view of them you forsake your integrity and chuse rather the smooth way of the world—let men praise you if they will—the great and good will not—the spirits of the just made perfect will not.[8] God cannot.

I said, in the *figurative* language of Scripture, *God waits,* for in truth, he cannot now reward you. He can if he please alter your condition according to your wish, but that might do you mischief. This discontented merit of yours shows the unripeness of the fruit. Genuine virtue was never grounded on the judgments of men and does not conclude itself abandoned because it is not honoured by them. Indeed it seems to me that in reading the lives of illustrious men the mind feels a sort of incongruity when, as sometimes though rarely happens, they chance to live in uninterrupted prosperity. Genius and virtue are out of place, and only half themselves, when they repose for fifty years upon chairs of state and inhale a continual incense of adulation. Their proper ornaments and relief are poverty and reproach and danger. These are the stern but wholesome guards that escort and give them might. Apply the same knowledge to your own condition and sufferings. The true reward of virtue is not praise nor wealth nor health but a freedom from the inquietudes of guilt, a clear head, a warm heart, and a growing preference of virtue to outward good whenever the desires of either interfere. As you persist in obedience, other good loses its attractions and so you lose your discontent. This is the reason why every promise is based on your perseverance. Blessed, saith St. James, is the man that endureth temptation, for when he is tried, he shall receive a crown of life, which the Lord hath promised to them that love him.[9]

Again. It is a common form which our discontent takes to suppose that the reason why we are no better is the fault of our circumstances. It will occur to an ardent spirit and he will find some self-justification in the thought that all his fortunes are cast in a vulgar mould; he wants the stimulus of great events. He thinks he could submit to martyrdom for his country or his faith but his temper and powers are filed and fretted away on little things. When will men learn the great lesson that Religion makes circumstances indifferent? that no condition can be low on which the approbation of God rests? Do I speak to any young man or young woman who considers his lot a hard one and ever finds himself comparing it with others, let me remind you that reason and faith direct you to esteem these your disadvantages—your mean and scanty fare, your wretched lodging, your hard and disagreeable work, and all the time spent in unsuitable

8. Hebrews 12:23.
9. James 1:12.

company—you are to esteem all these taken together as the rough outer casket suited to keep safe from all injury a precious and holy jewel—the character within—whose intrinsic value makes it a thing of no account whether its case be rich or poor. It is but for a span that we live here; and it is we ourselves who determine whether that life be great or trivial. So far from esteeming it a justifiable reason of complaint, that the duties cast upon us are common, I believe as much can be endured and triumphed over by you and me, as by Ignatius or St. Stephen, or any of all that noble army of martyrs.[10] This is as if a man should complain that because Newton had discovered the laws of light and the theory of gravity there was now no room for great attainments in knowledge, whereas the fact is the direct contrary. It was because former observers had made great discoveries that Newton, standing as it were on their shoulders, could see farther and show more truth. And all that he has done for us has been only to erect the observatory higher so as to command a wider view of the earth and bring the eye nearer to the heavens. So these great masters of virtue, these faithful disciples of the Cross, have carried humility and faith and love so far as to give the soul a greater confidence in the true divinity of these graces. They have shown us what man can do with God's aid. Their faults are seen by the light of their virtues. And we may adopt their good and shun their bad qualities and advance on the way to heaven with a trust made perfect by the history of all good men.

It is with all virtues as it is with one. They exist in the soul and not in the circumstances. He is not charitable who has much wealth to give away, but he whose soul disposes of all he hath so that it shall be of the most use.

And he lives over again the brave lives of Paul and Peter who carries their holy principles into the obscurities of a common life. He is the eminent Christian whom low company and bad example cannot prevail upon to part for one moment from the love of God and the hope of heaven; he who carries the desire of truth and the effort to become better wherever he breathes. He who cannot be brought to so low an opinion of himself as that possibly he can break his word, or forget his obligations to his Creator, or to so low an opinion of another as to speak a syllable of unkindness or contempt.

He who should hold these principles would begin to find that God had provided him with an ample domain in himself; that the wrinkles of a momentary discontent were smoothed on his brow by a nearer vision of God's perfections.

He would find that as his character rose, approaching to the stature of Christ, it would create love and veneration in those who knew him best and a progressive influence upon all men. But as the judgments of men grew more kind to his merits he would find himself more indifferent to their praise, lost in the anxiety to recommend himself by an absolute likeness of nature and oneness of will to his Father in heaven.

10. Ignatius, Bishop of Antioch, was arrested, taken to Rome, and martyred under Trajan in A.D. 107; St. Stephen (d. A.D. 36), a Hellenist and the first to proclaim the Second Coming of Christ, is regarded as a Christian protomartyr.

These are the considerations which every view of the disadvantages of our condition will suggest in a mind which never forgets the intimate presence of God in the soul. Each of us knows or may know that we are wholly derived from him. What hast thou which thou didst not receive?[11] And will he forget his work? Or shall we hesitate to trust in him? Let us cheerfully receive better views of Him at the hands of his Son. "Your heavenly Father knoweth what you have need of before you ask him." "And even the hairs of your head are numbered."[12]

11. I Corinthians 4:7.
12. Matthew 6:8, Matthew 10:30, and Luke 12:7.

CIX

Thus saith the Lord, Let not the wise man glory in his wisdom, neither let the mighty man glory in his might, let not the rich man glory in his riches; but let him that glorieth glory in this, that he understandeth and knoweth me, that I am the Lord which exercise loving kindness, judgment, and righteousness in the earth.

JEREMIAH 9:23-24

The unreasonableness of confidence in any good as our own is admitted by all men in theory and forgotten by almost all men in practice. No man probably when he is alone in his closet and alone in his thoughts, (that is, not considering his relations to other men) feels any very strong confidence in his own powers. He feels very sensibly the extreme weakness of his intellect to discover truth and the weakness of his will to perform his duty. He feels if he has grown old, the great difference between what he has done and what he once expected to do, for in solitude a man compares himself by no finite standard. He compares his knowledge with all that may be known and his virtue with the commandment. And if he cannot trust these immaterial faculties,—the strong part of his being,—much less can he say, to the fine gold, 'thou art my confidence,' or to his blooming health that the Consumption cannot waste it, or trust his influence of office or fortune or friendship over his fellowmen.

But when the self examiner comes out of his chamber and converses and deals with men, and compares himself with them, having wholly forgot the severe and infinite standard of his solitude, he continually pleases himself with the observation of advantages that belong to himself over others. There is no man that cannot find others below him. He plumes himself upon uncertain advantages, because they allow them to be such. In his closet he felt no pride of

---

Manuscript dated March 5, 1831, and September 9, 1832. Preached five times: March 6, 1831, at the Second Church, Boston; September 9, 1832, again at the Second Church; April 17, 1836, in East Lexington; May 1 in Lowell, Mass.; and August 14, again in East Lexington.

power, but he felt its uncertainty and vexations; but in society he is courted because of his power, and he takes a higher tone, and yields insensibly to false views of it. In his closet, he felt no pride of wealth, but its care and its fear; but now he readily accepts all the homage it procures him, and yields his speculative views, that is, his correct ones, to the ordinary customs by which wealth is administered. When alone, he felt no disposition to commend his knowledge or his wisdom, but felt only what they had disclosed to him,—their own littleness compared with what may be known. But when conversing with those who know less, he at once assumes importance.

Now no man can think with any attention to truth and not perceive that he has nothing of his own. Let him put his hand on the property, or the accomplishment, or the wisdom, or the virtue, that is his own. Human law calls that a man's own, which he possesses without any rightful claim from another. And in common speech we call that our own which is ours as not another's. But *creation* is the only immutable and absolute foundation of property. And which of your hands or your feet, is your own by that right? Which of your senses have you made? What truth have you that is any more yours than the sun and the moon? And lastly, except your moral freedom, except the elections you have made to do right and to do wrong, what is so much yours as to exclude God from partnership? And even here, though I know we tread dubiously on the last boundaries of knowledge, we feel that even virtue, God must somehow originate. When I chuse to do right, though unquestionable master of my choice, I do not make or do a new and arbitrary thing—I conform myself to an old and eternal law which I never made but which is God's nature. And moreover who opened my mind's eye to the excellence of that law so that I might choose? Who raised me above the elephant? Who raised the civilized above the savage man?

Well now if this be so, if God is the author of all, if there is nothing in you self-originated but all is derived, do you think it much to owe all your action, since you owe all your being, to Him? Let us consider ourselves and what are our most valuable possessions, that the truth of the prophet's declaration may more fully appear. Let not the rich man glory in his riches, nor the wise man in his wisdom, nor the mighty man in his might.

1. Let not the rich man glory in his riches. He did not get them by his own toil or skill unassisted. The assistance was more than his work and he cannot keep them, for he cannot put them out of the reach of fire, or storm, or waste, or war, or thieves, or the wants of his family, or his friend, or his own death, so that the ancient said of gold, "To have it was to be in fear; to want it was to be in sorrow."[1] Let him not glory in such a possession that is so little possessed. Let him not glory in it—if so, it would prove his shame. Let him be afraid of it rather and see well that it does not tempt him to sloth and pride and withdraw him from the source of good.

1. Samuel Johnson quotes this epigram in *The Rambler*, no. 131. See *The Rambler*, ed. W. J. Bate and Albrecht B. Strauss, 3 vols. (New Haven, 1969), 2:333. See *JMN* 6:24 and 6:172.

2. Let not the wise man glory in his wisdom. As little is there room for boasting of wisdom. 1. Proverbially, a little knowledge intoxicates, and the remedy to lead back to humility is to get a great deal. For that reveals to us the extent of our ignorance. Every fact is ascertained only as an avenue. 2. Eminently in wisdom is what is gained felt not to be our own. What is the object of wisdom? the acquisition of truth,—and truth is not *made,* but is only *seen.* It was, before we were. It was before the world. It was with God, it was God.[2] Therefore every man's wisdom is not a peculiar property; it is only what he sees of the common light. A French philosopher says, "It is no more according to Plato, than according to me."[3] It is God's truth. And the wise men and the prophets and apostles, yea, and Jesus himself are only vessels more or less filled with the eternal light. 3. In the next place it must be received according to God's law, or it is not received pure. A man must feel that wisdom comes from God or he cannot be truly wise. In God goodness and wisdom are one. He is perfectly wise because he is perfectly good, and he is perfectly good because he is perfectly wise. And therefore in his children every truth brings a man nearer to goodness and every right feeling brings him nearer to truth. Sometimes we see a mind, alas there have been many such, wholly averse from goodness yet ambitious of knowledge, and he appears half wise like a plant grown up in the dark, which is colourless, only half made. And sometimes we see the other extreme of good persons who, bred under the shadows of a false religion, have imbibed a fear of science, and who make goodness itself unamiable by this defect.

But the best minds in the world have got most of their wisdom from the heart. In the strictest philosophy as well as in the rule of religion, "the fear of the Lord is the beginning of wisdom."[4] Let not the wise man then glory in his wisdom except as it is to him an inlet of the infinite sea, and in profoundest humility he glories in the boundless wisdom of the Creator.

3. Let not the mighty man glory in his might. Any confidence in *power* not grounded in God as the source of power, is utterly groundless. Power guided strictly by right is indeed power. It works good like God's bounties of sun and rain and sense. Power used in the service of conscience is just and beneficent, and produces a sort of truer Providence. Innocence is safer. Earthly blessings are more closely linked to virtue, and pain stalks more closely after vice. But I am afraid that if it were fully understood in every breast that power must be administered strictly according to justice, power would not be so much coveted as now it is. If those who seek it now so long and so crookedly, knew that it could not be used to aggrandize themselves or their friends, that it was to be dealt by the line, that it was and could be nothing but a neglect of one's private good and quiet, for the sake of essentially serving your fellowmen in turning

2. Cf. John 1:1.

3. "Of the Education of Children," in *Essays of Michael Seigneur de Montaigne* . . . , trans. Charles Cotton (London, 1693), 1:225. See *JMN* 4:309; used in "Chaucer" (*EL* 1:285) and "Quotation and Originality" (*W* 8:193).

4. Proverbs 9:10.

their labor to their profit—I am afraid we should not have so many aspirants for power. It is for power that can yield private advantage; it is for power that instead of sternly confining its possessor to one act leaves many ways of determining what to do; it is for power that makes a man an object of anxious interest to hundreds and thousands because they do not know that he will be guided by his conscience, and do not know how he will determine; it is power that may be feared, and courted, and begged, and sold, that all this hot strife is for. Good power is never sought in a bad way, and bad power—the might of the community in one unprincipled hand—is not a thing to be gloried in. Let not the man of power glory in his power except as it is of God. If it is not of God it will bear fruit not of public good but public death.

Alas that Power is notoriously accounted a *prize* instead of a *trust*. Power is a plume that any body may strive to obtain with no more seriousness than any other ornament, with no fear of any other peril to follow its abuse than merely losing it. It is something to be enjoyed by the possessor because every body looks at it and esteems it highly.[5]

But truly considered there is nothing in the least arbitrary and capricious in the exercise of power by a good man. He surely will not regard it as a holiday clothing, but if it is put upon him he will gird himself with gravity and diligence to a severe and often thankless toil. He will not be the servant of public opinion or what is commonly so called, but which is the private opinion of the hour or the party, but he will obey implicitly the true public opinion of the whole world of good men in the body or out of the body. He will send the empire of good principles which govern him into the remotest vein and fibre of the state. Thus 'he will be,' in the language of the Apostle, 'instead of God,' for he will make God the heart of the state.[6] Far from thinking he is placed there to indulge himself and gratify his own whims, it will be seen that there is not so much arbitrariness or uncertainty in his councils as in the actions of the meanest slave. They are bound by laws as unchangeable as the laws of gravity; but freedom he has, for what he does he does with all his heart and all his soul. He is placed in a position of greatest ability to be useful and he realizes and fills the office.

But alas, far different is the popular understanding. And it is not regarded that the pages of history are full of this mistaken use of power. Alas! that men everywhere and here in our country as readily as anywhere look on power as an entertainment and a great lottery prize. The newspapers—let them furnish the commentary. Has any religious man—or I will say has any wise statesman—confidence in the good issue of many pending questions in our politics, grounded on his confidence of the conscientious administration of power? It is not regarded as a sacred trust in what should be the awful chairs of state, because it is not so regarded by every citizen. Men talk of a vote with levity. Men talk with

---

5. This and the previous sentence are used in Sermon CXXII; see n. 7 there.
6. No such phrase occurs in the New Testament, but see Exodus 4:16.

levity of a cunning politician, and if the fountains of power are corrupt no wonder the stream is also.

And so it is questioned whether this union of nations shall not be sundered by the explosions of party rancour, and that before all the generation that emancipated this country are yet laid in the ground. So much for the effect upon the state, and what is the effect upon the statesmen? The secret cannot be concealed—it will out—louder and more unanimous every month—that it is no longer desirable, scarce creditable, for one of good temper and good parts to mix in the conflicts of parties. Chagrin, odium, malevolence, and unfitness for peaceful and noble thoughts, follow the broken statesman home to his unwilling retirement, and sour and disgrace his closing years. All that is proper and elevating to the soul of man—the study of great truths at the foundation of things,—all noble sentiments,—all the triumphs of faith; all best actions—for all these he is disqualified—they have no savour to his depraved and belittled mind. Let not the mighty glory in his might; he has little disposition in his best day and less for every day of the dreary years of his servitude.

If then neither riches nor wisdom nor might may glory, if the way is shut up behind us, let us follow the way onward. "Let him that glorieth glory in this, that he understandeth and knoweth the Lord." This is true. If God is infinite (and we can find no bound) we who are his children have part in his infinity also. Here indeed is glory enough. It was well said of Homer "that it was weak in him to make his gods so mean; the less God is, the less we are."[7] Is rich, is strong, is sage, is king so great a title as child of God? Every thing else is dim to the glories of faith. In the loss of health or comforts; in the afflicting incapacity of thought; in the convulsions of states God abides, and in the darkest hour is nearest to every believer.

This great object belongs, my friends, to every one of us and to every soul of man. Not many of us are rich, not many mighty, not many wise, but every one of us was formed and filled by the spirit of God and so do inherit the hope of heaven.[8] Here in its connexion with him is the refuge and heaven of the soul. Keep it always turned to Him. Nothing so vast but feel that he contains it. Nothing so real or pure or great. If your idea of him is dim or perplexed pray and think and act more. The study of this thought is the education of the soul. It is the sure way of personal growth. Sincerity is always holy and always strong— Come good or ill, the pure in heart are in the right way. And presently and often you shall be rewarded with clearer perception, the sense of more intimate communion. Dear friendship or solitary piety is often conscious that God's approbation rests upon sincerity. That trust never comes to sensual thoughts, nor to the heart disturbed by love of money or when in the act of separating self-good from the good of the whole and laying out and fencing up a pleasure ground. It comes to the patriot when he thinks to hazard all freely; it comes to the martyr

7. Cf. "The greater God is, the greater we are. Homer was not grand in making his Gods so mean." In *JMN* 3:177 Emerson attributes the statement to Mary Moody Emerson, his aunt.
8. Cf. I Corinthians 1:26-31.

when he enters the dungeon door; it comes to the old when they yearn to die; it comes to the young when he considers that he has sources of happiness which in every possible change that may chance in his condition will remain unaffected; it comes to the dying in the joy of death; it comes to all who in simplicity take hold on the thought of God, relaxing their animal grasp on sensible things. God always waits to be gracious, to receive the soul. He endures—does not come to, or depart from. But we may apply ourselves to him more or less—not at all, and so perish—or so fully as to lose ourselves in rejoicing in the progress and the good of the Universe.

CX

Every good and every perfect gift is from above and cometh down from the Father of lights, with whom is no variableness nor shadow of turning.

JAMES 1:17

It is a received opinion that whenever a doctrine is received by large numbers of men and is observed to reappear in different ages and countries that doctrine is founded in truth. It is shown to be agreeable to the human mind. The plant is suited to the soil. This is the very best evidence we have for the existence of God, and for all the truths of religion, that they spring from the constitution of our minds, and so are found to be fundamentally the same, wherever there is a mind at all cultivated. A Revelation is credible or incredible according as it is consistent or inconsistent with the constitution of our minds. The reason why we know that the Koran is not a Revelation from God, is because some of its laws shock our sense of right and wrong, are at war with the constitution of our minds. And the reason why we receive the Christian Religion as the truth of God, is because it is agreeable to our moral constitution.

If there be any attribute ascribed to God, which good minds cannot approve, it must be false for only that idea of God can be true which the mind can receive.

It is of great importance to us, and the more improvement we have made, the greater is this importance, that our religious opinions should have the deepest basis. They should be felt to be solid, immoveable, though the pillared firmament were rottenness. And the only way to secure them from continual tottering is to have them rooted and grounded in the laws of our own mind.

The reason of any and of all infidelity among lovers of truth is always some contradiction between the religious views which the person has received and the laws of his mind. It is out of the question to receive a faith which is contradicted by a man's reason. He does not receive it. It is laid down at his door. It encumbers and hurts him, but it is not his faith.

Manuscript dated March 20, 1831. Preached five times: March 20, 1831, at the Second Church, Boston; March 27 at the First Church, Boston; April 10 at the Brattle Street Church; July 26, 1837, in Waltham; and August 6 in East Lexington.

118

It is the perception of this discrepancy that makes every degree of skepticism from which we suffer. Now there is, I apprehend, a good deal of uneasiness created in many minds by the commonly received doctrines concerning the Holy Spirit and its influences as in inspiration and in sanctification because those doctrines as received are inconsistent with natural Religion.

It is my present purpose to endeavor to state what is agreeable to reason and to Scripture on these points: What is the Holy Spirit? and what are its operations?

The word signifying *Spirit* is used in the Scriptures in as many as eighteen different senses; sometimes for *animal life;* as "the spirit of the beast goeth downward."[1] Sometimes for an *apparition;* as "they were affrighted and supposed they had seen a Spirit."[2] Sometimes for *meaning;* "not the letter but the spirit."[3] Sometimes for *angels;* "Are they not all ministering *Spirits*?"[4] Sometimes for a *frame of mind;* as "the spirit of a sound mind, the Spirit of wisdom and understanding."[5] Sometimes for the *soul of man;* as "Lord Jesus receive my Spirit."[6] Sometimes for *God;* as God is a Spirit.[7]

It may be observed that it is one and the same word which is sometimes rendered Ghost and sometimes Spirit. This variety of senses makes it necessary in order to learn what it means in any one passage to make a careful examination of the context. The most remarkable of these uses, is when it is equivalent to the *mind of God.* And this is the general use of the term Holy Ghost, Holy Spirit in the New Testament.

In these passages it is used as we use the word mind or spirit in application to men for the man himself, as when we say, It so appeared to the mind of Paul; for, It so appeared to Paul. This is shown from several passages where it is directly explained. As, "what man knoweth the things of a man save the Spirit of a man that is within him, even so the things of God knoweth no man but the Spirit."[8]

And in I Corinthians 6:19, Paul says, Know you not that your body is the temple of the Holy Ghost which is in you?—the meaning of which passage is explained in the third chapter, sixteenth verse—by his saying, "know you not that you are the temple of God and that the Spirit of God dwelleth within you?"

The custom of all Eastern writers to *personify* abstract ideas, that is, to speak of love as a person, of wisdom as a person, may be seen in every page of the Scriptures. Mercy and truth have met together; Righteousness and peace have kissed each other.[9] Poverty shall come as an armed man, Want as one that travelleth,[10] and especially in the remarkable description of Wisdom in the

1. Eccl[esiastes] 3.21 [Emerson's note].
2. Luke 24.37 [Emerson's note].
3. Romans 2:29.
4. Hebrews 1:14.
5. II Timothy 1:7 and Ephesians 1:17.
6. Acts 7:59.
7. John 4:24.
8. I Cor[inthians] 2.11. [Emerson's note].
9. Psalms 85:10.
10. Proverbs 6:11.

Proverbs. When he prepared the Heavens I was there—when he appointed the foundations of the Earth, then was I by him as one brought up with him,[11]— expressions which in truth are only equivalent to the words in the Psalms, By his wisdom he hath established the heavens, or, more simply, God made the heavens.[12] So in the introduction to St. John's gospel the Word or the wisdom and power of God are thus personified.[13] And in the discourses of our Saviour which St. John has recorded, the Comforter is promised—an expression which is explained by himself, "the Comforter—even the Spirit of truth."[14]

The idea of God is infinite in the human mind by its constitution and though it may ascribe supernatural power to stocks and stones and believe in dæmons and gods, yet push your inquiries a little and you force the mind to admit more. So that in the ancient nations behind the popular idolatry was the background of Fate, on which the mind of the populace reposed and the philosophers held a pure theism.

From the use of this figure of speech, from the personification of the powers or the operations of God, very considerable errors have sprung. The deity of the Holy Spirit has been maintained,—the separation of the spirit into a person, and that person a God. This error, if it had not been unhappily embodied in the word Trinity and so become in words the faith of great churches, would long ere this have disappeared—for among those Christians called Trinitarians little is said of the deity of the Spirit though much operation is given to the Spirit. The Father and the Son being the prominent ideas presented to the reverence of the mind. It is not this error that needs our attention; but there has often arisen, I apprehend, in the mind of liberal Christians an uncertainty as to the true meaning of this word and the true extent of its operations in what are called spiritual influences (as in inspiration or in sanctification) which make it very desirable that its meaning should be settled.

I believe that a careful examination of his own thoughts and of the New Testament will satisfy every sincere seeker of truth that the term Holy Spirit, Holy Ghost, signify nothing more than the uniform and universal operations of God upon men; that spiritual influences differ only in degree not in kind—that nothing more is meant, for this plain reason, that nothing more can be meant.

There is one passage however that deserves particular attention in this inquiry from the remarkable expressions that are used. I mean the language of our Saviour in Matthew 12:31-32, "All manner of sin and blasphemy shall be forgiven unto men, but the blasphemy against the Holy Ghost shall not be forgiven unto men. And whosoever speaketh a word against the Son of man, it shall be forgiven him, but whosoever speaketh against the Holy Ghost it shall not be forgiven him, neither in this world, neither in the world to come."

11. Cf. Proverbs 8:27-30.

12. Cf. Psalms 33:6 and 136:5, for example.

13. "In the beginning was the Word, and the Word was with God, and the Word was God" (John 1:1).

14. Cf. John 14:16-17.

Jesus had been working miracles in the sight of all men. He had restored a withered arm and sight and speech to a man blind and dumb. The Pharisees seeing this said it was done by power from the devil. Jesus speaks in this manner. If you are offended at me that I am of mean extraction, that I am a carpenter's son, that I am out of Nazareth, that I am surrounded by obscure men,—I will not much blame you, it is not an unpardonable offence. But if your minds are in such a state that you can resist the evidence of these miracles and think that this divine power is from devils—then I say to you your minds are in that state that no evidence can reach. I see not how you can ever become good either in this world or the world to come.

In this sense, which is the only one I believe which the passage can bear, it is plain that no power in any degree distinct from God is hinted at. The only distinction drawn is between his own character as a man, and the power derived from God which was exhibited through him.

I proceed to say that what are commonly understood as spiritual influences are chiefly three; Miracles, Inspiration, and the operation of God upon every mind in the Sanctification of the heart. And I wish to consider each in reference to our idea of God. Various explanations have been attempted of these peculiar phenomena. And many things are said to have been done by the spirit of God as distinguished from common effects. But to every view of this subject which goes to cut up and distribute into parts the agency of God in the education of the human soul a true answer may be furnished by my text. *Every* good and *every* perfect gift is from above, and cometh down from the Father of lights, with whom is no variableness neither shadow of turning.

God is every where present and active. There is no life that is not received from him as long as it is life. The Universe is his work, his manifestation, his creation from hour to hour. Without him was nothing made, that was made.[15] We hang on his attributes for the life of our bodies and of our souls as the plant gets sustenance from the ground, or the insect from the plant. All wisdom, all power, all goodness, is only larger reception from the same infinite source, whence the emmet and the fool draw their limited nourishment. It is by his energy that all things exist in order; and if he were not, nothing would be.

Now this great doctrine of the divine Unity, which is prescribed to us by the constitution of our own minds as well as by Revelation, exposes the falsity of the common notions concerning spiritual influences. For the idea of God rightly received is so omnipresent as to leave no room for any other agency. In the twelfth chapter of I Corinthians, St. Paul declares the true doctrine; "Now there are diversities of gifts, but the same spirit, and there are diversities of operations, but it is the same God which worketh all in all; . . . For to one is given by the spirit the word of wisdom, to another the word of knowledge, to another, faith by the same spirit, to another the working of miracles, to another prophecy," &c, &c. "But all these worketh that one and selfsame spirit, dividing to

15. John 1:3.

every one severally as he will."[16] And in the twenty-eighth verse of the same chapter, the same things are repeated with this change—"And God hath set some in the church, first, apostles, then prophets, then teachers, after that miracles, then gifts of healings," &c.[17]

He speaks rightly. There is one light through a thousand stars. There is one spirit speaking through a myriad mouths and working by a myriad hands. It will not do to divide or bound what is in itself infinite. Every word of truth that is spoken by man's lips is from God. Every thought that is true is from God. Every right act is from God. All these are as much done by his spirit as the miracle of Pentecost.[18]—I suppose they are of the same sort as that influence. The apostle who prophesied or who wrought a miracle, felt that his word or his act was as true to the occasion as he did when he lifted bread to his mouth that he might eat. The prophet understood his prediction, the apostle willed the cure of the cripple. I suppose that miraculous power is only more power not different power. I suppose it is strictly of the same kind, for I suppose there is but one kind. There is but one source of power, that is, God.

This is the reason why I can readily admit a well authenticated account of a miracle. It does not seem to me strange that since we exercise so much power which is all derived, (for no man I suppose imagines that he himself created the power by which he raises his own hand) that we should exercise a larger measure of power.

Wisdom and goodness are the great means of power, the communicable attributes of God, and as men more fully apply themselves to God they receive larger measures of these. He that wholly gives himself up to God, reaches the highest elevation, the most knowledge. And such men have grown wiser than the men who sought wisdom for bye ends, have outlearned the schools and have become conscious of the future as of the present and wrought miracles. Probably all men have the same capacity of prophecy and miracle. What is prophecy but more knowledge? What is miracle but more dominion of the soul over matter than is now evinced? (But a man can no more account for his power to raise his arm by a wish than the prophet can for his power to raise a mountain.)

Who knows the extent of the powers of the soul over matter? There are many well authenticated accounts of miraculous cures even in our own time. Probably these are the victories of faith. Jesus promises this effect to faith. When in a better age, men shall wholly do the will of God, they shall ascend to that moral elevation that they shall realize the force of their exalted wills, and shall say to this mountain, be thou removed, and shall not doubt in their hearts, and it shall be removed.[19]

As of miracle, so of Prophecy. I would offer to your consideration the question whether prophecy is not a state of mind more sagacious than that of other men only as that mind is more fully surrendered to God. Every day's experience

16. I Corinthians 12:4–11.
17. I Corinthians 12:28.
18. See Acts 2:1–4.
19. Matthew 17:20 and Mark 11:23.

shows us the different degrees of reception of wisdom by the same mind at different times. A man who does right and seeks truth has juster views than the same man when he does wrong and speaks falsely. The prophet in an exalted state of holiness therefore sees more truth than other men, but under the same conditions. It is not, as some of the fathers have imagined, that he utters he knows not what. He sees his predictions to be true and necessary, exactly with the same evidence that he discerns any other truth. If he did not, how could he, or how could those who heard him, distinguish his predictions from the ravings of a lunatic? The advice of a parent is prophecy to a child. The writings of Bacon and Newton contain truth out of the reach of other men, and therefore in philosophy are prophetic.

This view of prophecy harmonizes with what is said by St. Paul, that the spirits of the prophets are subject unto the prophets, that is to say, their foresight blends with all their knowledge, and is possessed in same way. He also charges them not to abuse their gifts.[20]

And so I understand the *inspiration of the Scriptures*. I believe when a man wholly opens his heart to the love of God and has no self-love, no motive but from on high, that man speaks with authority, and not as the Scribes;[21] he becomes passive to the influence of God, and speaks his words. And such a person I suppose in the highest degree of all born of women, was Jesus Christ of Nazareth who spake as never man spake. Such were the apostles, such were the prophets, in lower degrees. And such have been all good men, and all men in different degrees.

And whenever a man in the simplicity of his heart, endeavouring to do his duty, utters his honest conviction, I suppose that man speaks by the same spirit which filled Paul, and his words are made effectual by the same holy confidence in the right which Jesus intended when he declared to his disciples that when they were brought before kings and magistrates it should be given in the same hour what they should say.[22]

And lastly of spiritual influences upon us. I believe one law prevails throughout the moral universe. There is not an economy of spiritual influences different from the whole economy of the Creator. God does, to be sure, differently endow different souls. That is his prerogative by which one being is made a plant, and one a dog, and one a man. But having made us what we are, we are all subjected to one law of improvement, which is shortly this, Draw nigh to God and he will draw nigh to you.[23] Every promise in the Scripture is conditional on our effort. 'Ask and you shall receive.' 'Knock, and it shall be opened unto you.' 'Resist the devil and he shall flee from you.' 'Blessed are the merciful for they shall obtain mercy.'[24] It is thus in every promise that the condition, expressed or understood, is an inseparable appendix. And this is agreeable to

---

20. I Corinthians 14:32 and 9:18.
21. Matthew 7:29 and Mark 1:22.
22. Matthew 10:18–19 and Luke 12:11–12.
23. James 4:8.
24. Matthew 7:7; James 4:7; Matthew 5:7.

all we know. It is so of necessity. The Earth not only falls to the Sun, but the Sun falls to the Earth. All motion is reciprocal and so all influence spiritual influence. Wherein does Wisdom consist? What is Wisdom but laboring to become wise? What is goodness but laboring to become good?

Far be it from me to bring into question the reality of spiritual influences. I believe in them with my whole mind, but not in local, capricious, anomalous influences. God, God is always near. The soul that seeks to be holy and truly wise can always be so. There is no bar in the universe to progress towards him. But do not confine it to one season or one gift. Is there any good thing in your possession or in your history, any talent, any virtue, any friend, any occasion of good, any season of refreshment, any period of education, you do not ascribe to God? Was there ever a good man who did not ascribe every good thing to God? Then *all* is spiritual influence, and its omnipresence excludes every superstitious distinction. O yes, I believe in spiritual influences. I believe the reason why we are so weak and so ignorant is because we are so sinful. I believe that we shall see more, love more, do more, world without end.[25] I believe the heart of man hath not conceived the glory that shall be revealed.[26] I believe we stand waiting in the outer courts of knowledge and love. We do not realize the presence of our Father. In the language of Scriptures, we do not "walk with God."[27] Whenever we awake to the sense of sin, whenever we rise above the objects of sense in our motives, and give ourselves unreservedly to our maker, we shall then make progress in power compared with which our studies pursued for bread and praise shall seem ignorance indeed. We shall know as we are known;[28] we shall find the antidote to pain; we shall see the future as the present; we shall know our immortality—For how can it be otherwise? If we are more intimately united to God, or as St. Peter says, are *more fully partakers of the divine nature*,[29] what is that nature but infinite goodness, infinite wisdom?

Now does any one say, since this subject is so confessedly above our power to discuss with confidence, why attempt to explain away into common operations the agency so reverend in many pious minds as that of the Holy Spirit? Why disturb a faith which presents to many minds so helpful a medium by which they approach the idea of God?

It is not that I wish to lower your views of a part of the Spirit but that I would make your views of the whole more sacred, because I think the popular views on this head do harm by putting a medium; because it removes the idea of God one step further from the mind. It leaves some events, some things, some thoughts out of the power of him who causes every event, every power, every thought. It takes off the soul from seeing its Father's eye wherever it turns. Men are made to feel as if they ate their bread and committed every day's faults somewhere

25. Cf. Ephesians 3:21.
26. Cf. Romans 8:18 and I Peter 5:1.
27. Cf. Micah 6:8.
28. I Corinthians 13:12.
29. II Peter 1:4.

behind a screen, as if the spirit of God works in Jerusalem, or in churches, or in prayers, and not in the vulgar events of every hour. They do not feel as they ought that all is received, and that all good in us is the power of God; that not a star rolls in space, not a bird drops from the bough, not a pulse beats in a single heart, not an atom moves throughout the wide system, but is bound in the chains of his omnipotent thought. Least of all can we believe that the presiding Deity commands all matter, and never descends into the secret chambers of the soul. There he is most present. The soul rules over matter. Matter may pass away like a mote in the sunbeam, may be absorbed into the immensity of God, as a mist is absorbed into the heat of the sun; but the soul is the kingdom of God, the abode of love, truth, and virtue.

Let us feel that God is no respecter of persons[30]—that our difficulty in getting access to him accuses ourselves; that there is not one gracious motion, one pious desire in our heart, but God acknowledges as fully as in the heart of St. Paul; nor a false word on our lips but is as abhorrent to him, as alien from all his Nature as the lie of Ananias.[31]

30. Acts 10:34 and Romans 2:11.
31. See Acts 5:1-11.

CXI

The law of the Lord is perfect, converting the soul.

PSALMS 19:7

The law of the Lord is perfect. The understanding of man is imperfect. The religions of men, and every man has a religion in some respects peculiar to himself, are so many versions, more or less faithful, but all imperfect, of the Law of the Lord. That law is what is common to all minds. We approximate to the knowledge of it as our minds are purified. It is because of this omnipresent law, that all sects of Christians are agreed upon much more than that upon which they disagree. This fact is one of great importance, and when it is fully seen, might make us tremble. For it might show us, that many of us who are come up hither to worship, not pricked perhaps by any strong sense of sin and danger, do really stand condemned in our character by the law which all denominations from the most strict to the most lax acknowledge; that in the judgment of all we are unworthy and so cannot have any rational hope of present or future safety.

And this is the truth which I wish to present to your consideration at this time, that the sternest commandment is the most universal. It is a groundless imagination that by rising above the prejudices of a superstitious faith, you have escaped one real terror. All that ever gave life and power to alarm, to any false doctrine, was the true terror that lay under it. A hideous mask can only terrify when it is worn upon a living face. Show the mask separate, and it has lost all its frightfulness.

That which really causes anguish to a rational being for the commission of sin is older than his church creed, and survives in a good mind every human creed, and grows more dreadful on every offence in proportion to the elevation of the mind. It is this *law of the Lord,* or in other words, *the moral constitution of man.*

A wise man heedfully searching for truth wherever he goes, does not look upon every doctrine (in the form in which it is maintained by great sects,) as

---

Manuscript dated March 27, 1831. Preached eight times: March 27, 1831, at the Second Church, Boston; March 30, 1834, in New Bedford; March 1, 1835, in Waltham; April 5 in Plymouth; August 23 in Lowell; December 20 in East Lexington; January 22, 1837, in Concord, Mass.; and November 26 in Weston.

truth itself, but only as proceeding from truth. He looks upon the Catholic or the Methodist or the Friends' or the New Jerusalem Church as one manifestation more of the desires and opinions of the human mind (and if followed down to its principle,) based at last on the moral nature. It is another John crying in the Wilderness.[1] He is not the Light, but bears witness of the Light.[2] Every truth and every error refer to some reality. As every bud on the branch indicates the presence of vegetable life and every excrescence indicates it no less, though distorted by the worm that eats within. There never was a dogma received by multitudes, but, with sufficient diligence, it might have been traced down to some fact which gave to its perversions what semblance of truth they had,—to some eternal truth in moral nature.

In illustration of this remark, let me mention one or two doctrines that are urged by the church of Geneva, as peculiar to their faith. The Calvinist says, You reject the great doctrine of Christianity, which is *Justification by Faith*. You must give up your pride, and selfrighteousness, and be willing to be pardoned and saved only through the blood of Jesus Christ; that is, I must give up my selfrighteousness and look only for mercy to the righteousness of God, for such they think Christ is.—Now though this *language* is incorrect, the doctrine is bottomed in eternal truth. We *must* give up our selfrighteousness. We can have no merits to plead before God. Every pious man would be shocked at the thought of claiming the blessings of eternal life at the hand of his Maker, on the ground of his own good deeds. They would seem to him in the presence of God, "*filthy rags.*"[3] Every good man, every reasonable man sees that what we receive from God, is all free grace. The pious men of other denominations are mistaken in thinking there is any difference in the sentiment of good men on this point.

So of the doctrine of *Regeneration*. Let the doctrine be simply stated, that we must be born again, and all will admit it. That is to say, every good man admits the doctrine that in the worldly man the whole arrangement of his thoughts and purposes is from self as the principle; and in the good man the whole arrangement of the thoughts and purposes is from God, as the principle; and that this arrangement in every man from self-love, must be changed, and all his soul transformed to have the love of God for its principle, or he cannot be saved, because, the love of God *is* salvation.

Let me adduce as another illustration of this common basis of truth, upon which all slighter differences are builded, those crises which are esteemed as the practical effects of one doctrine and not of another. I mean what are called *Revivals of Religion*. If you love truth more than you love your party, go and converse with a pious man who believes in the divine efficacy of these occasions, and you will find that whatever dislike you may have to the manner in which it is executed, the whole *design* of these meetings can be defended on principles

1. Cf. Luke 3:4.
2. John 1:8.
3. Isaiah 64:6.

which you cannot reject. Thus the more exalted are your views of God, the more reasonable it will appear to you, that when the attention of any young person, wholly intent on the pleasures of the senses, is for the first time by good arts secured, and that sudddenly, to the idea of God and to an efficient faith in his own immortality, he must be startled, he must feel strongly.

Then it is the professed object of these assemblies to make earnest prayer for special influences of the Holy Spirit, which in common language, means, earnest desire of becoming better, and that through regard to our relation to God. And can any more rational request rise from the human heart? To be sure, it is for '*Special influence*.' But the true condition is regarded: it is *specially sought*. And we should never complain of our fellow men for praying.

Then it is the object of these meetings to make confession of sin and of suffering under the sense of a wicked heart. And will any humble believer of God speak with contempt or hostility of this feeling? No never. However alien from your habits, and unsuitable to produce effect on you, the excitement of these occasions may be, the principles on which Revivals are sought for, are perfectly sound. It *is* an objection to them that in all that I know of their history the Reason of man has not been addressed. Such representations of God have been made as keep down and hurt the mind and do not exalt it. Such representations of God as could be received only by an uneducated or else by a prostrate mind, but must forever keep aloof from their influences an enlarged intellect. With the progress of religious truth I should think the multiplication of such meetings might be expected. Men would meet to pray and exhort each other, but truth and devotion shall take the place of error and party spirit.

This defect is an objection to the manner of performance, but not to the plan. Among that portion of the community whose frame of mind makes them more open to rude than to gentle methods, to coarser than to finer influences, why should not these seasons of excitement have the happiest effect? If it save one soul from sin, towns and counties may well assemble for such a purpose. Besides, if really, to use their expression, they 'find religion,' they will not stop where they begin. If this faith which they first receive is erroneous, it is only the first stage of their education. The truth that is concealed in the impure food of a false doctrine will nourish them to a strength that requires, and an appetite that selects, a better aliment. The religious mind is always in the right road to truth. But let not knowledge be proud; let not those to whom God has given more truth look on without feeling the admonition of this fervor. In view of others' devotion let conscience do its office.

For what more natural, what more desirable to every wise and good man than a generous surrender of common employments to these impulses of the Soul? to the searching of the deep things of God?[4] What object more fitted to excite enthusiasm and suspend for a season the cares of a vulgar prudence?

The more it is considered the more it will appear, that there is a foundation in truth for the opinions and the practices which we are accustomed to call extrav-

4. I Corinthians 2:10.

agant. Let it teach that these differences which show so large and about which so much clamor is made are merely superficial. Let it show, (that I may return to the main subject,) that these are grounded in man's permanent nature, in the primitive fear of sin, and so let it teach that man does not get rid of his moral obligations by correcting his opinions. Let it be felt by us that there is a wide difference between opinion and duty; that opinions change, and advance, and recede; that Duty, this moral nature, is utterly independent of these fluctuations. Do you think because you do not receive the doctrines of Total Depravity and the Vicarious Suffering of Christ, that therefore you may unblamed indulge in any practice which a stricter brother would condemn? Do you think you may neglect a trust or forget a favor or lie later in bed, because you do not believe in Plenary Inspiration? Can you take an unjust advantage of your neighbor or slander him? Can you insult him in conversation by exhibiting contempt for his opinions or circumstances because you reject Transubstantiation and Trinity and Election? Or leaving these duties that the world with one voice demands, do you think your obligations are any the less sacred to charity and to gratitude and to an unremitted effort to change you heart, i.e., to substitute the love of God for self love, than if you were a Methodist or a Baptist? My brother, you know better by the misgiving that is in your mind when you condemn those practices as over religious. You may hold what views of ordinances you will; you may hold what views of the offices of Christ, it will never add nor diminish one jot in the obligation of these duties, nor, if you love truth, in the *pressure* of the obligation, for they belong to the constitution of your minds. These are written in lines that cannot be effaced. This is not a temporary law nor a covenant to a chosen nation. These are the laws that exist yesterday, today, and forever. They are not to be abolished, nor changed, nor shielded from. They make the substance of the soul. Heaven consists in keeping them. Hell consists in violating them; simply because they are the nature of God, the mould according to which he hath formed man, coupling praise to every right step and blame and pain to every wrong one.

It ought to be deeply felt by us that these moral obligations abide unchanged with the more or less of faith. It is one and the same law which one church writes in many and another in a few articles. It is not greater in a rigid church, it is not less in a liberal one. But I wish to remind you that more is true than this. It is an obligation that is not only equal to those of different Churches but to those of none. (It is not a Revelation that makes man religious. He is of a religious nature.) Are you inclined to skepticism? Has the truth such charms for you that you say you will not receive the belief of the miraculous until it is proved? You must put your fingers into the hands and side of your risen Lord or you will not believe.[5] If unhappily the Scriptures seem to want evidence, God has yet provided for your salvation, if you will only be true to yourself, in the beneficent influence of these laws of your mind.

All the moral obligations are perfect in the mind of the Atheist. "The law of

5. Cf. John 20:25.

the Lord is perfect." He has, it is true, renounced the central truth which gives harmony and explanation to all, but there still are the stubborn facts; *right* and *wrong* still exist, plainly distinguished in his mind; and there too are *good* and *evil,* their faithful followers. And there the royal Reason approves or condemns. 'The law is perfect,' and, as David adds, 'converting the soul.' If you will keep this law it shall convert your soul. It shall bring you to the Scriptures. The Works of God agree with his Word. I speak in conformity to the experience of many men. If unhappily early associations of faith with gross errors have made you dislike the name of *religion,* O then conform yourself to nature. *Speak the truth,* not because the Scripture says, 'Thou shalt not bear false witness,'[6] but because falsehood is unnatural. *Be just,* because dishonesty offends the nature of things. *Be temperate,* because excess tends to disease. *Do good,* because only by a mutual support can the greatest amount of natural good be produced. Presently by walking in this road, you shall see more truth. The fragrance of humility, the disgrace of sin shall appear to you; the love of your friends shall teach you to look for the fellowship of spirits—and the great First Cause will dawn again on your mind. In this way God always brings back by duty the humble heart to *Faith.*

It is always the effect of the practice of Right to increase the love of the Right—to quicken the Conscience. Men see by the light of their own virtue. "True wisdom," said Lord Shaftesbury, "comes more from the heart than the head;"[7] and those ancients who loved what was true and did what was right were led to very clear religious views, and learned to trust in God and pray to him and to speak humbly of themselves, and kindly to others, long before Jesus had yet brought immortality to light.

An observance of moral obligations has, further, the effect not to shut you up in a barren solitude of good deeds. It does not leave you an abstract religion, an empty heaven. It introduces you into a personal relation that may become all in all to you—to God the Father.[8] The faithful performance of our duties brings into exercise all your affections. The miser who shuts himself up with his purse may lose all love of men and all desire of God. But he that watches all the commands within and executes them, is brought into near relations with others; has an interest in their fate and would fain ask superior power to avert their dangers or bring them good. He learns thus to seek after God.

It not only produces the love of God, but it makes more amiable and venerable *all the means* which it pleases him to use in the Salvation of the Soul. It unites the soul to Jesus, the Head of the Church. Do I speak to any to whom that name does not convey a pleasing and an honoured idea? Do I speak to any to whom the love of Christ has an unamiable sound? Then you have not kept the law. The beginning and the ending of all love is *likeness.* You find sympathy, that is, you find something of yourself in your friend and so you seek his society.

6. Exodus 20:16.
7. See *JMN* 3:269.
8. Cf. I Corinthians 15:28.

You are continually brought to nearer resemblance by your intercourse. He that loves what you hate, he that hates what you love is not your friend but always according to the likeness of your pursuits and affections with those of another will be your mutual regard. The learned love the company of learned—gay of gay. Those who are humble and benevolent and who honour God supremely will find their hearts burn within them when Jesus Christ talks with them.[9] They will see beauty that they should desire in a character that to others was a root out of a dry ground without form or comeliness.[10] They have anointed eyes, they see what is spiritually discerned and see how it becomes the great God to manifest his power in external meanness.[11]

They can be his disciples, they can feel his friendship, they know his voice. They take pleasure in complying with his injunctions. They join heart and hand in his enterprize of mercy to lead men to the Father by truth and love.

9. Cf. Luke 24:32.
10. Isaiah 53:2.
11. I Corinthians 2:14.

CXII

Peace, peace to him that is far off and to him that is near, saith the Lord, and I will heal him. But the wicked are like the troubled sea when it cannot rest, whose waters cast up mire and dirt. There is no peace, saith my God, to the wicked.

Isaiah 57:19–21

The advancing season is bringing back the warmth of the sun to our soil, the sap is ascending in the vegetable tribes, the labors of men, interrupted by the cold, are again resumed, and we anticipate already the blossoms and the fruit of another year. The changes that there revolve, are only shadows of changes in us. Spring melts into summer and youth into maturity. But does the thought wake no alarm, that, the year that is come shall be like the last? That which hath been is now and that which is to be hath already been, and God requireth that which is past.[1]

And all of us who now see the bright return of the spring, does it find us as sanguine as in the last year? does it find us as happy? does it find us as good? does it find us as bad? It will be a shame to us, the months as they go by will seem to cry shame on us, if we let the periods pass without one pause of self-examination. Life is stealing on to the grave and it is unworthy of a reasonable creature never to descend into himself, never to take account of his loss and gain and see whether he is living or only growing old. The spring is wearing into summer. Life is wearing into death. Our friends are forsaking us; our hopes are deceiving us. Our riches are wasting; our mortifications are increasing. A few more winters, a few more friends, a few more hopes, a few more defeats and our thread of life will be snapped and men will throw a little dust on our breathless clay.

I hold it good for every man to ask himself occasionally the question whether life on the whole is a blessing; whether in his own experience the good or the

---

Manuscript dated April 3, 1831. Preached twice: April 3, 1831, at the Second Church, Boston, and April 17, 1836, in East Lexington.

1. Eccl[esiastes] 3.15 [Emerson's note].

evil preponderates;—in order that it may instruct him in his prayers, and in order that it may induce more careful inquiry whether he seeks his happiness at the right sources, and whether some of the chief occasions of vexation may not be removed or mitigated.

This question is very seldom asked. Truth is masked and kept at a distance by many causes. We live in a crowd that is in constant action. By the number and noise of the actors, we overrate the value of the prize. The great objects which the whole world pursue with such ardour will lose much of their lustre if examined. The deception is like that produced by the sight of the evening firmament. You go out in a clear night and the stars of heaven appear to be innumerable in their shining posts. The eye is bewildered with their multitude but the astronomer who has directed his telescope to every one, finds that not more than nine or ten hundred are visible to the naked eye, and that all the rest is illusion upon the eye, caused by the presence of so many cross lights.

It is just so with the objects of that life which man leads beneath their light. As soon as the telescope of Thought is directed upon them instead of a multitude of nameless attractions, they are found to consist of few and simple elements. A few pleasures and a few pains, often repeated, make up life. The ways to sorrow are manifold. The way to happiness is one, and straight, and narrow, and few there be that walk therein.[2]

In order to remove the illusion, in order to see things as they really are, the objects of life must be accurately observed, and for this end the wise have always insisted much on the necessity of *retirement* and *meditation,* of a voluntary truce imposed upon the tumult of care and hope, to the end that we might enter into that tranquillity which knowledge and goodness only can give.

To estimate truly what we ought to be and to do needs this solemn pause. We must plant our foot and refuse to follow the multitude. We must insist on knowing what is the road and what is the object of the journey. And we must judge whether the object is good, and the road is the right one. This can only be done by a firm resolve, a voluntary starting aside from the hurry of the crowd and a deliberate reflection.

In the use of the drugs that have been recommended to the victim of intemperance, as remedies, it surely was never expected that any drug in the world would of itself counteract that madness and produce temperance, it was only hoped to make the glass loathsome for a time, so that the moral sense of the victim, which, in the continual succession of appetite and gratification had no power to act, could now recover itself and operate; that the man might be himself again long enough to choose.

Precisely this good may be expected to come from a pause brought into the delusions of common life. There are other madmen besides the sot. A man may be—thousands are—as intemperate in their love of pleasure, of money, of office, of praise, as the drunkard in his love of wine. Surely they are more brutish

2. Cf. Matthew 7:14.

than men, surely they have not the understanding of a man. They need solitude, that revealer of the truth, solitude the parent of meditation, that hill that commands the wide prospect of life to make known things to them in true lights. It is related of the pious parent of a profligate son that on his deathbed he prevailed on his son to promise that he would spend one hour of every day alone. The son kept his word and found those uncomfortable hours at first painful enough, but wisdom grew out of them and he became an useful and virtuous man.

Now when this pause of consideration becomes habitual, it is Tranquillity of mind, and it is to the whole being, what an hour's consideration is to the whole day. See what advantage it will give you. Have you ever seen a man of hasty temper and confused utterance conversing with a man of perfect self-command? You have then seen the superiority of calmness over bluster; of clear head over a wrong head. Now just the advantage which the cool temper has over the hot one, just the same has the tranquil mind forever over the unthinking follower of custom.

In urging the benefits of a tranquil state of mind I certainly do not mean to commend any merely outward and unfounded tranquillity. The calmness of the calm I know is often only in the countenance and deportment whilst the thoughts underneath a marble brow are plying the same dusty vulgar roads as the most pitiable slave of fashion or of his appetite.

Sometimes it appears only in the temperament, and great and grievous changes, sickness, domestic calamities, and age will sour it. Sometimes it proceeds from languor and incapacity of being amused with common pleasures or pains. The gambler is calm when he is not playing for a deep stake. The soldier is calm in peace. The political partisan, the conspirator, the murderer are calm when no criminal work is to be done.

The easy and independent port of the man who seeks popularity may be traced to the same causes—a little greater extent of trifles. He meets with perfect equanimity the opposition of one man or of many men. It is because he depends on the number of those to whose favor he looks. If the praise of all is taken away he is miserable. But this is a calmness not worth recommending. I speak of that temporary repose which is sought as the entrance to duty and of that eternal tranquillity which belongs only to the good.

A bad man cannot be calm. Do you think the wretched man walks with a tranquil heart who enters the public Treasury at midnight with false keys and carries thence the heavy heavy load of other men's wealth? Does he much enjoy his riches now they are safe in his chamber, when the streets are full of eyes that fasten on him alone? He carries that consciousness within him that interprets every look and act into marks of guilt, and his few days' wealth is a weary estate. There is no peace, saith my God, to the wicked.

And it is not very much otherwise in those delusions that are not branded by the laws as guilt but that are no more founded upon principles. If a man makes a great adventure in this world, the greatest adventure he makes in it is his peace of mind. Had he set his heart on the tumultuous chances of an election? I am afraid the joy of success will hardly overpay the mortifications that precede and follow it, especially when it is remembered that success is only a new lure into farther adventures of your quiet and farther mortifications.

And is there any bold adventurer, not content with moderate gains but ambitious of sudden wealth, forgetful that the surest road to wealth without the pains of wealth is to conform our expenses to our means, and willing to hazard much to gain much? He puts more than property, he puts peace at stake; he ventures commonly into a whirlpool of business, into years of hurry and anxiety, which seeming to hold great satisfactions always before him, he yet never reaches. At the end of a year he looks back with imperfect gratification at what has been done and is still drawn on to greater distances from the real purposes of moral being.

But why need I enumerate these familiar instances? They are of no use without they make their moral clear, and this is to be read in one action as well as in a thousand.

For if a course of conduct is not right it will never produce a genuine satisfaction by multiplying its parts from ten to ten thousand transactions. This adds to the delusion, adds to the *appearance* of security, but does not add the least real security.

And the lesson that comes from all these instances is this, that no course of conduct can ever produce peace of mind, that is not pursued with a strict regard to moral principles—that no mind can be established, until it has rooted and grounded itself in what is eternal.

It is not enough that you do not kill or steal or bear false witness, you must break up the fountains of murder, of theft, of slander, by changing the heart. Until it has some love for truth and sought the pleasures of Religion, you are still of the same sort as the murderer, from whom an outward decency alone distinguishes you. Change your circumstances and you would do as he has done. And whilst you are of this mind, whilst you seek your happiness wholly in things present and never look beyond, you seek in vain because change and fear belong to these things—"Peace," saith the Lord, "let there be peace in the mind of him that is far off and him that is near and I will heal him. But the wicked are like the troubled sea when it cannot rest, whose waters cast up mire and dirt. There is no peace saith my God to the wicked."

Do you ask what are the treasures that lie hid from the great majority of men in the bosom of Tranquillity? They are simple and open to all: the love of truth and of right, the pleasures of religion, the love of God, love of Christ, and the hope of heaven.

Go alone, and converse with yourself, and the distinction of right and wrong so much overlooked and disguised and transgressed in the crowd will reappear and put a true face on every action. For the faces of those with whom you deal being absent, their example will not give a colour to wrong and your resentments fade and conscience that could not be heard in the stimulus of competition and the roar of business can speak and be heard.

Does any one to whom I speak think lightly of these riches of solitude? I say to you you have much to learn of yourself. You do not yet know that this principle, deciding on right and wrong within you, is the parent of all good that the Universe contains for you; is your league with God himself, and shall minister to your happiness and glory to the bounds of your being. This wonderful thought is that which makes all distinctions even. We cannot all be rich but we have this without which riches are curses. We cannot all be popular or healthy or well-favoured or learned but all, from the angel down to the poorest wretch that wears the form of man, have this transcendant thought which is the badge of immortal beings, which is the stamp of God on his own work. O my brother, congratulate yourself on this. Humble yourself before God in devout gratitude for it. O cherish it as your dearest guest. Honour it, it shall honour you. Trust to that prompting.

No man ever got above it. Men have transgressed and hated and gainsaid it but no man ever sinned but he felt this inward angel towering above him and threatening his well being.[3]

Go sit alone and think much of this feeling of right and wrong, you will soon perceive that the principles by which you measure actions are true and unfailing though you had never known a man who kept the law—oh yes, you feel that the nations are a handful before that multitude of beings for whom this law was made and whose destinies shall be administered upon it, for wherever rational nature exists there does this Law rule. He who thinks on this law of Right and Wrong thinks on truth compared with which History in its highest antiquity is young and recent. He thinks on that which ever was, which is, and which shall be, and so is the measure of all other things.[4]

Yet is this infinite idea but the introduction of the mind to the idea of God whose being this distinction implies and with whose nature it blends. It is in solitude of the closet but especially in a mind accustomed to solitary meditation that this great presence is realized. In solitude God is sometimes found as he is not in the world. The *secret* of the Lord is with them that fear him. He will be found of them that seek him.[5] The spirit of his son, the teacher, the prophet, the Saviour, shall come to you and be your companion and comforter as it was promised. And all the joys of piety shall be made known to you in course.

Now he that acts not by custom or caprice but by means of his clear insight into himself and his love and reverence for God, acts upon principles on which his being rests and sees clearly that he conforms to laws that must abide when the sun is quenched, may well be tranquil in his mind. The clouds are below him, "Eternal sunshine settles on his head."[6] He accustoms himself to a familiarity with infinite thoughts and this may well give elevation to his common intercourse. He may deal with the great without humiliation who lives among thoughts which weigh great men and empires and find them light in the bal-

3. Cf. *JMN* 3:244.
4. Cf. *JMN* 3:243.
5. Psalms 25:14; cf. Matthew 7:7 and Luke 11:9.
6. Oliver Goldsmith, "The Deserted Village," line 190.

ance. He may deal with the humble without pride for they are his fellows in the possession of this nature.

He may be calm who seeks truth, who practices virtue, who lives not for time but according to the order of the whole Universe, who loves God and so is loved by Him.

It is a steep descent my friends from this height to which the law of God and the example of Jesus bids us carry our nature, down to our practice. Yet every one of us has access to this mountain height. It shall be the Mount of Olives where Jesus learned to say, Thy Will be done.[7] And presently the hour of death will come to each of us and ask in tones of Judgment whether we have answered the purposes of life. There is not one of us so much removed from dangerous temptation but he needs all the aid that solitude and watching and prayer can give. And most of us in the daily warfare of the world are apt to come off conquered.

> "The world's infectious; few bring back at eve
> Immaculate the manners of the morn."[8]

Let us then seek by stated practices, the only safe mode, the assistance we require. Let us go alone daily. A little time for that purpose is of more value than can be told. Let us consider whether the day and the year and life are making us better. Let us seek the benediction by receiving the spirit of Jesus, the benediction of tranquillity. 'Peace I leave with you, my peace I give unto you. Not as the world giveth, give I unto you.'[9] The Peace of God which passeth understanding shall dwell in our hearts and minds forever.[10]

7. Luke 22:42.
8. Edward Young, *Night Thoughts,* "Night V," lines 142–43. See *JMN* 2:365.
9. John 14:27.
10. Cf. Philippians 4:7.

CXIII _____

Help, Lord; for the godly man ceaseth; the
faithful fail from among the children of men.
PSALMS 12:1

The civil authority calls us again this day to comply with the immemorial custom of New England, to keep a day of Fasting, Humiliation, and Prayer. 'Tis to be regretted it begins to be thought a burdensome custom. By many, and of course by many of those who need it most, it is neglected. It is looked upon as a relic of an ancient race, which has outlived its day. It is something which should be huddled aside by an informed generation as if it were a barbarous monument intruded into the new world of thought and religion which we inhabit.

Perhaps all do not thus regard it. Perhaps there yet remains in the bosom of society so much of the spirit of the fathers, or at least so much respect for them, as will not willingly see their venerable usages abolished and trod upon.

There are, it may be hoped, a great number yet remaining who hold in honour the memory of that old people, that selfdenying race, who redeemed England, and planted America.

The whole world runs after *living* fame. It is said a living dog is better than a dead lion.[1] But there is something noble in the love of the dead. And always where there has been any touch of a good nature, the departed have been kept in remembrance. Even the savages revere the land that contains the bones of their fathers. The Jews were taught that in their prosperous age, they should not forget the day of small things;[2] they should remember the distressed condition of the outcast Joseph, and say, "My father was a Syrian and went down a bondman into Egypt."[3] They were taught, when established in an ample domain to be kind to the stranger, and to say, "I was a stranger when the Lord brought me into this land."[4] And happy will it be for the children of New England if they never grow unmindful of their ancient stem, if the good family

---

Manuscript dated April 7, 1831. Preached three times: April 7, 1831, at the New North Church, Boston; again on April 7, at the Second Church, Boston; and April 6, 1837, in East Lexington. Notes and draft passages for this sermon occur in *JMN* 3:244-46. As Emerson indicates, this was a Fast Day sermon.

1. Ecclesiastes 9:4.
2. Cf. Zechariah 4:10.
3. Cf. Deuteronomy 26:5.
4. Cf. Exodus 22:21 and 23:9.

pride of being descended from men that loved God and freedom more than worldly good, does not fade out of their minds. Not that I think there is any danger that the names and exploits of the Puritans will be forgotten. It has become fashionable to praise them. Our selflove leads us to extol our ancestors. But far better would it be that we should praise them with understanding,—that we should inherit their sentiments. And whilst we give them good words not be in truth such alien descendants as to contemn their Religion.

I. Let us have juster regard to them and to their institution. Think of them as men whom God honoured with great usefulness. That solid sense, that expansion of the inner man to the truths of religion and of civil right—that greater reverence for history and for law which they had, may compensate for any arts of trade, and mechanical improvements, and fine houses, which they had not. He that thinks so profoundly, he that acts so habitually in reference to the principles of the first class as to give all his life and manners the expression of simple gravity, may be excused if he have little playfulness in his conversation, and little elegance in his circumstances.

What if their rigor was excessive in forms, and their seriousness was stern? All things are not trifles nor to be treated as such. Seriousness may be forgiven to those who languished in prison, that we might walk at large; who wore the sword that we might live without it. Seriousness may be forgiven to the Redeemers of suffering Liberty; to the defenders and practisers of Religion, in an unholy age.

That great body of Christians called the Puritans, from the time of their appearance in the age of Elizabeth, through their heroic war with Charles and James II in England, and their settlement at an earlier period of this country, have bequeathed great men and great thoughts to the world. 'The memory of the just is blessed.'[5] They were marked with faults as a party. They had great errors in faith and pursued some good ends by bad means, and some bad ends by bad means. But they atoned for their defects by their capital merit; they had *enthusiasm.* They thought life had something worth contending for. They lived and died for sentiments and not for bread only. To these apostolical men, to whom the cross was a dear emblem, who knew how to suffer themselves, their idea of Jesus was an indwelling thought, which manifested itself in every action— in the house; and in Church and in State.

When the near and the remote effects of that party are observed; the two revolutions which they wrought in England; the history of this country; and the effects of this example on Europe for forty years past and at this moment, to no party is the world so much indebted. They are vouchers for that just observation of history that nothing great was ever achieved without enthusiasm.[6]

---

5. Proverbs 10:7.

6. "[H]istories . . . confirm by irrefragable evidence the aphorism of ancient wisdom, that nothing great was ever achieved without enthusiasm." Samuel Taylor Coleridge, *The Statesman's Manual,* in *The Complete Works of Samuel Taylor Coleridge,* ed. W. G. T. Shedd, 7 vols. (New York, 1853), 1:433. See *JMN* 5:15. The quotation is used in "Circles" (*CW* 2:190).

We should honour their institution if only because it was theirs. Whatever precious relic of their customs has come down to us a good man would not scorn. He would respect this Fast as a connecting link by which the posterity are bound to their progenitors; as a trump through which the voice of the Fathers speaks to us.

II. But there is more reason that we should respect the institution than because it came to us from our ancestors. It belongs to a wider country than theirs, or ours. It is proper to man. Penitence, which originally means self-punishment, belongs to all who are frail and sin. It is needed for our public and our personal safety. It is wholesome to man to consider his sins. It is not amiss to humble himself by external acts. The house of mourning is better than the house of feasting.7 The hair cloth, solitude, and bread and water, are safer courses for tempted man, than much company, and rich clothes, and easy living. Jesus, it is true, says, "Anoint thy head and wash thy face"8—but he condemns hypocritical penitence in the view of inward penitence, and not an external fast in comparison with no fast at all.

In the first place it is a duty to humble ourselves as a people for the public sins. There is no excess of penitential service for this evil. But some will say there is no need: there is not a decay made manifest in our outward prosperity; there is a confident reliance in the heart of the people on the security of their good condition.

But read the warnings of the Old Testament. They were uttered under a sky that shone as bright as ours, and under walls of greater magnificence, and to a people distinguished by yet more signal favours. Yet those anointed eyes of Isaiah and Jeremiah saw in the corrupt character of the people the inevitable forerunners of outward calamity.

They saw the heaven darkened at noon. They saw the new wine mourn, the fenced cities already prostrate, and dragons and bats lurking in their prosperous palaces, and the same unnoticed admonitions and the same overthrow in other nations.9

And what evil can we discern impending over us? The flag of this country is hurrying over the ocean into every port and island of the globe. You see a great country only half explored; a fast increasing census; spreading cultivation; rising cities filled with every social institution. 'Tis the breath of life, the tumult of industry, and not the sound of falling ruins.

True; but it will not cost greater changes than have been often exhibited, to blow the trumpet of civil war from one end of the country to the other, and from the sea to the wilderness; to turn those fleets of merchantmen into privateers and pirates; to turn these pleasant cities into strongholds of cruel factions; and, in the end, every house into a bloody castle; and the friendships that tie us in one community, into murderous hatreds. It needs no strange or impos-

7. Cf. Ecclesiastes 7:2.
8. Matthew 6:17.
9. Cf. Amos 8:9, Isaiah 24:7, Jeremiah 5:17, and Isaiah 13:22.

sible foreign influence or marvellous series of external events. It needs only certain change in the speculative principles which we ourselves entertain. It needs a preponderance of passion over reason, a little more violent preference of selfish interest over honest shame than now we permit in ourselves, a little more casting off of the restraints of Puritan principles and Puritan manners, a little greater progress of unbelief which springs from a bad heart. It needs no more active causes. For when things have gone to a certain pass and strife begins, the antagonist parties goad each other on to indefinite mischief, and the atrocity of one is cause and plea of the atrocity of the other.

God grant we may be far, yes forever distant from these horrors that have made the history of nations as good as ours!—Yet the eye of good men have seen evil signs and their hearts are sad. Our treatment of the Indian in one portion of the country, a barefaced trespass of power upon weakness, and the vindication of that wrong by the law of the Land and the general indifference with which this outrage passes before the eyes of the whole nation, is a most alarming symptom how obtuse is the moral sense of the people.[10] In the language of the prophet, And judgment is turned away backward, and justice standeth afar off; for truth is fallen in the street, and equity cannot enter.[11] An indifference to a wrong as long as it does not touch ourselves, is one of the most certain marks of moral corruption.

The ferocity of party spirit which sees no crime but political difference and which enters even the halls of judicature. The low esteem in which the Union of this country stands, ready to be sacrificed to any momentary pique or trivial interest. The increasing habit of regarding power as a prize instead of a trust. The absence of stern uncompromising men of principles from the helm of power. The growth of vice with the growth of strength; the love of the present, the carelessness of the future; the desperation of our trade—a madness of avarice in the young and the adult greedy of wealth, impatient of the slowness of acquiring it by labor, plunges on from hazard to hazard staking on every chance not the property of the individual but of twenty confiding creditors. The love of display, of fine house, fine clothes, fine furniture—the ambition of the young to begin their housekeeping at the same rate of expense where their fathers left off. The hunger for excitement, the recklessness of the deep and solid foundations of a great character, which always must be laid in much solitude, in austere thought, and in a religious habit—the recklessness of all this whilst we rather rush into the crowd and take part with the successful, and sacrifice the holiest principles to any popular cry, and thence comes it that these atrocities which have been wrought in different sections of the country by mobs—Yes—we must blush to say it even in New England, the soil of the Forefathers, a spirit which even invades the houses of legislation, and it has come to be a familiar sound to

10. Emerson is likely alluding here to the well-publicized confrontations in Illinois and Wisconsin between white settlers and factions of the Sauk and Fox Indians under the leadership of Chief Black Hawk, which eventually led to the "Black Hawk War" in 1832.

11. Isaiah 59:14.

hear the will of the people proclaimed as a reason why something should be done contrary to law, to equity, and to faith.

These are bad tokens for the permanence of our institutions. Wo, wo for us, in the language of Jeremiah, for the day goeth away, for the shadows of evening are stretched out.[12]

And why are these evils occasions of humiliation and penitence to us? For the best of reasons, because we are the men. It is not the fault of the Constitution, or of any one or any few actions of public officers, that things have happened thus or so, but because every man is no better than he is: When the public mind is corrupt, the seat of the disease is in the corrupted private mind. The greatest of modern Philosophers, Lord Bacon, writes, "that the knowledge of the speculative principles of men in general between the age of twenty and thirty, is the one great source of political prophecy."[13] That is to say, what men think on principle, of peace and war, of free trade and monopoly, of what is lawful and unlawful in trade; and chiefly therefore what are their religious principles and to what degree these affect their practice—it is this knowledge of what passes in the conscience of the private man, and not what is the outward aspect of public affairs for the moment, or what may be the disposition of the persons who chance to exercise power for the time being—which alone can give any clue to the future, because it is this state of the soul, which, in the end, determines the intercourse of men, the elections, and the laws.

This truth cannot be too deeply fixed in our minds, that we may settle on our actions their full responsibility; that we may learn to feel that what is done in Congress, and at each extreme of the empire is only remote phenomena caused by springs that move in your own mind. It is not the State house nor the Capitol that give their shape and character to the destinies of the nation, but it is the Exchange, the tavern, the school house, the parlor, the nursery, the church, and the closet. It is what is done and taught and talked about and meditated and prayed at home in each individual mind.

Obvious illustrations of this important fact will present themselves to every thoughtful person. In every house, such liberties are taken, such a degree of vice is exhibited, as the moral sense of the family will permit, and no more. In every village, so much vice ventures to appear, as is not rebuked by the average virtue of all the families, and no more. If there be some eminently bad men in the community, vice will be more bold, if there are some eminently good, it will be less. Each mind operates exactly in proportion to its internal force upon all around it, and in accordance to the states of other minds. Here a good man wins the imitation of one mind; confirms the good habit of another; awes a third to conceal his vice; and is himself struck with admiration and desire by the merits of a greater soul. And such too is the force of the bad to corrupt.

But let it be considered the character of this influence mainly depends on the

12. Jeremiah 6:4.
13. Not located.

absence or presence of the religious principle or the idea of God. The importance of this principle will be felt if it be considered that most men are governed in many of their actions by no better motive than a *regard to society,* and if society would connive at them, would commit sins that now they do not. *They* have not much regard to God, but they stand in fear of those who have. Well then, it is those persons, wherever they are, it is each of us in proportion as we are those persons, it is the *fear of God* in the community, wherever it exists, which is the salt that keeps the community clean; or rather, which is the true foundation on which the permanence of society stands, and which failing, all the individual stones of the edifice leaning each on the other, and none standing by itself, the whole must tumble in ruins.

This principle is a spring which has no rival in force or good effect. It is at once spring and regulator. If you knew that principle was wholly gone from a community, you would know at once that society was disorganized. But let a society be in the worst possible plight—poor, small, oppressed,—and have that principle, if you knew every one of its citizens had become a devout worshipper of God, would it not give you a cheering confidence in the recovery of its prosperity? If the vitals were sound, health would pass into the extremities.

What a mighty refreshment comes to the heart in the heaviest hour of sorrow for our own, or others' desolation in this simple reference to Him. As in David's verse, Why art thou cast down and why art thou disquieted within me? Hope thou in God.[14]

Therefore, brethren, let us humble ourselves before God for the sins of the land as truly ours. Let not the Fast Day be a form with us. The fewer they be that keep it holy, the more imperative is the obligation on those few, though they be but ten or five. Let us repent of our sins. Open your heart to the eye of God, let him see all its long and painful record of evil words, evil acts, evil thoughts. Do not lay the flattery to your soul to consider yourself in comparison with others of less opportunity or light, but think what God has done for you; think of his perfect law within; of the Sacred Scriptures; of the instructions of Christ; of the promise of the next world. Consider that the bestowment of every gift imposed a new obligation; that every one of us shall reap what he hath sowed; that God's spirit is grieved by our offences; that for them the land mourneth and its laws are endangered because we have not borne our witness to the cause of right by every action of our lives.

My friends, if we go alone and examine ourselves, we shall soon find our attention withdrawn from the alarming sins of the times; we shall have no heart to censure the atheism and sensuality of other men under the nearer alarm of our own iniquities, our own estrangement from God. Let us not always avoid and postpone this work of self-examination. Let us for once be persuaded, here in God's house, now in the possession of his lavish gifts, and on this memorial-day of the fathers of the country, to search ourselves, and see how nearly we

14. Psalms 42:5.

conform to the law of Christ, and if we find any evil way in us, let us earnestly implore God to help our efforts to sacrifice it unto him. Let us be so true patriots and so true men as to keep the fast though all the world go away. They that sow in tears shall reap in joy.[15]

It will be effectual on our own characters in bringing peace into our souls, and according to the principles to which now our attention was directed, God may crown us with a mighty beneficence by extending the consequence of an individual's virtue to thousands and millions of his countrymen to their external honour, to internal peace, and to the generations to come.

15. Psalms 126:5.

CXIV

The Lord redeemeth the soul of his servants and none of them that trust in him shall be desolate.

PSALMS 34:22

There is no more frequent command in the Scriptures than the injunction to trust in the Lord;—one of the most sublime sentiments of which a man is capable, and one the most needed. Who is he that does not need this staff? Public and private events, the course of nature, and the perversity of mankind, and our own folly, are continually bringing a cloud over our prospect and tempting us to despondency. At this moment the civilized world rings with rumors of alarm. In one devoted country the martyrs of freedom are cloven down by hundreds and thousands under the dragoons of a despot, and their compatriots who yet survive seem only to wait a little longer the same doom.[1] In another country experience does not seem to have brought its just fruit and liberty is turned into a cloak of licentiousness—and in every country the stability of old institutions is threatened, and amongst us the favored people in former years are brought out with an outstretched arm, the good go mourning because judgment is turned away backward and justice standeth afar off, for truth is fallen in the street and equity cannot enter.[2]

Every day our vices threaten the good order of the community and not an institution but is weakened by this cause. Then time and chance happen to all,[3] and every man suffers in his person, in his affections, in his good name, in his property. Not a man is in the streets but some eye marks him to connect the recollection of some calamity with his form.

And how many secret griefs are concealed under pleasing manners? Where is he who has nothing to mourn? For one of these reasons, for the sorrow that has befallen them, for the evils they now suffer, and for the evils that are apprehended, the whole earth is clothed with sackcloth and is sad.

Manuscript dated April 24, 1831. Preached three times: April 24, 1831, at the Second Church, Boston; May 29, 1836, in East Lexington; and June 5 in Concord, Mass. Notes and draft passages for this sermon occur in *JMN* 3:249–50.

1. For Emerson's allusions to countries in political strife, see Sermon XCVII, nn. 5–7.
2. Isaiah 59:14.
3. Ecclesiastes 9:11.

For all these evils one and but one adequate remedy is to be found and that is the doctrine of the text, an entire trust in the Supreme Being,—a full belief that all events are observed and controlled by Him who seeth the beginning and the end, and can bring good out of evil.

Trials, good men say, are needed to develop the character and produce trust. The rain and the night are as necessary to plants as the light and heat. Our misfortunes direct upward, as shadows point always to the sun.[4]

Let us consider the reasons that lead us to this sentiment that it may be awakened or strengthened in our minds.

1. The first reason for unlimited trust in God arises from the very necessity of our condition. What else shall we do? Look at your state with attention and you see at a glance that in bringing to pass the whole number of actions and events in which you have had part your will has had very little to do; in far the greatest proportion of cases, you have been quite passive, indebted for your enjoyments and powers to an order of things which you did not create and can very little affect. For instance, your birth in this country; in a particular family; and in this age of the world; are circumstances of the first importance in their effect upon you, yet quite independent of your actions or wishes. These not only have affected your past condition but must continue to influence your lot.

Then your early associates, as well as the ties of blood, your opportunities of observation,—how much more have these depended on things out of your power than upon you! And must it not be so for the future?

Let a man consider what slight occasions determine usually the connexions of business, of friendship, of politics, of religious party which he forms and how fast the ties so slender in their commencement multiply and thicken into the strong cordage of habit and bind him for life.

Doubtless there are always those in the world who possess the intelligence you want, who are looking for the talent or means you have, or who are fitted by their friendship to make your happiness, but the chance of entering a different street, of visiting a friend's house a few minutes later or earlier may occasion your missing an acquaintance which will never be offered you again. What intelligence office can remove these barriers of time and chance? No human foresight can come up with all the chances that come from the motions of thousands and thousands of free agents. Certain facts being shown to you in a strong light, led you to adopt your present profession or join this association or reside in this place. Certain other facts exist which if they had been shown to you instead would have led to a very different course. And not only may this greater dependence on other than yourself easily be made clear in any particular case but all of life has this dependence on what is out of yourself because life itself has. What is life, but a mark that a thousand arrows always fly at? 'Tis a flame of lamp in the open air, which every gust may blow out. And who can tell from what quarter or when the puff of wind may come that shall extinguish it?

4. Cf. *JMN* 3:244.

Now what person in his senses would think of sitting down and reproaching these unalterable past events, and why any more should one sit and distress himself with the equally inaccessible causes by which he shall be affected here-after? It is vain to say too boldly I will do thus and so, leaving God's will out of the mind, for perhaps your reason will be taken away, or your friend's reason, or your life, or your friend's life. Who knows what unspeakable good the next hour has in store for him or what affliction? 'Tis obviously then the dictate of nature not to strive against the irreversible decrees of God but be calm and assume the port of a resolved mind that waits the coming hour but does not fear it.

2. The second reason why an unlimited trust in the arrangements of superior wisdom is becoming, is because when they are observed, they are found to be kind. Open your eye and heart to recollect the good you have enjoyed and say, whoever you are, if it would have been better that you had not been. I believe I speak to none—I believe I could speak to no living man, who has so far abused the riches of God's goodness as to have made the whole universe dark in his eye and life all bitter. The simplest blessings are so great—it is so noble a thing only to have seen the day and the night, and that not as they pass over the eye of a beast mere spots of bright and dark, but with the master eye of reason associat-ing us not to them, the works, but to the maker, and so looking down upon all matter as the footstool of our Father's throne[5] and to have had an insight into the machinery of this surrounding system. It is so noble a thing to have thought—it is so noble to have loved any fellow-being; it is so great to have had the eyes of the soul opened to the religious sentiment, to have entered the new world; it is such a happiness, where it has been bestowed, to have contributed in the small-est measure to carry on the scheme of God by doing good—by adding one hour's happiness to one of his creatures, that no reflecting person but will thank God for his being. But if the bare gift of being is of such price, see how it is enhanced in the experience of each of us. Leave the general view of God's creation and explore minutely its various parts. What is the impression given to the mind? is it a chaos? is it a house of pain? is it an unintelligible maze?[6] No; order every where appears; good is every where sought; souls are every where educated.

The only obstacle to our perception of the contrivances for happiness is our want of knowledge. The further we seek, the more kindness we find. The step of love has been before us everywhere. A great deal of the suffering which comes under our eye is capable of an easy explanation. Much of it is apparent only. Much of it is a small evil to prevent a greater—and probably a more extended insight would explain what is now unaccountable in a manner con-sistent with God's goodness. Order and one sovereign design meets us every where. Each tribe of beings keeps every other in check. Not a tendency but is

5. Cf. Isaiah 66:1.
6. "He has seen but half the Universe who never has been shown the house of Pain." Emerson to Mary Moody Emerson, March, 1827 (*J* 2:180).

guarded from excess by an opposite tendency, of which the best example is the familiar one that exactly as the force with which the earth falls to the sun is increased, exactly is the force by which it is dragged away from it increased.

Go out now in the budding fields and see if every tree and every bush and every sprouting blade is not pleasant, speaking of mercy, prophesying of immortality. A richer field, a plainer preaching of the wisdom and benevolence of the Maker is found in your families, in yourselves.

From all these his wonderful but familiar arrangements in society, the power of speech, the circulation of thought, the exercise of the affections—from all have no satisfactions arisen to you? Has no happy conversation enlivened your labor or sweetened your rest? Has no joyful friendship satisfied your heart? Has the dignity and delight of living for others and not for yourself alone—never cheered one day? The love of the parent to the child and of the child to the parent, of husband and wife, of friend and friend—have these affections never been felt by you? They might teach you, if you are not blind, that the Intelligence who established these relations in the human family, hath bowels of mercy and is worthy of an affectionate trust.

Well, if you have felt this beauty then do you not see that all you behold is ordered *kindly,* and why should you not believe that what you do not see is kind also? And why perceiving that things are in such good hands should you not feel a perfect trust that the future events will be wisely directed? But your hopes have been defeated. All that made life dear to you is gone. Still the proof of God's goodness from the very grief you feel at the loss might convince you that so tender a parent has not forgotten you; that good purposes are served by your grief and that he will yet provide an issue for you out of all your troubles.

3. The next consideration which should lead us to confide is that it is not only becoming and reasonable from a review of the facts, but prior to all consideration of the facts, the religious nature of man makes it a duty to trust in Infinite Wisdom. The heart of man seeks its Father and the Bible removes the cloud from his brow. We feel that a trust in God is a sort of duty for its own sake. I admire the words of a great poet,

> And Hope the paramount duty which Heaven lays
> For its own honor, on man's suffering heart.[7]

Will not the Judge of all the earth do right?[8] It is ungrateful to our Benefactor to doubt his designs. It is presumption to arraign before our ignorance his all-piercing sight, his all-befriending arm. When we have sat at the feet of Jesus, when we have realized our dependent and sinful condition and the character of God, we lose ourselves in the contemplation and love of his perfections—we

7. William Wordsworth, *Poems Dedicated to National Independence and Liberty* (1811), part 2, no. 33.
8. Genesis 18:25.

hang on his attributes, we are content to gain nothing, to lose all, to exist where he will, how he will—in pain, in disgrace, if need be, to fill the least place in our Father's Kingdom. This thought dwelt always in the mind of Paul and makes the eloquence of every page of the epistles—Paul who with Silas sang in prison, who rejoiced in tribulation, who counted it joy to suffer shame and stripes and bonds and death for Christ in the name of God.[9]

It comes sometimes to every Christian and as we grow in grace it will become more frequent in our thoughts till at last it shall take up its everlasting abode in the heart that is ready for heaven—that is entered into rest.

Here indeed is the true greatness of man. 'He that trusts in his own heart,' saith Solomon, 'is a fool.'[10] He that trusts in others leans on a reed, but 'blessed,' saith many a Scripture, 'is the man that trusteth in the Lord.'[11] He becomes great by leaning wholly on the greatest Being. It is a maxim of philosophy that "nature is commanded by obeying her laws."[12] So they become possessed of a divine power who calmly resign themselves to God. Acquaint yourself with your true position in the world. God has protected your freedom so carefully, that nothing compels you to throw yourself on him. Life is a festival to which we are invited. Nothing prevents us from pouting in a corner like selfwilled children and refusing to enter into the spirit of the occasion. But the loss is our own. The company is large and can easily spare us. But we should do more wisely to conform ourselves to circumstances intended kindly, not only to believe that our entertainer does not mean us harm, but to work with him to the utmost of our power to answer his beneficent ends.

Moreover the doctrine of the Future Life which Religion reveals can do more than all other things together to dispose the soul to endure with patience the light afflictions of the present life in the expectation of infinite compensations. In how short a time shall the curtain be withdrawn for us also, and we shall know all.

Let it be considered, lastly, that this Christian trust where it is possessed goes far to explain one of the purposes of pain—namely to bring out this highest grace of the character. An unshaken confidence in God's wisdom were cheaply bought by many disappointments. It more than replaces the good which is taken away for a time, if every good which is taken, is by the heart freely given up to God. What can we lose, what can we mourn, if fully we know that all things work together for good to them that love God?[13] What can we lose if in all our thoughts we see God in whom are all things?

And now consider brethren, I pray you, whether you find this trust in yourselves. Whether you do not yet lack one thing? In the varying and often disastrous aspects of public affairs, have you suffered your heart to sink and despair

9. Acts 16:25; II Corinthians 7:4; Acts 5:41.

10. Proverbs 28:26.

11. Cf. Psalms 34:8 and Jeremiah 17:7, for example.

12. Bacon, *Novum Organum*, "Aphorismi," no. 129, in *The Works of Francis Bacon* (London, 1857–1874), 1:222. See *JMN* 3:250, 3:269, and *English Traits* (*W* 5:241).

13. Romans 8:28.

of the cause of human right, unmindful that he who is higher than the highest regardeth,[14] and in his own time, ripens his own results? Or in your own toilsome way, when your own sky was overcast, when lover and friend have been taken from your side;—or when disease has withered your own strength; or when the hard times and fraud of others or misfortune threatened you with want; or in whatever present difficulty you may now stand—has your soul left its post, have you suffered yourself only to trust yourself and, failing what hope you had, all seems lost;—God forbid it, brethren. Oh, hasten to raise your eyes to that heavenly hill whence help cometh.[15] Trust in the Lord. Wait patiently for him.[16]

And remember I beseech you that this trust is no lazy fatalism, which would permit a man to relax his exertions and say, 'God will order all things and what have I to do.' A true trust will never cripple one muscle, but encourages the hands by the hope that is in the heart, that its labor is not in vain in the Lord. The very rule of David is 'Trust in the Lord and do good'[17]—And this is the confidence that we have in him, that if we ask any thing according to his will, he heareth us.[18] The most confiding Christian is the most active; he hears always the voice, and follows always the steps of Jesus, who carried trust to its perfection, by losing his own will in the will of his Father.

14. Ecclesiastes 5:8.
15. Psalms 121:1.
16. Psalms 37:7.
17. Psalms 37:3.
18. I John V.14 [Emerson's note].

*If any man would come after me,
let him deny himself and take up
his cross daily, and follow me.*

LUKE 9:23

The aim of the New Testament is to make us followers of Christ. But following must depend on the leading. To follow a soldier, is to fight; to follow a political party, is to vote in reference to a particular question of state; to follow a philosopher, is to speculate,—but what is it to follow Christ?

The main object, as it appears in the New Testament, which Jesus had in view, was, to establish the *moral* nature of man in its authority over him. There had been abundance of war in the earth to give exercise to the *senses* and the *passions*. There has always been sufficient seeking of *sensual comforts*. There had been *arts* to exercise the imagination and the *taste*. There had been *philosophy,* and very subtile philosophy too, to exercise the intellect, in the discussion of the nature and laws of the world, and there had been *religion,* but it was chiefly ceremonial, adapted to a young and ignorant race. Every faculty of man had found means and occasion of development and yet the moral nature of man had not assumed its place as his Lord. Virtue, that is, obedience to God, was seen to be a good, but it was not felt to be the chief good. It was not seen to be the head and top of all things, the law of the universe, without which nothing was made that was made. It was not seen that every forsaking of this law was a step downward bringing both unhappiness and degradation.

This Jesus came to reveal, to show with an authority none had yet exhibited, by plain appeals to what was in man, that the idea of God and duty was not only in the mind, but on the throne of the mind; that it was so deeply and universally the principle according to which God had arranged the system of nature that to receive this law was the first step to true wisdom, that the temple of God, which in the bible means a holy mind, was the only height from which a true view of the universe could be gained. It was by teaching this truth that Jesus gave light. It was thus that he threw light on all that was, and is, and shall be. It was thus

---

Manuscript dated May 1, 1831. Preached four times: May 1, 1831, at the Second Church, Boston; May 8 at the Hollis Street Church; May 22 at the First Parish, Framingham; and February 5, 1837, in East Lexington.

that by bringing out the inmost law, by giving authority to that which is the soul of the soul, that he makes us feel our immortality. It is thus that he giveth light to every man that cometh into the world.[1]

In short, it is by being nothing himself, but coming in his Father's name, by identifying himself with the moral law, becoming (so to speak) only a channel through which the moral Law flowed, that he possesses an eternal interest to the human heart.

Since this was the design of Christ, it is by often recurring to his principles, as they are eternal moral principles, that alone we can settle our duty as his followers.

My friends, we go along with the times in which God has given us our birth. Through his goodness these are Christian times, and as a nation, or as a city, or as a parish, or as partakers of his supper, we are reckoned followers of Christ. But you are aware there is a vast difference between the so *called,* and the so *being.* I propose to enumerate some of the marks by which a true follower of Christ may be known. By recollecting them, we may see how faithful we are to our duties.

1. The first mark I shall name, is the observance of a rule which meets every good mind, in the outset of his spiritual progress, and that is, that he ought not to confound himself in his progress or his backslidings with the church or the community. To any person who thinks he is a Christian because the community is good and he is as good as they are, I say—it is no merit of yours that society is more virtuous than it was. Neither do the vices of the day make any justification before God for your indulgence in them. God has made you distinct from all others. The thought that is in you, is not in others. The thought in your mind at this moment is in some respects different from any other act of any other being. And their temptations are not your temptations. And yet the common error of all the world, in which we rock to sleep our starting consciences, is this. Am I sought out of all and observed, whilst thousands are as bad and thousands are worse than I? I am not so bad as a great many in my own community, and yet the whole people among whom I live in New England, are, to a proverb, more virtuous than others. We are temperate, and industrious, compared with the countries north and south of us. We are chaste and righteous in life and conversation, compared with the whole population of the West Indies or the South of Europe. What of that? As far as it is true, it is your unspeakable blessing. It is the grace of God that has made you what you are. It is matter of gratitude—but no more. But is it an excuse for the indulgences you permit in yourself—this fact that these nations are sunk in sin? To answer this shortly by an extreme, and yet, I believe, a strictly parallel case—It is just as if you should quote the example of the *brute creation,* and say, behold the swine, the dog, and the bear,—and see how temperate, how chaste, how gentle am I!

God has set you on a mountain. God has made you for a light of the world,

---

1. John 1:9.

whilst they sit in a darkness that may be felt.[2] And so I say not to the community but to the individuals—and let the word of truth find its way to every heart in this house—Is there any one among us who has committed sins, or does every day meditate a sin on this plea, that your acquaintances do much worse? I say to you, my brother, before God you have no acquaintances. God has appointed you as different a trial from any other soul as if you lived in a separate universe. You live, as it were, in another world from the person who sits now at your side or dwells under your roof, such is the difference with which the moral obligations address themselves. Your conscience is a torch and his is only a taper. To you they are writ in light—not to be mistaken. You cannot withdraw your eye from them. To him the lines of virtue and vice are dimly drawn and he has never made many distinctions God has instructed you to make. Now every ray of light you have is an addition of duty. Do you ask what makes the difference?— what is your peculiar call to higher usefulness than others? "The delivery of the talent is the call."[3] You have the same call in one degree that Jesus felt in its fulness when he said, 'Wist ye not that I must be about my Father's business'[4]— the call of a capacity to know and do great things.

The sin you meditate and he commits has never appeared to him in the light in which God is showing it to you—That tender conscience, that power to pause and consider the sin, he has not possessed. And now instead of thanking God devoutly for the new organ, the wiser mind, the inestimable gift of a more tender conscience he has bestowed on you, will you throw away this higher nature and act as those who have it not? Having two eyes, will you walk as the blind into a ditch?[5] The good, all those spirits to whom God has equalled you by his gift, and who were watching to welcome every noble sentiment in you, shall mourn over your fall. Jesus pities his unfaithful follower who has done so much to unredeem, to uncreate himself—descended so far towards the second death.

It is not coming after *him.* As far as he is presented an example for us— consider that for one moment he is not identified with his contemporaries. He is always superior to those to whom he ministers—like a physician among the sick,—like a teacher among pupils,—like an angel among bad spirits.

2. Another consideration. The Christian must not only separate himself always in his thought from society—that is only half his work—he must also think for himself; he must not only not be confounded with others, but he must apply his own principles to things and courses of conduct. He must try the world, as by fire, with the principles of Christ. This is a very difficult and much neglected part of the Christian life. Yet the gospel will always be a form to you;

---

2. Cf. Exodus 10:21.

3. See *JMN* 3:223, where this sentence is attributed to Abraham Tucker (pseud. "Edward Search"), author of *The Light of Nature Pursued*, 7 vols. (London, 1768-1777). Used in "Ethics" (*EL* 2:147) and in "Spiritual Laws" (*CW* 2:82). See also Sermon XXXVIII (*Sermons* 1:294).

4. Luke 2:49.

5. Cf. Matthew 15:14 and Luke 6:39.

its promises must always remain unfulfilled to you; the kingdom of heaven will always be far off from you until the principles of truth penetrate the whole mass of your knowledge and your practice. These principles are the lifeblood, and wherever they cannot circulate from one extremity to the other, there health, and soundness, and life ceases. It is a mortified member.

It is, I conceive, the duty of a Christian above all men, as holding the highest and the best-founded theory of life that was ever holden among men, to consider himself at all times amenable to his principles. We should be ready to render a reason not only for the faith that is in us,[6] but for the practice of our hands, and for the practices we sanction. A true Christian will consider himself obliged to that person who points out a seeming inconsistency between his faith and the order of his household, or his modes of dealing, or of social intercourse,—and being pointed out will either explain it or remove it.

But he who waits for his friends or his enemies to do this, will be slow in his reform. He carries a torch himself that can show evils. He must be beforehand with reproof, or he is a slothful servant. It is your duty continually to call yourself to account; to state the principles of Christ to your soul; and obstinately to question every common usage of life, every received opinion; and take nothing for granted, with which you are expected to comply.

It has been said that a truly great mind is always recognized by the most ordinary men on a very short intercourse, simply by the method that runs through even the most trivial discourse. (But it will be allowed by all, that the more informed is the observer, the more apt will he be to discover these slight marks of superior intelligence.) It seems to me that a Christian will be known as a Christian by his most casual conversation, that by his look, even, it may be seen by an acute observer, that he is an accountable agent, that he believes in the immortality of the soul. If beggars, as is said, are skilful in detecting a merciful face and charity writes its name so plainly in the lines of the countenance that a practised eye can tell whom to ask, and whom to pass, certainly he whose principle is the love of God, which is the fountain of all virtues, should leave the impression of goodness writ every where on his works. He that deals with you, should feel that he has dealt with a rational and honourable and immortal being. He that eats your bread should feel that the cheerful and holy light of faith never deserts you.

You must carry your Christianity into every trifle as the sap runs into the smallest vein of the smallest leaf. You must adhere to truth in your compliments and by-words; you must not violate it even in expressions of civility in the subscription of a letter. An attention to principles in this trifling practice is laudable; but as I have alluded to it, I will add the remark, that on the other hand, words of politeness are not to be omitted when the omission would convey to your correspondent a false impression of disrespect. Every upright man will economize in his protestations of love and reverence.

6. Cf. I Peter 3:15.

Then it is better in our regrets at rain and cold to speak as believers in Providence than, as we commonly do, to speak as believers in Chance. It is not only useless to fret, but we all know, that if we knew more, we should not fret at any thing. Then we must do what it is hard to do—guard our lips throughout the day. We must not laugh at vice; we must not suffer ourselves to be carried into captivity by our complaisance—by the fear to offend. Nor must we, if we do not speak falsely, or do not slander, any more speak idle words without number.

I believe, to go back to the character of Jesus, it will be admitted that he governed his life by his principles.

3. He must then separate himself in his thought from others; and he must consider every thing in the light in which Christianity views it; and, *thirdly,* he must be a *worker* in the cause of righteousness and truth. This is the end not of Christ his Redeemer only, but of God his Creator. In the economy of nature God has made nothing in vain. All things pay a tax for being, in constant usefulness. The sun lights and warms; the air is the breath of animal and vegetable life; the sea instinct with tribes of life and navigable to men. Every plant is food or medicine, every stone is of service to the soil—nay every atom contributes its part to gravity and the vast attractions that hold the globe together and keep it in its orbit are made up of the separate attractions of all the atoms. And so every animal answers an useful end to the whole, imparts as well as receives benefit. And as God allows no cumberers of the ground amidst his lower works,[7] so neither was it his design that man should be idle. He has armed him with every faculty of all the rest in giving him reason by which he might conquer to his own service all other forces and faculties. He gave him the eye of Reason to see the toil of all so that the Universe might be an example to him. He gave him the law and hope of Religion that so he might have motive and order for exertion, and he gave him freedom by which he might act as a God and *choose* to do good.

An idle man is the greatest waste in nature. It is the squandering of indefinite power to produce good. But after man has received the light of Religion, then it is a heinous sin. For the whole force of Religion acts to wake him from sleep, to interest him in others, and to invigorate him to action. The test of Faith is Works.[8] And let us apply this truth to ourselves. Are we not only believers but workers? Are we making progress ourselves? Still more, are we workers for others? Do we make ourselves accessible to every call to be useful? Do we invite or do we reject opportunities of supplying the bodily wants, or of informing the ignorance, or of assisting the spiritual progress of our fellow men? Let every one of us consider with himself how many objects he pursues where the gratification to be gained does not end in himself; and how many where it begins and ends in others,—except the gratification of a good conscience, which is greatest

7. Cf. Luke 13:7.
8. Cf. James 2:17-18.

in those acts that afford no other. I am afraid these inquiries will press us sorely. To some I hope they will not come as an accusation but will echo the approbation of a good conscience. Yet who that might not have done more? And, alas! to most of us, I am afraid, Works of mercy are too strict for our religion. We had rather pray and commend our freedom from prejudice and error than seek the good of other persons. Well then let this be one more measure of our progress in Christianity; for when we are true Christians the idea of being useful and the exertion to be useful will not be irksome but will be the natural and pleasant course our actions will take.

And here again the example of Jesus is that of a workman of God.

4. Finally. The mark by which Jesus himself chose to distinguish his school was the Cross; the gloomy precept through which he invited men to glory was self-denial. He put no colour on the matter. He said frankly, If any man would come after me *let him deny himself, and take up his Cross.* And it behoves us who would be followers of the Son of God to see if we wear his badge; to see if we undergo his discipline. It has been in some degree anticipated in the last topic, for self-denial is the best of works,—and the measure of charity is the degree of sacrifice. But it is so important that it fully deserves a separate consideration.

The follower of Jesus, the good man, the child of God must be a denier of himself. It is very easy to discern the truth of this test of fidelity. We are born in such very different circumstances, some men apparently almost doomed to sin from the wretchedness and fatal example of their associations in infancy whilst others receive pure and virtuous desires with their mothers' milk and are born to be good—we are thus so differently born and placed that we are utterly unable to appreciate the merit of men by any given amount of service done. It is easier for you to build an asylum than it is for your brother to give a loaf to a beggar. It is easier for one man to spend all his Sundays in the religious instruction of children, which I esteem a great act of beneficence, than it is for another to abstain from some gross act of vice which would have chained him up in prison. Who can judge of another's circumstances and know the extremity of his temptation who fell, but God only? Therefore Jesus has not said, Do this work, but Deny yourself. If it is easy to do a good work, you are not virtuous in having done it. Do more. It is your task that is increased with your talent. Go on till you find it hard to serve him and then first you deserve praise and are entering on the glories of heaven. It is perfectly easy with this rule to ascertain how far each of us has followed our Master. Are we surrounded with every comfort and are not conscious of any obstacle in our path or any suffering for righteousness' sake? Then I am afraid we are lame followers. We must deny ourselves or there is no true discipleship. We must deny ourselves and not to add to our wealth or our praise or our power but to our goodness. We must suffer for God. Here is the summary of Christian morality. This includes all other marks of grace. And here I will conclude.

Come, brethren, today and tomorrow are yet new time, untrodden by sinful feet; time, that has not yet witnessed any fault of ours. Come, let us dedicate it to heaven, and our own souls' good. Let us set up crosses and denials in it. Let us appoint ourselves duties that we know will cost something. Let us approve ourselves followers of Christ by making this day a covenant that we will forsake some sin which we commit, or forbear some not quite innocent indulgence, or perform some difficult duty, in the coming days. And in the hour of temptation and of victory, thank God that he has made you capable of the sublime act of foregoing a pleasure that you may gain his approbation.

CXVI

The Sabbath was made for man.
MARK 2:27

By the Providence of God we are indulged with another opportunity of worshipping him on the Sabbath. The antiquity of this institution, if nothing else, should give it claims to our regard. It is near two thousand years that the followers of Christ—an ever-increasing multitude,—have paid honor to this day, so that now it is welcomed in every country under heaven by some men. But the Jews also set apart one day in seven, as we certainly know, for at least 1490 years before the era of our Saviour, because that is the date of the Mosaic history, in which the laws of the Sabbath are recorded. But in the very Commandment enjoining its observance, the language appears to indicate an institution already existing. "*Remember* the Sabbath day."[1] The expression implies that the Israelites understood how the day was to be sanctified. And so do all the precepts concerning it imply a *custom* by which it was already known what should be done, and what should be omitted. Moreover in the account of the gathering of the manna before the promulgation of the law from Mount Sinai, distinct reference is made to the peculiar honor paid to the Sabbath.[2] But far beyond this at an earlier period there are some traces of a division of time into seven days, and of course implying the preeminence of some one day. In the declaration of God to Noah it is said, after a week or period of seven days I will send rain[3]—near 4200 years ago according to our common computation. It is found that other ancient nations who knew nothing of Moses or his Law, yet divided the time in the same manner; as if it sprung from some primeval revelation that while yet the government of God in some familiar and visible form watched over the first families of the ancient world, and taught them language and the first arts of life—even then the Sabbath was bestowed, a beneficent provision that contained mercy for their innumerable posterity to the end of time.

An incomplete draft manuscript comprising portions of Part I and notes for Part II is dated May 15, 1831; the complete manuscript is dated May 29, 1831. Part I was preached twice: May 15, 1831, at the Second Church, Boston, and October 22, 1837, in East Lexington. Part II was also preached twice: May 29, 1831, at the Second Church, Boston, and, with "Part I," on October 22, 1837, in East Lexington. For an earlier treatment of the institution of the Sabbath, see Sermon VII (*Sermons* 1:100–106).

   1. Cf. Exodus 20:8.
   2. Exodus 16, 22–30 [Emerson's note].
   3. Cf. Genesis 7:4.

We celebrate then this day an institution whose origin is covered up under the mists and clouds of the morning of the world; or rather, we walk in a light whose source we cannot see, which runs back to mingle with the First Cause. It seems generally agreed by men whose opinions are entitled to weight, whether they receive the book of Genesis as a literal history or not, that the idea of God could not have been imparted without an original revelation. It seems reasonable to suppose that the institution of the Sabbath was coeval with that idea, and was given by God to the first men.

But with these indications of a truly divine antiquity, it has its own claims to our respect wholly independent of age. And I propose to ask your attention, my friends, to some considerations of its design, and its demands upon us as Christians. I shall attempt, in the first place, to show the uses of the Christian Sabbath; secondly, to show that we ought to keep it holy; and thirdly, to show how this may best be done.

I. The uses of the Christian Sabbath.

1. Its first mercy to man is Rest. Sabbath means *rest*. It was made, as Jesus declared, for man, for man who eats his bread by the sweat of his brow,[4] for the diligent, for the poor, for the dependent, for the slave, to rest his body from labor, that the health might not be destroyed nor the animal spirits wasted by unceasing work. This is its first and lowest but indispensable office, to administer repose to the exhausted frame, a purpose worthy of the care of the Creator.

This purpose of tender mercy is counteracted not only by those whom a too greedy love of gain induces to open their shops on Sunday, or keep their mills in operation, to open bar-rooms or places of amusement, wherein not only temptation is held out to the customer but labor imposed on the attendant, but it is violated by all those who in private business or domestic concerns demand of their laborers, or apprentices, or dependents, the least unnecessary work; and, lastly, by those who do not permit the beast of the field to enjoy that rest which God provided for him.

I would not ignorantly condemn innocent men. I have been told there are some sorts of business whose operations cannot be discontinued through the Sunday, without some injury, especially in the present state of competition. I am heartily sorry for it, but if this be so, it behoves those so engaged to bear always in mind if all would agree to discontinue their work none would be losers, and if every man is not very thoughtful the habit of allowing himself in taking away so much of the Creator's rest from his workmen, will make him insensible to the wrong he does them, and which, in some way, it is his manifest duty to repair.

2. The second use of the Sabbath is the interposition of a day of thought amidst days of business. The first use was to the body, the second use is to the mind. The body needs rest. The Soul is of another nature, and never needs rest. It requires no other refreshment than change of thought. It cannot bear too

4. Genesis 3:19.

steadfast attention to one object, or class of objects. And an occasional diversion of its thoughts from its usual ends to others, must be made, or the health of the soul will be sacrificed as surely as the health of the body that should be fastened for months in one posture.

No law of our nature is more familiar to us in our own experience and our observation of others than the fact that a long continued attention to a single object discovers continually new particulars, and so magnifies the importance of the object. This makes the value of the 'division of labor,' that a concentration of the attention to one out of many parts of a work enables the eye to observe many defects which it can remedy, many occasions and means it can lay hold of, for improving the processes of work. And, in this way, knowledge continually descends into nature on one side, as far as it ascends on the other. Man seems to stand midway on a stage that commands a view equally of the great and of the minute. And whilst on one side he is ascertaining new and vaster laws and systems than were known before, teaching that the planets observe the same law, and roll round the same centre, as the earth; and then going further to learn that the fixed stars bear relations to the Sun; yea, and noticing and recording and reducing to system the changes that have transpired in the face of the heaven for 3000 years; and still enlarging our acquaintance with these bodies and constellations in their inaccessible heights—On the other side, he is opening worlds of knowledge within the objects we have always looked upon, disclosing the habits of tribes of beings that dwell in a falling leaf, showing the pores in the firm texture of gold, and laying open the cunning texture of a hair. And the telescope does not more increase knowledge bringing down stars and systems into an orrery than the microscope which brings up mites and animalcules to aid the student in the anatomy of man.

But this beneficent law which enables us to increase our knowledge and power indefinitely among the most familiar things, is accompanied with this disadvantage to a finite being like man, that, because he can attend to only one thing at a time, the more his attention is given to a particular object the more must his attention be withdrawn from all other objects; and as we always learn to love what we habitually do, we come at last to magnify our particular pursuits to a very disproportionate importance. It is with the mind as it is with the outward eye. A pebble or a blade of grass held immediately before the eye appears larger than a mountain at a distance, nay, if brought still nearer, can shut out the view of the heavens and the earth.

Every one of us has doubtless seen many examples of this effect—a very undue estimation of things—in our daily life. Indeed every one of us does probably furnish an example of it in himself. We see men wound up to the highest key of feeling about things which, because we have never considered, seem to us trifles. Parties spring up in the state and we are utterly unable to account for the heat they exhibit in relation to subjects to which other men are cold. So it is with individuals. Every man thinks his house better than other people think it; or his quarrel one that should interest every other man; or his favorite book or his friend deserving of peculiar esteem.

And beyond this almost every man has some habitual theme of conversation which you know he thinks and speaks of much more than you should. Now what is this exaggeration but a tendency to insanity in every mind? If it were indulged, if nothing opposed it, it would produce a gradual inattention and finally an absolute ignorance of all other beings and things but this absorbing one. The lover would give himself up to his love, the hater to his hatred, the sick man to thoughts of his disease; every one would be a projector lost in his own affair, and instead of the common social ground on which we meet, the world would be a place of lunatics. The common remedy provided against this tendency in our nature, is in the variety of our faculties and the multiplicity of objects which solicit them; and in our mutual intercourse; one man's foible runs against another man's foible, and both are made ridiculous. So travelling is thought to have that good effect to enlarge a man's vision, to break up his associations and show him there may be noble objects of pursuit, great men, good laws and customs and wide countries which he had left wholly out of account while he thought of a few streets only at his own fireside. But these remedies do not go far enough. They can only set us right in a delusion in which many are not agreed. But perhaps others are wrong in the same way as we. Perhaps the great objects of pursuit by the whole world in all countries and times may have something of folly in them, may be elevated by the consent of mankind to an undue importance. Perhaps *power* is not really quite so great a prize, as by thinking so much upon it, we have come to esteem it. Perhaps *riches* are not the best possession in the world. Perhaps *health* of the body, and *life* itself of the body are not of that worth at which they are prized. If this should be so, and the suspicion that they are overestimated, has always existed in the world, how are these gigantic delusions to be exposed and overthrown? Only by arresting for a season the pursuit of them; by interposing a day of thought; by presenting the objects of another world. The glare of these torches of the earth is only to be diminished by breaking down the shutters and letting in the beams of the sun in heaven. For this the Sabbath is given—the day of God and eternity—to break the charm of things of time. It is interposed continually in the world's days to stop the headlong race of evil habits—to give us pause; time to make a new comparison of what we do and what we ought to do;—time to fall back on our principles; time to say No; time to plant our foot and resist the pressure of the Crowd; time to examine the direction of the road we follow, and see if it leads towards home, or from it.

My friends, if any of us have used the Sabbath well we shall gratefully remember this virtue in it, that it has undeceived us, that it has not only rested the body, but secured the health of the soul from an insane devotion to the world by the oft-returning respite and new direction given to our thoughts which it has afforded us.

3. A third great use of the Sabbath is that beyond the rest for the body, and the diversion for the mind, it is in its right use, a religious education itself. It is what man most wanted. See the hard lot of tens of thousands in every Christian country; see their scanty share of intellectual and moral advantages. Who in the six days has time to cultivate his mind by regular study? Not one in a hundred. Here comes in Sunday to give that opportunity to the poorest and most ignorant. Sunday—it is the rest not only of the weary, and the check of God on our extravagant delusions, but it is the poor man's college, the university of human souls. The simplest computation makes this very apparent. It is one seventh of our time. Of course the child that has lived seven years, has lived one whole year of Sundays. The young person that has lived fourteen years, has had in addition to all that the schools have taught him, two entire years of religious instruction. At the age of legal manhood, three years have been enjoyed. And which of you has lived fifty years—has been indulged with seven whole years of days devoted to meditation upon your duties to God.

This is one of those facts that ought to startle us in our sloth. Tell me not that this is so plain that the arithmetic of a child might show it. It is not plain or unimportant until we have each dwelt steadily upon the fact, that, whatever we may have done with the time, God has taken care to secure to us these many years exclusively appropriated to the care of the soul. We have been receiving ten talents, whether we have hid them in a napkin or spent them on our sins, and even now—today—he is renewing his provision.[5]

Part II

In the former part of this discourse I have spoken of the antiquity of the Sabbath, that it probably dates from the beginning of the human race. I proposed to speak 1. of its uses; 2. then to show that we ought to keep it holy; 3. to show how this may best be done. Under the first division, the uses of the Sabbath, we have considered three important ones. 1. Rest of the body. 2. Diversion of the mind. 3. Religious education. I go on to make a few more remarks on this topic before I come to the second main division of my discourse.

But I will first remark that I choose this subject and I particularly solicit the attention of each one whom I address, because I think it may and it ought to affect our conduct today, this month, this year. I believe practically in the free agency of man. If this means any thing, it means not that society is an unmoved and immoveable mass, one of whose customs we cannot hope to change in less than a century, but that the will of society may change the deepest rooted custom today. I speak to men and women who if they are made sensible that they have done wrong the last Sabbath or the last hour, may keep holy the remaining hours of this day. And I entreat your attention to the consideration of the Sabbath in the confidence that a reason will weigh more with a sensible

5. See Matthew 25:14–30.

person than a habit, and a duty will weigh more to a pious person than a temptation.

I have said that thanks to this institution one seventh part of every man's life in Christendom may be a period of distinct religious instruction besides all the time given in youth to school. All the cogent arguments therefore that in our times have been urged in favor of schools and of literary institutions of higher rank; all that can be said in the cause of books and all and any means of raising the minds of men by the diffusion of truth can be said with increased force in favor of the strict observance of the Christian Sabbath. All the politics of education or the use of education in civil society to fit men for freedom and at the same time to soften them and train good citizens, can be better said of Sunday. Hobbes, the famous defender of despotism said, "The Universities were the core of Rebellion."[6] That is, the existence of great institutions for the diffusion of knowledge are incompatible with the existence of despotism. I suppose it is universally true. But if a college opposes civil despotism a Sabbath exposes moral bondage. The Sabbaths are the core of that Revolt which good minds are always stirring up against the kingdom of darkness. The kingdom of Satan, in plain words the power of evil thoughts, can never subsist in the soul of a man who strictly and sincerely hallows the Sabbath day. And therefore much more can be said for this than for any other institution of merely civil and present use.

The Sabbath day is the celebration of the moral nature of man. It teaches the place and use of all other days and schools and means. Useful and excellent as are these political, scientific, social institutions, much as they are the ornament and instructer of society, yet in the view of a part of man's nature they are subordinate and cheap and local except as they are connected with Religion. Even the endowments of man—the upright form, the skilful hand, the speaking tongue, the Memory, the world of arts, all these only raise man to the head of the animal creation and are useful to secure to him his bread and clothes with more convenience and grace, and lay him at last in the ground with somewhat more decency than other lower creatures. But Reason—in whose right exercise Religion is taught—carries up this low creature to God and connects him with the Cause of Causes and interweaves his individual being with the great Order of the whole creation.

And the Sabbath is the festival of this Reason and this hope. A day appointed to look forward not for a few months or years, but to the whole being of the soul and around through the whole universe. A day to consider the sacred laws in the observance of which alone happiness can be found; a day to be pure in heart, poor in spirit; a day to be meek and forgiving; to speak the truth; a day to be sorry for our imperfections and eager for improvement, a day to be kind to our fellow men, to rejoice in the dear love by which God binds us to each other or to those souls that are not now here, but are with him in heaven. In short a day of rejoicing in God's beneficence and of seeking him.

6. Thomas Hobbes, *Behemoth* (London, 1682), 94; see *JMN* 6:82.

These are three general uses of the Christian Sabbath: Rest; the new and better direction given to the thoughts; and a religious education. But there are as many particular uses as individual observers of it. It is a magazine of good from which each selects what he wants. Every pious heart turns the day to good account in its own way, and the good use of the day has always made men better acquainted with its value. Great and good men have solemnly recorded their deep conviction that the Sunday was the sanctifier of the week, the leaven of the lump[7]—and as they had spent it to their spiritual profit, or otherwise, so were the remaining days prosperous or unprosperous.

II. We ought to keep holy the Sabbath day. I have spoken at some length of the uses of the institution. In these uses is contained the inference to which I proposed next to ask your attention, namely that it is our duty to observe it.

The obligation upon a Christian to keep it seems to me to rest partly upon the original Commandment given on Mount Sinai, which I think deserves great consideration from all Christians.[8] It was part of a miraculous dispensation manifestly designed for the instruction through the Israelites of the whole world. It is one *positive* or arbitrary precept joined with nine *moral* precepts; that is, every one will perceive his obligation is perfect to comply with nine of the ten commandments whether he believe this was intended to be binding on him or not, and when the purpose of this command is considered it approaches the nature of a moral law. Moreover, Jesus did not come to abrogate the Mosaic Law but to carry its moral precepts into force and to extend their reign over all men. "If thou wilt enter into life," he said, "keep the Commandments."[9] It is true, the day we observe is a different one from the Jewish Sabbath, yet did the disciples who followed their master transfer to the first day the careful religious observance they had used on the seventh. For these reasons I would put the obligation partly upon the fourth commandment, but I would chiefly in the second place derive it from the obvious expediency and justness of so doing. This is the way in which every obligation is made apparent to a rational being. How do I become acquainted with any of my duties? God does not write on the ground before me in so many words, Thou shalt. God gives to his children, yet ignorant and incapable of guiding themselves, a mere Commandment—Do thus or thus. But to his children, when instructed and made capable of self government, he exhibits the consequences of an action as a measure of the good or the evil.

And let the duty of keeping the Sabbath be tried by its value.

A day of rest, it will be admitted, is needed for the body. A suspension of our headlong labors and strifes is needed as absolutely for the mind. And the occasions and means of doing homage to the Father of the Universe and of calling in

7. Cf. I Corinthians 5:6–7 and Galatians 5:9.
8. The injunction to "Remember the sabbath day, to keep it holy" is the fourth of the Ten Commandments; see Exodus 20:1–17.
9. Matthew 19:17.

our thoughts and raising them above the earth is too vitally necessary to be questioned.

On this ground of expediency the obligation of the Sabbath is commonly urged and it is an expediency that appears greater as the mind is more informed till it becomes as sacred as the duty of speaking the truth. Let him who is accustomed to make little difference between his Sabbath and his workday, bring before him if he can the whole train of evils that would ensue if all men should do as he does and so the day be abolished. It was abolished once in Christendom; and in what time? and with what effect? In the midnight of the reign of terror; in days when men that walked about which way soever in the streets of Paris found the soles of their shoes red with blood of murdered men. That was no time for the Sabbath of Peace, and with every law and hope it was swept away. But mere reason of state and the clamor of the poor suffering for want of a day of rest speedily restored it to a part of its observance.

Even the French Sabbath, the half ritual half frolic day of the Catholics, will always be preferred to the gloomy week without a beginning or an end like a day without a morning or life without youth. But a Christian Sabbath, a New England Sabbath, the light of a good man's life is to these pagan Sundays what the conversation of a wise man is to the gossip of a buffoon, what a well organized school is to a mountebank's show-room.

O spare the Sabbath, the poor man's friend, the rich man's counsellor, the instructor of children, the comforter of the afflicted, the uplifter of the head and heart of wretched man to the glorious hope of heaven. Do I speak to any philanthropist who loves mankind and delights in the progress of the race? Do I speak to any friend to whom the welfare of his friends is dear? Do I speak to any parent to whom the earthly hope and advantage and the final salvation of his children is worth consulting for? To such I say, guard the order, the public worship, the private domestic observance of the Sabbath. Let the little fly and the creeping worm give you a lesson. The mason bee, the gnat, the ichneumon, and a thousand insects more that now are seeking their food in this day's sun-light will not cease from their labors until they have painfully collected and laid up securely a few seeds or eggs or mites as food for the young which they shall never see. When this provision for its unborn posterity is made, the careful parent dies contented. There is something wonderfully affecting in this lesson of nature. *Dum tacet, clamet.*[10] Its silence thunders. God gave you reason, and shall the instinct of the poor worm outrun your wisdom? God gave you reason and taught you that your children should not live by bread alone,[11] and will you provide them bread, and leave behind you no provision of reason for your child? no store of good institutions, no stock of good principles? Will you leave

10. "While he is silent he speaks." Apparently this is Emerson's version of Cicero's "Cum tacent clamant" ("By their silence they cry aloud") from *In Cantilinam,* I, viii; see *JMN* 4:96, 5:171, and 6:139.

11. Cf. Matthew 4:4.

them a declining church, a decaying public morality, public worship falling into contempt, and so the great barriers God enables you to build against a general profligacy all down under the trampling feet of dogs and swine? Then tie up the tongues of your church bells, and shut up the doors of the sanctuary, and make barracks and riding schools as a foreign soldiery have once done already of your houses of prayer, that the children may ride over the sepulchres of their fathers and God's name may be taken in vain in the very spot where it had been pronounced with repentance, and with overflowing praise and immortal hope.[12]

But if, as I trust in God, this would seem to you an alarming evil, an abomination not to be borne, then put it away. It is coming upon you by your own work, your own invitation, your own importunacy; or it is to be put away and abominated by your hands preventing it? If you think it desirable that the Sabbath should be kept, keep it. Come to church when the church is open and do not bring your body here to make a bed of your pew but bring your soul to be educated and sweetened and sanctified.

III. I have considered at some length the uses of the Sabbath and its general obligation. Let me now say something of the way in which it is to be kept holy by us. From the beginning of the world, in every nation under heaven, God has been honoured more or less rightly by public worship. That institution has come down to us in simple and beautiful forms. It is of all social rites the most worthy of our respect. Good men rejoice in the great and perhaps increasing honor this institution has in this community. Still I cannot think it was ever too much reverenced or is incapable of improvement here. It admits of improvement among us, my friends, in two respects; 1. in a more regular attendance of its external services; 2. in a more sincere performance of those services.

1. The public services of the Sabbath morning and afternoon usually occupy a little more than three hours out of the day. And shall we grudge this time to him that gave us time? Does it seem to you becoming that he whom neither sickness nor necessary labor hinders from coming to the church, whom the kindness of God has left master of his time, should hinder himself like a brute by an overloaded stomach, or a most unseasonable sleep, or should show a cold contempt of his highest duties that he may take his pleasure in an afternoon ride? Or if your regard for your reputation and for the well being of society avail to prevent this, is it suitable, is it on the whole the wisest bestowment of your time, to take a part of it for the sake of finishing the neglected business of the week?

Six days shalt thou labor and do all thy work, but the seventh is the Sabbath of the Lord thy God.[13]

Why should men who are so far enlightened that they believe in God absent themselves for slight cause from church? Or if all agree that the Sabbath worship is to be kept, why should the afternoon service be neglected?

12. Emerson alludes to the fate of several Boston churches during the Revolution; the phrase "the sepulchre of the fathers" occurs in *Nature* (C W 1:7).
13. Exodus 20:9-10.

Now it is sometimes said by people who would be esteemed conscientious persons, that they do not think it so very essential to go to church; to do their duty, to be kind, to be just, to be true, is the main thing and best part of religion. But public worship is a form and the substance can be had at home.

Now as far as this is a sincere objection it deserves and can easily receive an answer. And the answer will have most weight with the wisest man. I say then that it is no mark of a knowledge of human nature, no mark, that is, of self-knowledge, to despise forms. In this world, we need the form as much as we need the spirit of every institution and every thing. The form is the vehicle through which spiritual things address themselves to the senses, and through the senses to the soul. And therefore no man on earth can be superior to forms, any more than he can be superior to his senses. To answer the purposes of life, we must use our touch and taste, our eyes and our ears. And to be good, we must use the vulgar forms of goodness. Indeed strictly considered every action is only a form, and can we do without acting by only thinking right? It is a very dangerous symptom of a licentious thinking, when a man begins to refine to this excess as not only to undervalue outward forms, but to make them nothing. Those who would have the kingdom of heaven *wholly* within, have sometimes exhibited the kingdom of hell without. It is dangerous when a man begins to tamper with his nature, to be too wise for God, and being made up of body and soul, is foolish enough to affect to be all soul. Let us rather couple the body to the spirit, the outward act to the inward feeling. When we pray let us stand or kneel; when we feel respect for a friend whom we meet let us bow the head; when we feel pity let us embody the emotion in a deed. When we would make religious feeling habitual, let us embody and habitualize it (if I may say so) in a form of public worship.

Or to point the question, I will ask, have you found that when you staid away from church did you worship him? Did you find yourself in as humble and pious a frame of mind on the evening when for slight cause you had forsaken the church, as when you went there with a lowly grateful and prayerful attention?

2. In the next place, all will admit that the manner of our worship when we are in the church admits of improvement. It will suffice if we bear in mind that the time is not our own and give ourselves to the consideration of God as he has been and is to us with that fervor that shall make amends for any defects in the imperfect fellow-creature who is the organ through which the Scriptures speak or the petitions of men are uttered to God.

It remains to say something of the employment of the other hours of the day. It is Rest for the body, but the soul needs no Rest but action. Let it be spent agreeably to the faith of Christ. Let it be spent agreeably to the belief that God dwells in the soul. What then better can we do than form an acquaintance with this inmost and highest self in meditation, in reading as a help to meditation, in good works? The very way in which alone we can become acquainted with the best parts of our nature, the way in which alone they can be called into action, is in action for others. To do good then is a Sabbath office. It is lawful to do good on the Sabbath day,[14] to teach others. The Sunday School is a chosen service which makes the dark soul shine with light and which, like all that God approves, is twice blest: him that gives, and him that receives.

All cannot keep school; all cannot go to church; but all can hallow the Lord's day. Let us deny ourselves, brethren; let us resist our bosom sins; let us do what we can to build up the kingdom of heaven in our own hearts. Finally, to know by an unerring rule how to spend the Sabbath, fix your mind's eye upon the God of the Sabbath; Let him be in all your thoughts.

'Him first, Him last, Him midst, and without end.'[15] And you shall be sure of guidance, and right knowledge, sure that the Sabbath will shed light and goodness on the other days of the week, and be to your soul a sure prophecy of the everlasting Sabbath God appoints to his children hereafter.

14. Matthew 12:12.
15. Cf. Revelation 1:17-18.

CXVII

*Take unto you the whole armour of God,
that ye may be able to withstand in the
evil day, and having done all, to stand.*

EPHESIANS 6:13

Sentiments like this abound in the Apostle Paul. To rejoice in persecution, to count human judgment a small thing.[1] And surely nothing more fully shows the suitableness of Christian faith to our condition. Every day teaches us the instability of earthly good. The connexions we would have formed with those whom God seemed to have made to impart happiness are prevented by rudest disappointment. The connexions we have formed, just as they begin to minister delight, are snapped asunder by death; or those which seemed to promise as fairly, are soured by unexpected discords. This is the condition of human life. The very prosperity of the proud is promoted by a decay of the faculties, loss of the property or death of his friends. And if we stop at these facts it is certainly true that the earth is the graveyard of our ancestors, and wherever we go ourselves we only walk in a circuitous path towards our own tomb.

Observe the change in a man's spirits in the course of a single week. Flushed with a sudden success, gratified in his social affections by the company of his friends, flattered by a compliment, life looks pleasant before him, and he is deceived into sanguine expectations. But in some turn of his business, he meets a disappointment, he commits a mistake, he encounters opposition, and straightway the whole aspect of things is changed to him and he wonders where the cheerful light is gone that late he beheld in the sun, and the green earth, and in the faces of men, and in affairs. A man hears bad news respecting the elections, or meets with a loss in trade; or his friends backbite him; or his children dishonour him; or his health fails him; or the weaknesses of his character begin to show more evident; or advancing age breaks down some great hope that he has always cherished, and seems to fix him to a lower place than he hoped to fill; or

---

Manuscript dated May 29, 1831, and September 23, 1832. Preached six times: May 29, 1831, at the Second Church, Boston; September 23, 1832, again at the Second Church; February 16, 1834, in New Bedford; March 15, 1835, in Waltham; April 12 in Watertown; and June 19, 1836, in Concord, Mass. Some original matter may have been lost from the conclusion of the sermon in the course of Emerson's revisions.

1. See, for example, II Corinthians 12:10 and I Corinthians 4:3.

his sins begin to hasten to their reward; and seeing these things, his heart is filled with bitterness.

There is no external good which is not exposed to these injuries and not only exposed, but attacked by some of them. Do you say, these evils are very old and familiar? What matter how old they are, if you and I are now suffering under them from day to day? It behoves us to apply whatever of remedy or whatever of consolation there is in our religion to these evils. If it cannot remove or console them, what is religion for? I know it can do some in both ways, to remove or console.

It can do much more, I apprehend, for us than men are willing to believe, though not perhaps precisely in the way in which men expect it to serve them. It is a gross error, and yet a very popular one, to suppose that Religion can console bad men, that in the hour of great affliction Religion can administer comforting considerations to a heart not governed by its influence.

It is a great error to suppose that religion can heal any wound of an irreligious mind. The use of faith is to give more correct views of life; to arm the mind against adversity by giving different views of what constitutes success. It tends to keep the affections from being wounded by fixing them on indestructible objects. It tends to keep the hopes from being thwarted, by showing that man is always protected, that God's will is a benevolent will, and that it is always done.

But it cannot console a bad man, for he cannot receive the thoughts that should soothe him. He cannot rightly believe that God's will is done, for he has incapacitated himself by his vices from seeing the evidence of God's being. He cannot have the joys of faith for he has no faith. Its realities are foolishness to him, for they are spiritually discerned and he has no spiritual eye.[2]

To leave the consideration of miscellaneous evils and apply this observation to a particular case, there is one which is felt, I believe, by all men in the outset of their endeavours to form a religious character and long continues to darken their views, and whose influence is very seldom wholly got rid of, and that is, the error of expecting too much sympathy, and, in consequence, of being disheartened when we fail to find it. It is one of the hardest things in the world to pitch our expectations right, with regard to the nature of that success we ought to look for. What is called 'poetical justice' in poems and novels, the giving good fortune to the good, and bad fortune to the bad, is uniformly distributed with great accuracy by young people in forming their choice of ways of life. Every young person who is forming resolutions of leading a good life, represents to himself as the consequence, the approbation and love of all the wise and good, with as much certainty and fulness as if the wise and good were an organized association who enacted their will by vote. He anticipates the reward pressing impatiently upon every deed, love for his love; admiration for his magnanimity; health for his temperance, wealth for his industry.

He does not yet see that there are few wise, few good men; that they are

2. Cf. I Corinthians 2:14.

widely separated; unknown to each other; that he may never know any on terms of acquaintance gratifying to his self love. He does not know that progress in virtue is not often continuous, in regular degrees, but slow, irregular; that its reward is in like manner slow and irregular; that long after one of its triumphs, it may continue to pay the penalty of its past backslidings, and that outward prosperity is not its promised or its suitable reward.

Religion teaches quite otherwise. It teaches a reference to God and not to men, and that single rule changes the whole face of things. What seems much for a few days may seem little to an eternal Being. What seems success to man may be the worst of failures in the eye of God. He sees what is; man what appears. Blessed, said Jesus, are the poor. Blessed are they that mourn—Blessed are you when men shall revile and persecute you—why? because your reward is great in heaven.[3]

Christianity teaches us to set before our minds steadily the duty of regarding a good state of the soul as the highest success. There are abundant confirmations and will be more in our daily experience. We must not expect much sympathy. God has made every one differently. Nobody is constituted exactly like you, and therefore none can exactly think and feel with you. Indeed, if your acquaintance with men (which seldom happens) is unrestricted; if your situation allows you to mix with numerous individuals of every class, freely, and you are not disqualified by any social defect in your own nature from frank intercourse with all, yet you will find very few individuals with whom your views and feelings have strong affinity. In your own acquaintance can you reckon five? or three? or one?

But suppose there are several persons whose minds have been laid open to you, and have been your instructors, are they accessible to you, are they contemporaries, and countrymen?

It is often the case that those most suited, as it seems, to help us, live in another generation, or on the other side of the globe. Indeed a full and free sympathy is very rarely found in life. A person finds one who sympathizes with one part of his character, and another with another part. He is praised for that which he knows has little merit, and what is best in him is neglected. So that if the chief good seems to you, *to be fully appreciated and esteemed by other men,* you must not aim at very great excellence. It is very moderate merit which can be wholly understood. There is a shallow Italian proverb, that, 'to be fortunate you must not be too wise nor too honest.'[4] The biography of almost all distinguished men may shew you that in proportion as they have raised themselves to extraordinary acquirements and extraordinary virtues they have outstripped the affections of their fellowmen. If I may use the term, they fly out of sight. A

3. Matthew 5:3–4 and 5:11–12.
4. Cf. "So are there a number of little and scarce . . . faculties and customs, that make men fortunate. The Italians note some of them, such as a man would little think. . . . And certainly there be not two more fortunate properties, than to have a little of the fool, and not too much of the honest." "Of Fortune," in *The Works of Francis Bacon* (London, 1857-1874), 6:472-73.

very great man, a mind of powers far beyond the common measure of humanity, would be solitary. He would not enjoy his greatness, he would not much value the praises of others, for he would see that there are none who are fit to praise him.

Something like this is also true in this evil world of the good man, that he is lonely. Carry the virtues to any great height and you soon leave below you the common crowd of the good sort. Then the very severity of your virtues is a sort of standing accusation of the vices of others who will not fail to gratify a spite in casting doubt on your motives and thwarting you when their cooperation is necessary to the execution of your beneficent purposes.

It was a sad commentary upon this absence of sympathy under which the good man labors, which fell from the virtuous Phocion of Athens, when on one occasion the crowd applauded him in the midst of his speech; he stopped and inquired, "What have I said wrong?"[5]

The benefactor of his sphere though his heart embraces the whole human family is often despised and rejected of men,[6] and lives in solitude in the midst of his brethren. Jesus Christ was alone without any that understood him or entered into the great purposes that swelled in his bosom. He was in the world but the world knew him not.[7] And his disciples,—some they stoned, and some they beat, and some they slew.

In view of these facts Christianity sets before the mind steadily this duty of regarding a good state of the soul as the highest success. It tells you not to expect praise nor ease, from high virtue; that the very merit of it consists in the renouncing these things, and preferring an inward sentiment to outward pleasures.

It teaches you not to look for success but for virtue; to count virtue success enough. I speak to every one who has felt how much nobler it would be to act from generous principles than mean ones, but who has hesitated because nobody else acts from such principles. When you have looked around, life seemed to you a moral waste, where all your fellows act on low motives, and not only so but would pour out all the measures of ridicule upon the simple person who should undertake to govern himself by the impracticable precepts of Jesus Christ and his apostles. Even love and every high sentiment, viz., to love your neighbor, to speak the truth, to value God more than men, carried beyond a very moderate degree, are esteemed as becoming only in very young people, or in romances. Well now, what is the lesson God teaches you hereby as with an angel's trumpet? That you should sternly conform your life to the dictates of lofty sentiment; that you should be what you admire. But you say, 'Nobody can do thus; and no one will estimate my conduct—the sacrifices I make—the

5. Emerson's source may be Plutarch, *Phocion,* viii, 3, or *Moralia* 188A; or it may be "Apophthegms New and Old," no. 30, in *The Works of Francis Bacon* (London, 1857-1874), 7:129. See *JMN* 3:16.
6. Isaiah 53:3.
7. John 1:10.

purity of my intention.' Very probably, but that is exactly the scope and office of great sentiments, to enable you to stand without sympathy, to prompt you right against the voice, it may be, of the whole world. *Every feather* blows *with* the wind; the thundercloud sails *against* it, by its own current. All boats float well on smooth water, but the skilful pilot is known when the tempest rises and he conducts his bark in the face of the storm.

Feel a confidence in good and generous sentiments and if you do not desert them never be afraid that they will betray you.

Men take counsel in moments of peril of the deceptive face of things and not from themselves. But always listen to yourself; never be tempted to a word of vanity or of pride; persist in the old vulgar road of benevolence; make his good with whom you deal an omnipresent motive whenever you deal with him. Persist, only persist, in seeking the truth. Persist in saying you do not know what you do not know and you don't care for what you do not care. Persist in doing what you think right and be so true to yourself and to simplicity as not to expect notice, much less flattery.

The difference between what is called success, and virtue, is, that one regards this life, and the other all our being. And this is a consideration that I think, my friends, might be made a far more familiar and practical one, than it is. A Christian should never let the horizon of this life fall down over his prospects.

CXVIII

Draw nigh to God and he will draw nigh to you.

JAMES 4:8

I wish to invite your attention, my Christian friends, to some considerations that go to illustrate and establish the doctrine that spiritual influences are reciprocal; to show that nature and scripture both teach, that, there is nothing arbitrary in the administration of God's moral government, but that every gift partakes of the nature of a *reward,* that, in our spiritual progress, they that *ask,* receive; they that love, are loved again; they that show mercy, find it; and they that depart from God find that God departs from them.[1]

This is a great practical doctrine and it is quite important that we should have settled notions of its truth.

There is however one important statement to be premised. It is not to be contended that all men receive alike at first. It is very manifest that in the world men set out with very different advantages for knowing the truth and practising virtue. And we have confidence that he who sees from the beginning to the end, and who knoweth the infirmities with which we contend, will not require of us but according to what he bestowed. . . . exertion on my part, yea and an exertion exactly proportioned in force to the greatness of the good I am to obtain. I have no expectation of any happiness that is in store for me, in receiving which I am to be wholly passive. If I will not stretch out my hand, I do not believe it will be filled. If I will not work for the good, I must want it. It is always those who love men, that are loved again. It is always those who study that learn. It is always those who are meek, and upright, and diligent, who are at peace with themselves, and not the proud and dishonest and lazy. And not only in thus taking advantage of moral laws, but in what is strictly Religion, namely, the directing of the thoughts to God, the doing of what we suppose well pleasing in

Manuscript dated June 18, 1831. Preached fourteen times: June 19, 1831, at the Second Church, Boston; June 26 at the New North Church, Boston; July 10 in Charlestown; July 17 at the Purchase Street Church, Boston; August 7 in Dover, N.H.; October 9 in Concord, Mass.; October 16 at the Hollis Street Church, Boston; November 13 in Waltham; December 18 in Lynn; January 22, 1832, in East Cambridge; March 4 as a lecture at the Friend Street Chapel, Boston; April 15 in West Cambridge; July 1 in Fryeburgh, Maine; and November 1, 1835, in East Lexington. The manuscript is incomplete; the ellipsis points indicate loss of text.

1. Cf. Matthew 7:7, Luke 11:9; John 14:21, 14:23; Matthew 5:7; Matthew 7:23, Luke 13:27.

his sight, the abstaining from what we suppose moves his disapprobation, and the addresses of the soul to him whether in silent contemplation or in uttered prayer, we always know or always may know exactly how near is God to us and how acceptable is the tribute we pay him. The sun is not so apparent in the heaven as is the presence of God to the soul when fully he is revealed there. And He is always, in the language of Scripture, 'waiting to be gracious.'[2] He is always to be found of them that seek him and never of those who seek him not.[3] God's calls are man's endeavours. God called Abraham, I suppose, through the uprightness, the purity, the devotion to God that Abraham possessed. And whenever God has in the old or in recent ages shown favor to a man, I suppose it was because that individual, according to his light, did his duty. There is no arbitrary election, no special outpourings of the spirit of God upon one man or one community, in any other measure than the measure of their patient and unceasing efforts. There is no other known in Scriptures or in Men.

The reason of this strict proportion kept between our asking and our receiving is given in one word. Liberty. We are free agents. If God had made us as the brute creation without freedom though with more intelligence than they, his influences upon us would have been utterly independant of our action. He would have given us whatever impulse and direction pleased him, without reference to our state. But he has made us free—given us the power to choose—and made it our duty to choose the right. And of course he respects that freedom and withholds all influence that would take it away. If now he should impart floods of knowledge and good disposition to the mind it would be to make his other gift useless and interrupt the order on which his moral creation is administered. It is plain that the expectation of such a divine operation would be fatal to virtue—to all exertion. It would be the very error into which false theology has led some solitary fanatics who have sat and waited from year to year when the showers of divine grace should come and refresh and renew their perishing souls. This is not the way of God. God helps them that help themselves. Almighty as he is, and dust as you are, your free act is the only price on which his interposition can be purchased. All that you have, it is true, you have received.[4] There is nothing but *your free power to chuse,* that you can call your own; but that little all—that *free choice*—you must dedicate to him.

Let me illustrate this by one remarkable application to the doctrine of forgiveness of sins, as it is expressed in the Lord's Prayer. I have had occasion recently to refer to this topic in another place, expounding the sixth chapter of Matthew, but as the truth seems to me of great importance that has not received much attention I shall advert to it here.[5]

2. Cf. Isaiah 30:18.
3. Cf. Matthew 7:7–8.
4. Cf. Matthew 7:8 and Luke 11:10.
5. Emerson's allusion may offer a clue to the contents of the missing Sermon LXIV, delivered in Burlington, Vt., on June 5, though the reference may possibly be to an undocumented delivery of Sermon XXXII.

Jesus, teaching his disciples how to pray, joins to his other petitions this clause, "Forgive us our sins, as we forgive those that trespass against us"; and adds this remark,—"For if you forgive not others, neither will your Father forgive you." You observe, after saying *forgive our sins'* he departs at once from the form of petition, and introduces a remarkable assertion, *'as we forgive the sins of others.'*[6]

He seems to call our attention strongly to the import of our prayer. I hope I speak to no individual who has never yet offered this supplication, and I earnestly request that each one would ask himself what he understands by it. What do you mean when you say to God, *Forgive my sins?*—Do you mean to say, *'Though my motives have been wrong, yet approve thou them?* Enter into my feelings,—Love me as I am'?

Certainly this were a strange prayer for a sinner to address to God. God cannot approve your motives, whilst they are wrong motives,—wholly opposed to his will—and so are from the devil and not from God. This will be agreed on all hands. This cannot be your meaning. But if you would not say, *Approve my motives* do you mean, *Remit the consequences* of my sin? I am afraid this petition is no more reasonable than the other, for the greatest and worst consequence of sin is sin, and unless that is remitted and removed,—to save you from the less evils that flow out of it, such as the disapprobation of men, or a bodily inconvenience it has caused you, is to apply a momentary relief to a part when the whole is sick. It is to save a pin when the house is on fire. It is taking extraordinary pains to cleanse the skin when a mortal poison is raging in the blood.—Do you mean then, what is the only rational petition which the sinner can offer to God, *'O remove my sin from me?'*—But you feel whilst you speak, that because you are free agent God can only remove sin by means of your own will. God can only remove sin by the concurrence of the sinner. There must be in order to the divine forgiveness, the effort on your part to resist and remove the sin; and therefore Jesus inserts in the midst of this humble and dependant prayer, an assertion that goes the full length of human liberty and says, *'Forgive my sins, as I do fulfil my duty to my fellow men, or, exercise suitable affections toward them,* the part of duty of all others most comprehensive and difficult after duty to God, which, 'tis expressed in the words of the petition, had been violated;—very much as if he had said, *Forgive me my sins as I deserve to be forgiven;* or, *as I am a good man.*

So then it appears that we may ask for daily bread and ask to be delivered from temptation and ask blessings on others without hypocrisy, but ask forgiveness on ourselves without at the same time deserving it we cannot. It is vain. It is wicked. Jesus, full of mercy but full of truth, can find no way for the pardon of God to descend on men—no way for any spiritual influence to descend from God to men but through the voluntary act of man, calling down this mercy. It is

6. See Matthew 6:9–15.

the spirit of all his instruction. Draw nigh unto God, and he will draw nigh unto you.

Now, brethren, this doctrine that all spiritual influence is reciprocal we have seen to be confirmed by reason and by revelation. It is true in nature for I appeal to the experience of each one of you and ask if he has ever made a single virtuous exertion which he supposed was in vain. It is true in Revelation for it runs through the old and new Testaments. Perhaps you will say there is no dispute concerning its truths. He that runs may read.[7] It is admitted on all hands. So much the better. But if so, I say it is a practical truth of as solemn importance as any that can be stated to the human mind. It is one of those great truths which involve all other truth. For see what vast interest it throws on every action of a moral agent. If such is your relation to God—if every act draws down on you new favour or new disapprobation from the great source of all being; if every thought of ours on earth has this correspondency in heaven or in hell—then your fate is committed to you. To your weak hands God has given the keys of heaven and of hell.[8] Moreover it amounts to a revelation to us of all God's way and will concerning us. We know what influences exist. We may know exactly how far God will work with and for us and when he will stop. He will work whilst we work, he will stop when we stop.

And then what encouragement to virtue is in this promise! (The first expansion of the bud of goodness in you is watched and welcomed.) If we only apprehend the truth that every good wish and intention bears fruit, that on the first upward impulse of our soul, hands are outstretched from heaven to assist and guide us, I think it will give a mighty vigor to our fainting purposes.

All possible encouragement is held out to every good word and work in this certainty of speedy and assured effect joined to it by God. It gives an efficacy to prayer unknown before—in the language of the poet, "prayer,

> A stream which from the fountain of the heart
> Issuing however feebly nowhere flows
> Without access of unexpected strength."[9]

There are two objections, and but two, that occur to me which may be made by some pious minds to this view. I do not know but it will be said that too literal and strict application of these texts makes man sufficient unto himself and makes the agency of God so mechanical, so wholly dependent on man, that it is really dismissing that idea of God which is most precious to the mind and leaving the Universe with laws but without a Personal Intelligence.

But let it be considered by us that it is essential to any just idea of God that he

---

7. Habakkuk 2:2.
8. Cf. Matthew 16:19 and Revelation 1:18.
9. William Wordsworth, *The Excursion,* IV, 218-21.

be conceived immutable and necessary in his being—a living Law—without variableness or shadow of change.[10] At the same time the more steadfastly the mind is engaged in contemplating these holy laws the more distinct does its conviction become of the personal Creator who spoke it into life and by whose imparted presence it continues to subsist from one hour to another. Does the Atheist say, What operation have you left for God? What need of God? You are sufficient for yourself. Yes, but by permission. We did not make ourselves. We feel that our existence is wholly derived, and therefore God exists. It is arranged by laws of wonderful harmony and therefore God is good and wise.

Or the objection may be stated in another form. There are no two of us in like circumstances or placed in circumstances equally favorable to virtue. One is born to an inheritance of light, having pious parents, the advice and example of good friends, great advantages of education, and above all a happy temper and a clear head. Another is born perhaps to ignorance and corrupt example and a thousand early temptations. Will it be said that he who is most happily endowed had any part in the disposition of his own lot? Did he not receive freely, and have we not all received freely what we possess? Can we pretend to have paid the price of these blessings? Surely not. All these are God's allotment and infinite wisdom is the pledge that they are right. All these are the evidence to us of God's being and goodness. All that is maintained by reason and scripture, is, that with regard to those things which are the objects of our action,— those things which we are commanded to seek, this law of exact retribution takes effect. It is true as it regards what we do, not as regards what we have. "Whatsoever good thing any man doeth, the same shall he receive of the Lord."[11] Whatsoever a man soweth that shall he also reap.[12]

Therefore, brethren, I exhort you to make with me a careful self application of this command. Draw nigh to God and he will draw nigh unto you. In our studies, in our trade, in our conversation, in our charity, in our recreation, in our privacy, let us draw nigh and more nigh to God. It is the only happy, the only safe way.

---

10. James 1:17.
11. Ephesians 6:8.
12. Galatians 6:7.

*If ye do my commandments ye shall abide
in my love, even as I have kept my Father's
commandments and abide in his love.*

JOHN 15:10

These words contained in the discourse of our Saviour as recorded by John cannot be attentively read without suggesting some important religious truths. To some of these I wish to ask your attention. First, I propose to answer the question, What is the importance of the love of Christ to us? Second, I propose to show that to keep the commandments of Jesus is a necessary preparation to our abiding in his love. Third, I propose to show that this obedience and this love are both suitable to our immortal nature.

I. And first, it may be asked what is the importance of the love of Christ to us, that we should desire it? What is his true place in our regard?

The first commandment to the Jews from Sinai and through them to mankind is—'Thou shalt have no other gods before me,'[1] or as Jesus declares it, "Thou shalt love the Lord thy God with all thy heart and him only shalt thou serve."[2] And as this is the first commandment written on the table of stone so it is also first written in the mind. As the soul unfolds, it becomes anxious to know God. In exact proportion to every man's knowledge of himself is his interest to know his maker.

We repine at the disasters that befall us; we mourn our afflictions;—but I suppose every person will admit that if faith could become sight,—if he was as well assured of God's direct agency in the particular event as he is of his own existence, saw his life as discipline not as misfortune, he would not mourn, he would be overawed by the wisdom and power that dealt with him, and a perfect trust that all was well would take the place of his sorrow. The children of Israel said to Moses, "Speak thou with us and we will hear; let not God speak with us lest we die."[3] I suppose every good man in proportion to his goodness will say

---

Manuscript undated. Preached three times: June 26, 1831, at the Second Church, Boston; September 10, 1837 in East Lexington; and November 12 in Waltham.

1. Exodus 20:3.
2. Matthew 4:10.
3. Exodus 20:19.

exactly the reverse. He will say with Samuel, "Speak Lord, thy servant heareth."[4] He will with his whole heart beseech God to satisfy him of his agency that it is the Lord, that it is not man, that it is not chance, that it is the Beneficent Father himself, who has appointed his lot here,—his temptation, or has taken away his friend and laid his comforts low in the dust. Only make that sure and he will lay his hand upon his lips and rejoice in his tribulation.

We wish to communicate with God without any medium. He is the supreme object of all love. What we truly love in men, or in nature, or in thought, is the portion of God that is present in them. And as he is the true object of all affection, so he is our Governor, and from him alone comes every command-ment we are bound to obey. There is, there can be no rival to his claims on our love or our obedience.

Now what is the connexion of the soul with Jesus Christ, what is his claim upon my reverence to his commandment and my love to his character?

The bible presents him to us as declaring himself the Son of God—the Sav-iour of the world—who wrought miracles, and rose from the dead, and prom-ised immortal life to all who should keep his commandments. But why should I love and obey him? What is it to me that he exhibited wonderful power over nature, and over men, and over himself? that he was predicted beforehand, and raised from the dead? What has the mind that comes into being in these last days to do with Nazareth, or the Jews, with the prophecy or the miracle?—I answer; it is through my duty to God. As I read his life and listen to his word, I find that my love to God binds me involuntarily to love his Son. It is not that he was predicted for ages, or announced by angels, or clothed with power, but that he identified himself with the law of God; because he did not come in his own name: because he made himself nothing and God everything; was clothed with the power and spoke the voice of God; because he speaks what is as true in New England as in Judaea;—in earth as in heaven; to me as to him. I acknowledge his commandments because I feel there is nothing arbitrary about them. I ac-knowledge the voice that says, Thy will be done—Love your enemies—Deny yourself—Be poor in spirit; Be pure in heart;[5] for these words find an echo in the law which the Creator wrote in my breast. They are agreeable to the con-stitution of the human mind.

The very sayings of Jesus which are quoted to prove that he set up an indepen-dent personal claim to my reverence and love lead me to an opposite conclusion.

I suppose that it is because Jesus had lost all self-love, had made all subser-vient to God's will, because his will was done whenever God's was done, that he says, 'I and my Father are one'[6] and speaks with authority. The authority does not belong to him as a person, but to the truths which he uttered. The delivery of the same truth would invest the humblest created spirit with the same author-ity. And so he disclaims all merit, all wisdom, except as far as he is the organ of

4. I Samuel 3:9.
5. Cf. Matthew 26:42, 5:44, 16:24, 5:3, and 5:8.
6. John 10:30.

the All wise and Almighty. Why callest thou me good? he said, There is none good but one, that is, God, and he only asks his disciples to abide in his love.[7]

Let this truth then be fixed and settled in our minds, that the whole respect and love we owe to Christ is as the servant of the living God, the clearest Teacher of God's truth. That no embarrassment come to perplex our views out of a false theology, so long taught in the world, fix it deep in your mind that God is all in all, and as you worship him you will find that all your clearest conceptions of him run back to the words and the works of his Son—Jesus will then without effort take his place in your reverence, first among created beings, the faithful Son, and Teacher of Men, the chosen vessel of light and truth which God appointed for the cleansing of the nations.[8]

II. When we have fixed the right of Jesus to command, and his claim to be loved, because his command is God's command, and the love of him is love of virtue, the sentiment of the text becomes plain and important, that the keeping of the Commandments of Jesus is a necessary preparation to our loving him or to his loving us. I say to our love or his love; for the expression *abide in my love* may mean either, and it is indifferent which meaning we give it, because *love is mutual*. It is the same thing to say, that you abide in the love of Christ, as to say, that Christ abides in the love of you. For to say, that you love God, or that you love his son, is to say that you have all those dispositions which God delights in.

And what is more manifest than that obedience to the commandments is indispensable to the possession of this affection? Let it be borne in mind what was said before concerning these Commandments that they are not capricious nor arbitrary rules—appointed by Jesus on his sole authority for the observance of his friends. There is but a single commandment of that kind which has come down from him, to wit, The Lord's Supper;[9] all the rest had been our duty though God had never sent his son into the world. He calls them *Commandments,* but they might as well be called *facts.* It was true that the merciful obtained mercy; that the poor in spirit entered into heaven; that the pure in heart should see God, that those who hungered and thirsted after righteousness should be filled therewith[10]—it was as true before they had been uttered in the form of precepts as afterwards. And so with every rule of duty he gave. They are truths of yesterday, today, and forever. They are truths which apply directly to all moral action, and so do themselves take the form of laws. It were the same thing to say, If ye have goodness ye shall love me and I will love you. This is so of necessity. We cannot conceive how it should be otherwise. You cannot love God or a good spirit unless you know him.

You cannot form an idea of that to which there is nothing resembling in yourself. If there is nothing of God, no spark of goodness in you, I do not see how you can love him any more than an idiot may be said to love learning or a

---

7. Cf. Matthew 19:17.
8. Cf. Acts 9:15 and Revelation 22:2.
9. Cf. Luke 22:19 and I Corinthians 11:23–26.
10. Cf. Matthew 5:3–8.

deaf man to delight in musical sounds. Goodness *is* the love of goodness, and the more progress you make in it, the more amiable does all that is good and godlike become. But whilst you sin, you shut your eyes upon it; you destroy the very sense by which you should relish its sweetness, and therefore it is indeed true that to the darkened mind of the sinner Jesus hath no form or comeliness and when he shall see him there is no beauty that he should desire.[11] It is pearls before swine.[12] It is light wasted on the *sightless* eyeball.

On the contrary to the mind that has kept the commandments in some measure, the excellence of his life is revealed. Such a mind knows what is meant by the "beauty of holiness,"[13] a phrase wholly without meaning to others. Such a mind has 'entered within the veil,'[14] and has found a happiness springing from its religious frames of thought that it never knew before and which throws all other pleasures into the shade. 'The stranger cannot intermeddle with its joy.'[15] It has found out the *secret* of the Lord, which is with them that fear him,[16] and it has found that these enjoyments increase with its obedience. He finds that 'life which is hid with Christ in God.'[17] His ear is unstopped, his heart is opened. He becomes capable of understanding what is divine in Christ. The extent of his benevolence dawns upon his mind—the true dignity of his lowly manners and outwardly base condition and associations is felt—the perfect wisdom of those precepts which to worldly men have appeared paradoxical—such as the submission to injury and the extreme humility which he commends. His unerring moral judgments are acknowledged, which insisted on principles instead of forms, and on a heaven of thoughts and not of outward delights—finally his capacity to do and to suffer with unabated love, these will begin to be considered by us, not with a formal lip-honour which Christendom for hundreds of years has been wont to pay, but with a rational, discriminating, affectionate admiration, which seeks to imitate what it loves.

III. The next truth that will suggest itself out of this passage is that the obedience and the love are both infinite. "If you *keep* my Commandments—" but who keeps them? What man, what created spirit from the feeblest sinner to the purest angel ever kept them? Is it not true that the more we do, the more we find is to be done? Is it not true that the first mark of growing better is to know how bad we are, and the more improvement we make, the more faults we detect? Is it not true that the Commandments mean more, and extend farther as we obey them until they cover ground not known to exist at first? Thus the commandment 'Thou shalt not have any other gods before me,'[18] if announced

11. Isaiah 53:2.
12. Matthew 7:6.
13. The phrase occurs several times in the Old Testament; see, for example, I Chronicles 16:29 and Psalms 29:2.
14. Cf. Hebrews 6:19.
15. Proverbs 14:10.
16. Psalms 25:14.
17. Colossians 3:3.
18. Exodus 20:3.

to a pagan means that he should have but one idol, whichever was his chief god,—to the Jew it means, that he should have no idol at all; to the Christian it means, that his children or his power or his property should not rule him, and whatever idols he destroy and whatever progress he makes, he still finds some temptation, each less gross than the last, which tends to withdraw in a degree his affection from God.

The precept 'Thou shalt not steal,'[19] if uttered to a thief, means no more than that he ought not to pilfer. But to a man who is never guilty of theft it means, that he should not use or consent to *any frauds in his business* to obtain the property of others. As he keeps the commandment in this higher sense, it soon comes to mean—That *he should not steal in his heart;* he should not *desire* the property of others;—then, that he *should not withhold from others whatever bounty* God has enabled him to spare from his own store.

So it is with every Commandment. It opens itself to your obedience and every precept of Christ, the law of humility, of purity, of charity, of devotion, will disclose a new and loftier standard as we advance. It must be so with infinite beings. And with every degree we gain in holiness and with every step we make towards God, we get a more distinct apprehension of the character of Christ, and become more sure of his friendship, of his intercession, of his dwelling in us.

Is it not, brethren, a cheering truth that every day may unite you more intimately to the great head of the Church? and may draw over you more richly the influences of His spirit who was, and is, and shall be,—out of whom all life and knowledge and goodness go into the hearts of his servants. O let not these motives be urged on us in vain. It is not happy, it is not safe, to neglect the precepts of Christ, for they are God's precepts; nor be absent from his love, for it is to be averse from the love of all good spirits—from all peace of mind—from all inward health—from present comfort and from future hope.

---

19. Exodus 20:15.

CXX

Hear the words of the wise. Have not I written to thee excellent things in counsels and knowledge, That I might make thee know the certainty of the words of truth.

PROVERBS 22:17, 20–21

It has been said by an eminent living writer that the Scriptures are distinguished from all other pretended sacred writings by their frequent and earnest recommendation of knowledge, the search after truth. I do not know that many passages can be adduced from the New Testament containing express recommendations but by implication it certainly does commend inquiry. It is enjoined to follow after knowledge, to seek every good word and work, to improve the time, and the truth is proposed as the prize of effort, and the great Redeemer, which, according to the declaration of Jesus, *shall make us free.*[1]

And certainly Christianity has been attended in its progress by a wonderful progress in all kinds of learning. Religion and learning have ever aided each other; and in our day more than ever the products and the vessels of learning, that is *books,* treat of every subject and lie on every table.

They form so important and so active an agent in modern society, as to deserve a good deal of regard. The religious man, who never sees man arrive in the use of his faculties at a great good without acknowledging that this result was in the foresight and intention of that Providence who made the nimble hand and the accurate eye and the devising head, rejoices in this beneficent fruit of Divine Wisdom. Books form indeed a wonderful institution by means of which a private poor man may put all ages of the world under contribution;— by which in some sort he is enabled to make the eyes of thousands see for him and their hands work for him, and render account to him of their observations and their acts. He may sit in an obscure chamber and know what was done by Patriarchs before the deluge, and follow down the long line of human generations afterward, and understand better the lineage and fortunes of all the na-

---

Manuscript dated July 3, 1831. Preached once: July 3, 1831, at the Second Church, Boston.
   1. John 8:32.

tions that now people the earth, than his own experience would teach him the condition and history of the chief families in his own town.

But the history of the world is but a part of this treasury. The secrets of all science, of every art, of every mode of human thought; the jests of the witty; the arguments of orators; the fancy of poets; and every thing that is sweet, and every thing that is sublime in the human soul; not only the records of faith, but the prayers of devotion,—all are embalmed and laid up for an immortality on earth, in these lasting repositories. One of the best advantages is, they are so entirely at command. It is better to read the books for the most part, than it would be to have the power to converse with the authors. How much better in some respects is our intercourse with the dead, than with the living! Among the living, there is abundance of wisdom, and art, and benevolence. Perhaps as wise and as good men are now living as have ever died. But I cannot see whom I would; and there are a thousand impediments that spring up in living conversation, from mixture of company, or uncongeniality of minds, that obstruct our full acquaintance with another man's mind. Then most part of most men's time is spent with the companions of necessity, and not with the companions of choice.

But a man may select these silent friends with particular regard to his own convenience. He may give leave of speech to whom he will in the great family of the wise, and with far greater range of authority than ever the most absolute king could pretend to exercise over living sages.

But I pass over all the parts of this fertile subject, to speak of religious books and some uses that may come from them to our faith and our practice. And first of the Scriptures.

I. The Scriptures. The least consideration may show that these books afford a very valuable evidence of the truth of the facts they relate, which tradition could never have afforded. I do not think tradition is capable of bringing down such a narrative as would incline me to believe in the facts recorded in the New Testament. But this simple and consistent recorded account of miracles, this account of miracles sustained by a grandeur of sentiment in the miracle worker and communicated by him to the minds of his friends, and so animating every page of this wonderful book, persuades me to believe. The discourses of Jesus harmonize with his works. I can believe that he who speaks to me as no man spake, should also do what no other man has done.

This is a kind of evidence which is very strong and which requires the existence of books. Our sacred books furnish throughout indications of the prevalence of an exalted spirituality in the minds of the receivers of the new faith which distinguishes them as much from other men as did the possession of supernatural power. We are so familiar with the language of the bible from our infancy, that we do not feel the immense force of this evidence until in our own hearts and consciences we verify the sentiments of Christ. When in the progress of religion in the soul, the trite threadbare texts which millions of mouths have repeated, become the expression of living truth to us, become descriptions of solemn realities that are taking place in our own consciousness; when every commandment seems to be an echo of a voice within us; when no saying of Jesus seems to us a hard saying, and none indifferent; but all are full of meaning and of truth, then our faith becomes perfect; faith becomes sight. We find no difficulty in believing because the gospel no longer is a narrative of what was or what may be, but of what is. We are witnesses. Say rather in the words of Paul that then 'The spirit in us beareth witness that we are the children of God.'[2]

Like the Samaritans we say, Now we believe, not because of thy saying but because we have heard and seen.[3]

This evidence—the very highest—it will be seen, comes to us through means of *books.*

II. But, secondly, on some accounts it comes to us better from other books than the Sacred Scriptures. It is, as I said just now, not obvious to men generally, even when capable of generous sentiments, because of the familiarity of the Scriptures in our ears. The evidence is therefore more striking when it comes to us from books not sacred. As an example of this evidence to the truth of Christianity, I quote a passage from the epistle of St. Clement to the church in Corinth, which was written A.D. 80–90.

"You were all humble in spirit, nothing boasting, subject rather than subjecting, giving rather than receiving. Contented with the food of God and carefully embracing his words, your feelings were expanded and his sufferings were before your eyes—so profound and beautiful the peace that was given to you and so insatiable the desire of beneficence. Every division, every schism, was detestable to you; you *wept over the failings of your neighbours;* you thought their defects your own, and were impatient after every good work."[4]

This epistle was addressed, let it be observed, to the church in Corinth, a city famous for its luxury and unbounded vice. In such a city sentiments so exalted were entertained. Now I say it is no matter whether this epistle is canonical or uncanonical; or whether it should be shown that St. Clement's name was falsely set to it, and it was writ to that church by some one else. So it be shown as it may be shown. It is undoubtedly very ancient, and it establishes the fact that a new and powerful spiritual impulse had taken place in the world which makes the gospel history not improbable.

Let me quote one more passage from the 'First Apology,' as it is called, of Justin Martyr—written about A.D. 150—a defence of Christianity addressed to the pagans and appealing throughout to their knowledge of the character and acts of the Christians. "We," he says, "who formerly rejoiced in licentiousness now embrace discretion and chastity; we who rejoiced in magical arts now

---

2. Romans 8:16.
3. Cf. John 4:42.
4. ap. History of Church p. 28 in Library of Useful Knowledge [Emerson's note]. See George Waddington, *A History of the Church, from the Earliest Ages to the Reformation,* Published [for] . . . the Society for the Diffusion of Useful Knowledge (London, 1831–1833), 1:28. In fact Clement became fourth Bishop of Rome in A.D. 90 and wrote his Epistle to the Corinthians about A.D. 96.

devote ourselves to the unbegotten God, the God of goodness; we who set our affections upon wealth now bring into the common stock all our property, and share it with the indigent; we who, owing to the diversity of customs, would not partake of the same hearth with those of a different race, now, since the appearance of Christ, live together, and *pray for our enemies,* and endeavour to persuade those who unjustly hate us that by leading a life conformed to the excellent precepts of Christianity they may be filled with the good hope of obtaining the same happiness with ourselves from that God who is Lord above all things."[5]

Passages of this kind might be multiplied without end.

Observe, there are two evidences which I draw from these and similar passages—1. the *historical* evidence of a great change that had taken place in the lives of men; 2. the *internal* evidence that the truth and grandeur of these new sentiments give to their divine origin. It is the last which I have chiefly in view, and which is not I think considered as much as it deserves. This is an accumulating evidence which is presented to your mind anew whenever you meet a good religious work. Thus I think the celebrated work of Thomas A Kempis called the Imitation of Christ; The Meditations of Fenelon—; the Life of God in the Soul of Man by Scougal; to be among the best evidence of the truth of Christianity.[6]

Thus let the work of A Kempis be shown to a man of strong and candid mind, whose opinion is not made up respecting the truth of Christianity. He cannot choose but be affected by this great development of the religious feeling—by this great theory of action which is exhibited in this work so wonderfully adapted to make the peace and joy of the mind that receives it. He must reverence in this poor monk a grandeur of thought and principle which overawes and looks down upon all the greatness of this world. He must see in this system of thought, a resource for every exigency in human life; rebuke for its sloth; terror for its vice; solace for its grief; encouragement for its despondency; hope of life eternal in its death.

But where did this man get all these high and all-pervading sentiments? Out of the New Testament. That little book is all his school. The fishermen of Galilee are his masters in philosophy. It seems to me then whilst I read this book that it carries back to the gospel a part of that light and support it has received from it. It is a new voice proclaiming the excellence and sufficiency of the doctrines of the gospel, and so confirming me in the belief that they who wrote, wrote as they were moved by the Holy Ghost.

I have been led to make these remarks with a view to draw your attention, and so your gratitude to that beautiful provision of Providence, by means of which the past sages and saints of the human race are made the teachers of the

5. ap Hist of Church p. 31 [Emerson's note]. See Waddington, *A History of the Church,* 1:31.

6. Emerson owned Thomas à Kempis, *On the Imitation of Christ* (London, 1797); several titles by François de Selignac de la Mothe-Fénelon, including *Télémaque* and *Dialogues of the Dead* (London, 1797); and Henry Scougal, *Life of God in the Soul of Man* (Boston, 1823). Emerson canceled a reference in the manuscript to Joseph Butler's *The Analogy of Religion* (London, 1736).

present and the future; and then, with the wish to recommend to the attention of any who are not acquainted with it the little work to which I have referred by Thomas A Kempis called the Imitation of Christ. It seems to me, if read with a willing mind, it cannot but be useful to those who would form a Christian character. It seems to me, if allowances are made for the popular theology in which the author was born and bred, if allowance is made for some of the *language*, to contain no sentiment to which every Christian will not subscribe. Thus according to the strict Trinity of the Catholic Church, this writer uses for God often the name of Christ, and this may seem to some a grave objection to the usefulness of his book. But I think it ought not to be so regarded. Consider that whenever he used the word Jesus and worshipped—he presented to his mind precisely the same infinite idea that is in your mind when you worship God; and therefore there was no idolatry in his reverence. Only you two call the idea of God by different names. If this be borne in mind, I think the meditations of a Catholic may be read with equal edification by all. It is thoroughly imbued with the spirit of Christ. It breathes the air and speaks the language of the spiritual world.

Time will not permit me to enlarge upon the various uses to which our religious books and all books may be made subservient, or upon the cautions to be used in consulting them. I have only been willing to present fully to you this consideration, that not one thought of all the great treasury of recorded truth that is in the world, is there without God's knowledge and intention. If he formed the faculties by which this truth has been discovered and then transmitted in durable forms and made accessible to us—then he intended it should be at our use. We are accountable for its use. We are not to blame for not reading books when we are doing other needful and perhaps better things; but we ought all to bear in mind that God has, in a wonderful manner, provided for us an inheritance of the wisdom and virtue of all past ages, to which we may repair and so never waste the time which may be made richer then.

God seems out of this storehouse of wisdom to say to you in the words of my text, "Hear the words of the wise. Have not I written to thee excellent things in counsels and knowledge that I might make thee know the certainty of the words of truth."

CXXI

*The natural man receiveth not the things
of the spirit of God: for they are
foolishness unto him; neither can he know
them because they are spiritually discerned.*

I Corinthians 2:14

I invite your attention to some considerations upon the nature of spiritual discernment, and to notice some of the mistakes into which men are prone to fall upon religious subjects, from an inattention to the truth declared by St. Paul in the text.

A man is wonderfully placed in the possession of two worlds. By his body, he is joined to the earth. By his spirit, to the spiritual world. This is his natural condition, but by his own choice he becomes more united to one or to the other. Here are some persons who say—'he is all earth; there is no other world. How do you know there is heaven? how do you know there is hell? It is all delusion.'

Here are others,—here is St. Paul who says, 'There is a spirit in the Universe, that is, God, and we are made by Him and of Him, but spiritual truths are spiritually discerned.' And this seems to me the true account, and consistent with what I see. I observe that a good man has uniformly a strong conviction of God's being. I observe that a bad man loses the evidence of God's being, and doubts and denies that there is any such being. What is this but a devotion in one to the body, and in the other to the soul,—so that to one, the material world becomes all in all,—and to the other, the spiritual. A sensual man neglects his soul and attends to the gratification of his bodily appetites. He spends all his time in the pursuit of these pleasures, and, of course, all his thoughts. His attention is thus gradually withdrawn from spiritual objects, and imbedded in the senses. Is it strange that what he has ceased to see, he should cease to believe? that as he now knows nothing of God but the name, he should believe

---

Manuscript undated. Preached sixteen times: July 17, 1831, at the Second Church, Boston; July 24 at the First Church, Boston; August 7 in Dover, N.H.; August 21 in West Cambridge; September 11 in Charlestown; September 18 at the New North Church, Boston; October 9 in Concord, Mass.; December 18 in Lynn; January 15, 1832, as the Evening Lecture at the Castle Street Church, Boston; March 11 in Watertown; July 1 in Fryeburgh, Maine; March 23, 1834, in New Bedford; May 4 in Waltham; July 13 in Bangor, Maine; November 10 at the Second Church, New York; and April 3, 1836, in East Lexington.

that it is only a name? And, since the objects of sense are more real and dear to him, every day, by the growth of his habits, he may be said to *worship* them, he thinks they always were, and death, which, he sees, takes him from them, seems to him total annihilation.

On the other hand, here is a person who has preferred the law of his mind to the temptations of the flesh, and has resisted these temptations. He feels the pleasing peace and greatness which that victory gives, and repeats and increases his efforts. It becomes *easier* to subdue his body. He does not care so much for his meats and drinks, for his dress, his amusements, or the amount of his property as he did before. He holds these consideration at their true value; for example, the improvement of his estate second to the improvement of his character. By thinking much, his thoughts become more to him.

By keeping the commandments he learns them better. By drawing nigh to God, God draws nigh to him.[1] The pleasures of virtue are heightened. New and exalted sentiments begin to inhabit his mind. He begins to find he has some pleasures which common misfortunes cannot take away. The outward man perishes but the inward man is strengthened day by day.[2] Spiritual things begin to show more real than material things. The belief in God grows strong, whilst the whole world seems to him only an apparition—a temporary creation from the everlasting Wisdom. Having his eye fixed upon divine things he becomes more firmly convinced every day of the existence of an ever present parental Power that governs and guides and rewards him and all; and to whom it is his duty and his joy to commit his whole being. He finds these thoughts lend each other support, and one truth paves the way for another; he believes he shall always live by the same laws. Thus he becomes fit to receive all declarations of the scriptures—a believer in all the doctrines of a spiritual world.

This observation of these two sorts of men and their tastes may lead us at once into an insight into the manner of spiritual discernment. The whole secret is in one word, *Likeness*. The way to see a body is to draw near it with the eye. The way to perceive a spirit is *to become like it*. What is unlike us, we cannot perceive.[3] We cannot perceive the spirit of purity without being pure; of justice, without being just; of wisdom, without being wise. The only way to understand what love means, is to love;[4] and what envy and hatred mean, is to covet and to hate.

If this fact is borne in mind it will serve to explain many things which puzzle the unreflecting.

I. And first it will show the *certainty* of Faith; that the legitimate objects of

1. James 4:8.
2. II Corinthians 4:16.
3. Emerson alludes to the principle enunciated by Heraclitus that "Like can only be known by like," which he may have found in Coleridge's *Statesman's Manual* (*The Complete Works,* ed. W. G. T. Shedd [New York, 1853], 1:465) or in Marie Joseph de Gérando, *Histoire Comparée des Systèmes de Philosophie,* 4 vols. (Paris, 1822–1823), 1:486. See *JMN* 3:213, 3:236, 3:369–70, and 6:144.
4. "Si vis amari, ama": Seneca, *Epistulae Morales,* IX, 6. See *JMN* 3:236 and 6:144.

faith are not deficient in evidence, but are their own evidence. It seems sometimes to be thought that there is something of the imagination in faith, as if men
converted their wishes into belief. On the contrary, I suppose what we are
taught by faith, to be the most real and certain part of knowledge. Faith in the
gospel sense, is, the perception of spiritual things. It is itself fulfilment. It is not
hope, it is sight. As a man thinketh so he is.[5] A man who leads a devout life
knows without any shadow of doubt, that the principle of purity is better for
him, gives him more happiness than impurity would give. He knows without
doubt, that forgiveness of injuries is better for him, gives him more happiness
than retaliation would give, that industry is happier than sloth. When he has
given up his will to God and said, 'Thou art wiser than I; let me be obscure and
unhappy so that thy purposes are accomplished. I am wholly thine and I find
my good in the happiness of the whole,'—he is assured with a perfect assurance,
from the calmness and greatness of his own feelings, that this sentiment is true.

This is the meaning of that memorable language of our Lord, If they believe
not Moses and the prophets neither will they believe, though one rose from the
dead.[6] That is to say; if the commandments that they should not worship false
gods; that they should not steal; nor kill; nor bear false witness; nor commit
adultery; are not now plainly felt to be their duty,[7]—if the dead should come
back, they could not make it plain.

And the reason is clear. They do not see the force of these laws because they
have by their vices so depraved their understandings that they cannot see what is
true. And they must change their conduct, before their spiritual discernment
can be opened.

II. In the next place, the knowledge that spiritual discernment is likeness will
show why a bad man is skeptical and why a good man, (as we call good men)
never attains at any time a more distinct knowledge of God. I suppose it will be
admitted readily and with great sorrow by the most religious persons, that,
whilst the name of God, and some form of worship, and some imperfect ideas
of him, are found in all nations, yet nothing is more rare than consistent, distinct, steadfast views of his character and providence. Our communion with
Him is not face to face, as a man with his friend. But that very dimness with
which we conceive of him, is the necessary result of our sinfulness. We are not
good enough to know him better. We are not enough like God, to see God. He
is the source of our life, the Father of our spirits, the Perfection of those faculties
which are rude and impure in us. He will become present to us as these faculties
become more pure and perfect. When we are filled with benevolence, we shall
see that it is his character. When we have exterminated every impure desire we
shall feel that we have approached him. In short all the cultivation of our moral
and intellectual powers is teaching us to say, 'Thy will be done';[8] that our will as

5. Cf. Proverbs 23:7.
6. Luke 16:31.
7. See Exodus 20:1–17.
8. Matthew 26:42.

far as it is separate from the will of God is evil and pernicious, and as the soul comes to breathe that sentiment, the presence and the perfection of God is felt.

III. But besides this very imperfect faith in God, there are many specific errors widely prevalent among such as lead decent and in some respects religious lives, who believe in God and honour his word. And the reason why gross errors prevail in what we think the broad daylight of Christianity upon religious questions, is still the same, that is, for want of more religion. It marks a very sensual state of the Church, when things are understood sensually, or by pictures addressed to the senses, and not spiritually.

For example, we all know in what a number of minds the idea of Heaven and of Hell is still wholly a picture from the senses. I have heard a Christian who esteemed his views very elevated, describe the happiness of heaven in language wholly got from the eye. The saints are really to be arrayed in crowns and palms. There is to be a heaven of great pomp, of immense numbers, of vast space. All peoples, generations, worlds shall meet—We shall all praise and glorify God forever—with all the redeemed, with all happy spirits around his throne. The imagination is strained to present some adequate conception, and it gives no more pleasing or true result for the employment of human minds than that they are to utter commendations and anthems to a great king. Now this is a false picture—magnify it as much as you will.

Let the multitudes with which the prolific world has teemed now for sixty centuries, be a handful to the hosts of harmonious angels that should there be met. Let the throne be brightness before which the sun shall be black. Let the floor of this temple of eternal worship be "sanded with suns."[9] Carry out these thoughts to what visions of grandeur you will—it is all poor and mean at the last, it is all merely an image addressed to the eye and the ear, and what is addressed to the natural man can never satisfy one moment the desires of the spiritual man. God and man are alike dishonoured by these representations. To utter with the lips ascriptions—is a poor and unsuitable homage to glorify Him. The Source of all Being is not indigent and needy of our praise. The fault is, it is *unlike;* it is comparing spiritual things with sensual. The wants are spiritual, and so must the objects be.

The true heaven is, in the raising of this poor sinful soul to His love, knowledge, and likeness; to purity, to humility,—to kindness, to truth, to trust; to the possession of the treasures of unbounded truth; the fellowship and cooperation with all good minds in all works of love; and the enlargement of this soul to the great and increasing capacity for virtue. This is heaven.

The same attention to spiritual things corrects our false opinions respecting the manner in which the Judgment is passed and executed upon every mind. We take the parable for a literal description of facts. Men in general suppose that the separation of good and evil spirits is performed by a physical force; is really made in the way of a shepherd dividing his sheep and goats,—these are forced

9. Edward Young, *Night Thoughts,* "Night IX," Line 2312.

into one place, those are forced into another;[10] instead of interpreting this
Scripture by their own observation of what is done in the world every day and
by their spiritual eye. They would then find the real power of that solemn moral
law, by which, every where in the universe, the good seek the good, and the evil
seek the evil. They would find, that God does not need to appoint tormenting
whips and flames for the sinner,—for, *of their own accord,* they go down to
death;—they invite to them their own lusts; they indulge their own love of
falsehood, of anger, of evil speaking, of pride, of covetousness, of hatred, of
blasphemy; they seek, whilst in this mind, companions who love the same
things. They shun the society of good men precisely as the lustful, the glutton,
the miser, the robber, the murderer here shuns the society of wise and pious
men. It would not only be felt as insupportably tedious, but as a perpetual
accusation of their life.

And is it not as plain, that the good there, the pure, the lowly, the benefactor,
the martyr, the patriot, would seek the society of each other with the same
strong desire which here draws them together? It is a law of spirits, wholly
independent of time and place, that *like shall be joined with like,* and it holds of
the good, as of the evil.

Another of the errors which an attention to spiritual things might correct, is
the ungrounded expectation that when this world has failed to make us happy,
another will make us happy. How gross are the errors of men on this topic may
be every where noticed in conversation.

In this spirit men express weariness, disgust, hatred of life. I speak not of that
insanity which appears in suicide, but of the disgust of life expressed by men
esteemed sane and wise. One of the eminent writers and statesmen of the last
century says, "The best of life is but just tolerable 'tis the most we can make of
it."[11] And there are multitudes who, some in faith and some in infidelity, call the
grave a refuge, and look with gloomy satisfaction to the prospect of release
from the evils of life. Yet what shall be the bitter disappointment of such a mind
to wake up again after death the same wretched being he was—existence the
same intolerable burden,—with the added conviction that the future has now
no further resource from that hatred of life which made his head reel and his
heart sick. I say he finds himself the same, for what can a departure from the
body and from bodily circumstances do to heal and cheer a diseased *soul*? It is
the soul that is sick and gives the appearance of evil to external condition. The
true cause of the vexation we regret, is not in our peculiar circumstances, but in
a querulous mind, which is not humble, or diligent, or kind enough to be at
peace. And, as these are not disorders of the body, dying, i.e., passing out of the
body, will not cure them, and the same things will remain to be done, that now

10. Cf. Matthew 25:32–33.
11. Jonathan Swift, quoted in Joseph Spence, *Anecdotes, Observations, and Characters of
Books and Men . . .* (London, 1820), 74. See *JMN* 3:176, Sermon LXIII (*Sermons* 2:128), and
"Introductory" lecture on "Human Culture" (*EL* 2:219).

ought to be done, namely, to become pure and humble and industrious and kind.

My friends, no man can take the principles of the New Testament for his guide, without becoming alive to numberless errors that prevail in the life and conversation of men around us. He will become alive to his own errors of opinion and faults of practice. He will find that men do not listen to the secret instructions of their own inward Teacher. He will find that they are looking for heaven and for hell in an *outward condition,* instead of receiving that word of our Lord, 'the kingdom of God is within you.'[12] We sit still and hope that our salvation will be wrought out for us, instead of working out our own. We imagine that whilst we are under good influences, we are insensibly growing better, and *passively* too, instead of perceiving that our own effort is indispensable. The time will come, if in humble trust we will keep the commandments—the time will come when we shall see as we are seen, we shall know as we are known, and shall become wise unto eternal life.[13]

12. Luke 17:21.
13. I Corinthians 13:12; II Timothy 3:15.

CXXII

*As we have therefore opportunity
let us do good unto all men.*

GALATIANS 6:10

I have recently several times called your attention to the subject of Heaven or the future state of the good, because all men have the impression that happiness must be the object of every exertion and it seems important that we should rightly apprehend the nature of that which we seek. We ought to know that the reward is not something different from the labor, but will always be of the same kind. In this world, rewards are continually conferred, essentially different from the work done. As when a sum of money is given to a man for a scientific invention, or for a striking act of benevolence. And men generally think the same thing is true of heaven; as when a man reads literally the text that a saint is to sit on a throne and judge the twelve tribes of Israel,[1] instead of perceiving that virtue always by its own nature is superior to vice and judges and condemns it.

There is a common error that may be very frequently observed in conversation that the next world is a compensation of the outward inequalities of this, that a rich man will very hardly enter into heaven,[2] because he has been rich, and that a poor man will enter into heaven, because he has been poor. I have heard the Scriptures quoted to this end, as if the gospel preached originally by poor men to the poor were spiteful, partook of the envious feeling with which a wicked poor man observes the wealth of his neighbor, and so uttered the threat of a band of robbers. There can hardly be a more total misapprehension of the charitable Paul and John and Peter who never ceased to warn their humble brethren against envy. The poor man who thinks after this manner will be as poor in the future as in the present. Envy is spiritual robbery. To covet your brother's possessions is to prove that you would take them if men would let you.

If he is guilty in the sight of God of adultery who permits in himself the secret desire,[3] he is guilty of theft who is willing that by some change of affairs, (to

---

Manuscript undated. Preached three times: July 24, 1831, at the Second Church, Boston; February 2, 1834, in New Bedford; and April 9, 1835, in Waltham. Draft passages for this sermon occur in *JMN* 3:275–76 and 3:278.

1. Matthew 19:28.
2. Cf. Matthew 19:23.
3. Cf. Matthew 5:28.

which he will not be a party, only from the fear of man,) a rich man shall become poor, and he thereby rich. And this seems to be the very spirit of the doctrine that heaven is to provide a compensation for the physical sufferings of this world. The simple truth that *goodness is happiness,* is not enough for the perverted mind of worldly men and the reason is, we are incapable as yet of seeing the height and depth of that proposition how much meaning is contained in that word 'goodness.'

I have alluded to these subjects now, for the purpose of considering the fundamental mistake from which they spring. It all comes from thinking every thing is good as far as it benefits self and not as far as it benefits others. And this error prevails in all the popular views respecting the distinctions in this world. It is thought that the main use of riches is to afford delight to the rich man, and the same thing is thought of other distinctions. I deny not that other opinions may be found in books. Just sentiments have always existed in the world, but I speak of the opinions which are current among us in conversation and on which men act. I ask you, brethren, if our prevailing opinion is not that Riches are a prize; that Power is a prize; that Talents are a prize; are they not so accounted by men of honour and nominal Christians? All this is contradicted by the pure doctrines of the New Testament. In the eye of religion, they are all Trusts—and every good thing you have is a trust—committed to the individual for the greatest possible use. A few words on each of these points.

1. Riches are a Trust. This truth fully understood by a good mind will supply an unfailing test to show how wealth may be innocently and wisely gotten and spent. Receive the doctrine that you are God's steward and it will counsel the rich in possessing and satisfy the poor in the want of wealth. Let a man be penetrated with the truth of the gospel on this subject that use, that diffusion is the whole intent of wealth, that the whole purpose is to scatter as widely and effectually as possible the influence of his wealth, and not to contrive how best he can confine the good between the four walls of his own house. It is a great mistake to think that this sentiment would check industry or make men profuse. This view will sometimes add to his diligence in collecting, and sometimes make him frugal in his disbursing. This fact that the greatest possible use is the object of wealth, is the reason why it is not becoming in a good man to squander his property in what some men call charity. The worst charity is often to give alms. One of the poorest uses to which you could put a thousand dollars, would be to give it away in indiscriminate alms. It would probably occasion with some real good, a great deal of momentary luxury, some gross crimes, and speedily leave the receivers as poor as it found them, and less contented. Meantime, it would have taken from you the power to pay the wages of honest industry which in your hands it was paying, when it supported the families of laborious artisans, or sailors, or merchants. The Christian does not hesitate more than the Atheist to surround himself with the conveniences and elegancies which money will buy. If he has wealth he lives in a well built house, he wears good clothes, he uses handsome furniture. For he knows that it is better to his

part to support industrious men, than to support men in idleness. If he should refuse to buy the products of their arts he will be called to buy bread for them to sit idle.

But there is this wide difference between the pious man and the worldly man. One buys for himself, the other for all men. The good man is afraid himself of his ease—exercises himself in selfdenial. The principle of Love runs through every detail of his expenses. And that is the real regulator of every one. 'Shall I do more good by giving this direction to my expense or the other?' And not only in buying but in doing with what is bought. All possessions that end in self are odious. The man who affects to shut himself up in a reserved repelling splendour hath much of the devil in him and by the force of God's moral laws is always baffled. All selfishness injures the selfish man. The Exclusive in fashionable life excludes himself from social enjoyments in attempting to appropriate them as the Exclusionist in religion shuts the door of heaven on himself in striving to shut out others. The better your house is, the wider should its doors be flung open. Have you pictures? They are made to be seen, and are as if they were not, when they are in a dark chamber. Books are to be read, and the more excellent they are, the more you should circulate them.

And when the opportunity comes to visit the forsaken, to feed the hungry, to relieve a friend, or when a heavy burden by misfortune or misconduct of another is borne by you, do not represent it to others as your mishap, as is commonly done, but rejoice in it yourself and if others speak of it, speak of it to them as your privilege. Look on it with pleasure as the very end answered for which these means were provided. Nor ever in dispensing your wealth take the manner of giving your own, but always humbly account yourself what you are, an agent, a steward.

If the rich man give himself airs upon his riches—how ridiculous! for he too is a beggar fed from God's hand—the pensioner of a Providence which in seeming to give him all has yet far more richly endowed the Lazarus at his gate whose sores the dogs lick and whose thoughts the angels love.[4]

If the language of civility was sincere, all these cautions would be wholly unnecessary for it is remarkable that what are esteemed its exaggerated terms do really and faithfully express the rules of Christianity on this subject. A man who would be complaisant writes himself the humble servant of some person esteemed his inferior. This is precisely the gospel rule. If any man would be greatest among you let him be the servant of all.[5]

2. In the same manner we should think of Power. Power is notoriously considered even in this country where the words "that it is held for the people" are familiar[6]—it is here accounted a prize. See the struggles for office every day by incompetent persons.

4. Cf. Luke 16:19-31.
5. Mark 10:44.
6. Emerson is evidently alluding to the Constitution of the United States and to state constitutions which invoke the principle he cites.

See the language of the newspapers. An eminent and I hope an excellent man said, that he would not do something or forbear something, he would not truckle to some great party, no, not to be elected to the Presidency of the United States. Now though his sentiment might be highly praiseworthy, here is the mistake—he speaks of a great power as a great bribe and not a solemn trust. Men talk of seeking power as such. Power is a plume that any body may strive to obtain, with no more seriousness than any other ornament; with no terror of any other peril to follow its abuse than merely that of its loss. It is something to be enjoyed by the possessor because every body looks at it and esteems it highly.[7] It is esteemed as if it was a gratification to himself and not a means of benefitting other men.

To gratify one's self. This way of thinking of Power supposes that to have political power is to raise a man above these considerations that restrain the conduct of other men within the bounds of moderation, and is to enable him to do as he pleases. This is a mistake of fact as well as of principle. Few men do less as they please than men in power. They have courted some strong Party to carry them into office and they find they must court it still. They find that they are merely organs through which that strength acts and must be obedient organs or that strength will depart from them. So that most nominal kings and presidents and governors are merely clerks of some real power which stands erect at their side and does its will by them. They find themselves unable to do what they would but must serve another. But what the worldly man does unwillingly the good man does with his eyes open and with all his heart. In the most effectual service he believes he shall find his duty, his interest, and his happiness, and that these are thwarted by any endeavor to convert a public office to a private benefit.

It is remarked by physiologists that in the human body all the parts respect each other and have an action that refers to something else, the heart, the liver, the stomach, the brain; and the moment any organ begins to appropriate the nourishment received to itself, that moment commences obstruction and disease.

But there is nothing in the least arbitrary and capricious in the exercise of power by a good man. He surely will not regard it as an ornament, as a holiday clothing, and load the givers with impertinent thanks but will gird himself with gravity and diligence to severe and often thankless toil. He will not be the servant of Public Opinion, or what is commonly so called, but which is the *private* opinion of the hour or the party but he will obey implicitly the true Public Opinion of the whole world of good men in the body, or out of the body. He will send the empire of good principles which govern him into the remotest vein and fibre of the state. Thus will he be, in the language of the Apostle, instead of God, for he will make God the heart of the state.[8] Far from thinking

7. See Sermon CIX, n. 5.
8. See Sermon CIX, n. 6. This entire paragraph is borrowed from Sermon CIX.

he is placed there to indulge himself and gratify his own whims, it will be seen that there is not so much arbitrariness or uncertainty in his councils as in the actions of the meanest slave—they are bound by laws as unchangeable as the law of gravity; but freedom he has; for, what he does, he does with all his heart and all his soul. He is placed in the position of greatest usefulness and he realizes and fills the office.

3. The same error exists with regard to Talents, and is to be corrected by the same truth.

Men think in their admiration of a powerful genius how splendid is the distinction, how happy it would be to be possessed in one's own right of so much authority and honor as attaches to a masterly understanding. They think it good—why? Is it because that man sees things as they are, because he can avert a great deal of mischief from his fellowmen by timely information, seeing by his divine illumination the consequences of things in their causes, or can do a great deal of good by leading on the candid mind to greater insight into truth and good? Oh no; but because to be a man of genius, is, to be a man known and admired; it is thought the possession of eloquence or of brilliant imagination or penetrating sagacity will put the possessor quite at ease, contribute abundantly to his temporal good. And the *use* of genius, the *use* of Wisdom, which is its life and essential condition of being, is overlooked. Wo to the unhappy man of genius whom the common opinion has led into this fatal error! If he thinks his powers are his own, and were given him as means of procuring animal delights, he is a spiritual suicide. Learning, Talents, Genius, Wisdom, whatever name or form intellectual gifts may take—every degree of Wisdom is only a more or less excellent perception of truth which in its nature is more elastic and diffusive than light or heat. It must spread. It cannot be confined. As fast as a man becomes conscious of truth the more eager he becomes to make it known. The greater his gift the more plain and inevitable is his obligation to benefit men. He is a torch not lit for itself. If he attempt to confine his powers to his own good, to use spiritual light for sensual purposes, to sell out his birthright for pottage,[9] that moment his mind begins to be darkened and the glorious fire of truth to grow dim. He begins to wander from the source of goodness and truth, and his mind becomes perverted—his spiritual sight becomes imperfect and he is given over to his reprobate mind.

Wealth, Power, and Talents are all trusts given to no man for himself but as means of usefulness. What is true of them is true of every degree of them. I speak to no person who has not some property, if it be only his manual strength and skill, some power, if it be only his vote, and some wisdom. What is true of these is true of all we have. The great and common mistake which I have spoken of, arises from the evil heart, which seeks only a selfish, that is, an animal good. The great truth which the text teaches is the importance of cultivating that disposition of the changed or regenerate heart, which seeks not self, but the

9. Cf. Genesis 25:29-34.

good of all minds which is the will of God. Heaven consists in being most useful. Hell consists in being most hurtful to others.

Let us, brethren, receive from the word of God and from the voice of our own hearts this great truth—that we are not our own but God's children, that every moment we live by power received from him. Then our great duty will be ever present to our minds that we are not to live to ourselves but to the greatest good of the greatest number of our fellow beings.[10]

10. See Sermon XCVI, n. 10.

CXXIII _____

A good man shall be satisfied from himself.

PROVERBS 14:14

A great many errors prevail in the Christian Church. One of the most obstinate in keeping hold of the mind, and one of the most injurious, is, that it is the part of piety to receive the doctrines of religion without severe examination. It is thought to indicate pride if a man would measure by reason, religious truth. It is thought a mark of a disposition to infidelity, and blameable self confidence.

The zealot writes "Thus saith the Lord" upon every doctrine that is contained in the popular creed, and expects a good man to show his goodness by an unhesitating assent.

I think this a very prevalent and a very injurious mistake. There have been times when it operated upon all or almost all the minds of a whole age. Now it affects very deeply a large portion of the religious community and in some degree those who think themselves secure from it. If we look for truth I think we shall find that whilst on the one hand this opinion is a false one and tends to corrupt and degrade the mind, on the other hand, the objectors to self reliance in one sense, are perfectly right. There is always danger of pride and presumption—and of becoming wholly irreligious from an evil use of the understanding on religious questions. I shall endeavour to show the true distinction that should be made.

First then as to this opinion that it is more pious to receive religious truth, than to set out to think for oneself, I answer, that to think is to receive; that to think, to study, to verify in each one's own experience every doctrine, is the only way in which truth can in any real sense be said to be received.

The commandment is "thou shalt love the Lord thy God with all thy heart,"[1] not with thy neighbor's but with thy own. Go all lengths with this sentiment— fully trust yourself as the judge of truth. For suppose that which you try to believe differs from what you see. What can a man do against the truth? If himself, if his reason clearly say one thing, and the Scripture seem to say another, how can he receive that interpretation? Let him trust himself. Let him believe that whilst he honestly tries to know the true he shall not see the false. I

Manuscript dated July 31, 1831. Preached twice: July 31, 1831, at the Second Church, Boston, and July 30, 1837, in East Lexington. Draft passages for this sermon occur in *JMN* 3:279–80.
    1. Luke 10:27.

will believe that truth is stronger than I, and will prevail. I will believe that truth is good enough for me, and that I shall not be corrupted by knowing it. Yes, it seems to me that this distrust of human reason that cries out so loud upon *infidelity,* calls its own name; it is based on infidelity. It fears the light. It believes that free discussion, fair examination will show falsehoods in its religious system.

Are men afraid that their reason will outsee God? "lest their own judgments should become too bright"? that the faculties which God hath made will see sharper than is good? will find something more or different from what they should find? If they apprehend this, then I say, they do not believe in the true God, in God as he is, and the sooner their idol is overthrown, the better. And it is because men have been content to be religious by rote, to make piety to consist in giving a verbal assent to articles of faith, and in giving a bodily obedience to forms of worship, that theology has been so false, and that goodness has been so low. Religion has been asleep this thousand years. I do not speak of any one sect. I speak of all. I speak of us. I think almost all of us are content to be religious by education and not by realizing its truths. The only way for a man to become religious is to be so by himself. He is to go aside from all manner of society. He is to go into his closet and shut his door not only upon his household, and his friends, but upon the great association of believers with whom he is classed; upon the nations that are called of Christ; and upon the world that in some form worships God,—and he is to pray unto his Father who is in secret, and his Father who seeth in secret will hear him.[2] Yet it is not important that a man go into privacy and darkness to pray. Jesus only warns him against ostentatious prayer.[3] Let him pray if he will in thick of the crowd, but it *is* important that he go into a retirement of the spirit, from the subserviency to other minds that encourages at once both sloth and fear and shuts him out from a communion with God. To reflect—to use and trust your own reason, is to receive truth immediately from God and so it be humbly received from him, I know it may be trusted. It will do good, it will tell whence it came. What truth you thus receive is a living faith. To take on trust certain facts is a dead faith. A trust in yourself is the height not of pride but of piety, an unwillingness to learn of any but God himself.

But whilst this doctrine may be pressed to its full extent of trust in reason, and any denial of it is suicidal, there is a truth of vital importance which must be considered with it that it may be safe, and that is, whilst you trust in self—*the origin of self must be perceived.* The moment a man loses sight of the truth that he did not make himself,—that he is not a cause, but a mere effect of some other Cause, and so a mere manifestation of power and wisdom not his own—the moment he lets this truth go, he becomes a bundle of errors and sins. He sees all good that he is permitted to do as coming from himself and is proud. He sees all

2. Cf. Matthew 6:6.
3. Cf. Matthew 6:5.

good that comes from his exertions to be his own and is selfish. And when the doctrines of religion are presented to him, he wants that first truth which should open the door to them. Unaccustomed to feel his direct and total dependance upon God, though he may have assented always to his worship, he now asks the proof, he asks that it should be shown to his eye and his ear and his touch and smell. It cannot be shown to him without his perception of the truth that he has no existence by himself. And so his former nominal belief is exchanged for a real and professed unbelief.

It is the observation of this fact that has made good men fear trust in self. And this distinction is as firm as that of good and evil. This distinction is made in the text—"A *good* man shall be satisfied from himself." A *good* man knows that he is not his own. This distinction once seen is the perfect check. To a man who does not perceive this fact, the same doctrine is welcome but it inflames his pride and darkens his knowledge. To a man who sees that he has no other existence than that which he derives every moment from a power not his own, that is from God, the doctrine may be safely preached of a boundless reliance on himself because that is a reliance on God. He is great by the power, he is wise by the wisdom, he lives by the life of God.

I leave this doctrine, which amounts to no more in the end, than to say, God cannot make him perceive truth except by the use of his own faculties.

Akin to this is another doctrine on which I wish now to make a few remarks; viz., that it is only by our own affections that any object can be loved. This may seem so plain in the statement as it should never be doubted and yet I think it has been neglected by Christians in their regard paid to Jesus Christ.

There is a feeling that has caused a great uneasiness to many that they ought to pay a great and religious deference to Christ as designated by God to an eminent place and work in his creation. The opinion prevails that *God has made it their duty to love Christ.* They derive from this feeling of obligation an uncertainty in their views of him, and end perhaps in an open rejection of the faith or in a servile and hypocritical profusion of words of affection.

It is wholly wrong to attempt to require love and honour of a soul by representing it as an *obligation,* to compel affection. There is no power in the universe that can force a mind to revere another mind. The idea that dignity like that conferred by a king on a subject demands respect and love is the mistake in this case. God does not use *personal authority.* It is the direct effect of all spiritual truth to abrogate and nullify personal authority, to make us love the *virtue,* and the person exactly by the measure of his virtues. God is no respecter of *persons.*[4] Love is the reward of loveliness. Reverence is the reward of wisdom and goodness. Do not suppose attachment to him is to be *enjoined* on you.

It is not his office, it is not his power, his renown, but his moral and intellectual being that are the objects of your regard. And these—how are these to be loved? *Only by means of yourself.* Yourself must be the mean through which

4. Acts 10:34 and Romans 2:11.

only these exalted powers can satisfy your affections. For consider that any character can only be loved by likeness; whilst you are evil, you can never love him who is good.

But would you be his friends, keep his commandments.[5] And when you are filled with benevolence, you will discern new worth and beauty in his character; as you become meek, and true, and pure, and useful, you shall find his name dearer to you and a warmer fellowship arise between your souls.

This is suitable to the language of the New Testament where Christ is continually spoken of in the Epistles almost as an abstract name for those virtues that shone in him: Christ, the power of God and the wisdom of God; till Christ, who is our life, shall appear; we have the Spirit of Christ.[6] It was a name for moral perfection. To live is Christ.[7]

Thus, brethren, is a good man satisfied from himself, in his faculties and in his affections. And why is he thus perfect? It is written in the book of Genesis and it is written also in the mind. God said, Let us make man in our image and after our likeness and let him have dominion over the beast of the field and fowl of the air.[8]

It is because we are of God and only so far as we are of him that we find the whole creation both matter and mind coming under our dominion and able to yield us the riches of all its gratification. But the attempt to separate ourselves from him, to see knowledge and to get enjoyment by ourselves, destroys both. We become false and wicked.

Let us then feel, brethren, that we have our own work to do, that it is to no purpose that we are associated with religious minds, if we are not religious. Let us abstain from looking abroad or leaning on others, and go home. We must be satisfied from ourselves with truth or not at all. That only is our faith which is our own seeing, all the rest is shadows.

Let us feel also that the ground of all love is likeness, that the good love the good and with a degree always measured by the greatness of their virtues. That as the beatitudes that dwelt like so many angels in the bosom of Jesus Christ shall, by our own opening ourselves to the influences of God's Spirit, wax stronger in our minds, we shall find ourselves drawn to him in the only true way. We shall find ourselves filled with that spirit of God which makes all, as it made him, Sons of God. We shall then do the commandments and abide in the love of that glorious and excellent mind even as he does his Father's commandments and abides in his love.[9]

5. Cf. John 14:15.
6. I Corinthians 1:24; Colossians 3:4; Romans 8:9.
7. Philippians 1:21.
8. Genesis 1:26.
9. Cf. John 15:10.

CXXIV _____

For it is God which worketh in you both to will and to do of his own good pleasure.

PHILIPPIANS 2:13

The gospel represents men as under bondage, and it comes to deliver them from it, and make them free; it calls them to the glorious liberty of the sons of God.[1] Salvation is this deliverance—this gotten liberty. It speaks as if all or almost all were slaves or in servitude, that they are servants of sin whose wages is death, in the bond of iniquity.[2] And the truth of the Gospel is called Redemption, ransom. We call Washington the political Saviour of his Country because he was mainly instrumental in delivering it from political slavery. So then is Christ rightly the Saviour of the world in a higher sense if he delivers it from moral slavery. Brethren, I invite you to consider this great subject of Freedom. Are we free? It is of no account that we have political freedom if we have not moral freedom. It is of no account that we are free as a nation, if individually we are not free.

In attempting to show what is true on this question I am not speaking as a preacher of Christianity only and saying what is the meaning of freedom in the gospel sense but I shall try to show what true freedom is, that the only true freedom is freedom in the gospel sense and the only freedom a rational being can enjoy.

The elements of liberty are two, knowledge and goodness. The mind of man is made of two parts the intellect and the will, the power of knowing, and the power of doing. Knowledge, or, seeing things as they really are, redeems the intellect from slavery. Goodness redeems the Will from slavery. On reflexion it will appear that a man has only so much liberty as he has of truth and of Conscience, (and without them all boastful assertions of liberty are only a clanking of chains).

I. It will be admitted on a moment's consideration that knowledge is essential

---

Manuscript dated August 13, 1831. Preached ten times: August 14, 1831, at the Second Church, Boston; November 17 as the Thursday Lecture at the Second Church, Boston; February 16, 1834, in New Bedford; February 23 at the Hollis Street Church, Boston; May 11 in Watertown; January 18, 1835, in Lowell, Mass.; March 29 in Waltham; June 14 in Framingham; November 8 in East Lexington; and November 15 in Concord, Mass.

1. Cf. Romans 8:21.
2. Cf. Acts 8:23 and Romans 6:23.

to true liberty. We commonly say of the brute creation, of the elephant, of the horse, of the ox, if they *knew* their own strength they would not serve us. What is the reason why the barbarous and semibarbarous nations are in such a wretched subjection to the cruel institutions of their priests? Because of their gross ignorance. If they had true views of religion they would cast off their yoke at once.

Knowledge *is* Power, and he that has it is master of him that has it not. What is the progress of science but a continual emancipation of society from a bondage or state of fear and confinement under which it lay? Thus a savage beholds an eclipse or a comet with terror, a civilized nation with great satisfaction and reaps benefit from it. A savage is the servant and sufferer of inundations, insects, wild beasts, exhalations, rain, cold, diseases, and the like natural evils, which the civilized man masters by levées, clothing, houses, choice of ground, vaccination, medicine, police. The savage is the slave of these masters. The civilized is the master of these servants.

Every part of life is full of illustrations of this emancipating force of knowledge.

A man is on the stormy ocean and knows not how to steer; which way is the shore, and where are the currents, and where are the rocks? Let a friendly hand bring him a compass, and he knows his course. A quadrant and he knows his place; a chart and he knows his coast; and from what fears and horrid disasters is he not delivered out of bondage into freedom?

You are called to vote in a public assembly but upon a question of whose true merits you are ignorant. You are painfully perplexed. Every speaker sways you, every new view though false, because you do not see its face. What can make you free of this chain? Knowledge. Let the facts as they really are be shown to you and you will no longer be at the mercy of every speaker there. You will be your own man again.

And so it is in the daily history of every individual mind. Let two men converse on a subject on which one is well informed and the other is not, and you will quickly see which mind is master and who is servant of the other. Every new fact that he acquires, every error he corrects is, as we commonly say, opening his eyes. It is, strictly speaking, giving him freedom, for freedom is to do as he will, and the prejudice under which he labors hinders him from doing as he would if he saw how things stood.

Thus it is that in the intellect Truth makes men free.[3]

II. But a man may know what is right and approve what is right and yet do wrong. He is not yet free until he has the other element of freedom, that is, goodness. I call upon you, my friends, to consider within your own mind how many persons there are in all your acquaintance who can really be said to be free? It was this thought of the unknown extent of human slavery that led me to this topic. I have seen many persons in society whom when I meet I seem to see them led like a dog in a chain by a master. If you inspect narrowly the multi-

3. Cf. John 8:32.

tudes of your friends to see who are they whose vote or whose voice cannot be corrupted, who never give any thing to fear, nor any thing to favor, and never any thing to the subtlest devil that entraps human freedom, Self-love,—but who always cast a free vote—I am afraid those multitudes will melt away to a handful, to ten, to five, to one just man. Yea, if one be found.

Thus here is a man who seems to you a respectable member of society, a man of good temper and good education but he cannot control his appetites. See him at the table. He knows that he shall injure his health as well as his habits by this or that indulgence, but he yields to the temptation; and, knowing that, wherever you see him must you not feel that great as he is, or gifted as he is, his meat or his wine is his master.

Self indulgence is a tyrant of a great many subjects, among all men and among us.

Here is another man who is temperate and industrious,—but he does not venture a remark without looking to the company for assent and speaks not from himself but from his impression of their opinion on the subject in hand. His vote he would gladly give to the right side but the majority vote the other way and he has not firmness to resist them. Certainly no one will question whether this be true of thousands in this country so free and so jealous of its liberty. Let the importance so justly attached in our elections to the secret ballot over the hand-vote testify. Why is it better to vote by ballot? Because we really are not to be trusted as having courage enough to contradict the popular will.

Here is another man who is neither intemperate nor timid and who says—'I surely am free. There is no man in the world whom I esteem above myself. I do not associate with other men or but with few of other men. I surely am my own master.'—No. Pride is his master. He will put himself to the most painful inconveniences and does every day to avoid being out done by others. He will do wrong, he will be angry, he will be unjust, he will be extravagant to gratify that master passion. Is he then free? Here is another whom the prospect of a large gain will warp from his integrity, will shut his eyes and his ears and his heart, he will break his friendships and let go his good name. He is sold for gold.

Here is another who will do all for revenge. Are these men free? Now run over the names of your kinfolk and acquaintance and tell me, Who is? The popular expression that wicked men "are sold to the devil" or the more philosophical expression "the Ruling Passion"—what do these terms express but the observation of men through so many ages that Vice is a slavery? And therefore true is the other proposition that goodness is liberty; that every step to virtue is necessarily a step towards deliverance; that as he becomes better he escapes from these tyrants and becomes free. A good man is free in a twofold sense, 1. in his circumstances—outwardly—not hampered by evil obligations or by evil habits or by dangerous associates which happiness of condition he owes to his past life; and 2. in his mind or spiritually because he can choose to do what he knows is right.

It follows from this view of liberty, brethren, that liberty does not consist in doing what you please but in pleasing to do right. Liberty in the sense of arbitrary action does not exist. There is no such thing known in heaven or earth. There is no lawless particle in the material creation and no lawless thought. The more perfectly emancipated a man becomes from vice the more strict his adherence becomes to duty. The more perfect his freedom the more perfect his obedience, so that entire freedom is entire subjection.

> "— — — inspired by choice
> And conscious that the will is free
> Unswerving shall we move as if impelled
> By strict necessity along the path
> Of order and of good."[4]

But how then does it differ from mere subjection? How is the holy angel moving in the circle of his appointed duties better than the wretched victim of passion who walks in the chains of his own vices? Why herein; one acts with the whole consent of his own mind, the other is divided against self, that the one sees that his course is evil and hates and despises himself for being dragged along from sin to sin; the other sees that his course is wholly good;—all within him approves it; he acts with joy and exultation even before God. What if he feels that he is subject to a law? He is not a *servant,* he is a *son:* love has taken off the yoke and given him the spirit of adoption. He acknowledges that he lives not by himself, but by the Infinite Father, and to him he bows not by compulsion, but eager, trusting, devoted affection. His affection is inquisitive about its object. He believes there's more perfection than he understands. He opens his heart to receive more life. He perceives the great truth that God is in him, and that he is no longer his own; as he rids himself of his vices he becomes more and more instinct with life from the Vast Mind that animates and governs the whole Universe. Thus he becomes aware of the great sense of the passage, "God worketh in us both to will and to do of his good pleasure," and feels that what seemed to strike at human liberty becomes sovereignty. This service is perfect freedom.

Let me call your attention to one more distinction between the service of God and the service of sin. I shall do it in the remarkable words of an eminent foreign moralist.

"The most reckless sinner against his own conscience has always in the background the consolation that he will go on in this course only this time—or only so long—but that at such a time he will amend. We may be assured that we do not stand clear with our own consciences so long as we determine or intend or even hold it possible at some future time to alter our course of action. He who is certain of his own conduct, feels perfectly confident that he *cannot* change it,

---

4. Emerson misquotes William Wordsworth, *The Excursion,* IV, 1266-70.

nor the principles upon which it is founded, that on this point his freedom is gone,—that he is fixed forever in these resolves."[5]

This then is the liberty of the Sons of God. And now, brethren, I put it to you how far each of you have embraced the offer of salvation from the enemies of your spiritual country, the tyrants of your house, the destroyers of your peace, how far you have received the redeeming truths brought by Jesus Christ. It is a question growing in interest to you and me each hour we live whether we are free, because to work out our freedom is what God sent us here for. Only that soul is happy, is tranquil, is selfunited which is free. Examine your own heart. See whether you are master of your appetite. When you go to the family board to supply the wants of nature, consider whether you will transgress for a piece of bread. Then are you not free. Consider whether your lust has not enticed you to danger and ruin. Consider whether you ever speak falsely out of complaisance or the fear of man. Consider whether you indulge an illwill toward any brother and backbite his good name. Consider whether you have not put your free mind, your clean conscience, in bondage to your interest in your bargain. Consider if there is any prospect of gain which would tempt you to break the commandment. Consider whether you do not forbear the sincere actions to which your heart has often prompted you, whether you do not neglect your most generous sentiments and your wisest thoughts out of sloth or out of fear of the world. Then you are not free.

Come then let us gratefully go to the Son of God, the Redeemer, the Saviour. Let us learn of him to deny ourselves; to fear no man; to fear not death; but by following his great footsteps of humility, of justice, and of love, draw near in like manner to the throne of God; and feel that no longer we have a separate existence but that our will is swallowed up in his will, and that the words of St. Paul are verified—It is God that worketh in us both to will and to do of his good pleasure.

5. *Fichte* [Emerson's note]. This quotation occurs in "Specimens of German Genius, No. IV," *New Monthly Magazine* 29 (1830): 42; see *JMN* 6:107.

CXXV

*We know that all things work together
for good to them that love God.*

ROMANS 8:28

No one can read the epistles of St. Paul with attention without remarking that whilst they are written from and to persons whose condition was poor and despised, there is yet a strain of contentment, yea and of triumph running through them which is equally remote from the merriment of the frivolous, from the discontent of unfortunate and from the indifference of stupid persons. Poor and persecuted, hunted from city to city with stripes and tumults of the people, now imprisoned, now shipwrecked, in perils, in fasting, this brave follower of Christ opposes to all his unconquerable faith.[1] Not content with the hope of the next world he cheerfully claims all that is good in this. Godliness hath the promise of the life that now is and of that which is to come.[2]—If God be for us who can be against us?[3]—He glories not in his hopes alone or in the promises—We glory, he saith, in tribulations also.[4] And here in the text—We know that all things work together for good to them that love God.

This, brethren, has been the living principle that has kept Christianity alive so many ages. This is what it hath of divine. This is the seal and credentials it brings, that it is from God, and for the Soul. This strain suits our condition in the kingdom of God. It implies the great doctrine which Christianity declares in every truth that "no harm can befal the true disciple of Christ."

All things work together for good to them who love God. Let us see how far this will hold. All things work for good, nothing then works for evil. That is to say—No harm can befal a good man. I shall endeavor to illustrate the truth of this proposition.

Let it be considered that a good man is one thing and his fortunes or external condition quite another. The outward condition, the success or the miscarriage, is the crust or the shell, independent. The husks may be very coarse and meet

---

Manuscript dated August 28, 1831. Preached twice: August 28, 1831, at the Second Church, Boston, and November 27, 1836, in East Lexington.

1. Cf. II Corinthians 11:23-33.
2. I Timothy 4:8.
3. Romans 8:31.
4. Romans 5:3.

with rough usage too and the kernel within be very precious and very safe. Still he does much to form that crust. There it is true in the main, though it must be always received with qualification, that "every man is the architect of his own fortune." A man's condition depends very much upon his behaviour. If his situation is deplorable we suppose his conduct has not been wise and good. And yet I deny not that a man may be poor, and sick, and friendless, and deranged in his understanding who has not brought these evils upon himself, and this comes from causes that I shall presently consider. But in general I say, reserving the consideration of the exceptions—

I. The external welfare of a good man is not easily hurt. All things work together for good to him externally. It is agreed on the Exchange as well as in schools of morality 'that honesty is the best policy;' that industry will get on in this world faster than sloth; that temperance is more trusty than intemperance; and conciliatory manners better than violence.

Many of our misfortunes if we will deal honestly, we may trace back to our own imprudence or guilt. Have you lost the friendship of any worthy person? I suppose the fault is so far yours that it was in your power once to have preserved the confidence of that friend.

Have you lost your health? and are you sure that greater temperance might not have saved it? *Have you lost your reputation*? That is your own fault. For though it may be you are innocent of a crime or of crimes whereof you stand suspected, yet a good life such as you owed to God would have raised you above suspicion. Have you *lost property*? Consider if it was ever yours. It is very common for a person to appraise himself at a very high nominal value when really he is poor; for, the capital on which he reckons is really a borrowed one, and not the sweat of his own brow; or it is yet ventured in trade in hope of great returns at risks so great as in fact to be ruinous, and he was really poor, whilst he called himself rich. Or, if you once were rich, is it wholly the fault of the times that you are destitute? Would not a little more moderation in your desires have insured your wealth? Would not a little more knowledge or diligence which might have been acquired or used have insured it?

Take the world through, and I believe it will be found that a man who is very prudent, very honest, very diligent, very temperate, very amiable seldom or never fails in his business. Take the world through and such a man is far more likely to have health than a man of opposite qualities.

Such a man is sure to have a good name and influence among his fellowmen, and whatever else are the gifts of Providence are far more likely to be preserved by a man having these qualities than by one of opposite qualities. Yet must a man have all these qualities and more to constitute him a good man.

So that a good man can scarcely be hurt in his fortunes even; for they are made in obedience to the laws of God and so they stand by a divine strength.

The bad man on the contrary surrounds himself with distrust, hatred and contempt.

Certainly, I am not going to weaken the cause I plead by urging any overstatement. I do not deny that there is one event to the good and to the evil, that the same sun which scorches the field of the slothful scorches the good man's land, that the storm rends his ship, that fraud and violence do also afflict him as the knave and prodigal. But I wish to call your attention to the main reasons why he thus suffers and to the facts which are in their nature temporary and removeable. Most of the other causes of misfortune he is free from.

1. And the first is, he is obliged in the present state of society to depend much on bad men. It will be admitted, I suppose, that if all men were just men, commercial transactions would be carried on with much more security. But the necessary connexion and dependence of one man's affairs upon another's, make the honest man often the sufferer from the extravagance or the fraud of a third person which he could not foresee or prevent. So that this is a cause of injury to a good man, not resulting from the order of things as God made them, but from the depraved state of the world.

2. He is exposed to misfortune in the second place in common with other men by reason of his ignorance. A man sends out his ship into the sea and from ignorance of the coast it is lost; or from ignorance of the course of the currents and the prevalent winds it is delayed for months on the voyage; he uses a wrong diet in a new country, and falls a victim to a fever; his crop is cut off for want of knowing the habits of a worm, or the proper time of planting.

Every day we hear the observation; 'If I had known this fact at such a time, what losses, what disasters had I not been saved.' Now every year is increasing the dominion of man over nature and events by increasing science and as of all men so chiefly of the industrious and pure—of the good man who is always the candidate for knowledge.

So that the tendency of things is always to bring outward prosperity to the good according to the faith of David and of St. Paul.

In this manner, it will be seen the apostle had reason to say that godliness hath the promise of life that now is,—that all things work together for good for them that love God, even to the outward fortune.

And it is the perception of this fact that makes a great deal of the morality of men. This is the lowest degree of goodness—a subordinate and menial virtue— the practice of the laws of temperance, justice, industry and kindness not for their own sake but because they are the certain road to riches and honour. This is Prudence—a seeking of the good of the present estate. In the practices they enjoin, thus far the gospel and the wisdom of the world would perfectly coincide; but in the motive they would be wide asunder. For the man of the world is seeking worldly good as his end and the Christian is seeking the formation of his character as his end. The one is lost, if he loses his worldly good; the other never suffers with his fortunes, and though they perish he cannot be hurt; and this is the true meaning of the text.

II. No evil can befal a good man. Misfortune, we have admitted, can come to him as to others. His health or affections or power may suffer but with this difference from others, that he cannot be hurt. He bears a charmed life.[5] That which seems most hostile is as medicinal and wholesome to him as myrrh and salt. And this is highest sense of the doctrine of Paul. Goodness is invulnerable and what seems to threaten will only advance its good. Men in general seem to have some sense of this truth. A man whose soul is yet rude and unformed, who has nothing but wealth, in losing that, is said to be ruined. One who has nothing but bodily perfections, beauty and strength, as a wrestler or a belle—in losing them by disease or accident is said to be ruined. A general is said to be ruined when his military reputation is forfeited. But take the same things away from a great soul and it would not be ruined. But nobody would think of saying that Lafayette was ruined, because he had spent his property to establish the American and French Constitutions. No man would say that Socrates was ruined because he chanced to fall under the displeasure of his government or in the loss of health or reputation. Nor could St. Paul or St. John be ruined by all the poverty or persecution or torture or death that the malice of man could inflict. Their enemies beat the air.[6] These men are not animals but souls. The star that sets here rises as high on the other side. They have learned of their master that in order to rise in glory they must die in this world, that by suffering comes perfection.[7]

Let me show you how the soul purified and exalted by the principles of Christ is not to be injured but partakes of the Omnipotence of the Source of Goodness from whence it draws its supplies and like fire turns everything to its own nature. And as in our age the royal and imperial armies sent against the friends of freedom, when they approached them, cast down their colours and from enemies became friends, so do disasters of all kinds, as sickness, offence, poverty, bereavement prove unable to hurt the great spirit of a good man, but on the contrary are his instructers, comforters, and patrons.

Let there be a man who is penetrated with religious feeling, who has learned the difficult lessons of the discipline of the gospel.

His health is taken away—what is that to him but an advertisement that the beatitude of his nature draws near? He finds too that his thoughts of God give him the same or a sweeter satisfaction than formerly; that prayer has not lost its power; nor his affection for his friends abated. He is the same or hath more existence than before his body was weakened.

His property is taken away. He finds that half is better than the whole; that the care of money is taken with it; that his heart is not less large nor the satisfaction of kind feelings removed when the means of extended benefit are withdrawn. He finds that no part of his power or dignity is gone and he rejoices in the new perception of the soul's sufficiency.

He loses his friends. Do you think the faith of a Christian supplies no comfort

5. Shakespeare, *Macbeth*, V, viii, 12.
6. Cf. I Corinthians 9:26.
7. Cf. Hebrews 2:10.

here? He not only can say with the ancient patriarch, The Lord gave and hath taken and blessed be his name,[8] but he hath a faith beyond this—He believes not in death. The life of the soul satisfies his affection. The friend is not yet gone, is only veiled, perhaps is intimately present; and in the hour of solitude and silence something like society with the undying dead, is his solace and encouragement.

He is called to endure months of sickness. He sets himself with his whole soul to bear it well, and soon finds that strength is furnished to the humble mind according to its trial. And he looks upon that pain as the soldier looks at the strong frame of his conquered enemy, with new delight in his unexpected strength, acknowledging at the same time that his strength is from God. We have this treasure in earthen vessels that the excellency of the power may be of God and not of us.[9]

He is called to suffer disappointment, defeat, to uncommon degrees of obscurity and misfortune. He falls back on his faith in God. Do with me, he saith, even as thou wilt.[10]

He falls into temptation. Then he summons about him the invincible strength of his good thoughts, his dependence upon God, the intimate sight which God hath of every action, nay more, the stirring faith that every good man hath at the bottom of his soul, that he is not mortal, that he is not earthly, but draws his life from God; lives because God is within him and though now darkly and interruptedly seen,[11] yet every good thought and good work goes to dispel the clouds and darkness of his outer nature, and fill him with divine light. These thoughts are armies of angels which fight for him and resist temptation and then he rejoices in the beauty of right and the temptation which has once been resisted continually loses its force.

Thus doth pain, sickness, poverty, bereavement, temptation, prove unable to hurt the good man but all add to his strength and to his felicity. It is not so with the evil. As every event makes a good man better so it makes a bad man worse. Prosperity intoxicates him. Adversity sours him. He is full and denies God. He is poor and steals and takes his name in vain.

My friends, let us bring home this truth so full of comfort to our hearts. The character which the gospel aims to form in you, is the store of inexhaustible good. Every hour of this day and of every day, the years or months of life and the ages of eternity shall be your exercise in this truth that a soul governed by the principles of Jesus cannot be injured, and not only so but every event, seeming evil as well as good, brings new contribution to its peace and power.

8. Job 1:21.
9. II Corinthians 4:7.
10. Cf. Matthew 26:39.
11. Cf. Luke 17:21 and I Corinthians 13:12.

CXXVI

*Though a sinner do evil an hundred times
and his days be prolonged, yet surely I
know that it shall be well with them
that fear God.*

ECCLESIASTES 8:12

The author of the book of Ecclesiastes is a man of a melancholy and skeptical mind, who turning over in his thoughts the various fortunes of men in his experience, seems to be shaken by the observation that one event happens to all, to the good and the sinner,[1] and so is ever ready to conclude with the sensual that a careless and merry life is most coincident with reason and facts. But always, just as he reaches this conclusion, he is checked by a stronger impulse from his own heart, and contradicts his hasty thought by a sound judgment. His head brings him more arguments against Providence than his head can answer, but his heart controls his decision. Better is an untimely birth than the most prosperous of the children of men. As is the good so is the evil, and he that sweareth as he that feareth an oath. Eat thy bread. Walk in the ways then of thy heart and in the sight of thine eyes, *but know thou that for all these things God will bring thee into judgment.*[2]

There are times when every man takes the same gloomy view, feels the sentiment of St. James, What is our life but a vapor that appeareth for a little time?[3] Enter into it; follow hotly its objects, and it seems how real and minute in detail, but retire from it a little, and its solidest things seem pictures, and its most agitating struggles a delusion, and the very houses, and towns, and the globe itself in which we live, seem to have no more fixed existence than the rainbow that lasts half an hour upon a cloud.[4] And this it is, that casts a gloom over the hearts of men. This flitting frailty, this near expectation, after a few suns have risen and set, or a few winters have come and gone, of ceasing to be, withers the

---

Manuscript dated September 10, 1831. Preached twice: September 11, 1831, at the Second Church, Boston, and February 2, 1834, in New Bedford.

1. Ecclesiastes 2:14.
2. Ecclesiastes 9:2, 9:7, 11:9.
3. James 4:14.
4. Cf. William Shakespeare, *The Tempest,* IV, i, 148–56.

courage of the stoutest and turns pale the most cheerful cheek. It is felt as an inevitable evil winding into every part of human fortune. The youth exults in his advancing freedom till reason tells him that life wears out with youth. The landlord rejoices in his quarter day till he remembers that he has three moons less to live, that the years steal not his riches from him but him from his riches, for it is certain he shall carry nothing out of the world.[5] Indeed is it not matter of familiar observation that it makes a man grave to be reminded that he is growing old? And so it ought, and to terrify him unless at the same pace he is growing wise and virtuous; but if he is, he should bid the years speed, and smile with serenity at their flight, for he does not belong to any brief duration, but to God's time, whose moments are centuries, and the age of the heavens its morning prime, the same yesterday and forever and an eternal now.[6]

Men fear death because they love life. The rich and prosperous wonder what charm life has to the sons and daughters of poverty, who are deprived of almost all the joys which they value. But life's simplest pleasures are the best. The humblest laborer says truly, that life is sweet to him. Gloomy to him it seems to depart from the pleasant day-light and all his homely gratifications, from the joyful sense of vigor with which he starts from his bed in the morning; the moment's greeting he gives to the sun which contains perhaps a pious thought to the maker of the sun and of man; the relish of the repast eaten for strength in the morning of a working day; the pleasures of work itself,—for God has connected a delight with the exercise of every talent whether of the brain or the fingers; the consciousness of trustworthiness and respectability that accompanies patient labors; the sense of power which the mind derives from the fact that from a lot so hard it can draw out sweetness, (as those flowers please the eye best that grow on a rock); the regular action of the animal system giving health to the nerves and marrow to the bones; the equal ground of good humor and independence on which the laborer meets his fellow men; the satisfaction with which he returns under his own roof, greeted by smiles, a benefactor, a father, the giver of life a second time in daily bread; the manifold pleasures of conversation; and all the enjoyments of a growing experience; his skill in the politics of his country, in the history of families, and the fortunes of particular persons; and beyond and above all this whatever deep sentiment, whatever ardent love has enlightened and beautified his humble house; whatever good deeds he had done or good purposes he had set himself—to leave this wondrous web unfinished and at the time when it had grown to the largest extent—to go away he knows not where—but assured by the unvarying experience of millions of millions of fellow beings, that it is to close his connexion with earthly things forevermore—gloomy it is to him. It is sinking into an abyss their thoughts have never fathomed. They will not hover over and pry into that abyss until they are forced into it, and so it seems to them a land of horror.

5. I Timothy 6:7.
6. Cf. Hebrews 13:8 and II Peter 3:8.

Well now what relief did the human mind seek in all the ages of human history from this gloom? The idea of a future life has always been known.[7] It is like the idea of God which enters the human soul in all circumstances the moment it reaches a certain degree of cultivation. It is in it, and comes out, we know not how. It is true, some very obscure and absurd notions prevail among the vulgar in every nation, and among reflecting and good persons they become pure.

Let me enumerate briefly the observations on which this expectation seems to be founded.

In the first place all reflecting persons admit as a most important preliminary statement that it was originally more incredible that such beings as we should exist out of nothing, as we now do exist, than it is now that we should continue to live in another state. The lion and the bee and the whole brute creation arrive at once at the perfection of their faculties.[8] But man never arrives at the perfection of his faculties, but every step of his progress every day he lives only shows him how much more is to be known and done, that is to say, carries onward still farther the perfection of his being. He goes on increasing every day and at last all his acquisitions become only a starting post for new progress, until the decay of his body first retards and then interrupts the course of the mind by old age, sickness, death. Is it probable that having entered on this magnificent career with such advantages it is brought thus early to a final close?

Whence this difference between man and animals and what cruelty was it that revealed a perfection which in vain he seeks to reach?

Whence this unceasing education of man but because he is to be instructed by yet greater revelations?

2. An affecting argument that has led the mind in all ages to believe in its own perpetuity, is the observation that in nature nothing is lost;—that of the water that is spilled on the ground no drop is wasted, but it is received and used in the earth, then taken up again by evaporation, and circulates through the system of the world doing service wherever it goes; and so it is with every grain of sand, every globule of gas, every mote—nothing is lost; all is strictly economized by the frugality of nature. And shall we suppose amidst all this care that the capital work of works, a rational human soul, accomplished with so many powers, and with all its affections, the only intelligent being that appears in the world,— shall we suppose that this is lost, and goes out like the snuff of a candle, into useless and endless night?

3. But to include many arguments in one, I mention thirdly that all the proofs

7. Emerson seems to be reflecting Coleridge's position in *Aids to Reflection,* ed. James Marsh (Burlington, Vt., 1829), 209-10, that the doctrine of a future life is shared by all religions and is not unique to Christianity; see Kenneth Walter Cameron, *Emerson the Essayist* (Raleigh, N.C., 1945), 1:135.

8. Emerson's source for his comment on "the whole brute creation" may have been his gleanings from Coleridge's remarks on, among other scientists, eminent entomologists in *Aids to Reflection* (Burlington, Vt., 1829), 138-39; see Cameron, *Emerson the Essayist,* 1:89 and 1:166-67.

of God with which the Universe is filled, are proofs to a pious mind of its own immortal life. As soon as it believes in God it feels that his justice is holden to fulfil, as it has been termed, the promise of the faculties. Because we then come to see that this obstinate persuasion of the human soul through ages and nations of its great destination is the witness of God himself in us. When the mind is once satisfied of the being of God its anxieties about itself subside at once into an unlimited trust that all will be well with them who love God.

This leads me to speak of the doctrine as a revealed doctrine. There is something quite peculiar in the manner in which Christianity *brought immortality to light,*[9] as we say. Jesus, armed with miracles, teaches distinctly and with authority the immortality of the soul,—not a mystical existence of the soul absorbed into God, as some of the philosophers said; nor of resurrection after an interval of death, but a continuance of the individual being. God is the God of Abraham, he saith, and of Isaac, and of Jacob; and to him they live, i.e., Abraham as Abraham, and Isaac as Isaac.[10] This is plain. This is what we want.

But observe the fact that this information goes no further. It is most remarkable in this revelation that it has not answered one of the questions so embarrassing, concerning the state, and laws, and employments of a disembodied soul; its modes of action, and society, nor presented any interior view of the soul's abode. More than this, it does not insist explicitly and in the manner of declaring a doctrine hitherto unknown, on the fact itself that the soul shall live again. It is *incidentally* taught in the discourses of Jesus, as well as in the recorded sermons of the Apostles and in the Epistles. But instead of the express affirmation of this momentous truth and instead of gratifying the curiosity of the mind on all these points, what does it say? Repent, and be converted; love God; love thy brother; trample on your lusts; live above the world; redeem the time; be just; be merciful; put off the lower nature, put on the higher nature.[11] Here is all the emphasis, and you are left to make the inference, the assurance of life eternal involved in these instructions. And it is true that these precepts are given with an air of passion and triumph as if they were themselves the annunciation of the splendid truth, as if they were themselves the consolation and the power and the happiness which the heart of man sought in a gospel opening the future life.

Now, brethren, I suppose there is a deep wisdom, a faithful truth in this mode of making known this great fact. First; I suppose it never was meant to be communicated or received as a splendid and solitary truth that the soul should exist for ages of ages; it was not meant to be taught that bare existence was a blessing—a vast waste of unprofitable time, but always this truth was to be communicated in connexion with or rather as subordinate to the lesson of the soul's duties. Duty is the object of the soul, and the question in their minds is

---

9. II Timothy 1:10.

10. Much of this paragraph also appears in Sermon XCIV; see n. 5 there.

11. Acts 3:19, Luke 10:27, Galatians 5:16, Matthew 5:14, Ephesians 5:16, Philippians 4:8, Matthew 5:7, and Romans 8:9-10.

not how long we must live but how much is to be done. Not a single allusion is made by Jesus or by Paul to the idea of simple eternity; they dwelt so fervently on the actual progress of the soul, its sanctification, its redemption from lust, and pride, and hatred, and avarice, and falsehood; and its edification in love, humility, pureness, and simplicity, that they only perceived the duration by implication in the divine nature of these things. They wish to have it understood that it is to the mind as it becomes good, not as it lives longer, as it approaches God, not as it dies out of this world, that the revelation is made, that Time shall be no more.[12]

With regard to the other fact just now noticed that no account is given of the mode of being hereafter, I suppose it is because it would be of no use and probably is impossible that we should anticipate knowledge of this sort. That state is only to be known by being in it. The wiser sort of men have always inclined to the belief that it was a continuance not a contrast of this life. In the language of the noblest of Christian poets,

> "What if Earth
> Be but a shadow of heaven, and things therein
> Each to other like, more than on earth is thought?"[13]

Thus, brethren, the gospel teaches us, as the author of Ecclesiastes, not a direct assurance of life to come, but a direct assurance that we must keep the commandments and indirectly that we shall live. Surely I know it shall be well with them that fear God. Let us not then be greedy of life, but of living well. Let us cease to mourn for those who are gone to God; and let us not fear death ourselves, or prepare *to die,* but let us receive the great truth that the good never die, and let us awake to life. We are taught that because we have uses, great and endless uses, we have such a period. Whilst we fulfil them with a perfect love, that love shall cast out the fear of death.[14] Some Christians have believed, and as it seems to me with reason, that evil men fear to die in the spiritual world as much as they do in the natural world, not being conscious of any connexion with God.

Let us then draw this instruction from the gospel, no longer to look forward to a dubious future but feeling that the future is like the present, that what is true and good and beautiful now, will be true and good and beautiful forever, that the Eternity of God makes all things in heaven and earth the same, and that the whole of object of all being is usefulness; and whilst we pursue that singly, it will include life and happiness. Seeing all this let us begin to live now by exciting our faculties and exerting our virtues. Let me repeat to you the simple language of the moral poet—

12. Revelation 10:6.
13. John Milton, *Paradise Lost,* V, 574–76.
14. Cf. I John 4:18.

"Knowst thou Yesterday, its aim and reason
Work'st thou well Today, for worthy things
Then calmly wait Tomorrow's hidden season
And fear not thou, what hap so e'er it brings."[15]

It only echoes the language of the apostle, 'Now is the accepted time, now is the day of salvation.'[16] Godliness hath the promise of the life that now is and of that which is to come.[17]

15. Emerson evidently copied these lines from Thomas Carlyle's "Signs of the Times," *Edinburgh Review* 49 (June, 1829): 439, where they appear without attribution.
   16. II Corinthians 6:2.
   17. I Timothy 4:8.

CXXVII

For whosoever shall keep the whole law,
and yet offend in one point,
he is guilty of all.

JAMES 2:10

This text has been sometimes quoted in support of the extravagant opinion that there are no degrees in guilt; that vanity or excessive amusement or petty fraud are as bad as murder; that every man is a sinner or a saint. I suppose I need not insist on the falsehood of these doctrines.

What then is the true meaning of the passage? I understand St. James to declare, that, no virtue is found alone, and no vice is found alone, but virtue is joined with virtue, and vice with vice, so strictly, that he who has one good quality has more, and he who has one bad quality has more. For God is the author of the whole law, and he who is not deterred by the love of Him from breaking one commandment will not be deterred from breaking another whenever inclination and opportunity offer.

The unity of God has always been taught by the unity of design that reigns in all nature. It is because the author is one that every eye sees and every heart feels the harmony and relation of all the parts, of each to the other and of the mind of man to all. A sublime evidence of his Unity comes up from the strict correspondence of the outward to the intellectual world and of every truth to every other truth. There is a common bond betwixt the sciences and betwixt the arts; and so there is betwixt spiritual truths and betwixt the virtues, betwixt the virtues and the physical well being of man.[1]

All truth is related. The whole creation seems to be bound in so strict an unity that there is not an atom but has relation to all other atoms, is affected by all the laws of the whole, and is a sort of miniature and emblem of the whole. Thus take a pebble from the ground, and learn all that is true concerning it, and you would be an accomplished natural philosopher; nay, there is not science enough in the world to tell half that is true of a body so little. Who can tell me

---

Manuscript dated September 18, 1831. Preached six times: September 18, 1831, at the Second Church, Boston; March 2, 1834, at the Federal Street Church, Boston; March 9 in New Bedford; August 24 in Waltham; April 10, 1836, in East Lexington; and July 24 in Concord, Mass. Notes and draft passages for this sermon occur in *JMN* 3:281 and 283–84.

1. Canceled passages in the manuscript indicate that Emerson's source was Cicero.

what the light is, that shines upon it? Who can tell me what is the electric spark that can be drawn from its surface? Who can tell me why it falls to the earth? how old it is? how long it will last in its present form, and what will become of its particles when they separate? Every atom in the universe attracts every other atom. Who can measure the quantity of attraction that joins this pebble to the sun, or this pebble to the remotest star?—yet is that attraction as real, as its relation to the earth, or of one of its atoms to another. Oh no, 'What we know is a point to what we do not know,'[2] and if we could tell the history of one particle, we should know the history of all things. When Vanini was about to be burned for atheism he picked out a straw from the pile and declared that if it had been possible for him to doubt the existence of God the wisdom shown in the arrangement of that little structure would have demonstrated the fact.[3] It is from observing this intimate union that runs through all things, that a celebrated foreign teacher, in our own times, has built his system of instruction on this maxim, 'All is in all,' and requires of his pupils to learn something thoroughly— to study a single object in all its relations no matter what—and to refer every thing else to that, as if the principles of all things were contained in each one.[4]

And it is because this is so, that men grown up in so many different families and circumstances, can yet understand each other, and believe the same thing; for I suppose it will be allowed by all that we agree in far more things than we differ. And why? not because our circumstances have not been very different, but because all circumstances teach the same thing, give the same education. So true is this, that if you run over in your thoughts the names of those persons who have most fully sympathized with your opinions and feelings you will probably find they were not educated at your side, but in quite different circumstances— in different business, different constitution, other habits, other country; which shows, that the most diverse experience has read each of us the same lesson; and the deeper the thoughts the closer the coincidence we observe between them and those of other men. Indeed the fact is familiar to all that every man's trade or profession in the course of its processes furnishes him with an illustration of the same general truths, the sailor, as every one knows, drawing his illustrations of human character and human fortune from what he has observed in nautical life; and the farmer in like manner from his experience in agriculture. Thus is all truth related; a wonderful unity prevails in all that we behold. The law of God is every where the same. The law of God as it is observed in the intellect is truth; as it is chosen in the will is virtue.

2. Bishop Joseph Butler, as quoted in Robert Plummer Ward, *Tremaine,* 3 vols. (Philadelphia, 1825), 3:125-26. See *JMN* 6:64 and *Sermons* (1:283); used in "General Views" (*EL* 2:358), *Nature* (*CW* 1:25), and "Immortality" (*W* 8:341).

3. Lucilio (or Giulio Cesare) Vanini (1585-1619), Italian disciple of Averroë's and Pomponazzi and a victim of the Inquisition. Emerson may have read of Vanini in Victor Cousin, *Fragmens Philosophiques* (Paris, 1826). For the anecdote, see John Owen, *The Skeptics of the Italian Renaissance* (London, 1908), 396-97.

4. The allusion is to Johann Heinrich Pestalozzi. Emerson was reading Edward Biber's *Henry Pestalozzi and His Plan of Education* (London, 1831) in preparation for Sermon CXXVIII.

In following out the sentiment of St. James let us separate the two considerations; 1. That one truth prepares the way for all truth; 2. That one virtue prepares the way for all virtue.

I. It is because of this wonderful connexion and unity which reigns in all things, that no truth stands alone, but leads directly to the knowledge of other truths. Very slow and painful is the progress of the mind in truth. How little does each man discover for himself and how slowly he learns what is already known. Yet is all acquired by this law, that every truth which he receives prepares the way for other truth of which he is yet ignorant. All our learning advances step by step, what goes before making room for that which follows. So is every resolute searcher of truth a benefactor to men to a far greater extent than his own eye can see, for he is bringing them to a spiritual country which he is not permitted to behold.[5] The great saints and reformers of the Christian Church whilst they proclaimed to their times the new truths that filled them with joy, could not see the farther conclusions to which those truths would lead men in after generations. And yet were they the parents of our spiritual faith, because we see the relation that subsists between our teaching and theirs.

We never fully comprehend any one truth in all its height and depth. If we did, we should comprehend all. But the partial views we obtain of one truth, obtain for us a partial view of all the related truths which come in with it hand in hand. This gives an infinite value to every truth, that you are not only learning it, but you are learning a great deal more, introducing the leaders of an endless procession.

Especially is this manifest in spiritual truth. A clear perception of God's character or dealings, one just view of our own condition, of the way in which we are growing worse, or the way in which we must grow better, one true glance at the real heaven of goodness and the hell of selfishness,—casts at once a strong light through all the recesses of the mind, over all we know, and all we think, and does more to set us in the right road, than all the books upon human nature and human duty. This then is the reward and encouragement of every patient follower of truth, that his progress is indefinitely increased at every step—that the value of every fact depends upon the amount of his knowledge, for it throws back light upon all that he knows, and opens an unlimited series of new objects before him.

II. My second point is that as truths so neither do virtues stand alone but that every virtue you practise prepares the way for other virtues which you do not practise, that progress in any one virtue cannot be made without drawing with it a progress in all.

How stands the fact in your observation of men? If you were searching for an eminent example of excellence in any one virtue, as for a truly humble man or a truth-speaker or a charitable or a selfdenying or a just man, in what class of persons would such virtues be most surely found? Would it be among persons

5. An allusion to Moses, who was, however, permitted to behold Canaan (Deuteronomy 4).

who possessed the single virtue in question and were at the same time notorious for gross vices? If a man is marked for his true modesty is he usually dishonest? If he is scrupulously just is he likely to be intemperate? If he is of a pure mind will he be a liar or spiteful or covetous? On the contrary would not the individuals whom you would select as models of one virtue be found the possessors of much general excellence?

Is it not true in all our observation and experience that all the virtues mutually commend each other and commit the lover of one to the practice of all? There is in every generous mind a stimulus that gains strength by every exertion that prompts the soul to keep its virtue in repair by refreshing old merits with new ones.

And an act of great merit creates a sort of noble obligation under which the actor lies to all who behold and love his action that he will persevere and better it.

So obvious is this connexion of the virtues that some moralists have resolved all the duties of man into a single law, as that of justice or benevolence or enlightened self-love, for a man cannot be wholly just without fulfilling all duties; nor perfectly benevolent, nor true to self-good without complying with all the law.

For this fact that the virtues are generally found in company and not single and that the better knowledge and practice of one grace creates the power and the disposition to excel in every grace, there are two reasons: 1. because there is a natural connexion between virtuous *actions* on the one hand and between vicious actions on the other; 2. because there is a connexion of *principles* inasmuch as the right motive to one virtue is an equal motive to all the virtues.

1. There is a natural connexion between virtuous actions on the one hand and between vicious actions on the other. No one can doubt this who observes how fast in this world the virtues fortify themselves with external aids. A man who has exerted himself in any good cause is by that act thrown into association with all who esteem the same cause. He becomes pledged by his standing, by his associates, by his desire of confirming and advancing one good end, to labor for all good that is similar and congenial.

Everything in human nature is progressive: the bad to worse, the good to better.[6]

Besides to whatever good work a man may have committed himself he speedily finds that it is promoted by other excellent habits. He wants time for his work. Then he must rise early, and live abstemiously and guard his day and his life from unnecessary engagements, which are steps to the highest prudence and involve the whole Education of the Will. He must secure cooperation to his plan and this leads him into the most benevolent relations to fellowmen. A continual desire to fortify one's position to produce the full effect of the virtue we prefer leads directly to acts and forbearances which make demand on all the

6. Emerson's concise adaptation of Coleridge's definition of "Method" as "progressive arrangement" (Samuel Taylor Coleridge, *The Friend,* in *The Complete Works,* ed. W. G. T. Shedd [New York, 1853], 2:408–17). See *JMN* 3:299 and 6:222.

Christian circle. Every virtue precludes some temptations that oppose other virtues. Temperance makes purity easier. Industry repels all temptations.

It is very certain that one vice is a door to all the rest. What is the cause of all the dishonesty which produces so much suffering? There are those who will tell you that they could not get their bread if they did not use the petty frauds, the overstatements that are permitted in trade, so that the hard question seems to be between dishonesty and starvation. But if you search to the bottom you may find that not necessity but intemperance or sloth or cupidity or the love of display is the true cause of his being forced, as he says, to these arts.

Every one knows how fast the vices slide into each other. Envy leads to slander, slander to cowardice. Robbery often needs the seal of murder. Lust must have hypocrisy to shield it. Lies, according to the vulgar proverb, have no legs.[7] Fraud is patched up by perjury.

So on the other hand all the virtues are faithful allies to each other. Innocence is a protection. Truth is brave. Love is pure and generous and faithful. And from one good action a man finds his way open and easy to many so that it was anciently said, "When once a man has chosen noble ends then not virtues but divinities throng around him."[8]

He feels that the same love compels him to be just, that compels him to be kind; to be self denying as to speak the truth; to worship God, as to flee his lusts. And so Jesus who was the most meek was the most devoted; whilst the most thoughtful, was most active; asking nothing of others he yet indulged not himself; the most highly gifted, was the servant of all; and whilst he fulfilled the circle of the virtues, he taught men they should be perfect as God is perfect.[9]

The practical conclusion to which I come, then, is, that whilst it will not do to take any motive less than the highest, we may take advantage of this wonderful connexion of the virtues in concentrating our attention to a single work. Each of us, my friends, is, I suppose, by natural temper, or by circumstances, or by past sin, more exposed to the assaults of some one wrong desire than of others. We each of us have a bosom sin. It will be enough if with all our heart we set ourselves to fight this one. In the best of us, I fear, it will need all the strength we can command, and all the aid we can implore, to get a victory over that one. We must go for light to the bible, and study the precepts and the example of Christ and walk reverently and filially before the Father of us all. But whatever be your trial, rejoice in the sublime faith that whilst you have this motive, every step is a progress to all perfection.

7. See Sermon XCIX, n. 3.
8. Cf. "'Tis a noble but a true word of Bacon [in *De Augmentis Scientiarum*]—If once the mind has chosen noble ends, then not virtues but Divinities encompass it" (*JMN* 3:266–67). See the editors' notes to "Around the man who seeks a noble end," in *The Poetry Notebooks of Ralph Waldo Emerson*, ed. Ralph H. Orth et al. (Columbia, Mo., 1986), 735.
9. Cf. Matthew 5:48.

CXXVIII _____

Train up a child in the way he should go,
and when he is old he will not depart from it.

PROVERBS 22:6

I cannot help offering my congratulations to the honoured members of this charitable society whose thirty first anniversary we this day celebrate upon the wisdom with which they have selected the object of their benevolence. Whilst most of our duties lie at our door and are not to be chosen, a certain extent of choice is allowed us in regard to others. Whilst we owe the duty of kindness to all our fellow men, we are left at liberty to select for ourselves those few whom we are willing to engage in a strict friendship.

And whilst the crowd of benevolent projects with which the world teems demand our sympathy and respect, every one must select particular claims. And there is no charity of stronger claim, or more deeply concerning the wellbeing of the state, or of dearer interest to a good mind than that which has received your care. If the two hundred orphan children that have been trained by you in the way in which they should go, since 1801, had been left to grow up, the most part of them in the greatest dangers to which female weakness can be exposed, and all in extreme want and ignorance, who can estimate the amount of sin and suffering that had ensued?

It is indeed a noble work you have chosen,—but I need hardly tell you, it is a great responsibility you have assumed. Every thing that can affect the character has a high importance in the eyes of a Christian; but the charge of directing the minds of the young into the right road, and so of beginning for them courses that shall never end, is as grave a trust as any human being can assume. This subject comes so forcibly to the mind in connexion with your institution that I believe I need no apology for asking your attention to a few observations upon the objects of Education, and the manner in which they must be attained.

What is Education and how is it to be directed?

Manuscript dated September 23, 1831. Preached twice: September 23, 1831, at the First Church, Boston, and October 31 in Derry, N.H. Draft passages for this sermon occur in *JMN* 3:282 and 286. In the course of composing this sermon, on September 20 Emerson raised the following questions, which he subsequently answered in the sermon: "Is there not an education independant of the accomplishments? Is there not the making the moral agent an act? Is there not humility, gentleness, firmness, selfdenial, truth, sincerity[?]" (*JMN* 3:286). The occasion for the first delivery of this sermon was the celebration of the anniversary of the Boston Female Asylum, an orphanage.

I begin by repeating an observation that cannot, I think, be set in too strong a light, that *the accomplishments which are commonly taught children,* that reading, writing, ciphering, geography, chemistry and (in your institution what is added for girls) needlework and housework *are not an education but the means of education.* Let it be distinctly considered that all these accomplishments are wholly outward. They are the armour and not the man. They do nothing to explain their own use. They make the child learned and not wise.

If your instruction stops here, it is as if you gave a child a fortune, but gave him no discretion how he should spend it. It is as if you lengthened the child's arms, or nerved his hands, but did not teach him how to use them. A mere addition of skill in any or all these branches of knowledge does not give the slightest security that the child shall do well, that the child shall serve God and not Mammon.[1] They may be, and frequently are turned to bad account. A very fraudulent person may cipher well. A forger writes well. Many a sinner reads but too well in bad books. And it may be the effect of a too exclusive attention to the outer faculties of one of your pupils, that when she is grown up, she shall be a fairfaced enemy, an ingenious liar, a very dexterous cheat, or elegantly licentious,—which God forbid.

In saying therefore that this learning is overestimated, I do not depreciate the value of what are called the common branches—surely not—whilst *the first things,* the things needful are done I would not have these left undone. I only would have it felt, that they are subordinate; that they presuppose something else which, omitted, makes them worthless, and perhaps worse. You cannot forget that ages have rolled away and states of society passed in which noble men and women flourished, and exhibited great virtues, when these parts of learning now so indispensable were not possessed at all, or were confined to very few. The wives of the patriarchs of the ancient world were worthy women but could not read, or write, or cipher, and in geography, in which our children are so fluent, the greatest part of the globe, and the form itself of the globe was unknown to them. What renowned women,—very models of heroic virtue— have come down to us in the history of Sparta,—a people very rude in letters!

The fact is that there is an education wholly independent of these, a training of the mind itself, and where a good mind is formed, it will always clothe itself, as of course, in this learning, as the body clothes itself in the costume of the time and country in which we are born. I say therefore the accomplishments which are taught children with so much care and pains are not enough, will not serve them, are only exercises of the faculties but not an instruction that orders and illuminates the faculties themselves.

True Education is, as the name imports, a drawing out of the Soul itself. It is the awakening in their right order the natural powers of man. It has for its end not to add something to the soul but to make the soul itself expand. (As the parent bird does not carry the young on its back but teaches it to fly.) It goes on

1. Matthew 6:24 and Luke 16:13.

the presumption that the mind was made not to be a dependant, but to be free. It aims not to make a useful disciple, but to bring out in the mind a self-determining power. And so its main labor is bent, not to make the pupil docile and apt to put trust in other people, but to teach him his own strength, and to constitute the child a good man, or a good woman,—a judge of truth and falsehood, right and wrong, seeing with his own eyes, and acting from his own will.

This education recognizes that the soul is made up of two parts; reason and affection, or the mind and the heart. And in blending the action and nurture of both, it never forgets that true wisdom comes more from the heart than from the head.

Under the light of Christianity it is the aim of education to convince the child in its own experience that truth is better than falsehood; that kindness is better than selfishness; that it is better to be useful than useless; to make known to the young learner by his own consciousness, the unmeasured extent of powers of his own soul; and when he first feels the awful delight of this possession, to unfold to him that it is God who gave, nay, who is now giving its powers, to make him feel that goodness and truth have never been left alone in the world, but that God always provides for the instruction and salvation of his youngest child; that Jesus Christ was born and died to teach and save it, and to spread out before its wondering eye the sublime employment and opportunities of an endless duration.

It will be observed that the discipline of which I speak goes behind all that is commonly reckoned education in schools, and this discipline is fit and necessary for *every mind;* this is what must be taught previous to all consideration of the child's sex or condition, whether it shall command or obey, whether it is to study or to trade—whether it shall roll in riches, or beg its bread. This education goes on the presumption that God has ordained every creature he has made *for some use,* and this is to enable the child to show *what he was made for,* and to take that place.

But how is this education to be given?

1. By *negative provisions,* if I may so call them; by removing all impediments and all injurious influences as far as we can from the child, by secluding it from gross temptations, and bad language, and bad example, by supplying it with food and clothes and occupying its mind and hands; in short by keeping it out of harm's way, by doing what this Institution has done so carefully for these orphans. But there is a limit beyond which these precautions are not possible, and again a limit beyond which they are not wise.

For they cannot wholly keep out temptations. These leap over the wall, and join the children in their playground, and in the schoolroom, and at their household work, and in their morning meal. And if now they are exposed in your guarded retreat, what shall save them when they come out into unprotected places and duties, at a tender age, when there is none to answer for them but themselves, none to advise, none to warn, none to forbid the consequences of their own ignorance or folly or guilt from falling upon them?

Therefore you must not be content with negative provisions; you must give them actual strength. Otherwise you are doing them an injury in giving them crutches to lean upon, instead of teaching them how to stand and walk when the crutches shall be plucked away. Lest I should seem not to give sufficient importance to the excellent means you have here provided, let me quote to you the memorable words of the ardent friend of education, Henry Pestalozzi, who after having long endeavoured to change the characters of children by altering their situation, declared his solemn conviction in 1797, "that the amelioration of outward condition will be the effect, but never can be the means of mental and moral improvement."[2]

2. You must therefore add *positive provisions,* must give them instruction and practice in judging rightly and in acting well. You must aim to give them this inward strength by *actually possessing them with love,* and faith, and resolution. It will not do to cleanse the outside of the cup.[3] There must be more than the forms of education,—there must be the substance. And in order to do this, there must be a close companionship between the teacher and the child. To teach children, you must have the love of children. A good teacher must be the child's friend. A faithful instruction is like those sorts of work which cannot be done by machinery, but must be done *by hand.* Arithmetic and grammar may be taught well enough in classes but the moral discipline to be effectual must be given to each particular child. You must go and sit down with the child and win its love as well as command its respect. You must establish a living tie, a personal relation between you and it. You must make her see the good of order in her own little experience. You must lead the child to little acts of self denial on her own part, that she may feel its beauty. Her charity must always cost her something. They must see the majesty—let me call it—of telling the truth, and keeping their word. Nothing is unimportant. You must bear in mind the well-known fact that is little remembered, that the plays of children are not done in play, but are their most earnest work. And they must be shown that their sports are, as it were, recitations, where their principles must be practised.

But this teaching must be real and not verbal, after your experience, and not after books. And let me affectionately press it upon all those who have the government and instruction of children, that you must make them see and feel

2. Edward Biber, *Henry Pestalozzi and His Plan of Education* (London, 1831), 23; see *JMN* 3:286. This is the earliest edition of Biber's biography in English, and in Pocket Diary I Emerson included it in a list of books he wished to purchase; see *JMN* 3:347–48. However, since he withdrew the volume from the Boston Athenaeum March 23–May 8, 1832, he evidently had access to the book from another source during his preparation of this sermon. His first extended acquaintance with the work of the Swiss educator Johann Heinrich Pestalozzi (1746-1827) probably came from his reading of Mme. de Staël's *Germany,* in which Pestalozzi and Rousseau are treated comparatively.

3. Cf. Matthew 23:25.

that the being of God is a source of comfort, and pleasing thoughts and of commanding motives to you; that it is never absent from you, and that you are afraid of nobody so much as of yourself, that your own eyes are guards enough upon your hands and feet. They must see your hands make the commentary on your words. They must work with you and see and taste of your peace, and then *they have got something in them,* and can be trusted by themselves.

Let it not be objected to the application of these remarks, as it is sometimes said by teachers—Why, this is true, but these children are too young. They are not too young. No children are too young who have seen one summer and one winter, to receive a moral or an immoral impression. The only way to be safe, and begin early enough, is never to permit any other than a right impression to be given. It is recorded to the honour of that wonderful people, the ancient Spartans, that when Antipater would make a treaty with them, and demanded fifty children for hostages, they made answer that they would rather give him twice as many grown men, so much did they value the loss of their country's education to their infant children. And let that be the praise of this institution, that it secures to society whatever good it attempts by being beforehand with the enemy, by preventing with good the approach of evil. It is one of the most beautiful anecdotes in the life of Pestalozzi, that after he was compelled by misfortunes, to give up his asylum, which he had established for destitute children in his own house at Newhof, he yet comforted himself that all was not lost, that the seeds of knowledge and virtue had been planted in the breasts of a hundred poor children, go where they might in the mountains of Switzerland, and he calmly trusted their timely growth with God. And his confidence was as just as it was sublime.[4] "Never was a sincere word utterly lost."[5] And no work of true hearted kindness done to these little ones entirely fails of effect. It is present when you are absent. It is remembered when you think it forgotten. And when it cannot prevent a crime, it lessens it, or follows offence with repentance.

Neither let it be objected that these children are poor, and from the disposition that is to be made of them when they leave the Institution, are likely to remain poor. The education which I speak of, is anterior in the order of God to all circumstances, and will fit the soul alike to bear the extremes of good or ill as a rational being,—will fit your orphan to suffer with dignity, and do her duty though a bedridden patient in an alms house, if God in his Providence should appoint her to that condition.

But it may seem to you a question fit to be asked—Who is sufficient for these things?[6]—Where are the teachers? We can all point out defects in present systems—We can all say what it would be desirable to do—But who is competent to train a child, and, much more, sixty children in the way in which they should go? I know it is very difficult. I believe there is required a genius for instruction,

4. Biber, *Pestalozzi*, 52.
5. Mme. de Staël, *Germany* (London, 1813), 3:401. See *JMN* 6:61, 6:157; used in Sermon VIII (*Sermons* 1:112), "Religion" (*EL* 2:95) and "Spiritual Laws" (*CW* 2:92).
6. II Corinthians 2:16.

as much as genius for painting, and it is quite as rare. Yet many benefactors have arisen to the human race in our times. Bell and Lancaster, Miss Edgeworth, Mrs. Barbauld, Pestalozzi—might set us in the right way.[7] Read the life of Pestalozzi, or rather read in your own heart the love, which was Pestalozzi's teacher, and it will be a truer guide than any system.

Certainly a teacher cannot too strongly feel the importance of the charge. And the more elevated views the instructor or instructress holds of the office, the less drudgery will it become.

If however the task is hard, the object is great and the encouragements great. To train up a child in the way in which it should go—the way is long—it begins here—but it never ends; it rises higher and higher with every step, above sin and sorrow, into purer climes, and boundless prospects, to the walks of angels, the regions of truth, the presence of God.

I have wished to urge upon the attention of the guardians of this Seminary this important truth, because you have an opportunity and I know have the desire to fit these children not only to pass comfortable lives on earth but to give them to God forever. It will be much if this great fact is never lost sight of in the nurture they receive at your hands.

Let it be considered however by every person, not only every manager of this Institution but by every parent, and by every individual that feels an interest in the cause of education, the influence that every individual down to the very humblest exerts upon this cause. It is because the mature are no better that the prospects of the young are no better. It is said that a painter cannot give to a portrait the expression of more intelligence than he possesses himself. Sure I am that we cannot teach more than we know.

Do not say you have not the care of children. Do you live in society? Have you vices? Do you forget your duties and hopes as a Christian woman? Do you forget God? Then you are a hinderer of the progress of these children; you give to their box, but you defraud their souls. For if you consider what a highway society is for every influence; how wonderfully sympathetic; and that the average virtue is made up of the particular virtue of all the individuals, you will see the truth.

Not a note is struck in any part but vibrates all over it. What is done in the highest circle goes directly down to the lowest. What the king saith in his bed

7. Andrew Bell (1753-1832), Scottish clergyman and superintendent of an orphanage in Madras, India (1789-1796), originated the monitorial system of education, in which older pupils instruct the younger; Joseph Lancaster (1778-1838), British educator, member of the Society of Friends, who (to compete with Bell's system of education, which was supported by the Church of England) organized a corps of older students to instruct the younger ones in nonconformist schools and who emigrated to America in 1818, establishing schools in Philadelphia, Baltimore, Boston, and Washington, D.C.; Maria Edgeworth (1767-1849), British philanthropist and novelist, collaborated with her father, the inventor and educator Richard Lovell Edgeworth (1744-1817), on the popular treatise *Practical Education* (1798), which advanced the education theories of Rousseau; Anna Letitia Barbauld (1743-1825), prolific British author of verse and the frequently reprinted *Hymns in Prose for Children,* conducted an experimental boarding school for boys in Suffolk (1774-1785) with her husband, the Rev. Rochemont Barbauld.

chamber, he saith to mankind. The fashion that is set in the selectest circle of Vienna or London runs presently down to the beggars in villages of America. If therefore the leaders of society are bad, vice will be the fashion; if good, virtues will prevail. For are there bars in society? Is not society intersected every where by channels of communication that speed the doings of one circle to another on wings of wind? Is not every family served by those who see and hear, who faithfully relate to the poor and obscure every thing that is done by the rich and the beautiful and the celebrated?

Therefore let us take heed to ourselves, if we desire the prosperity present and eternal of these children, that we do not offend by our vices one of these little ones.[8]

Again I congratulate the managers and subscribers of this Charity on the measure of success that has attended your undertaking. Another year has witnessed, I hope, as much internal growth as external prosperity; has disclosed new talents and virtues in the children whilst it has shown the love of their friends. God in that time has called from their labors two of your number than whom none had the good of your institution more warmly at heart, but "their works follow them."[9]

In the death of Mrs. Elizabeth Dorr you have lost one of the original board of managers. She lived long enough for virtue and usefulness, long enough to be loved and honoured, and she is gone where a cup of cold water given in the spirit of charity is better than power or fame.[10]

A more recent providence has removed from your society one of its most devoted and efficient members, as well as one of the best friends and most munificent patrons of every good cause.

The memory of Mrs. Elizabeth Derby will not fade in the hearts of the good. In her death she has befriended the orphan whom she befriended in life; and yet, let me say, her example, living and dying, shall be her richest legacy to the Asylum and to her friends.

It remains briefly to remind this congregation to remember these orphan children. If you approve the object, and would extend the usefulness of this holy charity; if you would assist in saving poor forsaken little girls from the terrors of their lot, from want, from abuse, from ignorance, from crimes, and bring them within the walls of a secure Asylum, and within reach of that instruction that giveth life,—give according to your ability, and you shall have your reward in heaven.

8. Cf. Matthew 18:6.
9. Revelation 14:13.
10. Matthew 10:42.

CXXIX _____

Blessed is the man that endureth temptation,
for when he is tried he shall receive the
crown of life which the Lord hath
promised to them that love him.

JAMES 1:12

There are some views of life in which all men agree and which all systems sustain. Christians of different denominations may differ as to the terms and the nature of salvation but all agree that we need to be saved. Those who reject Christianity or who are ignorant of it do yet agree that the human character is capable of improvement, that individuals make great improvement, and that all ought to make some. And if in any thing we are unanimous it should be in this, that we should endure temptation when we are tried. We all know that temptations abound and believe they can be resisted.

This indeed is the professed object of all good men and receives the verbal approbation of all. From the text of St. James I ask permission to offer you a few practical counsels.

1. That we should always stick by the opinions of our soberest hours. And yet I fear every one of us has occasionally found a fatal slackness come upon his moral judgment and after the most earnest resolutions had been formed to persist in well doing he has found a sort of ague-fit chill the fervor of his purposes, and that in the most fatal manner. He not only became unwilling to keep them, but in the high tide of temptation they did not seem worth keeping. Now that he is full and merryhearted he remembers the thoughts of the closet as dull dreams, not binding on him, and wonders he did not take a more just and generous view of the day he is passing and of the customs of society than to seek to afflict himself with a lean self-denying temperance, an all forbearing humility, a stern unbending course of active usefulness, so foreign to the habits and expectations of this easy, selfsatisfied, self indulgent world. Under the clamor of appetite, or the impulse of the example and cheerful unrestrained converse of friends, the sharp distinctions of virtue and vice grow dim and indistinct. He

Manuscript dated September 25, 1831. Preached once: September 25, 1831, at the Second Church, Boston.

233

begins to think that virtue and vice differ only as shades of feeling, that he has made too much of them,—much more than other people;—and what right has he to be wiser than his neighbors? He begins to think that vice is only a harsh name for a sanguine temperament, or if it be as bad and dangerous as good men think it and he allow himself in sin, tomorrow will make all right again, by bringing back the freshness of his morning thought.

My friends, let each of us beware of this laxity of soul as of the gates of death. It is the confounding of eternal distinctions. If a man will really justify himself on this plea, and does really question whether the impulse of passion in that hour is not as good authority as the censure of reason in this,—I suppose he is as reasonable as if we should doubt whether we have not been in a mistake concerning sleep all our lives, and have really been awake when others thought us dreaming, and really dreaming when we thought we were awake.

But not many will carry this folly so far, and yet I suppose all men must be sensible in their experience of this variableness in the power of conscience. Therefore let me press it upon you as a good rule to set it down in our hearts, that, *we are to stick to the judgments of our soberest hours.* In those hours we should accustom ourselves to anticipate these periodical ebbs of moral force, and settle in our minds what we shall then do, so that those seasons may not take us unwarned and unarmed.

It is an important rule in morals, which may be worth remembering to all of us, that the merit of a good action is the greatest, when the motive to do it is most feeble in the presence of the most commanding motives to the contrary. It is greatest in our hearts and in the eye of God who is greater than our hearts.

And let me here add what is to my mind one of the most noble and one of the most thrilling truths in moral science, that we gain the strength of the temptation we resist. The savage in the Sandwich islands believes that when he overcomes and slays an enemy, the strength and courage of that enemy passes into him. The Soul instructed by God, knows, that whenever it resists and overcomes a temptation it becomes stronger by the strength of that temptation.[1]

A particular gratification is proposed to you, which you do not think it quite consistent with the good of your soul to seek. But the present advantage would be very great, and your friends think it no great harm; nay, they encourage you in strong terms to grasp it. And you say to yourself—what adequate return is there to me, if I forego this great and permanent advantage; I shall long regret it, and shall I sacrifice it for what is perhaps a foolish punctilio that would not stand in the way of any body else?

O say not so—there is a return, there is a compensation, not that follows after, but that accompanies and hallows every sacrifice of worldly good to principle; and that is, the power of principle itself; the sense that what is temporal has given way to what is eternal; the sense of heavenly elevation that seems to bring around the mind the society of angels and the presence of God. This

1. Cf. *JMN* 3:283.

will make a pleasant light in your thoughts in the gloomiest hour you shall ever spend. This if you persevere will cheer sickness and disappointment and age and solitude.

2. But secondly, Persist, Persist. One triumph is not enough; be not weary in well-doing.[2] Blessed is the man who endureth to the end.[3] It was the wise admonition of the ancient philosopher, to call no man happy until death—not to trust the most splendid prosperity, for, whilst life lasted, it might yet be changed to reverses.[4] It might be said with equal truth, Call no man virtuous until you have seen the end.—Trust not yourself because you have done well. In the very height and glow of virtuous triumph, there is imminent danger; the tempter watches his moment and on this very ground that you have done greatly, pleads for some abatement of the severity of your labor and zeal. You have given such dazzling proof of your worth, why should you be nice about trifles? But be not thou weary of well doing. O do not *for heaven's sake,* (to use a vulgar expression) do not *treat your resolution.*[5] Do not think the danger is past after one struggle; it is only begun. Simply persist in thinking what you have once been satisfied is true, and doing what you have once been satisfied is right. Humility is a brighter virtue on the brow of success and power. Self distrust, and trust in God, is the best offering of a mind determined to be faithful.

But to draw security and self complacency from success, and so think we may safely indulge ourselves in a sin we have proved it possible to vanquish, is the sad history of half the sinners of the world. For the vice comes back with accumulated power after a restraint, and carries away the strength we had collected, and the triumphs we had just reared, and therewith all our confidence in ourselves.

"When the unclean spirit is gone out of a man, he walketh through dry places, seeking rest and findeth none. Then he saith, I will return into my house from whence I came out; and when he is come he findeth it empty, swept and garnished. Then goeth he and taketh with himself seven other spirits more wicked than himself, and they enter in, and dwell there, and the last state of that man is worse than the first."[6]

3. But in order to any steadfastness in right thinking and good action, it is necessary in the third place that you should think for yourself, that you should realize your own great destiny as an independent accountable human soul. There is a false humility with which men clothe themselves who are strangers to their own minds. Surely, they say, it is desirable that religion be respected, and that the mind of society should be enlightened and converted, but that is not to be done by me. They dodge about wherever a whim or fashion calls them using

2. Cf. Galatians 6:9.
3. Cf. Matthew 10:22.
4. The formula appears frequently in Greek tragedy: see, for example, Aeschylus, *Agamemnon,* lines 928–29, and Sophocles, *Oedipus the King,* lines 1529–30.
5. Cf. *JMN* 3:283.
6. Matthew 12:43–45; cf. Luke 11:24–26.

the unfeigned apology that nobody notes what they think or do, and that it is really of no moment. And who are you, my brother, that thus you are exempt from the duties that belong to others—absolved from the ten commandments of Moses and the new commandment of Christ—by virtue of your insignificance? Alas you indeed know not what spirit you are of.[7] You have never entered into your own mind and sought to measure its unbounded powers. I fear you have used it only as a cunning servant to buy and sell and get gain for the body. You have never given scope and rein to the noble affections that belong to the human heart, and suffered them to transport you wholly from low calculations of selfish good into the region of lofty sentiments and to a life for others. And so you do not know your own treasure. What would it profit a man though he should gain the whole world, and lose his own soul, or what shall a man give in exchange for his soul?[8] Do I speak to any person who has attained years of discretion, and who thinks it of little importance what he does or omits? It is because you have been unfaithful to yourself. Because you have not yet manifested your own relation to virtue, which dignifies every thing which it touches, because you have not felt your relation to God, which makes all that is related to him partake of his infinity.

> "Teach me my God and king
> In all things thee to see
> And what I do in any thing
> To do it as for thee.
>
> All may of thee partake,
> Nothing can be so mean,
> Which with this tincture, *For Thy Sake,*
> Will not grow bright and clean."[9]

Consider that you are all the world to yourself; that by the eternal ordinations of God no real good can ever come to you but by your own instrumentality, that created and endowed as you have been by him, that you must take yourself for better for worse as your inheritance; that what you can get of moral or intellectual excellence out of this little plot of ground you call *yourself,* by the sweat of your brow—is your portion;[10] and though the wide Universe is full of good, not a particle can you add to yourself but by your toil bestowed on that spot. You must love others before you can be loved. You must open the virtues, in your own heart, before they will draw to you the precious friendship of the good. You must teach yourself, or the instructions of all the wise cannot teach you.

7. Luke 9:55.
8. Mark 8:36–37.
9. George Herbert, "The Elixir," lines 1–4, 13–16.
10. Cf. "There is a time in every man's education when he arrives at the conviction . . . that he must take himself for better, for worse, as his portion" ("Self-Reliance," *CW* 2:27–28). See also "The Protest" (*EL* 3:101).

Jesus cannot save you but by your own desire and cooperation—nor God bless you, if you will not be blessed.

Therefore go forth frankly and gratefully to your appointed duty, and do not repine that you are the child of an infinite being and made for immortal duties. Resist bravely your temptations, as one who has no slight stake at risk, but who contends for all the future, in this little present. Resist bravely as one who shall find auxiliaries when least expected. In the hour of our temptation, if the eye of the Spirit could be unsealed, what imploring countenances should we not see looking out upon us from the world of spirits and beseeching us to be strong, to quit us like men, in the firm faith that God approved our feeblest endeavour and that when presently the visible heavens should roll away from our eyes, the glories shall be revealed of that world for which we were made.[11]—Blessed is the man that endureth temptation, for when he is tried he shall receive a crown of life which the Lord hath promised to them that love him.

11. Cf. I Peter 5:1.

CXXX

*Ye have heard it said, Thou shalt love thy
neighbor and hate thine enemy. But I say
unto you Love your enemies; bless them
that curse you, and do good to them that hate
you and pray for them that spitefully use you.*

MATTHEW 5:43–44

Whoever considers attentively the history of the Christian Church will be struck
with the fact that the spirit of the gospel seems to have been better understood
and more consistent and more divine when preached to barbarous nations than
when by its influence the people had been refined. Its doctrine is less correct but
its spirit is more pure and more effectual. For it stands in such striking contrast
to the system it would supersede that there is no danger of its being contami-
nated insensibly by that. And the lives of the missionaries are far better than the
lives of the pagans and moreover are far better than they would be in their own
community. For the pagan becomes their teacher negatively as the gospel is their
teacher positively. Whatever vice the pagan practises, the missionary naturally
avoids: to use a humble illustration, as a well bred man in low company is far
more precise in his good manners than he would be in his own house. Besides,
as it most needs then, it is the spirit and not the letter of the gospel that is
insisted on. Men don't in instructing ferocious savages puzzle their heads with
fine speculative distinctions or learned criticism. They teach love and mercy,
righteousness, temperance and judgment to come, doctrines which are readily
understood and which it is plain as the sun in heaven will do them unspeakable
good. By keeping these benign rules before them they keep their own hearts in a
flame of love. And thus in that age of Christianity they are prompted to do more
than ever after. The early history of Christianity is full of the records of the
most decisive triumphs of principle over ease and all personal considerations, in
Asia Minor, in Rome, in Britain. In A.D. 596 the pious Augustine landed in Kent
in England with forty other missionaries sent by Gregory the Great to convert

---

Manuscript dated October 1, 1831. Preached twice: October 2, 1831, at the Second Church, Boston, and September 24, 1837, in East Lexington. Draft passages for this sermon occur in *JMN*
3:287–88.

the Saxons. After describing the horrible crimes of the Saxon race the historian writes, "Christianity brought with it some mitigation. The appearance of men who exposed themselves to a cruel death for the sake of teaching truth and inspiring benevolence was not without effect among the most faithless and ruthless barbarians. Liberty of preaching what they conscientiously believed to be divine truth was the only boon for which they prayed."[1] Nor had it lost its character four hundred years afterwards, for in recounting the events of that period he says, "It must be added that the Christian clergymen of that age surpassed their contemporaries in morality, which never fails in the end to resume some part of its natural authority over the most barbarous and even the most depraved."[2]

And if it could retain these principles in all their authority over the minds of its disciples for many generations it would go in triumph round the globe.

But when the gospel has operated for ages upon a nation, and affected by its moral influences even those interests and feelings that stand out in most pointed opposition to it, has qualified even the law of honor, and infused a mixture of sentiment even into the debauches of the voluptuary, and Christian precepts begin to be breathed from unexpected quarters, and Saul is found among the prophets,[3] why then the disciples of Christianity lose one of their strongest mementoes. When the whole world turns Christian the firm line of separation that secluded the disciple from evil men and joined him with good men is effaced. It is easier for him to sin without observation than before. Once if he had broken the Commandments it would have been to desert his party and become a pagan. Now it is only what many in this Christian community do, and so he does not lose *caste*.

Nay in the general sympathy the followers of the world and the professed followers of Christ often change sides, and the man of the world when it happens to suit his convenience argues warmly for his rights upon the ground of Christian love, whilst the Christian in poor extenuation of his own compliances strives to wrest the truth into a seeming sanction of some evil custom of the day.

Hence comes corruption of the church and an uncertainty as to what their duty demands of Christians. Not keeping the eye fixed solely on the principle but turning now to what custom (reputed good) sanctions, and now to principle, and vainly attempting to reconcile them, they cannot arrive at any settled conclusion.

This I suppose is precisely our condition. Christianity has made some real progress, and the whole civilized world where it has operated is very much the better for it. But it has made very little progress, and men have rested content

1. Vol 1. p 38 [Emerson's note]. See Sir James Mackintosh, Sir Walter Scott, and Thomas Moore, *The Cabinet History of England, Scotland, and Ireland,* 3 vols. (Philadelphia, 1830-1833), 1:38.

2. Mackintosh Vol I p. 47 [Emerson's note]. See Mackintosh et al., *Cabinet History of England, Scotland, and Ireland,* 1:47.

3. Cf. I Samuel 10:11.

with seizing and keeping the general fruits produced by it but have let the principle that bore them go and they cling to the customs established and instead of reforming them after the principle,—a process which would go on forever,—they measure the principle by the custom and pronounce it impracticable. Thus hath it fared for instance with the gospel rule of love to man. And leaving others I shall confine my remarks to this. The rule is "Love thy neighbor as thyself."[4]

And in the beginning of the reign of Christianity when men were penetrated with its spirit they eagerly sought to do each other all kind offices—quarrels were unknown—and they drew from their heathen neighbors the exclamation, "See how these Christians love one another!"[5] Then grew up as the first fruits of Christianity charitable institutions and these have attended it from their manifest beauty and use down to this day, a single effect of this golden rule. And what name or form of misfortune is there among us that has not some antidote following after it, if even, as sometimes happens, it has not outrun it?

But whilst the education which the world has received from Jesus manifests itself in this all embracing compassion and these institutions are no longer got up as *religious* but as *expedient* things, the principle on which they are founded, has as yet penetrated but a little way into the public mind. Let us inquire how far. Men do feel, and pretty strongly, the claims of extreme bodily want and suffering. They will help the helpless, the insane, the deaf and dumb, the blind, and the orphan. But there the principle stops and penetrates their conduct no farther. It has not yet taught them to commiserate error and vice. It has not yet taught them to love the soul of their neighbor. It has not yet taught you the great sum of your duty to him, made you feel that you have a concern in all his happiness, an interest to promote it all, that yours can never be complete whilst his is incomplete, and your work in the universe can never be done whilst there is suffering to remove.

To take an example—if you see a wretch in the street without clothes or food or fuel, you will do what you can to cover and feed and warm him. Perhaps from reasons of expediency or from the same reason that you would strengthen the police you will provide him with religious instruction, but beyond that mark you feel no obligation to love your fellowman. If he gets above his necessities and comes into your street to buy and sell, your love will not prevent you from hindering him if you can, or from taking some unfair advantage of his ignorance or his need. If he come into your company and advance opinions different from yours, the golden rule will not keep you—though the fear of men may—from overbearing contradiction in his presence and slanderous expressions when he is gone. It will not prevail with you, though it may be in your power, to forgive him, however poor, any part of a debt as long as you can extort a cent from his slender savings. Far less will it prevail with you to forgive him an injury

4. Luke 10:27.
5. See Sermon CVI, n. 6.

or an insult offered to you. Oh no. You must make the most you can of every affront—and thus are misunderstandings fomented that worry the unhappy parties and worry some of their neighbors out of sleep and appetite, each one standing out, to be sure, on his silly honor—he will not be trifled with—he will make it known, call in the whole congregation of the people through the public prints, he will go to law, yes and submit to every personal inconvenience and sacrifice before he will submit to draw back one inch from the ground he has taken. Whilst all the time he has perhaps known that he was in the wrong and adheres to it out of mere pride and folly.

Whilst the part called the better part of the community think and act thus, another part go one step farther, carry private hatreds to public brawls, and blows shall be given with the fist by a rational man to a rational man as if they were beasts, or they shall shoot at each other as you shoot a mad dog.

These extremes being permitted in society by the turbulent it is remarkable that in consequence of the same imperfect reception of the true doctrine of loving our neighbor general society have not made up a settled opinion as to what is the duty of men thus injured. How far resistance may be lawfully carried and whether retaliation does not become a Christian man are questions that embarrass the prudent and well meaning. And yet it seems strange that society should never get out of its boyish days and notions, that reason should never quite ascend to superiority over force. So manifest and beautiful is the virtue of forbearance. Glimpses of it may be noticed now and then as the dawn of the true day. Themistocles, even in pagan Greece, when struck by a rude fellow in the midst of his harangue calmly answered, "Strike, but hear me,"[6] and a poor novel that has gone the round of all the reading world in our day is yet distinguished by ascribing to its ruffian hero the utmost forbearance. Now let me revert to the true, the Christian rule, which in this conflict of opinion is thought extravagant, superhuman, *love thy neighbor as thyself,*[7] not submit to wrong, but submit to wrong, rather than avenge it. Avoid evil persons, not contend with them. Neither offend nor be offended, but rather than retaliate, give one cheek after the other to the blow; and coat after cloke.[8] The law of worldly prudence is—'be slow to enter any quarrel, but being in, bear thyself so as the opposer shall beware of thee.' The gospel advice is, 'Bear thyself so to him that is your enemy, as if your whole trade and business was to benefit him,—to bless him despite of himself.'

It does not stop with Forbearance,—that is but half, or it is but a little part. What is to distinguish the Christian's forbearance, which is sublime, from the coward's forbearance, which is base? Why manifestly, the *motive.* And what is the motive? The Christian does not strike you not because he fears you will return the blow, that were pusillanimous, but because striking you will do you

6. Plutarch, "Life of Themistocles," in *The Lives,* ed. John and William Langhorne (New York, 1822), 2:18.
7. Luke 10:27.
8. Cf. Matthew 5:39–40.

no good, and it is your good to which he is wholly engaged. Now, brethren, so far from the Christian rule's being extravagant and impracticable, it is the only practicable expedient. It is the only ground on which society possibly can stand. It is the only remedy that can reach the evil, and never until it has pervaded the minds of men can peace prevail. It is the impertinence of folly to pretend, as one may hear grave men pretend, that the Duel is necessary to keep the peace and civility of common intercourse. Let us go back to that practice. And what are its bounds? Who are amenable to it and who are not? In this country there is no privileged order of gentry, but every good man is a gentleman, and so that law of murder is to be binding on every man who values his character. It is not more abominable than it is ridiculous. If the king of England and the king of France having points at issue in their cabinet deliberations should propose to ascertain the right by wrestling or boxing in public, how would the civilized world ring with derision. Yet in the eye of just reason how mean an object is the throne of England and the throne of France compared with the knowledge and virtue to which every individual in the world may, if he chooses, lay claim.

In short every time another mind becomes imbued with the Christian principle it is an increased cement to human society. Every time that rule is violated it is one step to disorganization, to violence, to madness.

But it will be said this is all impracticable and if you take this quaker principle of non resistance why the Christian law applies to the case of property also and the unwise and impossible rule of a community of goods would also come in. And certainly the rule does apply to property, and no man can be a sincere Christian, who does not deal with all he has after the rule, Love thy neighbor as thyself. Not surely in the vain attempt to equalize what God hath made unequal in the condition of men, not to establish a vain community of goods, which tomorrow would be no more. No; it has been wisely said that "property is like snow, which if it should chance today to fall level, would be blown into drifts tomorrow."9 The skill, the industry of each to gain, and the discretion to spend are widely unlike and would defeat every attempt to continue an equality. But a better, a nobler, a juster division is made, a true equality, when the golden rule has gone home to the heart of every possessor of property. He then feels the whole burden of that distress which is within his reach as his own, he does not desire to shift off the burden upon other shoulders—and he sets himself with humanity and prudence to lighten it. Then the bounty of God is put into the hands of a wise steward, and does its utmost amount of good.

I need not take up more time to show the wide distance that now is between the practice of men and this principle of Christ. But I beg you to consider that the only way to carry farther on the triumphs of this pure principle is to let customs go—not to seek to defend them—but to keep the eye forever fixed on the principle. Trust to it with a boundless confidence through the opposition of

9. Source not located; used in *Nature* (CW 1:24).

friends and the laughter of the crowd. As God liveth, it will not betray you. Seek steadily another's welfare as your own. Be kind where you are known; be kind where you are not known. Seek another's convenience at the fireside; in a stage coach; in a crowd; in a bargain; in a quarrel. Let the good of others be felt by you to be your calling in the universe. And God who is Love shall bless you.[10]

10. Cf. I John 4:8.

CXXXI

Sing praises with understanding.

PSALMS 47:7

It is a natural idea that has always occurred to the pious man, that man is the tongue of the creation and is to utter praise not only for himself, but in behalf of all the irrational creatures, and of the inanimate works of God. He alone hath the music of speech. He alone can form the thought of praise into words. It is very hard to analyze music and say how much is intellectual and how much is material.

It is harder yet to analyze poetry and tell where the charm is lodged that pleases us in its measures. After the experiment is tried, after verses are made, we can tell what measures please and what offend. We can make rules describing them but who can go into the chambers of the ear, and tell why the order of syllables should be harmonious, and any change should hurt it? Hardest of all to analyze the joys of sentiment and imagination which make the soul of poetry. Only he that made the throbbing heart, the hearing ear and the speaking tongue, and the vibrating air, and to him let the music which results from them all be paid.

Music and poetry have come down together from an immemorial time. And

Manuscript dated October 2, 1831. Preached once: October 2, 1831, at the Second Church, Boston. Notes for this sermon occur in *JMN* 3:248.

Occasioned by the deliberation of a committee of the Second Church reviewing the adoption of a new hymnal, this sermon offers an early and rare formal statement by Emerson of attitudes toward church music and its relation to poetry. At issue in the Second Church was the possible replacement of Jeremy Belknap's hymnal by one recently published by Francis William Pitt Greenwood (1797-1843), minister of neighboring King's Chapel. Belknap (1744-1798), minister of the Church in Long Lane, Boston, later known as the Federal Street Church, compiled his *Sacred Poetry, Consisting of Psalms and Hymns, adapted to Christian Devotion, in Public and Private, Selected from the Best Authors, with Variations and Additions,* in 1795. Emerson's father, William, who published his own hymnal, *A Selection of Psalms and Hymns, Embracing all the Varieties of Subject and Metre Suitable for Private Devotion and Worship of the Churches,* in 1808, helped Belknap arrange some of the music for an accompanying tune book.

Emerson's candidate to replace Belknap's hymnal was Greenwood's *The Collection of Psalms and Hymns for Christian Worship* (1830). His laudatory remarks on the hymnal in this sermon are consistent with his praise of it in an unsigned review he wrote for the *Christian Examiner* 10 (March 1831); 30-34 (see Kenneth Walter Cameron, "An Early Prose Work of Emerson," *American Literature* 22 [November, 1950]: 332-38). The Second Church committee evidently agreed with its pastor's view, for according to Emerson's Preaching Record, on October 16 the congregation accepted the committee's recommendation to adopt Greenwood's hymnal.

from the earliest notices of them they were consecrated to religious service. The oldest records of every literature are religious odes. In every nation there appear to have been bards who were priests. The historians who take up the veil of time and show us the long pathway of our race leading back to the first seats of the human family, introduce us to the fathers of mankind, a simple race of shepherds and husbandmen duly meeting to honour the Deity in a true or false worship with hymns and dances. In ancient Egypt and in Europe it was a costly and gorgeous ceremonial. When purer religion displaced their idolatry, this natural species of worship remained; it has survived every revolution of opinion and held its place among Catholics and Protestants, among Episcopalians and dissenters, among Methodists and Shakers.

Some of the finest powers of genius have been exercised in providing this beautiful entertainment for the mind of the worshipper both in music and in poetry. For those who understand both it unites the finest pleasures of the Sense to the finest pleasures of the Soul. Psalmody is the union of sacred poetry to sacred music. I am wholly incompetent to speak of the first, of which few, I believe, understand less. But I am much interested in the last.[1] I wish to bring to your attention the subject of hymn books. I am anxious that our sacred poetry should be good; should be a worthy expression of our sentiments to the Creator. I am anxious that we should sing hymns which we can feel, and which can do the office of sacred poetry upon our minds—can arouse, thrill, cheer, soothe, solemnize or melt us. I desire that we should not sing hymns to God that we should be ashamed to compose in the praise of a man—flat, prosaic, unaffecting productions such as too many have been and are. I desire that on the altar of God, whilst eloquence brings its deepest truths, poetry should exhaust its powers.

It is but reasonable that the hymns which make so large a part of our religious service should be chosen and good ones. It must be perceived by any one who considers the subject that this part of our service admits of being made much more interesting than it is. A large number of every congregation have some taste for sacred poetry and perhaps a much larger number for sacred music. If this taste were taken advantage of in all cases by a diligent collection of the best hymns and a careful rejection of all inferior ones, the hymn would do much good in exalting devout feelings. Almost every person has at some time had opportunity to observe a very great effect produced upon an assembly by a pertinent hymn aided by the effect of fine music. This effect might be greater and more frequent if our hymn books were better.

1. In *Young Emerson Speaks* (Boston, 1938), 246, Arthur Cushman McGiffert, Jr. argues that Emerson inadvertently transposed the words "first" and "last" in this sentence and the one immediately above it, interpreting "Psalmody is the union of sacred poetry to sacred music" as the antecedent sentence to which Emerson refers here. If one follows the development of the paragraph along strict grammatical lines, McGiffert is correct. However, it is more likely that Emerson intended what he wrote, referring not to the sentence in which he defines psalmody, but to the first sentence in the paragraph. In effect, Emerson is disclaiming competency in music, but expressing interest, if not also competency, in poetry and in the entertainment function "for the mind of the worshipper" of music that is poetical.

It is very singular that in the English language, which contains some of the sublimest strains of poetry and of sacred poetry, the hymns sung in churches should have been until the last century so low and inharmonious, so sunk indeed almost below criticism. One would have thought it would have moved the ambition of great geniuses, of many a holy successor of David and Miriam, to give utterance to a nation's praise and pious rapture.[2] What work of learning or of imagination could ever hope for such permanent and precious fame, ever hope to enter into the heart and faith of a nation like the simple religious song that is in their mouth every Sunday aided in its effect by the reverence of the Bible, the power of music, the associations of the place, and the sympathy of a congregation? The best poet should have written hymns for those who speak the English tongue and whatever sublime bard has sung to any people could best have instructed them by doing this office, instead of permitting the unskilful versifiers who with whatever good intentions first turned the psalms of David into English metre.

Very great improvement however, though not so great as we could hope, has taken place. The stiff and wretched verses used in old times have disappeared.[3] Very many persons, some of them highly gifted, have turned their talents in this direction and some noble strains of devotion have been heard. Dr. Watts, though his mind was imprisoned in a dark and barbarous system of religious faith, did yet by the fervor of his piety and the freedom of his thought wonderfully raise the downtrodden muse of the English churches. Addison, Mrs. Steele, Doddridge, Cowper, Mrs. Barbauld—have enriched our collections and many living authors have added to our stock.[4]

The Collection of the late Dr. Belknap which is in use in this church was received with great satisfaction by enlightened men at the time of its appearance near forty years ago as being a very marked improvement upon the gloomy Calvinism of the old books. But many years have since elapsed in which the public attention has been intensely fixed upon theological questions and many errors then strongly suspected have been fully exposed. Much of its theology is

2. King David, second king of Judah and Israel, is the reputed author of many of the psalms. The prophetess Miriam, Aaron's sister, took up her tambourine and led the women in song to praise God in celebration of the Israelites' crossing of the Red Sea and the destruction of Pharaoh's army (Exodus 15:20–21).

3. The "stiff and wretched verses used in old times" probably refers to both the *Bay Psalm Book* (1640), the metrical psalter that, as an unpoetical rendering of the psalms, represented the Puritans' contempt for modern hymns, and *Psalms* (1652), edited by Thomas Sternhold and John Hopkins, popularly known as the "Old Version." Both had been widely used in New England.

4. The hymn-writers here include Isaac Watts (1674–1748), English theologian and composer of 600 hymns published in *Horae Lyricae* (1706), *Hymns and Spiritual Songs* (1707), and *Psalms of David Imitated* (1719); Joseph Addison (1672–1719), accomplished English essayist, poet, statesman, and composer of several paraphrases of the Psalms; Anne Steele (1717–1778), English hymnwriter, who published *Poems on Subjects Chiefly Devotional* (1760) under the pseudonym "Theodosia"; Philip Doddridge (1702–1751), English nonconformist minister and author of several hymns, including "O God of Bethel, by whose hand"; and William Cowper (1731–1800), English poet and, with the evangelical curate John Newton, collaborator on the *Olney Hymns* (1779), for which he composed 67 original pieces. For Anna Letitia Barbauld, see Sermon CXXVIII, n. 7.

therefore antiquated. No enlightened Christian can read many pages in that book without meeting confused views of God and many bad or at best ambiguous expressions concerning the offices of Christ, his Deity, his sacrifice and atonement, and his now exaltation as the central object of adoration to all beings in heaven as in the one-hundred-twenty-second hymn.

> "Jesus my God I know his name
> His name is all my trust
> Nor will he put my soul to shame
> Nor let my hope be lost."

My friends, it does not become us to whom God in his mercy has given his word in simplicity and in freedom to worship him with doubtful heart or with double lips. Let us not confound the reason he has given us by making two gods, or three; or two in one, or three in one. If we cannot measure the dignity of Jesus, and do not feel that our duty requires us to know of any other dignity than his truth and goodness, so let our hymn say, and let not our hymn book break the first commandment.

But besides this occasional Trinitarianism, sometimes express and sometimes by allusion, as grave a charge lies against many of these pieces as injurious to the character of God. Language is there applied to the Supreme Being that cannot be repeated without dishonouring him. He is represented as vindictive, greedy of praise and uttering threats in the poor passion of a man.[5]

Next to these great errors which ought not to be found in a book selected for such an use I may remark a confusion of thought and expression concerning the great doctrine of Christianity, namely the immortality of the soul, which in some of the psalms seems to be forgotten and in some misunderstood.

Another fault is a prevalence of unchristian sentiments of denunciation and bitterness which never flowed from the law of love.[6]

Again besides this utterance of unchristian sentiment there is a defect running through a great many of the hymns, that of a very gross material imagery. Heaven is always described as a land of rivers, of luxuries, of music, of crowns, God as a king sitting on a throne, Christ as a conqueror with sword and chariot, and the life of the Saint is painted in military hymns, and the mean descriptions of angels.[7] All which have a most pernicious tendency to mislead the mind in its understanding of spiritual things.

Let us not be unjust to this book so long and so generally used in the liberal churches of New England. It contains many excellent hymns which have served a pious purpose to many worshipping assemblies and many a private heart. But it contains numbers of indifferent and some bad ones, and does not contain a great many which ought to be introduced into our church. Much that is objec-

---

5. Ps[alm] 95 [Emerson's note]. Emerson left a space to quote some of the text, but did not do it.
6. See 101 Psalm called a psalm for a master of a family. [Emerson's note].
7. H[ymn] 13 [Emerson's note].

tionable in it arises from the division, now disused, into Psalms and Hymns. It is not wise to attempt to wrest and accommodate the peculiar language of David, originally suited to many temporary and private occasions, to the present wants of the Christian Church. In the attempt to do this, a great many inapplicable verses are made and what is worse a great many sentiments expressed utterly inconsistent with the Christian religion. The effect of this has been that one half of the versions of the Psalms in Belknap are now grown obsolete—are never or very rarely sung in our church. An obvious improvement would be to select the good versions of the many fine passages in the Psalms and incorporate them with other hymns adapted to our peculiar wants or to the wants of the church in every age.

The practical ill effect of these objections is of course not so obvious to any one in the church as to the preacher. It costs him much time to select pieces to be read and sung, and again out of the suitable pieces, to select what is unobjectionable. These faults exclude from use a very large number of the hymns and psalms in the book, so that out of 460 not many more than 200 are commonly used, and our church is as yet a stranger to a large number of excellent hymns, not included in this collection. And we fear that in our meetings the reading and singing of hymns grown so familiar to the ear fails of its desired effect.

I have thought it well to make these remarks to you, brethren, because it is in my opinion a great blemish on our service, and one admitting an easy remedy, and because, as you know, the expediency of introducing a new hymn book has long been and is before a committee of the Society, and the evil complained of is not mended by time. And before the report of that Committee is presented for your action, I desired to make a plain statement of what I esteem the faults of our service and what advantages we might hope to gain by a change.

There has now been for about a year a new Collection before the Christian public compiled by the Pastor of the Stone Chapel in this city. It has the suffrage of many good judges and almost of all sects in its favor. It is free from all the objections that lie against the old collections and contains near 600 hymns. I hope in these circumstances it may receive the examination, and, if found worthy, the approbation of every worshipper in our ancient temple.

We worship in plain walls. We have no tapestry, no pictures, no marble, no gold, no sacrifices, no incense. Let us at least have truth and piety. Let us have hymns worthy of God, the subject, and suitable for man, the singer. Let us not think this a light matter. Let us sing praises with understanding.

CXXXII _____

If thou wilt enter into life, keep the commandments.

MATTHEW 19:17

Whilst all sects of Christians agree in affirming the supreme importance of religion to the soul, it is strange that there should be so much discrepancy on the question what religion is. The one thing needful is described by different persons as being several very different things. Still it would be wrong to say that there is an irreconcilable difference. For there is some common ground which all descriptions cover. All agree that the religious man has goodness or must be a good man. Some think his goodness the consequence of his faith and some think his faith the fruit of his goodness; a third class think his goodness of no efficacy towards salvation, and a fourth destroy the value of his goodness by saying that neither faith nor goodness are got by man but are given by God. But all some way or other contrive to make goodness a part of his character. All would agree that a grossly vicious man is not pleasing to God. But men are slow, very slow, in perceiving that goodness is the one thing needful,[1] is not only what must be, but is all that must be; is not only the means, but the end; not only the work, but the wages; not only the way of salvation, but the salvation itself. Men are very slow in finding this out, simple as the truth is, but always men look for great and learned reasons for things first, and find the simple truth long afterward.

Let me offer a few remarks to show that the sum and substance of Religion is an obedience to the Commandments; that Christianity is only the interpretation of them showing their greater meaning; and that heaven, or salvation, is in them and not something more.

But this not only was contained in Christianity but was the object of Christianity. John who preceded and announced Christ, said, 'Repent,' 'for the kingdom of heaven (or the doctrine of truth) is at hand';[2] and Christ, when he came, said unto men, 'Keep the Commandments.' What is the course of his life? What

---

Manuscript dated October 16, 1831. Preached once: October 16, 1831, at the Second Church, Boston. Notes for this sermon occur in *JMN* 3:296.

1. For the expression "the one thing needful" here and in the second sentence of this paragraph, see Luke 10:42.

2. Matthew 3:2.

249

is the purport of his teaching? No penance, no sacrifice, no long prayers, no hatred, no persecution, no creed, but plain truth and reason instead,—the plain moral principles of humility, purity, temperance, fortitude, benevolence, resignation. From the beginning of the Sermon on the Mount, to the prayer on the Cross,—all one texture, all a desire to make better men. If he seems to ask more, if he seems as to some he does seem, to insist much upon something quite out of the way, namely a claim to divert a part of our religious veneration from God to himself, it is because we do not consider sufficiently the circumstances to which he spoke and which gave such a turn to the expression. Jesus came a Jew to the Jews, to the bigoted, selfish, oppressed, sanctimonious Jews, so depraved and barbarous that they expected for the Messiah such a person as Attila or Napoleon who should conquer and grind and kill their enemies; and therefore when a poor peasant presented himself, unarmed and attended only by poor men, distinguished only by his wonderful moral excellence and by miracles that were only a succession of kind actions, and not a weapon, no not so much as a word aimed by him at the Romans—this was not the Messiah they wanted: they hated him for calling himself so.

In the midst of these men of long prayers and many ceremonies and broad phylacteries, full of hatred and revenge, Jesus regards himself as the representative of the cause of truth and benevolence which in his actions and words he urged on men. Leave, he would say, these monstrous errors of opinion and fatal crimes and believe on *Me*.[3] None cometh to the Father but by *Me*,[4] that is, by these means or in this way which I show. And in the strong confidence that he had no will but God's,[5] and he being the only man who taught the truth, and the nation whom he addressed were wide of the mark, was not this language natural and unavoidable? It is familiar to us in the use of every eminent teacher, and the more striking is the contrast between the prevailing error and the truth which he presents, the more natural is this language. At the same time, to avoid misconstruction, Christ repeatedly and distinctly affirms that he has nothing and is nothing but what he has received from God.[6]

Now consider what is the way and the means which he recommends—the truth which he presents. Why, simple obedience to the Commandments—to the ten Commandments—simple goodness—nothing more—nothing less. Did he tell men what he *believed*? Did he encumber God's Providence with irreconcilable decrees? Did he practise the superstitions of his nation? No, he was kind, and true, and useful. He praised every thing that was good. He said, let the heart be right. Do the works—do the will of God, not say unto me Lord, Lord. Be known by your fruits. The humble publican is better in God's sight than the self-righteous Pharisee.[7]

3. Cf. John 6:35 and 7:38.
4. John 14:6.
5. Cf. Luke 22:42.
6. See John 17:1-26.
7. Cf. Matthew 7:21, 7:16, and Luke 18:9-14

When the question was put to him in direct terms, What shall I do to inherit eternal life? He answers in language beyond doubt or dispute, If thou wilt enter into life keep the Commandments.

And this was the understanding of Christian religion which the apostles received. Slow to give up their Jewish prejudices themselves, which they parted with piecemeal, yet did their eyes gradually open to this thought. What can be more satisfactory than Peter's discourse to Cornelius and the generous sentiment with which it is prefaced? "I perceive that in every nation he that feareth God and worketh righteousness is accepted with him,"8 and so it is with Paul, the great and consistent preacher of righteousness, temperance and judgment to come. It must be considered in all his reasoning with the Jews he is reasoning on their own premises, and so is best understood by us in his discourses to the gentiles. But every where he bursts out with the sentiment which he expresses to the Corinthians, "Circumcision is nothing, and uncircumcision is nothing, but the keeping of the Commandments."9

Even the author of the Epistle to the Hebrews, the most of a Jew in his opinions of all the converts, feels the overpowering genius of Christianity to be that of faithful obedience, and bids his brethren, "follow peace; and holiness without which no man shall see the Lord."10

But after this religion which demanded of men simple goodness had been in the earth a little while, men neglected that, its great work, and labored to find and to show that it taught something more. And even among us, though I believe a faultless obedience would always command reverence, yet in the minds of men the theory of religion is very much disturbed, and you may hear a moral life or mere morality spoken of with a sneer. There is an imagination that a man may be good and yet not religious. My friends, it is to sneer at God in heaven. Men want more than to keep the Commandments. I believe it is because they do not know how hard it is to keep the Commandments. It is as much as we can do. It is much more than we can now do. Who has done it so much as one day? Who ever kept the commandment to the letter and to the extent of the spirit? Was there ever man or angel? No, for the Commandment opens, as you obey it. It means more every time you read it. And every one of them will unfold a deeper sense, a higher use, a sweeter beauty to him who keeps it through all the future.

But what are these commandments in obedience to which Christianity places the whole duty of man?11 Our Saviour as we well know alluded to the Ten Commandments given on Mount Sinai.

To these laws Christianity has done the office of interpreter. These laws seem generally to have been understood by the Jews as having only a literal meaning. They were guiltless if they observed the letter of the rule. They kept the first if

8. Acts 10:34–35.
9. I Cor[inthians] 7.19 [Emerson's note].
10. Heb[rews] 12.14 [Emerson's note].
11. Cf. Ecclesiastes 12:13.

they did not worship Baal or Jupiter by name; and the second, if they did not make an idol with their fingers, and the third if they kept the terms of a vow, and so of the rest.

Christ came to teach them a true obedience; to open their eyes to the fact that the heart was the seat of heaven or of hell; and that these Commandments were then only obeyed when they were kept in the spirit as in the letter.[12]

Thou shalt have no other Gods before me,[13] i.e., neither the things thou lovest nor thyself who lovest them; thou shalt not love pleasure nor pride nor revenge better than God, thou shalt not take to thyself glory for any thing thou hast nor any thing thou art, but shalt truly think God gave me all and I must render all to him.

That the spirit of this command was to love the Lord thy God with all thy heart—but what is the love of God?—let St. John answer for his Master—"This is the love of God that ye keep his commandments."[14] Then the Jews and all future ages were taught that a true obedience to the first commandment was to feel, that we were not our own but so wholly another's work and property, that we were wholly engaged by every motive to do what he enjoins—and, once more, that we could only know and love that being by keeping his laws. This first command resolving itself into the rest will never be kept fully until all the rest are kept. Who of us keeps this and what more religion can there be on earth?

2. We should have no idols, neither ease nor money nor political power nor meats nor drinks nor luxury nor the praise of men, but should walk humbly before God.

3. We should keep our vows.

4. We should keep the Sabbath. We should join not only in general but in particular acts of homage to God.

5. We should honour our parents.

6. We should not kill, which in the explanation of Christ is *thou shalt not hate*.[15]

7. Thou shalt not commit adultery, which Jesus again refers to the heart, and says *thou shalt not lust*.[16]

8. Thou shalt not steal.

9. Thou shalt not bear false witness.

10. Thou shalt not covet.

Now take these commandments home to our daily life, home to our actions and conversation and thoughts, and keep them in the spirit which Christ has imparted to them, i.e., of the love of God and of our neighbor, and see how much they mean. Take, for example, the command, Thou shalt not steal. It

12. Romans 2:29.
13. The Ten Commandments are given in Exodus 20:1–17.
14. I John 5.3 [Emerson's note].
15. Matthew 5:21–22.
16. Matthew 5:27–28.

means first, Do not take away your neighbor's property clandestinely or violently. But when you have got above this temptation, it means more. Don't take it by means that are legal but yet iniquitous. Do not use any unfair advantage. Then, Do not withhold from him your aid whenever you can and ought to bestow it. And so the sense goes on as you follow it, till it comes to mean, Let no man seek his own, but every one another's good.[17]

Now, brethren, if these are the commandments do you think we shall not find work enough in keeping them? And must not duty so indispensable be the very work for which we were made? The Commandments are obviously the work of the same hand that made the heavens, and sun, and stars, and the Earth, and man. They are the work of which Christianity is the interpretation. While in one light they are *commands,* in another they are only descriptions of the true or right way of living for the creature Man so as to get the greatest degree of enjoyment his Creator intended for him. And to fear God, and keep them, is now, as always it was, the whole duty of man.

Brethren, I have one more remark to make concerning this simple truth that goodness or obedience to the commandments is the sum and substance of religion. And that is that goodness is its own reward. Among the many inventions with which men have covered the simplicity of God's truth is the doctrine that there is something besides goodness which is to be the reward of goodness. Sermons without end treat of salvation as something to come hereafter to a good man. Why should you keep the commandments? That you may be saved. Saved from what? from breaking the commandments. "In keeping the commandment is great reward," not after keeping them but in the obedience itself. For this plain reason, that to keep them is to live in the manner in which God made you to live, and the way in which Infinite goodness and wisdom made you to be, must be good and happy.

I need not, I think, expand this truth, which is familiar to every pious and thoughtful mind, that goodness is happiness; that to be good is the first and best way to learn truth; that to be good is the way to get the love and society of the good—and what other heaven can the Universe contain or the heart desire than to be perfect, to know the truth and to have the society of blessed minds and the love of God.

And now, brethren, are we keeping the Commandments? Have we learned to keep the first? To acknowledge in our hearts that we did not make ourselves but are another's work and are wholly engaged to live by his laws? Let us feel the immense obligation of these rules of life seeing that they gather new force and weight with every step the soul makes; that as the commandments are more commanding, the greater is the mind that obeys them; and that they shall sound in our ear as accusing witnesses and tormentors or the music of divine applause.

17. Cf. I Corinthians 10:24.

CXXXIII

If our gospel be hid,
it is hid from them that are lost.

II CORINTHIANS 4:3

I wish to speak from these words upon the reality and blessedness of religion; to show that religion is nothing uncertain or unintelligible, but is something which our minds can understand and our hands can do. To some of you, this may seem so plain as to need no explanation. And strange it is how the simple truth has been perverted and hidden. Strange—how gross and obstinate are the errors of men upon this subject. Ask men what they think religion means— Examine the language they use respecting it, and you find the strangest misapprehensions exist.

They speak of religion as a *profession*. They speak of it as something distinct from the character, that is to be worn like a dress, something not of the man, that is to be added to him. They speak of it as something that is to be got once for all, or to be done once and there is an end of it. Or they speak of it as if it were a duty to believe certain things to be true and so great a merit that a sound faith gets to be represented as of more importance than a sound practice—and even that a man may 'have religion' as it is termed, who is a bad man.

I speak not now of any class of unbelievers. Far be it from me, brethren, to impute to any sect religious views which they would disown. I do not say these mistaken opinions are entertained by any denomination of Christians. They are not entertained by the best men of any denomination. No, but you shall find among men of all sects traces of these prevailing misapprehensions of what religion is and aims at. And it is so general that we are all liable to be misled.

This general misapprehension may be reduced to two parts, as it respects what is believed and as it respects what is done. Religion as it respects the understanding or Faith is confounded with Credulity; and Religion as it respects the practice is confounded with a form. Pure religion consists in understanding and doing the commandments or in doing right from a right motive, but false religion consists in taking commandments without understanding them and keeping them outwardly and not inwardly.

Manuscript dated October 30, 1831. Preached three times: October 30, 1831, at the Second Church, Boston; June 12, 1836, in East Lexington; and June 19, 1837, in Concord, Mass. Draft passages for this sermon occur in *JMN* 3:296–97 and 3:301.

1. To consider this error as it affects what we believe. It is thought that the having more or less faith depends a good deal upon the strength of the imagination: that it is an acceptance as true of all things that are written in the Bible whether we understand them or not and that faith is required not only for things for which the understanding cannot see any evidence, but that such faith is meritorious, and gains great favor in the sight of God.

Now this I conceive to be great delusion. To receive religious truth on trust—it is impossible. It cannot be taken on the bare affirmation of any being in the Universe. You don't understand what Truth means. Truth is not crammed down the throat of men, but is something to be understood. Until it is understood, it is not truth to the mind. You may kill a child by thrusting bread into its stomach; it is not food, it is death. You may confound the mind by scaring it with the repetition of veracious but unintelligible propositions. The only way in which possibly truth can be received, is by the mind's own spontaneous affirmation that the thing is so. What else does it mean to *receive* truth, but to *understand* it? But when religious truth is thus received into the mind, does any one suppose that there is any less reality in that truth than in the rules of arithmetic or agriculture? For instance, it is a great religious truth that he who walks humbly with God is happy,—or, he who in all his thoughts acknowledges himself to be derived from power and wisdom not his own, is happy. Now some men clearly perceive that to be true, and some men do not. Is there any imagination about it in those who do? It is as real as the earth. It is as real as themselves.

Again, those are great religious truths that Jesus announces in the Sermon on the Mount;—that it is not only criminal to *kill,* but criminal in the same sort, to *hate;* that it is not only criminal to indulge in gross acts of sin, but to indulge the sinful desire.[1] Some men perceive these to be true sayings; some men do not. Is there any imagination in those who do? I say then that it is a gross error to confound faith with imagination. God never requires of any of his children to believe what they do not understand but has made the human mind to receive truth as much as the stomach to digest bread.

2. To consider this error as it affects our practice. Men not interested in religious truth think that those who are called religious men are in the same state of mind as they are, and only differ from themselves in this, that those persons are willing to bind themselves to live after a peculiar fashion, to use certain language and observe certain ordinances whilst they are not. They think that you may become more and more religious (as men take degrees in masonry) without affecting their character or way of thinking in the smallest degree. What is more strange, men not only hold this error as to religion in others but also as to themselves, and so there are multitudes of nominal Christians, and the Church is made up of unworthy members, and what is called religion is maintained as some great unmeaning ceremony. Is it not a wonderful, is it not a pernicious, a fatal error? All society would fall to pieces if its great

---

1. Matthew 5:21-22, 5:27-28.

interests were managed as that is which is called religion. It would be a dreary scene of emptiness.

Men treat religion with respect. They go to church, they pray, they read the bible; they do all these things with reluctance—are glad when they are done, and they get back to what they love, and think this will serve them in the sight of God, will do them some good,—win them some interest in heaven. They serve an idol. They never knew God. It can do them no good. A religion that dwells in the tongue or the brain or the custom is no religion. It must have the heart; and to affect the heart it must be a substance and not a shadow.

For God has so constituted the human race that they must deal with realities. What sort of a farmer would he be who talked of cultivation but never planted a seed? What sort of merchant who talked about commerce but never bought or sold? What sort of a chemist who discoursed on the probable effects of caloric or of azote without an experiment? And therefore a religion of outward respects, a religion consisting in a decorous regard for the institutions of worship, a lip service, an eye service, an ear service, it is all vanity.

Oh no. It is a spirit that must make these dry bones live, or they are dead.[2] It is the heart that must come in to every human work that is really to be done. The heart must become religious or religious hands or lips will profit nothing.

Only compare the things that men do heartily with those they do in this formal way. See the lover sick with passion for the society of his friend; is it of any consequence to him how long is the way, or how sad the sky, or how poor is the house? Does he need to put on any face, or make up any speech? No, the very delight of the connexion is, that it is all unaffected, that he gives himself up without restraint to the enjoyment of his feelings, and the mere pleasure of admiration and trust is enough for the heart.

Or here is a philosopher seeking a conversation on subjects which he lives to study, with a wise man. The hope of it comforts him when he wakes in the morning, and enters into all the arrangements of the day. Does it trouble him that it rains, or that the times are hard, or that he loses a gay party when he posts away at the appointed hour to the house of the sage? Here is the scholar who has got the book that for years he has desired and steals away into his chamber to read it. Here is the artist seeking a picture; or the mechanist a model; or the botanist a plant; or the huntsman a horse. The merchant in the prospect of a great bargain leaves no land unsearched and no sea—he cannot think too much upon it. Wherever he goes it goes with him, and as his plan matures and succeeds, his spirits rise, and he is never weary of any conversation or work that will help it to a good issue.

Well is there any affectation in these things? No, they have what they seek; and they draw a solid satisfaction from them. There's no sham at all about it, no effort to be pleased or to appear pleased, but they go about their several doings

2. Cf. Ezekiel 37:1-14.

with manifest goodwill. "The heart is the sole world, the universe," and, if its wants are satisfied, no defect is perceived.

These men enjoy these things because they have them and not imagine them.

And the truly religious man enjoys his religion because he has it; and no man can ever have any use or good out of it, who has it not. It must be a reality to him.

And so it is. Look at the fervent Methodist stealing away from every occupation and pleasure that other men pursue, to the obscure street where his humble class meet to sing and pray. Look at the sectarian of each New Church that arises in the bosom of Christendom and see what an absorbing reality religion is to them.[3] It gives them a solid contentment. These new sects teach under a new name always the same truth, namely, that religion has become merely formal with the bulk of society, and they feel it to be real. But why go so far? Each of you when you have done right, from the first hour of your recollection to this day, have felt the truth and excellence of so doing, which was the dawn of religion in the soul.

If therefore you find any difficulty in it; if religion is disagreeable to you and what you call your religious services are done against your will, why shut your eyes to the fact that you have no religion at all, and that all your views of it are false?

When the truth of the commandment is seen in the *understanding,* and when it is obeyed by the *Will,* then comes the peace and joy which the world cannot give. The pleasure of obedience increases precisely with the fidelity of obedience. Our respect for our own souls, our religious veneration for conscience, our regard for the souls of others, our hope in the future, our love of the truth, increase in the same measure. These spiritual goods in the New Testament are called the *Kingdom of Heaven.* It is not surely an imaginary heaven; then it would not be any at all. But it is the only real peace, the only unmixed satisfaction human nature knows.

It will be seen that the question as to the truth and reality of religion is very different from the question as to the truth of the records of our faith. A man may be religious in Asia, or Africa, or the remotest islands where the Bible never went. When the bible comes to him it will be one thing to perceive the eternal truth of its moral doctrines, which if he is a good man he will perceive, and another thing to settle in his mind the credibility of the historical facts therein recorded.

Therefore, my friends, would any of you truly reckon with his conscience and his Maker and know whether Religion is any thing to you? You have only to consider whether you are keeping the Commandments out of a simple regard to their own eternal goodness, for that it is to keep them out of love to God. The question is a plain one—We can put it to ourselves.

---

3. Emerson refers here to the Church of the New Jerusalem, the Swedenborgians.

But after we have examined ourselves by this test and found that we are not
religious persons there still may remain in the thought of some who do not find
that religious truth has much hold of their affections the further question—
Since this is not a reality to me, is it to any one? The world of sense is manifest
enough. I see and understand the value of the operations of men in it. They eat;
drink; marry; get gain; build houses; make war; sail on the sea; suffer; sicken;
and die. These things I see and sympathize with; I have a relish for the pleasures
of sense, and a horror for pain. But not well can I understand what you tell me
of spiritual things. I doubt of the soul. I doubt of judgment. I doubt of immortality. I doubt of God.

If any whom I address have doubts that reach to this extent, I believe it is
because (what is a common case,) they have not rightly weighed facts that speak
from within us concerning our spiritual nature.

There is something awful in the attributes of a human mind. You doubt of the
immortality of the Soul;—and well you may, for the mind staggers under a
thought so vast; but consider, I beseech you, the nature of your soul: that no
truth can be announced to you of any kind but the soul immediately takes it up
into itself and seems to recognize it as already known. See how strangely all
things seem in their principles to be contained in your mind.

Do you doubt of the reality of the *Judgement*? Consider, I pray you, that in
every human mind there is that peremptory decision upon every action that is
done under its eye, upon every action of every man. Every child in all the great
families encamped under the broad vault of heaven all round the globe, every
individual in all the past nations from Adam until now, hath had this eye opened
within him upon all actions. Every man contains within him this wondrous
tribunal by which truth is affirmed and wrong condemned, by which laws and
institutions are sustained or overthrown, by which nations are defended. He
contains it in him without surplus or diminution, as one form of the omnipresence of God. Is it not a glorious provision for his government that has put
the governor into every soul that he hath made?

And thus is Reformation secured for the corruptest church; thus is religion
provided for in the cruellest idolatry; thus is Liberty seated behind the last
bulwark of Despotism, yea, in the soul of every soldier that fights for a tyrant;
thus is Virtue planted under the foulest vices in the worst bosom that is defiled
by lust or pinched by selfishness or fired by revenge. Is not this a living Judgment Seat from which in a voice clearer than the archangel's trumpet God
pronounces and ever shall pronounce judgment upon every soul of man?[4] And
seeing these things, conversing with the human soul, and beholding the never-
ending wisdom and beauty of the world, can you doubt that the Law which
overrules it all and forms it day by day must be real?

I beseech you therefore, brethren, to consider with new attention the claims
of the gospel. For if it is hid from you, ye are lost. For these things which

4. Cf. Romans 2:9.

Religion teaches and does are real and eternal. Many ways are wrong; only one can be right. If this be what all who have tried it know it to be, a way of peace, all others are ways of sorrow. Religion, as it is taught in the heart, Religion as it is taught in the gospel of Christ, as it is taught in his life, consists in keeping the commandments. If we keep them they will keep us. If we do not keep them they will be still right and we shall be wrong. If they do not work us good they will oppose us and work us wo. If our gospel be hid it is because we are lost.

CXXXIV

Thou desirest truth in the inward parts.
PSALMS 51:6

To name Truth is to praise it. There is no man, however corrupt, who will not admit that truth is better than falsehood. Yet almost as soon as this comparison is taken out of the abstract proposition and presented in a practical shape, as soon as conversation offers the opportunity of chusing the true or the false, most men begin to dissemble. A very close scrutiny, who can bear? A very close scrutiny of the sincerity of men will perhaps make us see too much truth in what David said in haste, that all men are liars.[1]

I would not, my friends, begin an exhortation to follow the truth, with rash and exaggerated charges upon society for its violation, and therefore before I offer what I have to say upon the larger sense of truth which is called *truth of character* and which may be meant by the words in the text 'truth in the inward parts,' I will speak of the truth of conversation and specify some of the occasions on which it is violated by our customs.

I propose to consider 1. Truth of conversation, and 2. Truth of character, which is the source of truth of conversation.

It is very hard to speak the truth amidst the temptations of bad customs. In the world where all of us live and which we make up, truth is a secondary thing. In heaven it is the first thing. Who can withstand the expectation of society? You are expected to say smooth things first, and true things no longer than they are pleasant; and to make assurances of regard which you do not feel; and to pay visits which are disagreeable to the maker and the receiver; and to talk when you have nothing to say; and nothing is less expected, than that a man should have made up his opinions on the ground of simple truth. How many men or women do you meet who are in earnest to know what is true and never lose sight of that end in their discourse? Some leave it from courtesy; some from contradiction; some from laziness; some from vanity; some, to be amusing;

Manuscript dated November 6, 1831. Preached nine times: November 6, 1831, at the Second Church, Boston; November 27 at the Purchase Street Church, Boston; December 4 at the New North Church, Boston; March 25, 1832, at the Castle Street Church, Boston; July 12, 1835, in Lexington; July 26 in Waltham; August 9 in Chelmsford; January 17, 1836, in Weston; and June 26 in West Cambridge. Some portions toward the end of the sermon probably represent revisions done after the first delivery; see the Textual and Manuscript Notes.

1. Psalms 116:11.

some, from interest; some, from example; some for party; some for the sake of talking.

It was said of one of the Roman Emperors that at nineteen he put on the cloke of dissimulation which he never put off.[2] And we meet people for whom simple truth never seems enough. If you talk to them they afflict you with an excess of interest in all that you say and add to their exclamations surprize, grimace and gesticulation. You wonder that the fatigue of acting a part does not become intolerable to them. This remark may be extended to much of that profusion of words in which in writing or in speech we express civility. I know that here many persons would find the chief difficulty lie. It was petulantly said of the French language, which is most copious in forms of civility, that one could not speak twenty words in it without lying.[3] And many well meaning persons who speak the honest English tongue do yet surrender their integrity to what they think good nature demands, a compliance with deceitful forms of speech.

I believe there is more courtesy in words of truth than in words without it. I believe that neither justice nor benevolence ever require flattery.

There are others almost as numerous, in whose conversation the love of truth is always subordinate to the desire of making out a good story for themselves, and if they do not falsify yet their object is not to show what is or what ought to be but to show what part they bore in every occurrence, and that they bore an important part, ignorant that this egotism cannot impose upon any sensible person, but he thinks more meanly of them by every fact they add in their own praise.

Then how many there are who neither know nor care for the truth but their whole conversation though very plausible is feeling after the opinion of them with whom they deal, and they are content, when they have found it, to echo it. You may find this heartless talk which seems to think that there is nothing worth living for. You may find it among people of good understandings in every place. But to me it seems worst where it is apt to intrude in the chambers of sickness, in the desolate house of mourning.

The nearer any thing is to the heart the more impatient we are of insincerity. We can bear that people should exercise their loquacity upon things indifferent to us but they might forbear idle prating about that which is sacred to us. I speak of the mourner. When men are afflicted they want truth. Only truth is tolerable to the petulance of grief. He that does not speak it insults you with every word. He is not seeking truth and therefore what you say and feel has no interest to him and you will not molest yourself by uttering it. He is thinking only of himself, and how he shall come off. Let him be silent. We learn from him the sad difference between words that are things and words that are words. The mourner is suffering now under a privation of the affections and this insincerity adds a privation of the whole spiritual world.

2. The allusion is to Tiberius, second emperor of Rome (A.D. 14–37). See Bacon, "Of Simulation and Dissimulation," in *The Works of Francis Bacon* (London, 1857–1874), 6:387.

3. Used in "Truth," *English Traits* (W 5:118).

Every thing seems fading away from him, all but this hungry, thirsty, diseased, perishing flesh. What we mourn for is the loss of a friendship so near and intimate that it was wholly sincere. It had no need of the drapery of courtesy and this hollow talk makes him feel the loss the more. It suggests to us the disapprobation which the departed would feel or feels with us and draws us nearer to the dead and farther from the living.

These are but a few particulars out of all the violations of truth which might be named—violations of truth of conversation. The source of all these falsehoods is the same. The vice at the bottom of all these follies is a defect which it is possible has never presented itself to some young persons who hear me, as a defect—but which all of us must perceive before ever any progress can be made toward the formation of a religious character,—I mean the want of a reverence for truth itself. Vulgar minds value whatever knowledge they have as a means to some end of their own, as if you should read a book for the sake of talking about it, or should learn nothing that would not help you to get bread.

Great minds value the truth as the end, that it is a worthy and sufficient object for an intelligent mind, that it should desire to know and in all companies and at all times should seek what God has actually done and established. In all conversation, therefore, he seeks not to *say* what he can, but to learn what he can. If you know less than he, he sets you right. If you know more, he receives information.

And I think I cannot too strongly urge this consideration upon the attention of all, that we are not here as merchants to make a petty advantage of what we know, nor as Rabbis, who are expected to know all things, and who have a reputation for learning to keep; but we ought to feel that God has put us here, from the oldest to the youngest, as little children, to be instructed by his Providence and by his Word in things necessary: that here he is unrolling before the eyes of each one of us, the great map of his creation, that we may rightly learn its extent, and our true place in it. He is leading each one through a series of instructive events—now placing you in one company, now in another; now appointing you to labor, then to rest, then to sickness, then to honour; drawing out your affections, gratifying them, disappointing them—he is leading each one through this sunshine and shade—as so many lessons in his school to call out successively each of the faculties and fit every mind for the duties now unknown to us of the next world.

This, as far as we can see and as far as we are told, is the design, and it becomes us to live and think accordingly. This will direct us to what is a right conversation. We are not angrily to take sides upon questions, but to find what is true. We are not to find what people think but what God thinks, that is, what is true. We are not to be ashamed of being ignorant of what we could not know but to own it in order to remove it.

Let it be remembered that truth is what we were made to know and serve. All excellence in every kind is approach to truth. Truth in things is skill; seeing truth is wisdom; speaking truth is eloquence; loving truth is holiness; acting truth is power. The cunning tradesman is he who is most faithful in applying himself to the laws of nature, i.e., the truth of things. The eloquent orator is he who adheres closest to the truth of the facts and the truth of the feelings. The wisest statesman is he that best knows and touches closest the actual state of things in the Commonwealth.

The powerful reasoner does not make his reasons, he merely sees and repeats them. As Jesus saith, "it is not I that speak but my Father." It is not I that speak, but Truth through my lips, and so he promises his disciples that if they will not think too fearfully how much can be said but take for their guide the truth of the time and the cause it shall not be they but God that speaks.[4]

This doctrine that truth is our main object, and not a means to any end but the end itself, (unless you please to say that truth becomes a means when considered in relation to virtue, which I shall not dispute) this doctrine being fully understood leads directly to what is called *truth of character,* the larger sense of truth on which I proposed to remark. It is that habit of mind which we denote by the word 'singleness' or 'single mindedness.' It is 'truth in the inward parts'— truth pervading the whole man. It is the character of that mind which does what it does with its own full consent; a man who does not look one way and walk another; a man in whom there is no rebellion of so much as a gesture or a word from the single purpose which all his powers conspire to fulfil. This, it will be admitted, would be the perfection of the human character.

It is the habit of that character which is seeking to know itself, to discover what is the use for which God designed it in his kingdom, i.e., what is that employment in which every power of his mind is in full exercise and none is demanded which he has not. It is that habit of character which we mean when we say a man is *true to himself,* who knows what he can do and what he cannot and as freely acknowledges his defects as he exerts his talents.

Yet something like this is seen in great and good men that from time to time God has raised up in the world as if to cheer and stimulate us. It is from such a person that we learn the value of words. And it is only in such a character that we discern what truth of conversation imports. From such a man would be heard, as from every man ought to be, no idle words. There are words that are felt to be as forcible as actions, and whenever the word comes from the heart it is so. A man should not utter a word he is not willing to act. A man should not utter a word he is not willing to die for. He should be of that singleness throughout, that his whole being is guarantee for every act, and his speech should be counted as one of his acts.

It is a common proverb that, 'actions speak louder than words'; but it is only true when the words and the actions are at variance; when they are alike, words speak louder than actions, are a higher class of actions.

Such a person would be slow to speak, for Silence, says the old maxim, is the candidate for truth.[5] And when he spoke every word would tell,—would be

4. Cf. John 14:6–14.
5. Francis Bacon, *The Advancement of Learning,* in *The Works* (London, 1857–1874), 5:31; see *JMN* 6:121.

uttered for a distinct purpose, and would execute that purpose and so would be as necessary and as much a part of the man as his most serious and long continued undertaking. Words are things or nothings. By such a mind nothing is said for show, nothing is said for by-ends, nothing for self love, nothing from want of thought, but all is dictated from the great principles which lie at the bottom of all the actions.

This is the state of mind that in the sight of God is of great price. The offering of this mind he will accept. For the offering is the mind itself. He that closely follows truth in thought will follow it in action. But truth in action is right, or virtue, or obedience to the Commandments. And every sin is a violation of truth in action. My friends, are we the friends and followers of truth? It is our natural element. As light to the eye is truth to the mind, if it lose it, it becomes diseased and dies. Let the example of Jesus Christ, who was himself the bright example I have considered of unity of character, whose words went with his actions and so he spake as never man spake,[6] save us from offending against it. Let the love of God, who desires truth in the inward parts and who hath declared that the lip of truth shall be established forever,[7] make us constant to our convictions, cautious in departing by the least word or sign from the straightforward path of integrity.

Permit me in conclusion of this discourse to make a practical application of its doctrine. I have endeavoured to show that in the best man there are no idle words but his words are things. Is there any more plain duty than this, that we ought to set out with the sublime purpose never to violate the truth? Is this not an object important enough to be worth some sacrifices? If a man would own a county, he must not spend for trifles. If a man aspires to speak the truth, if he would have every word he utters pass for entire fact he must not make compliments. It will cost you much consideration and some sacrifices. You must be careful when you dispute. Be careful with those whom you would please. It will cost you many self-denials and possibly some unjust reproaches to hold your tongue when a talker looks in your face for assent, or a flatterer expects his payment in praise. Let it cost something. It is worth all. Would not the value of that man's words be presently known? Would not he be blessed in heaven and earth who could not frame an untruth in his mind, whose lips refused to utter it?[8] Would not his soul be filled with sublime peace? He would repose on the rock of Ages, upon all that is good and enduring in the Universe, upon the God of Truth Himself.

6. Cf. John 7:46.
7. Cf. Proverbs 12:19.
8. This is apparently an allusion to Emmanuel Swedenborg, *The Apocalypse Revealed,* 3 vols. (London, 1832), 1:255; cf. *JMN* 4:342–43: "Very philosophical was their tale that in the other world certain spirits tried to pronounce a word representing somewhat which they did not believe. They twisted their lips into all manner of folds even to indignation but could not utter the word." Cf. "Spiritual Laws" (*CW* 2:91).

CXXXV _____

*Let every man be fully
persuaded in his own mind.*

ROMANS 14:5

I had occasion recently to offer to your consideration some thoughts upon truth of character or upon that excellence which is called single mindedness.[1] It is obvious that singleness of character must depend on simplicity of motive, and I have now to ask your serious attention to some remarks in opposition to the common opinion, yea and to an opinion of great authority, (if ever any authority in support of a false opinion can be called great) that we ought to do and to forbear many things out of regard to the effect of our example. I believe the truth is you must act from the naked purpose to do right and not mix other motives therewith.

It is commonly thought that a great many things ought to be done for the sake of example. That many indulgences in which we might permit ourselves safely, it will not do to use on account of the effect of our example; that especially in religious observances, at times when we could well dispense with attendance on church or on prayer or on almsgiving on our own account, it will not do to neglect them because of setting a bad example. I believe this motive an improper one. I believe we ought never to do any thing for the sake of an example. And I desire to present as distinctly as I can the reasons which ought to forbid the use of such language and remove such an opinion from among Christians.

1. It is wholly unsuitable to that humility which befits a child of God. Who are you that have attained such an exaltation of virtue that you have no longer need to consult for your own salvation, your rescue from pressing temptations, but may look complacently round to see how you shall fittest walk to lead your fellow men into ways that are safe for them? You are safe from danger, quite relieved from any apprehension of harm, quite absolved from any obligation to go forward and condescendingly interfere and play a trick to save your neighbors. It seems to me it is an insult upon your fellow men to intimate that there is

Manuscript dated November 20, 1831. Preached twice: November 20, 1831, at the Second Church, Boston, and February 18, 1838, in East Lexington. A draft passage for this sermon occurs in *JMN* 3:303–4.
    1. In Sermon CXXXIV.

one law for you which is easy and another law for them which is hard, and it betrays a surpassing ignorance of the great and ever increasing task which God has appointed to yourself and which so far from being capable of being done and leaving you leisure, is never done, never can be done, and is always becoming more instead of less.

2. It is a departure from simplicity of action. It is a duplicity. It is a deception. It is a hypocrisy. It is acting to be seen of men and attended with all the dangers of such a course to the soul that admits it. According to the common way of thinking, things which I do not think wrong for me I am to affect not to do and affect to think wrong lest another should do them whom they will hurt. You see it is plainly to forsake that great light which God set up in our breasts for our guide and to trust our course to very uncertain lights. One thing I know well, that it is right for me to do thus and wrong to do thus, so written by eternal laws.

Why should I quit this plain statute and embarrass myself by the perplexing question of what may be the effect of my conduct upon others? If once you set out to act from that motive, from a calculation of the probable or possible consequences of your action upon the conduct of others, you need omniscience to go right, for every action is liable to misinterpretation, and to be copied by those who should not copy it; and you would never act at all, lest a wrong handle should be made of your action.

3. Moreover it is followed by the natural consequence of all duplicity or deception: it cheats nobody; it defeats itself. For the only reason why men respect your example, is, that they think you are speaking sincerely and acting heartily; the moment they find, as they infallibly will find, that you are *acting a part,* they lose confidence in you and will only regard those actions as your example which they think speak your real sentiments.

4. But, fourthly and chiefly, it is wholly superfluous. The obligation to do right for right's sake is perfect in every individual mind. And in general and in almost every particular, if punctually followed out, will be found to command the observance of the same things that a regard for one's example is now supposed to enjoin. Now it is of immense importance to every man who would establish a character that can stand forever, that he should act with the full consent of his own mind in every thing he doth, from the highest down to the most insignificant performance, that he should mean to be believed in every word he speaks, and esteemed as acting heartily in every thing he does.

Let the good man leave these crooked roads and take the shortest way. To seem good let him be good. Let him use his own judgment and calmly determine whether the action is in itself right or wrong, and act accordingly, and let the example follow as it may. Of a good tree the fruit is good.[2] Cast thy bread upon the waters.[3] Cast thy good action upon the world, and leave its appear-

2. Matthew 7:17.
3. Ecclesiastes 11:1.

ance and its issues with God. Surely a good example is a most persuasive argument which you can address to the minds of your fellow men. A good example is the richest gift you can bestow but the only way to make your example truly good is to have it genuine, not from the desire to have a good example, but to do good actions. There never was a good action since the world began but God and good angels followed it out with good consequences to the end of its effect. There never was an evil action how plausible and varnished over with whatever appearances but it was poisonous in its effects. Whilst you act with your whole mind, from the best light he has given you, he will be responsible for the consequences.

> "This above all to thy own self be true,
> And it must follow as the night to day
> Thou canst not then be false to any man."[4]

But it will be asked, is it so easy to dispose of this grave question and am I really absolutely free from the restraints I have so long imposed upon myself, (as I thought) out of an imperious regard to the wellbeing of the community; and need I never look beyond my simple duty to myself, in so many questions of practice as occur, where my way of acting will certainly influence some others? What, then, is the use of the consideration of others in my actions, which I cannot get rid of and which surely presents itself sometimes with commanding force?

Thus here is a pious man who scruples to engage in some employments which he regards as very suitable and proper for him, which others think very frivolous and disgraceful, or suppose one who scruples to attend the theatre to hear some fine declamation because others will think it very unsuitable for him to go, or suppose one man thinks it right to occupy the hours of the Sabbath in conversation and works which another man thinks profane the day, and so abstains. One man regards dancing as a pleasing and innocent recreation; his neighbors think it would be very indecorous in him.

As soon as it comes to the point when one of these things on which we have meditated is to be done do you not see with what force this consideration of the effect upon others will present itself? What is the advantage of this scruple and hesitation which rises in every man's mind, if it is not right to regard it?

I conceive there is an use, a great use, in that consideration. It is a wise and beneficent order of Providence to give us a new and better view of the whole thing. Our attention is forcibly called to the effect, to the consequence of the action, and so the whole shown us as in a glass by which we may better judge of its true character. If we see that real dangers appear, why it stimulates our attention more keenly to review the action itself, and very likely we find that it is in itself something foolish or wrong for ourselves, for I see how it is going to

---

4. Shakespeare, *Hamlet,* I, iii, 78–80.

injure my neighbor and on reflection I perceive perhaps that it tends to injure or is injuring me in the selfsame way. Thus a man indulges, as he thinks, innocently, in the occasional use of ardent spirit. He is perfectly sure that it has never done him any injury and such his selfcommand that it never can. Still he is prompted by regard to his neighbor who sits with him to abstain, for fear he, having much less prudence and selfcommand, should drink, encouraged by his example, and become a sot. These thoughts lead him to inquire whether really it is useful or safe or innocent *for himself,* and presently perhaps to the conclusion that it is not; that it is a foolish and dangerous self-indulgence.

If, however, on this consideration, on these calm second thoughts, the action seems to you perfectly innocent and right for you, then do it (without any unseasonable fear that God shall not take care that his children shall not harm each other); if it does not, forbear; but, doing or abstaining, act with your whole heart, in simple reference to the moral quality of the action itself.

And, if you consider it well, nothing is more needless than any fear of the bad effects of the example of a good man. There is no danger of its being misinterpreted. One part of his example will explain another part of his example, and no one in good faith will appeal to the act without considering also the principle.

A Swedenborgian believes that it is right to join in public worship only on Sunday morning and that he receives this instruction by a revelation. Would there be any reason why a pious member of that sect should constrain himself to attend what he reckoned an unsuitable service in the afternoon for fear lest his example should induce others to stay away who did not hold his opinion? If he was conscientious in this, men would expect he would be conscientious in practice of all his opinions and would judge him by his own law.

Nor will a man who strictly adheres to the rules of his conscience come under suspicion from the peculiarities of his deportment any more than a suspicion attaches to Jesus because he was the associate of publicans and sinners.[5]

Finally, do not suppose, my friends, that in ceasing forever to act from a regard to our example and acting from simple regard to the good or the evil of the action itself, do not suppose that in so doing we should be relaxing the obligations to virtue. We should be coming under a more not a less strict law. We have the dangerous habit of reading our duty in the eyes of others; and others judge by the false standard of custom; but if we will cast down this and every idol, and let God speak by his word and by his Representative in the human heart, and allow ourselves only in such freedom as that allows, and do all which that enjoins, we shall find the day is not long enough to leave us leisure, nor a saint's life pure enough to satisfy its law. It will not do to leave undone the good actions we now perform from example, without also doing those which our Conscience approves, that now we leave undone, because society gets along without them.

5. Cf. Mark 2:16.

If we take the indulgence of the law we must also take its strictness. We shall then I believe find ourselves led by a new and purer motive to do the same things for their real good, for the salvation of our souls, which now we are hypocritically doing, as we say, *for the advantage of other men*. We shall find that the praise of God and the love of all good minds and the admiration of the young and the desire to imitate and equal it follow and rest upon the single and true heart that acts entirely when it acts at all, and from the love of right and not to be seen of men.

Textual and Manuscript Notes

In these notes, a physical description of the sermon manuscript is followed by a record, keyed to the text by page and line number, of all of Emerson's insertions, cancellations, variant passages, and transpositions, as well as all editorial changes not covered in the categories of silent emendation outlined in the Textual Introduction. The text given here is a literal genetic transcription of the manuscript and therefore differs in some respects from the edited version above. Editorial matter is enclosed in square brackets, while Emerson's brackets are represented as curved. All inscription is in ink unless otherwise noted.

The symbols used in these notes are explained in the list below. Matter that immediately follows a cancellation without space or symbol of insertion, as in "⟨i⟩It" or "⟨we⟩you," should be understood as having been written directly over the canceled matter.

Symbols

⟨ ⟩	Cancellation
↑ ↓	Insertion
/ / /	Variant
[ ]	Editorial insertion
{ }	Emerson's square brackets
¶	Paragraph

Sermon XCI

Manuscript: Four sheets folded to make four pages each; folios nested and sewn with white thread around the left edge; pages measure 25 x 20.1 cm. A leaf (14 x 18.6 cm.) containing an added passage, verso blank, is tipped to the recto of leaf 6.

[Two variant Bible texts are in light pencil partly overwritten by the final text in dark pencil:] / As sorrowful, yet always rejoicing II Cor. VI. 10/Come unto me all ye yᵗ labor & are heavy laden & I will give you rest Mat. 11. 28./

Lines	*Page 13*
5–6	if the ⟨assertions⟩ doctrine↑s↓ which these miracles /accompanied/ were wro't to attest/,
11–13	miracle p answer . . . end that /it/the purpose of it/ . . . come to ⟨attes⟩ prove . . . or any thing ⟨trifling⟩↑in↓different
22	¶ Now ⟨it seems to me that⟩ I wish . . . attention to /what seems to me/a . . . brings/

24-(14)2   consolation ⟨If a religion⟩ to human suffering. ⟨If the course of these
                remarks shall seem to speak the truth of the gospel to any who
                especially need consolation it would be the best confirmation of their
                ⟨truth⟩ justice.⟩ ["If the . . . justice." canceled in pencil] ¶ A . . .
                man↑,↓ ⟨would⟩ we . . . misery. ⟨The world is⟩ Man

                                        Page 14
9-11   individuals, of ↑the devastation of pestilence, the scourge of war↓
                hard . . . sea, ↑of ⟨insurrection⟩ the rising of slaves on their masters
                or the oppression of colonies by their gov.t↓ of gross [additions and
                cancellations in pencil rejected as late emendations on the supposition
                that Emerson's allusion is to Nat Turner's rebellion of August, 1831]
                . . . parties↑,↓ . . . of the ⟨w⟩few by the many↑,↓ [commas added in
                pencil]
16   who ⟨are nearest him⟩ ↑stand around his bed,↓
18   defeated & ⟨loneliness⟩ the house
21-23   death & ⟨I find them⟩ ↑tho' . . . things↓
27-30   man / you have lost your ⟨w⟩ / estate / property / / you have failed in yr
                applic /, [last variant in pencil] . . . of it, ⟨but⟩ ⟨and⟩ ↑or↓ . . . you
                ⟨that⟩ ↑as↓ . . . it. [Emerson's caret, but no inserted text] You . . . if
                ⟨you⟩ he
30   your ⟨father⟩ ↑parent↓,
33   with ↑a↓ chronick ⟨c⟩malady
34-35   desired. [Here follows a passage in pencil which, in revised form,
                occurs in ink as Insert "A" below:] ↑False Religion attempted to
                alleviate suffering by mending the circumstances of the sufferer
                ⟨without reference⟩ his character remain⟨s⟩ing the same. true
                religion proposed to change his character without any attention to yᵉ
                circumstances↓ ¶ ↑This . . . other.↓

                                        Page 15
3   ¶ Now the ⟨New Testament⟩ gospel
5-7   what ⟨a⟩rewards . . . speaks to ⟨your⟩ ↑the human↓ . . . you ⟨rest.⟩
                ↑principles.↓
8-10   will / be religious / believe / . . . shall be ⟨glorious⟩ well
11   ↑worldly↓
13-14   ↑Forsake all.↓
14-15   follow me. ⟨What then were the requisitions & what the consolations
                that spring from them He gave all in this Love the Lord thy God in
                with all thy heart & thy neighbor as thyself⟩ [canceled in pencil and
                ink] ↑ie Love . . . ↑means of↓ . . . God.↓
18-19   ↑And . . . them?↓
20   say, ⟨S⟩Let your affections ⟨upon⟩ ↑receive↓
23-24   ↑Let . . . primal ⟨principle⟩ love↓
30   uplifting ⟨peace of enjoying⟩ ↑assurance of↓ [emendation in pencil]

                                        Page 16
3-10   God. ¶ ↑{Insert A.}↓ [At the bottom of the page, a passage marked
                "A.":] ↑{The ↑sum of this↓ distinction then ⟨that I wd show⟩

between . . . & Xty ⟨was⟩ ↑is↓ . . . alleviate ⟨the⟩ suffering by ⟨atte⟩↑me↓nding . . . same. ⟨t⟩True religion . . . circumstances.} ↑This . . . soul↓↓ ["This . . . soul" is added in ink over a pencil version that reads:] ↑This . . . a sword. I bring . . . peace to within↓

12   apostles ⟨and⟩ which
17–18   philosophy. ¶ ⟨I wish to⟩ ↑Let me↓ add ⟨a few⟩ ↑one or two↓ [emendations in pencil]
23   revolve⟨s⟩ in their [word obscured by sealing wax] orbit and ⟨all⟩ every
26–27   ↑It is the unfailing . . . God—down to the least↓
28–37   ↑It is simply . . . what↑,↓ no doubt↑,↓ [commas added in pencil] . . . first, so ↑is↓ he . . . pleasures of virtue.↓ [On a leaf affixed with sealing wax over "It is the health of the Soul. Happiness . . . orbit"]

Page 17

1–2   known the ⟨s⟩ true
4   inward ⟨ & that his s your soul is capable⟩↑.↓ [period added in pencil]
6   ↑now . . . is↓ [addition in pencil]
7–8   regard ⟨your⟩ those
12–15   perfections that /the faith may grow into your souls/when . . . gone,/ [variant in pencil] . . . connexions of [end of line] of affection . . . glorified—in ⟨heaven.⟩ the

[Following the end of the sermon are these notations:]
    The God of hope fill you with all joy & peace in believing—Rom 15.13

   ↑If you are good you will love them If you love them you cannot spare them without pain.↓ [addition in pencil]

Sermon XCII

Manuscript: Six sheets folded to make four pages each; folios stacked and cross-stitched with white thread around left edge; pages measure 25 x 20.1 cm.

[Below the Bible text:]   Salem [in pencil]

Lines	*Page 18*
3	falsehood? He
6	calamity. ↑to mankind.↓
7	dispraise, ⟨first⟩ and
11–13	truth. ⟨These⟩ By these falsehoods, ⟨the⟩ ↑many↓ . . . been ⟨its⟩ ↑the↓ warmest friends ↑of the Christian faith↓
15–16	proportion to /what/the degree of/ independence
20	is ⟨v⟩much
23	diminishing ⟨its⟩ ↑the strength of its↓
25–27	it. ¶ ⟨The points ⟨in⟩to which I mean to ask your attention at present are two. ⟨first⟩ [end of line] ⟨I.⟩ In the first place there is thought to be⟩ ↑It . . . is↓ . . . faith. ⟨a⟩ many

Page 19

1–3   reason. ↑a false . . . up↓ [in pencil] . . . where ⟨we⟩ this
7–12   There ⟨↑still↓⟩ / prevail / are ⟨throughout⟩ to a great extent / [emen-
            dations in pencil] . . . heathens / & that there is something unfriendly
            to the virtue of the natural heart / & secondly . . . ↑dearest↓ privelege
            . . . prejudices. /
18   ↑this↓
21–23   ↑this . . . but↓ something . . . unfairness ⟨is seen⟩ ↑may be con-
            tinually observed↓
27   ↑at once↓
30–33   reason. ⟨I would look at the administration.⟩ The ↑perfection of the↓
            . . . ↑the perfection of↓ . . . another,—but th⟨is⟩e ↑gospel↓ . . .
            ↑trembling↓ . . . ↑glowing↓
35   receive ⟨but⟩ ↑and↓ which ⟨must⟩ ↑are to↓
36   whole ⟨force⟩ ↑credit↓ . . . lies in [end of line] i⟨ts⟩n the
38   which ⟨Socrates or Plato⟩ ↑any . . . heathen↓

Page 20

1   would ⟨hail⟩ [end of line] hail
3   Eden in the [end of page] the
5–6   brethren, and . . . gleam of / truth / the light of nature /,
14   We ⟨are⟩ have
19–22   unclean. ↑& from . . . respecter &c &c.↓ ¶ More [The allusion is
            completed from Acts 10:34–35. The following addition appears oppo-
            site this passage on the otherwise blank preceding and facing page:]
            ↑"I am not come to call the righteous but sinners to repentance."↓
24   some the old ⟨Stoic⟩ heathen
26   most ⟨valuable⟩ ↑important↓
28   heathens, that . . . only [end of page] ⟨can⟩ be
31   dependance & ⟨g⟩ instructer ⟨&⟩ than
32   humble, that
35–38   made. ¶ ↑X↓ [At the bottom of the page, a passage marked "X":] ↑↑It
            . . . humility—reference to Gods strength.↓ {Who . . . God.}↓

Page 21

5   the ⟨opinio⟩ idea
12–13   him. ¶ ⟨However it⟩ ↑Whatever the cause may↓
15   interesting [end of page] men,
19   gospel, ⟨& p⟩ explores
24   consider a ⟨dangerous & pernicious⟩ ↑mischievous↓
26   adverse to the ⟨oppressing⟩ ↑hoodwinking↓
28–30   dogmas. ↑X↓ [On the preceding and facing page, a passage marked
            "X":] ↑{But . . . ↑The power of↓ . . . articles.↓
39–42   account, that ⟨every⟩ ↑the↓ pure ↑in↓ . . . him that we are spiritual,
            that

Page 22

1   is the ⟨ge⟩ direct
20–22   mind that . . . effectual ⟨love⟩ ↑support↓.

Sermon XCIII

Manuscript: Seven sheets folded to make four pages each; folios stacked and sewn with white thread along the left edge; pages of first folio measure 24.3 x 20.3 cm, and those of remaining folios measure 25 x 20.1 cm. The first folio contains what is apparently a revised fair copy of the first one and a half paragraphs. The text, which is without revisions, occupies MS pp. 1–2; pp. 3–4 are blank.

Lines	*Page 23*
Bible Text	observation neither
17–20	imperfectly comprehended by most of those who heard him [end of MS p. 2] comprehended by most of those who heard him, . . . them, ⟨as⟩ ↑when↓ . . . minds to ⟨a f⟩ the use

	Page 24
1	that ⟨so⟩ they
8	¶ Yet ⟨is⟩ this
11–17	its ⟨great⟩ ↑main↓ . . . is ⟨not⟩ ↑very slowly↓ [addition in ink over pencil] received by us. ⟨T Let that great hope which it upholds to the ⟨faithful⟩ ↑obedient↓, be the measure.⟩ ↑{A}↓ [On the facing page, the following passage:] ↑⟨{A}⟩ ↑For to measure the real / prevalence/ power/ . . . obedient. i.e.↓ Let . . . gospel. ↑Let any intelligent person ask himself ⟨how generally he supposes this doctrine of heaven ↑is understood↓ the true nature of the future happiness the gospel promises, is understood or⟩ how . . . gospel.↓↓ ["Let any intelligent . . . gospel." is added in ink over the following passage in pencil:] Let any intelligent person consider [one or two illegible words] how generally ↑he supposes↓ this doctrine of the ↑nature of↓ future happiness it promises is understood. Who knows what the kingdom of Heaven means?
18	itself⟨?⟩,—⟨unveil its glory to our eye⟩ ↑be . . . is↓,
20	saying⟨?⟩— . . . you?"
21	condemns ⟨our want of faith⟩ ↑therefore . . . Christ↓
31–35	Jesus & ⟨to⟩ whom . . . world. ↑{Insert B}↓ [On the preceding page, the following passage marked "B":] ↑though . . . want.}↓ [This passage is preceded by a rough draft in pencil:] ↑B {though we call it spiritual because we refer it to the soul after death yet it is substantially carnal because it a is an image of external goods an image of thrones & splendor & outward joy ¶ It ⟨is imagined⟩ ↑commonly tho't↓ that *faith* in the Christian sense of that word has an alliance with the imagination that it is a conversion of our wishes into belief. In ⟨the⟩ truth ⟨the⟩ what we are taught by our faith is the most real & exact part of our knowledge. It is what we think & what we are}↓
36–(25)4	warmth ⟨who d⟩ as . . . ↑bright↓ light & ↑sweet↓ . . . they /give/ hold out/ [variant in pencil] . . . ↑(↓they . . . desireable . . . thither↑)↓ [parentheses added in pencil] . . . ↑something beyond . . . love↓ [addition in ink over pencil]

Page 25

14–19   belief ⟨that virtue⟩ that . . . meaning ⟨has⟩ ↑is↓ . . . which ↑is↓ . . .
         Eastern ⟨philosopher⟩ ↑moralist↓,
24–26   ¶ ↑And . . . itself.↓
27–28   been ⟨that⟩ observed . . . likeness ⟨th⟩ so . . . from ⟨the same⟩ ↑a
         similar↓
37   object ⟨a⟩illuminates
39–(26)3 ¶ {A man's . . . of its processes ↑of his business↓, . . . augmented.}

Page 26

12–20   ¶ ↑In these . . . them.↓
12–13   mind ⟨is⟩ has . . . be ⟨improved⟩ benefitted
15–19   may ⟨admin⟩ furnish . . . action but ⟨its action its ⟨be⟩well being or
         ill being mu⟩ as . . . give ⟨shelter⟩ & food . . . send ⟨up its plumule
         into the air⟩ ↑down . . . nourishment↓ Out of it. So ⟨the⟩ all the
         stores of ⟨wi⟩ knowledge
22–30   indulge ↑{Insert X}↓ [On the preceding and facing page, a passage
         marked "X":] ↑You hear . . . weakness↑;↓ ⟨and⟩ ↑he sneers↓ . . . he
         has ⟨the⟩ an . . . ↑On the contrary, . . . tormentor.↓↓ ["On the
         contrary, . . . tormentor." added in ink over pencil]
31   envious, ⟨quarrelsome⟩ ↑suspicious,↓
34–36   courage & ⟨generosity⟩ & . . . happiness. ⟨Indeed it is like saying
         there is brightness in the sun to say so.⟩ ⟨I⟩Certainly . . . eagerly
         ⟨sought to⟩ render↑ed↓ him ⟨a⟩ ↑very important↓ service↑s,↓
37–38   angel ⟨in heaven⟩ ↑with God↓, . . . love⟨d⟩s . . . ↑& lives . . .
         benefactor↓,

Page 27

1–2   which ⟨we know is⟩ ↑is a guarantee . . . for it is↓
3   ↑Such . . . possible.↓
7   face of the ⟨soul⟩ mind,
12   con⟨n⟩joined
14   which ⟨it is⟩ flesh
25–32   ¶ ↑Certainly . . . ↑& unknown↓ . . . & it ⟨is impossible for us⟩ ↑we
         cannot↓ . . . us ⟨to⟩ speak . . . knowledge ⟨But⟩ when . . . in the
         ⟨sovereign importance⟩ ↑eternity↓ of spiritual /distinctions/⟨char-
         acter⟩/ ⟨which must always regulate condition⟩ & in the fact . . .
         character.↓
34   tends to ⟨set all our religious⟩ undeceive us of all ⟨religious⟩
         ↑dangerous↓
35–(28)4 as ⟨he⟩ ↑it↓ becomes ⟨good⟩ ↑virtuous⟨.⟩,↓ in proportion . . .
         within ⟨him⟩ ↑it↓.—Only one ⟨side it⟩ ↑hand, this truth↓ . . .
         happiness ⟨&⟩to . . . one,—⟨beseeching all to enter;⟩ on the other
         . . . themselves. ⟨or⟩ If . . . goodness and ⟨what belongs to goodness
         bad men cannot⟩ ↑& the . . . goodness↓ . . . reformation ⟨& self
         denial & prayer⟩ & justice

Page 28

6–11	¶ {I wish . . . *God*,↑'↓ *&* ↑'k.↓ *of* . . . reveal to us.}
13	that ⟨th⟩heaven
16	into ⟨farther⟩ ↑interior↓
17–21	↑Then . . . faculties↓ [in pencil]

Sermon XCIV

Manuscript: Eight sheets folded to make four pages each; folios stacked and cross-stitched with white thread around left edge (from which the eighth folio has torn away); pages measure 24.9 x 20.1 cm. An additional sheet, folded to make four pages, is laid in between leaves 14 and 15; pages measure 23.9 x 19.7 cm. A strip (verso blank), 12.4 x 19.2 cm., is tipped to verso of leaf 14.

Lines	*Page 29*
Bible Text	⟨h⟩He
1–2	↑which↓ ↑The Scriptures . . . remove↑,↓ ⟨the fear of death.⟩↓ always . . . the mind⟨.⟩ that
3–10	house ⟨& would rejoice in the social comfort it promises him⟩, . . . shall ⟨here rejoice⟩ ↑rejoice . . . please,↓ . . . ↑their↓ . . . trained, ⟨joys & sorrows shall multiply⟩ they . . . to ⟨p⟩school . . . shall ⟨die⟩ ↑be dead↓ . . . beside him & ⟨others⟩ ↑strangers↓ shall stand ⟨i⟩on his ⟨place⟩ hearth
11–15	to ⟨the mind of⟩ him . . . begins to ⟨count his ⟨pr⟩ money⟩ ↑reckon his interest↓, & to ⟨think if he⟩ ask . . . he ⟨mourns⟩ ↑sighs↓ . . . day ⟨that⟩ ↑which↓
16–17	came ⟨I⟩ ↑he↓ out of ⟨my⟩ ↑this↓ . . . must ⟨I⟩ ↑he↓

	Page 30
11–13	It is the /grief/age/ . . . ↑new↓ . . . infirmity. ↑it is . . . all.↓
13–14	It ⁽²⁾checks . . . tames ⁽³⁾our pride. ↑it withers . . . strength.↓ It ⁽⁶⁾threatens the intellect ⟨it ⁽⁵⁾demolishes strength it ⁽⁴⁾withers beauty It ⁽¹⁾touches us all.⟩ And thus
19–21	↑an↓ . . . condition. ¶ ⟨I wish to ask your attention⟩ ↑Let us inquire↓, my friends, ⟨to the question⟩ whether . . . the ⟨power⟩ ↑yoke↓
22–23	And what ⟨it behoves us⟩ ↑we ought↓ . . . . ourselves from ⟨its ⟨cruel fear.⟩ thraldom⟩ ↑it.↓ ¶ ⟨As there are two kinds of ignorance—an abcedarian ignorance before any knowledge can be and a learned ignorance which is the conclusion after much study that we fully know nothing so it ⟨may be said⟩ must be noticed there are two kinds of ⟨fear⟩ courage or overcoming of fear one merely brutish proceeding from want of thought & one wholly moral proceeding from a superiority to the cause of danger, when it is fully known.⟩ ¶ It has been said by ⟨a great philosopher⟩ ↑Lord Bacon↓
26–32	know that ⟨daily⟩ ↑some↓ . . . ↑constant↓ . . . ↑without loss of ⟨spirits⟩ cheerfulness↓. ⟨The⟩ ↑The savage . . . wolf.↓ ↑The↓ . . . march up ⟨to⟩ ⟨the⟩ a [end of line] ↑against↓ blazing ⟨battery for six pence per day⟩ ↑artillery without emotion↓; and ⟨⟨↑very ignorant↓⟩ men & women continually amongst us ⟨in⟩ ↑of the↓ lowest class

↑are↓ dying ↑every day↓〉 ↑↑without . . . persons↓ we know . . .
every day↓ . . . alarm. 〈↑So with savages.↓〉 ¶ Now

34–35   It 〈is said〉 ↑has been observed that↓ . . . ignorance; an 〈abcedarian〉
↑childish↓

38–(31)7 merely 〈brutish〉 ↑passive & animal↓, . . . moral, proceeding from a
〈perceived〉 conscious . . . known. ↑{X}↓ [On the facing page, a
passage marked "X":] ↑{〈I conceive that the essence of t〉The fear
. . . mind 〈is〉 ↑seems to consist in 〈a〉↓ the doubt . . . gloom↑y↓
[end of line] 〈y〉 apprehension of annihilation;—〈that〉 the sun
↑indeed↓ . . . this 〈fear〉 ↑doubt↓, . . . death} ↑There is . . . this↓↓
[last addition in pencil]

Page 31

11   through a 〈g〉 dogged
18   stronger 〈I suppose〉 ↑in general↓ . . . become. 〈Every one knows
that Dr Johnson a man of strong religious feeling indulged this gloom
〈a〉 whenever the idea of dissolution was presented〉 Men
20–22   attention. ¶ 〈Now h〉How shd . . . ↑that is,—made . . . life↓ [in ink
over pencil] shd be 〈the〉 〈subject〉 ↑more than others subject↓
27–29   learned 〈to〉 that there is a 〈deeper〉 ↑richer↓ . . . than 〈ever〉 ↑any↓
. . . life 〈↑worth↓〉 more 〈precious〉 to him〈self〉 than
32–41   of 〈vast〉 ↑profound↓ . . . who 〈has cultivated his moral powers〉 ↑is
engaged . . . character↓ . . . ↑purest &↓ . . . learned the 〈deep
delight〉 ↑serious pleasure↓ [addition in ink over pencil] of medita-
ti〈on〉ng . . . to him 〈infinitely〉 more . . . selfish. 〈Life to him〉 He
lives in ↑an↓other earth ↑than they;↓ 〈&〉 other heavens 〈than〉
↑shine over his head.↓ [end of line] they; life to . . . world of 〈sweet
& holy〉 ↑pure & pleasant↓ . . . it, 〈is〉 〈whenever

Page 32

3   ↑higher↓
7–14   doubt 〈the〉 ↑whether . . . is↓ real↑ly↓ independant 〈being〉 of their
〈moral nature.〉 ↑body.↓ [Apparently in conjunction with this revision, Emerson wrote the following on the blank facing page:] 〈↑He
supposes his Will in its connexion with love & virtue & God not
independant of the body↓〉 [in pencil; canceled in ink] is 〈perfectly〉
unavoidable that 〈they〉 ↑a man↓ . . . whilst 〈they f〉 ↑he↓ sees that
↑in . . . others↓ . . . to the 〈the〉 animal . . . of the 〈soul〉 ↑body↓;
. . . act /nobly/energetically/ . . . & have 〈honour〉 & abundance
15–18   the 〈outward〉 flesh 〈& fleshly lusts〉 ↑& its gratifications↓ . . .
mind, 〈sh〉 that
23   independance
23–24   sentiment 〈to〉of love to 〈th〉 him who has never felt〈.〉 ↑it.↓
24–25   be 〈felt〉 ↑believed↓
25–27   ↑as the . . . so↓ . . . fact of 〈submitting the body to the soul & living
to spiritual purposes.〉 executing
29–30   confirm th〈e〉is . . . by 〈use〉 the use of 〈it by bringing〉 our spiritual
nature, 〈by bringing it into exercise,〉 that

31–36   to ⟨long⟩ ↑much↓ . . . as upon ⟨the⟩ human liberty, . . . upon the /
         law of compensation / perfectness of the retributions that take place /,
         or upon the ⟨great conclusions that flow from⟩ the analysis of the
         affections,—or ↑upon↓ any ⟨kindred⟩ question ↑of simple right↓;—
         ⟨that after such study⟩, if, . . . have ⟨at such moments⟩ a far
37–38   And this ⟨is⟩ because . . . by ⟨being in⟩ their
38–40   action. [end of page] ¶ ⟨↑We have all probably heard or known of the
         ↑godly lives &↓ godly deaths of such upon which the world may look
         with supercilious doubt but no serious mind can look at them without
         awe↓⟩ ¶ ⟨↑Tho then they had neglected their intellect they had
         cultivated the moral power till it stood out to their mind a living soul
         uneffected by the change in the body↓⟩ [all in pencil; end of page] ¶
         There is a⟨nother class of facts that go also⟩ ↑higher . . . inwardly↓
         to prove ⟨it, the⟩ ↑the same doctrine—↓a life
42   see ⟨whom⟩ ↑such persons↓
43–(33)1 faith ⟨left⟩ bequeathed . . . gone. ⟨The country⟩ New England yet
         ⟨smells⟩ savors

                                    Page 33
2–8   generation who ⟨had al⟩ living . . . almost no↑ne↓ ⟨books⟩ but their
         bible & ⟨psalter⟩ ↑hymnbook↓ & ↑⟨had⟩ burning within↓ . . .
         ↑among us↓—died ⟨y⟩ ↑not only↓ . . . Christ. ¶ ⟨⟨{I have often heard
         the story of an excellent Christian long since departed who lost
         apparently all power of / moving his limbs / speech, / in the approach
         of death yet when his ⟨minister⟩ beloved minister came to his bed-
         side & said ⟨to him⟩ ↑in his ear↓ "If Jesus is with you in the
         dark valley, hold up your hand"—even in that hour, when the mists of
         death were already on him he instantly raised both his arms in signal
         of his faith and died in triumph.}⟩ ¶ ⟨I⟩ ↑We↓ have . . . flesh.
         The⟨y⟩irs
11–(34)19 Lords. ¶ ⟨⟨It is the direct tenden⟩ To produce this state of mind, was
         the direct intention & effect of our Saviours mission. {I know there is
         a painful interest given by the evangelists to his own ↑last↓ sufferings
         by which many ⟨minds⟩ Christians think that the hideous circum-
         stances of of his arraignment & death overwhelmed him with fear.
         that the bitterness of the cup was the bitterness of fear. ↑lest life
         should expire in his bloody grave. But we have continual instances of
         minds of great power who suffer with disappointment at their failure
         but without doubt of the truth of their principles↓ ["lest life . . .
         grave." in ink over pencil; "But we . . . principles" in pencil.]
             There are many considerations that may direct us to an under-
         standing of our Saviours state of mind without resorting to the idea
         that it involved any doubt of his continuing to exist ↑the whole lesson
         of his life & death is inconsistent with such a supposition & there are
         many considerations↓ [addition in pencil]
             In the first place, moral considerations cannot overcome physical
         pain, which is most acute to systems of the greatest sensibility. ⟨He
         was⟩ Jesus was subjected to excruciating torment, & the prospect of

this were enough to sadden his spirit without the farther suffering
⟨to⟩ which he partook

There was the moral ⟨gloom⟩ ↑suffering↓ that rose from considering his manifest ill success; the seeming total failure of ⟨his⟩ all his
instructions & all his works,—the ⟨entire⟩ hatred of his nation, the
flight of his disciples, the treachery of Judas; & his foreknowledge of
these events could not hinder a mind of deepest love from feeling them
sorely. The dreadful solitude in which he was left could not ⟨hi⟩ help
producing in him in the next place a fear of another kind namely lest
he might fail.

Let it be remembered that he was conscious that he was acting for
the world; that the truth he was commissioned to teach was to work a
mighty revolution in the whole history of the race of man. Yet was he
who was to seal this truth tempted in all points like as we are, [cf.
Hebrews 4:15] & now ⟨the⟩ death in ⟨the⟩ circumstances of horrid
aggravation, was at hand, and as he was wholly free there was yet the
doubt that he might wholly fail, & the hope of mankind be buried in
the loss of his faith & perfectness.

⟨I think the more fully we⟩ ↑We cannot↓ [emendation in pencil]
enter by meditation into the thots of Christ /the more reason we shall
find/without learning/ [variant in pencil] to ascribe his agony to
other causes than any doubt of his own truth of the eternity and self-
sufficiency of the Spirit which dwell in him without measure, & in
less degrees dwelleth in all men. His declaration to the thief at his
side—'This day shalt thou be happy with me' [Luke 23:43]—indicates
his abiding conviction in the truth he had taught.}

⟨The great doctrine of Xty ⟨wa⟩is that God is life & obedience to
God ⟨makes⟩ ↑giveth life↓ by making us part of God These truths
were that the Father hath life in himself & hath given to the Son also
to have life in himself & the Son imparteth life to who⟨m⟩ ever
cometh to him [cf. John 5:26–27]. Verily verily I say unto you, if a man
keep my saying he shall never see death. He that cometh to the son
hath everlasting life [John 8:51; John 3:16]. Indeed throughout the
New Testament this I understand to be the constant burden of all the
instructions of our Saviour & his apostles that the spiritual life which
he showed them was ↑itself↓ happiness and was immortal⟩

[The following addition, a revision of the preceding paragraph, is
part of the longer cancellation and is added on a quarter-sheet (verso
blank) tipped to the verso of leaf 14:] ⟨↑The great doctrine of
Christianity is that sin causes the death of the soul, & ⟨who⟩ that
only those who sin fear death; that God is life, & obedience to God
giveth life, by making us *part of him.* that if we ⟨were so wholly
conformed to God, that his Will & ours were one⟩ ↑free from sin↓,
we should no more doubt our immortal life, than we doubt our
present life. And it is by the communication of this law to our hearts,
that Jesus is the Resurrection & the life [John 11:25]. The Father hath
life in himself & hath given the Son also to have life in himself. & the
Son imparteth life to whosoever cometh to him. Verily I say unto you

if a man keep my sayings he shall never see death. He that cometh
unto the son hath everlasting ⟨life⟩ life.↓⟩
    whenever you keep your word to your cost⟩
    [The following addition appears on the folio laid in between leaves
14 and 15:] ↑III I have spoken . . . be no more.'↓

22–23   want. ¶ ⟨But I observe that⟩ But observe
25   soul; its

Page 34

13   lust ⟨from⟩ ↑&↓ pride
20   the ⟨brutal⟩ indifferency
22   bring ⟨it⟩ any
23–26   But ⟨the⟩ I . . . mortality /by/thro/ its own /consciousness/enjoy-
             ment/
27–28   but ⟨with⟩ by
33–35   death, to ⟨create in you⟩ ↑stablish your mind with↓ the ⟨feeling⟩
             ↑assurance↓ . . . die, ⟨though⟩ ↑though↓
37   just ⟨relations to God & man⟩ ↑performance of duty↓ [addition in
             ink over "performance of our duty" in pencil] . . . make ⟨our⟩ the
             light

Sermon XCV

Manuscript: Six sheets folded to make four pages each; folios nested and sewn with
white thread along the left edge; pages measure 25 x 20.1 cm. A leaf, 24.9 x 19.6 cm, is
attached to recto of leaf 7 with red sealing wax to replace the original leaf 6, which has
been cut out, leaving a narrow edge sewn in the left margin.

[Above Bible text:]   Salem [in pencil]

Lines   *Page 35*
2   of ⟨true⟩ religion.
4   ↑Roman↓
9   hell ↑as↓
10   ↑they contain↓ as we ⟨would⟩ ↑desire to↓ [emendations in pencil]
13–14   written, ↑though↓ they may ⟨have⟩ ↑receive↓ . . . ↑the sake of↓ their
             contents ⟨but⟩ they ⟨p⟩ are
21–22   persons↑,↓ [addition in pencil] . . . ↑wives↓

Page 36

2   beat, ⟨ & the countenance feel⟩ ↑& the feet . . . work↓
5   is ⟨constantly⟩ ↑always↓ [emendation in ink over pencil]
8   ↑too closely↓
10   consider ⟨in the first place⟩ what
11–12   or, in ↑an↓other place⟨s⟩, "⟨Christ⟩ ↑God↓ . . . world." ↑in righ-
             teousness . . . ordained↓ ⟨What is meant by "Christ" in this
             expression⟩ Before

14   import ⟨in which⟩ ↑th⟨ey⟩at belongs to↓ the name of Christ ⟨is
            used⟩ in
16–17   is ⟨often⟩ used . . . epistles, ⟨in⟩ with . . . latitude↑.↓ ⟨it is con-
            tinually. Thus i⟩In
19–21   *religion.* ⟨So when⟩ It . . . life" ⟨in which no one will pretend that
            can substitute his person was the light or the life⟩ W⟨as⟩hat . . .
            light? ⟨C⟩Not
25–30   accuseth you." ¶ ↑So . . . passages {see X}↓ [On the preceding page, a
            passage marked "X" in which the entries are separated from each
            other by short rules in the left margin:] ↑The law . . . Christ ¶ If
            Christ . . . sin ¶ I live . . . me ¶ —till . . . you ¶ but ye . . . Christ ¶
            {Arise . . . light ¶ {When Christ . . . appear ¶ Christ . . . God.↓
32   men are meant.
34   how ⟨this is done [illegible word]. In the first place,⟩ the . . . judge
            ⟨every man⟩ the

                              Page 37
4   with ⟨those⟩ ↑that↓ law⟨s⟩, we
6–8   with a ⟨key⟩ better ⟨key⟩ test for detecting the ⟨soundness of other
            knowledge.⟩ truth of other opinions. ⟨¶ Especially ⟨is this true⟩
            ↑may this be said↓ of religious truth. The doctrine of [several illegible
            words] Enjoy good principles condemn bad ones⟩ ↑Especially . . .
            less excellent.↓
12–18   action. ⟨It [several illegible words]⟩ It . . . condemns every ⟨or⟩
            thing that will be ⟨hurtf⟩ displeasing . . . soul. ⟨And nothing else but
            the religion of Christ will render this service.⟩ Every ["And . . .
            service." canceled in pencil and ink] respecting ⟨manners⟩ ↑study↓,
            . . . man ⟨s⟩ himself
21   ↑of *love*↓ from which good ⟨breeding⟩ manners spring, & the
            ⟨duty⟩ ↑sentiment of right↓
23   a ⟨mistake⟩ ↑corruption↓
27–(38)12   soul. ¶ [MS pp. 11–12 cut out; text continues on MS p. 13:] ⟨⟨The
            Reformation⟩ What is the Reformation but the judgment of Christ
            upon the falsehood & crimes of the Romish church. It was bro't up to
            the light & seen to be false. Its place was filled by the Reformed
            Church & that again is ⟨y⟩ bro't to the light & shown to contain
            much falsehood in its c⟩ [On a leaf attached with red sealing wax to
            MS p. 13 (recto of leaf 7) is the following passage:] ↑I. Christ . . .
            earth.↓
29   it ⟨ever⟩ shall be⟨.⟩ at
40   ¶ The ⟨grinding⟩ oppression

                              Page 38
12–18   ↑"Neither do . . . country."↓
20–21   escape; In each . . . ↑the↓
22   try ⟨him⟩ it
25–27   was ↑Love all men↓ Be . . . all; ⟨love all men;⟩ and all . . . the ⟨light⟩
            ↑brightness↓ of his ⟨rule⟩ ↑law↓.

34   obeyed ⟨to⟩ ↑if we would↓

Page 39

3–4   to ⟨lay the m⟩ collect . . . ↑as the Scriptures speak↓
8   that ⟨promises⟩ intimates
10–13   ↑in this world↓ . . . us, &, ⟨further⟩ ⟨more than⟩ ↑beyond↓ . . . of
                      m⟨e⟩an⟨.⟩kind.
20–29   evil. ⟨Thus may these ⟨go⟩ accomplish a future punishment [one
                      illegible line of inscription]⟩ [Emerson concluded the sermon at this
                      point by adding the date: "Chardon Street. November 13, 1830." On
                      the same day, however, before the first delivery, he canceled the
                      dateline and added the following paragraph:] ¶ Brethren, ⟨we⟩ ↑Let
                      us↓ . . . ↑as . . . may,↓ . . . principles ⟨is⟩ may . . . horror is not that
                      we [Emerson's revision of this passage (see below) shows that this
                      superfluous "not" was a careless error.] ↑ever↓ . . . reap.
                      Chardon St.
                      November 13, 1830.

[The following revised conclusion belongs to a later delivery of the sermon; it replaces
the last (added) paragraph of the first-delivery text, which is canceled in the MS:]

⟨Brethren there is a consideration of greatest importance to us, which I can only now
suggest & leave with your tho'ts because the subject is imperfect without it, and, that is,
that the judgment of God upon individuals is not made manifest in this world The
material world in which we live in which our temptations & education lie⟩

Brethren, there is a consideration of greatest importance to us which I can only now
suggest & leave with your tho'ts, because any examination of this subject would be very
imperfect without it. It is that the judgment of God upon ⟨us is⟩ individuals is not made
manifest in this world. The judgment is taking effect & will take effect around us, but
our eyes are not yet opened ↑to see it but in part↓. [addition in pencil] The material
world in which we live, in which our temptations & so our education lie⟨s⟩↑,↓
[emendation in pencil] operates as a screen or an illusion. They who have its blessings are
tho't ⟨to⟩ by others & are taught to think themselves happy, ⟨and wh⟩ whether they
have or have not the blessing of God↑.↓ ⟨& whilst⟩ and they who are poor, or sick, or
lose their friends, are thot ⟨by others⟩ to be unhappy, though they may be good. And
whilst we live in a material body ⟨it will continue⟩ the judgment will continue to take
effect ⟨but will not be seen⟩ in the mind↑,↓ [addition in pencil] but will not be seen in the
whole condition but when the body passes away to the elements the we shall be seen by
men & by ourselves as we are seen by God. We shall then not have a twofold nature of
body & mind but shall be subject only to spiritual good & spiritual evil. But *now*, every
day, every hour this judgment is working, & forever will work; it is setting the good on
one side, & the evil on the other. Let us not then shut our eyes to it. Let us ⟨not as do
others postpone our⟩ work with God. Let us beware lest any action is habitual to any of
us, any language, any desire that cannot stand before the judgment of the law of Christ.

O consider most of all whether the general habit of all our life the general level of our
principles may not be condemned by that law, whether the reason why our conscience
doth not fill us with horror is that we skulk into the dark because our deeds are evil & do
not ever bring our principles to the trial. Be not deceived God is not mocked; whatsoever
a man soweth that shall he also reap.

[The following notes occur in pencil after the revised conclusion of the sermon:]

↑That judgmt consist ¶ every hour is increasing yᵉ strength of yᵉ love wh. we bear for what is good or for what is evil. every act of the ⟨mind⟩ ↑will↓, every thot is doing its part to determine our real place in the universe, our friendship for good or for evil minds—And when the body passes away the choice we have made will be manifest & this is judgment↓

Sermon XCVI

Manuscript: Five sheets folded to make four pages each; folios stacked and sewn with white thread along the left margin (from which the first, second, and fourth folios have torn away). One sheet, folded to make four pages, is attached with red sealing wax to the recto of the first leaf; its four pages contain the substitute opening written for the second delivery of the sermon. Pages measure 25 x 20.1 cm. A strip (verso blank), 12.5 x 20 cm, is attached to the verso of leaf 2 with red sealing wax.

[The following variant opening, written for the second delivery on January 1, 1832, replaced the Bible text and the original first paragraph, which is bracketed in ink:]
                    Thy will be done. Luke 11.2
↑{↓The last day of the old year casts its eye backward The first day of the new looks forward. The last day is the day of remembrance The first day is the day of hope. Man has been characterized as the being who looks before & after. We have /performed one part in its season/given ourselves in their to the reflexions due to the past./ [variant in pencil] Let us now seek those tho'ts that appertain to the new season.

Let us rise with new thoughts on the new day Let us rise if it please God wiser & better for the experience of the past Let us abate no jot of heart or hope but salute with good resolutions & Christian wishes the opening year.↑}↓ [brackets in pencil]

It is related of Chilo one of the seven ⟨wise men⟩ whom antiquity distinguished for / wisdom/the wise men/ [variant in pencil] that when he was asked wherein the well educated differed from the uneducated man he answered "In a good hope." And it seems to me a very just sentence for with all our pretended progress in knowledge no man takes any very large strides beyond the rest: no man gets so far but the plainest questions still puzzle him: ⟨⟨I⟩No man g⟩ The man who gets farthest is forwardest to see & lament his ignorance The causes of the most common appearances are buried in night to the most learned as well as the unlearned eye. No man has found out what a Fever is. No man has found out why the heart beats, or by what process the hand is lifted to the head. Much less has any human penetration been permitted to lay open the divine secrets of the mind & explain how it is that the fact which has been hidden from me for years starts into my thought the moment a question is asked to which it is an answer, & is called remembrance. And

And still less has any been able to answer the questions which all do or can ask concerning the author of this nature & of this world Who can by searching find out Him? Who can find out the Almighty unto perfection? ⟨At the same time⟩ All men stand very nearly upon a level in their research into the unfathomable depths of nature human & divine

Still there is a difference between those who have learned to think who certainly are the well educated & those who do not think whom I call the uneducated though they have got all the learning of the schools. These have—a good hope—they expect well of themselves & of society & of the order of things. They see reason for cheerful anticipations. They have an obstinate conviction that things work well in the world; that however unfavorable present appearances may be, there is always kindness at the bottom of things; that opportunities are always presenting themselves to the diligent & the just

Whether they have been able distinctly to express to themselves the grounds of their hope or not, it amounts in every such mind to an assurance clear or obscure that the administration of the world flows from Design & ought to beget in us an unlimited trust, to make us contented when we do not succeed in the belief that we were aiming at wrong ends or by wrong means & ought not to succeed. ↑nay yᵗ yᵉ good man in yᵉ midst of ill success is always succeeding.↓

The Gospel gives distinctness to this occult faith, gives reason for this instinct. "All is for the best," is the creed of simple nature. "Thy will be done" is the sentiment of the gospel.

Lines	Page 40
1	¶ {When . . . said ⟨Le⟩ "Not
2	only ⟨said⟩ prayed
3–4	↑in your memories↓ [emendation in pencil] . . . men. ⟨It is⟩ ↑Is it . . . perceive↓ [addition in pencil]
7	this ⟨pro⟩ sentiment
8–9	law & health [imputed ampersand obscured by red sealing wax] end.
15	heaven.}
18–21	will he . . . better than [end of page] than ⟨of⟩ all
21	up ⟨{& is mortified to find that he does not obtain the same notice elsewhere that he finds at home.}⟩ [brackets and cancellation in pencil] He
26–(41)8	young ⟨& old⟩ [cancelation in pencil] men . . . earliest /impressions/views of things/ [variant in pencil] . . . Paris. ¶ ⟨The only reason why the childs preference of his own house & his own friends was /ridiculous/wrong/ [variant in pencil] was that he loved himself in them that he tho't things good in proportion as they were near to him, that he preferred ⟨the⟩ his own to another's, & not that he preferred /them/his own village/ [variant in pencil] to London & Paris. And now that he ⟨fl⟩ pleases himself with his great superiority to his prejudices↑,↓ /he has yet/it may be/ [added comma and variant in pencil] the same mistake the same proud self-regard from which that ignorance sprang.
	Is there no one to make the discovery to him that he is opposing his own nature & his happiness & the whole Creation by preferring himself to God his will to God's will.}⟩
	↑But . . . serve it. ¶ The time shall come &c &c↓ The time shall come sooner ["But . . . &c &c" appears on the strip attached to MS p. 8, concealing the canceled paragraphs above; following "&c &c" is a mark pointing to the bottom of the page for the paragraph that follows.]

	Page 41
11–12	↑is↓ . . . season. ¶ ⟨⟨What is⟩ Let us⟩ 'Thy
13–14	say? /Let us consider/I invite yʳ attention three points of considerat/ [variant in pencil] ⟨What is⟩ ↑how↓ God's will ⟨how it⟩ is
16	¶ ↑What is↓ [in pencil]
18	↑The solid earth↓ The

19   place ⟨The planets⟩ Our
21   good that ⟨in⟩ the
23–24   eternity. ↑We . . . heat↓ [addition in pencil]
26   with ⟨delig⟩ confidence
28–(42)2   cloud ⟨wets⟩ lowers . . . ↑or we . . . to want↓ . . . comprehended in
              ⟨h⟩ Gods . . . foolishly. ¶ ↑⟨If we consider what would follow⟩
              ↑What wd. become of us↓ if . . . ours, ⟨if⟩ how . . . ↑man's↓ . . .
              another ↑earth rent . . . spices↓ ↑zones . . . start into ⟨chaos⟩↓
              [addition in ink; "chaos" canceled in pencil; cancellation rejected for
              grammatical reasons] here one . . . nation & the ⟨rivers⟩ [canceled in
              ink] overflowing . . . would [Except as noted, the paragraph thus far
              is in pencil; the inscription continues in ink] drown . . . kings to
              ⟨obey the mob⟩ ↑serve their subject↓ & strike the people to ⟨avenge⟩
              ↑wreak↓ the kings ↑spite↓ [emendations in pencil] and ↑the tendency
              of↓ . . . world.↓

Page 42

3   hold ⟨on⟩ these
4–5   ↑main↓ [in pencil] . . . dependant
12–16   ↑For if /a man declared he came from God & bid us/it . . . & bid
              us/ [variant in pencil] steal & murder & shd. work a miracle to prove
              his commission it cd. not prove it. ↑hate our brother or take our own
              life; or if . . . persons; they . . . them.↓↓ [The addition "hate our . . .
              them." is in pencil.]
28   ¶ ↑And↓ So the ⟨whol⟩ united
30   of ⟨any⟩ ↑the↓
32–34   ↑He may reveal . . . being but {any . . . us} but lay hidden↓ [in pencil]
36–38   God⟨,⟩ only, or what ⟨is⟩ determines . . . inquire ⟨beyond⟩ the

Page 43

1   basis of of every
1–6   ↑This . . . omnipresence.↓ ↑He . . . of all↓ [last addition in pencil] ¶
              ⟨How⟩ ↑The will of God↓ is ⟨that⟩ to be . . . exigency. ↑⟨II⟩2.↓ ["II"
              is added in pencil.] And What is it? ⟨It is the stern judgment of right.⟩
              Universal . . . good of the ["Universal . . . good of the" written over
              "It is the law of love. It commands us to love all men as children of
              God"; "It . . . It" in pencil]
9   is ⟨love⟩ ↑mercy↓
11   good of ⟨eternity⟩ the
13–17   always ⟨it issues u⟩ the . . . ↑the will . . . another↓ [addition in
              pencil] it is . . . ↑and that . . . authority.↓
20–21   he is↑,↓ [addition in pencil] is an ⟨outrage⟩ an insult
23   scourge & a↑n↓ ⟨men⟩ outrage
26   that ⟨man's⟩ ↑self↓ will . . . it ⟨fights⟩ is
31   envy these

Page 44

3–4   desireable the moment we ⟨apply it to⟩ measure

6–7	Religion↑,↓ that is↑,↓ . . . being↑,↓ our life↑,↓ . . . Gods Will↑,—↓ . . . world↑,↓ [additions in pencil]
10	Religion ⟨teache⟩ changes
17	health↑s↓
24–26	↑The . . . done↓ ↑{Insert X}↓ [At the bottom of the page, a passage marked "X" that is rejected from the text as belonging to the second delivery:] ↑{Let us set out on a new year with this divine purpose to do the will of one greater & better whose will makes the law & the doing of whose will is the prosperity of the Universe.}↓ Let
29	God's↑,↓ ⟨as Jesus Christ is the first⟩ it

[The following notation occurs in pencil following the end of the sermon:] ↑We are willing his will shd be done in France & England but not with us↓

Sermon XCVII

Manuscript: Eight sheets folded to make four pages each; folios stacked and sewn with white thread along the left margin (from which the fourth and fifth folios have torn away); pages measure 25 x 20.2 cm.

Several clues allow for a reasonably certain identification of revisions introduced for the second and final delivery of the sermon, on December 1, 1836, at East Lexington. The Preaching Record shows that Emerson's insertion of a lengthy passage from Sermon XII was done at this time. His cancellation of original matter (making room for the borrowed matter) is in pencil. One other revision, also in pencil, and clearly designed to adapt the sermon to an East Lexington audience, is the substitution of "commonwealth" for "town," an effort to generalize a reference to the Boston setting of the first delivery. On the basis of this evidence, the editors have concluded that most of the pencil revisions were made in 1836, and have therefore not adopted them in the clear text.

[Above Bible text:] ⟨Praise ye the Lord blessed is the man that feareth the Lord, that delighteth greatly in his commandments. Ps. 112.1⟩ Thanksgiving. 1830

Lines	*Page 45*
Bible Text	men ↑Ps. 107. 21↓ . . . loving [end of line] kindness of the Lord 107. 43.
2	to ↑discharge↓ the [in pencil, rejected as a late emendation]
5–9	every ⟨eve⟩ dealing . . . the /common/universal/ [variant in pencil, rejected as a late emendation] . . . general↑,↓ [comma in pencil]
12	mercy↑;↓ [addition in pencil] . . . rain ⟨& sun⟩ to
14–16	the ⟨infinite⟩ love of God ↑that it is infinite↓ [addition in pencil, rejected as a late emendation] & the wisdom which ⟨gives⟩ ↑knows how to↓ multipl⟨ies⟩y every . . . to ⟨multitudes⟩ towns

	Page 46
1–15	house ↑of our happiness↓ [addition in pencil, rejected as a late emendation] & show . . . the /Assyr/Babylon/ian, [variant in pencil, rejected as a late emendation] . . . Him. ¶ ⟨And first, . . . cheered you⟩ ¶ ⟨↑Or↓⟩ To [The paragraph is canceled in pencil, its cancellation rejected as a late emendation.]

7–13 and ↑has she↓ brought ⟨you⟩ no fruit ⟨from her ample⟩ ↑to your↓
. . . medicine in her / materia medica / herbs & balsams & drugs / for
your sickness; [end of page] has the ⟨rain⟩ cloud . . . ours? & the
wind . . . his fire; has

20–24 The ⟨meanest bird⟩ [canceled in pencil] ↑humblest note↓ . . . paradise ¶ / And / But aside from the general order of nature / [variant in
pencil, rejected as a late emendation] has

27 ↑Has not the fear . . . removed↓

28 Has no ⟨instruct⟩ knowledge

30 soul rejoicing

31 Have you had no↑t had the highest favor, any↓

33 happiness—⟨not⟩ the

35 ¶ Secondly. ⟨Let us remember⟩ ↑We have↓

36 of {this metropolis & of} New

38–(47)1 ↑We are natives or ⟨citizens⟩ ↑inhabitants↓ . . . pilgrims.↓

Page 47

1–4 joy in the⟨s⟩ two . . . ↑this simple↓ useful . . . Christian ⟨honour⟩
⟨↑town↓⟩ ↑commonwealth↓ ["town" canceled and "commonwealth"
added in pencil, rejected as a late emendation] We . . . greatness ²We
have ⟨been to⟩ ↑studied in↓ her schools ¹We have worshipped . . .
churches.

4 have ⟨dwelt in her streets⟩ obeyed

5–7 streets. ¶ ⟨Far more favoured⟩ Compare . . . our ⟨righ⟩ personal
independance with those ⟨crowded⟩ ↑thronged↓

8–10 ↑on the day↓ . . . ↑sworn↓ . . . broken. ↑by her princes.↓

11–27 ¶ But ⟨we are freeborn.⟩ ↑We have . . . patriots↓ At . . . freeborn. ¶
⟨Akin . . . acknowledgments. ↑& so the whole / moral / social /
political order in which we live is a part of our private store↓⟩ ¶
⟨Thirdly.⟩ We [Cancellation of the paragraph and of "Thirdly" is in
pencil and is rejected as a late emendation; the addition of "& . . .
store" in pencil is likewise rejected.]

14 that ⟨is writ⟩ ↑may be read↓ in ↑the present condition of↓

15 the ⟨general health of⟩ knowledge

17 us. / The . . . this. / In proof of this let that singular fact be con / We
[variant in pencil, rejected as a late emendation]

20–21 goodness ⟨has bee⟩ reflected upon the⟨m⟩ir ↑ / evil ways / deprav / ,↓
[variant in pencil, rejected as a late emendation] . . . ↑& life↓

22 these ⟨gloomy⟩ painful instances, as if ⟨the earth⟩ ↑devils . . . men↓

24 exhibited ⟨here⟩ ↑among us↓

25–26 ↑And . . . acknowledgments.↓

33 as ⟨an⟩ a

33–34 He ⟨sympathizes⟩ occupies

35–36 with the / Cherokee / N. A. savage / . . . camp & the / Chinese /
Tartar / [variants in pencil, rejected as late emendations]

38–40 ↑The cause . . . their cause↓ they . . . color; ⟨↑The↓⟩ as

41–(48)14 brother ¶ ⟨It is . . . sons of men. ¶ A yet⟩ [Cancellation of the
paragraph and of "A yet" is in pencil; cancellation of the paragraph is

rejected as a late emendation.] ¶ [The following addition is rejected as belonging to the second delivery:] ↑We have our share in that good which is not confined to us in that advancement & multiplication of all the arts of life that lightens labor & increases pleasure. We have abundant cause for gratitude for the progress of man, for the facilities of knowledge & enjoyment which the accumulation of so many centuries of labor has furnished us The Arts have arrived in our day at that perfection & have made the dominion of man over nature so considerable as to deserve admiration. Man has emerged from the woods where once he shivered under the storm & the cold. The sheep is sheared the loom is contrived & mines vegetables & fishes lend to his raiment their splendid dye. Granite & marble are quarried for his structures. He descends to the margin of the sea & launches his little bark into its unfathomable waters a bauble a particle on the interminable waste I see it mount the ridges & sink into the vallies of the ocean [At this point, the paragraph breaks, with Emerson adding the following note:] {&c &c—from Sermon XII as far as to the words— "separate taught from untaught man by an almost infinite interval"↓ [For the pertinent passage from Sermon XII, see *Sermons* 1:137–38.] ¶ ⟨An event . . . destroying the ⟨throne⟩ despotism de stayed . . . not as ⟨before⟩ ↑in former revolutions↓ . . . Europe & ⟨s⟩confirm . . . well to ⟨the hu⟩man ⟨race⟩ ↑kind↓. . . . praise.⟩ [cancellation of paragraph in pencil, rejected as a late emendation] ¶ In short brethren

Page 48

21   distinction ⟨/that should be made/which forces itself upon our attention/⟩ among

25–26   For ⟨if it⟩ ⟨I wish it might be impressed on our minds brethren⟩ ↑Do . . . secondary?↓

37   what [end of line] to end

38   for ⟨other⟩ the

Page 49

1   ¶ So ⟨it⟩ we

3–5   ↑The mechanical . . . laid up↓ In . . . accommodation ⟨we⟩ ↑&↓ swim↑s↓

7   than /this/the steamboat/—

10   ↑This . . . good.↓

12–16   government. ⟨We turn⟩ ↑Insert A↓ [addition in pencil; on the preceding page, a passage in ink marked "A" in pencil:] ↑{⟨France⟩ [canceled in pencil] ↑Portugal↓ or Spain or /Belgium/Mexico/ [variant in pencil] . . . dragoons.}↓ [brackets in pencil] kingdoms are ⟨pu⟩ turned to desarts; ⟨n⟩ a

17   No; ⟨nor yet for the⟩ but

20–33   good. ↑B ↑Insert B↓↓ [addition in pencil; on the preceding page, a passage in ink marked "B" in pencil:] ↑{And . . . al⟨l⟩most . . . itself.↑} ¶ There is much instruction in an old story↓ [in pencil; rejected as a late addition] . . . victory? Pyrrhus replied↑, "↓⟨t⟩To

⟨be⟩ ↑make himself↓ . . . ↑sd yᵉ counsellor "↓To . . . sure" ↑replied
the king.↓. . . . ↑recover↓ . . . then⟨—⟩? Why . . . him ⟨always⟩ all
. . . & ⟨losing the⟩ forgetting . . . means.}↓ [brackets in pencil; end
of Insert B]

37–38   ↑This . . . crown the others↓

Page 50

3–4   away. ¶ [The following paragraph, in pencil, is rejected as a late
addition:] ↑Come then, my friends, let us praise God that we are alive;
that we are thus elevated in the scale of being; that he has enabled us to
attain such a sovereignty by art over the world where he has set us. Let
us praise him yet more for the great endowments of the understanding. Let us praise him ↑for↓ the affections which bless us. Let us praise
him for the revelation of his son; for the example of Jesus. Let us
praise him for the resurrection from the dead & for the eternal life we
have already begun. Let us thus praise him with our lips & in our
hearts by giving as we have opportunity to the poor—by all the acts of
a holy life.↓ ¶ There

11   we ⟨have⟩ are

Sermon XCVIII

Manuscript: Eight sheets folded to make four pages each; folios stacked and sewn with
white thread along the left margin; pages measure 25 x 20 cm. A strip, approximately 3.5
x 20 cm, has been torn from the bottom of the first leaf of the fourth folio. This leaf is
blank, recto and verso.

Lines   *Page 51*

3   fears ⟨his⟩lest . . . ↑his↓ stocks ⟨fall⟩ ↑depreciate,↓
8   ↑loss↓ [in pencil]
9–10   ↑The first words in which↓ It . . . heaven ⟨by these first words⟩ ↑were↓
15–16   ¶ ↑In . . . doctrine↓ . . . person↑,↓ ⟨present⟩ whether
28–(52)2 fear. ¶ ⟨I.⟩ Perfect . . . out ⟨the⟩ fear↑.↓ ⟨of God⟩ ¶ What

Page 52

5   say No man
8   ↑Tis true↓ We
11–13   ¶ Yet ↑it . . . we↓ are ⟨we⟩ fitted for his love ⟨ & advanced in his love
indirectly⟩ by ↑whatever↓ acts ⟨that⟩ make . . . his ⟨c⟩nature
16   him.}
19–20   & /strong/vigorous/ . . . have ⟨physical⟩ power & ⟨external⟩
wealth & influence—↑Tis↓ Not
21–22   world ⟨the Caesars & ²Bourbons & ¹Bonapartes⟩ ↑whose . . .
mouths↓
25   God he
28   vicious one ⟨makes⟩ removes
33   upon ⟨our sins⟩ us
35   be /swept/passed/
37–38   friend. ↑it will conquer our sharpest sorrows with↓ [incomplete
addition in pencil] ¶ II.

40   ↑love↓
41–(53)1   two ways; *first*, ["1" is added in the margin, beside "two ways"]

Page 53

1–3   we have ⟨/injured/wronged/ them⟩ ↑sinned. . . . so↓. ↑Violent . . .
                           rare↓
5–6   bloody ⟨feuds⟩ ↑quarrels↓ which /{in every country attend a period
                           of gross vice}/ rise . . . places/ & which /give/fill/
8–11   of ⟨that⟩ generosity ⟨they have.⟩ they . . . enemy—I ⟨wish⟩ ↑know↓
                           this ⟨were⟩ ↑is not↓ universally true. ↑There . . . us.↓ ¶ ⟨But t⟩There
12–13   ↑sometimes↓ . . . those ⟨dark bosoms⟩ ↑unhappy individuals↓ /
                           which/who/ . . . pleas⟨s⟩ure
15   as de⟨st⟩testable
17–18   the ⟨bursting⟩ ↑overflowing↓ bounty of the ⟨G⟩ benevolent . . . that
                           /was/seems to have been/ lighted ⟨in⟩ ↑from↓ hell.
18–21   Its ⟨fruits⟩ ↑coals & smoke↓ . . . murder. ⟨And⟩ ↑If you . . . for↓
                           ⟨t⟩⟨T⟩this, . . . skilful ⟨sophist⟩ ↑deceiver↓.
22   seldom ⟨or never⟩ a
23–24   ↑on . . . any↓
30   ¶ But ↑there . . . whom you⟨r⟩ ↑have↓ feelings ⟨have⟩ of declared
                           hostility↓
31–33   fear? ⟨I⟩ let . . . breasts⟨?⟩. You fear the ⟨man⟩ ↑person↓ who↑m↓
                           ⟨has⟩ you have injured⟨.⟩, ↑or↓ You
37–39   principles ⟨from⟩ ↑than↓ . . . you & ⟨feels your⟩ must . . . sensible
                           some
40–42   people? is . . . the /overseer/agent/ afraid of his /principal/
                           employer/; . . . her /husband/servant, master./?
43–(54)11   office. /Their own compunction is the power that distorts the
                           countenance of their neighbor into an expression of reproach or
                           contempt. Every/ ¶ It is their . . . have ⟨neglected⟩ ↑wronged↓ . . .
                           compunction ⟨to⟩ finds . . . Every/ good ⟨book⟩ ↑word↓ . . .
                           conscience. ↑/In all these cases it is plain that sin is the cause of fear &
                           that the love of God which casts out sin will remove your anxiety./ ¶ It
                           is wonderful . . . ↑to . . . dreams↓ . . . anxiety./↓ ¶ 2. Secondly,

Page 54

18   fear. ⟨He⟩It ⟨c⟩ removes
20   that ⟨perf⟩ image
23–24   ↑not only↓ . . . Pennsylvania ⟨& extorted⟩ but
28   fear. ⟨P⟩ It
31   ground ↑& wiping . . . his ⟨brow⟩ face,↓ & said
35   has a ⟨balsam⟩ ↑salve↓
38–39   prejudices, a
40   ¶ Thus [A draft of this paragraph—or notes for it—appears three
                           pages later in the MS on an otherwise blank leaf:] ¶ There is one more
                           application I wish to make of this doctrine & that is to religious
                           disputes. Religion was never made for disputes. ⟨Rel⟩ The essence of
                           Religion is love. ¶ Here are two great parties in Christs church called
                           the Orthodox & the Liberal party, & very often you may hear them

expressing fear of one another ¶ Now in this sectarian feeling there is great danger that people will lose sight of the first great principle of the Christian religion Love It is to be feared that people will be such zealous Baptists or such zealous Unitarians or such zealous Calvinists that they will not be zealous Christians

Page 55

2	to ⟨one fault⟩ ↑a particular↓
7	a ⟨certain⟩ fear
9–10	↑Here then↓ It
14	they ⟨reasonably⟩ think
14–15	↑But . . . discern↓ It
25	↑¶ We . . . these↓
27	partisan. ⟨One⟩ ↑He↓
28	He ⟨see⟩ is calm
30	lies ⟨lies⟩ parallel
37	¶ Scattered ⟨amongst⟩ ↑under↓
37–(56)1	↑It . . . separates↓ The pious Unitarian ⟨&⟩ ↑from↓ the pious Calvinist ⟨are far more alike⟩ It

Page 56

3	¶ This ⟨man⟩ ↑true Christian↓
4	love. ⟨Do not think he is⟩ ↑He cannot be a↓
7	Whatever sect [end of page] ⟨The sect that can have any permanent superiority in our country must be that which contains the greatest number of these ⟨tr⟩ Christians. And⟩ whatever sect ⟨that⟩ may be ↑feared↓
17	↑so↓
22	feed the ⟨le⟩ small
25	And ⟨so⟩ this
30–32	↑O carry . . . by. & . . . is.↓
33	church at ⟨Thessalonica⟩ ↑Ephesus↓ [addition in pencil and ink]

Sermon XCIX

Manuscript: Eight sheets folded to make four pages each; first six folios stacked, seventh and eighth folios nested, and all cross-stitched with white thread around left edge; pages measure 25 x 20 cm.

Lines	*Page 57*
1–2	¶ I. ⟨S⟩Evil . . . other. ⟨However [illegible letter]⟩ It
3	in ⟨Persia⟩ ↑Asia↓ [emendation in pencil]
6–8	↑They . . . subsist↓
10	there↑with↓
12	retire ⟨f⟩to
15–16	↑The truth is↓ It . . . tenacious ⟨unremoveable⟩ ↑/& intimate/ & dangerous/↓ [first variant in pencil]
17	it ⟨appears⟩ ↑originates↓.

	Page 58
1–3	some ⟨laudable⟩ *innocent* . . . gained. ↑grow selfish & fretful↓

4–7   *good* like ⟨your intellectual⟩ ↑the↓ improvement ↑of your mind↓, . . .
        other good⟨,⟩ being omitted, ↑read books . . . duties.↓ or that a
        ⟨vain glory will⟩ foolish pedant⟨ry⟩ic

11–18   ↑Great . . . quarrelled about [end of line] because . . . [Possibly
        Emerson neglected to cancel "about" here.] . . . mouth.↓ ¶ Or you
        ⟨achieve a great exploit⟩ ↑on some occasion, you display great↓ of self
        devotion . . . pride ⟨when⟩ because . . . self-love. ↑related of . . .
        officiated ↑with great success↓ in a ⟨strange⟩ church . . . prayer he
        . . . desk.↓

19   hand of ⟨Satan⟩ the

23–24   triumphant ¶ ⟨If⟩ This . . . been ⟨a⟩ hard

26   the ⟨gospel⟩ ↑Christian↓ [cancellation in pencil; addition in ink over
        pencil]

31–33   this, that ⟨a great p⟩ we . . . ↑moral↓ . . . temptations—⟨and⟩ ↑that
        we make↓ . . . worst. ↑of them↓

35   every ⟨thing⟩ good should lead to ⟨things⟩ better. ⟨{A very sore
        temptation is felt only in extreme circumstances which prudence &
        virtue might in all probability have avoided.}⟩ [cancellations in
        pencil and ink; brackets in pencil] We

37   a ⟨just⟩ ↑wise↓

41   a↑n↓ ⟨crime⟩ enormous

Page 59

4   inevitable. ⟨In⟩ Where . . . terrible ⟨punishments⟩ examples

6–8   And in ⟨individual⟩ the vices of individuals, ⟨the bar-room is the
        porch to the gambling table to the brothel & the jail.⟩ ↑it . . .
        workyard, nor ⟨in the⟩ round the ⟨domes⟩ fireside↓ it . . . that
        ⟨high⟩ violent

10   the ⟨gambling house⟩ ↑gaming table & the brothel↓

11   pray be ⟨carried⟩ ↑put↓

15–16   more. ↑A↓ [On the following page, a passage marked "A":] ↑Consider
        . . . us.↓ [additions in pencil]

17   statement ↑a ⟨calumny⟩ slander, for example↓.

18   ↑a↓

19–21   more /humiliating/mortifying/ . . . so ⟨dirty⟩ ↑low↓ a thing as a⟨s⟩
        lie? The lie ↑then↓

22   ↑Now . . . legs.↓

23–26   on ⟨the⟩ ↑your neighbor's↓ reputation↑.↓ ⟨of another.⟩ But these
        irrecoverable words ↑cannot be won back; they↓ fly ↑nimbly↓ . . .
        injured ⟨toward⟩ ↑against↓ . . . temptation↑,↓ [comma added in
        pencil] ⟨to which you more easily yield.⟩ ↑& a greater one↓. [last
        addition in ink over pencil]

29   ¶ ↑Perhaps . . . different↓ Or . . . ↑species↓

31–(60)1 want. ⟨It is because you have a handsome watch, that you must buy a
        handsome chain; because you have got a better horse that you must
        have a better carriage. The old furniture will not suit the new house.⟩
        ↑{Insert B}↓ ↑B ⟨An earthen lamp gives as much light as a silver one
        but /the/one/ expense we have permitted seems to us to make /

more/another/ [variants in pencil] necessary.⟩ {A very . . . comfort.
↑You have got↓ A costly . . . good.}↓ [addition in ink over erased
pencil] ¶ /The falling merchant/The embarrassed tradesman/ . . .
this, ↑who but↓ . . . temptation strong↑?↓ ⟨himself⟩ ¶ Or

Page 60

3–6   temperance. ⟨And th⟩ ¶ And . . . sin. ⟨If⟩ Let . . . the ⟨road⟩
            downward
7–8   him ⟨shall⟩ that . . . he that ⟨sins⟩ is
11   ↑& indigestion↓ &, the
14   habit to ⟨a quicker & fuller sympathy⟩ ↑an acquaintance↓
15–20   many. /These . . . loath⟨e⟩some . . . progress./ ¶ These are helps—
            that make us ambitious to do better. And as you become worthier why
            you receive important trusts & enter into new connexions and these
            bind you as it were to virtue and are like a wall between you & a great
            many temptations. You all know that there are some things which are
            severe trials to one man & no trial at all to another merely because
            one has made a greater progress than the other. One man cannot
            resist the temptation to drink liquor that is offered him. The other has
            used himself to refuse it ⟨it⟩ till it has become loathsome/ [variant in
            pencil, rejected as a late addition]
27   force. ↑{↓As Alexander . . . competitors,↑}↓ [additions in pencil]
30–31   ↑¶ We . . . cure.↓
36–(61)9   imperceptible ⟨d⟩advances, . . . threaten you ⟨to be safe⟩ [canceled
            in pencil] ¶ ⟨Watch; for "sin to be hated needs but to be seen." & it is
            knowledge only that can[end of line] for there is no more perfect cure
            of the desire of vice than a distinct apprehension of the consequences
            of vice & this knowledge is to be got by watchfulness.⟩ Do you . . .
            again. ¶ ↑{Insert X}↓ [On the preceding page, a passage marked
            "X":] ↑{Watch, . . . perfect ⟨valu⟩ ↑cure↓ . . . would you have ⟨We
            have con⟩put your . . . burden.↓

Page 61

11–18   overcoming ↑a↓ sin⟨s⟩. ¶ ↑{Insert C.}↓ [On the following page, a
            passage marked "C":] ↑{Watch . . . the ⟨voice⟩works of . . .
            selves.}↓ [A pencil draft of this passage occurs, canceled in pencil,
            three pages earlier:] ⟨↑Watch & pray For the great temptation of most
            of us is not any particular evil as the general habit of our life the ⟨low⟩
            misdirection of our love averse from God, addicted to the world.
            Watch then the things within & those without, the works of nature
            the dealings of Providence the voice of Christ, what is close to you yet
            unseen. Watch the wanderings of your own Soul. Sin watches for you
            God watches for you & shall we not watch for ourselves.↓⟩
24–26   capable. ↑{Insert D}↓ [On the following page, a passage, in pencil,
            marked "D":] ↑{True . . . angels.↓
27   desireable
29   weilds

34–36   for ⟨it is more of⟩ God ↑has . . . it↓ than of man. ↑Yet . . . state↓ [last
             addition in pencil]

Page 62

3   leads↑,↓ ⟨to⟩ as

Sermon C

Manuscript: Six sheets folded to make four pages each; folios nested and sewn with
white thread along the left margin; pages measure 24.9 x 19.9 cm. An additional sheet,
folded to make four pages, is attached to the recto of leaf 3 with red sealing wax; these
pages measure 24.2 x 19.9 cm.

Lines   *Page 63*
1–4   ¶ ⟨The year . . . Christ. ↑As . . . disseminated↓ A more . . . round
             ⟨this commemoration as the world grows older⟩ ↑the religious . . .
             Nazareth↓.⟩ [Canceled in pencil, this opening sentiment is clearly
             appropriate to a Christmas sermon. Since Sermon C was first deliv-
             ered on December 26, 1830, the cancellation is rejected as a late
             emendation.]
5   stable, ⟨is the king of a kingdom that⟩ increases ↑his power↓
8–9   for ⟨its⟩ ↑this↓ . . . ↑& slain↓
13   ↑now building ↑them↓ . . . righteousness,↓
15–23   by the ↑outward↓ [addition in pencil] . . . now it⟨'s increases⟩ ⟨↑great
             & increasing sway↓⟩has greater sway ⟨from year to year⟩ in the
             world ↑than at any former period.↓ [The words "great & increasing
             sway" added in pencil; "than . . . period." in ink over pencil.
             Emerson's outline notation here follows at the bottom of MS p. 2, set
             off by a large square bracket to the left:]
                     1. Christianity exactly coincident with morals
                     2. Its progress not opposed by infidelity but by sin
                     3. It is the greatest good.—
             ¶ [Because the following paragraph, canceled in pencil and ink, is
             appropriate to the first delivery of the sermon, its cancellation is
             rejected as a late emendation:] ⟨It will . . . ↑of the religion↓ . . .
             ↑without this↓ [addition in ink over pencil] . . . decoration &
             ⟨games⟩ ↑festivity↓ [addition in ink over pencil] & ↑solemn↓ . . .
             Christ ⟨to [illegible word]⟩ to all men, & to us.⟩ ¶ It . . . defended; It
             is

Page 64

2   in the ⟨possess⟩ hearing
2–5   us ↑{↓improve the time by↑}↓ consider↑{↓ing↑}↓ [brackets added in
             pencil] ⟨on an⟩ a few . . . faith ↑in its↓ [addition in pencil] &
             ⟨correct⟩ ↑bring↓ [addition in ink over pencil] our practice. ↑nearer
             to its rule.↓ [addition in ink over "nearer to it" in pencil]
10–(65)3   Conscience. ⟨It is like the light of the moon & stars by day that so
             mixes with the light of the sun that they are not themselves perceived.
             The mere moralist wd teach the same things as Christianity without

perceiving that he owes them to Christianity.⟩ [Although Emerson
did not include the following in this cancellation, the passage is fully
repeated in the addition that follows, and is therefore treated here as if
it had been canceled.] It enjoins what that enjoins & condemns what
that condemns It teaches every sober & every elevating principle, &
militates against no man, & no society, & no interest, & no motive,
that is ⟨safe &⟩ desireable or safe. It condemns war, & slavery, &
intemperance, & every vice; every unsocial & injurious practice.
⟨Now this is very different⟩ ↑Herein it differs↓ from other teachers
pretending to come from God The religion of Mahomet teaches what
is contrary to the conscience, it is sensual. [end of page] ¶ ⟨T[manu-
script torn]igion of the Hindoos is cruel violation of natural duties; &
so ↑are the religions↓ of the savage nations of the North & South— ¶
But the law of Christ teaches nothing inconsistent with the moral
constitution of man so that a man cannot be at odds with Christianity
without being at odds with his own moral being. ⟨↑Herein is its
evidence. It demonstrates more than a miracle its divine origin.↓⟩ ¶
Further, Christianity is not only strictly coincident with morals but it
⟨carries⟩ enlightens ⟨the⟩ & confirms the moral law. The moralist
since the coming of Christ, teaches more & better than he taught
before. He not only teaches to respect mens rights & to abstain from
evil, but he shows whence men's rights flow out of a common
parentage in God; he teaches to abstain from evil *as sin,* a distinction
of infinite value. Repeat to yourself the main precepts of Jesus Love
God love men ¶ Raise yourself above men by serving them Conquer
your enemies by benefits Serve God by a ↑↑godly life↓ & you lead life
of yᵉ spirit not of yᵉ flesh↓ ["& you . . . flesh" added in pencil] ¶ What
is a godly life? not one of sacrifices or of solitude but a life of
humanity & active duty ¶ You [manuscript torn] that Christianity
prepares its own way enlightens the soul that receives it, & when it
has kept its lower laws, teaches the Conscience to be more scrupulous,
to aim at higher & harder virtues, & shows that to be plainly grand
& godlike which the worldling regards as mean & disagreeable,
namely to love your enemies, to give to them that ask you, & to
despise riches & honour in comparison with spiritual things. ↑{a}↓
[On the following page, a passage marked "a":] {Is not this fact, i.e.
the coincidence of the Christian rule with the moral law as far as the
moral law went, & the coincidence with the moral law beyond what
that had ever taught before by carrying ⟨a⟩the conscience along with
it & making it raise its standard & teach all that Christianity
teaches—is not this an evidence a demonstration beyond all the force
of miracles that it came from the same hand from which moral nature
came.}↓ [The passage marked "a" is added in ink over the following
passage in pencil:] ⟨Ar⟩Is not this fact the coincidence of the Christian truth with the moral /law/nature/ as far as the ⟨conscience⟩
↑moral law↓ went & the coincidence with our ⟨conscience⟩ ↑the
moral law↓ beyond what the ⟨conscience⟩ had ever taught, but
carrying the conscience along with it & making it raise its standard

an evidence a demonstration beyond all the force of miracles yᵗ it came from the same hand that nature came from} [end of passage in pencil] ¶ In this manner then, it appears Chrᵗʸ not only does not contradict our moral nature but enlightens ⟨it⟩ & perfects it. ¶ A word now to that part of the Christian law which is not *moral* but *positive*. Has it encumbered us with cruel or needless ceremonies. It is understood to enjoin the observance of the Sabbath ⟨to⟩ ↑the rite↓ of baptism & of the Lords Supper. One of these is ⟨th⟩confessedly the most salutary & useful institution of modern times the others ⟨of⟩ ↑not only innocent, but have↓ the best ↑practical↓ effect upon the life & the heart of Christians. ¶ ↑Repent [this word may be "Repeat" or "Repeal"] these & you see that tho' now urged by the moralist they were never urged before with any thing like the same assurance↓ [addition in pencil] ¶ ↑↑{a great sign of progress in a Christian is the discerning some thing to be a sin that before, he did not consider such.}↓↓⟩ ¶ ↑The conscience . . . nature came?↓ [This lengthy revision occurs on the inserted folio attached with red sealing wax to leaf 3 recto.]

11	term, ⟨is a very difficult one to define⟩ ↑⟨It is not easy to define⟩ is used . . . looseness↓.
12	man ⟨& is⟩ according
15–19	wisdom. ⟨& Increase a man's light & he sees things to be wrong which he esteemed innocent⟩ ↑Conscience ↑strictly speaking↓ . . . ↑be↓ . . . more, viz ⟨yᵉ⟩ not . . . observance.↓
20–22	has ⟨been⟩ gone, . . . ↑i.e. with . . . persons.↓.
22–23	It ⟨cer⟩ commends
32–33	with ⟨morals⟩ what . . . confirms ⟨it⟩ ↑the conscience or moral sight↓.
34	upon obscure field of duty & ⟨throws brightness ⟨upon⟩⟩ ↑along↓
36	others rights↑.↓ ⟨& to abstain from evil.⟩ The Christian moralist ⟨te⟩ shows
43–(65)1	the ⟨moral law⟩ ↑conscience↓ . . . law &, ⟨th⟩ further, . . . with⟨e⟩ it

Page 65

7	second ⟨consideration⟩ ↑point↓ ⟨I⟩to which
8	us ⟨hungers⟩ waits
10	which passes⟨s⟩
10–11	↑Public↓ Sin ⟨in States⟩ opposes Christianity in states, ⟨sin⟩ private
13	his ⟨sin⟩ ↑moral guilt↓. [emendation in ink over pencil]
19	commands of ⟨conscience⟩ ↑duty↓
20–23	then ⟨doubts⟩ finds . . . if ⟨there is⟩ it . . . bosom? ⟨Thou hypocrite! f⟩First
25–27	↑a practical . . . former↓ [in ink over pencil] . . . revelation is ⟨an infinite blessing⟩ ↑the greatest ⟨good⟩ external good of man,↓ [emendation in ink over pencil] . . . to ⟨seek⟩ ↑hear & obey↓
31–32	or the ⟨gr⟩ law of gravity it ⟨lay⟩ ↑passes↓
36	tongue, & ⟨teeth, & a palate⟩ ↑⟨voice⟩ ↑& eye↓ ear↓,

41–(66)2   better. ¶ ⟨Herein is the true distinction⟩ Without ⟨it⟩ ↑this distinc-
                tion↓ . . . life. ⟨the⟩ He

                                Page 66

5   us ⟨gratitude &⟩ joy
6–8   nature. ↑{Insert A}↓ [On the following page, a passage marked "A":]
                ↑{It . . . pleasure.}↓
8–11   you. ⟨The⟩ ↑Let a↓ principle come⟨s⟩ from . . . ↑such as Jesus
                presented,↓ . . . *God.* ↑If . . . soul↓ Forthwith, . . . of ⟨ground⟩ the
                earth, ⟨he⟩I become⟨s⟩ associated with God, ⟨he⟩ I
15   principle to ⟨its own⟩ ["its" is partially restored] height and have ⟨a⟩
                by
16   communicates ⟨emb⟩ applies
21–28   love⟨.⟩; ⟨In strict connexion with these he taught that the soul of man
                doth not perish⟩ that the end ⟨of all things⟩ ↑for . . . exist↓ . . .
                right. ¶ ⟨And if we knew our own souls↑'↓ [apostrophe in pencil]
                good, we should pour out our hearts to God in gratitude for this
                mercy.⟩ [canceled in pencil] My friends, . . . rights↑.↓ [addition in
                pencil] ⟨We⟩ ↑Men of Science↓ . . . of ⟨old error⟩ ↑pedantic specula-
                tion↓.
29–30   Newton who ⟨taught us that all bodies fall towards each other by
                certain laws⟩ ↑disclosed . . . matter↓ & so saved us from ⟨the⟩
                ⟨errors in important cases⟩ ⟨We are never weary of commending⟩
                ↑mistake . . . praise the↓ the name
33–36   good⟨s⟩) nothing but a↑n↓ ⟨corollary from the⟩ ↑inference↓
                ⟨c⟩flowing . . . Jesus. ⟨The⟩ ↑Political↓ ["The" incompletely can-
                celed] . . . received; ⟨the⟩ freedom ⟨of⟩ ↑to↓ the subject & ⟨the⟩
                freedom ⟨of⟩ ↑to↓
39–40   grieve. ⟨T⟩He . . . mere ⟨w⟩ absence
41   of ⟨the mind⟩ ↑sin↓.
41–(67)1   planets ⟨he will tell us &⟩ the ["&" accidentally canceled]

                                Page 67

5   The ⟨o⟩eldest
8–10   things ↑1.↓ . . . strictly ⟨af⟩ consistent . . . ↑2.↓ . . . ↑& 3.↓ & that
                . . . it is ⟨so⟩ ↑an↓ infinite a ⟨bless⟩ good
13–19   love. ⟨We shall ⟨greet⟩ welcome . . . Man.⟩ [cancellation rejected as
                a late emendation] ¶ ⟨↑We shall abide in his love by keeping his
                commandments↓⟩↑We shall value ["We shall abide . . . command-
                ments" in pencil, overwritten by the text in ink] . . . apostle in his
                ⟨earnest declaration⟩ ↑continual thankfulness,↓ . . . Christ.↓

                            Sermon CI

Manuscript: Eight sheets folded to make four pages each; folios stacked and sewn with
white thread along the left margin; pages of the first seven folios measure 25 x 20.2 cm,
and those of the eighth folio, from which the bottom has been cut off, measure 23 x 20.2
cm.

[Above Bible text:]   Last night of the year 1830.

Lines	Page 68
2	age ⟨in all⟩ is the approach of ⟨death⟩ ↑dissolution↓ to animated & ⟨of dissolution⟩ to
5	lifted ⟨till⟩ ↑to be↓
9–10	under ⟨rivers⟩ floods . . . ↑have been swallowed↓ [addition in ink over pencil]
11	that intomb
16	stayed in ⟨the East⟩ ↑Asia↓ & War in ⟨the West⟩ ↑Europe↓
18	urn. ⟨In his brightest hour as the sun rolls on his bright ecliptic it is but a funeral fire lighting men & animals & plants to their graves.⟩ The
20–21	light, ⟨it⟩ to . . . of ⟨that⟩ all
24–(69)3	of ⟨waste⟩ ↑destruction↓ . . . that ⟨every wind⟩ the . . . proves ⟨a⟩ poisonous ⟨simoom⟩ [both cancellations in pencil] to . . . rheumatism. ⟨Every east wind that blows the sails of the seas to our shore breaks up the life of vigorous men The year that is gone slain its hosts & loosened the hopes broken the heart⟩ ¶ ⟨↑The year that is gone has dismissed its nations from the earth. And it has ⟨sh⟩ undermined the health or stolen away the senses or broken the hearts of those ↑multitudes↓ [addition in pencil] who remain. ↑And meantime the sword is drawn already↓↓⟩ [last sentence in pencil] ¶ ⟨Therefore⟩ In . . . man ⟨re⟩ hears . . . turn. ↑to die?↓ ⟨And at the close of a year, when the last sands are running out of another ↑of the few & evil↓ periods of life God & man seem to ⟨call upon⟩ ↑ask↓ each of us as with a trumpet, How old art thou.⟩ ¶ It is ¶ ⟨We do right my friends in this hour sacred to ⟨death⟩ ↑tho'ts of mortality↓ to come up to⟩ ↑The true . . . is↓

	Page 69
5	God / scared / affrighted / [variant in pencil]
5–12	↑⟨↓To the . . . also in God↑⟩↓ [parentheses added in pencil] ↑{D}↓ [On the following page, a passage marked "D":] ↑¶ What . . . not ⟨impair⟩ put . . . not.↓
14–32	hourglass. ⟨There is a creation⟩, ⟨w⟩Whilst all perishes↑, there is a creation↓ ⟨is s⟩as fresh . . . prime, ⟨when⟩ ↑before↓ . . . the heaven ⟨When the wheels of nature drag with age. We have within & around us a world which is our real home but of which few men are yet conscious It is amidst us yet we know it not. The cause of all order, the source of all good it is in the world & the world was made by it yet the world knows it not. As ⟨one⟩the world is but the house of our bodies and as our body is but the house of our souls, so all these changes are only the occasions the admonitions the instruments ↑the body,↓ of this spiritual nature. There is a life of the soul the entrance into the kingdom of truth peace righteousness the knowledge & the love of God and in the opening of the interior senses to ⟨this⟩ the perception of this kingdom does true life consist. The Scriptures are

the message from this world to the soul of man which was native there
but has wandered ⟨& lost the memory of his home. The Scriptures
teach the necessity of a new birth as the body was born into this world
so must the soul be born into that.⟩⟩ ↑There is . . . daily↓

21–23   is ⟨incorruptible⟩ ↑immutable↓ . . . incorruptible [struck through in
pencil] & cannot grow old. ⟨The vast majority of mankind tread
upon its borders unconscious of it.⟩ The

29   the ⟨s⟩closing

34–36   care & ⟨busy work⟩ ⟨↑↑close↓⟩ ↑keen↓ competitions↓ . . . ↑no
better than↓

36–(70)1 ↑in itself↓ . . . Himself. ⟨a⟩And . . . means? ⟨nothing but the truth
he taught.⟩ ↑His truth alone.↓

Page 70

1–6   you, ↑said he↓—*they* . . . life." ↑{Insert X.}↓ [On the following page,
a passage marked "X":] ↑{That soul ⟨of all of us has only⟩ ↑only has↓
. . . out, [Emerson added a caret, but no text.] that . . . better than
↑to seek↓ . . . a perfect ⟨faith gives more joy⟩ trust . . . {These facts
. . . soul.}}↓

7–9   ear for the⟨n⟩re ⟨it⟩they . . . soul as we receive

10–11   Then ⟨is the being⟩ ↑does man↓ emerg⟨ing⟩e

13–15   us ⟨with all the ⟨life⟩ energy & sense the gospel can give it.⟩ do not
. . . you are ⟨of ↑in↓⟩ in ⟨this⟩ ↑any true↓ . . . ↑for your Almanack.↓

20   thoughtfully & ⟨notice⟩ observe

23   you /burdensome/mean/ [variant in pencil]

28   rule? ⟨How many⟩ Have

30   ↑now↓

31–32   burst ⟨from⟩ its bond⟨s⟩age

34   sloth, ↑covetousness↓ [addition in pencil]

37–38   children. ¶ ⟨The harvest is past the summer is ended & we are not
saved. [Jeremiah 8:20] ¶ Honourable age is not [space left in manu-
script] neither is measured by number of years but wisdom is grey hair
unto man & an unspotted life is old age⟩ ¶ My friends,

Page 71

9–24   ¶ {These . . . good."}

9   our ⟨being⟩ action.

20–28   leaf ⟨in⟩ nor . . . of souls,. When . . . thus ⟨lose⟩ [canceled in pencil]
find . . . good."} ¶ ⟨Now, brethren, . . . he who does ↑not↓ . . .
permit ⟨y⟩ me {in . . . term} to . . . you.⟩ ↑Is it not fit o my friends
that we should make the life of ⟨G⟩the soul in us or the life of God in
the soul coextensive with the term of our natural life.↓ [cancellation
and addition rejected as a late emendation] That ↑whole↓

29–30   make up ⟨your all of preparation⟩ ↑human life↓.

30–33   up in ⟨boy⟩↑child↓hood; [emendation in pencil] . . . real ⟨time⟩ life
. . . much of ⟨manhood⟩ ↑maturity↓ [emendation in pencil] . . . is
⟨shuffled⟩ ↑shoved aside↓

34   soon ⟨bu⟩And

35	↑delay↓
37–39	allows ⟨us⟩ ↑to each,↓ . . . commandments, to ⟨choose our⟩ ↑make↓ . . . men, ⟨to talk together,⟩ to choose . . . character, ⟨is now ours.⟩ That

Page 72

1–3	that ⟨Socrates⟩ ↑saints & heroes↓ had. ⟨It is all that Plato had.⟩ It . . . Luther or ⟨Calvin or Fenelon⟩ or Newton ↑or Washington↓ [emendations in pencil] had, to lift ⟨↑&↓⟩ themselves . . . ↑& sublime energy↓ [addition in ink over pencil] . . . world & ⟨teach⟩ ↑help↓ [emendation in ink over pencil]
4	↑of life↓
4	independance
9	truth ⟨that⟩ may [Opposite this sentence on the otherwise blank facing page is the following notation in pencil:] Can crowd eternities into an hour / Or stretch an hour into eternity [Cf. Byron, *Cain*, I, i, 536–37; cf. *JMN* 7:140; used in "The Oversoul," *CW* 2:162.]
10–11	men to ⟨see good & evil, to make their election & begin their progress to truth & good, or it is long enough to do evil to deny our Maker & tempt the souls of our brethren⟩ ↑be . . . lost↓.
11–14	↑to make our election;↓; ↑all . . . exist↓ {the . . . eternity,} the choice . . . advancement ⟨from⟩ towards . . . love ⟨forever & ever⟩, or ⟨wo & folly & hatred & madness & despair⟩ ↑the ⟨refusal re⟩ rejection of all these ⟨or spirit of our souls⟩↓ are
15–16	choose ⟨the⟩ principles ⟨of the gospel of Jesus Christ⟩ for the /law/ rule/ [variant in pencil] . . . little ⟨dirty good⟩ gratifications
20–21	consideration ⟨of this serious truth with more than common force It⟩there is ⟨a⟩ ↑another↓ fact /worthy of our most intense attention/ that may increase interest/ ⟨that⟩ the
22	law of ⟨the⟩ ↑this↓ moral ⟨world⟩ ↑order↓
23–24	↑Every . . . rest↓
25–30	judgment & ⟨various⟩ rich . . . not wise in [end of line] ⟨himself. But these are means of helping those that help themselves. ↑And yet more clear is this true of anothers virtue. He is virtuous to himself⟩ {Insert B}↓ [On the following page, a passage marked "B":] ↑{And yet . . . nor ⟨anothers⟩ ↑one man's↓ . . . themselves.}↓
30–33	given. ⟨Else⟩ ↑If . . . law↓ . . . teach ⟨ushim⟩ ↑every . . . ruin. ↑and . . . doubt↓↓ [end of page] in thunder. The convictions
36	brother all
37–38	directs it ⟨and so we can only teach who will be taught we can only present⟩ ↑But . . . presenting↓ excitements suggestions ⟨we can only⟩ ⟨↑that⟩ to . . . attention &↓
40–41	¶ {One . . . speaks to ⟨your souls⟩us. Th⟨is⟩e shadows

Page 73

1	to ⟨you⟩ ↑us↓
2	outspeak ⟨y⟩our

3–4   time has [end of line; the following addition replaces the text cut from
             the first leaf of the eighth folio:] ↑any . . . do,↓ [end of page] or
8   that ⟨some you⟩ ↑the flesh↓ ha⟨ve⟩s yet
9   ↑not be deaf to this ⟨Word of truth⟩ ⟨↑Voice↓⟩ ↑Voice↓↓ save
10–11   ↑Let us repent⟨s⟩ of our sins.↓
12   more. ⟨t⟩These

[The following notation in pencil appears below the end of the sermon:] The summer

Sermon CII

Manuscript: Five sheets folded to make four pages each, and a single sheet folded to make
four pages laid in between the fourth and fifth folios but not included in the sewing; original five folios stacked and sewn with white thread along the left margin, from which the
fifth folio has torn away; pages of the original five folios measure 25.1 x 20.2 cm, and those
of the inserted folio measure 24.1 x 19.6 cm. Additionally, a stray leaf containing material
consistent with the tone and substance of Sermon XCIII has been found with the manuscript; however, thread holes along the left margin of the leaf do not match those of either
Sermon XCIII or any other sermon from this period. The stray leaf measures 25.1 x 20.3 cm.

Lines   *Page 74*
2–5   It ⟨is⟩ ↑has been↓ . . . accurate ⟨examination⟩ ↑comparison↓ . . .
             ↑in human life↓.
5–7   th⟨e⟩is sour philosophy in th⟨is⟩e general . . . good, ⟨all the hazards
             of⟩ a new year. ↑↑We . . . year↓ . . . hazards.↓
7–10   other that / we are yet alive / the simplest goods a sufficiently desire-
             able in themselves / [variant in pencil], . . . labor. [end of page] the
             ⟨dedu⟩ hunger ["hunger" in pencil over ink] pain &
11–13   not a ⟨Christian⟩ ↑traditional↓ faith ↑in life after death↓, . . . who
             ↑by . . . age↓ . . . live ⟨in sickness & old age⟩ would
17   ¶ ↑Who . . . pain?↓ [in ink over pencil]
18–(75)3   ¶ To the ⟨most⟩ largest . . . are ⟨closely⟩ knit . . . ↑to the laborer
             . . . passing day↓ [in pencil] to . . . walls of ⟨great⟩ ↑a↓ librar⟨ies⟩y,
             [emendation in pencil] . . . time ⟨a work of such⟩ an ample

                                 Page 75
4   ¶ ↑And↓ ⟨T⟩these↑,↓ ⟨are⟩ I suppose ↑are↓
4–7   ↑This↓ We should expect ⟨that it would be so⟩ ↑in . . . Cause↓; . . .
             ↑observed↓ between the ⟨gr⟩ powers . . . such ⟨unceasing⟩ [can-
             celed in pencil] attention
13   happy ⟨new⟩ year
15–23   in the⟨ir⟩ face; . . . encountered; ↑they see ⟨that the days of⟩ what
             the last year has done that its days have been the tombs of their
             friends↓ [in pencil; rejected as an addition for the second delivery on
             the supposition of an allusion to the death of Edward B. Emerson,
             October 1, 1834] they are . . . what ↑the↓ last . . . restore, ⟨or they
             see⟩ and . . . they see ⟨sor⟩ troubles ⟨ripening⟩ which . . .
             ↑ripening↓ . . . the ⟨year⟩ ↑season↓ [emendation in pencil] . . .
             overcome the ⟨Circumstances⟩ difficulties
24   these sufferer⟨er⟩s

29	↑not↓
35–37	↑I say . . . are natural they . . . his nature.↓ [in pencil]
38	↑make↓
43	many a ⟨man⟩ ↑sluggard↓ has been ⟨formed to usefulness⟩ ↑made a workman↓ by the very ⟨sternness⟩ ↑desperateness↓
44	must ⟨exert himself with ⟨the⟩ ↑this↓ whole vigour⟩ ↑put out his might↓,

Page 76

2	shall ⟨wake⟩ ↑arouse↓.
3	poverty? ↑it . . . little,↓
4	Is it a ⟨trial⟩ severe
6	pride↑?↓ ⟨in some rivalry⟩ ↑Your . . . friends.↓
7	that you ⟨have scorned to⟩ ↑are ashamed of, before↓
9	friend ⟨for⟩ with
13	may ⟨strengthen⟩ ↑arm↓ the ⟨whole⟩ ↑entire↓
15–17	↑in his heart↓, . . . his ⟨soul⟩ ↑mind↓ . . . has ⟨imagined⟩ ↑believed↓; . . . variety of ⟨exert⟩ discipline
18–22	¶↑By . . . spirit ↑In the multitude of your thots↓ . . . dignity, ⟨whether it be⟩ ↑as much in↓ a menial as ↑in↓ a commanding ⟨place⟩ office. . . . dwelling↓ [paragraph added and emended in pencil]
24–26	by /destroying/impairing in mature minds/ . . . surely ⟨act⟩ ↑operate↓ [emendation in pencil]
28	take off the ⟨deceitful lustre⟩ ↑false colors↓
30	¶ ↑And . . . trials.↓
32	favour, ↑or,↓ according to ⟨the⟩ ↑a good↓
33	Unexpected ⟨trials⟩ difficulties
39–(77)1	let ⟨them⟩ ↑it↓ bear ↑me↓ . . . hour when ⟨they⟩ ↑it↓

Page 77

5–6	particular ⟨art b⟩act . . . seem ⟨incredible⟩ wonderful . . . ↑every . . . heart↓
12–13	have ⟨brightened⟩ ↑made a little light↓ for us ↑in↓
14	witness, ↑Nor↓ [This sentence is written over the following notation in pencil:] There is no winter to the warm heart
19	will ⟨better⟩ more
20–28	affections? [For either the second or third delivery, Emerson canceled the first paragraph of heading III and substituted a lengthy revision inscribed on pp. 2–4 of the folio that is inserted, but not included in the sewing, at this point. The revision is not adopted in the clear text.] ¶ ⟨III. There . . . intended ⟨being⟩ duration . . . end.⟩ ¶ ↑III. There is yet a third way in which God strengthens us for our trials, & that is by the gift of an infinite nature, infinite in duration as in capacity. This consideration gives an extent of meaning to the promise, that will infuse a mighty virtue into our souls. As thy days, shall thy strength be. But the days of the soul are without end. When the sun of the spiritual world hath risen upon it, it can never fear a night. One day is as a thousand years. So then, according to this appointed duration is

thy strength. God has formed us, as these affections & faculties may declare, not for seventy summers, but for day without night, for ⟨duration⟩ action without end. ¶ It seems to me brethren as if we ought solemnly to congratulate one another that we exist not that we have begun another twelvemonth of mortal measure but that we live embosomed in the love of God ⟨that out of all our vexations & wants we can withdraw into a shelter of peaceful & divine thoughts⟩ that whilst our feet walk & our hands work in the material world, & our lungs breathe material air, each one of us does at the same time inherit an entire spiritual world of thought & affection that hither out of all our vexations & wants ⟨we can⟩ we can withdraw into a shelter of peaceful & divine thoughts. Without, we have wants & fears & pains. Within, is nothing mean or transient. ⟨To its duration a century is but the turning of an hourglass. This creation is this moment as fresh as it was in its morning prime before the stars were launched on their orbits & shall be as fresh when the stars have fallen out of heaven.⟩ For each of us can retire to the presence & communion of God in his own heart, can dress himself in such thoughts & affec-tions as to feel the company of that friendly Eye following him with love in all his steps, can learn to live amidst men practising the necessary details of mortal life ⟨agreeably to⟩ ↑upon↓ principles that ⟨rule⟩ ↑govern↓ the angels of heaven, & so introduce eternity into time↓

30   wretched, ⟨is⟩ the
32   formed ⟨for⟩ to

Page 78

1   ↑We shall feel . . . with us.↓
3   seek ⟨in⟩ first
4–7   ↑And if . . . them good.↓
13   be ⟨as it⟩ what it will. As ⟨is⟩ our

[The following is inscribed on a stray leaf found with Sermon CII:] & deliver the very truth itself instead of circuitous oriental representations of it & this by the development of the great Christian doctrine I have alluded to, that the kingdom of God is within us.

{"The kingdom of God is within you." It only needs to meditate on a few particulars comprised in that proposition to see how significant it is. A man contains all that is needful to his government within himself. He only can do himself any good or any harm. Nothing can be given to him or taken from him without an equivalent. The benevolence that bestows a cup of cold water is itself enlarged enriched by the act; the malevolence that refuses the same is contracted & impoverished ⟨by⟩ thereby. Every act puts the agent in a new condition. The purpose of life seems to be to acquaint a man with himself & whatever science or art or course of action he engages in reacts upon & illuminates the recesses of his own mind. Thus friends seem to be only mirrors to draw out & explain to us ourselves; & that which draws us nearest to our fellow man, is, that the deep Heart in one, answers to the deep Heart in another,—that we find we have ⟨a common Nature⟩—one life which runs through all the individuals, & which is indeed Divine. But there is no time to venture upon this expanding subject.}

⟨Then [two illegible words]⟩

Sermon CIII

Manuscript: Seven sheets folded to make four pages each; folios stacked and sewn with white thread along the left margin; pages measure 25.2 x 20.1 cm.

[Emerson rewrote the beginning of this sermon, retaining the Bible text, but canceling the introduction and most of the text under the three numbered divisions (designated I, II, and III in the earlier version). The substitute text, which employs arabic numerals for these divisions, incorporates uncanceled portions of the earlier version. In the interest of clarity, the text of the earlier version is here given down through the first paragraph of division III. The presence and position of uncanceled passages belonging to the earlier version are indicated, though revisions within them are treated as these passages appear in the revised version. The editors have retained the roman numeral division markings, both because Emerson reverted to that system with division IV, and because his use of arabic numerals appears to have been a mere convenience in keeping the revised text distinct from the unrevised.]

> The same came to Jesus by night, & said unto him Rabbi We
> know that thou art a teacher sent from God for no man can do
> these miracles that thou doest except God be with him.
> III chap John, 2.

⟨It is my present purpose to offer a plain account of the state of the question respecting the miracles of the New Testament. A miracle is not essentially incredible in some circumstances, in others it is.⟩

⟨In the first place, I would observe that a miracle is not the highest kind of evidence A miracle cannot prove any fact by itself. A miracle cannot prove that a falsehood or a command to do a vicious act came from God. If a man declared that hatred & murder were agreeable to God and should at the same time cause stones to speak & confirm his word would any good man believe this wondrous work came from God, & that it was right to hate & to kill men & that the messenger came from God? Certainly not it would indeed bewilder & unsettle our convictions, but the wonder would not be ascribed to the same power which made our moral constitution but to an evil Spirit. To make a miracle of any effect it is plain it must accompany ⟨a⟩ ↑the↓ declaration of a truth;

Therefore a miracle is not the highest kind of evidence to a revelation. Its internal evidence is the highest kind⟩

⟨I. It is /plain/agreed/ [variant in ink over pencil] that we can conceive of no communication from God to man to be known as such that does not involve a miracle.⟩ [The following uncanceled sentence is marked "X" for inclusion in the revised version:] To deny ↑therefore↓ [in ink over pencil] that there has ever been or ever can be any miracle, is to deny that there has ever been or can be any communication from God to men. ⟨The readiest way to prove the credibility of a miracle seems to be to show a man the evidences there are of design & of a moral government, for the moment the idea of God is fully received into the mind, nothing is more reasonable than the doctrine of miracles.⟩

⟨II. The goodness of God in his ordinary operations seems to have the effect of making men tho'tless of him; for the invariableness of his laws makes the mind ⟨rest in⟩ ↑stop at↓ the law, & take that for cause enough, & ⟨it⟩ the only way by which men's

attention can be aroused to the tho't, that th⟨is⟩ere is a presiding intelligence, is to
startle them by a plain departure from the common order as by causing the blind to see
& the dead to awake.⟩ [The following uncanceled passage was included, with further
revisions, in the revised version (see the notes below):] There are thousands of men who
if there were no histories & if the order of ⟨eve⟩ natural events had never been broken
would never ask in the course of their lives for anything beyond what they saw But
astonish them with a miracle & their minds instantly inquire why things keep one order
rather than another, & the same inquiry instantly suggests itself to every mind who hears
of the miracle

⟨⟨III.⟩ ↑I↓ ⟨I say⟩ l⟩Let a man receive the belief of a God & a miracle ⟨s⟩ ceases to be
incredible for God is the great miracle ⟨in which all⟩ whose being is beyond our
conception & which explains all else. ↑It does not require more power than is always
exerted in & around us.↓ I am obliged to suppose his existence by what I already know,
& his existence supposed, a miracle is an easy thing.⟩ [The following uncanceled
sentence marks the convergence of the earlier and revised versions of the opening of the
sermon:] Does the unbeliever, who

Lines	*Page 79*
2–5	credible. ⟨It will be admitted by all, that as soon as one miracle has been shown to be credible it is enough for our faith.⟩ ⟨↑It is not the evidence of a particular miracle which is to be laboured. After once supernatural power has been shown we have seen ⟨m⟩one miracle wro't we have no difficulty in believing that the same hands may do more. It is only the first miracle that is denied.↓⟩ [canceled in pencil] ↑It will . . . proof.↓
8	existed ⟨at⟩ in
11	that ⟨it is impossible⟩ a . . . which ⟨g⟩God
13–14	suppose ⟨a⟩ million↑s of↓
16–18	God. To deny therefore, &c {Insert X} [Emerson has drawn a hand pointing to the right to indicate the inclusion of the uncanceled passage from the original version, now marked "X":] To deny ↑therefore↓ [in ink over pencil] . . . men.
19	requires ⟨a little⟩ more ⟨detail⟩ ↑words↓
20	to / mankind / the human mind / ,
22	with⟨r⟩draw

	Page 80
1–3	what ⟨aris⟩ the . . . the [end of line] whole [end of page] whole furnishes . . . makes ⟨him⟩ ↑man↓
6–17	enough. ⟨The li⟩ ⟨↑It is enough for them to say that stone falls or earth falls in orbit by Gravity without asking why gravity↓⟩ Now . . . them ⟨well⟩ by . . . arise. There are thousands, &c [Emerson has drawn a hand pointing to the left to indicate the inclusion of the uncanceled passage from the original version:] There are thousands . . . of ⟨eve⟩ natural . . . / anything beyond what they saw / a secondary cause & never ask for a first /. [variant in pencil] ↑It . . . *by Gravity*; [underscored in pencil] . . . asking ⟨why⟩ ↑whence↓ Gravity & / whence / what is / [variant in pencil] Life?↓ . . . the miracle

[Here at the end of the uncanceled passage from the original version, Emerson has written "Now does not this" and drawn a hand pointing right to signal resumption of the revised text.]

17   furnish a ⟨very⟩ ⟨reason that will make⟩ suitable
18–20   ↑If . . . both?↓
21–23   that ⟨may⟩ make↑s↓ a miracle ↑not in↓credible, . . . than ⟨he⟩ ↑we↓ ha⟨s⟩ve . . . around ⟨him.⟩ ↑us,↓ And
24–25   what ⟨I⟩he now behold↑s↓ . . . more. Does the unbeliever, &c. [Emerson has drawn a hand pointing left to indicate resumption of the uncanceled text from the original version:] Does the unbeliever, who
31–32   day. ⟨I⟩ A wise . . . story that ⟨an insane man⟩ ↑reason↓
36–37   ago. ⟨We live by⟩ ↑All our life is a↓ miracle⟨s⟩.
42   In ⟨fine,⟩ ↑other words;↓

Page 81

3–5   ¶ ↑IV.↓ In the ⟨second⟩ ↑fourth↓ . . . the ⟨i⟩Intelligence . . . evidence ⟨to⟩ ↑of↓ a moral ⟨end.⟩ ↑truth.↓
6–7   law↑—that . . . is a ⟨good life⟩ moral life↓.
8   ↑The↓ Love ↑of others↓
10–11   with ⟨some varia⟩ no . . . in ⟨every⟩ ↑the↓
12–15   moral. ↑& therefore . . . a ⟨peculiar⟩ special . . . *purpose* ⟨does not⟩ conforms . . . him.↓ ¶ ⟨It is a very important consideration⟩ I . . . ↑from↓
18   cannot ⟨commend⟩ ↑approve↓ [emendation in pencil]
19   before our⟨e⟩ eyes
27–28   miracle ⟨throw light on⟩ ↑mutually confirm↓ each other. ¶ These ⟨circumstances make⟩ ↑considerations . . . general↓
33–35   same ⟨a⟩wisdom . . . its ⟨us⟩ customary . . . reason, ⟨t⟩ very [The sentence is written over a two-line pencil notation, partly erased, from which the phrases "incredible yᵗ" and "be common till one true many false" have been recovered.]
39   would ⟨put⟩ defeat

Page 82

1   would ⟨fall to the ground⟩ be
2–7   miracle. ¶ ⟨These considerations may show us that it is not unreasonable to believe that in some circumstances miracles have been wrought.⟩ I wish . . . Testament. ⟨↑There is one general circumstance⟩ ↑↑In so doing↓ . . . consideration↓ . . . that is, ⟨the nature of⟩ the . . . revelation.↓ ¶ ⟨There is this great distinction belongs to the evidence of these miracles that belongs to none other that the moral truths which these were wrot to establish are utterly incompatible with the supposition of imposture in those who declared them & lived by them.⟩ It
9–10   Christians. ⟨The i⟩Internal evidence ↑far↓
10–11   reasoning ⟨man⟩ ↑Christian↓ . . . by the ⟨inter⟩ fortifying
12   history of ⟨Christianity⟩ the

19-21   or not. ⟨If I did not acknowledge the doctrine as true, I should yield to
               the skeptic that this story of miracles like other such stories was false.
               But as the doctrine is true, the miracle falls in with & confirms it.⟩
               [canceled in pencil] ¶ The truth↑s taught in N.T.↓ will . . . itself.
               [faulty emendation] ↑In other words,↓ [addition in pencil] Many

24-26   that . . . them. [On the blank facing page, Emerson wrote the
               beginning of what appears to be an extension of this sentence:]
               whether they do not wholly exclude the sup.

35   which the⟨y⟩se men
36-37   imposture↑.↓ ⟨without⟩ ↑To . . . admit↓
39-40   sincere seeker for
43   make a ⟨thousand⟩ ↑multitude↓ credible, as one ⟨report of a can-
               non⟩ ↑clap of thunder↓ has a ⟨thousand⟩ ↑hundred↓
44   account ⟨of⟩ that

                                    Page 83
10   affirmative

                              Sermon CIV

Manuscript: Six sheets folded to make four pages each, and two single leaves, the first
between leaves 4 and 5, the second between leaves 8 and 9, both included in the sewing;
folios stacked and sewn with white thread along the left margin; folio pages measure
24.7 x 20.1 cm; the first single leaf measures 24.7 x 20 cm, and the second measures 24.6
x 20.2 cm. The sermon is numbered "104" at the top of MS p. 1.

[The following notation, in pencil, appears below the Bible text:]

                         Eternal & Almighty King
                         All nature feels attractive power

Lines   *Page 84*
1   to present ⟨&⟩the
12   in ⟨others⟩ the
15-(85)2   ¶ ↑{↓Especially should ↑these↓ . . . good.↑}↓ [brackets in pencil]
17   expedients, ⟨'⟩to
20   which ⟨is such⟩ makes

                                    Page 85
8   calculated. ⟨But⟩ ↑This is not true.↓ ⟨s⟩Self-love
12   act. ⟨It⟩They ⟨is⟩are . . . action ⟨& will⟩ ↑as . . . its↓ not hav
               ⟨e⟩ing
25-28   England Scotland Wales ⟨& Ireland⟩ ↑included in isl of GB↓ [emen-
               dation in pencil] . . . them ⟨a⟩each a perpetual garrison ⟨ar⟩ upon
               . . . all the ⟨ex weary⟩ expenditure . . . which ⟨such⟩ war
29   that it ⟨does not ⟨eat or drink⟩ ↑cost↓ a single soldier's ration⟩ ↑costs
               nothing↓. [cancellation of "does . . . ration" in pencil; "costs noth-
               ing" added in pencil]

Page 86

3	↑I find↓ You
6	↑sort of↓
10	which is ⟨heard at inte⟩ so . . . the ⟨prosperous⟩ rich
11–12	the ⟨advantage⟩ ↑interest↓ . . . ↑of↓ society . . . true & ⟨yet⟩ ↑much↓
14	the ⟨duty⟩ ↑law↓
32–33	wants? ¶ Nor can the love of our neighbor in that degree [followed by a long blank space] ¶ Nor can the love of our neighbor in that degree ⟨in⟩of
44–(87)5	elegant. [end of page] ⟨the elegant, the modest, & the good.⟩ ¶ But that . . . commonly ⟨the⟩ unlovely, . . . diseases⟨,⟩. ⟨↑{↓—as . . . observe.↑}↓⟩ [brackets added in pencil; cancellation rejected as certainly belonging to a later delivery]

Page 87

6–8	higher ⟨love⟩ ↑principle↓, . . . would be a ⟨wretched⟩ ↑bad↓ . . . ↑sickly↓
9	the ⟨rich⟩ ↑selfish↓ . . . nuisance; ⟨that they must thank themselves for their misery⟩ ↑that↓
13	it ⟨act⟩ really
18	not ⟨able⟩ ↑sufficient↓
23	through God; ⟨He⟩ ↑God↓
26–27	principle for ⟨to⟩ the ⟨spring⟩ ↑motive↓ of actions ⟨of⟩ ↑that . . . done↓
30–31	to ⟨present themselves from⟩ ↑meet us ⟨in the⟩with . . . of↓
31–33	↑Yes & it . . . duties↓ [in pencil]
34–36	↑from our minds↓, . . . life. ↑& dims . . . itself.↓
40	than ⟨men⟩ ↑we↓
41–(88)1	*not that ⟨ye are the temple of God His.⟩ ↑the spirit . . . you↓*

Page 88

6	↑by it↓
7–9	right, we ⟨cooperate with him we perceive our union with him, we are sensible of his presence & favor⟩ ↑consent . . . our hands↓. ⟨We draw nigh unto God & God draws nigh unto us It is I who do wrong, it is God in me who does right. And it is the perception of this living in God that makes the /truth/propriety/ of the command Be perfect as your father in heaven is perfect. ¶ Now whilst I see this to be true in my nature I see that my fellow man is made in the same mould & of the same substance. Every man you meet seems to repeat yourself⟩ ¶ When
15–17	perfect.↑, commandments . . . nature.↓
19–21	me. ⟨I beseech you my friends that this faith may not ever [end of page; thus far canceled in pencil] seem less welcome as it may happen to have been represented as a favourite doctrine of one sect of Christians, thus to exalt human nature. In the sense & for the reason that I have given, it cannot be exalted too much It is not the doctrine

of a sect but of all devout Christians. I may say not the property of Christians but of men. Are you an unbeliever The pious men of the Stoic sect that lived before Christ yet received this ⟨tr⟩doctrine saying that the wise man differed from God in nothing but duration ↑They also had the maxim that the mind was God in man.↓ ¶ If I speak to any member of the Church of Rome let me remind him of the saying of Fenelon that God is in our souls as our soul is in our bodies. ¶ If I speak to any member of the Church of England, Abp Leighton (↑Sel. Works↓ Vol I. p. 257) writes yᵗ by yᵉ love of God yᵉ soul is made divine & one with him quoting St Austins words "Si terram amas terra es Si deum amas quid vis ut dicam Deus es." ¶ Are you a Calvinist. That great light of the Calvinistic Church, Henry Scougal, says in his sermon on the excellency of the⟩ [end of page; canceled in ink and in pencil] Religious, "Learn to adore your nature" For all . . . found ⟨that⟩ this . . . life as Paul said The

23–(89)7   ↑¶ This great . . . there ⟨lives⟩ is . . . exist; so . . . One, is . . . any / set of opinions/church/ . . . all /opinions/churches/ . . . sect ⟨of⟩ but . . . before Christ⟨ianity⟩ had . . . divine ⟨& quotes⟩ and . . . you ⟨are⟩ ↑become↓ . . . your nature." ¶ ↑It was the favourite doctrine of Geo. Fox, & Wm Penn & of the society of Friends that the whole growth of man was by direct communication imparting of the Divine Spirit↓↓ [The last sentence added in pencil, perhaps for the second delivery, in New Bedford, February 9, 1834, is rejected as a late emendation (Emerson's interest in Fox is scarcely documented before the summer of 1832: see *EL* 1:164). The entire addition ("This great . . . Spirit") occupies both sides of the second inserted leaf.] ¶ ⟨When we do right it is not our act it is that we receive God into our souls & submit to be his organ. We are then conscious of acting upon a greater will & to a greater end than self-good. ¶ God said to the Jews Be ye holy because I am holy, & by Jesus Christ Be ye merciful as your father is merciful Be ye perfect as your Father in heaven is perfect. Commandments which would be wholly incomprehensible but for this great truth that men in the words of St Peter /*are partakers of the divine nature*/rejoice in this divine origin/⟩ ¶ Now [Emerson has so written this sentence as to incorporate the word *nature* (the first word on a new line) from the previous sentence; since the underscoring relates to its previous context, the editors have not reproduced it in the final context.]

Page 89

9   the same↑.↓ ⟨differing⟩ We

16–21   present God ²{Are we not . . . entrance? ¹{Must not . . . tender ⟨sacred⟩ reverence . . . disguised by ⟨selfish⟩ ↑selfishness in both of us.↓

26–28   would /remember/not forget/ . . . necessities ⟨&⟩ of his . . . sin ⟨&⟩ ↑I would↓ . . . sin I

29   him ⟨in the only⟩ for

38   is not ⟨a piece of bread which⟩ a

Page 90

8   the ⟨Universe⟩ ↑Creation↓

11–12   accomplish. ¶ ⟨Bretheren I have stated as I hope truly & plainly the
                     principle on which Christianity founds our duty to others. I cannot
                     stop to show its applications to the multitude of human circum-
                     stances. It rebukes the spirit of War the spirit of Party the spirit of
                     Covetousness & every form of self-seeking. It says to the human race
                     with an angels voice Little Children love one another. It says Whoso
                     would be chief among you let him be the servant of all. I have only⟩
                     [canceled in pencil; end of page] ¶ The

15   ↑long↓ . . . world? ↑or↓

19–20   adverse↑,↓ the fears & ⟨un⟩vexations . . . peace↑,↓ [additions in
                     pencil]

22   life↑?↓ [top portion of question mark in pencil over a period in ink]

26   admonition, ⟨& which though⟩ a soul

30   ↑from an infinite superiority↓.

38   evil ⟨angels⟩ ↑influences & his own will↓,

Page 91

2–6   ↑{In . . . an ⟨evil⟩ ↑unkind↓ . . . him o . . . world less?}↓

Sermon CV

Manuscript: Four sheets folded to make four pages each; folios stacked and sewn with
white thread along the left margin; pages measure 25.1 x 20.2 cm. A single leaf, 24.8 x 20
cm, containing a variant opening, is attached with red sealing wax to the upper and
lower left margins of the recto of the first leaf. Another leaf, 24.8 x 20 cm, is attached to
the recto of leaf 3 with red sealing wax, and a strip (verso blank), 20.3 x 6.9 cm, is tipped
to the verso of the same leaf. Finally, a sheet folded to make four pages (25 x 20.2 cm.),
containing a variant conclusion, is attached with red sealing wax to the recto of leaf 8.

[The following substitute introduction, lacking hymn citations, occupies both sides of
the added leaf, and was written for the second or third delivery; it was apparently meant
to replace the sermon's first paragraph, which is bracketed:]

CV.

And whatsoever ye do, do it heartily as ⟨un⟩to the
Lord, & not to men Col. 3. 23

I suppose there is no thinking person in this house who loves what is right & honours
the Bible & loves the example of Jesus Christ, who has not sometimes felt very sorry in
observing how few persons among his acquaintance are genuine Christians,—faithful to
every jot & tittle of their master's law—Perhaps in reckoning over the individuals you
love best ↑& respect most,↓ you cannot be sure that any one comes quite up to that high
mark & as to the greater number of men they do not pretend to obey it. As the scripture
says, 'They will transgress for a piece of bread.' [cf. Proverbs 28:21] The great multitude
of men seem to have no ⟨hig⟩ strong desire to know or do their duty. They never sit
down & think for themselves & pray to be shown what it is. They are content to be as
good as they see other people—of a great many it is true I am afraid that they are willing

to be as bad as their fear of other people will let them be. The Bible they hear or perhaps read without thinking that it speaks to them. Its principles are so high & hard that & do so condemn their practice, that instead of ⟨affecting their lives⟩ ↑making them hate themselves↓ it makes them hate the Bible ⟨instead of⟩ until ⟨they begin to believe⟩ God gives them up to their hard heart, & they begin to believe that the Bible is not true, & nobody can be so good as it teaches. Seeing this the Christian begins to suffer from doubts. It seems strange to him that a religion so sweet to him in ⟨his⟩ times when without it he would have felt forsaken & despairing—it seems strange that it should disgust men. He feels that there is a sore side to human nature—Men call evil good, & good evil

Lines	Page 92
Bible Text	↑And . . . heartily↓ As ⟨un⟩to . . . not ⟨un⟩↑un↓to men. ⟨Eph. 6. 7⟩ Coloss. ⟨23⟩3. 23.
1–14	¶ ↑{↓Every . . . ↑even↓ to . . . soul; ⟨the⟩ its . . . nature; ⟨the Calvinist seems to be justified in his too literal use of the complaint of the Psalmist, that, they are all gone astray—there is none that doeth good—no, not one.⟩ [cf. Psalms 14:3] ↑that men . . . good evil.↓↑}↓ [brackets in pencil]
19	pleasures of⟨f⟩ believing,
22–24	principles ⟨are so⟩ differ . . . marked. ⟨It should have the odour of sanctity. From our⟩ In childhood . . . upon ⟨the example⟩ our
27	are /his/that/

	Page 93
2	↑the↓ English
9–10	is ⟨dreadful⟩ dangerous
12–16	talk as ⟨a⟩ [end of line] ↑of one that is absent↓ [end of page] [canceled word obscured by sealing wax] ⟨then⟩ in short, . . . ruin. ¶ ⟨This is the reason why⟩ For . . . stumble, ⟨why⟩ the
19–39	men. ¶ ↑⟨Immortality—Aids to Reflection p. 211⟩ ¶ ⟨It takes one life to learn how to live.'⟩ ¶ I have seen an ⟨affecti⟩ old . . . Unchangeable Refuge.↓ [Immortality . . . Refuge." inscribed on inserted leaf attached to recto of leaf 3.]
22–23	fields /but his ears always open/but his soul ever on the wing/,
30	God-believing /animal/mind/. [variant in pencil]
32	by natural [manuscript torn]nces ↑of this habit↓ [addition in pencil] ⟨and what a monument of wretched deception is that beautiful character if there be no future. I think with pain what havock wd a moment's skepticism [end of page] ¶ It is an objection to yᵉ denomination "Unitarian" yᵗ [manuscript torn] yᵉ Orthodox, Trinitarians, because people end in being w[hat th]ey [manuscript torn] are accused of being. Vide Donne's story of girl catechized⟩ ¶ nor can / he/such a man/ [variant in pencil] ⟨b⟩seen
37–38	guide than ⟨the⟩ ↑whatever↓ feeling ⟨that comes⟩ ↑is↓ uppermost it needs to be ⟨steadied⟩ ↑made fast↓
40	discovery of ⟨g⟩ imperfections

Page 94

I   ourselves. ↑When we have↓ [incomplete addition in pencil] 'Experi-
    mental

4–7   have ⟨forsaken⟩ ↑quitted↓ . . . ↑(↓& no common place↑)↓ [paren-
    theses in pencil]

11   persons. ⟨And therefore⟩ We have tasted pleasures ⟨we see to be real
    we have felt pains⟩ of the

13–18 ↑We begin . . . perish ⟨We begin to feel that the soul⟩ The more . . .
    grows the ⟨more⟩ greater . . . sure he grows ⟨he⟩ that . . . die↓
    [addition on strip attached to verso of leaf 3]

19–20 ↑imperfections . . . unworthiness↓ in th⟨e⟩ose ↑we had↓ . . . God
    ⟨gross unworthiness⟩, though

24   professions ⟨may⟩ ↑should↓

27–32 conscience. ¶ ⟨↑This lesson then it ought to teach us, that no faith is
    good that rests on any but God, & no ⟨morals⟩ ↑character↓ ⟨are⟩is
    good that is not formed ["is not formed" written over several illegible
    words] any but God↓ One lesson it ought to teach us by the very
    disturbance & sorrow it occasions us, that only we have come up to
    the Christian mark, that only we can have a well grounded hope of
    final salvation, when all we do, is done *as unto the Lord & not unto
    men.*⟩ ⟨m f The gospel teaches us this lesson, wh. is enforced by yᵉ
    consideration I have now presented that no faith is good yᵗ rests on
    any but God & no other character is good yᵗ is formed on any
    principle but yᵉ love of God, yᵗ only he⟩My friends, . . . unto men
    ["My friends, . . . men" in ink over "m f The . . . only he" in pencil]

36–37 ↑And so . . . friends↓ [in pencil] You ↑are↓ ⟨can⟩not ⟨be⟩ a

39   name ⟨He did not speak⟩ He

Page 95

2   He ⟨ask⟩ sought

14–17 sin⟨. It may⟩, which . . . sinful. [end of page] ⟨which⟩ It . . . are
    ⟨the⟩ ↑not unfounded falsehoods but↓ exaggerations

22   why? ⟨i⟩Is

24–27 is ⟨nothing more than⟩ ↑mere . . . of↓ . . . necessary. ⟨It proceeds
    from a horror of sickness & death.⟩ It flows . . . hungry &
    ⟨in⟩dishonest

35–36 unhappy. ¶ ⟨But once more, t⟩The reason

38   out of ⟨love⟩ regard

38   ↑& a thousand↓

40   ↑secret↓ unhappiness. The reason ↑why . . . sorts↓ [in pencil]

Page 96

3–5   The /rebuffs/opposition & injuries/ he encounter⟨s⟩ed would . . .
    & not /his spleen./make him cross./ ⟨↑{↓⟩Consider [all emenda-
    tions in pencil]

11–12 condition. ¶ ⟨I have only⟩ ¶ Consider

14–15 this ⟨motive⟩ rule . . . us. ⟨Our⟩ The

[The following variant conclusion is inscribed on the first two pages of an inserted folio attached with red sealing wax to the recto of leaf 8:]

My friends do I speak to any one among you who sometimes finds his or her situation in life wholly disagreeable? Are you sometimes so sensible to the unpleasant circumstances of your lot that you find yourself fretful to your children or your friends? Permit me to give you such advice as the Apostle himself furnishes out of his text. The next time that hour comes to you—only stop & think carefully over the last three or four days, & you will somewhere find lurking the secret occasion of all this ill humor.—⟨namely⟩ Bring it to the light, & you will be surprized to find it is not any evil sent on you by God but some particular fault of which you have been guilty yourself. Take out that splinter— Correct this fault ↑or repent of it↓ & you will find the wound heal over, & soundness restored to the whole ⟨body⟩ of your tho'ts & feelings. Consider who is yᵉ most contented person you ever knew. I am sure it was a religious person.

⟨B⟩ My friends, if the Bible gave us nothing else but this one rule it would have ⟨richly⟩ provided us an unerring law for every situation. The situations of those who are now in this house are widely various—our duties our fears our temptations, our prospects. Some of us are beginning life; some will shortly leave it. Some of us I hope are entering & some making progress in the spiritual life—are learning to pray—& to resist temptation. Some perhaps are departing from God & have already meditated sin. But there is not one who if he will open his understanding & his heart to this commandment will find it strictly suitable to ⟨h⟩ our particular occasions & an everlasting benefit Let us carry it home in our hearts & not forget it tomorrow & it will bless the week Whatsoever ye do do it heartily as unto the Lord & not as unto men.

Sermon CVI

Manuscript: Four sheets folded to make four pages each; folios stacked and sewn with white thread along the left margin; pages measure 25 x 20.3 cm.

Lines	*Page 97*
4–7	notice ⟨our own⟩ ↑a boastfull↓ disregard of any /superstition/ opinion or practice/ [variant in pencil] . . . sacred↑.↓ ⟨and t⟩The particular . . . eat ⟨"meats⟩ the
13	him & ⟨you⟩ ↑us↓
16	↑¶ 1. Have . . . God ⟨when thou goest to the house of God⟩ ↑first in acts of worship↓.↓
17	to ⟨goodness⟩ ↑piety↓,
18–19	crutches of ⟨our⟩ weakness. ⟨If⟩ It . . . dependant
20	life. /Who does not not know/Is it not true/ [variant in pencil] that a mere toy, ⟨the⟩ a

	Page 98
1	soul is /a young child/not yet mature/, his soul
2–6	dies? [Emerson's paragraph symbol added.] But . . . but the ⟨fire⟩ temptations
8–10	forms ⟨which⟩ of . . . new. ⟨They are⟩ Forms . . . have ⟨been⟩ done,
13–14	growth. ¶ ⟨t⟩They . . . of ⟨great men⟩ learned

19	commenced. ⟨We must⟩ Indolent worship ⟨⟨Re⟩ will not do⟩ ↑is none↓.
20	not ⟨need this begging⟩ ↑have this mendicant faith↓
23	A ⟨good⟩ ↑truly devout↓ man at church ⟨does⟩ ↑would↓ not / see the walls nor the passing multitude / feel yᵉ interruption of / trifles / inconveniences / / .
25	to him / is / would be /
27–29	sounds ⟨pa⟩ that . . . valuable, seems to him ⟨a hollow brass⟩ a . . . ↑or a breath of mist↓.
31	independant
35	alliances ⟨&⟩ of
36–37	when it ⟨enters into⟩ ↑subordinates↓ . . . ↑to its great perceptions↓. ⟨Now the evil that comes from any dependence in this all important ⟨is twofo⟩ possession, is twofold.⟩ Have it
38	patron↑, no partner↓.
39–40	↑You . . . another.↓ ¶ Most . . . dependant

Page 99

1	they ⟨are⟩ ↑stand↓
3–4	We can⟨not⟩ ↑hardly↓
7–9	dependance. first that you allow [end of line] ⟨yourself in practices as low as theirs⟩ [end of line] ↑adopt . . . speculation↓ . . . ↑in prac-tice↓. ¶ ⟨1. It will be admitted⟩ We
12	↑of thinking, of believing↓
14	is ⟨thus⟩ transmitted
20	for ⟨he⟩ ↑it was↓
24–25	got to [end of page] to be . . . surprize & ⟨every body⟩ men
26	This ⟨was⟩ ↑is↓ [emendation in pencil]
27–28	agreeable to the ⟨prayer⟩ description . . . principles ⟨by the⟩ in
37	was the ⟨for⟩ preparation

Page 100

2–3	↑It is time↓ to forsake the ⟨guides⟩ ↑interpreters↓,
4–8	God. ¶ ⟨My whole purpose in these remarks will be answered if you will⟩ consider . . . time. ¶ ⟨3⟩ ↑↑2↓ We . . . others↓ ["We . . . others" added in pencil] When these
29	privelege
30	assisted by ⟨the⟩ our
33–34	must ⟨be in⟩ have and independant connexion with God ⟨that⟩ in
36	increase & it & be increased

Sermon CVII

Manuscript: Six sheets folded to make four pages each; folios stacked and sewn with white thread along the left margin, from which the fourth folio has been torn out; pages measure 25 x 20.2 cm. A single half-sheet, 25.2 x 20.1 cm, at one time attached with red sealing wax to the recto of leaf 9, has torn away. The sermon is numbered "CVII" in pencil at the top of MS p. 1.

Lines   *Page 101*

3–6   disease to the ⟨House⟩ ⟨death⟩ tomb, . . . all ⟨duration⟩ ↑time,↓
             . . . man ⟨enlarge⟩ ↑through that extent;↓

8   find its ⟨happin⟩ perfection

9   ¶ But ⟨with⟩ these . . . ↑to be sought↓

12–16   one.— ¶ ⟨It is joined by ties of [illegible word] & kindness to many
             more souls who suffer in its suffering & lose their sufferings when it
             passes out of their company.⟩ A thousand . . . them. ⟨But to all God
             sends this general consolation of saving truth.⟩ And . . . Testament.
             ["And . . . Testament." written over the same in erased pencil]

19–21   crowd ⟨b⟩in . . . ↑an↓ end.

21   no ⟨part⟩ ↑interest↓

                                       Page 102

1–3   two ⟨remarks⟩ ↑counsels↓ . . . cases are ⟨unjustifiable⟩ ↑thrown
             . . . truth;↓

4–8   the ⟨afflicted⟩ ↑bereaved↓ . . . not ⟨murmur⟩ repine . . . Almighty.
             [end of page] ¶ ⟨*it never occurs to a* mind of⟩ ↑Let . . . *occurs to a*
             [The underscoring below "to a" has been canceled.] mind↓ . . . ↑at
             all↓ acc⟨c⟩ustomed to observe ↑& admire↓ [addition in ink over
             pencil] . . . ↑that, on every hand↓ reach⟨ing⟩ far . . . sight, ⟨[illegible
             letter]⟩ when

10–15   ↑who reigns in all↓ [added in ink over "who governs all" in pencil] . . .
             receiving ⟨this⟩ ↑such an↓ [emendation in ink over pencil] . . . him
             ⟨that the earth⟩ ↑not to fly, or that↓ . . . his ⟨head⟩ ↑thoughts↓.
             [addition in ink over pencil]

20–21   hope is. ↑'and . . . good.'↓ [in pencil]

22   faith⟨.⟩?

26   mind ⟨of correct perceptions⟩ ↑that seeks truth↓

30   himself ⟨with⟩ to

34   but ⟨pity him &⟩ do not

36–38   ¶ ↑I have said that↓ The mind . . . his ⟨laws⟩ ↑commandments↓, will
             not ⟨murmur at⟩ charge . . . at the ⟨un⟩happiness

                                       Page 103

3–7   weep. [end of page; the following appears inverted in relation to the
             rest of the text:] Boston Jan. 28. 1831. Dear Edward [end of page] ¶ ↑I
             . . . that↓ The Christian faith ⟨raises the⟩ removes . . . those who
             ⟨have fallen asleep.⟩ ↑die, . . . survive. 1.↓ The . . . ↑who leave this
             world↓ . . . doubt ⟨w⟩ as

9   ↑unaided↓

13   ↑'mansion,' ie. the↓

18   thought⟨,⟩ of

22   habits, ⟨growing into the knowledge of God⟩ &

27–(104)1   soul [end of line] and [end of page; leaves 7 and 8, which follow, have
             been torn out, and canceled text continues on the recto of leaf 9:] ¶
             ⟨But the blessing of the Christian hope enters with alleviation into
             every degree into every thought of sorrow. The Christian faith teaches

us that the soul does not die but is separated from the body & enters into a nearer relation to the Father of Spirits The Christian faith teaches this & the Christian soul as it departs out of life affirms it cheerfully to those who weep. ¶ In this manner it removes the gloom of the grave.⟩ [On a half-sheet once attached with red sealing wax to the recto of leaf 9, the following addition:] ↑and you have not . . . way in⟨to⟩ to . . . leave the sou[MS torn] with . . . suited to the sou[MS torn] in . . . ↑may↓ think he sees enough ⟨⟨w⟩ within his reach⟩ in . . . death. It peoples every solitude↓ [end of page] It peoples every solitude; ⟨I⟩it animates

Page 104

7	spirit to the ⟨entire⟩ clearer
11	to ⟨the living⟩ his
12	or in ⟨the streets⟩ ↑the open day↓,
18	child. ⟨And the spirits have not forgot any good work any upward effort of their brother on earth There is joy in heaven over one sinner that repenteth.⟩ [Luke 15:7] Jesus will not forget a ⟨faithful⟩ ↑humble↓
21–22	The ⟨friend⟩ ↑soul↓ . . . preferred ⟨us to him⟩ our . . . well ⟨our⟩ what
28	is th⟨is⟩ese contemplation↑s↓ which make⟨s⟩ what ⟨Young⟩ ↑has been well↓ call⟨s⟩ed
30–31	us. ⟨It now seems to⟩ When we have ⟨walked [two illegible words] in [three or four illegible words] chamber &⟩ ↑explored . . . seen↓ we ⟨o⟩ return . . . to ⟨the⟩ the ⟨thought of death⟩ ↑tomb,↓

Page 105

3	When ⟨we⟩ the
9	friends ⟨we love⟩ who watch over us [end of line] would
12–13	excellence ↑the . . . source.↓ [in ink over "the . . . goodness" in pencil]
14–20	claims of ⟨m⟩ others . . . tribute ⟨of⟩ the . . . our ⟨station⟩ place . . . defeat, of ⟨gr⟩ ↑reproach, of↓
22	↑be↓
31	↑in . . . Testament↓ [ink over pencil, expanding "N.T." in the pencil layer]

Sermon CVIII

Manuscript: Five sheets folded to make four pages each, and a single leaf attached to the verso of leaf 7 with red sealing wax but not included in the sewing; folios stacked and sewn with white thread along the left margin; folio pages measure 25.1 x 20.3 cm, and the single leaf measures 25.2 x 19.3 cm.

Lines	Page 106
Bible Text	Lord x x x x that
2–6	grief. ↑& the . . . face↓ [addition in pencil] ⟨Who⟩ ↑No one certainly↓ . . . appear, ⟨or who will⟩ ↑None can↓ . . . an end⟨? No one⟩ Good

8   now ⟨it⟩ ↑pain↓ . . . life—⟨that what we suffer⟩ that whatever
11   him to /think/dwell/ [variant in pencil] more of the ↑few↓
16   heart↑.↓ ⟨& work out the misery of him that cherishes them.⟩ Youth
18-20   pain. as . . . invite ⟨the wind &⟩ the lightning, ↑& the wind,↓ & the
             worm⟨s⟩.
21-(107)1   other,' and ⟨Young says ⟨of⟩ truly⟩ ↑it has been ⟨truly⟩ ↑pointedly↓
             said↓ . . . is ⟨a⟩the

                              Page 107
7-8   ↑{↓In the . . . temple↑}↓ [brackets added in pencil]
15   ↑are or↓ . . . ↑tis not these↓
17-18   common /measure/degree/ [variant in pencil] . . . sustain. which
21   persons ⟨whose⟩ over
28   lot; ⟨they are short⟩ opportunities
31-38   them, ⟨with⟩ blest . . . malady; ↑{Insert X}↓ [At the bottom of the
             page, a passage marked "X":] ↑{⟨well placed themselves, life is
             rendered miserable by the guilt or by the misfortunes of their nearest
             friend;⟩ hating depend⟨en⟩ance, . . . & conscious themselves of
             superior powers, &c.↓ [end of Insert "X"] or conscious of ⟨great⟩
             superior powers, . . . ought & ↑to↓

                              Page 108
1-2   them ⟨read the⟩ find . . . Jesus. "Our
5-6   afflictions & I will . . . sympathy that
8-14   ↑In a ⟨spirit of⟩ pious ↑&↓ docil⟨ity⟩e ↑temper↓, . . . find it
             ⟨out⟩↑over↓runs . . . griefs↓ [end of page] ¶ ⟨Let me appl⟩ ↑{Insert
             A}↓ [On the facing page, otherwise blank, a passage marked "A":]
             ↑{Let . . . in whom ⟨is⟩ ↑when↓ . . . straitness of of . . . to appear↓ ¶
             ⟨As y⟩You go along
15   forsaken ⟨y⟩You feel
17-20   good ⟨things⟩ ↑actions↓, . . . for /them/your fellow man/; . . .
             sacrifices that ⟨carry⟩ ↑blow↓
23   poverty, ⟨its fear⟩ but
25-29   ↑"Who . . . particulars↓
31   judgments. ⟨T⟩God

                              Page 109
6   these ru⟨bs⟩de rubs
13   the ⟨u⟩↑un↓ripeness
15-22   them. ↑{A}↓ [On the recto of a half-sheet attached to the verso of leaf
             7, a passage marked "A":] ↑{Indeed it . . . ↑sometimes though↓ . . .
             might.} . . . sufferings}↓
30   which ⟨th⟩ our
32   ↑self-↓justification . . . he ⟨t⟩ wants
34-(110)5   his ⟨spe⟩ temper . . . filed & fr⟨i⟩ette⟨red⟩d away on little things.
             ↑{Insert B}↓ [On the verso of a half-sheet attached to the verso of leaf
             7, a passage marked "B":] ↑{⟨Th⟩ When . . . rough outer ⟨crust⟩ ↑cas-
             ket↓ [emendation in pencil] . . . determine ⟨the⟩ whether . . . trivial.}↓

Page 110

5-6	esteeming /this/it/ . . . ↑that . . . common↓
11	because ⟨Gilbert & Kepler⟩ ↑former observers↓
13	he ha⟨d⟩s done
19	qualities ⟨with a trust⟩ &
25	he ⟨it is wh⟩ lives
28	moment ⟨to⟩ from
30-32	bro't to ⟨think⟩ so low ↑an opinion↓ . . . speak a⟨n unkind word⟩ ↑syllable . . . contempt.↓
39	praise ⟨&⟩ lost

Page 111

5	better ⟨thr⟩ views

Sermon CIX

Manuscript: Five sheets folded to make four pages each, and a single leaf laid in between leaves 7 and 8 but not included in the sewing or in the pinning; folios stacked and sewn (thread now missing), and later pinned (pin now missing); folio pages measure 25 x 20.3 cm, and the single leaf measures 24.3 x 20 cm. A stray single sheet folded to make four pages has also been found with the manuscript; the folio bears pin holes that do not match those found in the folios of Sermon CIX, nor does the content of the inscription match that of the sermon; pages measure 24.9 x 19.8 cm.

Lines	*Page 112*
Bible text	↑⟨Let him⟩ ↑He↓ that glorieth ↑let him↓ glory in the Lord. I Cor. 1.31—↓ [rejected as a late variant]
5	very ⟨strongly⟩ ↑sensibly↓ [emendation in pencil]
7-15	do. ⟨And much⟩ ↑for . . . commandment↓ [addition in pencil] And . . . to his ⟨precarious⟩ ↑blooming↓ health ⟨thou art firm⟩ ↑that . . . it↓ or t⟨o⟩rust his . . . ↑or friendship↓ over his fellowmen↑.↓ ⟨this is my Rock⟩ ¶ ⟨A man is apt to be sad alone, who is cheerful whenever he is seen.⟩ But when ⟨a ma⟩ the . . . men, & ⟨me⟩ compares

	Page 113
1	↑he felt↓ its ⟨abundant⟩ uncertainty & ⟨abundant⟩ vexations; but ⟨now⟩ ↑in society↓
3-4	but its ⟨fear⟩ care . . . readily ⟨takes⟩ ↑accepts↓
15	*creation* [underscored (italics here) in pencil]
16	senses ⟨is yours⟩ have
20-21	dubiously on /this extreme & shaking ground/the last boundaries of knowledge/
24	↑moreover↓
31	not the ⟨wise⟩ ↑rich↓
35-36	or ²waste or ¹storm or war, or thei⟨f⟩ves, . . . ↑or his own death↓
38	possession i.e. so

	Page 114
1-4	for ⟨glor⟩ boasting of wisdom ↑1.↓ . . . is to ⟨take⟩ ↑get↓ a great

deal. ↑⟨1.⟩ For . . . ignorance ⟨All⟩ Every fact ascertained . . . avenue 2.↓

6   wisdom↑?↓

8   property it

10–11   And ⟨Newton & Bacon & Socrates & Franklin⟩ ↑the . . . himself↓

12–13   ↑3. In the next place↓ . . . pure. ⟨It mus⟩ A man

17   every ⟨good⟩ right

18   mind ⟨like the french philosopher Voltaire⟩, ↑alas . . . such↓ [emendation in pencil]

19–20   he ⟨grows up⟩ ↑appears half wise↓ like a ⟨colourless⟩ plant grown up ⟨without light⟩ ↑in . . . colourless↓, only half ⟨wise⟩ ↑made↓. ⟨a⟩And

21–22   persons who ⟨⟨have⟩ growing up⟩ ↑bred↓ . . . this ⟨disease⟩ defect.

24   ↑the rule of↓

28   might. ⟨I shall try to show th wisdom of this saying that a⟩Any

36–(115)1   long & ⟨laboriously⟩ ↑so crookedly,↓ . . . to be ⟨rea⟩ dealt . . . their ⟨stre⟩ labor to their profit [end of page] I

Page 115

2–4   advantage ⟨I⟩ it . . . ↑instead . . . act↓ . . . of determin↑in↓g . . . makes ⟨men⟩ ↑a man↓

8   for—Good

9   in. ⟨In this country there can be no more important public lesson than a diligent imprinting on every heart in the people of this simple text⟩ Let not

12–33   ¶ ↑Alas that power is [end of page; beginning of inscription on leaf laid in between leaves 7 and 8:] Power is . . . the office. ¶ ↑But . . . regarded↓↓ ["But . . . regarded" added in pencil; end of inscription on inserted leaf. "And . . . regarded" is a variant, replacing "Wo for us ⟨if⟩ ↑that↓" in the original inscription.]

12   notoriously /considered/ accounted/

17   least ⟨more⟩ arbitrary

21–22   is ⟨so⟩ commonly . . . obey ⟨the⟩ implicitly

36   them ⟨bu⟩furnish

37   has any ⟨philosopher⟩ ↑wise statesman↓

39–40   not ⟨so⟩ regarded ↑as a sacred trust↓

Page 116

2–5   also. ⟨Hence what issues come?⟩ ⟨↑Now mark the effect.↓ in the face of the world & ⟨in⟩ ↑under↓ the Eye of Supreme Providence, it is yet questioned whether the Indian tribes shall be banished from their remnant of [end of line] of the↑ir↓ whole territory to barren wilds without water & without grass⟨,⟩. ⟨& that before the generation who emancipated this country is wholly gone.⟩⟩ [last clause canceled in ink; the whole passage canceled in pencil] ¶ ↑And so↓ [addition in pencil] It . . . sundered by ⟨boys & boyish⟩ ↑the explosions of↓ ⟨fun⟩party rancour. ↑& that . . . ground.↓

8   desireable

11	years. ⟨He feels no disposition in his last days to glory in his might, & less, every day, that adds a thorn to his crown. It⟩ All
21	was ⟨m⟩weak
22–23	Is ⟨king is⟩ rich, is strong, is ⟨king is proud⟩ sage,
23	to the ⟨lustre of religion⟩ glories
24–32	afflicting ⟨sense of⟩ incapacity . . . believer. ⟨The only way of constancy for the soul is to secure itself here. Keep the soul always turned to God ¶ Nothing so vast but feel that he contains it⟩ ↑{Insert A}↓ [On the facing page, otherwise blank, a passage marked "A":] ↑{⟨The only way of constancy⟩ This . . . heaven. Here i⟨s⟩n its . . . contains it. Nothing so pure, &c↓ Nothing so real or pure
37–38	solitary ⟨b⟩piety . . . rests upon. That trust

[The following is inscribed on the first two pages of the stray folio found with the manuscript:]

The series of helps which are provided for the education of the soul are precisely analogous to those which ⟨are furn⟩ the body requires. Look at yonder new-born man He is destined it may be in the Providence of God to set his shoulder to uphold the falling mass of an empire He is to be an active benefactor by his sense & energy to a great community his commerce is to make his ⟨influence felt in ever⟩ name respectable & his influence felt in every port which the ships of this country visit on all sides of the world. Yet see this future laborer & upholder of men a helpless ⟨naked⟩ ↑soft↓ babe whom his nurses arm might overlay & kill His limbs ⟨have not strength for their own support. His limbs his feet cannot bear his own weight⟩ ↑cannot bear their own weight.↓ He lies relaxed on the lap of the mother A few days a few weeks hence by continual care & exercise his limbs can support their own weight & the head is erect. A few months more & by the aid of the arms ⟨&⟩or of the cradle⟨s⟩ side he can stand on his feet

Come again & he has learned to stand without aid & to go alone, & in due time not only to ⟨stand⟩ walk but to labor & to help others to stand & labor. So is it with the human soul. It is not sent adult & full grown into the world but it is sent a seed a babe & provided with a like series of ⟨crutches⟩ supports & crutches which are successively withdrawn as ⟨if⟩they have answered their purpose & enabled it to lean on its own strength.

Sermon CX

Manuscript: Eight sheets folded to make four pages each; folios stacked and sewn with white thread along the left margin, from which the first three folios have torn away; pages measure 25 x 20.2 cm. A leaf, 11.7 x 12.1 cm, is laid in between leaves 3 and 4; a strip, 6.1 x 19.2 cm, is attached to the verso of leaf 7 with red sealing wax; and a leaf (verso blank), 19.7 x 18 cm, now laid in between leaves 12 and 13, was once attached to the verso of leaf 12 with red sealing wax. A false start for this sermon, including the Bible text and first two sentences, occurs with the MS of Sermon CXX; see the Textual Notes on page 364.

Lines	*Page 118*
Bible Text	↑Every good &↓ Every perfect gift ⟨cometh⟩ ↑is↓ . . . ↑& cometh down↓

1–2   opinion ⟨among thinking men⟩ that whenever a doctrine ⟨a⟩is
         received . . . ↑of men↓

3   be agre⟨a⟩eable

5–7   God, & ⟨so,⟩ for . . . a [end of line] ↑a mind at all↓ cultivated↑.↓
         ⟨mind.⟩ A

7–8   it is ⟨agreeable⟩ ↑consistent↓ or ⟨disagreeable to⟩ ↑inconsistent
         with↓

9   because ⟨it shock⟩ some

11   Religion as [end of page] as

13   any ⟨character⟩ ↑attribute↓

20–21   laws of ⟨his⟩ ↑our↓ own mind↑.↓⟨, to be afraid of error⟩ ¶ The . . .
         ↑among lovers of truth↓

                              Page 119

4–6   sanctification ↑because . . . Religion↓ ¶ ⟨I shall endeavor to state the
         scripture doctrine on these points What is the Holy Spirit & what are
         its operations⟩ ↑⟨It is my present purpose to⟩ [added in pencil;
         canceled by being overwritten by "because . . . Religion"] It is my . . .
         state↓

7–17   operations? ¶ ⟨πνευμα The word Spirit is used⟩ ¶ The word . . .
         many as ⟨twelve⟩ ↑eighteen↓ different senses↑; sometimes for
         ↑animal↓ . . . Spirit;" Sometimes for ⟨the mind of⟩ *God;* . . . a
         Spirit.↓ ¶ ⟨The most remarkable of these is when it is used as
         equivalent to the *mind of God.*⟩ ↑It may . . . Spirit↓

18–19   learn ⟨the particular sense of⟩ ↑what it means in↓ any ↑one↓ passage
         to ⟨judge of it by⟩ ↑make↓ a careful ⟨comparison⟩ ↑examination↓

19   these ⟨senses is⟩ uses,

24   to Paul. ⟨That t⟩This ⟨appears⟩ ↑is shown↓

26   him↑,↓ even [comma added in pencil]

27–30   I. Cor. ⟨3. 16⟩ 6.19. . . . Ghost which ⟨dwelleth⟩ ↑is↓ . . . yᵉ Spir-
         it⟨s⟩ of

31–32   of ⟨the⟩ all Eastern writers to ⟨person-⟩ [end of line] *personify* . . .
         in ⟨all⟩ every

33   truth have ⟨embraced⟩ ↑met together↓;

34–35   ↑Want . . . travelleth↓

                              Page 120

1–3   he ⟨ordered⟩ ↑prepared↓ . . . with him. [end of short line]
         expressions . . . Psalms↑,↓ By [comma added in pencil]

5–6   So . . . personified. [In ink over the following in pencil:] ⟨So in the
         Proem of St John yᵉ Word And in the discourse of our Saviour in the
         ad⟩

9–14   [Paragraph on leaf loosely laid in MS:] ↑¶ The idea . . . nations
         be⟨yond⟩↑hind↓ . . . theism.↓

15   of the ⟨faculties⟩ ↑powers↓

17   of ⟨it⟩ ↑the spirit↓

20–21   Trinitarians ⟨the⟩ little . . . ↑tho much . . . Spirit↓.

25–26   operations ⟨⟨as in⟩ in inspiration⟩ in . . . influences (⟨or⟩ ↑as in inspiration or in↓ . . . desireable
30–31   more ⟨&⟩than the ⟨ordinary⟩ ↑uniform & universal↓ . . . ↑that spiritual . . . kind—↓that
35   Saviour in ⟨⟨3⟩12. chap⟩ Matt. 12. 31–32

Page 121

1   ¶ Jesus ⟨before⟩ had
7–8   state that [end of line] that . . . from ⟨the⟩ devil↑s↓—
12   that no⟨thing⟩ power
15–17   ¶ ↑I proceed to say yᵗ↓ What . . . Miracles, ⟨Prophecy⟩ Inspiration, & the ⟨effect on individuals⟩ ↑operation . . . mind in↓ in the
18   the↑se↓
20   common ⟨gifts⟩ ↑effects↓.
21–22   God in the ⟨formation &⟩ education . . . soul ⟨the Scripture makes this plain statement⟩ ↑a true . . . text↓.
23–25   gift ⟨cometh⟩ ↑is↓ . . . turning. ¶ ⟨Now to every view of this subject which goes to cut up & distribute ↑into parts↓ the agency of God in the education of the human soul, the Reason of man answers in the words of St James, '*Every* good & *every* perfect gift cometh from above, from the Father of lights, with whom is no variableness, nor shadow of turning.'⟩ ¶ God
28–29   ↑for . . . souls↓ . . . or the ⟨bee⟩ ↑insect↓
29   wisdom, ⟨all genius,⟩ all
33–(122)4   ↑¶ Now . . . Revelation ⟨makes⟩ exposes . . . agency.↓ [Written on a strip attached with red sealing wax to the verso of leaf 7, as a variant for the following passage, which the strip covers:] ¶ {Now where do we get this idea of God? I answer from the laws of our minds which will not permit us to describe God in any thing less than absolute expressions. And, as I have said, it is the coincidence of the Scriptures with these views of the Divinity that make their best evidence, for the evidence of miracles I look upon as altogether secondary to that of the conscience.↑}↓ ¶ ⟨Now apply to this first doctrine of the divine Unity the common notions concerning spiritual influences & the falsity of those notions will be felt ↑{Insert X}↓⟩ In the 12 chap. I Corinthians, St Paul ⟨at some length⟩ declares . . . all; [Emerson's ellipses] . . . prophecy &c &c "But . . . healings, &c."

Page 122

6   ↑speaking↓ . . . ↑& . . . hands↓.
17   ↑can↓ [addition in pencil] readil⟨l⟩y
25–26   than th⟨em⟩e
30–31   ↑(↓But . . . mountain.↑)↓ [parentheses in pencil]
32–33   There ⟨is no⟩ are . . . ↑even in our own time↓. [addition in ink over pencil]
36–37   shall ⟨see⟩ realize . . . their ⟨volitions⟩ ↑exalted wills↓, [addition in ink over pencil] , . . . removed⟨;⟩ &

41–(123)4   God. ↑{Insert X}↓ [On the preceding page, a passage in ink over
                erased pencil, marked "X":] ↑{Every . . . falsely.}↓ [end of Insert "X"]
                ↑T↓He ↑prophet . . . holiness↓

Page 123

5   as ⟨has been⟩ ↑some . . . have↓
7–8   could he ⟨know⟩ or . . . him ⟨know⟩ ↑distinguish↓
13–15   unto the prophets ↑that is to say ⟨are possessed in the same way as
                their⟩ ↑their foresight blends with↓ all . . . gifts.↓
16–17   man ⟨is⟩ wholly
21   ↑who spake . . . spake↓. [in ink over pencil]
23–27   degrees. ¶ ⟨But⟩ ↑And↓ . . . ↑same↓ holy ⟨courage⟩ ↑confidence in
                the right↓
31   There is ⟨no separation of spiritual influences⟩ not
33   different ⟨being⟩ souls.
36–37   Scripture is ⟨thus reciprocal⟩ ↑conditional on our effort↓.
38   ↑'Resist . . . you'↓
39–40   condition↑,↓ ⟨is an inseparable appendix⟩ expressed

Page 124

2–4   reciprocal [end of page] ↑and . . . good↓ [addition in pencil]
5–6   I ⟨freely⟩ believe in them ↑with my whole mind↓
9–10   ↑good↓ . . . ↑any friend,↓
12   ascribe ⟨any⟩ ↑every↓
13   ↑its omnipresence↓
14–27   ↑O yes, . . . sinful↓ [in ink over pencil] ↑{Insert D}↓ [On the leaf now
                laid in between leaves 12 and 13, a passage marked "D":] ↑{⟨In
                spiritual influences⟩ I believe . . . shall be re⟨lived.⟩vealed. I believe
                . . . language of Ss. we . . . Whenever we ⟨see⟩ awake . . . unreserv-
                edly ⟨& with cordial love⟩ to . . . We shall ⟨then⟩ know . . . known;
                ⟨for how⟩ we shall ⟨see th⟩ find . . . goodness infinite wisdom?↓
33–35   ↑a part↓ the . . . views of / all operations / the whole / . . . views ⟨of⟩
                ↑on↓
39–(125)1   somewhere ⟨in the purlieus of the creation⟩ behind a screen, ⟨for⟩
                ↑as if↓

Page 125

3   that all ⟨but our vices⟩ ↑good in us↓
6–7   presiding ⟨d⟩Deity
11–12   virtue; ⟨say rather it is his own child—and the bringing all minds into
                union with him is the work which God worketh from age to age.⟩ ¶ Let

Sermon CXI

Manuscript (earlier version): Four sheets folded to make four pages each; folios stacked
and sewn with white thread along the left margin; pages measure 25 x 20.2 cm. A single
leaf, 25 x 20.2 cm, is attached to the recto of leaf 1 with black sealing wax but not
included in the sewing; a single leaf, 25 x 20.1 cm, laid in between leaves 1 and 2 is
included in the sewing.

[The text of the earlier version, apparently an incomplete draft of the sermon, follows:]

CXI.
Th⟨y⟩e law ↑of the Lord↓ is perfect, converting
the Soul. Ps 19.

↑The law of the Lord is perfect. The understanding of men is imperfect. The ⟨re⟩ religions of men & every man has a religion in some respects peculiar to himself are so many versions more or less faithful but all imperfect of the law of the Lord. That law is what is common to all minds, of men & of angels. We approximate to it ⟨by studying the minds of good men⟩ ↑as our minds are purified↓↓ [emendation in pencil]

The fact that all sects of Christians are agreed upon much more than that upon which they are disagreed, is a very important one, & when it is fully seen might make us tremble. For it might show us that / we/ many of us/ [variant in pencil] who are come up hither to worship not pricked perhaps by any strong sense of sin & danger ⟨are⟩ do really stand condemned in our character by the law which all denominations from the most strict to the most lax acknowledge, that in the judgment of all we are unworthy & so cannot have any rational hope of safety. And this is the truth which I wish to present to your consideration at this time, that ⟨it⟩ the sternest commandment is the most universal. It is a most groundless imagination that by ⟨escaping⟩ ↑rising above↓ from the prejudices of / orthodoxy/a superstitious faith/ you have escaped one real terror. All that gave life & ⟨a face⟩ ⟨of alarm⟩ ["of alarm" canceled in pencil] ↑power to↓ to any false doctrine was the true terror that lay [end of page; below the last line are the canceled phrases "this made" and "living fear"] under it. ⟨If it had no truth under it, it would / give no more terror than the tales of the Roman or Indian Gods/ ⟨show the mask separate from the living body & it is ludicrous⟩⟩/ ↑{Insert A}↓ [On the following page, a passage marked "A":] ↑{A hideous mask can only terrify when it is worn upon a living face. Show yᵉ mask separate & it has lost all its terror.↓ But that which really causes anguish to a rational being for the commission of sin, ⟨survive⟩ is older than his church creed & survives in a good mind every human creed and grows more positive on every offence in proportion to the elevation of the mind. ↑It is the moral constitution of his mind.↓

⟨Now a wise man heedfully searching for truth wherever he goes will regard every doctrine sect that he finds as one manifestation more of the human mind & always founded on truth ⟨the excresce⟩ as much as every bud on the bough indicates the presence of sap & life & every excrescence indicates it no less though distorted by the worm error that has found lodging within. In this manner, as I have heretofore intimated, there is no doctrine that has been received in the Church but its foundations if we grope we shall find eternal in the nature of man⟩

↑A wise man heedfully searching for truth wherever he goes does not look upon every doctrine, ⟨as truth⟩ in the state in wh. it is maintained by great sects, as truth itself, but as remotely proceeding from truth. He looks upon the Catholic or the Methodist or the Friends ↑church↓ as one manifestation more of the desires & opinions of the human mind based ⟨on⟩ somewhere on its moral nature, its disapprobation of sin. ↑Tis another John crying in the wilderness↓ ⟨This⟩He is not the light, but ⟨it⟩ bears witness of that Light. Every truth & every Error refer to some reality. As every bud on the branch indicates the presence of vegetable life & every excrescence indicates it no less, tho' distorted by the worm that eats within. There never was a dogma received ↑as I have heretofore↓ by multitudes but it could be traced down to its eternal foundations in this moral nature

The doctrine of election is there, inasmuch as God gives means & temper & example to one which he denies to another. He makes one the Son of a wise man & another the son of a sot.

The doctrine of Regeneration

↑I extreme belief

II. unbelief.↓ ["I . . . unbelief." added in pencil]

↑In yᵉ next place I remark up not only doctrines but yᵉ practical of those who believe most are founded in moral obligation↓↓ [sentence added in pencil]

Let me adduce as another illustration of this common basis of truth upon which all the slighter differences are builded the ⟨or⟩ crises which are the practical effects of one doctrine & not of another. I mean what are called Revivals of Religion. If you love truth more than your party, go & converse with a pious man who believes in the divine efficacy on these occasions & you will find that whatever dislike you may have to the manner in which these meetings are managed the whole design can be defended on principles which you cannot reject. Thus the more exalted are your views of God the more reasonable it will appear to you that when the attention of any young person wholly intent on the pleasures of the senses is for the first time by good arts secured ⟨ & all at once⟩ ↑& that, suddenly↓ to the idea of God & to an efficient faith in his own immortality he must be startled. he must feel strongly

Then it is the professed object of these assemblies to make earnest prayer for special influences of the Holy Spirit which being translated into common language means earnest desire of becoming better, & that through regard to our relation to God. And can any more rational request rise from the human heart? It is for special influence, but ⟨it is on⟩ the true condition is regarded, it is specially sought. And I will never quarrel with my fellowman for praying

Then it is a confession of sin & of suffering under the sense of wickedness And will any humble believer of God speak with contempt or hostility of this feeling? No never. However alien from your habits the exterior of them may be, the principles on which Revivals are sought for are perfectly sound. My only want of sympathy with them is that in their history, the reason of man has not been addressed Such representations of God have been made as keep down & hurt the mind & do not exalt it. Such representations of God as could be received only by feeble & slothful minds but must forever keep aloof from the assembly an enlarged intellect. Among that portion of the community whose frame of mind makes them more open to this influence than to any other, why should not these seasons of excitement have the happiest effect? If it save one soul from sin ⟨it will pay for the assembling of⟩ towns. & counties may well assemble for such a purpose. This faith which ⟨no⟩ they first receive tho' ⟨now⟩ erroneous, is only the first stage of their education. The truth that is concealed in this impure food will nourish them to ⟨su⟩ a strength that requires & an appetite that selects a better aliment. The truly religious mind is always in the right road to truth. ⟨Only I hope that as they gain knowledge they may not lose⟩ ↑But let not knowledge look on without feeling the admonition that its coldness is reproached by↓ their fervor. ↑↑In view of others devotion↓ Let conscience do its office.↓

For what more natural what more deeply desireable to every wise & good man than a generous surrender of common employments ⟨ & pru⟩ to the sole searching of the deep things of God. What object more fitted to excite enthusiasm and suspend for a season ⟨his pr⟩ ↑the cares of a↓ vulgar prudence than the contemplation of God? What sublimer thot can occupy yᵉ man yⁿ thot of God?

⟨Thus it appears that t⟩There is a foundation in truth for the ⟨extravagant⟩ opinions & the ⟨extravagant⟩ practices which we are accustomed to call extravagant. Let it show that these differences which show so mighty, & about which much clamor is made, are merely superficial. Let it show (that I may return to the main subject,) that ⟨a⟩ ↑⟨these⟩ these are grounded in his permanent nature, in the primitive fear of sin, & so let it teach that↓ man does not get rid of his moral obligations by altering his opinions. Do you think because you do not receive the doctrines of total depravity & the vicarious suffering of Christ that therefore you may unblamed indulge in any practice which a stricter brother would condemn. Do you think you may ↑neglect a trust↓ lie later in bed because you do not believe in ⟨literal⟩ plenary Inspiration? Can you take an unjust advantage of your neighbor or slander him? Can you insult him in conversation by exhibiting contempt for his opinions or his ⟨feelings⟩ circumstances, because you reject Transubstantiation or the Trinity or ⟨Total Depravity.⟩ Election.

Do you think that your obligations are any the less sacred to prayer & to Charity, to an unremitted effort to change your heart, i.e. to substitute yᵉ love of God for self-love, than if you were a Methodist or a Baptist? My brother, you know better by the misgiving that is in your mind when you condemn these practices as over religious. You may hold what views of ordinances you will; you may hold what views of the offices of Christ it will never add nor diminish one jot in the obligation of these duties, nor if you love truth, ↑in↓ the *pressure* of the obligation, for they belong to the constitution of your minds. These are written in lines that cannot be effaced ⟨These are a covenant that cannot be altered.⟩ This is not a temporary law nor a covenant to a chosen nation These are the laws that exist yesterday today & forever They are not to be changed nor evaded nor shielded from. They make the substance of the soul. Heaven consists in keeping them. Hell consists in violating them.

Simply because they are the nature of God, & the mould according to which he ⟨th⟩ hath formed man coupling praise to every right step & pain & blame to every wrong.

⟨2. I have said all our moral obligations are independent of the differences in creeds. But more is true than this.⟩ ↑2. I wish it to be felt that th⟨is⟩ese ⟨nat⟩ moral obligations abide unchanged with the more or less of faith (It is not the Revelation that makes man religious He is of a religious nature.) And as this obligation is not greater in a more strict faith neither is it less in a more liberal one. If you give up all the faith it will remain.↓ It should be deeply felt by us that they never desert us. Are you inclined to skepticism? has the truth such charms for you that you say you will not receive the ↑belief of the↓ miraculous until it is proved. You must put your fingers into the hands & feet of your risen Lord, or you will not believe; if unhappily the Scriptures seem to you to want evidence⟨—⟩; God has yet provided for your salvation, if you will only be true to yourself, in the beneficent influence of these laws. All the moral obligations are perfect in the mind of the Atheist. ↑The law of the Lord is perfect↓ He has renounced the central truth which gives harmony & reason to all but there are the stubborn facts; *right* & *wrong* ⟨ar⟩still exist & there too are *good* & *evil* their faithful /consequences/ followers/. And there the royal Reason approves or condemns. And here let me use the words of ⟨Gods⟩ ↑David "The↓ law⟨,⟩ is perfect converting the soul." If you will keep this law it shall convert your soul. ⟨Duty⟩ ↑It shall bring you to yᵉ Scriptures The Works of God are faithful to his Word.↓ If early associations of faith with gross errors have made you dislike the name of religion O then conform yourself to nature *Speak the truth*↑; not because God has said "*Thou shalt not bear false witness*," but↓ because falsehood is unnatural. *Be just,* because dishonesty offends the nature of things. ⟨*Eat only to live*⟩ ↑Be temperate↓; because excess tends to ⟨si⟩ disease. *Do good;* because only by a mutual support can the greatest amount of natural good be produced. Presently by walking in this road, you shall see more truth, the fragrance of humility, the disgrace of sin shall appear to you; the love of your friends shall teach you to look for the fellowship of spirits—& the great First Cause will dawn again on your mind. In this way God always brings back by duty the humble heart to faith.

It is always the effect of the practice of Right to increase the love of the Right to quicken the conscience ⟨Virtue unseals the blind eye⟩ Men see by the light of their own virtue "True wisdom" said Shaftsbury, "comes more from the heart than the head." And thus those ancients who loved what was true & did what was right were led to very clear religious views—& learned to trust in God & pray to him & to speak humbly of themselves & kindly to others long before Jesus had yet brot immortality to light

It has further the tendency not to shut you up in a barren solitude of good deeds It does not leave you an abstract religion; an empty heaven. It brings you into a personal relation that may become all in all to you—to God the Father. The faithful performance of our duties brings into exercise all your affections. The miser who shuts himself up with his purse may lose all love of men & all desire of God; but he that watches all the commands within & executes them, is brot into relations with others has an interest in their fate & would fain ask superior power to avert danger or bring them good He learns thus to seek after God

Further it has a tendency to ennoble the whole mind so that nothing imperfect can satisfy it & so it seeks to find its parent & realize the presence of God He cannot be acquainted with the sublime order ⟨w⟩& feel the necessity of a Mind without involuntarily beseeching the protection & favor of that Mind. [end of page]

[The following notation is in pencil:] ↑The learned love the company of the learned the gay of the gay↓

Manuscript (revised version): Five sheets folded to make four pages each, and a single leaf laid in between leaves 8 and 9 that is included in the sewing; the first four folios are nested, followed by the single leaf and the fifth folio, all sewn with white thread along the left margin; folio pages measure 25 x 20.4 cm, and the single leaf measures 25 x 20.1 cm.

Lines	*Page 126*
5-6	purified. ⟨⟨The⟩ Hence⟩ It . . . ↑than↓
10	conde⟨n⟩mned
19-20	all ⟨terror⟩ ↑its↓ frightfulness.
23	more / positive / dreadful /
24	*Lord,* ⟨which is⟩ ↑or in other words↓,

	Page 127
2-3	Friends' ⟨Church⟩ or . . . mind ⟨based⟩ (&
5	not ⟨that⟩ ↑the↓
11	some ⟨fact⟩ eternal
13	to th⟨is⟩eir
21	hand of ⟨God⟩ ↑his Maker↓, [emendation in pencil]
34-35	salvation. ¶ ⟨In the next place I remark that not only peculiar doctrines but peculiar practices of those who believe most are founded in ⟨m⟩this common moral nature.⟩ Let

37   mean ⟨Re⟩ what

Page 128

7   which ⟨being⟩ in
10   regarded, it
17   sound. ⟨My only want of sympathy with them is⟩ ↑It . . . them↓
21–24   enlarged ⟨mind⟩ intellect. ↑{With . . . party spirit.}↓
25   is ⟨my⟩ ↑an↓
26   community ⟨that⟩ whose
36   others [Emerson's apostrophe is directly above the *s*.]
38   desireable
41–42   prudence, ⟨than the contemplation of God?⟩ [canceled in pencil] ¶
                          ↑The . . . that↓ ⟨T⟩there

Page 129

1   it ⟨show⟩ ↑teach↓ [emendation in pencil]
5   by ⟨altering⟩ ↑correcting↓
6   duty; ⟨Let us fe⟩ that opinions change, & ⟨modify⟩ advance,
11   ↑forget a ⟨k⟩favor or↓ lie later in ⟨your⟩ bed,
13   by ⟨expressing⟩ exhibiting
15–17   Election? ⟨D⟩Or . . . charity & to ⟨prayer⟩ ↑gratitude↓ . . . sub-
                          stitute ⟨yᵉ⟩ the
26   be ⟨changed⟩ abolished,
29   step & & blame
35   but ↑to↓ those
37–38   that you say will
40   evidence; God

Page 130

1   has↑, it is true,↓ renounced ⟨that⟩ the
8   men. If [end of page] If unhappily
33   ↑their↓
34–35   God— ¶ ⟨Further it has a tendency to ennoble the whole mind so that
                    nothing imperfect can satisfy it & so it seeks to find its parent &
                    realize the presence of God. ⟨⟨He⟩ ↑A pure mind↓⟩ ↑A sincere man↓
                    cannot be acquainted with the sublime order ⟨& feel⟩ that reigns in
                    all things & feel the necessity of a⟨↑n ⟨i⟩Intelligence↓⟩ mind,
                    without involuntarily beseeching the protection & favor of that
                    mind.⟩ [paragraph canceled in pencil] ¶ ⟨[two illegible words] the
                    law or the keeping of the law converts the soul⟩ It

Page 131

3   your ⟨desires⟩ pursuits
4–5   ↑The learned . . . of gay.↓

Sermon CXII

Manuscript: Four sheets folded to make four pages each, and a single leaf laid in between leaves 5 and 6 but not included in the sewing; folios stacked and sewn with black thread along the left margin; folio pages measure 25 x 20.2 cm, and the single leaf measures 24.9 x 20.2 cm. A strip, 7.8 x 12.4 cm, verso blank, is attached to the recto of leaf 2 with red sealing wax.

Lines	*Page 132*
5–8	↑But does . . . that,↓ The year that is ⟨to⟩ come . . . last. ⟨Let this truth sink into the heart⟩ That which . . . already been. ↑& God . . . past (Eccl. 3.15)↓
12	let the /seasons/periods/ [variant in pencil]
13–20	of a [end of page] of a reasonable creature ⟨not⟩ never . . . old. ↑{Insert A}↓ [On the strip attached to the recto of leaf 2, a passage marked "A":] ↑{The spring . . . wasting our . . . ↑of life↓ [in pencil] will be ⟨spun⟩ ↑snapped↓ [emendation in pencil] & men will throw a little dust on our ⟨silent⟩ /bodies/breathless clay/.↓ [variant in pencil]

	Page 133
2	induce ⟨th⟩ more
5	asked. ⟨The⟩ Truth
6–9	number & ⟨diligence⟩ noise . . . prize. ⟨Instead of a multitude of nameless attractions it is found to consist of few elements.⟩ ↑The great . . . lose ⟨their g⟩much . . . examined.↓ The ⟨i⟩deception
10–14	↑in their shining posts↓. ↑The eye . . . multitude↓ [second addition in pencil] . . . upon th⟨is⟩e eye,
15	which ⟨he⟩ ↑man↓
16–17	upon ⟨it⟩them . . . attractions, /it/they/ is found
18–19	pains↑,↓ often repeated↑,↓ . . . manifold↑.↓ the way . . . one↑,↓ & straight↑,↓ & narrow↑,↓ [punctuation in pencil]
23–26	voluntary ⟨cessation⟩ ↑truce↓ . . . give. ¶ ⟨Now t⟩To estimate . . . ↑to be &↓ to
28	↑the↓ road . . . ↑of the journey↓.
31	↑a deliberate↓ [in pencil]
32–40	↑use of the↓ . . . expected ⟨by⟩ that . . . ↑of itself↓ counteract ⟨a diseased habit ⟨that could only⟩ ↑& effect the cure↓⟩ ↑that madness↓ ["& effect the cure" canceled in pencil] & produce . . . victim ⟨could recover itself⟩ ↑which, . . . gratification↓ . . . recover itself. ↑& operate; . . . choose.↓ ⟨The man slept whilst the house was burning it only needed to wake him & his escape mt. be made.⟩ ¶ Precisely . . . delusions of ⟨the besotted lover of trifles⟩ ↑common life. There . . . sot.↓
41–42	are as . . . love of ⟨gold & trifles of time &⟩ ↑pleasure, of money of office of /dress/praise/↓, [variant in pencil]

	Page 134
2–3	that ⟨overlooks⟩ commands
4–5	son that ⟨he⟩ on his deathbed ⟨he made of him the single request⟩ ↑he prevailed on hi⟨m⟩s son to promise↓ that he would ⟨go alone much⟩ spend

6	son ⟨complied with the request⟩ ↑kept his word↓
15	over the ⟨follow⟩ unthinking
17–18	¶ ↑In . . . ↑to commend↓ any ⟨ou⟩ merely . . . tranquillity.↓
19–22	deportment ⟨but⟩ ↑whilst↓ . . . ↑a marble brow↓ [addition in pencil] . . . roads as ⟨statesmen & sinners walk in⟩ ↑the most . . . appetite.↓ ¶ Sometimes it only
26–28	partisan, ⟨is⟩ the . . . no ⟨deep⟩ ↑criminal↓ . . . done. ⟨But this is a calmness not worth recommending⟩ ¶ The ⟨calm⟩ ↑easy↓
32–34	↑But this . . . speak {of . . . which ⟨is the⟩ sought . . . duty &} of . . . good↓
36	the /house/pub. Treasury/ [variant in pencil] ↑at mid night↓
41	↑There . . . wicked.↓ [in pencil]
44	↑in this world↓,
45	mind. Ha⟨ve⟩d ⟨you⟩ ↑the↓ set ⟨your⟩ ↑this↓

Page 135

1–2	mortification ⟨of defeat⟩ ↑that precede & follow it↓
4–7	bold ⟨merchant⟩ ↑adventurer↓ . . . sudden wealth⟨, & willing to hazard much to gain much⟩ forgetful . . . wealth ⟨is⟩without . . . gain much⟨,⟩? he puts
10–12	reaches. ⟨& is drawn on⟩ At . . . purposes of ⟨life⟩ moral
13–16	use without . . . clear ↑and . . . be ⟨s⟩ read . . . thousand.↓ ¶ ⟨The deception in all Ask The deception in all arises from the idea that tho' happiness is not to be found in one⟩ For if
22–35	established, ⟨th⟩ until it has rooted ⟨g⟩& . . . eternal. ¶ ⟨The peace I speak of not only refuses to spring up in the heart of Napoleon, or of the smaller plunderers & slayers of mankind but it ref will not grow in many bosoms for it is a holy fruit a tree of life & the cares of this world & the deceitfulness of riches & the lusts of other things entering in choke it & it becomes unfruitful.⟩ ¶ ⟨↑{The ⟨principle⟩ ↑reason↓ is this yᵗ no course of conduct can produce peace of mind yᵗ is not pursued with a regard to moral principles, yᵗ no mind can have peace wh. does not rely upon what is eternal}↓ ¶ ⟨The deception is here that that course of conduct which is not pursued with a regard to moral principles⟩ ↑For if a course of conduct is not right↓ ⟨it⟩ ↑You↓ never can produce satisfaction ⟨and the⟩ ↑by↓ multiplying its extent from ten to ten thousand transactions, ↑for↓ whilst it gives an *appearance* of security does not add the least, for as there is no foundation, it is all alike perishing. ↑And yᵉ lesson yᵗ comes from all is this yᵗ no course of conduct can ever produce peace of mind yᵗ is not pursued with a regard to moral principles yᵗ no mind can have peace wh. does not only rely on what is eternal ↑(Insert X)↓⟩ ¶ ↑⟨X {⟩It is . . . wicked"⟨}⟩↓ ¶ ⟨And now let me speak of what I deem⟩ ↑Do . . . are↓
26–27	Until it /has been turned to God,/has some love for truth/ ↑& sought . . . Religion.↓ you . . . murderer ⟨but⟩ ↑outlaw↓ from [variant and additions in pencil; the superfluous "outlaw" may have been influenced by the "but" that was canceled in ink and looks like "out"]

36–38   ↑They . . . all. ↑the love . . . heaven↓↓ ["the love . . . heaven" added
               in pencil]
45   the↑se↓ riches

Page 136

1   learn. of
11   for ⟨this⟩ it.
14   no man [end of page] no man ever
16–21   alone & ↑think . . . wrong↓ you ⟨feel⟩ ↑will soon perceive↓ . . .
               though /all your acquaintance tho all men had fallen short of the
               standard/you . . . law/ . . . made ⟨for⟩ & whose . . . Law ⟨e⟩ rule.
23   was, ⟨& is⟩ which
28   great ⟨thought⟩ ↑presence↓
30   seek him. ⟨And from your conversation with your Maker a peace
               shall take possession of your mind that passeth understanding.⟩ The
32   promised. ↑and all . . . course.↓ [addition in pencil]
34–35   upon ⟨these⟩ principles . . . sees ⟨tha⟩ clearly

Page 137

6   a ⟨far⟩ steep
8–9   ↑It . . . done↓
15–16   ("The worlds . . . morn.")
18–19   ↑A little . . . told↓ [in pencil]
20–23   benediction 'by [Emerson failed to cancel the quotation mark when
               going on to write the additional introductory phrases.] . . . tran-
               quillity Peace . . . you ↑The . . . forever.↓

Sermon CXIII

Manuscript: Five sheets folded to make four pages each, and a single leaf laid in between
leaves 6 and 7 but not included in the sewing; folios stacked and sewn with white thread
along the left margin; folio pages measure 25.1 x 20.2 cm, and the single leaf measures
25.2 x 20.1 cm. A strip, 18 x 18.6 cm, is attached to the verso of leaf 8 with black sealing
wax.

[Above Bible text:] FAST DAY, 1831.

Lines   *Page 138*
Bible text   [lacks punctuation]
2–3   ↑Tis to be regretted↓ It [addition in pencil]
3–4   many & ⟨as⟩ of course by ↑many of↓
4–5   looked upon ⟨as by many⟩ as . . . day, ⟨and is only a curiosity⟩.
6–7   ↑were↓ [in ink over pencil] a barbar⟨ity in⟩↑ous monument intruded
                into↓ ["intruded" in ink over pencil] . . . which ⟨they⟩ ↑we↓
8   the ⟨prese⟩ bosom
12   of ⟨those⟩ ↑that↓ old people, that ⟨generous⟩ ↑selfdenying↓ [addi-
                tion in ink over pencil]
14–15   ↑It . . . lion↓

15–16	always whe⟨n⟩re
17	savages ⟨value⟩ ↑revere↓
21	bond- [end of line] man
22	domain to ⟨remember⟩ be
24–(139)2	unmindful [end of page] ↑of their↓ . . . ↑being↓ descend⟨ing⟩ed . . . minds. ⟨I do n⟩Not ↑that I↓

Page 139

5–6	But ⟨what I think desireable is⟩ ↑far better would it be↓ . . . we should / value what they valued. / inherit their sentiments. /
6–8	words ↑not↓ . . . such ⟨degenerate⟩ ↑aliens↓ descendants . . . their / Fast day / Religion /. ¶ I. ↑Let us have juster regard to them. ↑& to their institution.↓↓
11	law which ⟨distinguished the people of this country from the time of its settlement down to the Revolution⟩ ↑they had,↓ . . . ↑any↓
14	his ⟨face⟩ ↑life↓
21	practisers of ⟨pure⟩ Religion⟨;⟩, ⟨to the pious men who held fast to their integrity⟩ in
23–24	↑the time of↓ . . . Elizabeth, t⟨o⟩hrough
27	with ⟨great⟩ faults
28	faith & ⟨great cruelty in some⟩ pursued . . . bad end↑s↓
29	↑they atoned . . . merit;↓
31–39	men, ⟨to whom⟩ ↑⟨to whom⟩ the cross . . . themselves,↓ . . . thot, which ⟨was never absent from yᵉ mind—⟩ ↑manifested . . . State.↓ ¶ ↑⟨To no party in England⟩ ↑When the . . . party are observed; ⟨when they [two or three illegible words]⟩ the two . . . past; & . . . much indebted.↓ ⟨We should⟩ They are . . . enthusiasm↓

Page 140

3–4	respect ⟨their⟩ this . . . their ⟨Fathers⟩ ↑progenitors↓;
7	it ⟨belo⟩ came
9	our ⟨safety⟩ ↑public↓
12–13	safer ⟨fare⟩ ↑courses↓
14–17	he ⟨distinguishes⟩ ⟨↑promises↓⟩ ↑condemns↓ hypocritical penitence ⟨from⟩ ⟨↑before↓⟩ ↑in yᵉ view of↓ inward penitence, & not ⟨between⟩ ↑an↓ external fast ⟨&⟩ ↑in comparison with↓ . . . all. [The following pencil notations are inscribed at the bottom of the page:] ¶ ↑Even the reli schools of the philosophers fasts were used & ¶ No man who owns his frailty but may see the duty of seasons of penitence for public & personal sins & for public sins because they are his own.↓ [end of page] ¶ In
18–20	↑But⟨,⟩ ↑some↓ will ⟨any⟩ ↑some↓ [addition in pencil] say there is no need⟨?⟩↓ There . . . prosperity there
23	that sh⟨i⟩one⟨s⟩ as
25–26	inevitable ⟨signs⟩ ↑forerunners↓
27–30	¶ ↑They . . . nations.↓
31	us? ⟨The ocean⟩ The
33	explored; ⟨rising cities⟩ ↑a fast increasing census;↓

36   ¶ ↑True; but↓ It will not ⟨take⟩ ↑cost↓

2   principles ⟨of⟩ ↑which we↓ ourselves ↑entertain↓.
5–7   ↑a little greater progress of ⟨skepticism⟩ ↑unbelief↓ . . . heart.↓. ↑It
                      . . . causes.↓
7–9   pass & ⟨hostilities⟩ ↑strife↓ begin↑s↓, the⟨y⟩ ↑antagonist↓ . . .
                      ↑indefinite↓ [addition in pencil] . . . one is ²plea & ¹cause
14–18   of that ⟨crime⟩ wrong ⟨in⟩ ↑by↓ the ⟨⟨govmt⟩ Govᵗ.⟩ ↑law of the
                      Land↓ . . . symptom ⟨that⟩ ↑how obtuse is↓ the moral sense of the
                      ⟨nation is obtuse.⟩ ↑people↓. ↑In lang. of prophet, {⟨[two illegible
                      words] find the [three illegible words] text from [illegible word]⟩And
                      judgment . . . cannot enter.}↓
19–20   wrong ⟨that do⟩ as . . . marks of ⟨insane selfishness⟩ ↑moral
                      corruption↓.
22   The ⟨lax⟩ low
24–30   ↑The increasing . . . trust,↓ The absence of stern uncompromising
                      ⟨heroes from the public councils⟩ men of principles from /the helm
                      of power/its ordinary administration/. ↑the growth . . . the
                      ⟨blindness⟩ carelessness of the future;↓ ⟨These are bad tokens for the
                      permanence of our institutions Wo wo ↑for us,↓ for ↑in the language
                      of Jeremiah↓ the day ⟨is far gone⟩ ↑goeth away↓, for the shadows of
                      evening are stretched out.⟩ the . . . trade a madness . . . chance the
                      not the
34   in ⟨s⟩much
40   has ⟨b⟩ come

7–10   men. ⟨Because i⟩It is . . . actions of ⟨in⟩ public . . . he is: ↑↑When
                      pub. mind is corrupt,↓ The seat . . . private mind.↓
11   ↑Lord Bacon↓
13–21   ↑on ⟨the⟩ principle,↓ . . . ↑& unlawful↓ . . . & ↑to↓ what ⟨hold⟩
                      degree the⟨y⟩se . . . time being—⟨it is this knowledge⟩ which . . . of
                      men, the⟨ir⟩ elections, ↑&↓
22–27   minds, ⟨to⟩ ↑that we may↓ settle ↑on our actions↓ their full responsi-
                      bility; ⟨on our actions; to make us⟩ ↑that we may learn to↓ . . . own
                      mind. ⟨It should direct all your actions.⟩ It is not ⟨Faneuil Hall⟩ ↑the
                      State house↓ . . . that ⟨determine⟩ ↑give . . . to↓ . . . ↑the Exchange,
                      the tavern,↓
28   ³talked about & ²taught & ¹done
31   thotful ⟨mind⟩ ↑person↓. In ⟨a⟩every
35   ↑more↓ bold⟨er⟩, if
37–40   around it. & in accordance to the⟨ir⟩ states of other minds. Here
                      ⟨the mind of⟩ a good . . . & is ⟨itself⟩ ↑himself↓ . . . greater ⟨mind⟩
                      ↑soul↓.
41–(143)12   considered the ⟨degree⟩ ↑character↓ . . . ↑or the idea of God↓.
                      ⟨{The duties of life will be very differently discharged by one who
                      acts from a regard to men & by one who acts wi⟨h⟩th an eye to God.

The first acts out of the respect which the last mediately or immediately commands.}⟩ ↑{Insert X}↓ [Two pages preceding, on the verso of the strip attached to the verso of leaf 8, a passage marked "X":] ↑↑The . . . felt↓ If . . . ↑no better motive than a↓ regard to *society,* & ⟨in other circumstances⟩ ↑if . . . at them↓, . . . have ⟨no⟩ ⟨↑little↓⟩ ↑not much↓ . . . they ⟨have fear⟩ ↑stand in fear↓ . . . keeps ⟨it⟩ ↑the community↓ . . . which failing↑,↓ ⟨to⟩ all . . . tumble⟨.⟩ in ruins.}↓ ¶ This ⟨last is a⟩ principle ⟨of mighty efficiency in human society. It⟩ is

Page 143

16	principle, ⟨you would be sure it would recover itself⟩ if
19	¶ Wh⟨y⟩at a
21	down ⟨o my soul⟩ &
23	us ⟨go⟩ humble
30	of the SS;
36–38	alone & ⟨consider⟩ examine . . . times; ⟨from⟩ ↑we . . . censure↓ . . . men ⟨by⟩ ↑under↓
41–(144)2	house, ⟨here⟩ ↑now↓ in the possession of ⟨the⟩ ↑this↓ . . . help our ⟨struggles⟩ ↑efforts↓ [last emendation in pencil] . . . unto him. ⟨If only ten men should fast let us abstain from⟩ Let us

Page 144

3–8	↑They . . . joy↓ [in pencil] ¶ ⟨The work⟩ It will . . . souls, and ⟨we shall have the satisfaction by considering⟩ ↑according to↓ . . . directed ⟨to rejoice in a glorious reward of⟩ ↑God . . . mighty↓ beneficence ⟨by which God⟩ ↑by↓ extend⟨s⟩ing . . . of individuals

Sermon CXIV

Manuscript: Five sheets folded to make four pages each; a single loose leaf once included in the sewing, containing the original opening; a sheet folded to make four pages, included in the sewing and containing a revised opening; a single leaf following the revised opening, included in the sewing and torn from the folio that contained the original opening; a single sheet folded to make four pages and a single leaf, nested in the original fourth folio and included in the sewing; except for the single leaf containing the original opening, all stacked and sewn with white thread along the left margin; the original folio pages, including the two single leaves, measure 25 x 20.2 cm; the folio pages and single leaf nested in the original fourth folio measure 24.8 x 19.8 cm.

[The following variant introduction, occupying all four pages of the first folio in the resewn gathering, was written for the second delivery of the sermon; the addition and cancellation of "122" suggests a confusion on Emerson's part between Sermons CXXII and CXIV:]

↑⟨122⟩ ↑114↓↓ [additions in pencil]
The Lord redeemeth the soul of his servants & none
of them that trust in him shall be desolate Ps. 34 22

The scriptures abound with injunctions to trust in the Lord.—one of the most sublime sentiments of which a man is capable and one of the most needful. Who is he that does not need this staff? Public & private events the course of nature, the perversity of mankind & our own folly are continually bringing a cloud over our prospect⟨s⟩, & tempting us to despondency.

The labor of your hands will not at all times afford you pleasing occupation the toil of the eyes in study will not carry with it peace of mind nor will the multitude of amusements↑,↓ ⟨,⟩no, nor social pleasures always gratify. There are times when the spirit in man will obstinately question itself & will not be pacified by anything but truth. Every one sometimes calls himself to account & compares the present day with the past hope & sees very clearly a great difference between the promises of his youth & the performance of his manhood—sees distinctly that thro' all the pretention & apparent activity of his life, his soul is not becoming more mature or more happy

But beside this obstinate self scrutiny which occasionally comes to all & which makes all things bitter all men are exposed & in turn suffer from misfortunes. Their peace of mind their self satisfaction is put to severe trial That which they most prize is taken away Unforeseen & bitter mortifications await them in the prosecution of that which they have most at heart. They have enemies who hinder them from sleep. They lose their employment & livelihood Their health is wasted; or dear friends are removed from them by death or the⟨ir⟩ altered character of their friends has ceased to make their life a source of happiness to them

I see around me in the world a great many persons who are called unfortunate who have lost their friends on whom their earthly ⟨p⟩hopes rested or who have grown up to that age which is expected to provide for itself & whom yet circumstances prevent from so doing. I see those who far removed from want are yet from leisure & the opportunity of comparing their situation with others, far more keenly sensible of a solitary or dependant condition. I see people who, without any fault of their own, are yet excluded from the sympathy of others. I see disappointed men, in whose hands every project fails. I see lonely & unhappy women. I see age left childless, & the invalid of many years. I see the oppressed, the suspected, the friendless, & the mourner.

Lines	Page 145
Bible Text	⟨↑O Lord I know that the way of man is not in himself it is not in man that walketh to direct his steps Jer. 10.23.↓⟩ ¶ The Lord
1	frequent ⟨injunction⟩ ↑command↓
4	man↑kind,↓ [addition in pencil]
6–16	↑{↓At this . . . ↑In one devoted country↓ The martyrs . . . despot↑,↓ . . . licentiousness—↑}↓ . . . stability of ⟨its⟩ ↑old↓ . . . people ↑↑in former years↓ brot out with an outstretched arm↓ . . . enter. ¶ ⟨And⟩ ⟨e⟩↑E↓very [all additions and emendations in pencil]
17–20	↑Then . . . all↓ [addition in pencil] And every . . . property. ⟨You cannot⟩ Not a . . . him ⟨as⟩ to connect ↑the recollection of↓ [addition in pencil]
21	griefs ⟨t⟩are
22	↑one of↓ th⟨i⟩ese reason↑s↓,
23–(146)3	apprehended, the [end of page] ⟨whole . . . sad.⟩ [cancellation rejected as late emendation] ¶ For ⟨the⟩all . . . adequate ⟨relief⟩ remedy . . . in ⟨God.⟩ ↑the Supreme Being,↓—a . . . all ⟨the course of⟩ events ⟨is⟩are

Page 146

5	↑good men say↓ are ⟨then seen to be the parent of trust⟩ needed
6	The ⟨shade⟩ ↑rain↓ . . . as the ⟨sun⟩ light
7	misfortunes /lead/direct/ [variant in pencil]
12–14	see ⟨with⟩ ↑at↓ a glance ⟨that in most things you have been passive⟩ ↑{Insert X}↓ [On the preceding page, otherwise blank, a passage marked "X":] ↑{that in ⟨far the greatest⟩ ↑bringing ⟨about⟩ to pass the whole↓ . . . do, in quite passive,}↓
17–18	this ⟨particular⟩ age . . . yet ⟨wholly⟩ ↑quite↓
19–21	continue to ⟨determine⟩ ↑influence↓ your lot. ⟨↑very much↓⟩ ¶ Then your early associates, /the ⟨connexions⟩ ⟨↑marriage ties↓⟩ [last cancellation in pencil] you have formed/ as well the ties of blood/, [variant in pencil] ⟨the⟩ ↑your↓ opportunities of observation ⟨you have had⟩,—how much more ⟨th⟩have
23–30	slight ⟨accidents (as he terms them)⟩ ↑occasions↓ . . . connexions of ⟨friendship⟩ of business, . . . party ⟨th⟩which he forms and ⟨what⟩ how fast the ⟨slight⟩ ties ⟨he first assumes become⟩ ↑so . . . into↓ . . . life↑.↓ [period in pencil] ¶ ⟨You think perhaps⟩ ↑Doubtless↓ [addition in ink over pencil] ⟨t⟩↑T↓here are ↑always↓ . . . world ⟨whose society would ⟨con⟩⟩ ↑who . . . friendship to↓ . . . chance ⟨as you call it⟩ of ⟨turning down one⟩ ↑entering a different↓ [emendation in pencil] street ⟨instead of another⟩, [canceled in pencil] of
31–32	↑What . . . chance?↓ No ↑human↓
35–36	profession or ⟨parish⟩ ↑join this association↓ or ↑reside in this↓
37	led to very
38–42	dependance . . . this ⟨alien⟩ dependance ↑on . . . yourself↓ . . . has. ⟨↑{↓What . . . always fl⟨ie⟩y at? . . . may ⟨put⟩ ↑blow↓ . . . extinguish it?↑}↓⟩ [passage lightly canceled in pencil; brackets added in pencil; cancellation rejected as a late emendation]

Page 147

1–3	down & ⟨bemoaning⟩ ↑reproaching↓ [emendation in pencil] . . . distress ⟨the⟩ himself . . . inaccessible /providences/causes/ by which ⟨you⟩ ↑the↓
4–6	↑too boldly↓ . . . ↑leaving . . . mind↓ . . . life. ⟨I⟩ Who
8–11	to ⟨kick⟩ ↑strive↓ . . . waits ⟨an enemy⟩ ↑the coming hour↓ . . . fear ⟨him⟩ it. ¶ ⟨⟨⟨1⟩2. The second reason why we should trust ⟨in⟩God is the very obvious one that not only can we not controul the order of events, but that order is *kind,* & ⟨we st⟩ when it is observed, we acquiesce in it, & love it.⟩ He who understands much of natural science knows that there is a perpetual operation of checks & balances that each tribe of beings keeps every other in check; that a guard against excess is everywhere provided. And all things set to a tune. He who sees how system is kept from running into system how centrifugal & petal counteract he who sees the care to produce pleasant sensations he that looks into the field nowadays & sees the budding year & hears the birds—he who sees man & woman mother

& child the armchair of age & ⟨rattle⟩ ↑drum↓ of boy will not
question the Beneficence.⟩ ¶ 2. The

12   ↑is↓ because
18–21   seen the ⟨sun⟩ day . . . not ⟨will⟩ as they pass ⟨a⟩ ↑over the eye of a
             beast↓ . . . dark↑,↓ ⟨upon the eye of cattle⟩, but . . . footstool of
             ⟨his⟩ ↑⟨the⟩our Father's↓
23–27   any ↑fellow-↓being; ↑it . . . world↓ it . . . adding one ⟨moment's⟩
             ↑hours↓
28   ↑of↓ such
36   everywhere. ⟨Every seeming suffering All the suff⟩ A
38   greater—⟨⟨And all⟩ Ever⟩ and

Page 148

1–3   opposite tendency. of . . . by which ⟨it departs from⟩ it
4–5   every ⟨flower⟩ tree . . . prophe⟨c⟩sying
6   field, a ⟨more⟩ plainer
11   or ⟨digni⟩ sweetened
11–12   ↑Has↓ The dignity
14   friend have
15–17   They might [end of page] teach . . . these ⟨hum⟩ relations . . . mercy
             & ⟨may be⟩ is . . . trust. [The inscription at the top of the page is
             written between the lines of a pencil notation:] beauty of the social
             institutions love of yᵉ parent to the child & of yᵉ child & yᵉ parent
25–(149)10   troubles. ¶ [The following large cancellation and selected cancella-
             tions within it (as specified below) are rejected as late emendations. At
             the page break within the large cancellation, the folio and single leaf
             which contain the substituted text are nested in the original fourth
             folio and included in the final sewing (see below for the substitute
             text). The inscription that follows the cancellation here, clearly part
             of the original text of the sermon, now follows the added folio and
             single loose leaf, but was not canceled when these were inserted.] ¶
             ⟨3. The next consideration which ⟨I have to offer⟩ ↑shd lead us to
             confide↓ . . . ↑from a review of the facts,↓ but ↑prior to all considera-
             tion of the facts↓ . . . brow. ↑X↓ [At the top of the page, a passage
             marked "X":] ↑We feel that a trust in God is a sort of duty for its own
             sake I admire the words of ⟨the⟩ a great poet
                 ⟨And Hope the ⟨sovereign⟩ ↑paramount↓ duty wh.
                 Heaven lays
                 For its own honor, on man's suffering heart⟩↓
             [cancellation of the two lines of verse rejected as a late emendation]
             . . . all piercing . . . have ⟨rea⟩ sat . . . dependant . . . in the
             contem⟩ [end of page] plation . . . ↑to gain nothing, to lose all↓ . . .
             the epistles ⟨rejoi⟩ who . . . God. [sentence written in ink over the
             "Xn hope of immortality" in pencil] ¶ It ⟨is⟩comes . . . become
             ⟨hab⟩ more . . . rest ¶ ⟨Moreover ⟨the⟩ Religion reveals to us the
             eternal life⟩ ¶ Here

             [The following passage, inscribed on the added folio and single leaf

nested and sewn in the original fourth folio, was written for the
second delivery of the sermon, May 29, 1836, following the death of
Charles Chauncy Emerson. It was meant to replace the text given at
page 148, lines 26–38:]

↑It may be you have been called to mourn the loss of a dear friend
⟨under⟩ connected with yourself by all those bonds that make
friendship dearest & its loss sorest. And what is ↑it↓ that such events
say? Why this, certainly. The chasm of the loss, these bursting tears,
this broken voice, this wearisome sense of privation,—what is it but
so much eulogy of the departed? What is it but, under another form, a
thanksgiving to God that he had so highly blessed us? It is an
acknowledgment (how unsuspicious) of the ⟨immense blessing⟩
↑privilege↓ of being associated with a noble character. Indeed,
brethren, I prize above all prosperity that which is sometimes called
the joy of grief. I value ⟨the⟩ every tear that is shed for departed men,
because it is a certificate of the excellent endowments, the graces, the
character which have dwelt with us. What good shall we compare
with this good? ↑with↓ the reverence & love which human character
↑has inspired↓ seen in closest intimacy where all hypocrisy & veil
were impossible,—seen in the practi⟨s⟩ce of common duties, & in
the gaiety & vexations, the plans & failures, the opinions & actions
of daily life, passing from duty to duty, ⟨having friends⟩ at home, &
abroad⟨,—the reverence & love which this has inspired⟩. When we
have been made acquainted in our own familiar circle with one who
was so severe an adorer of truth that it would have been as easy for
him to steal as to dissemble; ⟨when⟩ with one who so reverenced the
oracle in his own mind that he held all men's opinion light in the
balance with its softest whisper; with one who had such a value for
time that he thought men's ⟨es⟩ frugality of it the measure of their
worth; with one who adding to his virtues the finest accomplishments, had no vanity, and never added to his necessary discourse one
word for the sake of display; with one who amidst all the attractions
which the world offered had so high a standard of ⟨life⟩ ↑action↓
[emendation in ink over pencil] & character that /mere life/⟨am-
bition⟩/ [variant and cancellation in pencil] had nothing to charm
him & ↑{↓in his most ambitious hour↑}↓ [brackets in pencil] held the
world very cheap; ⟨by reason of his familiarity with the /noble life &
thoughts/greatness/ [variant in pencil] of David & ⟨P⟩ ↑divine life↓
[addition in pencil] Jesus & ↑fiery soul↓ [addition in pencil] Paul.⟩
⟨↑as scorn of life increased↓⟩ ["as . . . increased" added and canceled
in pencil] ¶ ⟨Of⟩With one who prized the religious sentiment as
God's greatest gift to man, & was impatient of any discourse or
speculations in the Church which led the mind away from this,
because it was the basis of human strength the succor in trouble, &
especially the right of the great number who have almost no education
but that which the ⟨Church⟩ ↑Sabbath↓ supplies them. ↑one who had
true wisdom & pure philosophy without its cant↑;↓ ⟨&⟩ who prized
at their true rate the scriptures stimulated by his love of the greatness

of David of the divine life of Jesus & the fiery soul of Paul.↓ My
friends, I say that when we have been made acquainted with such
character, we ought not to be too curious in counting the months or
years of its presence, the circumstances in which it pleased God to
bring it, or to keep it, or to take it, but we ought to consider how
immense a blessing has been made visible unto us as a Vision out of
heaven—to encourage what is good in us, to suppress & ⟨eradicate⟩
root out what is bad—to call up our hopes the sentiment of piety, of
gratitude of trust in short to see the whole ⟨gift⟩ ↑benefit↓ in God—as
his gift, as his admonition, as his love to us—and ⟨as⟩ ↑as↓ an
assurance not to be questioned that who has ↑once↓ given us so much,
can give us the like or greater blessings. ¶ What is true of this calamity,
this loss of friends, who made the value of the world to us, is true of all
losses, of all calamities, that an unseen & infinite blessing lies hid
under the sorrow. ¶ they are all found to be kind.↓ [At the bottom of
the page the following, written upside down relative to the balance of
the page:] ⟨Dear William ¶ Thanks⟩ [end of fourth page of the
inserted folio] ¶ ↑Thus↓ We must trust, because we are ⟨helpless⟩
weak & ⟨powerless⟩ unable to interfere in the management of the
world; then, because ⟨as far as we can see⟩ our experience teaches us
that Providence is kind. 3. The next consideration which should lead
us to confide, is that ⟨i⟩so to do, is, not only becoming & reasonable
from a review of the facts, but prior to all consideration of the facts,
the religious nature of man makes it a duty to trust in Infinite
Wisdom. The heart in us seeks the Father and the Scriptures unveil his
face. We feel that a trust in God is a sort of duty for its own sake. I
admire the words of the a great moral poet
    Hope is the paramount Duty which Heaven lays
    For its own honor on man's suffering heart.
When we ⟨can⟩ are perplexed with doubt as to what duty requires—
we can stand & wait. When we are enervated by grief, we can yet say
to the spirit & the event—Accomplish thy mission, finish thy will,—I
shall yet see that it is good ¶ There is underneath all our fears &
agitations & regrets an ineradicable belief in the human mind that All
is Well that a Will which is perfect that a Wisdom which is Love
overrules the world. We will not then arraign before our ignorance
⟨his⟩the all pe↑i↓rcing sight, ⟨his⟩the all befriending arm? Let us
read the Evangelists Let us read the Epistles There we are instructed
in a better school There we learn the philosophy of suffering. When
we have sat at the feet of Jesus, & owned in the face of God our
dependence & sin,—we lose ourselves in the contemplation & love of
the divine perfections↓

Page 149

10   man ⟨He is great by leaning wholly⟩ 'He
11   others ⟨i⟩leans
15–16   God. ⟨Realize⟩ ↑Acquaint yourself with↓ your true ⟨situation⟩
          ↑position↓

21–24   kindly, ⟨to c⟩not . . . entertainer ⟨will take care⟩ does . . . ends. ¶ ⟨It will be observed that in the considerations which approve a Christian trust there is nothing which can excuse a foolish fatalism. Nothing is more irrational than the foolish sluggard who lolls out his tongue at defeat and at success & says "it is all for the best"—And many ¶ No man can have a trust in God who does a vicious action. It does not cripple a muscle. It is promised only to vigorous endeavours to discharge all our duty. And to the mind that does labor faithfully it is a shield against every enemy and ⟨s⟩a solace to every wo. Indeed without this support no man can⟩ ¶ Moreover

28–36   all. [The following cancellation is rejected as a late emendation:] ¶ ⟨Let . . . character ⟨It has⟩ An unshaken . . . replaces /what/the good which/ . . . lose if ⟨we⟩ in . . . God of in whom . . . things?⟩

38–(150)3   ↑varying & often↓ disastrous aspect↑s↓ . . . he ⟨th⟩ who . . . results. [The following addition, written for the third delivery, June 5, 1836, at Concord, where Charles Chauncy Emerson had taught Sunday School, is rejected as a late emendation:] ↑⟨[illegible word]⟩ ↑When↓ sickness ⟨visited⟩ laid a heavy hand on one who was honored & loved? Is the Teacher removed from his place & the lips sealed for a time from which you gladly received the word of truth.↓ Or

Page 150

4–9   way h when . . . when ⟨your⟩ lover . . . ↑or when disease . . . strength; or↓ . . . ↑of others↓ . . . lost;—⟨O, then, more is lost than ²fortune or ¹health or friends—your own soul is lost.⟩ ↑God forbid it, brethren.↓

12   fatal⟨s⟩ism,

16   The ⟨r⟩very

16–18   good'—↑↑And↓ This . . . thing acc. his . . . us. 1 John. V. 14↓ The

18–19   hears alway . . . trust to ⟨a⟩its

20   Father. [The following addition, written for the closing of the second or third delivery, is rejected as a late emendation:] ↑Let us listen to his voice animating us in every grief & difficulty—'Let not your heart be troubled ye believe in God believe also in me. Do not think that th⟨e⟩is evil⟨s you have felt are the⟩ ↑life↓ is all your being. In my Father's house are many mansions.—↓ [Cf. John 14:1–2]

Sermon CXV

Manuscript: Six sheets folded to make four pages each; folios stacked and sewn with white thread along the left margin; pages measure 25 x 20.3 cm. A strip, 10.8 x 20.1 cm, is attached to the recto of leaf 4 with red sealing wax.

Lines   *Page 151*

Bible Text   him ⟨take⟩ deny . . . cross ⟨&⟩ ↑daily, &↓ follow me. Luke 9.23 Luke 9.23 [second citation in pencil]

1   Christ↑.↓ ⟨↑{↓& so children of God.↑}↓⟩ But [brackets in pencil]

3   vote ⟨as you are told⟩ ↑in ⟨in⟩reference to ↑a↓ . . . state↓;

5–6   in N.T. which . . . was, to ⟨reinstate⟩ ↑establish↓ [emendation in ink over pencil]

7	give ⟨authority⟩ exercise
8	of *sens*⟨ible⟩↑ual↓ *comforts.*
10	subt⟨le⟩ile
13–14	man ⟨was⟩ ↑had↓ not assumed ⟨at⟩ its
19	show ↑with . . . exhibited↓,

Page 152

3–6	world. ¶ ↑In short↓ [addition in pencil and ink] It is by ⟨identifying him⟩ being . . . ↑becoming . . . only ⟨the⟩ ↑a↓ channel . . . flowed,↓
8–9	Christ, ⟨to follow him must be to work in the same cause. And⟩ it . . . ↑as . . . principles↓ [addition in pencil]
13	↑or as partakers of his supper↓
14–22	between ⟨being⟩ ↑the↓ so *called,* & ↑the↓ so *being.* ⟨And so, let us devote our earnest attention for a little while to a few practical considerations upon the duties that become the followers of Christ.⟩ [canceled in pencil and ink] ↑{Insert A}↓ [On the facing page, a passage marked "A":] ↑¶ ⟨I propose to name some of the marks by which a true follower of Christ ⟨is know⟩ ↑may be known,↓ & which are known from a consideration of his own character Let us devote a little serious attention to these practical considerations that we may see how faithful we are to our duties⟩ [passage in partially erased pencil; the following written over it in ink:] I propose to ⟨consider⟩ ↑enumerate↓ some of the ⟨chief⟩ marks . . . known. ⟨And let us, I pray you, devote our serious attention to these practical considerations, that⟩ ↑By recollecting them↓ we . . . duties.} ⟨The indications of a true Christian which ⟨I propose⟩ are essential to any faithful obedience are 1. that he do not confound himself with others. 2. that he ⟨view every action by the light of Christian principles⟩ ↑carries Xn principles into ⟨his⟩the ⟨principl⟩ judgment of smallest actions↓. 3. that he be a religious worker as well as believer 4. that he deny himself.⟩↓ [end of Insert "A"] ¶ ⟨1. A⟩ ↑1. The first mark I shall ⟨↑consider↓ very important⟩ name, is the observance of a↓ rule which meets every ⟨person who has a sincere desire to do right⟩ ↑good mind↓, . . . ↑and that↓ is, . . . community. ⟨It is not your tho't⟩ ↑To . . . yours↓
23–24	day ⟨need⟩ ↑make↓ any justification ⟨in⟩ ↑before↓ God⟨'s ear⟩ for
24–25	distinct. ↑from all others↓.
25	not in ⟨them⟩ ↑others↓. The thought in ⟨this⟩ your
28–31	this. ⟨↑{↓Why need I fear that I am the mark of all eyes in the spiritual world? There are ↑in yᵉ world↓ [addition in pencil] ⟨5⟩600 000 000 men.↑}↓⟩ [brackets in pencil] Am . . . than I. ⟨Indeed⟩ ↑I . . . yet↓ [emendation in ink over pencil] . . . proverb, ⟨a⟩ more
34	↑the West Indies or↓
36–37	↑It is matter . . . more.↓ [in ink over pencil]
37–38	yourself⟨?⟩—this . . . sin? To ⟨illustrate it⟩ ↑answer this shortly↓ [addition in ink over "answer this" in pencil]
41–(153)9	am I! ⟨So little are their means of virtue to be compared with yours And so ⟨let⟩ I say ⟨to⟩ not to the community ↑but to the indi-

viduals;↓—⟨but⟩ let the word of truth find its way to every heart in this house↑—↓⟨that has contemplated⟩ ↑is there any one who is conscious that he has meditated a↓ sin on this plea that ⟨your⟩ ↑his↓ acquaintances do much worse? ↑Let him consider that God makes a different trial to every different soul↓ I say to you, my brother, you live as it were in another world from the person who ↑eats at your table or who↓ sits now by your side, such is the difference with which the moral obligations address themselves to you & to him.⟩ [The following addition is inscribed on the strip attached to the recto of leaf 4:] ↑¶ God has set . . . themselves↓

Page 153

6	in a ⟨d⟩ separate
9	↑Your . . . taper.↓
11	them. ⟨You feel guilt in dreams even.⟩ [canceled in pencil] To
13–14	↑what makes the difference?—↓ . . . others—?
16–18	business.' ↑the call . . . things↓ ¶ The ⟨vice⟩ ↑sin↓
21–22	↑more↓ tender⟨er⟩ conscience
27–29	↑to unredeem, ⟨to⟩↓ to . . . death. ¶ ⟨Brethren there are few things more dangerous to our character more fatal to our imbibing the principles of the Saviour than this lowlived huddling into a crowd this making twenty sinners twenty apologies for our crimes.⟩ ¶ It is
30–32	for ⟨2.⟩ one . . . his ⟨times & h⟩ contemporaries. He ⟨stands aloof from them like an angel among the bad ↑spirit↓⟩ ⟨↑is always superior to those to whom he ministers↓⟩ ["spirit" added in pencil; "is . . . ministers" added in ink over pencil] ↑is always . . . ministers↓— . . . pupils⟨.⟩,—↑like . . . spirits.↓ [addition in ink over "like an angel among bad" in pencil]
34–36	society ⟨but⟩ that . . . not only not ↑be↓ . . . must ⟨form his⟩ apply

Page 154

7	best founded
8	should ⟨no⟩ be ready ⟨not only⟩ to
11–13	out ⟨a def de⟩ an ↑seeming↓ . . . intercourse.—and . . . it or ⟨alter⟩ ↑⟨amend⟩ remove↓
22–24	trivial ⟨remarks⟩ ↑discourse↓. ↑(↓But . . . intelligence.↑)↓ [parentheses added in pencil]
25	casual ⟨observation⟩ ↑conversation↓. that
28–31	lines of the ⟨face⟩ ↑countenance↓ . . . whose ⟨fountain of moral life⟩ ↑principle . . . which↓ . . . every [end of line] where
34–36	you. ¶ ⟨So y⟩You . . . into ⟨every⟩ ↑the smallest↓ vein of the ↑smallest↓
37	↑in expressions of civility↓ [addition in ink over "in expressions" in pencil]
40–41	words of ⟨course⟩ ↑politeness↓ . . . impression ⟨↑of disrespect↓⟩ ↑of disrespect.↓

Page 155

1–2	↑in our . . . cold ⟨to speak⟩↓ to speak ⟨*divinely* than to speak⟩ ↑as . . . than↓ as we commonly do ⟨*humanly* of the *weather.*⟩ ↑to . . . Chance.↓

4   what—⟨o! how hard⟩ it is ↑hard↓
5-7   must not⟨, as we constantly do,⟩ suffer . . . by our ⟨social kindness⟩
                     ↑complaisance↓— . . . offend. ⟨&⟩↑nor must we↓ . . . slander, ⟨yet
                     at least⟩ ↑any more↓
9-10   ¶ ↑I believe . . . principles↓
14-29   Creator ↑{↓In . . . good.↑}↓ [brackets in ink over pencil]
15-16   constant ⟨labor⟩ ↑usefulness↓.
19-20   vast ⟨forces of⟩ attractions . . . ↑separate↓
21   animal ⟨& s⟩ answers . . . whole imparts
34-36   ↑Are we not . . . others?↓
41-(156)1   greatest in ⟨s⟩those

                     Page 156
2   To ⟨a few of us⟩ ↑some↓ I ⟨doubt not⟩ ↑hope↓
7   Christians ⟨such ex⟩ the
10   ¶ ↑And . . . God.↓
11   The ⟨tes⟩ mark
13   ↑He put . . . frankly↓
16-17   last ⟨c⟩topic, for ⟨ne this⟩ ↑self-denial↓
27   build a↑n↓ /hospital/asylum/ [addition and variant in pencil]
28-30   man to ⟨forgive⟩ spend . . . in the ⟨care⟩ ↑religious instruction↓ of
                     ⟨poor⟩ children↑, wh I . . . beneficence↓ [emendations in pencil
                     except for the cancellation of "forgive"] . . . vice ⟨for⟩ which ⟨you⟩
                     would
34   more. i⟨n⟩t is . . . ↑with your talent↓.
36-37   easy ⟨f⟩ with . . . followed ⟨the Lord⟩ our
41-(157)1   power but ⟨to add to the wealth or the praise or the power of others
                     or at least to our own goodness. We must suffer for God.⟩ ↑/Here is
                     the summary of the Xn morality. This includes all the other marks of
                     grace. And here I will conclude/to our . . . conclude./↓ ["Here . . .
                     conclude" added in pencil before cancellation of "to . . . God"] ¶
                     Come↑,↓ brethren↑,↓ [commas in pencil] . . . not ⟨wi⟩ yet

                     Page 157
1-2   Come↑,↓ . . . heaven↑,↓ [additions in pencil]
5   ↑not quite↓
6-7   days. ⟨It is a sublime act⟩ ↑And . . . victory↓ Thank

Sermon CXVI

Manuscript (draft version): Five sheets folded to make four pages each, and a single leaf
used as a title page, now loose but at one time included in the sewing; folios stacked and
sewn with white thread along the left margin; folio pages measure 25.1 x 20.3 cm, and
the single leaf measures 25 x 20.2 cm.

[It seems unlikely that Emerson delivered any part of the present draft version on
May 15, 1831, despite the presence of that date at the end of the MS. The text is casually
written and fragmentary in places, and lacks a Bible text. More probably Emerson had

the revision of Part I ready for delivery at that time, and finished Part II by the time he next appeared in his home pulpit on May 29, the date which appears at the end of the revised version. The following draft contains significant portions of the first part and lesser portions of the second part of Sermon CXVI:]

CXVI.

I shall attempt, in the first place, to show the uses of the Christian Sabbath; secondly; to show that we ought to keep it holy. thirdly; to show how this may best be done.

↑I.↓ 1. The uses of the Christian Sabbath. Its *first* mercy to man is Rest. Sabbath means *rest*. It was made for man, for the ⟨po⟩ diligent, for the poor, for the dependant, for the slave. to rest his body from labor, that the health might not suffer nor the spirits be broken down by unceasing work. This is its first & needful & lowest ⟨work⟩ office to administer rest to the body. It is violated—its purpose of tender mercy is counteracted ↑not only↓ by those whom a too greedy love of gain permits to open the shop on Sunday, or keep the↑ir↓ ⟨distillery⟩ ↑mills↓ in operation, to open bar-rooms or ⟨stables and⟩ ↑places of amusement but↓ by all those who demand of their laborers or apprentices, or dependants, the least unnecessary work; and lastly by those who do not permit the beast of the field to enjoy that rest which God provided for him.

2. The second use of the Sabbath is the interposition of a day of thought amidst days of business. The body needs rest. The soul is of another nature & never needs rest. It needs no other refreshment than change of thought. It cannot bear too steadfast attention to one object or class of objects. And an occasional diversion of its thoughts from its usual ends to others must be made or the health of the soul will be sacrificed as surely as the health of a body that should be fastened for months in one posture.

No law of our nature is more familiar to us in our own experience & our observation of others, than the fact that a long continued attention to a single object discovers continually new particulars & magnifies the importance of the object. This makes the value of the 'division of labor,' that confinement of the attention to one out of many parts of a work enables the eye to observe many defects which it can remedy, many occasions & means it can lay hold of for improving the processes of work—And in this way knowledge continually descends into nature on one side, as far as it ascends on another. Whilst one class of philosophers are ascertain-[end of line]↑ing↓ new & vaster laws & systems than were known before another class are opening worlds of knowledge within the objects we have always looked on.

Telescope brings down stars & systems into our orrery

Microscope brings up mites & animalcules into anatomy

But this beneficent law which enables us to increase our knowledge & power indefinitely among the most familiar things is accompanied with this disadvantage to a finite being like man. that because he can attend to only one thing at a time if he confines his attention to a small class of phenomena, he loses the memory of the rest of things, & magnifies the objects of his attention to a very disproportionate importance. A pebble or a shred of wool held ⟨be⟩ immediately before the eye appears not only larger than a mountain but shuts out the whole prospect of a county.

Every one of us has doubtless seen many examples of it in our daily life. Indeed every one of us is an example of it ourselves. We see men ⟨heated⟩ ↑wound up↓ to the ⟨greatest extravagance⟩ ↑highest key of feeling↓ about things, which because we have never considered, appear to us trifles. Parties spring up in the state and we are utterly unable to account for the heat they exhibit in relation to ⟨things⟩ ↑subjects↓ about which other men are cold. So in individuals, ⟨This is what is meant when men are vulgarly⟩ ↑A man is vulgarly↓ said to have ↑this↓ hobb⟨ies⟩y. Any object to which a man's attention has been directed with that intensity as to exclude every other. ⟨Well now the vulgar objects of attention the supply of our daily wants the acquisition of competence, of independance, of opulence, are, in the eye of a truly wise man, pursued with an ardour & neglect of other things wholly unsuitable to their value. And if there was no remission given it would lead to an insanity. Thus a miser is insane. The lovers of power who wholly destroy their peace for the sake of ambition are insane.

And many more

Now see in this the necessity of the Sabbath day. It thrusts in an opportunity to interrupt this excessive devotion to one thing. It sets other objects before you & permits the prisoned soul to rest itself by a new attitude⟩

The steadfast attention to a single object producing a total neglect of other objects ⟨pr⟩ brings about at last a perfect insanity. And we frequently see men who have a love of something or an aversion to something which is perfectly unreasonable in its extent over their ⟨m⟩Minds. The common remedy provided for this in the world is the multiplicity of objects & one man's foible runs against another man's foible & both are made ridiculous. So travelling is thot to have that good effect, to enlarge a man's vision to break up his associations, & show him there may be noble objects of pursuit; great men; good laws⟨,⟩ & customs; & wide countries; which he had left wholly out of account in his former estimates of human life. But these remedies do not ⟨wholly⟩ go far enough. Perhaps the great objects of pursuit by the whole world in all countries & times may have something of folly in them, may be elevated by the consent of mankind to an undue importance. Perhaps *power* is not really & truly quite so great a prize as by thinking so much upon it we have come to esteem it. Perhaps *riches* are not the best possession in the world. Perhaps *health* of body & *life* itself of the body are not of that ⟨unutterable⟩ price that they are counted. If this should be so, & the suspicion that they are overestimated has always lived in the world, how are they to be exposed? ⟨B⟩ Only by presenting the objects of another world. The glare of torches of earth is only to be shamed by breaking down the shutters & letting in the beams of the sun in heaven. For this the Sabbath is given—the day of God & eternity to break the charm of things of time.

The Sabbath is interposed by Gods mercy continually to check this running tide of habit & enable us to fortify to give us pause time to make a new comparison of what we do & what we ought to do time to plant our foot & resist the pressing crowd—time to say No; time to examine the direction of the road we follow & see if it ⟨e⟩leads ⟨us⟩ ↑towards↓ home or from it.

3. A third ⟨& main⟩ great use of the Sunday is not only that it interrupts our worldly cares but it is in its right use a religious education itself. It is what man wanted. Look at the hard lot of thousands, at the inequality of civil & literary advantages. Who, in the six days, has time to cultivate his mind? Almost not one. Well here comes in Sunday to give that opportunity to the poorest & most ignorant Sunday tis the rest not only of the weary & the check of God on our extravagant delusions but it is the poor mans college the university of [end of line] of human souls. A simple computation will make this very apparent. One seventh of our time is separated to the Soul. Of course, the child that has lived seven years, has lived one whole year of Sundays. He that has lived to fourteen, has had besides all his schools ⟨2⟩two ⟨yrs⟩ entire years of religious instruction. At the age

of legal manhood three years have been enjoyed. And which of you has lived 50 years has spent seven years of meditation upon his duties to God

All therefore the cogent arguments that can be urged in favor of schools, of literary inst⟨u⟩itutions of higher rank all yᵗ can be said in the cause of books & all & any means of raising the minds of men by the diffusion of truth can be said in favor of the Christian Sabbath. All the politics of Education or the use of Education in civil society to soften men & make them good ⟨subjects⟩ citizens can be said for Sunday. But more & better can be said

All that is solemn & affecting

It is the celebration of the moral nature of man. It is the day which undervalues all institutions Sunday is the religious day. Useful & excellent as all these political scientific social institutions are much as they are the ornament & school ↑the↓ tamer of society yet compared with a part of man's nature they are subordinate & cheap local except as they are connected with Religion. The memory, the skilful hand, the speaking tongue, the upright form, the world of arts,—all these only raise man to the head of the animal creation & are useful to secure to him his bread & clothes with more convenience & decency & lay him at last in the ground with more grace than other lower creatures. But Reason, the faculty wherein Religion resides, carries up this low creature to God, & connects him with the Cause of Causes & ⟨joins⟩ interweaves his individual being with the great Order of the whole Creation It teaches us that we have a longevity beyond that of mountains or sun or stars; that when new revolutions shall break up the surface of the globe, we shall renew ⟨ou⟩an eternal youth; that while we look back to nothing on one side, we behold heavens & earth forever new on the other; And why? on what foundation does it rear this hope? It speaks to the heart within us as the child of God & the heart answers the appeal

And the Sabbath is the festival of this hope. On The day ⟨of⟩ not of a commemoration but of a hope. A day appointed to look forward not for months or years but to the whole being of the soul & around through the whole universe. A day to consider the sacred laws through which alone happiness can be found; a day to be pure in heart to speak truth; a day to be meek & forgiving a day to be sorry for our imperfections & eager for improvement a day to be kind to our fellow men to rejoice in the dear love by which God binds us to each other or to those souls that are not now ⟨hear⟩ here, but are with him in heaven. A day of rejoicing in fine in Gods beneficence that we are under his protection & that his Providence

Who that has a heart will not rejoice in beholding this day? He who has kept the commandments so that h⟨e⟩is ⟨can⟩ willing mind can understand the excellence of Jesus will gratefully remember his holiness, will welcome the peaceful hours of prayer of reading & of social worship and will go up gladly with the multitude of them that keep holy day to the sanctuary.

↑These are three general uses ↑of↓ the Christian Sabbath; Rest; suspension of common tho't; & a religious education. But there are as many particular uses as individual observers of it. Every pious heart turns the day to ⟨its own⟩ good account in its own way & the good use of the day has always been the teacher of its own value. Great & good men have ⟨rep⟩ declared their deep conviction that the Sunday was the regulator of the week,—& as they had spent it to their spiritual profit, or otherwise, so were the remaining days prosperous or unprosperous.↓

II. I have spoken at some length of the uses of the Christian Sabbath. In these uses is contained the inference to which I proposed next to call your attention, namely, to this, that it is our duty to keep the Sabbath holy. I ⟨do not⟩ put the obligation ↑partly↓ upon the original Commandment to the Jews, ⟨though⟩ ↑which↓ I think ⟨that⟩ deserves great consideration ↑from all Christians, so nearly does the institution of yᵉ Sabbath ↑from its purposes↓ approach to a moral law↓, ⟨for⟩ ↑and↓ Jesus did not come to abrogate the law, but to carry its moral part into force; and he said, "if ⟨I⟩thou will enter into life, *keep the Commandments.*" ↑I know↓ The day we observe is a different one from the Jewish Sabbath, yet did the disciples who followed the steps of their master transfer to this day a careful religious observance. But I would ⟨rather⟩ ↑chiefly↓ rest the obligation of keeping this day sacred upon the obvious expediency & justness of so doing. A day of rest is needed for the body. A suspension of our headlong labors & strifes is needed as absolutely for the mind. And the occasions & means of doing homage to the Father of the Universe and of ⟨qu⟩ calling in our thoughts & raising them above the earth is too vitally necessary to be questioned

Let him who is accustomed, if I speak to any such, to make little difference between his Sabbath & his workday ⟨cons⟩ bring before him, if he can, the whole train of evils that would result from the abolishment of that day. Spare the ⟨last hope of humanity⟩ ↑Sabbath↓ the poor mans friend the rich man's counsellor the ⟨ed⟩ instructor of the children the comforter of the afflicted, & the uplifter of the head & heart of wretched man to the glorious hope of ⟨life to come⟩ heaven. Every patriot every ⟨serious⟩ ↑wise↓ man ⟨may⟩ know↑s↓ that the best legacy that he can desire for his children or his country is a sacredly kept Sabbath. ↑[hand pointing right] *mason bee &c*↓

III. Let me now speak in the last place of the way in which the Sabbath is to be kept holy by us. From the beginning of the world in every nation under heaven God has been honoured more or less rightly by public worship. That institution has come down to us in ⟨a⟩ simple & beautiful forms. It is of all social rites the most worthy of our respect and does not deserve to fall into neglect among us. Good men rejoice in the ↑great & perhaps increasing↓ respect this institution has ⟨am⟩ in this community. Still I cannot think it was ever too much reverenced or is incapable of improvement here. It might easily be a more acceptable service from us, my friends, in two ways, first; if it↑s external services↓ were always attended, &, secondly; if it were made a more sincere service. The service of the morning & afternoon together occupy about three hours out of the Sabbath; and is it right to grudge that time to him who gave us time. Is it becoming in those whom neither sickness nor necessary labor hinders from coming to the church to hinder themselves like a brute by an overloaded stomach or ⟨an⟩ ↑a most↓ unseasonable sleep or a profane & most ungrateful neglect of his maker that he may take his pleasure in an afternoon ride. Or if you are too correct & regardful of opinion & of your conscience to do thus, yet is it a just return of Gods goodness & the wisest bestowment of your time to rob a part of your holy time for the sak⟨ing⟩e of finishing the neglected business of the week. Six days shalt thou labor & do all thy work, but the seventh is the Sabbath of the Lord thy God.

⟨⟨I know very well how much⟩ ↑It↓ may be said in defence of not going to church.⟩ God is a spirit & everywhere present & may be worshipped at home or on the road. Truly he is—but have you staid away from church to worship him—and was He the subject of your conversation or of your solitary meditation And did you find yourself in as humble & pious a frame of mind on the evg when for slight cause you had forsaken the church, as on the day when you went there with a lowly grateful prayerful ⟨mind⟩ attention

And so with regard to the manner of our worship When we are here it will suffice if we bear in mind that /we are/the time is/ not our own & give ourselves to the consideration of God as he has been & is to us with that fervor that shall make amends for any defects in the imperfect fellow creature who is the organ through which the Scriptures speak or the p⟨r⟩etitions of men are uttered to God.

My brethren to be acceptable to God—to be of any use to *us,* to be anything but sounding brass & tinkling cymbal, the service of Sabbath must be a solemn reality. It will not do for sinful men to come up hither with all their sins on their heads & be present only in body & absent in mind nor to be present & merely passive without in their secret soul asking forgiveness of one sin or resolving on one struggle with appetite.

I am not a lover of morose religion I do not find it in the bible nor in reason You may be as full of joy as the doctrine of Immortality can make the soul but if you are conscious of any sin if you are conscious that the eye of God as it dwells on you here sees any thing hostile to him in your heart any enmity to your brother any delight in evil then the Sabbath should be a day of gloominess to you till you have thoroughly repented of your sin. Finally to know how to spend the Sabbath, fix your minds eye upon the Lord of the Sabbath Let him be in all your tho'ts

Him first, him last, him midst, & without end, & you shall be sure of guidance and right knowledge sure that the Sabbath will shed light & goodness on the other days of the week & be to your soul a sure prophecy of the everlasting Sabbath that God made you for hereafter.

May 15, 1831

Manuscript (revised version): Eleven sheets folded to make four pages each, and a single leaf between leaves 11 and 12 and included in the sewing; folios stacked, except for the sixth folio (which is nested in the fifth folio and included in the sewing), and sewn with white thread along the left margin; folio pages measure 25 x 20.2 cm; the single leaf measures 25 x 20.1 cm. A single loose leaf, 25 x 19.9 cm, lacking thread-holes, has also been found with the manuscript.

Lines	*Page 158*
Bible Text	Mark 7.27
4	multitude—, have
8	which the ⟨common⟩ laws
9	to ⟨refer to⟩ ↑indicate↓
11–15	all the ⟨laws⟩ precepts . . . ↑already↓ . . . omitted. Moreover ⟨in⟩ ↑(↓Exodus 16, 22–30↑)↓ . . . . Sinai, ⟨the S allusi⟩ distinct
16–17	this ⟨in the morning of the world⟩ ↑at an earlier period↓ . . . ↑implying↓ the pree⟨e⟩minence of
18–19	after a ⟨seven days⟩ week or period ↑of↓ . . . rain. ↑⟨4178 years ago.⟩ near . . . acc. our . . . computation↓ It is
24	a ⟨merciful⟩ ↑beneficent↓

	Page 159
3–6	Cause. ⟨As in the opinion of most philosophers⟩ ↑It . . . by ⟨the⟩ men . . . literal ⟨accou⟩ history or not, that↓ . . . . revelation, it seems
10	independant
19	dependant,
22–28	frame. ↑a purpose . . . the ⟨Former of our bodies.⟩ ↑Creator.↓↓ ¶ ⟨It⟩This purpose ⟨is violated⟩ of . . . temptation is ⟨aff⟩ held . . . on the ↑at↓tend⟨er⟩ant↑,↓ ⟨from⟩ but . . . dependants,

31–38   I ⟨know⟩ ↑have been told↓ . . . competition↑. I am . . . so,↓ [emen-
           dations in pencil] ↑it . . . mind↓ but if all . . . losers and . . . way, it
           his

Page 160

9   work⟨,⟩ enables
16–25   ↑then . . . that↓ . . . recording & ⟨bringing in⟩ ↑reducing↓ . . .
           ↑bodies & constellations in their↓ . . . objects ⟨that are familiar to
           the eye,⟩ ↑we . . . upon,↓ . . . leaf, ⟨counting⟩ ↑showing↓ the pores
           in ↑the firm texture of↓ . . . hair. ↑And↓ The telescope ↑does not
           more increase kno↓ brings down . . . into ⟨t⟩ an orrery; ↑than↓ The
           microscope brings
29–33   attend [end of page] attend . . . more ⟨close is⟩ his attention ↑is
           given↓ . . . what we ⟨constantly⟩ ↑habitually↓ . . . magnify ⟨the⟩
           ↑our↓ . . . importance. ⟨A⟩ It is
35   nay, ⟨can shut out the⟩ if
42   subjects ⟨about⟩ to
43   thinks ↑this↓

Page 161

3–4   some ⟨general⟩ habitual . . . should. ⟨Well⟩ now
9   disease every
14   runs ⟨again⟩ [end of line] against
19–20   which ⟨both⟩ ↑many↓ . . . But ⟨P⟩perhaps
26   that ⟨inestimable⟩ worth
28–29   Only by ⟨interposing⟩ arresting
31   only to diminished
36–37   principles ²{time to plant our foot . . . Crowd;} ¹{time to say No;}
           time
41–42   the ⟨ret⟩ oft-returning respite ⟨it has⟩ &

Page 162

5–6   a ⟨thousand⟩ hundred. ⟨Well⟩ here
7   rest⟨,⟩ not
12   ↑all↓ . . . him, ⟨has had⟩ two
14   has ⟨spent⟩ been
16   sloth. ⟨We have been v⟩ Tell
18   have ⟨all⟩ ↑each↓
21–23   talents, ⟨if⟩ ↑whether↓ . . . hid ⟨it⟩ ↑them↓ . . . spent ⟨it⟩ ↑them↓
           . . . provision. [end of page] [The following lines are inscribed in
           pencil between the conclusion of the first part of the sermon and the
           beginning of Part II:]
               ↑Resort to sermons but to prayers most
               Praying's the end of preaching O be drest
               Stay not for the other pin Why thou hast lost
               A joy for it worth worlds Thus hell doth jest
               Away thy blessings & extremely flout thee
               Thy clothes being fast but thy soul loose about thee

> Judge not the preacher for he is thy judge
> If thou mislike him thou conceivst him not
> God calleth preaching folly. Do not grudge
> To pick out treasures from an earthen pot
> The worst speak something good if all want sense↓

26 ↑1.↓ . . . ↑2.↓

28 Sabbath ⟨I⟩ ↑we↓ have ⟨shown⟩ ↑considered↓

32–34 ¶ ↑But . . . that↓ I choose this ⟨topic⟩ ↑subject↓ . . . conduct ⟨now,⟩ today,

36–37 ↑one of↓ whose customs ⟨slowly change fro⟩ we . . . change ⟨a⟩ ↑the deepest rooted↓

39 hour ⟨of this⟩, may

Page 163

3–5 ¶ ↑I have . . . institution we one . . . school↓

12–21 Hobbs . . . Rebellion." ⟨The Sabbath still more will teach men to be free even freedom by truth as Jesus pronounced it but will teach also the lesson of love.⟩ ↑{Insert X}↓ [On the facing page, a passage marked "X":] ↑Universities were the core of Rebellion ie ⟨w⟩ the . . . But ⟨the Sabbath still more will teach men to be free even freedom through truth. And⟩ ↑If a college . . . bondage↓ ⟨t⟩The Sabbaths . . . always ⟨making⟩ ↑stirring up↓ . . . Satan in plain ⟨English⟩ ↑words↓ . . . sincerely ⟨keeps⟩ ↑hallows↓ the Sabbath day ⟨holy.⟩. And therefore . . . than↓ [end of Insert "X"] But much more can be said for this than for . . . use. ⟨The Sabbath⟩ [end of page] ¶ The Sabbath

22 means. ⟨Sunday is the religious day.⟩ Useful

27–29 ↑all these↓ . . . secure ⟨in⟩to him . . . with ⟨a⟩ somewhat

30–36 But Reason ↑& Religion↓—in whose [addition rejected for sense] . . . creation. ⟨It teaches us that we have a longevity beyond that of mountains or sun or stars; that when convulsions of nature shall break up the surface of the globe, we shall renew an eternal youth; that whilst we look back to recent beginnings & to nothing on the one side, we behold heavens & earth forever new on the other. And why? On what foundation does it rear this hope? We are so constituted as to receive it The heart of a good man knoweth its maker & with gladness hear⟨s⟩eth his voice.⟩ ¶ And . . . ↑Reason & this↓ hope. ⟨The day not of a commemoration but of a hope.⟩ A day

37 alone ⟨ca⟩ happiness

42–(164)1 beneficence & ⟨that we are under his protection⟩ ↑of seeking him↓ ¶ ⟨Who that has a heart will not rejoice in beholding this day? Who will not feel his own want of these advantages which it offers or will not remember the good he has already derived from it. Who that will not welcome the day of hope to human nature, the resurrection of Jesus, and ⟨his⟩ ↑keep↓ the peaceful hours of prayer ⟨of reading⟩ of ⟨social worship⟩ ↑secret study↓ & go up gladly with the multitude of them that keep holy day to the sanctuary.⟩ ¶ These . . . Sabbath, Rest;

Page 164

4   selects ⟨his own⟩ what
14   Sinai ⟨where it is a single *positive* precept joined with nine *moral* precepts⟩ which
17   ↑or arbitrary↓
28   place ⟨rest⟩ derive
30–31   ↑How . . . shalt↓
33–34   self govern- [end of page] ⟨to his Son, to the angels, to wise & good men⟩ he
36   let the ⟨value⟩ duty

Page 165

4   that /is/ appears/
7   would ⟨result from⟩ ensue
8–9   once ⟨for a time⟩ ↑in Christendom↓;
10–13   terror; In ⟨the⟩ days . . . ↑which way soever↓ . . . murdered men ⟨At that time to get rid of the Sabbath ten days were assigned to the week⟩ ↑That . . . away.↓
14   restored it ⟨in⟩to
19–20   what a ⟨s⟩ well . . . to a ⟨circus⟩mountebanks
26–27   ↑earthly↓ . . . consulting. ↑for?↓
29   ↑the ichneumon↓
31   until they [At this point in the manuscript, the following is inscribed at the bottom of the page, upside down relative to the remaining inscriptions:] ¶ ⟨There are three general uses of the Christian Sabbath, Rest; the new & better direction given to the thoughts; &, a religious education.⟩ [end of page] ⟨have⟩ have painfully
35   nature. ⟨It⟩ *Dum*
38–39   behind you ⟨no store⟩ no provision ⟨from⟩ ↑of↓ reason for your child⟨,⟩↑?↓

Page 166

1–3   morality, ⟨ser⟩ public . . . against ⟨atheism⟩ ↑a general profligacy↓
5–7   schools as ⟨was done once before⟩ ↑a foreign . . . already↓ of ⟨the⟩your . . . spot where ⟨his name⟩ ↑it↓
9–10   you ⟨a far off⟩ ↑an alarming↓ . . . then ⟨do⟩ put
11   ↑to be↓
12   desireable
17–18   now ⟨speak⟩ say . . . us. ⟨Rest & Public Worship are two of its principal purposes. Of the first I shall speak presently⟩ From
21–22   increasing ⟨respect⟩ ↑honor↓
24–25   respects; ⟨first⟩ 1. in . . . services. 2.
31   ↑should show↓
34   is it ⟨the⟩ on
40–41   Or if ⟨they come once in⟩ ↑all agree that↓ the Sabbath ↑worship is to be kept,↓

Page 167

1   is ⟨often⟩ ↑sometimes↓

4	But ⟨worship⟩ public
17	↑not only↓
19	begins ⟨to be too wise for God⟩ to
37	employment of the ⟨h⟩ other
43	into /light/action/,

Page 168

2	all ⟨on which⟩ ↑that↓
3–4	blest him . . . receives. ¶ ⟨But a⟩All cannot

[The following is inscribed on the loose single leaf found in the manuscript. Its theme, Sabbath rest, clearly relates to a major theme developed in Sermon CXVI, yet because the leaf lacks thread-holes, its actual service in either the first or second part of the sermon is doubtful:]

¶ It seems to me of little importance what ⟨are the⟩ is a man's vocation, what are his advantages, what is his society, so that only he have the opportunity & the habit of occasional self communion. A man—a young man, a young woman,—must sometimes be at home, at home from the world, at home from even their nearest friends, at home in the secret chapel of their own ⟨thoughts⟩ ↑mind↓. The soul is hardly yet entitled to be called a soul, that does not sometimes give account of itself to itself and quite aloof from conversation, from custom, from the routine of daily action, ask and answer the question What manner of person am I? What does ⟨t⟩all this life I have been leading amount to? Whither do I drift in this great sea of time? Give me leisure for this scrutiny and I have the right & the power to entertain all noble thoughts all heroic purposes, to cleanse & hallow a Temple for Almighty in my breast. Give me leisure & awake in me the will to this reckoning, & it seems to me indifferent how my other days are spent, whether in turning over books or ploughing in the field whether in casting the pages of a ledger or in wielding the hammer & the axe. And herein I see the value of the Sabbath Day.

Sermon CXVII

Manuscript: Five sheets folded to make four pages each, a single leaf laid in between leaves 3 and 4, a single leaf between leaves 4 and 5 included in the sewing, a single leaf laid in between leaves 6 and 7, two separate leaves between leaves 9 and 10 included in the sewing, and a single leaf following leaf 10 included in the sewing, making 32 pages in all; folios are stacked and sewn with white thread along the left margin; folio pages measure 25.1 x 20.2 cm, and with the exception of the single leaf between leaves 6 and 7, which measures 24.6 x 20.2 cm, single leaves measure 24.2 x 20.2 cm.

A number of lengthy added passages occur on the inserted leaves, usually in conjunction with the cancellation of proximate original matter. The handwriting in these additions is distinctively smaller than that of the original text. Evidence from the dates supplied at the end of the MS ("29 May, 1831" and "23 Sept, 1832") suggests that the revisions were done for the second delivery of the sermon, and are therefore rejected in the clear text. Some original text may have been lost in the course of revision at the conclusion.

[The following variant opening, for a later delivery of the sermon, occupies MS pp. 1–2, while the remainder of the first folio is blank:]

↑CXVII

Forasmuch then as Christ hath suffered for us in the flesh,
arm yourselves likewise with the same mind. 1 Peter. 4. 1.

Exhortations of this sort abound in the epistles of St Peter & St Paul. The⟨y⟩ ↑early
Christians↓ were champions & sufferers for righteousness sake. Their lives & liberties
as well as their reputation & comfort were in hourly danger. They cheered each other by
generous sentiments, by the example of Christ, & by the hope of Gods grace to stand
fast—to withstand in the evil day—& to endure to the end. They drew copiously &
easily from their faith these ⟨exalted⟩ ↑high↓ sentiments—to rejoice in persecution to
count human judgment a small thing, to appeal always to the sentence of God.

And nothing shows more plainly the suitableness of Christianity to our mortal condition than its power to sustain & reward these men. Those days of danger & blood are
passed. But the necessity of this Comforter is none the less. The evils of life are only
changed in form. Each of us has his own cross to bear, & we need ↑to be armed with↓
the same mind. Every day teaches us the instability of ⟨worldly⟩ ↑earthly↓ good. The
connexions we would have formed with those whom God seemed to have made to
impart happiness are prevented by some ⟨frightful casualty⟩ ↑rude disappointment↓
The connexions we have formed, just as they begin to minister delight, are snapped
asunder by death, or those which seemed to promise as fairly are soured by unexpected
discords. This is the condition of human life The very prosperity of the proud is
promoted by a decay of the faculties loss of the property or death of his friends. And if
we stop at the outward facts, it is certainly true that the earth is the graveyard of our
ancestors & wherever we go ourselves we only walk in a circuitous path towards our
own tomb.↓

[The original opening of the sermon, the Bible text and first paragraph has been
canceled, on MS p. 5, the first page of the second folio. The sermon number has been
excised by a small semicircular tear at the center top of the page.]

Lines	Page 169
Bible Text	/ Take . . . Eph. 6. 13. / Not with eye service as men pleasers but as yᵉ servᵗs of X doing will of God from heart 6.6/ [variant in pencil from Ephesians 6:6 probably added for later delivery] ⟨[two or three illegible words]⟩
1–13	¶ ⟨⟨The connexions of life are so short & uncertain. A great deal of life is a sort of aenigma to us. The instability⟩ ↑Sentiments . . . judgment ⟨an⟩ ↑a↓ . . . condition↓ . . . have ⟨formed⟩ ↑made↓ to impart ⟨peace of mind⟩ ↑happiness↓ [last emendation in ink over pencil] . . . life. ⟨t⟩The very . . . ↑a↓ decay . . . friends. ↑And . . . that↓ The earth . . . we ⟨walk⟩ ↑go↓ ourselves ⟨it is only⟩ ↑we only walk in↓ [last emendation in ink over pencil] . . . tomb.⟩ [end of page] ¶ Observe
15–16	compliment, ⟨he is⟩ life . . . deceived. into
18–20	where the ⟨glory⟩ ↑cheerful light↓ . . . ↑in the faces of↓
20–24	man ↑hears . . . or↓ meets . . . always ⟨n⟩ cherished, & seems to ⟨chain⟩ ↑fix↓ him ⟨down⟩ to

2–14   bitterness, [end of page] ¶ [The following cancellation is rejected as a
        late emendation:] ⟨There is . . . its influence.⟩ [The following para-
        graphs were added on the first of the inserted leaves in place of the
        canceled paragraphs for later deliveries of the sermon:] ¶ ↑In short
        there is no external good which is not exposed to these injuries & not
        only exposed but ⟨attacked⟩ ↑wounded↓ by some of them. ¶ Since
        ⟨this is so,⟩ ↑these calamities exist,↓ it would be of great service to
        ⟨us⟩ ↑men↓ if they would ⟨settle⟩ ↑⟨write⟩ record↓ it as a settled fact
        in their minds, that this is the invariable order of human life; that this
        is what, if they live, they are to expect; ⟨it is the property of⟩ ↑that
        evil floats in↓ the air ↑& grows in the grain↓ & impregnates the
        waters of this world; it is the elementary form of all benefits⟨:⟩. And
        then, secondly, that they would inquire in what manner the religion
        which has come from God proposes to prevent or to cure these
        calamities. It must be a remedy or a consolation, or men will say—'if it
        cannot remove or console them what is religion for?' ¶ And this is my
        object in the present discourse, to consider what may justly be
        expected of religion what it actually teaches us in reference to these
        evils. in what manner it ⟨inculcates the duty of⟩ ↑animates us to↓
        endurance. ¶ I know it can do something in both ways—something to
        remove, something to console the evils we suffer. It can do much
        more, I apprehend, for us than men are willing to believe, though not
        ↑perhaps↓ precisely in the way in which men expect it to serve them.
        Thus it is a gross error & yet a very popular one to suppose that
        religion can console bad men; that in the hour of great affliction
        Religion can administer comforting thoughts to a heart not governed
        by its influence.↓

3   external ⟨condition⟩ ↑good↓ . . . these in⟨roads⟩↑juries↓

4   very ⟨ancient⟩ old

6   apply ⟨the⟩ whatever

8–9   do some⟨thing⟩ in both ways. ↑to remove or console↓

10–11   more I ⟨believe⟩ ↑apprehend↓ [emendation in ink over pencil] . . .
        believe ⟨and they do not use it in the right way. Men⟩ ↑though . . .
        them.↓

12–13   console ⟨irreligious⟩ ↑bad↓ . . . affliction ⟨for the loss of a friend⟩
        Religion

15   ↑an↓

16–17   give ⟨very different⟩ ↑more correct↓ . . . by ⟨placing⟩ giving

20–21   Gods will ⟨is always done.⟩ ↑is a benevolent . . . done.↓ ¶ ⟨b⟩But
        ⟨not⟩ it

25–29   spiritual eye. ¶ [The following paragraphs were added on inserted MS
        p. 11 for later deliveries of the sermon:] ↑To see this rightly, it is
        necessary that we should consider that ⟨the⟩ as far as we can discern
        the object of our Creator in setting us here, that object is, the
        formation of our character; not that we should make a fortune; not
        that we should get a recipe for comfort; not that our assistance is
        anywise necessary to him in carrying on his glorious beneficence, but

simply he has placed us here for our discipline. ↑& know↓ that these
evils of which we complain, neither come by chance nor by destiny
nor for torment, but are our ²tutors & ¹nurses to convey instruction
that could no otherwise be gained ¶ But ⟨the⟩ ↑it is our↓ [emendation
in pencil] great evil ⟨the pressing danger under which we labor⟩
↑from which our innocence is always in danger,↓, is, that we ⟨are a⟩
recognize this fact so slowly, that we are always grasping at temporal
good in ⟨contradiction to⟩ ↑violation of↓ the voice of conscience.
Brethren we do not rely boldly enough upon the principles within
when they are opposed to some vulgar gratifications.↓ [end of page] ¶
⟨Among these constantly returning /occasions/sources/ of regret⟩
↑To leave . . . case,↓ . . . felt ⟨be⟩I believe . . . character & ⟨is very
seld [end of line] &⟩long continues . . . & ↑whose influence↓ [in
pencil] . . . wholly ⟨outgrown⟩ ↑got rid of↓,

32   right↑,↓ [addition in pencil]

33–39   look for. [With the exception of one cancellation, the emendations in
the following sentence, as well as the revised version inscribed on
facing MS p. 12 belonging to the second inserted leaf, are rejected as
late emendations:] ⟨↑In poems and novels↓ What is called ⟨in⟩
'poetical justice' ⟨in poems & novels⟩ ↑is required↓, the giving good
fortune to the good, & bad fortune to the bad, is uniformly ↑sup-
posed to be↓ distributed ⟨in⟩ with great accuracy by young people in
⟨forming⟩ ↑making↓ their ⟨notions of their⟩ choice of ways of life.⟩
[On the preceding page:] ↑{In poems & novels what is called 'poetical
justice' is always required; that is, we require that good fortune should
be given to the good & bad fortune to the bad. If this is not done we
say the moral is bad. Now what we require in the romance young
persons uniformly suppose may fairly be expected in real life. In
↑making↓ their choice of ways of life they act on this presumption.}↓
Every young person who re- [end of page] ⟨deliberates upon good⟩
↑is forming↓ . . . who ⟨trans⟩↑en↓acted their

40–41   ↑his↓ magnanimity; health for ↑his↓ temperance, wealth for ↑his↓
industry.

Page 171

4   ↑in like manner↓

6–16   suitable reward. [The additions and, except for its internal emendations, the cancellation that follow are rejected as late emendations.
The following line was added for later deliveries of the sermon to
effect a transition between this paragraph and the addition that
immediately follows the canceled material:] ↑Experience will read
him another lesson.↓ ¶ ⟨{Religion teaches . . . in heaven.} ¶ {⟨We
are⟩ ↑Christianity teaches us↓ . . . experience.}⟩ ↑It will teach him
that↓ We must not expect

21–22   ↑in your . . . intercourse with, all,↓

23   affinity. ⟨Can you find⟩ ↑In . . . reckon↓

25   ↑persons↓

27–29   countrymen? ¶ [The following addition, on the recto of the third

inserted leaf (the verso is blank), is rejected as a late emendation:]
↑Instead of esteeming it much to discharge those duties from which
you cannot escape, remember that it is a rule in morals that the merit
of a good action is th greatest, when the motive to do it is most feeble
in the presence of the most commanding motives to the contrary. The
merit is measured by the difficulty encountered↑.↓ ⟨not⟩ Furthermore
it is to my mind one of the most noble & one of the most thrilling
truths in moral science, that we gain the strength of the temptation we
resist. The savage in the Sandwich Islands believes that when he
overcomes & slays an enemy the strength & courage of that enemy
passes into him. The soul instructed by God knows that whenever it
resists & overcomes a temptation, it becomes stronger by the strength
of that temptation. Not in a remote heaven not in a future hour but in
the hour & moment of the contest the compensation the power & the
peace of God enter into & possess him.↓ [end of MS p. 17] ¶ ↑It is
. . . globe.↓

31   with ↑an↓other

35–39   understood. ↑There is . . . too honest' [addition to this point in ink
                    over pencil] The biography . . . you that↓ In proportion as ⟨you⟩
                    ↑they have↓ raise↑d↓ ⟨yourself⟩ ↑themselves↓ . . . virtues ⟨you⟩
                    ↑they have↓ outstrip↑ped↓ the affections of ⟨your⟩ ↑their↓ fel-
                    lowmen. ⟨You⟩ ↑If . . . they↓

                                        Page 172

1–3   man ⟨an⟩ ↑a↓ mind . . . common ⟨run⟩ measure of humanity ⟨is⟩
                    ↑would be↓ solitary. He ⟨does⟩ ↑would↓ . . . he ⟨does⟩ ↑would↓ . . .
                    he ↑would↓ see⟨s⟩ that

7   of ↑the↓ good

7–10   ↑very↓ . . . purpose↑s↓

11–16   commentary ⟨which fell⟩ upon . . . from the ⟨great⟩ ↑virtuous↓ . . .
                    ↑in the midst . . . inquired↓ [addition in ink over "in midst of speech"
                    in pencil] . . . wrong?" ⟨he inquired.⟩ ¶ The ⟨good man⟩ ↑bene-
                    factor of his sphere↓ [emendation in pencil] . . . embrace↑s↓ . . . men,
                    ↑{↓& lives

17   him ⟨n⟩ or

20–32   slew. ¶ ⟨Now in view of these facts religion teaches us two great
                    lessons applicable to the experience of every mind. ¶ The first is⟩ ↑In
                    view . . . stead⟨a⟩ily this ⟨fact⟩ duty . . . these ⟨very⟩ things, . . . to
                    ⟨these⟩ outward pleasures. ¶ ↑It teaches you↓↓ . . . virtue; ⟨T⟩to
                    count . . . enough. ⟨You act alone.⟩ I speak . . . from ⟨a⟩ generous
                    . . . else ⟨th⟩ acts from such principles. ⟨You would act alone.⟩
                    When . . . but ⟨very⟩ would . . . impracticable ⟨refinements⟩
                    ↑precepts↓

33–34   love ⟨beyond⟩ and . . . ↑viz. to . . . men ⟨carried⟩ ↑carried↓↓

38   admire. ⟨b⟩But you say, '⟨n⟩Nobody

                                        Page 173

2   ↑to enable . . . sympathy,↓

4   *against* ↑it,↓
6–17   storm. [The following notations are inscribed at the bottom of the
             page:] ¶ 'But no one will estimate your conduct;' if no one else doth,
             God will. ¶ "In whose pure sight all virtue doth succeed." [end of
             page; the following cancellation and addition are rejected as late
             emendations:] ¶ ⟨Feel a confidence . . . less flattery.⟩ [end of MS
             p. 24; the following added matter is inscribed on the two consecutive
             inserted leaves:] ¶ ↑You cannot make a sacrifice however little,
             however great, to your sense of right, that shall go unrewarded. He
             that made the world & the soul of man & wrote his law therein, hath
             done his work too well, hath guarded his divine government too
             surely, than that any creature should come by loss by keeping his
             commandment. But the gain is to be measured by ⟨the truth⟩ ↑true
             scale↓ & not by ⟨error⟩ ↑a false one↓. You are here to form your
             character, & not to enjoy sensual pleasure & your true reward ⟨real
             gain⟩ is ⟨of that kind⟩ ↑corresponds to the task↓. By every sacrifice
             you make to duty not your reputation, not your present ease, but your
             moral & intellectual strength are increased; you are not made a more
             prosperous but a more noble & useful being. ¶ ↑This is a truth that is
             not to be confirmed by authority. It is attested by every mans soul.↓
             [addition in pencil] ¶ I rejoice to add from the most popular writer of
             our times a pleasing testimony to the same truth. "I think," he says, "a
             character of a highly virtuous & lofty stamp is degraded rather than
             exalted by an attempt to reward virtue with temporal prosperity. Such
             is not the recompense which Providence has deemed worthy of suf-
             fering merit & it is a dangerous & fatal doctrine to teach young
             persons ⟨(the most common readers of romance)⟩ that rectitude of
             conduct & of principle are either naturally allied with or adequately
             rewarded by the gratification of our passions or attainment of our
             wishes. In a word, if a virtuous & selfdenied character is dismissed
             with temporal wealth, greatness, rank, ⟨(—)⟩ the reader will be apt to
             say, 'Verily, virtue has had its reward.' But a glance on the great picture
             of life, will show that the duties of self denial, & the sacrifice of
             passion to principle, are seldom thus remunerated; & that the internal
             consciousness of their high minded discharge of duty produces on
             their own reflexions a more adequate recompense in the form of that
             peace which the world cannot give or take away." (Ivanhoe.)↓ ¶ ⟨The
             next lesson⟩ The difference
11   pride persist . . . vulgar ⟨way⟩ ↑road↓
18   this is ⟨the⟩ ↑a↓
20   prospects. [The following addition, which extends onto the last single
             leaf, is rejected as a late emendation. The uncharacteristic abruptness
             of the ending that results suggests that the MS may have once included
             a last folio, now lost, which contained the original ending that this
             addition was designed to replace for the second delivery.] ↑Virtue is
             best, because it is good forever. ⟨Vice⟩ The pleasures of sin are really
             poor pleasures now, & will presently come to nothing. Let me
             beseech you then brethren to enter into the divine plan, to cooperate

with God in the saving of your souls, to consider attentively the apparent purpose of our life, & seeing that the state of the soul & not the circumstances of the body constitute real happiness, let us learn to look at the evils that menace us, as our real friends. Let us borrow faith & patience from the benevolent sufferings of Jesus Christ & forasmuch as he hath suffered for us, let us arm ourselves also with the same mind. Let us feel a confidence in good & generous sentiments & be assured if you do not desert them, they will never betray you. ⟨Feel receive b⟩Believe the sublime prophecy that comes from within you when ever you prefer a principle to a temptation. It speaks to you of a sublime an omnipresent Friend. It ⟨predicts to you⟩ ↑foretells↓ immortality. Let us take then a wise survey of the ground before us. Expect privations; expect opposition; expect poverty; expect disease; expect death. Lay yourself out for these things & long before trouble comes whilst your friends smile kindly upon you make up your mind to be no fair weather friend to your friends to your master to your God, but one who shall endure when he is tried, who is unshaken & immoveable because he does not rest upon mutable men but upon the rock of Ages.↓ ¶ [The following notation in pencil:] ↑In yᵉ daily conflicts with temptation ⟨as well⟩ ↑not less than↓ as in serious questions of duty accustom yourselves to rely generously on a principle↓

Sermon CXVIII

Manuscript: Six sheets folded to make four pages each; folios stacked and sewn with white thread along the left margin from which the first and sixth folios have torn away; pages measure 25 x 20.3 cm.

Lines	Page 174
Bible Text	nigh ⟨un⟩to . . . nigh ⟨un⟩to
2–4	illustrate & ⟨perhaps⟩ establish the doctrine /that spiritual influences are reciprocal/yᵗ influences of God upon yᵉ human mind neither given nor withholden without cause/ [variant in pencil rejected as a late emendation]; ⟨that the gifts of God⟩ ↑to show that↓ . . . ↑moral↓
14	knoweth ⟨o⟩the
15	bestowed. [End of MS p. 2. MS p. 3 contains only a quotation from Romans 1:28, inscribed as an insert:] ↑X {'And even as they did not like to retain God in their knowledge, God gave them over to a reprobate mind,'—}↓ [MS p. 4 blank. MS p. 5 begins in midsentence, indicating the loss of some text:] exertion
17	↑receiving↓
22	dishonest ↑& intemperate↓ & [rejected addition in pencil]

	Page 175
4–6	pay him. ⟨↑I believe↓ The sun . . . there. ↑It shall remove all darkness & the Lord God shall be the light thereof↓⟩ ⟨↑And so in every less degree. You may always judge of the nearness of your mind to God—

of the likeness between your will & his will by the distinctness of your
faith in Him.↓⟩ [additions and cancellations in pencil; rejected as late
emendations]⟩ And ⟨h⟩He

7	him & ⟨not⟩ ↑never↓
8–9	endeavours. ↑When the ancient prophet relates↓ God [rejected addition in pencil] . . . uprightness↑,↓ the purity↑,↓ [commas in pencil]
16	is ⟨answered⟩ ↑given↓ . . . ↑Liberty.↓
29–31	themselves. ⟨The⟩ Almighty . . . purchased. ⟨You can only will but that little all you must pay.⟩ All that you have ↑it is true,↓
35–38	Prayer. ⟨↑{↓I have . . . VI ⟨Ma⟩Chap. . . . importance & that . . . here.↑}↓⟩ [brackets in pencil; cancellation rejected as a late emendation]

Page 176

5	petition, & ⟨⟨declares⟩ makes⟩ ↑introduces↓ . . . *forgive* ⟨our⟩ *the*
7–9	import ⟨intent⟩ of our prayer. ↑I hope . . . by it.↓
10–12	↑to God↓ . . . *them.* Enter . . . am.'
15–16	↑This . . . meaning.↓
17	mean, ⟨'⟩*Remit*
22–23	It is /to decorate the person/taking . . . skin/ when a ↑mortal↓
26–27	sin ↑⟨through⟩ ↑by means of↓ your . . . remove sin↓
32	↑part of↓ . . . ↑& difficult↓
40	men—↑no way↓
41	of man. calling
41–(177)1	is ⟨his⟩ the

Page 177

9–10	it is the ⟨most important⟩ a practical truth ↑of . . . any↓
11	truth. ⟨It amounts⟩ For
14–16	in hell ⟨it will not do for us to slight actions & thots which God regards.⟩ ↑then . . . hell.↓
17	us. ↑If as has been stated that the forgiveness of sins must always depend.↓ We [rejected addition in pencil]
19–20	stop. ↑A ⟨A revival of very⟩revival of religion in one man or in a community may always be sought & found, may be at any hour checked or promoted.↓ ["A revival of very" in pencil; addition rejected as a late emendation] ¶ And
21–24	only appre⟨ciate⟩↑hend↓ the ⟨fact⟩ ↑truth↓ . . . first ⟨lifting of our wil⟩ upward . . . guide ↑us↓,
26	by /God/prayer/. [rejected variant in pencil] It gives ⟨a value to prayer⟩ an
31	¶ There ⟨is one⟩ ↑are two↓ objection↑s↓ & but ⟨one⟩ ↑two↓ that occur⟨s⟩ to
34–35	dependant . . . dismissing th⟨e⟩at
37	it is ⟨a⟩essential

Page 178

| 4 | ↑personal↓ |
| 5–7 | another. ⟨Then continually are we reminded of one sovereign will |

that ⟨placed us in ⟨different⟩ circumstances how different!⟩ ↑ordered the varieties of human condition↓ Does the Atheist say, What operation have you left for God?⟩ ↓Does . . . make ourselves↓

10   ¶ ↑Or . . . form.↓

13   friends ⟨in⟩great

15–16   temptations. ⟨Did not⟩ Will . . . part in ⟨his⟩ the

23   ↑It . . . have.↓

24   ↑good thing↓

25–30   reap. ¶ ⟨Therefore, brethren, I exhort you to make with me a ⟨d⟩careful self application of this command. Draw nigh to God & he will draw nigh to you. In our studies in our trade in our conversation in our charity in our recreation in our privacy, let us draw nigh & nigher to God. It is the only happy the only safe way.⟩ [cancellation in pencil; addition that follows in ink between the lines in pencil] ↑Therefore, . . . safe way.↓

[The following variant ending for a later delivery of the sermon is inscribed after the conclusion:] ↑Let me exhort you if you are slumbering in a foolish belief that because God is merciful he will save you when he pleases ↑without your effort↓, to consider whether he feeds you when he pleases without any exertion of your own. If you should act a single day on that presumption you would perish. If you act on the expectation that he will save you, make you wise without your /labor/reflexion/, or useful without your labor, or holy without your /labor/prayers/, or happy without your /labor/obedience/ you will be lost undone. Work out saith the Apostle Work out your own salvation with fear & trembling.↓ [Philippians 2:12]

Sermon CXIX

Manuscript: Four sheets folded to make four pages each, two single leaves between leaves 2 and 3 included in the sewing, and a single sheet folded to make four pages containing Insert "A" (recto of first leaf), included in the sewing but now torn away; folios stacked and sewn with white thread along the left margin; folio pages and single leaves measure 25 x 20.2 cm, and pages of folio containing Insert "A" measure 17.4 x 20.2 cm.

[Above Bible text:] ↑[two illegible words] Salem↓ [addition in pencil]

Lines   *Page 179*

3–7   attention. ↑{Insert A}↓ [On the recto of the first leaf of the loose folio, a passage marked "A":]

                                 ↑119

              {1. I propose . . . ¶ 2. I propose . . . ¶ 3. to show . . . nature.}↓

8   ↑it may be asked↓

10–12   commandment ↑to t⟨o⟩he Jews . . . mankind↓ . . . me.' ↑or as Jesus declares it↓ "Thou shalt ⟨have⟩ love

15   every [end of page] ⟨kn⟩ every man's

17–20   ¶ We ⟨e⟩ repine . . . ↑saw . . . misfortune↓

                                Page 180

2   will ⟨say⟩ with

5–6   ↑only make . . . tribulation↓

11–29   ↑There . . . obedience.↓ ¶ Now ⟨how⟩ what . . . character? ¶ ⟨The
bible presents ⟨us with a person who calls⟩ him⟨self⟩ ↑to us as
declaring himself↓ the Son of God—the Saviour of the World who
wrought miracles & rose from the dead & promised immortal life to
all who should keep his Commandments. ⟨Now⟩ ↑But↓ why should I
love & obey him? ⟨If he⟩ ↑What is it to me that he↓ exhibited
wonderful power over nature, & over men, & over himself,—⟨if⟩
↑that↓ he was predicted beforehand & raised from the dead ⟨what is
he to me or I to him? What have I to do with Nazareth, or the Jews or
miracle or prophecy?—⟩ ["what is . . . prophecy?—" canceled in
pencil] ↑What has yᵉ mind yᵗ comes into being in these last days ↑the
prophecy↓ ["the prophecy" added in pencil] I answer it instructs me
of my duty ⟨& my love⟩ to God. As I read his life & listen to his
word I find that my love to God binds me ⟨to a love⟩ ↑involuntarily↓
to love his son.↓ It is not that he was predicted for ages, or announced
by angels, or clothed with power, but that he identified himself with
the law of God;—because he did not come in his own name; because
he made himself nothing, & God everything; ⟨but⟩ was clothed with
the power, & spoke the voice of God, because he speaks what is as
true in N. England as in ⟨Israel⟩ ↑Judea↓, in earth as ⟨to⟩ ↑in↓
heaven, to me as to him. I acknowledge his command-⟩ [end of page]
¶ ↑The bible . . . his command-↓[end of page]ments because

29–31   acknowledge the ⟨law⟩ voice . . . heart for

34–37   of ⟨his⟩ ↑Jesus↓ [emendation in ink over pencil] . . . ↑personal↓ claim
to my ⟨love⟩ reverence . . . conclusion. ¶ ⟨I ack ¶ If ye keep my
Commandments ye shall abide in my love.⟩ I suppose . . . will, ⟨that
he speaks a⟩ because

Page 181

2   God. ↑and he . . . love↓ [addition in pencil]

4–5   ↑servant . . . God, the↓ clearest ⟨Pr⟩Teacher of Gods truth. ⟨Let⟩
↑That↓

7–18   him /&/you will/ . . . his Son—⟨⟨you⟩ ↑he↓⟩ ↑Jesus↓ will . . .
beings, the ⟨chosen⟩ ↑faithful↓ . . . Men. the chosen . . . nations. ¶
⟨II. Another and very important fact is expressed or suggested by the
text, that⟩ ¶ ↑II. When we . . . virtue, the ⟨next⟩ sentiment . . . that↓
. . . preparation ⟨for⟩ to . . . us. ⟨I may here state the general law
that⟩ ↑I say . . . because↓ love is *mutual.* ⟨that⟩ it

20–22   in. ¶ ⟨I proceed to say⟩ ↑⟨a⟩And . . . than↓ that ⟨the⟩ obedience
. . . affection↑?↓

31–32   before ⟨Christ came as it was⟩ ↑they . . . precepts as↓ after↑wards.↓

32   every ⟨Commandment⟩ ↑rule of duty↓

33–38   forever. ⟨It is to say⟩ ↑They . . . to say↓ If . . . love you. ↑This is . . .
know him.↓ [addition in ink over pencil] ¶ ⟨{It is sometimes said Is
God so good as you represent—they why should the bible describe so
strongly his hatred of sin, his disapprobation of sinners. It would
rather seem that he should love them, & so I will not believe my

danger is so great as you declare it. I would rather believe that God will
love those who do not have goodness. ¶ But let it be considered that
⟨you ca⟩ ↑love must have↓ an object. You cannot love that which is not.
You cannot love that which is the proper object of hate. Goodness is the
proper object of love.}⟩ [canceled in pencil and ink] You

40–(182)1   more ⟨↑{↓than you can be said to love food which you never tasted
or↑}↓⟩ [brackets in pencil; passage canceled in pencil] than an ideot
. . . ↑or a deaf . . . sounds.↓ [ink over pencil]

Page 182

3–5   it; ⟨d⟩you . . . mind of [end of page] of . . . Jesus ⟨is⟩ hath
7   light ⟨poured⟩ ↑wasted↓
8–9   measure, the ⟨beauty of holiness is apparent⟩ ↑excellence . . .
reve⟨i⟩aled↓.
12   frames of ⟨mind⟩ ↑thot↓ that it ⟨was stranger to⟩ ↑never knew↓
16   ↑His . . . opened↓
17   understanding ⟨the greatness of his character⟩ ↑what . . . Christ↓.
20–21   such as ⟨Resist not⟩ ↑the submission to↓
24–29   ↑these↓ . . . a ²discriminating ¹rational . . . seeks to [end of page] to
. . . loves. ¶ ⟨Thirdly.⟩ ¶ III. . . . love ⟨ar⟩ are
30   them? ⟨Who ever kept⟩ ↑What man,↓
32   true that ⟨the better⟩ the first
35   not /thought of/ known to exist/ at first? ↑Thus↓ The [The addition
of "Thus" appears to eliminate a paragraph break at this point.]
36–(183)8   ↑if announced to a pagan↓ means ⟨one thing to⟩ [end of line] a
⟨⟨⟨Pagan⟩ ↑Jew↓⟩ ↑Pagan↓⟩—that he should ⟨not w⟩ have but one
idol⟨;—⟩ ↑whichever . . . god,—↓to . . . that his /appetites or his
passions or his affections/ children or his power or his property/ . . .
↑tends to↓ withdraw⟨s⟩ in . . . God. ¶ ⟨So it is with every Commandment.⟩ The precept . . . not to ⟨plunder his fellow men⟩ ↑pilfer↓.

Page 183

8   guilty of ⟨frauds which the law condemns⟩ ↑theft↓
22–23   Church↑? &↓ may . . . influences of ⟨h⟩His . . . be,—⟨the source
of⟩ ↑out of whom↓
28   health from [end of page] from

[Following the end of the sermon is an illegible word, heavily canceled, followed by
Emerson's bracket.]

Sermon CXX

Manuscript: Four sheets folded to make four pages each, and a single leaf between leaves
2 and 3 included in the sewing to replace a leaf torn out; folios stacked and sewn with
white thread along the left margin; folio pages and the single leaf measure 25 x 20.1 cm.

Lines   Page 184
Bible Text   ⟨The preparations of the heart in man—are from the Lord Prov 16.1.
¶ Commit thy works unto the Lord & thy tho'ts shall be established

16.3⟩ ¶ ↑⟨Have⟩ Hear . . . Prov. 22;—17–20 21 ⟨[one or two illegible numerals]⟩↓

3   knowledge. the search after truth,

4–5   ↑from N.T.↓ containing express recommendations ⟨I⟩ but . . . ↑commend inquiry.↓.

7–10   time and ⟨it is decl⟩ the truth . . . great ⟨liberator⟩ ↑Redeemer↓ . . . *free.* ⟨↑& no man can faithfully keep the Christian laws without finding his mind excited & improved to that degree as to raise an inextinguishable thirst for all truth↓⟩ ["& no . . . truth" in erased pencil] ¶ And

12–13   other; and /now/in . . . ever/ the products & the ⟨vehicles & tools⟩ ↑vessels↓ . . . *books,* ⟨enter into every house⟩ ↑treat of every subject↓

14   ↑and so active↓

15–23   ↑never↓ . . . arrive ⟨&⟩in . . . faculties at ⟨no⟩ a . . . was in the ⟨in⟩ foresight . . . Wisdom. ⟨They⟩ ↑Books↓ . . . ↑by which↓ in some sort is . . . acts. ⟨h⟩He

Page 185

7   —all, ↑are↓

8   ↑One of↓ The best advantage↑s↓ [additions in pencil]

10–11   How ⟨different in this manner⟩ ↑much . . . respects↓

12–13   ↑Perhaps↓ As . . . ↑are now↓ liv⟨e⟩ing

18–19   choice. [At the bottom of the page, the following false start for Sermon CX is inscribed upside down relative to other entries on the page:]

CX.

⟨Every good & every perfect gift cometh from above from the Father of lights with whom is no variableness nor shadow of turning   St James.

     It is a received opinion that no opinion can be received by any great number of men & reappear in different times & places without being founded in truth. It shows that the soil is fit for the plant.⟩ [end of page] ¶ But ⟨in⟩ a . . . particular ⟨attention⟩ ↑regard↓ to his ↑town↓

22–25   sages. ¶ ⟨I wish to speak of religious books⟩ ↑But . . . speak of ⟨certain wo⟩ religious . . . practice.↓ and . . . Scriptures.

28   could ⟨not equal.⟩ ↑never have afforded.↓

30–33   ↑simple &↓ consistent ↑record↑ed↓↓ [Emerson seems first to have written "record" as a variant for "account."] . . . book ⟨disposes⟩ persuades

37   books. ⟨These⟩ ↑Our sacred books↓

44–(186)1   ↑to us↓, . . . of ⟨o⟩solemn

Page 186

5   what ⟨wh⟩ was

12–13   ¶ ↑II But, . . . SS.↓

15   ears. ⟨B⟩ The

16–17   ↑As an . . . Xty↓ ⟨Let me⟩I quote

21–22   words, ⟨{⟩your feelings were expanded {& his . . . eyes—} so

27–28   ↑In . . . entertained↓

30	it, ⟨but⟩ ↑&↓ it
30–31	↑So . . . may be shown↓
31	ancient, ⟨&⟩ ↑it↓
34–35	from the '⟨Second⟩ ↑First↓ . . . ↑written about AD 150↓

Page 187

1–2	goodness we . . . wealth [end of page] "now
9	¶ ↑Passages . . . end.↓
10–12	passages—⟨first⟩ ↑1.↓ . . . men; ⟨& *secondly*⟩ ↑2.↓
16–17	called the ⟨im⟩Imitation
18	Scougal; ⟨{The Analogy of Natural & Revealed Religion by Bishop Butler}⟩ to . . . evidence⟨s⟩
20–21	strong & ⟨but⟩ candid mind, whose ⟨mind⟩ ↑opinion↓ . . . up ⟨I⟩ respecting
21–23	He ⟨will⟩ cannot . . . ↑which . . . work↓
31	↑little↓
32	are ⟨the⟩ his
34	proclaiming the ⟨divine⟩ ↑excellence &↓

Page 188

2–3	↑to which . . . T. A Kempis↓
9	Christ, ⟨but⟩ and
10–11	But ⟨it seems to me⟩ ↑I think↓ . . . so ⟨considered. Reflect⟩ ↑regarded. Consider↓ . . . Jesus ⟨he⟩ &
13	↑two↓
15–17	↑It is . . . Christ It ⟨speaks the⟩ breathes . . . world.↓
20–21	been ⟨anxious⟩ ↑willing↓ to present ↑fully↓ to you⟨r⟩ ↑this↓ consideration, ⟨this tho't⟩ that
27–29	us ⟨a sort of⟩ an . . . so ⟨no⟩ never . . . richer than.

[These notations are inscribed following the closing of the sermon:]
    See yᵉ passages in Advancement of Learning
            & in Seneca marked Books
    ↑I am tired of talking now the lust of talking is over & only want to excite the rest of the body & so quiet the lungs↓ [addition in pencil; written over the following in pencil:] pew no 1 D

Sermon CXXI

Manuscript: Four sheets folded to make four pages each, and two single leaves, the first between leaves 2 and 3, the second between leaves 6 and 7, included in the sewing; folios stacked and sewn with white thread along the left margin; folio pages measure 25.1 x 20 cm, and the single leaves measure 25 x 20.2 cm.

The lack of emendation in the manuscript strongly suggests that portions were revised and replaced. The manuscript further reveals two distinct sorts of inscription, an earlier one in lighter ink, occupying MS p. 1 and pp. 5–9, and a later one in darker ink and a generally smaller, more careful handwriting, occupying MS pp. 2–4 and pp. 9–20. The earlier inscription, itself a fair copy, apparently corresponds with the first delivery of the sermon, as evidenced by the hymn citations on MS p. 1. This inscription comprises the Bible text, the first paragraph, and the fifth through the middle of the eleventh paragraph, down to "character & providence" (see text, p. 191).

Lines	*Page 189*
10	'There is ⟨no other world⟩ ↑a spirit in↓

	Page 190
7	pleasing ⟨peace⟩ [end of page] peace
10	before. ⟨By thinking much, his thoughts become more to him.⟩ He . . . value; ⟨second that is to the improvement of his character⟩ for
15	exalted ⟨feelings⟩ ↑sentiments↓
21	present ⟨P⟩parental
35	to ⟨prove⟩ explain

	Page 191
8	than ⟨retaliation would give⟩ impurity
11	said '⟨t⟩Thou . . . I ⟨am⟩; Let
20–24	plain. ¶ {And . . . opened.}
34	better, We

	Page 192
6–7	Christianity ⟨is still the same⟩ upon . . . same [end of page] that
9–10	spiritually. ⟨The world has not made such progress as to learn to compare spiritual things with spiritual.⟩ ¶ For
13	eye↑.↓ ⟨& the ear⟩ The
16	spirits a⟨b⟩round
23	met⟨,⟩. Let
35–36	cooperation ⟨of⟩ ↑with↓
41	force; [end of page] ⟨that the separation of good & evil spirits⟩ is

	Page 193
5	to ⟨p⟩ appoint
12	↑insupportably↓
14–15	↑the benefactor↓ . . . would ⟨take the same⟩ seek
17	independant . . . place, ⟨& is⟩that
20	is the ⟨expectation⟩ ungrounded
22–23	conversation, ⟨↑{↓& the pistol of the suicide ↑from time to time↓ only adds new evidence to this gloomy mistake.⟩ ¶ In [bracket in pencil; cancellation in pencil and ink]
23	not ⟨now⟩ of
27	multitudes, who some
30	↑after death↓
34	to ⟨purify⟩ heal

	Page 194
7–8	for ⟨a⟩ heaven

12   ↑too,↓ . . . that ⟨we can only grow better by⟩ our own ⟨action⟩
              effort
15   known, ⟨we⟩ ↑&↓

Sermon CXXII

Manuscript: Five sheets folded to make four pages each, and a single leaf following leaf
10 included in the sewing; folios stacked and sewn with white thread along the left
margin; folio pages and single leaf measure 24.9 x 20.1 cm. Two sheets folded to make
four pages each containing a variant opening have also been found with the manuscript;
folios stacked and pinned (pin now missing); folio pages measure 24.9 x 19.5 cm.

[The following variant opening, which seems to refer to the crisis over the Bank of the
United States, was probably written for the sermon's second delivery, February 2, 1834,
at New Bedford. Further, Emerson's use of arabic numerals to identify the sermon in this
variant is consistent with the practice he developed after his resignation from the Second
Church. The revised opening was intended to replace the original Bible text and first four
paragraphs of the sermon.]

122

None of us liveth to himself & none of us dieth to himself
Let us therefore follow after things which make for peace &
things whereby one may edify another. Rom. 14 7 & 19

⟨The evils from which our community now suffers & the worse evils which we fear
cannot fail to awaken a more than ordinary attention to the⟩ In the worst seasons of
public or private distress the highest consolation is that which is to be derived from moral
considerations: because, if an evil which afflicts us came without cause, it may come
again or it may last forever; but, if we can see how we are ourselves the authors of our
own misfortunes ⟨we discern⟩ ↑there is then some hope↓ that they may be avoided in
future. Besides, if a man feels the dignity of his nature as a reflecting being, he will enjoy
amid the sorest trials a quiet delight in perceiving what rich resources remain to him in
his moral nature when his outward comforts are removed.

↑And so I trust↓ [addition in pencil] The evils from which our commercial community
now suffers & the anxiety which overspreads it from the fear of worse ↑will↓ ⟨can⟩not
[emendation in pencil] fail to awaken a more than ordinary attention to the moral causes
of such calamities. We hear enough & more than enough of the influence of individuals
of ↑the↓ monied institutions & of the government in producing the public distress. But
the primary cause, the character—the actions of all the individuals in the country,—that
great society of which we are a part & which made the government & made the monied
institutions & which breathes into them the breath of their life & determines the spirit in
which they shall be administered—this influence is quite overlooked in the discussion.
Yet is this the original all commanding influence on which whatever is good or evil in our
social estate depends.

Certainly, it is not for me & least of all in this place to express any opinion on this
particular question or impute blame to any party. But it is my duty to express my
conviction that ⟨it⟩ it is of much less consequence to determine ⟨to⟩ what error or crime
was the immediate occasion of the present suffering than it is to see the share which every

citizen has had remotely but efficiently in causing it. For neither the government nor the commercial institutions of the country stand alone they are neither selfcreated nor single handed. They were created by the people and are now supported each by ⟨great⟩ the sympathy of great masses of the people. Both the political & the commercial institutions were made by the people the people is composed of individuals & every individual has his full share of influence not by his vote only but by all the ways in which each of us acts on society in determining what the character of the government & what the rules & customs of the exchange shall be. It is ⟨as⟩ certain all the individuals taken together make up the community & it is just as certain that what is thot & done by that community is made up of what is thot & done by each of the members

Our great institutions then of every kind are necessarily only concentrated representations of the virtues & the vices which the individuals possess. We may see our own principles carried out in them. Each of the conflicting parties at this day ⟨m⟩charges the other with interested motives with that extreme & reckless selfishness which burns down its neighbors house to bake its own loaf. And is there not some colour for this mutual recrimination in what we see & know in private life. ⟨Is it any more than a natural exaggeration⟩ Can we not recognize something of ourselves in what we blame most harshly Is it any more than a natural exaggeration of that narrow self-love which we ↑ought↓ continually to blush for in our own dealings.

Therefore if we would apply the axe to the root of the tree is it not the surest way of reforming nations & restoring a prosperity that should be invulnerable in all time to come, ⟨woul⟩ to reform ourselves & begin life anew in obedience to principles which cannot mislead

⟨↑There can never be a virtuous community so long as the views of individuals upon practical questions are radically false↓ It becomes us to settle in our minds the limits of selflove & the love of our neighbor, to perceive ⟨in⟩the evil influence which selflove breathes into every act & thought, so that love is a name for almost all virtue & selfishness for almost all vice⟩ By the want of right feeling on this subject the sources of action are corrupted & all our views of this life & the next are coloured.

⟨I make⟩ ↑In further illustration & support of↓ these remarks, ⟨to⟩ ⟨↑I↓⟩ ⟨introduce to⟩ ↑I invite↓ your attention to some considerations upon the different view which is ordinarily taken of th⟨e⟩ose ⟨gifts of Providence⟩ ↑blessings of life↓ which are unequally distributed by ⟨Christianity⟩ the Christian & by men of the world /I wish to exhibit/A careful selfexamination will perhaps show us in ourselves/ [variant in pencil] the strong contrast that exists between the view that *is* taken, & that which *ought* to be taken It is the vulgar error to think every thing good as far as it benefits self. It is the true the Christian view to think every thing good as far as it benefits others.

[At the top right corner of MS p. 1 is the remnant of a strip attached with red sealing wax and bearing the inscription "us die"—clearly part of the first line of the Bible text as given in the variant opening. It was thus probably for the second delivery that the original Bible text, from Galatians, was canceled:] ⟨As we . . . Gal. 6.10.⟩

Lines	*Page 195*
2	because ⟨I th⟩ all . . . impression ⟨that⟩ that
6–7	kind. ⟨Men think⟩ In . . . work ⟨paid⟩ ↑done↓.
9	as⟨,⟩ when a man ⟨supposes⟩ ↑reads literally the text↓

11–12 it. ¶ ⟨Akin to this is the⟩ ↑There is a↓ [emendation in pencil] common error that ⟨is⟩ may

15–19 ↑I have . . . end↓ ↑with a malevolent.↓ [additions in pencil; apparently Emerson abandoned his intention of extending the addition] as . . . ↑originally↓ . . . poor ⟨partook⟩ were . . . ↑a↓ ⟨r⟩band

20 charitable ⟨meek⟩ [canceled in pencil] Paul

25–(196)1 theft ⟨who permits in himself the desire⟩ who . . . man,) ⟨tha⟩ a

Page 196

2 rich. ⟨¶Now the gospel surely does not countenance such But it is not only false⟩ And

4–11 *goodness* ⟨will necessarily make men happy⟩ *is* [Emerson first underscored "is" (italics here) and then underscored the whole phrase, leaving "is" underscored twice.] . . . proposition ⟨of⟩ how . . . contained in ⟨those few words⟩ that word 'goodness.' [Below this sentence at the bottom of the page the stray phrase "They will" is inscribed in ink.] ¶ ⟨Now this way of thinking not only shows wrong views of heaven ⟨but w⟩ false views respecting external⟩ ↑I have . . . now, ⟨not that I intend to⟩ for . . . respecting the↓

12–13 man, & /so/ the same thing is thot/ of other distinctions. I ⟨speak not now of what⟩ ↑deny not that other↓

15–16 opinions ⟨on which men live & act.⟩ ↑which . . . act.↓

18–20 Christians. ⟨Whereas⟩ ↑↑All this is contradicted by [addition thus far in ink over pencil] . . . Testament.↓ ⟨i⟩In . . . religion,↓ . . . every ⟨species of⟩ good ⟨distinction⟩ ↑thing you have↓ . . . to the⟨y⟩ individual

21–22 points. ↑This is the doctrine taught in the text that we do not live to self but to God & to render account to Him how we have edified one another. To consider this in three particulars. We dont live to self but to God & to render acct to him how we have edified one another consider this 3 ways↓ ["This . . . ways" added in pencil; "This . . . particulars." traced over in ink; addition rejected as a late emendation.] ¶ 1. Riches

24–25 spent. ⟨It is the⟩ ↑Receive . . . will↓ counsel⟨lor of⟩ the rich in possessi⟨on⟩ng ⟨it is the⟩ ↑&↓ satisf⟨action of⟩y the poor

29 can ⟨wall up⟩ ↑confine↓

29–31 ↑It . . . profuse↓

31 add ⟨d⟩to

32 This ⟨reaso⟩ fact

41–44 merchants. ⟨He s⟩ The Christian . . . buy⟨, to⟩. ↑If ⟨his⟩ he has wealth he↓ live↑s↓ in a /handsome/ well built/ house, ⟨to⟩he wear↑s↓ ⟨has⟩ good clothes ⟨&⟩he

44 better ⟨to purchase the labor⟩ to

Page 197

3–6 idle. ¶ ⟨But⟩ ↑But there . . . selfdenial.↓ the principle of Love ⟨must⟩ run↑s↓

7 that ⟨must be⟩ ↑is↓

7–8   'Shall I ⟨be⟩ do
10–12   who ⟨shuts⟩ affects . . . him ↑& by . . . selfish man↓.
13–15   life ⟨&⟩ ↑excludes . . . ↑social↓ enjoyment↑s↓ . . . them ↑as↓↓ . . .
           religion ⟨both act from the same sinful error; they are cowards &
           afraid to be measured, & they wish to keep their supposed advan-
           tages strictly to themselves. In pr⟩ ↑shuts . . . others.↓
19–23   ↑↑to↓ [addition in pencil] visit . . . hungry,↓ . . . is ⟨th⟩ borne . . .
           ↑& if others . . . them↓
29   has ⟨⟨yet withheld⟩ does⟩ yet . . . endow [end of line] the
39   here ⟨consi⟩ accounted

                            Page 198

3–5   the U. States. ↑Now . . . praiseworthy↓ Here . . . ↑he speaks of↓ a
           great power ⟨is⟩ as
7–8   ↑than any ↑other↓ ornament;↓ with no terror of ⟨any other responsi-
           bility⟩ ↑any other peril↓ [emendation in ink over pencil] to follow
           ⟨↑as consequent upon↓⟩ [emendation in pencil] its . . . merely
           ⟨losing it⟩ ↑that of its loss↓. [addition in ink over pencil]
11–12   men. ¶ ↑To gratify ones self.↓ ¶ This
19–20   kings & ⟨generals⟩ ↑²governors↓ & ¹presidents ⟨by title⟩ are
21   ↑do↓
23   ↑does↓
25   to ⟨live⟩ convert
28   have a [end of line] ⟨common⟩ action ↑that . . . else↓,
30–32   disease. ¶ [Emerson's notation in pencil:] ↑? I ⟨can't leap over⟩dont
           like these chasms in discourse↓ But there . . . least ⟨*more*⟩ [under-
           scored in pencil] arbitrary
37   *private,* ⟨*party*⟩ opinion of the hour, ⟨& the neighborhood⟩ ↑or the
           party↓

                            Page 199

2   not ⟨more⟩ ↑so much↓ . . . councils ⟨than⟩ as
5   greatest ⟨capacity of use⟩ ↑usefulness↓ [Emerson underscored the
           phrase "greatest capacity for use" and wrote "*ugly expression*"; all in
           pencil.]
7–8   Talents. ↑& is ↑to be↓ . . . truth.↓
10   in ⟨his⟩ ↑one's↓
12–14   why? ↑is it↓ . . . ↑from his fellowmen↓ . . . seeing ⟨farth⟩ by
18   sagacity ↑not will profit others but↓ will [addition rejected for sense]
20   being is ⟨little esteeme⟩ overlooked.
22   him ⟨for the good of his belly⟩ ↑as . . . delights↓,
23–25   ↑Learning, Talents,↓ Genius↑,↓—Wisdom . . . ↑excellent↓ [in pencil]
           . . . ↑more↓
27   becomes to [end of line] to
27–28   The ⟨more⟩ ↑greater↓
30–31   ↑to use . . . purposes,↓ . . . pottage ⟨for his belly⟩ that
35   but ⟨for⟩ as
37–38   ↑strength &↓

39   have↑.↓ ⟨ & ⟩ The
41–42   which the ⟨gospel⟩ ↑text↓ teaches / arises from the/is the import^ce
                . . . of the/ [variant in pencil]

Page 200

5–6   duty will / flow from this truth/be ever . . . minds/ [variant in pencil]

Sermon CXXIII

Manuscript: Six sheets folded to make four pages each; folios stacked and sewn with white thread along the left margin, from which the sixth folio has torn away; pages measure 20.1 x 24.9 cm. A strip (recto blank), 12.4 x 19.8 cm, containing a revised opening, is attached to MS p. 1 with red sealing wax.

[The following addition, found on the strip attached to MS p. 1, was evidently written for the second delivery, July 30, 1837, at East Lexington:]

↑A good man shall be satisfied from himself.

These words express a sentiment as full of delight as it is of truth, the ⟨self⟩sufficiency of goodness to the soul, or rather the sufficiency of the nature of man to make his happiness without addition from without when once it is under the direction of religious principle. I wish to present two topics to your consideration ⟨th⟩to which the sentiment may be naturally divided 1. That a man's knowledge of the truth shall be satisfied from himself 2. That a man's affections can be satisfied only by a good state of his own mind.↓

Lines   Page 201
1–2   ¶ ⟨A great . . . Church.⟩ One . . . obstinate ↑errors y^t prevail↓ in . . .
                is, ↑the opinion↓ that [The cancellation of the first sentence and the
                additions in the second are rejected as manifest accommodations for
                the substitute opening of the second delivery.]
4   reason, ⟨the⟩ religious
5–6   confidence↑.↓ ⟨to⟩ ¶ The
6–7   contained in ⟨⟨the⟩ whatever is⟩ the
9   this ⟨a great⟩ a
14–19   ↑the objectors . . . right,.↓ ⟨t⟩There is ⟨danger in⟩ always . . .
                questions. ⟨Meantime I think the truth on this question may be made
                plain to every candid person.⟩ ↑I shall . . . made↓ ¶ ↑1.↓ First [last
                addition rejected as late emendation]
20–22   ones'self, . . . study, to ⟨prove⟩ ↑verify . . . experience↓ ⟨the⟩
                [canceled in ink over pencil] ↑every↓ [addition in ink over pencil] . . .
                ↑in any . . . to↓
23–29   heart" not . . . own. ⟨Are you prepared to⟩ go all lengths with this
                sentiment—⟨Are you⟩ fully to trust . . . truth. ⟨↑You are a judge &
                ye only judge ↑⟨with⟩⟩ X↓↓ [emendations in pencil] ⟨Yes implic⟩
                [end of line] itly. ↑{Insert X}↓ [A passage marked "X" on the facing
                page to replace the following sentence added in ink over pencil and
                canceled in pencil:] ⟨↑You are a judge of the truth or falsehood of any
                proposition the terms of which you understand.↓⟩ ↑X {For . . .
                false.↓ ["For . . . see." added in ink over pencil; pencil layer has
                "receive" for "try to believe"]

Page 202

3   that this ⟨doctrine⟩ ↑/preaching/⟨contempt⟩ distrust of human
      reason/↓ . . . ↑so loud↓

7–9   God? ↑"lest . . . bright"↓ . . . good; will

14   worship, that ⟨the belief⟩ ⟨or⟩theology

16   ↑one↓

19   society he

23–24 him. ⟨To⟩ Yet it is not ⟨so⟩ important

24–25 ↑Jesus . . . prayer↓

26–27 ↑it *is* important↓ . . . from the ⟨a⟩ subserviency . . . ↑encourages
      . . . fear &↓

29–30 God ⟨without any intervention⟩ [canceled in pencil and ink] ↑and
      . . . came↓

33–34 himself. [The following addition is rejected as a late emendation:]
      ↑Let a man therefore prove all things, and hold fast that which is
      good. [I Thessalonians 5:21] Let him not use any duplicity with
      himself. Let him never fear to reject that view of God which his heart
      tells him is wrong believing that it is God in his heart who bears
      witness to Himself.↓ ¶ But

34–36 be ⟨safely⟩ [canceled in pencil] pressed . . . ↑that it may be safe,↓
      [ink over pencil]

37–40 man ⟨cuts off from his consideration⟩ [canceled in pencil and ink]
      ↑loses sight of↓ . . . ↑other↓ . . . manifestation of ⟨other⟩ power . . .
      moment he ⟨quit⟩ lets . . . becomes ⟨a n⟩ bundle

41   himself & ⟨grows⟩ ↑is↓

Page 203

6   without ⟨this medium of⟩ [canceled in pencil and ink] his

7–9   so h⟨e⟩is . . . unbelief. ¶ ⟨And hence the fear that men have of⟩ ↑It is
      . . . men fear↓

10–21 ↑This . . . text—"A *good* man &c A *good* . . . own↓ ↑This . . .
      check.↓ [last addition in pencil; below this sentence is the phrase
      "entire security" in pencil][2] To a man who sees . . . on God [1]To a man
      who does . . . knowledge. ↑He . . . God.↓ ¶ ↑I leave↓ [addition in ink
      over pencil] This doctrine ↑amou↓ [addition in pencil] ⟨↑{↓which
      ⟨would seem plain enough for it↑}↓⟩⟩ [brackets and inclusive can-
      cellation in pencil; "would . . . it" canceled in ink (effectively restor-
      ing "which")] amounts . . . end↑,↓ than to say↑,↓ [commas in pencil]
      ⟨↑{↓a man must use his own eyes to see↑}↓⟩ [brackets in pencil] God
      . . . faculties. ¶ ↑2.↓ [rejected as a late emendation] Akin . . . another
      ⟨po⟩ doctrine

27–29 creation. ⟨They feel as if they did not enough love & honor ⟨him⟩
      one whom God thus loves & honors.⟩ ↑The ⟨doctr⟩ opinion . . .
      Christ.↓ They derive /hence a greater incapacity to love him/from
      this . . . him/, & end perhaps in ⟨a⟩ ↑an open↓

32–33 affection. ⟨No person was ever loved by⟩ There . . . can ⟨engage⟩
      ↑force↓ . . . another mind. ⟨⟨If⟩Let God endow⟨ed⟩ his Son with
      what authority it pleases him⟩ The idea

39–(204)3   on you ⟨or expect that you should feel for him that personal regard
                 you entertain for one⟩ [end of page] ¶ ⟨As only yourself can be the
                 medium thro' which religious truth comes to your mind, so only
                 yourself must be the medium through which your affections flow. It is
                 in vain to command you to love Christ. It is not his office It is not his
                 glory it is his transcendant character & this can only be loved as any
                 character must be loved by likeness to it. It is impossible for avarice to
                 love generosity; it is impossible for lowliness to love pride or⟩ ¶ ↑It is
                 . . . his ⟨fame⟩ ↑renown↓, . . . For ⟨whilst you can⟩ consider . . .
                 likeness, whilst . . . good.↓

                              Page 204
8–11   language of N. T. . . . him Christ . . . God till . . . appear We
12–13   Christ ¶ ⟨Why is this⟩ Thus,
20   gratification ⟨As⟩ But
22–23   wicked. [end of page] ¶ Let ¶ [The following notation is added, in
                 pencil, beside the false start of the paragraph:] ↑"When I am unhappy
                 I am untrue to my principles."—Richter↓ [cf. *JMN* 6:94] ¶ Let us
24–25   ↑Let us abstain . . . home↓
26   which ↑is↓
31–32   ↑shall by . . . Spirit↓ . . . minds we
34   him ⟨a⟩ Son↑s↓
35–36   do th⟨is⟩e commandments . . . as he d⟨id⟩oes . . . & ab⟨o⟩ide↑s↓

Sermon CXXIV

Manuscript: Seven sheets folded to make four pages each; folios stacked and cross-
stitched with white thread around the left edge. The seventh leaf has been torn away
leaving an irregular stub. A single leaf and a sheet folded to make four pages are laid in
after leaf 13. Folio pages measure 24.9 x 20.2 cm, the single leaf measures 24.7 x 20.1 cm,
and the pages of the additional folio measure 24.7 x 20 cm.

[Below the Bible text:]   Salem [in pencil]

Lines   *Page 205*
2   free [end of line] it
3–6   liberty. ⟨I wish to come to an understanding on this matter of
                 Freedom, brethren.⟩ It . . . servitude, ⟨and as if this was⟩ ↑that they
                 . . . wages ⟨a⟩is . . . Redemption ⟨↑by the del↓⟩ ransom↓
6–7   ↑was mainly instrumental in↓ deliver⟨ed⟩ing
8   ↑in a higher sense↓ if he deliver↑s↓
9   ↑Brethren, . . . Freedom, ⟨to weigh the sublime sense of the text⟩.↓
                 [canceled in pencil] ⟨↑Insert X↓ [On the top of the page, a passage, in
                 erased pencil, marked "X":] ↑Brethren [several illegible words] are
                 striking for political liberty [several illegible words] the hostile field
                 [one illegible line] & they will prevail [two illegible words] political
                 liberty is but the outward shadow of a higher liberty of which life is
                 [several illegible words] must be striven for by nations but by souls↓⟩
                 Are

10–11   we ⟨have⟩ are . . . if ⟨w⟩ individually
15–16   ↑that . . . sense↓
18–20   ↑The mind . . . will. ↑the power of knowing, & the power of doing↓↓
           [second addition in pencil]
20–21   redeems the ⟨mind⟩ intellect
21–24   slavery. ⟨I suppose⟩ ↑On . . . that↓ . . . chains.⟩

Page 206

1–7   liberty. ²{What is . . . why the ⟨Hindoos⟩ ↑barbarous & semibar-
           barous nations↓ . . . If /you can give them the/they had tr/ true
           views ⟨of those priests & institutions the whole nonsense would go
           ⟨d⟩ to pieces at once⟩ ↑of religion . . . at once↓ ↑¹{We commonly
           . . . us.}↓ [end of page] ¶ [The following addition, in pencil, is
           rejected as a late emendation:] ↑↑It is related of↓ The ancient stoic
           Philosopher Epictetus was ⟨a Thracian⟩ ↑that he was sold as a↓ slave
           and when ⟨his master⟩ ↑he was↓ offered ⟨him⟩ for sale at the market
           in Athens Epictetus cried out to the competitors for the purchase
           "Who wants ↑to buy↓ a master?"↓ [see *JMN* 7:361–62; end of page] ¶
           ⟨{What is the reason ¹As we commonly say of the brute creation of
           the Elephant the horse the ox if they *knew* their own strength they
           would not serve us.}⟩ ¶ Knowledge . . . it is ⟨*free* from⟩ ↑master of↓
           . . . not ⟨& free *with* him⟩. What
11   reap benefit
12–14   cold, ⟨&⟩ diseases, ↑& . . . evils,↓ . . . levées, ⟨h⟩ clothing, . . .
           ↑police↓.
16–17   knowledge. ¶ ⟨You are⟩ ↑A man is↓
18–21   ↑Let↓ [addition in pencil] A . . . bring⟨s you⟩ ["s" canceled in pencil]
           ↑him↓ a compass, & ⟨you⟩ ↑he↓ know↑s↓ /your/his/ . . . quadrant
           & ⟨you⟩ ↑he↓ know↑s↓ /your/his/ place↑;↓ a chart & /you/he/
           know /your/his/ coast↑;↓ [semicolons in pencil] . . . disasters ⟨are
           you⟩ ↑is he↓
23–24   You are ⟨bewildered &⟩ painfully perplexed. ↑Every speaker sways
           you every . . . false because . . . face.↓
26–27   will ⟨stand again on your⟩ ↑be . . . again↓
28–35   ↑Let . . . see wh⟨o⟩ich ↑mind↓ . . . other↓ . . . acquires, a every . . .
           eyes. ⟨It is making him free from some prejudice which fettered him
           & hindered him from doing as he would if he saw how things stood.⟩
           It is↑,↓ strictly speaking↑,↓ [commas added in pencil] giving him
           freedom, ⟨for the prejud⟩ for . . . would if ⟨that were removed⟩ ↑the
           . . . free.↓
38–(207)4 friends ⟨(in solemn sadness)⟩ to . . . free? [The following cancella-
           tion is rejected as a late emendation; changes in person and number
           within the cancellation are also rejected as late emendations:] ⟨{It was
           ⟨a⟩ ↑this↓ tho't ⟨of this kind⟩ ↑of the ↑unknown↓ extent of human
           slavery↓ . . . topic.} I have seen⟩ [canceled in pencil] ↑We see↓
           [addition in pencil] . . . society ⟨that⟩ ↑whom↓ when ⟨I⟩ ↑we↓
           [emendation in pencil] meet ⟨I⟩ ↑we↓ [emendation in pencil] seem to
           see ⟨them led . . . master.⟩ ↑the chain by wh they are led as the

culprit is led by his jailer↓ [emendation in pencil] ↑Insert A↓ [A
passage in pencil marked "A" on the facing page, rejected as a late
emendation:] ↑{If in his inmost mind a man determines that one
⟨thing⟩ ↑word↓ is fit to be spoken or ↑one act↓ fit to be done & then
out of regard to ⟨lower considerations⟩ ↑fear or interest or passion↓
he speaks a different word or does a different act, then ⟨it must be
admitted⟩ he is not free He cannot or he says he cannot do as he
would}↓ If . . . they ⟨whose vote . . . corrupted⟩ [canceled in pencil
and ink; rejected as a late emendation] ↑who speak what they think &
act as they & not others chuse↓, [added in ink on the line below an
erased pencil version of the same; rejected as a late emendation] who
never . . . entraps ⟨our⟩ human freedom, ⟨the devil of⟩ Self . . .
always ⟨a⟩ cast

Page 207

7–8   ↑See . . . table↓
10–11   gifted as he is, ⟨he is th⟩ ⟨a sweet⟩ ↑this↓ meat or ⟨a glass of⟩ ↑this↓
             [all emendations after the first cancellation are in pencil]
13–14   us. ¶ ⟨Y⟩Here . . . he ⟨is⟩ does
17   give to ⟨one⟩ the
19–20   in ⟨our free⟩ ↑this↓ country ↑so . . . liberty.↓ Let the ⟨sacred⟩
             importance so justly /given/ attached/
29–31   another who↑m↓ ⟨will do all for covetousness⟩ ↑the prospect . . .
             friendships & ⟨lose⟩ let . . . name.↓ he
33–34   ↑Now . . . is?↓
37–39   And ⟨equally⟩ ↑therefore↓ true is the ⟨contr⟩ other . . . as he
             ⟨grows⟩ ↑becomes↓
40–(208)12. free. ↑I have alluded &c↓ [addition in pencil; see *Note 1* below. The
             following cancellation is rejected as a late emendation:] ⟨A good . . .
             associates ⟨2⟩ which . . . is right⟩ [canceled in pencil; the following
             three paragraphs, added and canceled in pencil, are rejected as a late
             emendation:] ⟨↑Allow me to quote to you the ↑memorable↓ language
             of a Christian addressed to the army of Cromwell 200 years ago, but
             which ⟨are⟩ ↑is↓ the language of a Christian a freeman of Christ to
             the human race {Turn back to A [end of page; see *Note 2* below]

             First then I fear no party or interest for I love al[inscription runs off
             the edge of the page] I am reconciled to all & therein I find all
             reconciled to me I have enmity to none but the son of perdition. It is
             enmity begets insecurity

             But we being enlarged into the largeness of God, & comprehend-
             ing all things in our bosoms by the divine spirit, are at rest with all, &
             delight in all; for we know nothing but what is, in its essence, in our
             own hearts."↓⟩ [end of page]

             [The cancellation of the following sentence is rejected as a late
             emendation; see *Note 3* below:] ⟨It follows . . . right.⟩ [The addition
             of the following, in pencil, is rejected as a late emendation:] ↑{X↓ [On
             the preceding facing page, a passage marked "X":] ↑There is nothing
             capricious or arbitrary about the doings of a good man. He before

was under dominion of pride now under meekness before he was ruled by lust now by a good affection before by love of mischief now by desire of usefulness [several illegible words] he has only passed from one yoke under another. How then can you say he is free.↓ [The cancellation of the following is rejected as a late emendation:] ⟨Liberty in . . . or earth ↑There is no lawless . . . lawless tho't↓ . . . so that ⟨the height of⟩ ↑entire↓ freedom is ⟨the height⟩ entire . . . of good.—"⟩

[*Note 1:* In the passage above, "I have alluded &c" is Emerson's reference to matter found in the folio inserted after leaf 13; the addition is rejected as a late emendation:] ¶ ↑I have alluded to some of the passions that are commonly observed to abridge our liberty. It is however important to observe that there is a mighty difference in the moral character of the various checks & obstructions that interfere with our freedom. Some of these are virtues compared with others. They stand in an ascending & descending scale. No man becomes suddenly free, nor suddenly good & wise. He passes from a worse to a milder thraldom—thence to one more mild—more nearly approaching freedom. Thus the chains that fetter thousands ⟨are⟩ ↑are of the grossest sort—↓ those of animal appetite. ⟨These are of the grossest *sort.*⟩ As, by resistance, a man ⟨rises⟩ breaks these,—he comes into ↑a↓ subjection far less gross, as the fear of opinion, the fear of poverty, the fear of death. In the progress of a virtuous mind as each of these in succession is overcome, he finds a yoke remaining, ⟨still⟩ [end of page] still more gentle & plausible than the last There is the fear of offending the fear of being misapprehended & misjudged the fear of consequences that may arise from strictly following our conscience & using all the liberty our conscience allows us, these are fears which embarrass the best men. ¶ ⟨And the progress of the soul in goodness is a continual emancipation.⟩ Entire freedom perhaps no man attains in this world—alas how few to any high degrees of it— but the progress of the soul in goodness, yes, every step, every ⟨good⟩ intrepid right action every benevolent desire is a continual emancipation a loosening & removing of a chain.↓

[*Note 2:* In the passage above, "Turn back to A" is Emerson's reference to matter found on the single leaf inserted after leaf 13. The two paragraphs that follow the note in the passage above are Emerson's paraphrase of the quotation, while the paragraph which includes the note is clearly a draft version of the first paragraph below; all of this matter is rejected as a late emendation:] ¶ ↑As an illustration of the tranquillity & happiness that belongs to this deliverance let me ⟨read⟩ ↑repeat to↓ you the memorable language of a Christian soldier addressed to the army of Cromwell 200 years ago ↑in times of great disorder & terror↓ but which ⟨are⟩ ↑utters↓ the sentiments of a Christian—a freeman in Christ's sense—addressed to the human race. ¶ "I have no life but truth, & if truth be advanced by my suffering, then my life also. If truth live, I live. If justice live, I live. ⟨&⟩And these cannot die, but by any man's suffering for them, are enlarged, enthroned. Death cannot hurt me. I sport with him; am above his reach. I live an immortal life. What we have within, that only can we see without. I cannot *see* death; & he that hath not this freedom is a slave. He is in the arms of that, the phantoms of which he beholdeth, & seemeth to himself to flee from. ¶ Let me be a fool & boast, if so I may show you a little of that rest & security which I & those of the same spirit enjoy & which you have turned your backs upon, self like a banished thing wandering in strange ways.

First then I fear no party or interest for I love all. I am reconciled to all & therein I find all reconciled to me. I have enmity to none but the son of perdition. It is en⟨em⟩mity begets insecurity. ¶ But we being enlarged into the largeness of God, & comprehending all things in our bosoms by the divine spirit, are at rest with all, & delight in all for we know nothing but what is in its essence in our own hearts."↓

[*Note 3:* Having revised the introductory paragraph and written out the quotation cited in *Note 2* in order to replace the added drafts of the same, for later deliveries of the sermon Emerson went on to revise the paragraph from the original version of the sermon that then followed the added quotation. He probably wrote the rejected pencil addition "X" ("There is . . . free.") within the original paragraph for the delivery in which he first incorporated the rough introductory paragraph and paraphrase replaced by the addition in *Note 2*. Not satisfied with the paragraph as it then stood, Emerson extensively revised it as indicated below. This addition, rejected as a late emendation, occurs on the second leaf of the folio inserted after leaf 13:] ¶ ↑I proceed to another very important fact which ⟨demands⟩ is that a state of liberty is not a state of uncertainty of action. Liberty does not consist in doing what you please but in pleasing to do right Liberty in the sense of arbitrary action does not exist. No such thing is known in heaven or in earth. As fast as these yokes of tradition, of custom, of regard to unworthy considerations fall from him, he finds a new law in their place. By escaping from bondage he does not escape from law. Before, he was under dominion of malice, now under love once he served his lust now he serves his reason once he lived for wealth now for the desire of improvement once for self now he loves the adamantine law of justice ¶ Every tie that snaps as flax in the flame only discovers beneath it an inconsumable unchangeable natural bond of more perfect command & when he becomes wholly free it is that he may be wholly a servant because the highest state of the soul is the clear perception & hearty acknowledgment that we exist from God and a total self surrender to his guidance. ¶ ⟨↑This is the sublime sense of the Apostle. God worketh in us both to will & to do of his own good pleasure.↓ [addition in pencil] ¶ The more perfectly emancipated a man becomes from vice the more strict his adherence becomes to duty. The more perfect his freedom the more perfect his obedience so that entire freedom is entire subjection

       inspired by choice
     And conscious that the will is free
     Unswerving shall we move as if impelled
     By strict necessity along the path
     Of order & of good.—↓⟩ [canceled in pencil]

Page 208

13	¶ But ⟨it is no⟩ how
14–15	↑of passion↓
15–16	↑one acts . . . against self↓
21–22	He ⟨feels & rejoices to feel⟩ ↑acknowledges↓ . . . himself, ⟨by⟩but . . . bows not ⟨with reluctance⟩ ↑by compulsion↓,
23–24	↑His affection . . . understands.↓
25–27	life ⟨It is⟩ He ⟨feels⟩ ↑perceives↓ . . . longer hi⟨mself⟩s ↑own↓ ⟨but one with⟩ ↑as . . . from↓
28	he ⟨feels⟩ ↑becomes aware of↓
30	becomes / liberty / sovereignty /

30–34   freedom ¶ [The following additions are rejected as late emendations:]
⟨↑I have said that ⟨the servic⟩ obedience to the law contrasts with
obedience to passion in this, that in one case there is consent from all
within & in the other discord.↓ Let me . . . moralist. ↑I quote them
the more readily because of their invaluable practical lesson.↓ ¶ "The

31–32   more ⟨remarkable⟩ distinction . . . in the ⟨memorable⟩ ↑re-
markable↓

35   on in th⟨e⟩is

Page 209

2–3   resolves." *Fichte* ¶ ⟨This then is the liberty of the Sons of God.⟩ ↑To
be wise & to be good to know & to do right. But the beginning of
knowledge is goodness↓ [addition in pencil; addition and cancellation rejected as a late emendation. The following revision, added on
the facing page, is likewise rejected as a late emendation:] ↑This then
is the liberty of the sons of God—to be wise & to be good. To know
& to do right. But the beginning of knowledge is goodness. Certainly
my brethren there is no need that I should praise the advantages of
freedom to you or tell you how base it is to be a slave. To every man
who has ever reflected in earnest upon his condition & hopes as a
man, it must be an object of determined pursuit to redeem himself
from the bondage of his passions & walk forth in the world a freeman
Every one who reflects knows too well what his own chains are. ⟨↑If
lusts made one good affections rule another Tis only passing out of
one into another h[ea]d↓⟩ ["If lusts . . . another hd" in erased pencil
is visible between the lines at this point in the addition.] It needs not
to praise the liberty but it does need ⟨to reflect⟩ reflexion to
comprehend fully our own condition & dangers↓ And now

5   ↑spiritual↓

8–10   free? ⟨Examine you own⟩ ↑because . . . your own↓ heart↑.↓ ⟨& see
if you have wrot out your freedom.⟩ See . . . appetite. ⟨w⟩When

12–13   free ↑Consider . . . ruin.↓

16–28   your bargain⟨s⟩. Consider if ⟨you could⟩ there . . . commandment—⟨Then you are not free.⟩ ↑Consider . . . forbear ⟨to do⟩
[canceled in pencil] the sincere . . . free↓ [The cancellation of the
following paragraph, the original conclusion to the sermon, is rejected
as a late emendation:] ¶ ⟨Come then . . . God the ⟨Deliverer⟩
↑Redeemer↓ . . . existence but th⟨ou⟩at . . . pleasure.⟩

[The following variant conclusion is inscribed after the end of the sermon:]
¶ ⟨It deserves consideration that if we do not choose to live by *the law* of the Universe it
yet will have its way and the men that oppose it are overthrown by it & tho' dementated
(prius dementat) are to the⟨y⟩ eyes of all clearsighted persons monuments & demonstration of that power which they deny. Vices prove God as shadows point to the sun.⟩
[canceled in pencil] ¶ Amid the heats vexations fears of the times ⟨is it⟩ were it not well to
remember that absolute freedom, unchangeable freedom is offered—the freedom of
God—a union of mind with the source of our being that shall not unfit us for the world
but that shall descend into & elevate the least & obscurest actions. Were it not well in a

day of public despondency & private alarm to go alone & seeking counsel of highest
Wisdom see that we do what we shall never repent. Were it not well for every soul, in
whatsoever condition, that has found out that existence is a blessing—that God is
good,—to consider seriously what hindrances obstruct its freedom—compare its views
of duty with its daily life—by selfexamination expose its own bonds & by meditation &
prayer invite God into the soul to dispose of it entirely—to act through it in the
perfectness of his wisdom & love forevermore.

Sermon CXXV

Manuscript: Eight sheets folded to make four pages each; folios stacked and sewn with
white thread along the left margin; pages measure 24.9 x 20.1 cm.

Lines	Page 210
3–5	contentment↑,↓ . . . stupid ⟨people⟩ ↑persons↓. [emendations in pencil]
6–7	stripes & ⟨imprisonment⟩ tumults . . . fasting th⟨e⟩is [emendation in pencil] ⟨unconquerable⟩ ↑brave↓ [addition in pencil]
14–15	alive ⟨this⟩ ↑so↓ many ages. ⟨in the world⟩ This
17–19	It ⟨goes on the⟩ implies . . . Christ" ⟨And this truth I shall endeavour to illustrate.⟩ ¶ All
21–23	say—⟨nothing can harm the good man.⟩ No . . . man. I ⟨propose to consider⟩ [canceled in pencil and ink] ↑shall endeavor to illustrate↓ . . . proposition. ¶ ⟨1. I⟩ Let it be considered ⟨in the first place⟩ that . . . fortunes ⟨another⟩ or
24–25	↑The outward condition↑,↓ . . . shell independent↓ [addition in pencil except for the comma] The ⟨crust⟩ ↑husks↓ may be very ⟨/rough/mean/⟩ ↑coarse↓

	Page 211
2–4	↑he does much ⟨He⟩to forms that crust↓ ⟨t⟩There ↑it↓ [addition in pencil] is ⟨a good deal of truth in the proverb⟩ [canceled in pencil] ↑true in the main↓ [addition in pencil] ¹{that "every . . . fortune"} ²{though it . . . qualification.} [Emerson clearly marked these phrases for transposition, though his numbering, evidently in error, leaves their order undisturbed.] ⟨We all admit the fact & act upon the presumption that⟩ ⟨a⟩A man's
6–8	↑I deny not that↓ . . . himself, ⟨for reasons⟩ ↑and this comes from causes↓
9–16	exceptions—⟨A good man cannot⟩ ¶ ↑I. The external ⟨condition⟩ welfare . . . not↓ easily ⟨be⟩ hurt↑.↓ ⟨in his fortunes.⟩—All . . . for ⟨his external ⟨welfare⟩⟩ good. to him externally. ↑{Insert X}↓ [On the facing page, a passage marked "X":] ↑It is agreed . . . violence.↓ [end of Insert "X"] ¶ ⟨Most⟩ ↑Many↓ [emendation in pencil] . . . ↑deal↓ honestly↑,↓ ⟨try⟩ we . . . imprudence or ⟨our⟩ guilt. Have ⟨we⟩you . . . ↑worthy↓
20	saved ⟨you⟩ ↑it↓?
25–42	is ⟨yet ventured⟩ really . . . ventured ⟨on the seas⟩ ⟨at great risks⟩ ↑in trade↓ . . . be ⟨fatal⟩ ↑ruinous↓, . . . rich. ⟨o⟩Or, . . . more

m⟨e⟩oderation . . . it? ¶ [The following cancellation, made in ink over pencil, is rejected as a late emendation:] ⟨Take the world . . . amiable ⟨& very amiable⟩ seldom . . . qualities ¶ Such . . . good man. [end of page] ¶ So . . . strength.⟩ [last paragraph canceled in ink only] ¶ [The following additions are rejected as late emendations:] ↑↑Health follows temperance; wealth industry; power knowledge;↓ All things work together for good to the good. He builds his success upon ⟨diligence justice⟩ ↑fidelity industry↓ prudence benevolence which are the laws of God, & so his success stands upon foundations of divine strength & will endure when the hasty structure of evil men is beat down by the winds & the floods. The good mans reputation goes before him like a footman & makes way for him. Humility makes friends. The benefits he has conferred make friends. His self-command inspires respect His truth inspires trust. All things work for good to him These qualities do not make enemies. ⟨The bad man on the contrary surrounds himself with distrust hatred contempt His hand is against every man⟩ ¶ How has the soldier acquired his ⟨indomitable⟩ ↑formidable↓ courage? By a rare occasional action? No but eating his daily bread in danger of his life by having seen a thousand times what resolution & combination can accomplish. How is a firm cheerful conversation acquired not by one effort but by spending days & years well & so having a divine support for such a frail nature to lean upon a divine support of all the virtue in a mans life What makes the majesty of a good & great man, those men who are in deed the pillars of society? The consciousness of an innocent & beneficent life & the cumulative glory of so many witnesses behind. When we hear ⟨them⟩ ↑him↓ speak, when we see ⟨them⟩ ↑him↓ act we see behind him the faces of former ⟨benefits⟩ brave & just acts. There they all stand & [end of line] & shed an united light on the advancing actor. He is attended as by ⟨an⟩ ↑a↓ ⟨in⟩visible escort of angels to every mans eye.↓ ¶ The bad

44–⟨212⟩2   any ⟨extravagant⟩ ↑over-↓statement. I do not ⟨sa⟩ deny that ⟨as⟩ there . . . which ⟨b⟩scorches

Page 212

4–5   to /two/the main/ . . . ↑& to the fact↓ which
6   ↑Most . . . from↓ [in pencil]
9   more ⟨confidence⟩ security.
10–11   dependance . . . another's, ⟨⟨& the⟩ unu⟩ make . . . fraud of [end of line] of a
14–20   depraved ⟨condition which men themselves have bro't on⟩ ↑state of↓ the world. ¶ 2. ⟨Beca⟩ He . . . ↑in common with other men↓ [addition in ink over pencil] . . . ignorance ⟨He b⟩ ↑A man↓ . . . from ig- [end of page] ignorance . . . & the ⟨monsoons⟩ ↑prevalent winds↓ . . . worm; or
26   ↑outward↓
32–33   lowest ⟨step⟩ degree . . . justice ⟨labor⟩ industry
38–39   seeking the ⟨virtues⟩ ↑formation of his character↓

39–41	good the . . . suffers ⟨for⟩ ↑with↓ his fortunes, ⟨are not himself⟩ ↑& tho' . . . hurt↓; . . . the ⟨second topic⟩ ↑true meaning of the text↓. [addition in ink over pencil]

Page 213

3–4	↑And . . . Paul↓ Goodness is invulnerable ⟨& the night is light about it⟩ ↑& what . . . good↓. [emendation in pencil]
5–7	whose ⟨character⟩ ↑soul↓ . . . that↑,↓ [comma added in pencil] . . . ruined. ⟨A man⟩ ↑One↓ . . . perfections ⟨as⟩ beauty
9–10	↑But take . . . be ruin.↓ But
14–15	all the ⟨persecution or⟩ poverty
17–19	↑They . . . perfection.↓
22	& ↑like fire↓
23–24	↑in our age↓ the ⟨⟨imp⟩ native⟩ ↑royal & imperial↓ . . . against the ⟨Poles⟩ ↑friends of freedom,↓
31	near. ⟨that heaven⟩ He
33	affection⟨s⟩ for . . . ↑hath↓

Page 214

4–5	veiled perhaps is [the spacing is the only guide to the placement of the comma, greater between "veiled" and "perhaps" than between "perhaps" and "is"] . . . ↑undying↓
7	endure / severe pain / months of sickness /
8	furnished ⟨from above⟩ to
10–11	in the his unexpected strength ⟨The Christian refers all to God.⟩ ↑acknowledging . . . God.↓
16–17	wilt ¶ ⟨Once more,⟩ he
18	dependance upon God, ⟨his⟩ the
22–23	to ⟨disencumber him of his⟩ dispel . . . nature, ⟨& to make the light ⟨w⟩appear within⟩ & fill him with ↑divine↓
30–31	full ↑& denies . . . vain↓

[The following paragraph is inscribed, in pencil, on the page facing the concluding paragraph of the sermon:] As God liveth, it shall be well with the soul Every hour the most tedious & the most distressing you may do something to set this seal on your happiness to bring God on your side & make him the security for your welfare. Every event alike the great & trivial may by your exertions to ⟨lead⟩ obey the precepts of Jesus contribute to your peace & power & happiness

Sermon CXXVI

Manuscript: Seven sheets folded to make four pages each; folios stacked and sewn with white thread along the left margin; pages measure 25 x 20.2 cm.

Lines	Page 215
1–4	melancholy ⟨s⟩& . . . conclude ⟨that⟩ with ⟨Epicurus⟩ ↑the sensual↓

7–11   His ⟨is⟩ head . . . heart ⟨corrects⟩ ↑controls↓ his ⟨inference⟩
            ↑decision↓ ⟨Better he saith are the dead than the living⟩ ↑Better is
            . . . bread↓

12–15   *know thou* &c [The allusion to Ecclesiastes 11:9 has been supple-
            mented from that source. The following addition is rejected as a late
            emendation:] ¶ ↑And all his epicureanism comes to this result. Hear
            the conclusion of the whole matter Fear God & keep the command-
            ments And in the text ↑⟨Eat thy bread & drink thy wine with a merry
            heart⟩ & after all his foreboding & complaints↓ whatever I may have
            said or may say concerning the expediency of playing the fool surely I
            know it shall be well with them yᵗ fear God. ¶ ⟨We welcome t⟩This
            conclusion ⟨whilst⟩ ↑is cheering↓ our varying life ⟨confirms in our
            feeling his melancholy thot that all here is vanity. All is unreal.⟩ Let us
            hold it fast when our experience whispers that all is vanity & unreal
            & a dream↑.↓ [period in pencil] ⟨I shall aim to show that Christianity
            gives us the same instruction⟩ ↑⟨for⟩And our experience like his,
            teaches us that life is vanity & when we are evil & unthankful, it is
            worse than in vain The words of a poet in our times respond to his
            view

                         For know whatever thou hast been
                         Tis something better not to be.

            ¶ But the voice of Christianity ↑the corrected decision of reason↓ yes
            & all that is good & hopeful in the profound depths of our own
            hearts, cries out against the forlorn conclusion They say also surely
            We know that it shall be well with them that fear God.↓↓ ["⟨for⟩And
            . . . God." is in pencil; end of rejected addition and end of page]
            ⟨What a dream is life what a vanishing vapour,⟩ ↑There . . .
            ⟨a⟩every man ↑takes the same gloomy view↓ [addition in pencil] feels
            . . . little time↓

16   real & ⟨infinitely⟩ minute
20   cloud. ⟨But⟩ And

                         Page 216

1–3   pale the ⟨cheek of the⟩ most cheerful ↑cheek.↓ ⟨T⟩It is . . . part ⟨of
            the trunk & branches & killing every leaf of joy⟩ ↑human fortune↓.
            The youth ⟨rejoices⟩ ↑exults↓ in his advancing ⟨years⟩ ↑freedom↓
4–5   ↑that he . . . live↓, . . . steal ⟨from him⟩ not
7   that ⟨men are alarmed at being⟩ ↑it . . . be↓ reminded that ⟨they are⟩
            ↑he is↓
8–10   terrify ⟨them⟩ ↑him↓ . . . pace ⟨they are⟩ ↑he is↓ growing ⟨good⟩
            ↑wise & virtuous↓; but if ⟨they are⟩ ↑he is↓, ⟨they⟩ ↑he↓ . . . their
            ⟨course⟩ ↑flight↓, for ⟨they⟩ ↑he↓ . . . but ↑to↓
12–13   now. ¶ [The following addition is rejected as a late emendation:] ↑The
            love of life is a universal passion. The rich & the poor young & old
            those who have much to live for & those to whom life is a long disease
            & every day a new aching all cling to it↓ ⟨They⟩ ↑Men↓ fear
14   sons ⟨of⟩ &
17–39   pleasant ⟨light of the sun⟩ ↑day-light↓ . . . from the [end of page] the

. . . man; the ⟨sweetness⟩ relish . . . fact that ⟨out⟩ from . . . rock.)
the . . . nerves & ⟨the bones⟩ marrow . . . independance . . . bread;
the ⟨pleasures⟩ manifold . . . sentiment whatever . . . house whatever . . . go away ⟨we⟩he know↑s↓ . . . close ⟨our⟩ ↑this↓ . . . it is to
⟨them⟩ ↑him↓.

40   hover ⟨&⟩over

Page 217

5–6   ↑It is true,↓ Some . . . among ⟨philosophers⟩ ↑reflecting ⟨persons⟩↓
        & good ⟨men⟩ ↑persons↓ ⟨if⟩they

8   ¶ Let me ⟨mention⟩ ↑enumerate↓ briefly the /grounds/observations/
        [emendations in pencil]

10–13   ¶ ↑In . . . it ⟨is⟩ ↑was originally↓ . . . state↓ [addition and emenda-
        tion in pencil]

14–17   faculties. ⟨A swallow builds her nest this summer as well & no better
        than a swallow in the time of Caesar or of Aristotle,⟩ but man . . . . . .
        say, ⟨removes him⟩ ↑carries onward↓ still farther ⟨from⟩ the perfection

18–19   his ⟨progress⟩ ↑acquisitions↓ . . . body ⟨checks⟩ ↑first retards↓ &
        ↑then↓

21–22   close. ¶ [The following notation is added in pencil between the
        paragraphs:] ↑worst life mendable↓ ¶ Whence

24   because ⟨we⟩he

28–30   it is ⟨us⟩ received . . . through ⟨nature⟩ ⟨useful⟩ ↑the system of y^e
        world↓

33–35   works, ⟨that miracle,⟩ a rational . . . candle⟨?⟩, in to

Page 218

1–2   own ⟨fut⟩ immortal

3–9   faculties. ⟨The⟩ ↑Because the we . . . us.↓ When . . . well [end of
        line] them who love God. ¶ ⟨This leads me to speak of⟩ ↑This leads
        . . . something ⟨most⟩ quite peculiar ⟨extraordinary⟩ in the↓ the
        manner

12   said⟨,⟩; ⟨but ⟨an⟩ a continuance⟩ no⟨t⟩r of

16–19   ¶ But ⟨I wish to call your attention to⟩ ↑observe↓ the fact that ⟨it⟩
        ↑this information↓ goes no further. It ⟨is one of the⟩ ↑is↓ most . . .
        ↑interior↓

22–23   in the ⟨Epistles⟩ recorded

26   world; ⟨improve⟩ ↑Redeem↓

28   inference the assurance

31–33   truth. ↑as . . . ↑themselves↓ . . . which the ⟨thot⟩ ↑heart↓ . . . gospel
        ⟨br⟩ opening . . . life↓

36   that ⟨w⟩ the

40–(219)1 ↑Duty . . . done.↓ [in pencil]

Page 219

2   to the ⟨mere⟩ idea

6–8   ↑They . . . that↓ It . . . ↑as it ⟨grows⟩ ↑becomes↓ . . . longer,↓ . . .
        not as it ⟨leaves the body⟩ ↑dies out of this world↓

18–26   thought" ¶ ⟨And so brethren if the gospel teaches us that there is no
               death but sin let us not prepare to die but let us die no more & awake
               to life. ⟨It seems from what we have considered that the only true
               revelation of immortality is contained in the precepts of the New
               Testament, that⟩⟩ ↑Thus brethren . . . assurance that ⟨virtue is
               eternal.⟩ ↑we must . . . live.↓ . . . Let us ⟨ne⟩ cease . . . to life.↓ we
               are taught that ↑because↓ we have uses↑,↓ ⟨as⟩ great & endless
               ↑uses,↓

27–38   death. ⟨It is the doctrine of one sect of⟩ ↑Some↓ Christians ↑have
               believed, ⟨as⟩ & as it seems to . . . reason,↓ that evil ⟨spirits⟩ ↑men↓
               [In the space between the lines, "seems to" is written over "men"
               prompting Emerson to rewrite "men" for clarity.] . . . world↑, not
               . . . God.↓ ¶ ⟨↑Therefore the moral that I draw from Xty is not how
               to die but life.↓⟩ [addition and cancellation in pencil] Let us . . . earth
               ↑the same↓, ⟨⟨let us begin to live now. let us⟩ God lives & we by him
               Christ is our life the Commandment is life Let us then obey God &
               receive the truth of Christ & keep the commandment⟩ ↑and that . . .
               poet—↓

                                    Page 220
4–5   brings." ⟨Or in⟩ ↑It only echoes↓

                                 Sermon CXXVII

Manuscript: Nine sheets folded to make four pages each; folios stacked and sewn with
white thread along the left margin; pages measure 25 x 20 cm. in the first, second, third,
and ninth folios, and 23.9 x 19.4 cm. in the remaining folios.

It would appear that all the matter on MS pp. 11–32, from the middle of the third to
the end of the eighth folio, represents revised text, the original having been lost. Doubts
may be entertained about the originality of the ninth folio as well, based on the
appearance and placement of the date ("Chardon St. Sept. 18, 1831"), which may well
have been copied from the last page of a lost original MS. The text presented in this
edition is the earliest that can be derived from the MS, but may not exactly represent the
sermon as first delivered.

Lines   *Page 221*
2   amusement or ⟨an idle word⟩ ↑petty fraud↓
9   love of ⟨h⟩Him
11–12   offer. ¶ ⟨The law of God as it ⟨lat⟩ is observed ⟨in the natural world
               is science.⟩ ¶ as it is observed in the intellect is truth ¶ as it is observed
               in the will is virtue ¶ Every eye sees, every heart feels the harmony &
               relation of all the parts. of each to the other & of the mind of man to
               all. Cicero observed long ago that there ⟨was⟩ ↑is a common bond↓
               betwixt the sciences ⟨a certain common bond⟩ ↑betwixt spiritual
               truths & betwixt the virtues.↓ To express this as generally as I can, I
               propose to show the important practical truths of this passage by
               showing ¶ 1. That every truth we receive prepares the way for the
               reception of others of wh. we are ignorant. I suppose this is obvious
               to every one. All our learning ⟨goes⟩ ↑advances↓ step by step, ⟨the

former⟩ ↑what goes before↓ making room for that which follows till results the most abstruse & great are as plain as abc⟩ ¶ The

15-17   all. ⟨Cicero observed long ago⟩ ↑A sublime . . . truth.↓ [addition in pencil]

18-20   spiritual truths. & betwixt the virtues. ↑betwixt the virtues & the ↑physical↓ well being of ⟨⟨the⟩ out⟩ man.↓ [addition and emendations in pencil] ¶ ⟨↑A higher ⟨ev⟩ knowledge of his Unity we get from the concord in the intellectual world No fact is insulated. Every thing is a cause & an effect & is related to all other facts↓⟩ [addition and cancellation in pencil] ¶ All

20   whole ⟨universe⟩ ↑creation↓

23-25   pebble ⟨or a chip of wood⟩ ↑from the ground↓, . . . ↑enough↓ [addition in pencil] . . . little. ⟨T⟩Who

Page 222

4   universe ⟨draws⟩ ↑attracts↓

5-6   pebble ⟨&⟩to the sun, or this pebble ⟨&⟩to ⟨a⟩ the remotest star⟨;⟩?—yet

8   could ⟨exhaust⟩ ↑tell↓

9-12   was ⟨accused of⟩ ↑about to be burned for↓ . . . picked ⟨up⟩ ↑out↓ . . . from the ⟨ground⟩ ↑pile↓ & //proved/said/ the being of God from the /wisdom/existence & arrangement/ shown in that structure, before his judges./declared . . . fact./ [emendations in pencil]

14-17   has ⟨for⟩ ↑built . . . on↓ . . . all,' & ⟨teaches⟩ ↑requires of↓ . . . ↑to study . . . relations↓ [addition in pencil] . . . that. ↑as . . . one.↓

21   because ⟨any of the⟩ ↑our↓ circumstances have ⟨been alike⟩ ↑not been very different↓,

23-29   this, that ⟨I am persuaded by my own experience that⟩ if . . . persons ⟨with⟩ who⟨m you have found the most perfect sympathy upon moral & religious subjects which are the deepest we ever consider, you will find them to be persons who have been bro't up often in circumstances widely different, in different business, different habits, different constitution, different country.⟩ ↑have most . . . were not ⟨those who were⟩ educated . . . ↑we observe . . . other men.↓↓ ["we . . . men." added in ink over pencil]

30-35   ↑or profession↓ . . . processes ⟨is⟩ ↑furnishes him with↓ [over "furnishes him" in pencil] an illustration ⟨to him⟩ of . . . truths. ↑{Insert X}↓ [On the facing page, otherwise blank, a passage marked "X":] ↑{the sailor, . . . agriculture}↓ [end of Insert "X"] ⟨↑In this manner all truth related a wonderful unity prevails in all that we behold the law of God is every where the same↓⟩ [added in pencil; the following is written over it, in ink:] ↑Thus is . . . same.↓

36-(223)4   it is ⟨observed⟩ ↑chosen↓ [emendations in ink over pencil] in the ⟨mind⟩ ↑will↓ is virtue. ⟨I proceed to say ↑1. in following out yᵉ sentiment of St James,↓ that one truth prepares the way for all truth↑; 2.↓ and that one virtue prepares the way for all virtue.⟩ ¶ ↑In following . . . us ⟨divide⟩ ↑separate↓ [emendation in pencil] the ↑two↓ . . . virtue.↓ ¶ I. It

Page 223

5   truth ⟨is alone⟩ stands

6   truths. ⟨And this ⟨makes⟩ ↑gives↓, you see, an infinite value to every
             truth, that you are not only learning it, but you are learning a great
             deal more I suppose we never fully comprehend any one truth in all its
             height & depth, for, if we did, we shd. comprehend all. But the partial
             views we get at one truth, ⟨g⟩obtain⟨s⟩ for us ↑a↓ partial view of all
             the related truths, which come in with it, hand in hand. This gives a
             sublime pleasure to every sincere inquirer after truth. This makes one
             mind receive the being of God the immortality of the Soul & kindred
             facts with ease because they naturally cohere to truths which he
             receives.⟩ [end of cancellation on MS p. 10] Very

7   slowly ²learns ¹he

10–13   follows. ↑{B}↓ [On the facing page, a passage marked "B":] ↑{So . . .
             he is ⟨introducing⟩ ↑bringing↓ [emendation in pencil] . . . which
             ⟨his eyes⟩ he . . . behold.}↓

17–18   theirs. ¶ ⟨I suppose w⟩We never . . . depth↑.↓ ⟨for i⟩If

23–24   procession. ↑Insert A↓ [On the facing page (the first of folio 4), a
             passage marked "A" that is rejected as a late emendation:] ↑{And
             what man of reflection but ↑can↓ remember seasons in his life when
             he was uncommonly affected by a single truth. Under the influence of
             one commanding thought the whole world took an altered face to his
             eye. That thought seemed the key to the whole; it explained all
             mystery. It seemed to promise infallible guidance for the future.
             There was no view of life to which it was not applicable. ¶ It so
             seemed because it really was related to all, & only seemed infinite in
             its extent & consequences because the mind was excited to extraordi-
             nary attention. Every thought, every truth has the same depth of
             meaning & universality of application Every thought is one face of the
             world.}↓ ¶ Especially . . . truth. /One ⟨pure⟩ idea/A clear percep-
             tion/ [cancellation and variant in pencil]

29–35   books ⟨of all the learned.⟩ ↑upon . . . duty.↓ [addition in pencil; the
             following cancellation is rejected as a late emendation:] ⟨This then
             . . . progress i⟨n⟩s indefinitely . . . opens ⟨a great⟩ an . . . before
             him.⟩ ¶ [The following addition, on the second page of folio 4, is
             rejected as a late emendation:] ↑This then is the reward & encourage-
             ment of every patient follower of truth that his progress is indefinitely
             increased at every step that the value of every fact /depends upon the
             amount of his knowledge/is not measured by ⟨notion⟩ its own
             importance/↑,↓ [emendations in pencil] for it throws back light upon
             all he knows & opens an unlimited series of new objects before him
             ↑So that every person in whatsoever condition ↑whose mind is only
             open by a spirit of entire docility↓ may be satisfied in seeing that he is
             on the right track to all ⟨knowledge⟩ ↑wisdom↓—in the most
             obscure place infinite opportunities open before him. Nothing hin-
             ders the sincere inquirer from the immensity of knowledge.↓↓ ["So
             that . . . knowledge." added in pencil] ¶ II. My

37   practice. that ⟨eminence⟩ progress

39   ↑in your observation of men↓ [in pencil]
40–41   of ⟨an⟩ excellence . . . ↑a truth-speaker or↓

Page 224

1   question ⟨but⟩ ↑and↓ were ⟨equally⟩ ↑at the same time↓
4   liar or ⟨a hater⟩ ↑spiteful↓
6–7   much /character/general excellence/ [possibly the variant is intended
            to replace "much character"] ¶ ⟨Do not all⟩ ↑Is it . . . that all↓
9–13   by every ⟨good act that leads the soul to⟩ ↑exertion . . . keep ⟨his⟩its
            . . . by↓ refresh↑ing↓ . . . ones↑.↓ ⟨& make good the ground it has
            taken⟩ ¶ And ⟨a good action⟩ ↑an act of great merit↓ . . . which
            ⟨you⟩ the . . . love ⟨it⟩ ↑this action↓
14   some ⟨eminent⟩ moralists
17–23   true to ⟨him⟩self↑-good↓ . . . law ¶ ⟨I take it as I have said to be a
            fact that⟩ ↑For this fact that↓ . . . found ⟨joined⟩ in . . . grace↑, . . .
            reasons↓ ¶ ⟨And this in two ways ⟨first⟩⟩ ¶ 1. because . . . on other ¶
            2. because . . . *princ↑i↓ples*
25–26   ¶ ↑1.↓ There . . . actions ⟨on the one hand & between vicious actions
            on the other⟩. [Emerson's cancellation, made in pencil, signals the
            beginning of a substantial revision of the latter portions of the sermon
            for later deliveries. The cancellation is rejected as a late emendation.
            In the earliest version of the sermon, Emerson developed the connec-
            tion between virtuous actions and vicious actions with parallel para-
            graphs, as will be clear in the text and in the notes that follow. In the
            version of the sermon as revised for later deliveries, however, he may
            have reduced his treatment of vicious actions by eliminating a major
            paragraph on the subject (see the note to "↑Every virtue . . ." below).
            Furthermore, in the revised version he treated more extensively the
            power of virtuous action to generate yet more virtue by elaborating on
            point 2 raised in the text ("there is a connexion of *principles* inasmuch
            as the right motive to one virtue is an equal motive to all the virtues"),
            a point that he virtually ignored in the earliest version of the sermon.]
29–31   ↑He . . . of ⟨ad⟩ confirming . . . congenial↓
32   progressive the
34–38   ¶ Besides ⟨if a man devotes himself to a cause⟩ ↑to whatever . . .
            himself↓ . . . habits. ⟨If h⟩He . . . work↑. Then↓ . . . guard his
            ⟨lips⟩ ↑day↓ [emendations in pencil] . . . engagements↑,↓ [addition
            in pencil] . . . ↑whole↓
38–39   ↑He . . . fellowmen.↓

Page 225

1–10   ↑Every virtue . . . all temptations Patience↓ [addition incomplete] ¶
            ↑{↓It is . . . rest. ⟨Every vice is the effect of one vice & the cause
            again of more.⟩ What . . . intemperance or ⟨imprudence⟩ ↑sloth↓
            . . . display ↑is↓ . . . being ⟨driven⟩ ↑forced↓, . . . these arts.↑}↓
            [brackets in pencil] ¶ ↑On the other hand↓ [addition, in pencil,
            rejected as a late emendation] Every one
11–12   Lust ⟨needs⟩ ↑must have↓ hypocrisy to ⟨cover⟩ ↑shield↓ it, Lies,

13–14   perjury. ¶ ⟨So on the other hand⟩ ↑But↓ all [emendation, in pencil, rejected as late]

19–20   [The following paragraphs, which include a variant ending of the sermon, are rejected as a late addition. In these paragraphs Emerson elaborates on point 2 raised in his text (the "connexion of *principles*"), a point he neglected to develop in the earliest version of the sermon.]

↑Thus there is a connexion between virtuous actions whereby one induces another.

But it will occur to the minds of many that there are individuals who have given evidence of uncommon merit in a / particular / single / [variant in pencil] virtue who yet were very far from consistent excellence A hairsplitting integrity in pecuniary matters has been sometimes combined with licentious principles & practice. Many a man has been much praised for his charity who was luxurious & unjust "It is more easy to be beneficent than to be just" Then the miser is a martyr of temperance & diligence & the murderer is a man of courage & fortitude.

⟨In answer to⟩To remove this objection, & to make the vital distinction which divides right actions that are always connected, from right actions which are disconnected with the character, it becomes necessary to state the second & chief reason why one virtue leads to all virtues. It is shortly this, The principle of all virtues is one & the same.

The principle of virtuous actions is simple is one The actions to which I have alluded,—the good actions of bad men,—flow from many motives. A man thinks it a sufficient motive for his action that it is the custom; that it secures his personal safety & peace; that it secures the good opinion of particular friends or of the community; or it is reckoned a good example; & to one act is annexed the promise of reward, & to another act is annexed the threat of punishment.

Good actions that flow from such sources are not virtue. They are the works of tradition, of fear, of calculation. There is no security for the continuance of that man's virtue. Worst of all there is no earnest of improvement. Over his torpid soul, days & years, & opportunities & instruction, trials & happiness pass in vain.

⟨In society the action is regarded not the source of the action But w⟩We may be sure we have made very little progress in a holy life, if we see various motives to various duties. We have made but little use of the wonderful discipline of God's world upon the human mind, if we are practising what we call right actions from a regard to external considerations. All true religion tends to restoring simplicity, unity, to the character. It is the supplying us with a principle instead of enjoining an act upon authority. The soul is not yet alive until it is conscious of one principle from which all its actions proceed. And now a few words as to the nature of that principle.

All men who have attained a certain stature in their spiritual growth, become impatient of words & demand realities. They must have a better reason for their action than because it is enjoined. They begin to demand truths which are their own evidence. They seek no longer for a God of tradition, nor laws of authority, but for the Creator as he is; as he speaks directly to them through nature & the providence manifested in their life. They are ceasing to act from external motives, & learning to find their spring of activity within. The soul begins to realize the sublime doctrine of Christianity, that it is instinct with God, lives from God; draws wisdom, power, & grace from Him, & needs but to renounce its own will, & resign itself to the highest influence, in order to secure the wisest & happiest direction. There is a time when a man becomes ashamed of his vices & ↑his↓ weakness & is no longer content with exemption from blame, but is smit with ⟨a⟩the desire of absolute excellence, apprehends the divine distinction of his nature that God has set no limits to its improvement.

He looks upon himself as the promise of what he shall be, & enters on the task of setting in order his spiritual house, of combatting one by one the enemies of his peace. In that state of mind he perceives that the motives to duty are simple unchangeable permanent; that the principle of the virtues is not a desire to decoy other people out of harms way; nor to preserve ourselves from punishment; nor to be esteemed good & wise; but the love of the truth itself, the love of ⟨the⟩virtue itself, the incessant endeavor to be a more excellent & useful creature,—so simply & thoroughly obedient that God speaks by his voice & works by his hands.

Is it not plain that he who has come to this faith will be equally pledged to every virtue? If he is humble, he will be just. If he is just, he will be generous. This faith will open his eyes to the perception, that there is no duplicity in duty; no preference in virtues; that in surrendering the direction of his conduct to the ↑inward↓ Monitor, ⟨that speaks ever from within his soul⟩ he cannot be misled.

The practical conclusion to which we come, is, that, whilst it will not do to act upon any motive less than the highest, we may take advantage of this wonderful connexion of the virtues in concentrating our attention to a single work.

Let us meditate on the encouragement which issues from this truth to the devoted heart. It teaches us that the circumstances of our lot however unfavorable we may think them are no hindrance to the soul touched with the love of truth & goodness, that the study of truth in our own narrow sphere, is the beginning of universal wisdom, & that the humble endeavor to serve God in the particular duty this moment assigns to you, is a step taken toward all perfection.↓ [end of eighth folio] ¶ He feels . . . truth; to ⟨serve⟩ worship

23	↑the most . . . all;↓
27	virtues ⟨by⟩ in . . . single ⟨law⟩ ↑work↓.
29	one ⟨sin⟩ ↑wrong desire↓ [addition in ink over pencil]
31–34	all the ⟨aid⟩ strength . . . one. [The following cancellation, made in pencil, is rejected as a late emendation:] ⟨We must . . . us all.⟩ But
35	faith that ⟨every step in⟩ ↑whilst you have↓ . . . ↑every step↓

36   perfection. [Following the conclusion of the sermon, Emerson, having canceled the sentence noted above, added the following for what must be regarded as an intermediate version of the conclusion. The addition is rejected as a late emendation:] ↑↑Think of these things as Christians.↓ When we are ⟨↑{↓resisting sin & striving to plant in ourselves the peaceable fruits of righteousness↑}↓⟩ [brackets added in pencil] ↑engaged in acquiring truth & doing our duty↓ we are dealing with a wonderful an unfathomable nature. ⟨T⟩In attempting to discharge our duties to the few fellow beings whom God has placed next us, we are not only acquiring a claim to their love & respect but to the love & good offices of spirits that are now undergoing the same education in other countries or in other worlds or in other states of being. ↑{Insert D}↓ [At the bottom of the page, a passage marked "D":] ↑{In getting one truth by prayer & self examination we do not become richer by one fact but by an increased value in all that we have, & an increased power to know all things.}↓ In ⟨attempting to⟩ withstand↑ing↓ a temptation that besets us before few witnesses or none & leaving every thing undone that we may conquer that, we are withstanding all temptations & getting peace & power that every day & every age shall renew.—↓

Sermon CXXVIII

Manuscript: Nine sheets folded to make four pages each; folios stacked and sewn with white thread along the left margin; pages measure 25 x 20.2 cm.

[Above Bible text:] Anniversary of Female Asylum. 1831.

Lines	*Page 226*
2–9	whose ↑⟨3⟩thirty first↓ . . . the wis⟨e⟩dom . . . selected ⟨as well as the success which has followed⟩ the . . . benevolence. ⟨A certain extent of choice is allowed us.⟩ Whilst . . . we ⟨bind⟩ ↑are . . . for↓ ourselves ⟨in a strict ⟨union⟩ friendship only with a few.⟩ ↑those . . . friendship.↓ ¶ And ⟨of all⟩ ↑whilst↓ the ↑crowd of↓ . . . teems ⟨we⟩ ↑demand . . . respect↓, . . . particular ⟨ones, or help none.⟩ ↑claims.↓
10	charity ⟨can⟩ of . . . or ⟨so⟩ ↑more↓
12–17	↑200↓ [addition in pencil in a space left for it] . . . up, the ⟨greatest⟩ ↑most↓ . . . who can ⟨⟨say what had been⟩ ↑measure↓⟩ ↑estimate↓ . . . ensued? ¶ [The following addition, belonging to the second delivery of the sermon, is rejected as a late emendation:] ↑It has given me great pleasure to attend with others a part of the exercises of the pupils of this academy. In offering you some remarks this evening I thot I cd. not do better or choose a subject of more interest to you than that one which has called us together ¶ ⟨And⟩↓ [emendation in pencil] ¶ It . . . have ⟨espoused⟩ chosen,—
19	has ⟨an⟩ ↑a high↓ . . . but the ⟨education⟩ charge
22–25	connexion ⟨of⟩ ↑with↓ . . . ↑I believe↓ . . . attained. ¶ ⟨What⟩ ¶ What . . . be ⟨conducted.⟩ directed?

Page 227

3–10   ciphering, ⟨needlework⟩ ↑geography, ↑chemistry↓ ["chemistry"
        added in pencil] . . . housework↓ . . . *of education.* ⟨These accom-
        plishments admit their natural strength & skill, as if you lengthened
        their arms or gave cunning to their hands but they do not teach how to
        use them⟩ ↑{Insert A}↓ [On the facing page, a passage marked "A":]
        ↑{Let it . . . wise. ¶ ⟨It is⟩ ↑If your . . . it is↓ . . . them.}↓

14   fraudulent ⟨man⟩ ↑person↓ . . . forger ⟨must be a good penman⟩
        ↑writes well↓.

15–17   of a ⟨labored⟩ ↑too exclusive↓ . . . pupils, ⟨↑which God forbid↓⟩
        that . . . ↑a ⟨fairfaced⟩ [canceled in pencil; rejected as a late emenda-
        tion] enemy,↓ . . . cheat, ⟨and⟩or

19–21   ¶ ↑In saying . . . overestimated,↓ . . . surely not—⟨I would have them
        not left undone⟩, whilst . . . ↑I . . . undone↓.

25   exhibited ⟨worthy lives⟩ ↑great virtues↓,

30   women,—⟨what⟩ ↑very models of↓

32   independant

35–39   born. ↑{Insert B}↓ [A passage marked "B" on the facing page that
        appears to have followed the paragraph ending "God forbid." in the
        original inscription:] ↑↑I say therefore↓ The⟨se⟩ accomplishments
        . . . ↑↑are not enough,↓ ⟨do⟩ will not serve them↓ . . . themselves.↓ ¶
        ⟨True Education is as the name imports a drawing out of the Soul
        itself—it is the awakening in their right order the powers within,
        having for its end to constitute the pupil a living soul—a judge of
        action a distinguisher of truth & falsehood of right & wrong teaching
        him to see with his own eyes, & act ⟨with⟩ ↑from↓ his own will.⟩ ¶
        True

41–42   ↑(↓As . . . fly.↑)↓ [parentheses in pencil]

Page 228

2   not to ⟨b⟩make a useful ⟨satellite⟩ ↑/follower/disciple/↓, [cancella-
        tion and variants in pencil]

5   constitute ⟨him⟩ ↑the child↓

9   blending ⟨the⟩ [end of line] the

14–21   known to ⟨them by their own⟩ ↑the young learner ⟨his⟩ by his own↓
        . . . powers of ⟨their⟩ ↑this↓ . . . when ⟨they⟩ ↑he↓ . . . unfold to
        ⟨them⟩ ↑him↓ . . . for ⟨its⟩the . . . ↑of his youngest child;↓ . . . eye
        the ⟨vast⟩ sublime

24–27   ↑in schools,↓ . . . consideration ⟨whether⟩ ↑of↓ the child↑'s↓ ⟨is to
        command or obey, to be a scholar or ⟨to⟩ tradesman; ⟨a⟩ ↑be↓ rich
        or a pauper.⟩ ↑sex . . . it is is ⟨to⟩ study . . . bread.↓

29–30   child to ⟨declare⟩ ↑show↓ . . . & to ⟨find⟩ ↑take↓

33–37   from ⟨bad⟩ gross . . . supplying it⟨s⟩ . . . clothes ↑& occupying . . .
        way,↓ ⟨in short⟩ /by . . . orphans./And so many parents are very
        solicitous to remove ⟨every tempta⟩ evil influence bad example from
        their children & think they have done all their duty & insured their
        improvement when they have put them out of the reach of temptation/
        But [variant in pencil, rejected as belonging to the second delivery]

41–42   exposed / in your guarded retreat / with all yʳ care / , [variant in pencil, rejected as late emendation]

Page 229

2–4   them? ¶ ⟨Therefore⟩ ¶ ⟨2. In the second place,⟩ ↑Therefore↓ . . . them ⟨positive⟩ ↑actual↓ strength. ⟨You must⟩ Otherwise

7–10   means / ↑{↓you have here provided,↑}↓↓ / provided in schools / [brackets and variant in pencil; variant rejected as a late emendation] . . . you the ⟨solemn conclusion⟩ ↑memorable words↓ . . . situation, ⟨published his belief in 1797⟩ ↑declared . . . in 1797↓

13–16   ¶ ↑2. You . . . *provisions.* ↑must . . . well.↓↓ You must ⟨therefore⟩ aim . . . resolution. ⟨There must be the forms⟩ It

17–23   substance. ↑{Insert X}↓ [On the facing page, a passage marked "X":] ↑{And in . . . children. ⟨This⟩ ↑A good . . . friend↓ . . . sorts of ⟨business⟩ ↑work↓ which cannot ⟨don⟩ be done by mach↑i↓nery, . . . *by* ⟨*the*⟩ *hand.* . . . ↑to be effectual↓ must be given ⟨in private⟩ to ⟨the⟩ ↑teach↓ particular child.}↓

24   love ⟨&⟩ as

24–25   ↑a personal relation↓

28–29   ↑let me↓ call⟨ing⟩ it— . . . word. ⟨Then you must⟩ Nothing

32   ↑as it were↓ . . . must be ⟨shown⟩ practised.

33–34   ¶ But ⟨you cannot teach more than you know.⟩ ↑this . . . books.↓

34–35   upon the all . . . ↑& instruction↓

Page 230

6–7   themselves. ⟨Of the lessons of which I speak every day & every company & every⟩ ¶ Let . . . to ↑application of↓ . . . remarks ⟨th⟩ as it is ⟨commonly⟩ ↑sometimes↓

12–18   given. ⟨Th⟩ It . . . their ⟨babes⟩ ↑infant children↓. And ↑let↓ that ⟨is⟩ ↑be↓ the ⟨beauty⟩ ↑praise↓ . . . attempts by ⟨⟨anticipating⟩ ↑preventing↓ with its good influences⟩ ↑being . . . good↓

19–24   anecdotes ⟨recounted⟩ ↑in the life↓ . . . after he ⟨had re⟩ [end of page] he . . . ↑go . . . Switzerland↓ & he / serenely / calmly /

26–35   ↑entirely↓ fails of ⟨all⟩ effect. ↑It ⟨lives⟩ ↑is present↓ . . . cannot ⟨save⟩ prevent . . . it. ↑or follows offence with repentance.↓↓ ¶ ↑{↓Neither . . . fit the⟨m⟩ ↑soul↓ alike ↑to↓ ⟨to suffer or to rejoice⟩ ↑⟨⟨bear adversity⟩ persevere⟩ bear . . . ill↓ as ↑a↓ rational being⟨s⟩,—will fit ⟨them⟩ ↑⟨her⟩ your orphan↓ . . . & do ⟨their⟩ ↑her↓ . . . condition↑}↓ [brackets in pencil]

38–39   desireable to do—⟨b⟩But . . . to ⟨teach⟩ train

40   believe ⟨it⟩ ↑there is↓ require⟨s⟩d

Page 231

1–2   Yet ⟨our times have been fruitful in this way⟩ ↑many . . . times.↓

2–3   Edgeworth, M⟨iss⟩rs

4–6   or ⟨wi⟩rather read ↑in your own heart↓ . . . system. ⟨But let me earnestly press on the consideration not only of every patroness of this⟩ [end of MS p. 26; the continuation of this sentence occurs, uncanceled, at the top of MS p. 29 (see below) after the interpolation of two pages of new matter] ¶ Certainly . . . feel the ⟨weight⟩ importance

8–9   become. ⟨But ⟨I am not⟩ perhaps it does not become me to offer advice⟩ ¶ ⟨I wish however to call your attention briefly to one point of practical importance to all of us & that is that we are all instructors, let your connexion with this asylum of orphan children be near or remote all of us are by the constitution of society teachers of good or of evil.⟩ ¶ If

11   ↑with every step,↓

14   upon ⟨your⟩the attention ↑of . . . Seminary↓

19–(232)11   ¶ ↑{Let . . . little ones.} [Here as elsewhere in this sermon the brackets undoubtedly indicate omission of text in the second delivery.]

19–21   ¶ ↑{Let . . . Institution↓ [end of MS p. 28; the addition replaces the first half of the sentence canceled on MS p. 26 (see above); Emerson failed to alter the wording to match the revised syntax:] {Institution⟨,⟩ but on every parent, & on every . . . education, the ⟨steady power that all⟩ influence

23–24   better. ⟨We cannot teach more than we know.⟩ It is said . . . give ⟨more expression⟩ to . . . more ⟨genius⟩ intelligence . . . himself. ⟨I believe our incapacity as teachers⟩ Sure

26–27   children ⟨Ha⟩Do . . . society? ⟨&⟩ Have you vice↑s↓?

28–29   children you . . . but you ⟨take⟩ defraud

31   virtue is [end of page] is made

34   lowest. ⟨The fashion that is set in the selectest⟩ What

Page 232

6   family ⟨attended⟩ ↑served↓ by ⟨domestics⟩ ↑those who see & hear↓

11–12   little ones.} ¶ ↑The cause of education is the cause of all. Our happiness depends so much on others that every ⟨child of God⟩ one ↑must↓ desire⟨s⟩ that others may be trained well. But not for ourselves if we are Christians not for ourselves let us do what we can to educate the souls of our brethren but that they may be happy Let us seek the good of others because they are Gods children & we desire to add to the amount of well being in the universe↓ [in pencil, rejected as a late addition] ¶ Again

12–13   on the ⟨succes⟩ measure

13–15   has ⟨strengthened your hands⟩ witnessed . . . love of ⟨its⟩their

17   none ⟨cheris⟩h⟨e⟩ad ⟨y⟩ the good

18–19   them." ¶ ↑In the death of↓ Mrs Elizabeth Dorr ⟨was⟩ ↑you have lost↓ . . . original ⟨managers⟩ board

20–22   ↑long eno' to be loved & honoured,↓ . . . than ⟨the wealth⟩ ↑power↓

24–25   friends ↑& ⟨&⟩most munificent patrons↓

28   ↑let me say,↓ . . . shall be ⟨her ⟨a⟩the⟩ ↑her↓

30–31   remains ⟨to say⟩ briefly to ↑remind↓ . . . children↑.↓ ⟨to⟩ If

Sermon CXXIX

Manuscript: Four sheets folded to make four pages each, and a single leaf, containing the sermon number with the Bible text (recto) and insert "A" (verso), included in the sewing;

folios are stacked and sewn with white thread along the left margin; folio pages measure
25 x 19.9 cm; the single leaf measures 24.9 x 20.1 cm.

Lines	*Page 233*
Bible Text	which ⟨God⟩ the Lord
1–2	↑in↓ which all men /take/agree/ [emendations in pencil] . . . sustain. ⟨We may differ⟩ Christians of diff denom
4–7	↑human↓ . . . ↑that individuals make great improvement↓ & that ⟨we⟩all ought to ⟨be mended.⟩ make some. ⟨We all at⟩ And . . . this that
7–12	↑We . . . resisted ⟨that every day shd. witness some improvement in our character.⟩ ¶ This . . . approbation of all. {Insert A}↓ [On the facing page, a passage marked "A":] ↑{From . . . I ⟨wish⟩ ↑ask permission↓ . . . hours.}↓
17–22	keeping. ⟨He⟩ Now . . . seek to ⟨bind⟩ ↑afflict ⟨himself⟩↓ himself / to/with/ . . . stern ⟨unrelenting⟩ ↑unbending↓
24	cheerful ⟨con⟩ ↑unrestrained converse↓

	Page 234
4–5	it be ⟨more al⟩ ↑as bad . . . think it↓
7–8	¶ ↑My . . . distinctions.↓ ⟨Now i⟩If
9–13	↑does really↓ . . . impulse ⟨to vice⟩ of passion in th⟨is⟩at . . . as if ⟨he⟩ ↑we↓ . . . whether ⟨he⟩ ↑we↓ ha⟨s⟩ve . . . sleep ⟨also⟩ ↑all our lives,↓, & ha⟨s⟩ve . . . awake when ⟨he was⟩ ↑others thot us↓ . . . dreaming when ⟨he⟩ ↑we↓ tho't ⟨he was⟩ ↑we were↓
15–16	conscience. ⟨↑1.↓⟩ Therefore
21–22	which ⟨is⟩may . . . merit of ⟨that⟩ ↑a good↓
23–24	↑It . . . than our hearts.↓ [ink over pencil]
27–28	savage⟨s⟩ . . . strength & ⟨prowess⟩ ↑courage↓
31–34	you↑,↓ [addition in pencil] . . . soul to ⟨attain⟩ seek. But ⟨it⟩ ↑the present advantage↓ [addition in ink over pencil] . . . you ⟨by⟩ ↑in↓
35	me↑,↓ [addition in pencil]
38–40	return↑,↓ [addition in pencil] . . . ↑of principle↓
42–(235)3	↑This . . . This ↑if you persevere↓ . . . solitude.↓

	Page 235
4	↑One triumph is not enough↓ [in ink over pencil] be
5	↑Blessed . . . endureth. ↑to the end.↓↓
8	said with ⟨almost⟩ equal
11–12	very ⟨plea⟩ ↑ground↓ . . . abatement of /your/the severity of your/
14–16	↑thou↓ . . . expression) ↑do not↓ . . . *resolution.* ↑⟨T⟩Do not think . . . begun. ⟨ & do not hasten to indulge⟩↓ Simply
18	virtue ⟨i⟩on
18–19	↑Self distrust . . . of a ⟨determined⟩ mind . . . faithful.↓
20	so ⟨indulge⟩ think
27	& find⟨ing⟩eth
34	independant
35	who ⟨have⟩ are

36–(236)1   desireable . . . me. ⟨You⟩ ↑They↓ . . . calls ⟨you in an⟩ ↑them using
               the↓ unfeigned ⟨feeling⟩ ↑apology↓ . . . what ⟨you⟩ ↑they↓

Page 236

6–7   ↑I fear↓ You
10   ↑& to a life for others↓
13   soul? ⟨⟨It is because—⟩ Is⟩ Do
15–16   ↑yet↓ manifested ⟨to⟩ your
18   his infinit⟨e⟩y ⟨character⟩
25   *For Thy Sake,* [double underscoring (italics here)]
28–30   instrumentality, ⟨that though the wide universe is full of good⟩ ↑that
               ⟨gifted⟩ created . . . him,↓ . . . your ⟨portion⟩ ↑inheritance↓; [last
               emendation in pencil]
34–35   open ⟨goodness⟩ ↑the virtues,↓ . . . draw ↑to you↓
36   cannot ⟨te⟩ teach

Page 237

1   ↑desire &↓
7   ↑In . . . temptation↓ If
11–14   eyes, ⟨&⟩ the glories ↑shall↓ . . . made.—⟨Blessed is yᵉ man yᵗ
               endureth temp for when he is tried he shall recve a crown of life wh yᵉ
               Lord hath promised⟩↑Blessed . . . love him.↓ [addition in ink over
               pencil]

Sermon CXXX

Manuscript: Eight sheets folded to make four pages each; folios stacked and sewn with
white thread along the left margin; pages measure 25 x 20.1 cm.

Lines   Page 238
Bible Text   ↑Ye . . . said↓ . . . neighbor a⟨s⟩nd thy hate thine ⟨self⟩enemy. . . .
               Matt. 5. 43–44. [Bible text in pencil; "Matt. 5. 43–44." in ink over
               pencil]
2   that the /spirit/instructions/ [rejected variant in pencil]
4–5   ↑Its . . . effectual↓ [in pencil]
6   danger ↑of↓
9   commu- [end of page] munity.
11   avoids↑.↓ ⟨& as naturally⟩ ⟨⟨& finds a pleasing triumph in showing
               the superiority of his system,⟩ ["& finds . . . system," canceled in
               pencil and ink] to use . . . man in ⟨vulgar⟩ ↑low↓ [emendations in ink
               over pencil]
15   ↑speculative↓ [addition in pencil]
18   keep ⟨alive⟩ their
19–22   love. ↑And↓ [Addition in pencil in the left margin, serving as a key to
               the following passage on the preceding facing page, also in pencil:]
               ↑And . . . of record the . . . considerations In Asia . . . Britain↓ In
               ⟨5⟩A.D.

Page 239

6–8   prayed." ↑Vol 1. p 38↓ ⟨And in recounting the events⟩ ↑Nor had
        ⟨they⟩it lost ⟨their⟩its character↓ . . . ↑for in . . . period↓
13   disciples ⟨as⟩ for
14–18   nation↑,↓ . . . to it↑,↓ . . . honor↑,↓ ⟨yes⟩ & . . . quarters↑,↓
        [emendations in pencil]
20–21   Christian ⟨the believer⟩ the . . . separation ⟨that so⟩ ↑that↓ [addition
        in pencil] secluded ⟨him⟩ ↑the disciple↓ [emendation in pencil]
23   had ⟨deviated from⟩ broken
33   ↑(↓reputed good↑)↓ [parentheses in pencil]
36   some ⟨pro⟩ real
38–(240)3 progress↑,↓ . . . general /advantages/fruits/ . . . them go [end of
        page; the leaf that follows is blank except for the phrase "hath made
        wise" inscribed upside down at the bottom of the verso] & they . . .
        principle↑,—↓a [addition in pencil]

Page 240

5   with the ⟨l⟩ ↑gospel↓
5–6   ↑And leaving . . . this↓ [in pencil]
8   of ⟨its⟩ reign of
13   day, ⟨and as one⟩ ↑a single↓ [emendation in pencil]
14   what ⟨rare⟩ name [cancellation in pencil]
17   this all /searching/embracing/ [variant in pencil]
21   helpless, the ⟨d⟩ insane, . . . dumb, ⟨&⟩ the
23   farther. ⟨They⟩ It
24–25   taught ⟨them⟩ you the great sum of [end of line] of your
37–38   you ↑tho' the fear of men may↓ from
40   debt ⟨whilst⟩ ↑as long as↓

Page 241

3–4   parties & ↑worry↓ . . . his ⟨spotless⟩ ↑silly↓
9–10   it ⟨from⟩ ↑out of mere↓ [emendation in pencil] pride & folly. ⟨Who⟩
        ¶ Whilst
11   ↑go one step farther↓
17–19   injured. ⟨One p⟩ How . . . well ⟨intentioned⟩ ↑meaning↓.
22–23   ↑Glimpses . . . day.↓
23–25   ↑pagan↓ . . . me," and ⟨the⟩ ↑a↓ [emendation in pencil] poor novel
        that /goes/has gone/ [variant in pencil]
26–28   forbearance ⟨The Christian rule⟩ ↑Now let me ⟨state⟩ ↑revert to↓
        ["state" canceled and "revert to" added in pencil] . . . which↓ . . .
        extravagant superhuman ⟨⟨submit to wrong⟩ ↑rather↓⟩, *love* . . .
        thyself ↑not↓ submit ⟨not⟩ to
29–30   ↑{↓Avoid evil persons↑,↓ . . . them.↑}↓ [additions in pencil]
31   blow; & ⟨cloke⟩ coat
32   'be ⟨not sud⟩ slow
33   advice⟨,⟩ is,
38–39   *motive* [underscored in pencil (italics here)] ↑and what is the motive↓
        [addition in pencil].

39–(242)1   you ⟨because⟩ not . . . blow↑,↓ . . . good↑,↓ [commas added in pencil]

Page 242

6   pretend, ⟨&⟩ as
7–8   practice & what
12   points ⟨of⟩ at
15–16   mean ⟨is their pomp & place⟩ ↑an object . . . France↓ compared with the ⟨glory of⟩ /reason/knowledge/ [variant in pencil] & virtue ↑to↓
17–18   claim. ¶ ⟨Let that be your principle & it will be sword & shield about you preventing foes by turning all men into friends. No man would ever come under the imputation of cowardice who was animated by this spirit. It would swallow up in its divine flame the meaner fires of self love & resentment which ⟨teach⟩ make men quarrelsome. It would show a courage in every days conflict that would make the courage of the mere soldier ridiculous It would show Christians ready to do all, to endure all, to rejoice over all for the sake of the good of others⟩ [canceled in pencil] ¶ In short every ⟨increase of⟩ time
21–22   impracticable & ⟨the same reason of quaker⟩ ↑if . . . of↓ non resistance ⟨would⟩ ↑why the Xn law↓ appl⟨y⟩ies
24   certainly ⟨it⟩ ↑the rule↓ . . . ↑sincere↓
26–27   unequal [end of line] the condition
28   ↑No;↓ It
31   unlike & ⟨the⟩ would
34–36   ↑as his own,↓ . . . with ⟨care &⟩ humanity
40–41   let ⟨the⟩ customs

Page 243

1   will /bring you out ⟨right.⟩ ↑safe.↓/not betray you/ [emendations in pencil] ⟨P⟩ Seek
3   anothers ⟨comfort⟩ ↑convenience↓

Sermon CXXXI

Manuscript: Six sheets folded to make four pages each, and a single leaf following leaf 12, included in the sewing; folios stacked and sewn with white thread along the left margin; folio pages measure 24.9 x 20.1 cm, and the single leaf measures 25 x 20.3 cm.

Lines   *Page 244*
1   ¶ ⟨Let every thing that hath breath praise the Lord.⟩ [cf. Psalms 150:6] It
5–6   much is ⟨bodily⟩ material.
8   experiment is /made/tried/, ↑after verses are made↓ [emendations in pencil]
10   of the ⟨minds⟩ ear,
11–12   it ↑hardest . . . poetry↓

13   ↑the throbbing heart,↓ the ↑hearing↓ ear ⟨& the air⟩ & the
                    ↑speaking↓

Page 245

4–5   pathway ⟨by which⟩ of ⟨the human⟩ ↑our↓ . . . mankind a
8–11   In ⟨the⟩ ancient . . . ceremonial. ⟨A⟩ When . . . ↑Methodists &↓
14–17   ↑For . . . both↓ It . . . Soul. ⟨I understand⟩ Psalmody . . . music. ⟨I
                    understand⟩ I am . . . ↑I believe↓
17–18   last↑.↑—↓I wish . . . books. I am↓
21   can ⟨soothe awake⟩ arouse, ↑thrill,↓
22–24   I ⟨am⟩ desire . . . man. ↑flat, . . . & are.↓
33   exalting ⟨the⟩ devout

Page 246

3–6   ↑until the last century such low & inharmonious↓ so ⟨flat &
                    prosaic,⟩ ↑sunk↓ . . . criticism. ⟨However⟩ One . . . Miriam, to
                    ⟨have⟩ give
11–14   congregation. ⟨Milton⟩ ↑The best poet↓ [emendation in pencil] . . .
                    permitting the ⟨wretched⟩ ↑unskilful↓
17   verses ⟨of⟩ used
18   have ⟨contributed⟩ turned
23   collections & ⟨now⟩ [canceled in pencil] many
26–27   recieved . . . by /the American churches/enlightened men/ [variant
                    in pencil] . . . ↑near forty years ago↓
28–30   elapsed ⟨of⟩ in . . . the public /mind/attention/ . . . have ↑been↓

Page 247

2–9   meeting ⟨false & injurious⟩ ↑confused↓ . . . as the ⟨prominent⟩
                    central . . . ↑as in yᵉ 122 hymn. . . . lost." H. 122↓
14–19   do not ⟨desire⟩ ↑feel . . . us↓ . . . our hymn ⟨call him⟩ ↑say,↓ . . .
                    commandment. ¶ ⟨And if⟩ But . . . God. ⟨There is⟩ ⟨l⟩Language
                    ↑is↓
29   hymns ⟨a⟩that
32–33   hymns. ⟨w⟩ ↑and . . . angels.↓
35–36   liberal [end of line] churches [Between these lines "A less defect" has
                    been inserted and canceled.]
38–39   contains ⟨many⟩ ↑numbers of↓ . . . church. ⟨Many⟩ Much

Page 248

6   Christian ⟨spirit⟩ religion.
14   sung, ⟨&⟩ and ↑again↓
16   ↑many↓ more than ⟨1⟩200
20–23   well to ⟨state these facts⟩ ↑make these remarks↓ . . . ↑because . . .
                    remedy, and↓ [emendations in pencil] . . . been ↑& is↓
24–26   time. ⟨I doubt not you will determine wisely⟩ ↑& before ⟨it is
                    presented⟩ the report of yᵗ Com . . . action↓ & I . . . what I ⟨th⟩
                    esteem . . . of ⟨Belknap.⟩ ↑our . . . change.↓
27   ¶ There ⟨a⟩has . . . ↑Christian↓

28–29	suffrage of ⟨all⟩ ↑many↓
32–33	temple. ¶ ⟨We do not buil⟩ We worship
33	no ⟨hangings⟩ ↑tapestry↓
35	↑God↓ . . . for ⟨the⟩ man,
35–36	not ⟨rest till this⟩ think

[The following list is inscribed after the end of the sermon:]
Faults of Belknap
1. False views of God
2. False views of Christ
3. Loose notions about immortality
4. Unchristian sentiment
5. Material imagery, gross notions of Spiritual things; & low & flat expression
6. ⟨Want of good hymns⟩ ↑Bad method of Ps & H.↓

Sermon CXXXII

Manuscript: Eight sheets folded to make four pages each; folios stacked and sewn with white thread along the left margin; pages measure 25 x 20.2 cm.

Lines	*Page 249*
5	irreconcileable
5–6	which ⟨ev⟩all descriptions cover. ⟨Goodness though⟩ All
8–9	↑think . . . fourth↓
11–12	↑All . . . God↓
13–14	that ⟨th⟩ goodness . . . be; ⟨&⟩ is
19–21	that ⟨Ch⟩ the sum . . . to the ⟨w⟩ Commandments; . . . them⟨, giving⟩ showing
24	↑preceded &↓

	Page 250
4–5	↑From . . . Serm. on Mount . . . Cross all . . . men↓
7–8	namely a ⟨personal⟩ claim to ↑to divert a part of our↓ . . . veneration ⟨I⟩ ↑from God to himself↓ [emendations in pencil]
9	came ⟨to⟩ a
12–17	kill ⟨his⟩their enemies [Emerson here skips a line.] and . . . miracles ⟨all done⟩ ↑that were only↓ . . . weapon, no⟨t⟩ not . . . Romans this . . . wanted they
23–25	↑And in . . . Gods↓ And ⟨if⟩ he ⟨were⟩ ↑being↓ [emendations in pencil] . . . were wide wide of
34–35	irreconcileable

	Page 251
5	jewish
6	thought. ⟨Peter⟩ What
8–9	nation ⟨whoso⟩ ↑the that↓ . . . accepted ⟨of⟩ ↑with↓
16–20	the ↑Ep. to the↓ Hebrews . . . Lord." (Heb. 12. 14) ¶ 1 John 5.3 ¶ James ¶ But

25–26   or ⟨pu⟩ mere . . . sneer. ↑⟨There⟩ there is . . . religious↓
26–27   heaven. ⟨They⟩ ↑Men↓
29   now do. ⟨To⟩ Who
32   ↑of them↓ will ⟨op⟩ unfold
37   Sinai⟨e⟩.
40–(252)4 first ⟨& second⟩ if they did not ⟨make an idol with their fingers nor⟩
         worship Baal ↑or Jupiter↓ . . . vow. ¶ & so of the rest. ¶ Christ

Page 252

8   shalt not ⟨not⟩ love
16   ↑not our own but↓
18–21   ↑This . . . rest [end of line] & will . . . earth↓
22   idols neither
24–30   God. [Emerson reverses the next two paragraphs by renumbering
         them:] ¶ ⟨3⟩4. We shd . . . homage to God. ¶ ⟨4⟩3. We should
         ⟨honour our parents⟩ ↑keep our vows↓ . . . ¶ 6 We . . . hate. [The
         following notation is added at the end of the line:] ↑Whosoever is
         angry with his brother without cause↓ [Having turned the page,
         Emerson neglected to number the seventh through the tenth com-
         mandments; the numbers have been editorially supplied.]
36–39   home to ⟨the⟩ ↑our↓ actions . . . neighbor. ↑& see . . . mean↓

Page 253

1   clandestin↑e↓ley
3   iniquitous. ⟨Then⟩ Do
8   them? & ⟨is⟩must
11–15   interpretation. ⟨& more than this they are their own reward⟩ ↑While
         . . . ↑for the creature ⟨m⟩Man↓ . . . him↓ & so . . . was, ⟨mans⟩
         the whole
18   religion. (If thou wilt enter into life keep the commandments,) [Text
         in parentheses rejected as the false start of a transition into what
         follows:] & that is
35   we d⟨o⟩id
38–40   makes that the⟨y⟩ commandments . . . them & . . . or the ⟨appl⟩
         music⟨e⟩ of divine applause ⟨↑You↓⟩ [addition and cancellation in
         pencil]

[In addition to the canceled "You" that would seem to be the beginning of another
sentence in the last line of the text, Emerson drafted the following, in pencil, after the
closing:] ¶ ↑⟨You⟩ ¶ There is no more fitting or sublime employment than ⟨to seek⟩ to
keep these rules for a day. Every ⟨step⟩ transgression of them the least as well as the
largest in private or in public is a wrong step & must be retraced, & that with shame &
sorrow. God in heaven beholds each of our hearts↓

Sermon CXXXIII

Manuscript: Six sheets folded to make four pages each, a single leaf, containing the
sermon number, Bible text, and opening paragraphs, included in the sewing but now

torn away, and two single leaves, the first between leaves 6 and 7, the second between leaves 8 and 9, both included in the sewing; folios stacked and sewn with white thread along the left margin; the folio pages and the second and third single leaves measure 25.1 x 20.2 cm, and the single leaf containing the opening matter measures 25 x 20 cm. The text on this first leaf (down to the middle of the last sentence in the fifth paragraph) appears to be the revision of a lost original opening, and was probably written for the second and third deliveries in June 1836. Additionally, following leaf 12 and containing several draft passages, but not included in the sewing, are a loose single leaf, 24.9 x 20 cm, another loose single leaf, 18.2 x 20 cm, and a single sheet folded to make four pages (of which only the recto of the first leaf is inscribed), measuring 24.9 x 20.1 cm.

Lines	*Page 254*
7–8	↑the strangest misapprehensions exist.↓ [addition in pencil]
10	like a⟨n⟩ dress,
16	¶ ↑I speak . . . unbelievers↓ [addition in pencil]
19	entertained [manuscript torn; end of page] the
21–22	that we /ought all to /clear/settle/ our thoughts on the subject/are all liable to be misled/ ¶ This general /error/misapprehension/ [variants in pencil]
24–25	respects the /will/practice/

	Page 255
5–6	faith is [end of MS p. 2] is meritorious, [At the top of MS p. 3 is the notation "CXXXIII" in green pencil, probably not by Emerson.]
10	but ↑is↓
14	is by ⟨its⟩ ↑the mind's↓
17–18	↑the rules of↓ arithmetic or /chemistry/agriculture/? [emendations in pencil]
23	¶ Again, th⟨ey⟩ose
27–30	↑I say . . . bread.↓ [in pencil]
31	practi⟨s⟩ce.
33–35	that ⟨they are⟩ those . . . ↑to use certain language↓ [addition in pencil]
38–40	only ⟨have⟩ ↑hold↓ . . . ↑unworthy↓ ["unworthy" added in pencil]

	Page 256
10–13	realities. ²{What sort of merchant would he be who talked . . . sold? ¹{What sort of a farmer who ↑talked of cultivation but↓ [addition and transposition markers in pencil]
19–21	↑The heart . . . nothing↓ [in pencil] ¶ ⟨Pure religion I understand to consist in *doing right from a right motive*. It is not only, to keep the commandments,—but to keep them from love to the goodness & wisdom that made them & us that is—from love to God. ⟨Its⟩The operation of religious truth is twofold,—upon the *understanding;* & upon the *will*.⟩ ¶ Only . . . this ⟨ceremonious⟩ ↑formal↓ [emendation in pencil]
21	for ⟨a fellow mortal⟩ ↑the society of his friend;↓ [addition in ink over pencil] is it ↑of↓

23   he ⟨have⟩ ↑need↓ to ⟨assume⟩ ↑put on↓
24–25   delight ⟨he⟩ of . . . ↑the enjoyment of↓
27–28   on ⟨topics⟩ subjects . . . lives ⟨for⟩ ↑to study↓,
30   gay /ball/party/ [variant in pencil]
34   botanist a ⟨flower⟩ ↑plant↓;
35–38   ↑he cannot . . . & he ⟨has the⟩ is . . . issue.↓
41–(257)1   or ↑to↓ . . . with ⟨sheer⟩ ↑manifest↓

Page 257

2   wants [end of page; on the next page, otherwise blank, is the
                following notation in pencil:] ¶ ↑Now is it any different with our
                possession of religion My brethren it is not. That also must be seen &
                felt to be a reality, must be loved with the whole heart to be of any
                use↓ [end of page] are satisfied
3   them & ⟨know⟩ ↑not imagine↓ [addition in ink over pencil]
5   have ⟨it or⟩ any
5–16   ↑It . . . him.↓ ¶ ↑↑{Insert↓ X}↓ [Emerson originally placed the insert
                after "has it not." and moved it after he added the next sentence. Four
                pages before, on the recto of leaf 8, a passage marked "X":] ↑{And so
                . . . see ⟨with⟩ what ↑an↓ . . . ↑It . . . contentment↓ [addition in
                pencil] . . . religion has ⟨got to be⟩ ↑become↓ . . . far each . . .
                doing. ↑which . . . soul↓↓ [last phrase added in pencil; end of "Insert
                X"]
20–23   false. ¶ ⟨Truth is also received into the *Will*. And unless it be so, a man
                is not a religious man.⟩ ¶ ⟨But⟩ when . . . give. ⟨It is a⟩ The
28   only ⟨solid⟩ ↑unmixed↓
30–31   that the ⟨operation⟩ ↑question . . . reality↓ . . . question ⟨of⟩ ↑as
                to↓
33   him ⟨he will embrace with joy a revelation of truth⟩ it

Page 258

2–4   some ↑who . . . affections↓ the further question—⟨Is⟩ Since
5   understand the ⟨me⟩ value . . . it they
11–12   doubts /of this nature/that reach to this extent/, . . . ↑(what . . .
                case,)↓ . . . facts ⟨within the reach of every one⟩ that
16–20   soul↑.↓ ⟨that . . . mind.⟩ [emendation rejected as late] [The following
                four paragraphs are rejected as late additions:] ↑¶ Go study the
                wonders of your spiritual nature; see how might⟨y⟩ily it works in the
                breast of the humblest & vilest men. Go to a great public meeting that
                calls together all classes to debate a question of common interest
                Listen to the orator ↑when he rises to eloquence,↓ & see the means by
                which he works. What is it that sways that stormy multitude to the
                will of one & leads them as with a thread? ↑What is it goes to the
                bottom of the heart?↓ What is it that brings the blood in an instant to
                a thousand faces? ↑Not ⟨me⟩appeals to mean passions↓ Not the
                promise of plunder or of any present advantage—but the announcing
                of a great ⟨sentiment⟩ & generous principle the utterance of a lofty
                sentiment—the determination to be free—the determination to abide

by the right—this knits into one all the discordant parts of that ⟨great⟩ ↑living↓ mass, in a breathless silence or a thunder of acclamation. An assembly of men *are searched by principles* as an assembly of angels might be. ↑↑A principle↓ ⟨&⟩seems to ⟨impart⟩ ↑swell↓ a sort of omnipotence to so slender a creature as man.↓ ¶ Moreover in your own private tho'ts have you not found yourself thrilled to the bottom of the soul by an anecdote of virtue? ¶ Then did it never strike you as mysterious & show the greatness of your nature that every truth the ⟨strangest⟩ the most novel ⟨&⟩ and amazing that is advanced has nothing strange in it but seems old & familiar ↑We seem to recognize a truth the first time we hear it.↓ The universe seems to contain no ⟨truths⟩ knowledge of which the principles are not laid up in the soul, no facts whose laws are not. ¶ But what is this in us so quick to hear so wise to judge?—What is this that so stirs at a noble ⟨& divine⟩ truth, as a traveller at ↑the sound of↓ his own language in a foreign land? Is it not the spirit of God in us? & is such an inmate to perish like a worm under the foot.↓ ¶ Do

21–23   there is ⟨the Conscience⟩ that . . . man. ⟨Under the broad vault of heaven e⟩Every ⟨individual⟩ ↑child↓ . . . under the ⟨great⟩ ↑broad↓ . . . globe Every

26   which ⟨nations are def⟩ truth

30–35   made. ¶ {And . . . revenge.}

42–(259)3   ↑{↓For these . . . wrong only . . . sorrow.↑}↓ [Brackets in pencil, probably indicating the substitution, in a later delivery, of the following text, which is inscribed in pencil on the otherwise blank facing page:] ↑1. that there are truths which you ought to receive. It is unworthy of a mind to which God has imparted Reason to live in yᵉ world without using it—without reflection without asking itself whence it came & whither it goes. Who is its Maker & what are his laws. Go read them in the SS. Go study them in the life & death of Christ & you shall find they are all plain & easy to be understood by those who are ready to hear. ¶ 2. that yˢe truths being recd are commandments wh. ought to be obeyed, that they teach something which all can do, which will promote our happiness if obeyed, & which will certainly make us unhappy disapproved of God hateful to man hateful to ourselves if disobeyed↓ Religion

Page 259

5   we ⟨do not⟩ keep them ⟨m⟩they

[Following the close of the sermon, a notation in pencil:] ↑the more you know↓

[The following passage, possibly rejected draft material, is inscribed on the loose sheets and folio following the close of the sermon:]

↑⟨My friends⟩ But St Paul says in the text If our gospel is hid it is hid from them that are lost, ⟨or, if⟩ that is, 'if we do not see the reality of this good wo unto us!'

And what is it which he & so many other fervent men in every age have ⟨so e⟩ used such earnestness in commending to us. Let our best hours declare—↑The religious life—

the gospel—&c, is, the reception of true views of ourselves & our duties The world is governed by one set of principles, namely, the satisfaction of the lower desires Jesus & God teach us another set of principles & the reception of these makes this new view of all things↓ [addition in pencil]

The Scriptures call the entrance of the religious sentiment into the soul a passing from death unto life, they call it a being born again; they compare the change from the life of sin to the life of holiness to the passing away of the heavens & the earth and to the appearing of new heaven & earth. Its effects are descr↑i↓bed by all terms of sweetness & fragrance & delight

And truly ⟨friends⟩ ↑no description can be extravagant↓ it deserves all this love & praise. It is the great revolution in the mind, ↑the parent event in the history of each man,↓ an event which apprises us for the first time of the worth of being and the nature of the soul. The natural birth of man into this world, as it is ⟨merely⟩ ↑no more than↓ the opening of the senses to the sights, sounds, smells, tastes, & touches of surrounding things, is merely the arrival of the best of animals into his pasture & stall; & cannot compare in importance with the awakening of the religious sentiment in the Soul; for that is the arrival of the Soul into its own world, into a more glorious nature, where, as from a high place, it sees the poverty of the bodily nature, and sees ⟨that⟩ how much itself is better, sees that itself ⟨is⟩ hath all things, that for it all things were made. My friends we spend so much time upon the life & comfort of our bodies ⟨that⟩ that when at times we remember the perfections of its inmate, they strike us with awe & surprize [end of page; the appearance of the handwriting and the allusion to Swedenborg suggest that the next two paragraphs, which occur on the second loose leaf, are of a later composition, and probably date to 1836]

The Religious Sentiment is one. it is a life out of which many virtues flow as out of one body many members. All these virtues are the practice of principles precisely contrary to those which are popular in the world. It desires peace with all men. It desires the good of all men & reckons nothing good for itself but that ⟨b⟩which carries equal benefit to others. It is lowly. & counts him greate⟨r⟩st who is humblest. In the eye of the soul he who serves most commands most. God is the servant of the Universe and if there were any being whom he did not benefit he would not be the God of that being. In like manner the oldest & wisest are the most childlike, so that it was well said by a spiritual seer that "in heaven the oldest angel appears the youngest" [Swedenborg, *The Apocalypse Revealed* (London, 1832) 1:255; see *JMN* 5:115 and *CW* 4:71] In the growth of its affections, it perceives its whole being to be a receiving & giving, that no man can truly say "this is mine" but he is rich who yields the most good. he richest who feels & acts as if nothing were his own.

A man discovers that he has invisible riches which make all others vile. that he has a felicity incorruptible which neither loss of health nor of property nor of friends can bereave him of—that ↑it↓ is father mother friends house & home to them who are destitute of all. [end of page]

It counts prosperity dangerous. It embraces a lowly lot. It accepts the lowest place. It hates flattery. It loves reproof.

In short it aims at perfection. It perceives that where worldly men think is profound darkness, there is indeed perfect light that upon the private thoughts of our heart the whole spiritual world opens its eye. These indeed are more manifest than any public action for an action is but one & finite; being done, it ends; but a thought is the seed & parent of many actions & seeks continually to publish itself in action. It retires from the discordant noise of human censure & praise ↑as from confusion & twilight↓ to find in itself a clear public & universal verdict upon all actions↓

Sermon CXXXIV

Manuscript: Six sheets folded to make four pages each from which the last leaf has been torn away (leaving only its stub in the sewing), a single leaf between the fourth and fifth folios included in the sewing, and a single loose leaf once included in the sewing following leaf 12. A single sheet folded to make four pages, containing an early draft of portions of the sermon, is not included in the sewing. Folios stacked and sewn with white thread along the left margin; pages measure 25.1 x 20.2 cm.

The detached thirteenth leaf contains on the verso what is clearly the original conclusion of the sermon (the last sixteen words of the last sentence and the inscription "Chardon St. 6 November, 1831."). The recto, which was probably blank in the original version, now contains what appears to be late rewritten material, most probably a revision of the text on the removed leaf from folio 6. While the physical evidence of the manuscript does not allow for a firm determination of the presence or extent of late additions to the text, the editors regard all but the final sixteen words of the two concluding paragraphs as most likely to have been written after the first delivery. If, as the editors believe, the final paragraph contains an allusion to Swedenborg, the inscription could hardly have been made before the fifth delivery.

Lines	Page 260
1	name ⟨the word⟩ Truth
6–7	make us ⟨apply the language of David—'There is none that doeth good,'—so is there none that speaketh truth, no, not one.⟩ [canceled in pencil; cf. Psalms 53:3] ↑see . . . liars↓
8–15	begin ⟨th⟩ an . . . will ⟨specify⟩ speak of truth ⟨in the sense of *sincerity*⟩ ↑of conversation↓ . . . customs. ¶ ⟨The more important is any interest event the nearer any thing is to the heart the more impatient are we of insincerity We can bear that people should exercise their loquacity upon things that do not interest us & to which we need not give heed, but that which touches us to the quick they must not scratch with idle prating⟩ ¶ ↑↑I propose to consider↓ 1. . . . conversation ¶ 2. Truth . . . convers.↓
19–24	expected to ⟨make of⟩ say . . . maker & ↑the↓ . . . expected ⟨of a man⟩, than that ⟨he⟩ a . . . truth. ⟨W⟩How . . . you ⟨know⟩ ↑meet↓ [last emendation in pencil]
25–26	↑some from contradiction;↓

	Page 261
6	their ⟨expressions⟩ ↑exclamations↓ ⟨of wonder the⟩ ↑surprize↓
8–16	to them. ↑{Insert X}↓ [A passage marked "X" on the following page inscribed in ink over the same in pencil:] ↑{This . . . to ⟨all⟩ ↑much of↓ [emendation in pencil] . . . demands, ⟨since custom has once established⟩ a compliance . . . flattery.}↓
17–21	others ⟨more⟩ ↑almost as↓ numerous↑,↓ ⟨than these,⟩ ↑in↓ whose . . . occurrence ↑and . . . important part,↓ . . . ↑cannot↓ impose⟨s⟩ upon ⟨no⟩ ↑any↓

25   is ⟨exploring⟩ feeling
28–29   living for, ⟨among those who have good understandings⟩. ↑You may
                . . . But to me it seems worst where it is apt to intrude↓ [addition in
                pencil on the facing page] ↑But to me it seems worst where it is apt to
                intrude↓ [addition in ink]
33   but ⟨idle prating⟩ they
38–39   silent. ⟨There are⟩ ↑We . . . between↓ [emendation in pencil]

Page 262

1   thing ⟨good⟩ seems fading away ↑from him↓,
2   we ⟨d⟩ mourn
4   makes ⟨us⟩ ↑him↓
7–12   all the ⟨forms of⟩ violations . . . conversation ⟨Now⟩ ↑The source
                . . . same.↓ [addition in ink over pencil] the vice . . . defect ⟨a want⟩
                which . . . us ⟨have got to learn somewhere somehow⟩ ↑must
                perceive↓ . . . —↑I mean↓
15   ↑or should . . . bread.↓ [ink over pencil]
18   times ⟨des⟩ should
20   more he
24–26   but ⟨Go⟩ we . . . from the ⟨yo⟩ oldest . . . as ⟨childre⟩ little . . . his
                ¹Word & by his ²Providence [although the numbering of these words
                seems to leave their order intact, one can only suppose that Emerson
                meant to transpose them]
28–33   each ⟨of us⟩ one ⟨of us⟩ through . . . placing ⟨us⟩you . . . fit ⟨each
                one⟩ ↑every mind↓
38   God ⟨has made⟩ ↑thinks↓,
41   know & ⟨seek⟩ serve.
42–44   skill; ⟨in⟩ seeing . . . ↑acting truth is ⟨wisdom & goodness⟩ power.↓
44–(263)1   in ⟨m⟩ applying . . . nature, i.e. the

Page 263

1–4   orator is ⟨is⟩he . . . feelings. ⟨↑{Insert X}↓ [At the bottom of the
                page, a passage marked "X":] ↑{The wisest statesman is he that best
                knows & touches closest the actual state of things in yᵉ Common-
                wealth.↓⟩ [In the text the addition is repeated with the first words
                written over "Insert X":] The wisest . . . Commonwealth.↓
8   much ⟨shd⟩ ↑can↓
10–11   ¶ This ⟨understanding⟩ ↑doctrine↓ . . . truth ⟨is a means to virtue,⟩
                becomes
17–19   ↑a man who . . . another;↓ . . . from the /full/single/
19–20   This↑, it will be admitted,↓
21–26   ¶ ↑It is . . . itself, ⟨↑{↓by steady endeavours at self-improvement↑}↓⟩
                [brackets and emendation in pencil] to discover . . . kingdom i.e. . . . .
                his ⟨in⟩ defects as ↑he↓ exerts his ⟨pow⟩ talents↓
28–31   has /sent/raised up in/ ⟨a man into⟩ the world . . . us. ↑⟨The⟩ It
                . . . imports↓ ⟨In⟩ ↑From↓ such a man ⟨it⟩ would be ⟨seen⟩
                ↑heard↓ as ⟨in⟩ ↑from↓ every man ⟨it⟩ ought to be↑,↓ ⟨seen that
                there are⟩ no

33–34	not ⟨say⟩ ↑utter↓ . . . not ⟨say⟩ ↑utter↓
35	guarantee ⟨&⟩ for
38–41	when ⟨actions⟩ the words . . . than actions, ⟨inasmuch as speech is better than pantomime.⟩ ↑are a higher class of actions.↓ ¶ ⟨It is plainly necessary that to ⟨such a⟩ the exhibition of such a character much silence is ⟨necessa⟩ fitting. ↑A great part of truth is the art of being silent. Silence, said an old maxim, is the ca↑n↓didate for truth.↓ It was said of Epaminondas, who was a sort of image of the ancient hero⟨e⟩is↑m↓, that "no man spoke so well or so little." And St ⟨Pauls⟩ ↑James's↓ rule is "be slow to speak"⟩ ¶ ↑Such a person would be ⟨very silent⟩ ↑slow to speak↓ . . . is the ca⟨d⟩ndidate for truth.↓ ⟨In this person⟩ ↑and when he spoke↓

Page 264

3	nothings. ⟨In⟩ ↑By↓
7–11	¶ (This is . . . truth in action.)
11	truth? ⟨Let the⟩ It
13	who was ⟨the⟩ himself
18–20	↑the least↓ . . . integrity. ¶ ⟨Will you pardon me if I detain you⟩ ↑Permit me↓
22–24	things. ⟨Now I wish to ask if this⟩ ↑⟨Suppose⟩ ↑Is there . . . this↓ that we ⟨should⟩ ↑ought to↓ . . . truth.↓ is not an [Addition in ink over the following in erased pencil:] "Suppose we shd set out with the supreme purpose never but the truth"
25	not ⟨buy /sugarplums/toys/⟩ ↑spend for trifles↓.
26	pass for ⟨simple truth⟩ ↑entire fact↓
27–28	↑It will . . . please↓
31	praise. ⟨↑Be careful when you dispute. Be careful with those whom you wd please↓⟩ Let it
31–32	↑Would not . . . known?↓
34	Would not ⟨God fill⟩ his soul ↑be filled↓

[The following is inscribed in pencil after the end of the sermon:] ¶ ↑*Addenda* That every man would be interesting as a *new man* if he spoke the truth & so we shd not fear company. ¶ That Truth does not demand a puritanic sanctimonious literalness of speech but admits of irony, fable, wit, metaphor provided simple truth be the omnipresent end.↓

[The following passage, an early draft of portions of the sermon, is inscribed in the additional folio found with the manuscript:]

The reason why we neglect truth so much is because the senses are much more attended to than the soul. ⟨Ou⟩ Thoughts are not much esteemed by us This is the reason why we think less of the order of the inner world than we do to be surrounded by the conveniences & splendor of the outward world. If we were more good & wise we should feel it to be a far greater violation of our peace that the truth should be violated to us or by us than that we were poor or sick.

Men think much more of the body. ↑In a world supposed to be gov^d by chance↓ Wealth is called the main chance. They keep th⟨is⟩eir interest always in view & are willing to get amusement & dignity from accidental goodness. They are willing that thought & the tongue which is its instrument should be the servant of interest & so withdraw it from its true calling & profession which is Truth & make it tell the lie of flattery of malice & of fraud.

Where truth is felt to be a paramount interest, right which is truth in action will be so regarded. And then we should not see the spectacle now seen with indifference

God desires truth in the inward parts. Man does also. Especially when we are afflicted we want truth. Only truth is tolerable to the petulance of grief. He that does not speak it insults you with every word. He is not seeking truth & therefore what you say & feel has no interest to him & you will not molest yourself by uttering it. He is thinking only of himself & how he ⟨appears⟩ shall come off. Words that are things & words that are words. You are suffering now under a privation of the affections & this insincerity adds a privation of the whole spiritual world. Every thing seems fading away. ↑all but the eating, drinking, coughing, wretched body.↓

What we have lost is a friendship so near & intimate that it was wholly sincere. It had no need of drapery of courtesy. And this hollow talk makes us feel the loss the more. It suggests to us the disapprobation which the departed would feel or feels with us & draws us nearer to the dead & farther from the living.

↑The lip of truth shall be established forever & honoured↓

It is very hard to speak the truth. In the structure of society custom has grown a hypocrite & expects you to say smooth things & to make assurances of regard which you do not feel & pay visits which are disagreeable to the maker & the receiver & to talk when you have nothing to say, & nothing is less expected than that a man should have made up his own opinions.

If every man would think before he speaks if every man would speak what he thinks we should never fear the approach of our friends No conversation would be tedious, no man would be uninteresting. Every mind would be instructive to us for it would be a mind & not the poor mimic of the whole neighborhood of men. Every remark of the learned or unlearned would contribute something ⟨to help you to the truth⟩ ↑to your wisdom.↓

Sermon CXXXV

Manuscript: The sewn gathering consists of a single leaf and five sheets folded to make four pages each; the first three folios are stacked and the remaining two are nested. All are sewn with white thread along the left margin; the folio pages measure 25.1 x 20.2 cm, and the single leaf measures 25 x 20 cm.

Lines	*Page 265*
3	↑singleness . . . on↓ simplicity of motive ⟨is essential to singleness,⟩ and [emendation in pencil]
11–13	we mt permt ourselves . . . ↑of the effect↓ of our example; that ⟨⟨many⟩ then⟩ especially . . . we ⟨h⟩ could
18	language ⟨or⟩ &
24	into ⟨saf⟩ ways

	Page 266
1	hard and
7	↑It is acting . . . men↓
8–9	↑According . . . thinking↓ Things [addition in pencil]
12	lights. ↑I do not well know what may be yᵉ effect of any particular

action of mine upon others. It may excite one man to imitate &↓
[addition in pencil; rejected as incomplete] One

18–19   omniscience to ⟨act⟩ ↑go↓

23   deception ⟨it defeats itself⟩ it

25–27   will ↑find↓, that . . . regard ⟨y⟩ those actions ↑as your example↓

28–37   ↑4. But, . . . does.↓ ¶ ⟨These three reasons seem to me sufficient to
show that it is an insufficient & a vicious motive to act from regard to
example.⟩ Let ⟨him⟩ ↑the goodman↓ leave

39   ↑in itself↓

Page 267

1–8   God. ↑{Insert X}↓ [On the following page, a passage marked "X":]
↑{↑Surely . . . but ⟨act from⟩ to . . . actions↓ ["Surely . . . actions"
added in pencil] There . . . in its effects}↓

19   and ⟨may⟩ ↑need↓

21   which ⟨surely⟩ I

23–30   force. ¶ ⟨My friends I conceive there is a use a great use in that
consideration. It is this.⟩ ¶ Thus ⟨suppose I regard⟩ ↑there is a
⟨scrupulous⟩ pious . . . in↓ some employments ↑which he regards↓
. . . for ⟨me⟩him, . . . suppose ⟨I wish⟩ ↑one who scruples↓ . . .
declamation ⟨but⟩ ↑because↓ . . . for ⟨me⟩him to go, or suppose ⟨I
⟨s⟩think⟩ ↑one man thinks↓ [over "one man" in pencil] . . . which
⟨others⟩ ↑another man↓ think↑s↓ profane the day↑, & so abstains↓
[emendations in pencil]

30   recreation his

34–35   ↑What . . . it?↓ [ink over pencil]

38   thing. ⟨My⟩ ↑Our↓ [emendation in pencil]

40–42   that /any/real/ . . . more ⟨closely⟩ keenly . . . see ⟨where⟩ how

Page 268

2–3   man ⟨is in the habit of occa⟩ ↑indulges as he thinks innocently↓ [end
of line] ↑in the occa↓sional /indulgence in drinking/use/ ardent
[emendations and variant in pencil]

5   neighbor⟨s⟩ ↑who sits with him↓

7–8   to ⟨think⟩ inquire . . . really it⟨s⟩ is

11–14   it (⟨without⟩ [cancellation rejected for sense] any . . . fear ⟨lest⟩
↑that↓ . . . other)↑; if . . . act ⟨in⟩ with . . . itself.↓

16–17   ↑There . . . misinterpreted↓

18–19   example↑, & ⟨every one will feel the folly of ⟨y⟩⟩ [canceled in ink
over pencil] ↑no . . . will↓ ["will" added in ink over pencil] appeal-
⟨ing⟩ . . . principle.↓

21–22   revelation. ⟨Now is there any danger⟩ Would . . . why a ⟨me⟩ pious

29   the ⟨friend⟩ associate

37–38   such ⟨license⟩ ↑freedom↓ . . . all ⟨that it⟩ ↑wh that↓

39–41   do to ⟨omit⟩ ↑leave undone↓ . . . without ↑also↓ . . . we ⟨do not⟩
↑leave undone↓, [all three additions in ink over pencil]

Page 269

2   I ⟨imagine⟩ ↑believe↓ [emendation in ink over pencil]t

INDEX